Odysseus Unbound

Where is the Ithaca described in such detail in Homer's *Odyssey*? The mystery has baffled scholars for over two millennia, particularly because Homer's descriptions bear little resemblance to the modern island called Ithaki. This highly illustrated book tells the extraordinary story of the exciting recent discovery of the true location of Homer's Ithaca by following a detective trail of literary, geological and archaeological clues. We can now identify all the places on the island that are mentioned in the epic – even the site of Odysseus' Palace itself. The pages of the *Odyssey* come alive as we follow its events through a landscape that opens up before our eyes via glorious colour photographs and 3D satellite images. Over a century after Schliemann's discovery of Troy, this breakthrough will revolutionise our understanding of Homer's texts and of our cultural ancestors in Bronze Age Greece.

ROBERT BITTLESTONE was educated in classics and science before reading economics at the University of Cambridge. He is the founder of Metapraxis Ltd, a company specialising in the detection of early warnings for multinational companies. He is the author of many articles about the importance of visualisation and he has applied these principles to the enigma described in this book. He is married with four children and describes himself as an enthusiastically incompetent skier, sailor and windsurfer.

JAMES DIGGLE is Professor of Greek and Latin at Cambridge and a Fellow of Queens' College. His publications include *The Oxford Classical Text of Euripides* (Oxford, 1981–94), *Euripidea: Collected Essays* (Oxford, 1994) and *Theophrastus: Characters* (Cambridge, 2004). He was University Orator at Cambridge for eleven years and has published a selection of his speeches in *Cambridge Orations* (Cambridge, 1994).

JOHN UNDERHILL is Professor of Stratigraphy at the University of Edinburgh. His primary research interest lies in the use of geological fieldwork and geophysical methods to investigate the structure and stratigraphy of sedimentary basins. He has been investigating and elucidating the geology of the Ionian Islands of western Greece since 1982. He is a Fellow of the Royal Society of Edinburgh. He also referees professional football matches and in 2001 was promoted to the FIFA List of International Referees.

Head of Odysseus: Tiberius Grotto, Sperlonga

Excavated from the cave at the foot of Mount Ciannito between Rome and Naples, where Tiberius (Roman Emperor from AD 14 to 37) is thought to have entertained his dinner guests beside his fish farm.

[Image: photographed by the author with the kind permission of the Soprintendenza per i Beni Archeologici del Lazio, Ministero per i Beni e le Attività Culturali, Roma.]

Odysseus Unbound

The Search for Homer's Ithaca

ROBERT BITTLESTONE

With James Diggle and John Underhill

CAMBRIDGE
UNIVERSITY PRESS

CAMBRIDGE UNIVERSITY PRESS
Cambridge, New York, Melbourne, Madrid, Cape Town, Singapore, São Paulo

Cambridge University Press
The Edinburgh Building, Cambridge CB2 2RU, UK

Published in the United States of America by Cambridge University Press, New York

www.cambridge.org
Information on this title: www.cambridge.org/9780521853576

First published 2005

Printed in the United Kingdom at the University Press, Cambridge

A catalogue record for this book is available from the British Library

Library of Congress Cataloguing in Publication data
Bittlestone, Robert, 1952–
Odysseus unbound : the search for Homer's Ithaca / Robert Bittlestone;
with James Diggle and John Underhill. – 1st ed.
    p.   cm.
Includes bibliographical references and index.
ISBN 0-521-85357-5 (hardback : alk. paper)
1. Homer – Knowledge – Ithaca Island (Greece)   2. Homer. Odyssey.   3. Ithaca Island
(Greece) – In literature.   4. Cephalonia Island (Greece) – Antiquities.   I. Diggle, James.
II. Underhill, John, 1961–   III. Title.

ISBN-13   978-0-0521-85357-6 hardback
ISBN-10   0-521-85357-5 hardback

Extract of *Helen* taken from *George Seferis: Complete Poems* translated by Edmund Keeley and
Philip Sherrard. Published by Anvil Press Poetry in 1995. Reproduced by permission of Anvil
Press Poetry and Princeton University Press.

For the people of Kefalonia
Great suffering had desolated Greece.
So many bodies thrown
into the jaws of the sea, the jaws of the earth,
so many souls
fed to the millstones like grain.
And the rivers swelling, blood in their silt,
all for a linen undulation, a filmy cloud,
a butterfly's flicker, a wisp of swan's down,
an empty tunic – all for a Helen.

George Seferis, *Helen* (1953)

And for Jean
From women's eyes this doctrine I derive:
They sparkle still the right Promethean fire;
They are the books, the arts, the academes,
That show, contain, and nourish all the world.

Shakespeare, *Love's Labour's Lost*
IV.iii.297 (1593)

Contents

Acknowledgements

This book could not have been written without the advice of experts in many different spheres of classical and scientific knowledge, nor without the support of friends both on and off the island of Cephalonia. In every case I have received unfailing courtesy and assistance from those who have no vested interest in this project apart from a commitment to excellence and the open exchange of ideas. I have listed here the names that I remember and I apologise to those who may have been inadvertently omitted.

James Diggle is Professor of Greek and Latin in the University of Cambridge and a Fellow of Queens' College. His involvement with this enterprise started with the provision of a crucial expert opinion concerning the Homeric description of Asteris and since then he has been a delightful and untiring source of inspiration, expertise and philological advice. His willingness to devote serious consideration to alternately ridiculous and radical proposals from an amateur whose Greek was half-forgotten has been remarkable. He has combined the eye of an eagle with the pen of a poet and I owe to him more than I can describe.

John Underhill is Professor of Stratigraphy at the University of Edinburgh and an international expert on Cephalonian geology. His enthusiasm to solve the riddle of Strabo's Channel has been boundless and he has visited and revisited the island in order to unravel the mystery of its transformation. He has devoted extraordinary energy to this quest while simultaneously acquitting himself as a Scottish Premier League referee.

Anthony Snodgrass is Laurence Professor Emeritus of Classical Archaeology at the University of Cambridge. He has acted as mentor to many of today's classical archaeologists and he and his wife Annemarie have provided encouragement and expert advice at crucial points in this venture. Their personal involvement in the summer of 2004 resulted in fundamental new interpretations and insights.

Tjeerd van Andel is Honorary Professor in Earth History, Quaternary Science and Geo-archaeology at the Godwin Institute of Quaternary Science within the Department of Earth Sciences at Cambridge University. Internationally recognised as the author of *New Views on an Old Planet* and the discoverer of geothermal vents, his work on *terra rossa* and the interaction between human beings and their physical environment has been of great importance to this project.

Michael D'Souza was a co-explorer on the second and third expeditions: *inter magna alia* he constructively challenged the Asteris hypothesis and thereby injected more rigour into this proposal. His interests range from Bronze Age marine warfare to the Dorian Invasion and beyond: he has been an invaluable and enjoyable companion and sage.

Chris Goodger filmed with great professionalism key moments of the first expedition as the discoveries were taking place and simultaneously refused to be blinded by Homeric research, obliging me to check and recheck the interim findings for real-world credibility.

John Bennet is an expert on Pylos, Knossos and other classical sites. He was latterly the Sinclair and Rachel Hood Lecturer in Aegean Prehistory at the Institute of Archaeology at Oxford University and is now Professor of Archaeology at Sheffield University. He has given generously of his time and knowledge in interpreting the project's photographs and experiences: he also has the rare ability to detect and correct mistakes in Linear B.

Christopher Bronk Ramsey and Jean-Luc Schwenninger of the Oxford Research Laboratory for Archaeology and the History of Art (RLAHA) visited the island with both professionalism and enthusiasm to conduct carbon-14 and optically stimulated luminescence dating trials. Their associate Daniel Miles of the Oxford Dendrochronology Laboratory provided expert advice on tree dating.

Gregory Nagy is Francis Jones Professor of Classical Greek Literature at Harvard University and Director of the Center for Hellenic Studies in Washington DC. He and his colleagues Jennifer Reilly and Douglas Frame have provided welcome support and practical advice on the pursuance of this venture and the publication of this book.

Professor James Jackson is based at the Bullard Laboratories of the Department of Earth Sciences at Cambridge University and is a leading researcher on seismology and neotectonic movements. He patiently explained that soil erosion alone would not have acted rapidly enough to infill Strabo's Channel over only two or three thousand years and hence prompted the search for a more catastrophic mechanism.

Per Wikstroem of Radarteam in Sweden surrendered a holiday in order to deploy his advanced ground-penetrating radar antenna, which was instrumental in identifying former sea level contours and also in profiling a famous collapsed cave.

James Whitley is Director of the British School at Athens and an authority on Greek archaeology. His extensive knowledge and thoughtful guidance have been of major benefit to this project.

C. H. Goekoop is the former Burgomaster of Leiden, Holland, and belongs to a family with impressive Homeric investigative credentials. His tenacity in analysing the *Odyssey* and using it to identify specific place names provided an outstanding model for the approach used herein, although the conclusions I have drawn differ from his.

Manolis Pantos of the Daresbury Laboratory Archaeometry Unit has been a source of rare reference materials and he has also cooperated with C. H. Goekoop in preparing an English translation of his book. The generosity of his spirit in encouraging me to pursue a competitive theory has been extraordinary.

Gilles le Noan is an indefatigable Homeric researcher whose publications on this subject are thought-provoking and controversial. He provided me with access to some recondite source material and his inquiry into the history of today's island of Ithaca has been of considerable value. Although our views differ on the central question of the geology of ancient Ithaca, we nevertheless find ourselves in agreement regarding several of the Odyssean locations.

In 1998 Babis Katsibas of Lefkas alerted me to the possibility of historical changes in the sea levels on mainland Greece as a basis for reassessing an archaeological site in Acarnania and this became a catalyst for the present project.

Peter Kuniholm of the Malcolm and Carolyn Wiener Laboratory for Aegean and Near Eastern Dendrochronology at Cornell University in Ithaca (NY) clarified the relationship between claims and reality in the matter of Greek olive tree aging.

Andreas Delaportas of Livadi personally experienced the 1953 earthquake on Cephalonia and provided an eyewitness account of its effects. He and his family always responded knowledgeably to my endless questions and they escorted me to remote parts of the island with unfailing kindness and good humour.

Tim Severin is an intrepid explorer whose *Ulysses Voyage* proposed that the *Odyssey* describes real sea journeys and places: his adventures sparked my interest in this endeavour and also helped me to focus on small-scale topography rather than long-distance voyages.

Professor Anastasia Kiratzi at the Department of Geophysics in the Aristotle University of Thessaloniki identified key research papers that explained the history of local sea level changes. The earthquake catalogue of over 20,000 tremors dating back to 550 BC and related researches by her, together with Professor B. C. Papazachos and others at the University's Geophysical Laboratory, have provided essential information on historical continuity.

Dr Paolo Pirazzoli of CNRS in Paris and Professor Stathis Stiros and colleagues at the University of Patras conducted the research into the effects of the 1953 earthquake on the local land levels of Cephalonia which helped in the quantification of vertical land thrust.

Dr G. A. Papadopoulos of the Institute of Geodynamics at the National Observatory of Athens created the catalogue of historical tsunamis which supported the discussion towards the end of this book.

Takis Patrikarakos, a long-standing friend and CEO of KeySystems SA in Athens, obtained and despatched the fourteen indispensable 1:5000 Greek Army surveying maps of the key locations in time for them to be scanned and digitised prior to the first expedition.

Menelaos Antoniou of Geotritikes Ergasies in Cephalonia is a professional driller of water boreholes and he advised me of the unexpected finding of salt water in the buried marine channel at a considerable distance from the sea.

Professor Ioannis Koumantakis of the Department of Mining Engineering and Metallurgy in the Section of Geological Sciences at the National Technical University of Athens and Professor T. Mimides of the Laboratory of Agricultural Hydraulics at the Department of Land Reclamation and Agricultural Engineering of the Agricultural University of Athens performed the original research on the composition of these underground inland sea water reservoirs and they also identified an important hydrological anomaly.

Elias Toumasatos of the Corgialenios Library in Argostoli provided resourceful and cheerful assistance in the location of rare reference material on the 1953 earthquake and other textual researches.

John Walker, founder of Autodesk and co-author of AutoCAD, wrote the astronomical programs that enabled the exact positions of Mars and Venus at dawn on specified dates 3,200 years ago to be determined.

Professor William Murray of the University of South Florida provided expert advice on the depth of the former coast around Lefkas and also on the tactics of ancient naval warfare.

Peter James thoughtfully explained to me his theory of *Centuries of Darkness* and thereby facilitated some of the speculative considerations presented in this volume.

Andrea Celentano and Ilaria Tramacere of Eurimage in Rome obtained high resolution Digital Globe Quickbird satellite images of the critical locations and their colleague Axel Oddone patiently manipulated the data involved to provide image resolution to an accuracy of 70 centimetres from an orbit 450 kilometres away.

Des Newman of D&L Software created the OziExplorer 2D and 3D programs which made possible the integration of satellite, survey, geological and digital elevation imagery with on-site GPS data values.

Alistair Dickie is the author of OziPhotoTool which synchronised the timestamps from digital photography with those from GPS location information.

Dennis Johnson and Michael Jeffords of Geophysical Survey Systems provided the ground penetrating radar control equipment and the analytical software that enabled the radar scans to be interpreted.

Ray Gardener is the author of Leveller, a volume sculpting tool for three dimensional digital elevation models which helped in the recreation of the former channel contours.

Simon Bittlestone recalled C. H. Goekoop's reference to the potential ambiguity of the Greek word 'nesos' at a crucial moment and applied it to the identification of Asteris when exploration time was running out and no windy heights were to be found. He also acted as the project's on-site coordinator in the summer of 2004.

Nicola Bittlestone's penetrating question about the proximity of the sea at Palairos in 1998 launched a chain of thought which led to the Schizocephalonia hypothesis.

Matthew Bittlestone realised that there would be no point in developing a theatre for the inhabitants of a deserted city and he also alerted me to the implications of the fact that Odysseus, Penelope, Telemachos and Laertes are the only witnesses to much of the action described in the *Odyssey*.

Mark Bittlestone discovered the second well of Arethousa Spring and worked out why Telemachos would have chosen to land at a bay as small and unknown as Agni Cove.

In London my solicitor Lawrence Cartier provided support and advice well beyond the call of purely legal duty. He also suggested an additional reason for the relatively high population of Doulichion, in view of its proximity to the Greek mainland as a first port of call for visitors.

In Argostoli my solicitor Nellie Constandaki-Hioni provided invaluable assistance and guidance in connection with the people and the places of this beautiful island.

The library of the Athenaeum in Pall Mall has been an outstanding source of rare volumes and I am most appreciative of both the quality and the quantity of the books that I have been permitted to borrow, particularly in the case of those that were donated by their authors.

I am especially grateful to all of my friends and colleagues at Metapraxis for their support during a period of major changes for the company.

Michael Sharp and his team at Cambridge University Press adopted and adapted my typescript with great professionalism and they also had the courage and the confidence to commit to a full colour publication from an author unknown in this field.

Finally, writers need families and I am no exception. Simon, Nicola, Matthew and Mark have humoured and encouraged me throughout this undertaking and as for Jean, who married me in 1979 in the teeth of much prevailing advice: well my dear, you will note that I have dedicated half of this book to you. I realise that this will represent little compensation for all those solitary evenings but at least your half is still heavy enough to satisfy your urge to throw it at me from time to time.

Prologue The *Odyssey* is Homer's story of the return of Odysseus from the Trojan War to his palace on the island of Ithaca and his battle to regain the kingship there after a long absence. The *Iliad* describes certain events towards the end of this war which is believed to have taken place in the twelfth century BC. Although these poems are thought to have been set down in writing several centuries later, the *Iliad* and the *Odyssey* nevertheless represent two of the world's oldest surviving texts.

These are long epic poems of magnificent style and breathtaking sophistication. They were pivotal in defining the language and culture of classical Greece and these in turn have fundamentally influenced the development of Western Europe. Many aspects of our own spoken and written word, democracy, philosophy, politics, mathematics, architecture, painting, sculpture, drama and other facets of Western culture derive from the Greek civilisations of the fifth and fourth centuries BC.

The Greeks regarded Homer as their teacher and the Homeric poems made an immense impact upon the whole of ancient literature. Socrates, Plato and Aristotle studied the *Iliad* and the *Odyssey* as a precursor to the development of their own ideas and for the last 2,500 years the Homeric poems have been required reading for every serious writer and philosopher. That legacy remains with us: in fact it is difficult to compose a significant paragraph in Italian, French, Spanish or English without using at least one word that was first articulated by Homer.

Ever since classical antiquity there has been considerable speculation about who Homer was, when and where these poems were written, whether there was a single author and whether the people, events and places that are described are real or imaginary. Although some of the place names that are mentioned in the *Odyssey* continue to exist today, including an island called Ithaca in the Ionian Sea to the west of Greece, attempts to relate this location to Homer's descriptions have proved unsuccessful. Despite continuing claims, excavations on modern Ithaca have failed to reveal the ancient city or Odysseus' Palace and its geography cannot be reconciled with descriptions in the *Odyssey* itself. This represents a marked contrast with the *Iliad*'s description of Troy, which was located by Heinrich Schliemann on the north-western coast of Turkey and extensively excavated since the 1870s.

However, new geological research into the location of the ancient seaway which I describe as Strabo's Channel has now suggested an alternative location for Homeric Ithaca. At an early stage of its development this theory implied that researchers over the centuries have been looking for Ithaca in the wrong place because the channel no longer exists. The evidence in support of this former seaway has been evaluated by John Underhill and his summary of the scientific findings is contained within an appendix to this book.

This new location for Homeric Ithaca agrees very closely with descriptions of the island in the *Odyssey*. Specific sites for Phorcys Bay, Asteris, Ithaca city, Odysseus' Palace, Hermes' Hill, Raven's Rock, Laertes' farm and other Ithacan locations have been identified and visited and the results of this preliminary on-site exploration are very positive. This is particularly evident in the case of those well-known Homeric passages that have previously appeared topographically inconsistent. In every case this new location supports the view that Homer's geographical descriptions of ancient Ithaca in the *Odyssey* were exact. James Diggle has reviewed and retranslated from the Greek all the crucial passages which provide us with these clues and his expert assessment of this material is referred to in the text and presented by him in a further appendix.

The essence of the theory presented in this book was compiled before my first visit to present-day Ithaca or Cephalonia, although I was familiar with other areas of Greece and its islands. The solution that emerged therefore represented the first phase of a 3,200 year old detective story: an *ab initio* attempt to identify the site of Homer's Ithaca based on an evaluation of off-site evidence. This consisted primarily of seismic research, geological considerations, textual analyses, Internet-based photographic repositories, satellite images, previous researchers' theories and responses to e-mail or telephone inquiries. The task was to try to fit together all these different clues so that the historical jigsaw made sense.

Once the first draft of the theory was complete, a series of visits was arranged to see if its predictions were supported by the reality. Although some important aspects of the theory were modified in the light of these visits, the central thrust has remained the same and I have tried to echo this in my title, which draws on Aeschylus' and later Shelley's reference to the plight of Prometheus tied to a rock. In this case Odysseus and his homeland have been tied to the rock of Same by earthquake-induced landslip: I hope that these present researches may represent an initial step towards their liberation.

As an amateur in their disciplines I am conscious of the blunders of interpretation that I have doubtless made in deploying material from the expert domains of seismologists, geologists, classicists and archaeologists. I ask them to forgive me for these mistakes and also for my use of everyday language in the presentation of these findings. However, even if I possessed the skills to convey this material in the language of experts, I am not sure that I would have used them, because this is a story that affects us all and it is perhaps therefore appropriate that all of us should have the chance to absorb it.

I hope that some of those who read this volume will agree that sufficient progress has now been made on preliminary research to justify the organisation and funding of professional investigation. This project will always belong to Greece but the sites involved are very extensive and it will take a major international effort for them to reveal their secrets. Consequently it is hoped that some form of conduit for information and resources can be established to facilitate contact with those organisations and individuals who wish to support this endeavour and thereby become associated with the further discoveries that may emerge.

Finally, anyone involved in a venture such as this cannot fail to be aware of the extensive history of prior attempts to solve this ancient puzzle, of the debt that is owed to those great researchers and to the ever-present possibility of failure. It will take time for this proposition to be tested independently and inevitably some disappointments will ensue. I hope that these will be offset by the excitement of new discoveries but if that should not be the case then I can do no better than to refer to Shelley once more and quote from his own Preface:

Whatever talents a person may possess to amuse and instruct others, be they ever so inconsiderable, he is yet bound to exert them: if his attempt be ineffectual, let the punishment of an unaccomplished purpose have been sufficient; let none trouble themselves to heap the dust of oblivion upon his efforts; the pile they raise will betray his grave which might otherwise have been unknown.

Kingston-upon-Thames, October 2004

Text, translation and images

While writing this book I have been conscious of two distinct audiences: amateurs and experts. As an amateur I have tried to learn from experts in disciplines such as geology, archaeology and classical studies. When I introduce material from their domains I aim to explain the underlying concepts as I have tried to understand them myself. This approach may help other amateurs but it runs the risk of irritating experts, so that is one reason why James Diggle has composed Appendix 1 and John Underhill Appendix 2. I have been very fortunate to be advised by them and other authorities; the resulting text is intended to stand up to the scrutiny of their peers. Expert readers are encouraged to refer to their appendices at an early stage as an antidote to the layman's descriptions elsewhere.

Because this book is both an explanation and also a chronology of the search and the discovery, I have from time to time exposed the reader to some of the blind alleys that I unwittingly entered as this adventure unfolded. It might have been simpler to have omitted these false steps but the result would have been less true to life. If you are an expert reader you will probably be horrified by some of these naïve presumptions; fortunately they were in most cases detected and the resulting correction is then discussed in a later chapter.

Some of these false steps involved my misunderstanding of the text. My own ancient Greek is decidedly rusty, although when armed with a magnifying glass and Liddell and Scott's Greek dictionary I can attempt a word-by-word translation. I based my preliminary research into the *Odyssey* on the translation by Robert Fagles published in 1996. Fagles' intention was to turn the poem into an accessible vernacular and in this he succeeds remarkably well; but this success is of necessity sometimes achieved at the expense of textual fidelity. From time to time I have therefore reverted to a more traditional translation, mainly that of A. T. Murray published in the Loeb Classical Library (1919) and revised by George E. Dimock (1995).

After reading a first draft of the initial chapters of this book in which I had quoted Fagles' translation, James Diggle persuaded me that since I was building much of my case on the text of the *Odyssey*, I needed to use a translation which reflected as precisely as possible the nuances of the original Greek. At the same time he felt that a literal prose translation would fail to convey the poetic qualities of Homeric verse. He therefore volunteered to translate into verse all the passages upon which I relied. This rapidly became a major undertaking since those original 260 lines soon turned into over 700, but I believe that he has achieved what I thought to be impossible: a translation of great elegance which simultaneously retains an exceptional level of fidelity to the original Greek. I have used other translations of the *Odyssey* for the passages that I quote at the beginning and the end of this story, where the reverential awe of Murray's Victorian English seems appropriate.

I also owe to James translations from the *Iliad* and from other verse and prose authors; those translations for which he is not responsible are acknowledged in the text. He has added notes to his own translations where he felt that they required them, drawing attention to problems in the Greek text and in its interpretation. These notes are designed to be accessible to the reader who knows no Greek. The index at the end of the book includes line references to these and other Homeric translations; the line numbers throughout refer to the Greek version of the text.

In modern Greek I am about as speechless as the average tourist and therefore most grateful to Karen Rich, who managed not only the normal complexities of translation but also tackled some arcane phrases from geophysical electrochemistry. With the benefit of hindsight I suspect that my cheerful words of encouragement that most of these terms were derived from ancient Greek in the first place may not have been as helpful to her as I imagined at the time. The remaining translations from French, Italian and German are my own except where otherwise indicated; in some cases I have made use of computerised translations.

Concerning the English spelling of Greek proper names I have generally followed James Diggle's advice to remain faithful to the original except where established convention makes that awkward. Odysseus is the familiar English spelling of the name which in Greek is *Odusseus*. The Roman version of his name is *Ulixes* and from this comes the English spelling Ulysses. So I have kept to the familiar spelling for him and a few other well-known individuals but used the Greek form for the remainder.

There are many maps, diagrams and photographic images in this book. The use of satellite and other digital imagery has been fundamental to these researches and the appropriate credits have been provided throughout. Almost all of the photographs were taken by me on-site and so where an alternative source is not listed then I am responsible for the image.

Much of my professional life has been spent in emphasising the importance of visualisation within business circles and so I make no apology for bringing the same techniques to bear in this rather different inquiry. I hope that they will help the reader to visualise Homer's Ithaca, both as it was in the time of Odysseus and as it is today. They also serve to lighten the impact of what might otherwise have been a rather intimidating sequence of unbroken pages of text.

Finally I must point out that the island on which most of the following action takes place is variously spelt as Cephalonia, Cephellenia, Kefalonia, Kefallenia and Kefallinia. In general I have adopted the first of these except when referring to the 'great-hearted Cephallenians' who live there. That adjective is a Homeric epithet (*Iliad* 2.631) which I have found to be as true of the people who inhabit the island today as it was over 3,000 years ago.

PART 1 Speculation

Nothing feebler does earth nurture than man,
of all things that on earth breathe and move.
For he thinks that he will never suffer evil in time to come,
so long as the gods give him success and his knees are quick;
but when again the blessed gods decree him misfortune,
this too he bears in sorrow with such patience as he can,
for the spirit of men upon the earth is just such as the day
which the father of gods and men brings upon them.

Odyssey 18.130–7 (transl. Murray)

CHAPTER 1

Catastrophe

A bad earthquake at once destroys our oldest associations: the earth, the very emblem of solidity, has moved beneath our feet like a thin crust over fluid; – one second of time has created in the mind a strange idea of insecurity, which hours of reflection would not have produced.

Charles Darwin (1839)[1]

Midnight in Manhattan: Andreas Delaportas awakens bolt upright in his bed. Sleep-shot ears have not yet learnt the noises of his new home but this is a sound that he can never forget. The deep rumble grows louder and the room begins to shake. A shrill keening bursts from his dry throat and he curls into a foetal knot back under the bedclothes. The roar comes yet closer and now Andreas knows that he cannot escape. Poseidon has followed him across the ocean, he has followed him across the land, he has found out where he is living and he is coming for him again from five thousand miles away. Awakening is not an end to this nightmare: it is only the beginning. As the crescendo builds his screams pierce the night and now his sister is beside him: 'Don't worry Andreas. That's just the subway train: it passes right underneath us. It's not the earthquake.'

Cephalonia, 22 May 2003: *In 1953 I was six years old when we had the earthquake. 80% of the houses on the island were destroyed. All the rocks came tumbling down the mountainside (Figure 1.1): it was a terrible thing to see. I remember it from that day: I will remember it all my life. It was something for which your mind wakes up, when you realise the power of nature. I was in the village: we were lucky because we were having lunch outside, it was the summertime. If it had been night-time with people asleep in the houses there would have been a lot more deaths.*

And we saw all the stones – big stones, they were loose at the top of the mountain and we saw them just rolling down the mountainside into the ocean. It started on the Sunday with the small earthquakes and then there was the big one.

I tell you that it is a strange experience for your life to find out how weak the human being is. Very few people have experienced a catastrophe like this. You might think that living near a volcano would be similar, but it's not. Because with a volcano you see it's coming, and it's coming in one spot, and you have plenty of time to protect yourself. But with an earthquake, you don't have any time and you don't see it: it happens too fast.

And everyone was so frightened: nearly everyone left. The population of Cephalonia was 125,000 before the earthquake and about 90% of the people left. Even now it is still only about 25,000 people.

FIGURE 1.1
The mountains of
Kondogourata
*Andreas Delaportas was born
in the village of Livadi in the
foreground.*

Look – we had the Second World War. Then we had the Civil War. Then we had the earthquake. Put those three things together: how are you going to survive? It was impossible to survive on the island. The economy was hopeless: you have no work, you have no home: how can you survive? So we all left: 100,000 of us left.[2]

1953 has already been a memorable year. On 20 January Dwight Eisenhower is sworn in as US President, the first such ceremony to be broadcast live on television. Stalin dies on 23 February at his Black Sea dacha and on 26 February Francis Crick and James Watson discover the structure of DNA. In South Africa Nelson Mandela is organising his first anti-government protests and on 29 May Edmund Hillary and Tenzing Norgay reach the summit of Mount Everest. On 2 June Queen Elizabeth is crowned before another live television audience and on 25 June *The Times* devotes a leading article to Michael Ventris' achievement in deciphering Mycenaean tablets written in a language called Linear B.[3]

FIGURE 1.2
Andreas Delaportas
*Photographed on the
Livadi–Atheras road: the
Mesovouni quarry lies behind
him and the summit of
Kastelli is to the right.*

The southern Ionian Islands lie off the western coast of Greece (Figure 1.3: for their location in the Mediterranean see Figure 3.1). At 07:41 GMT on Sunday 9 August seismographs record an earthquake with a surface magnitude of 6.4 at latitude 38.43N, longitude 20.50E, a location in the sea off the north-western peninsula of the largest of these islands, Cephalonia.[4] Over the next few days many smaller earthquakes impact the same area in quick succession, but the next major quake strikes on Tuesday 11 August at 03:32 with a magnitude of 6.8 at 37.85N 20.45E: this time its epicentre is off the north-west coast of the neighbouring island of Zacynthos (also known as Zante). Throughout that day the islands continue to be shaken by further tremors.

These are very serious earthquakes, but how much do these numbers matter? The Richter magnitude is based on the amount of ground motion recorded by a seismograph, using a logarithmic scale. This means that a gap of 1.0 between two earthquake magnitudes corresponds to a tenfold increase in the movement of the ground where the seismograph is located, which is typically many kilometres away from the earthquake's actual epicentre. Although ground motion is an important indicator, the actual energy released by an earthquake increases even faster: there is thirty-three times more energy for every 1.0 increase on the scale. To put this in perspective, the 6.4 magnitude quake of 9 August released the equivalent of about 4 million tons of TNT high explosive, while the 6.8 magnitude quake of 11 August was comparable to an explosion of 16 million tons.[5]

The citizens of Ithaca and Cephalonia were used to frequent seismic movements. The earthquake catalogue shows that there had already been significant tremors that year, just as there had been for most of the years in living memory and throughout history. Although these earthquakes created very

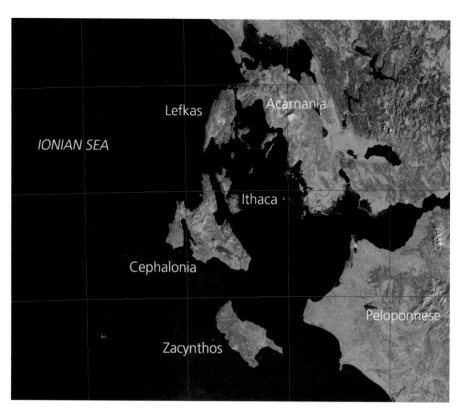

FIGURE 1.3
The southern Ionian
Islands
*Colour interpretation:
vegetation → green; water →
black or dark blue; urban
areas → lavender; bare
soil → magenta. Grid: 50 km.*
[Image credits: Landsat-7
false colour satellite
mosaic (SWIR 7,4,2)
courtesy of NASA Applied
Sciences Directorate –
John C. Stennis Space
Centre. Processing:
OziExplorer. Websites:
https://zulu.ssc.nasa.gov/
mrsid/mrsid.pl,
www.oziexplorer.com/]

significant damage, the Greeks had long since adopted the philosophy of their ancestor Zeno and learnt to be stoic: to accept the power of nature, to endure hardship without complaint and without trying to circumvent whatever the future might hold.

But at 09:24 GMT on Wednesday 12 August 1953 something happens to Cephalonia that is both unthinkable and unendurable. To understand this we need to consider the geography of the island (Figure 1.4). The central land mass is shaped roughly like a tilted rectangle with sides of about 30 km by 20 km and with two long peninsulas to the north and the west. Much of this terrain is mountainous, with height varying from sea level to the peak of Mount Ainos at 1,640 m (Figure 4.2). A very conservative estimate based on an average height above sea level of not less than 200 m results in a volume of rock (mainly limestone) above the waterline of at least 120 billion cubic metres. Using a similarly conservative figure for the density of limestone at 2,000 kg per cubic metre, this equates to a mass above sea level in excess of 240 trillion kilograms, although obviously this mass also extends below sea level in order to join up with the earth's crust.

Running through Cephalonia there is a complex system of fault lines. On that day an earthquake of magnitude 7.2 pushes this mass upwards by about

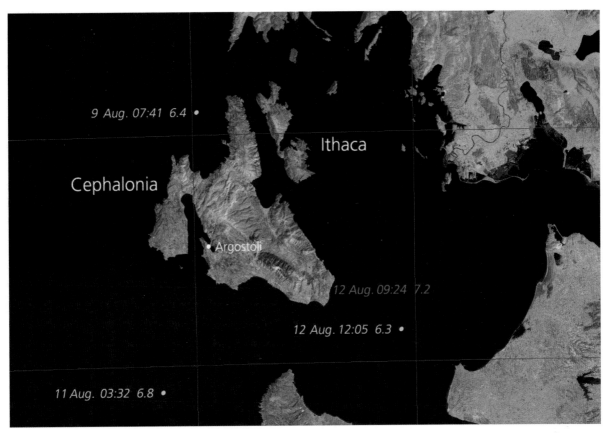

FIGURE 1.4
Epicentres of the major
August 1953 earthquakes
*Colour interpretation: as
Figure 1.3. Grid: 50 km.*
[Data source: Papazachos
et al. (2000); also see
endnote 4. Image credits:
as Figure 1.3.]

60 cm within the space of a few seconds and with the force of 63 million tons of high explosive. Most of the island is now simply that much higher than it was before, as the rock markings of the previous waterline all over the island reveal (Figure 1.5).

When you look at Figure 1.5 your immediate perception is that the sea level has lowered, but that is because your brain initially rejects the outrageous alternative that it is not the sea that has gone down but the land that has risen up. And by this I do not mean just the mass of this particular rock, which resides in a rather interesting bay near the capital town of Argostoli that we shall visit later, but the land mass of the entire island that is visible in the background as well. To add shocking insult to terrible injury, later that same day at 12:05 another earthquake struck off the eastern coast of the island with a magnitude of 6.3 – a mere 3 million tons of explosive.

The effect of the magnitude 7.2 earthquake is literally catastrophic: it is as if a thermonuclear bomb were to be modified so that instead of exploding at a single point, its energy is radiated evenly from the surface of a huge blanket lying underneath the island. In fact the largest H-bomb ever exploded

FIGURE 1.5
Cephalonian land level
prior to August 1953
*The boundary between the
light and dark rock marks the
former sea level. On 12
August 1953 the island was
uplifted by about
60 cm.*

had an energy of only 15 million tons of TNT and it created a crater over a mile across and 240 feet deep in Bikini Atoll the following year,[6] so it is as if four such modified bombs were simultaneously detonated under Cephalonia. In his eyewitness report 'The Drama of the Ionian Islands' Jean Savant said:

At 9.40 the ground shakes. Corfu and Paxos are not affected, but Lefkada, Ithaca, Cephalonia and Zante are in dire straits. The ground continues to tremble. The houses and the cafes are emptied. The roofs fly off and are crushed on the ground. Whole sections of wall fall down. Within the space of a few minutes, entire districts are no more than a pile of rubble. Suffocating dust is everywhere. The cries of terror and horror, of wounded and trapped people resound: 'Dipso, Dipso' (Water, Water), the same cry as of Jesus on the Cross. We hear it, this pitiful cry, on the days that follow, and always louder and louder.

From the top of the mountains (because these islands on volcanic ground are very mountainous) blocks of rock detach themselves, start to roll and then hurtle down and crush into pieces the farms in the villages, the public buildings and the pretty low-lying houses in the towns. And simultaneously, the sea stirs. A tidal wave submerges the interior of Cephalonia over a distance of three hundred metres inland. In Ithaca and in Zante, the spectacle is the same. The reckless sudden advance of the sea makes the islanders believe that their island is being swallowed up by the ocean.[7]

A journalist on board the troop transport *Alpheios* in Argostoli harbour observed that 'the people on the bridge of the ship jumped up by 30–40 cm'; the ship 'rolled heavily, broke its mooring ropes and seriously damaged its radar installation'.[8] Newspapers the next day said that 'the bedraggled survivors, with pitifully few possessions, reported that the quake caused hundreds of huge landslides which blocked the roads and trapped many islanders . . . Landslips sent whole neighbourhoods crumbling into the sea. Some reports said entire inland villages were swallowed up by huge fissures. Tidal waves swept the port of Vathy, capital of Ithaca.' Eyewitnesses said that the disaster scene 'looked like the end of the world. Tremors shook up geysers of dust like bomb explosions. Wells were muddied. Seas and inland streams were shipped to a steady boil.' The Cephalonian police transmitted the frantic radio message 'We are all sinking. Send the navy to take off the inhabitants. They are mad with fear. All is crumbling down.'[9]

Around 450 lives were lost and when the rescue ships arrived to help the survivors they were met by a surreal spectacle. Captain P. D. Gick of the destroyer *Daring*, the first British ship to reach the island, radioed that 'the tremors were shaking its hull like depth charges'. He described his experiences on the BBC Home Service while launching the Greek Earthquake Appeal four days after the disaster struck:

We anchored off the little town of Argostoli – there was not a building standing, and I could see thousands of people clustered in the open space by the jetty . . . I went ashore at once, and as my boat came alongside, none of them moved. They sat in little groups, with a few belongings salvaged from their homes. Then a few men came slowly towards me, they shook me by the hand and said nothing. The whole situation was quite uncanny, the people were alive but absolutely stunned. Gradually more people came forward and started to talk.

For three days the earthquake had gone on, destroying their homes, killing their relations and friends and even as I stood there you could feel the tremors still shaking the ground. They felt no need for food or water, or anything else – all they really wanted was to get to a piece of land that stayed still. I had to explain to them that I couldn't take them away. My first job was to care for the wounded and to land all the

FIGURE 1.6
Argostoli after the
earthquake
*Photographed looking west
from above the town bridge.
For a modern comparison see
Figures 15.2 and 15.5.*
[Image credits: Gerasimos
Galanos, reprinted in
Odusseia (2000) p. 39.
Reproduced here courtesy
of Evridiki Livada-Duca,
Argostoli.]

supplies that I had. They turned sadly aside, and walked back to their family groups and sat down to go on waiting as they had done for days.

During that morning sailors poured supplies ashore. They set up a hospital in tents and rescue squads went into the town and worked furiously to drag anyone they could find alive out of the wreckage of the buildings. All through the first day and those that followed more and more ships arrived, Greek ships laden with supplies, Israeli, American, Italian, French and New Zealand ships – all offering everything they had to help; it became perhaps one of the most wonderful combined operations in history.

The sailors and marines set up field kitchens to feed the townspeople, and on foot or in whatever transport they could find, battled and blasted their way along broken roads to bring help to isolated villagers.

There were and still are tens of thousands of people without homes of any kind and with all their possessions lost. They must have, and have as soon as possible, the tools and the materials with which to rebuild their houses, their farms, and their shops, and in doing so, their lives. And this help must come before the winter.

The Greek nation alone, recovering as they are from the devastation of the last war, can't hope to provide everything that is needed. And that's why the National Greek Earthquake Appeal has been started in this country, to get money with which to buy supplies which these people need so urgently. The Navies have done all they can. And now it's up to you, every one of you, to give all you can to the Greek Earthquake Appeal.

Most of you are sitting comfortably in your own homes, and soon you'll be going to bed – before you do, think of all the people in the Ionian Islands with no roof but the branches of an olive tree, and no bed but the hard earth – no light but the moon, or the stub of a candle left by a passing sailor – and please send every penny you can spare, and please send it now – they need it.[10]

Fifty years later the island still bears the scars. Because almost every building was destroyed, the houses are now mainly of modern construction, with the exception of the northern peninsula (Erissos) which was much less affected for reasons that we shall discuss later. Elsewhere a casual walk along a village path often leads the tourist past the abandoned shell of a pre-1953 building that was uneconomical to rebuild or remove.

Some important questions are raised by this terrible tragedy. Why did this earthquake happen? Has it happened before and, if so, how often? Do these earthquakes always raise the island? What are the main effects, apart from death and the destruction of buildings? Will a similar earthquake happen again and, if so, when? Apart from our natural sympathy for loss of life and livelihood, why should an earthquake in Cephalonia have any wider implications than an earthquake anywhere else in the world? Questions such as these are usually rhetorical: we ask them without expecting an immediate answer, or indeed any answer at all. But as it happens the answers to all of them are now known with some precision.[11]

The earthquake happened because Cephalonia is poised precariously at the edge of the continental plate where Europe collides with Africa. An earthquake of this magnitude has occurred in the Ionian Islands on average every fifty years since records began in 1444 and very probably for many centuries beforehand as well. The only earthquake that is known with certainty to have raised the land mass of Cephalonia itself is that of 1953 but there is evidence that several others before this also did so. One of the main effects of earthquakes in mountainous regions is to dislodge large quantities of rock and earth which fall down on to the land or sea below. Other effects can include tidal waves.

Statistically speaking the next major earthquake in Cephalonia is not due until about 2048, but there is a very wide degree of variation in these predictions.[12] For example, there was one major quake in 1766 and another in 1767, then a gap of 100 years until 1867, then a 86-year gap to 1953 and then a major offshore quake in 1983 which did much less damage to the island. But the underlying mechanism indicates that these earthquakes have taken place for many millennia and that they will continue into the indefinite future.

In later chapters we will be looking at the rationale behind these answers since there is indeed a special significance to earthquakes in Cephalonia. In terms of their impact upon Western civilisation they are perhaps the most important such tremors in the world, because it was the earthquakes of Cephalonia that destroyed the identity of Odysseus' island and buried the evidence there for nearly three thousand years.

Notes

1 Darwin (1839) ch. 14, diary entry dated 20 February 1835 at Valdivia, Chile.
2 Videotaped interview with Andreas Delaportas: 22 May 2003, Livadi, Cephalonia. The population statistics quoted are indicative but unverified.
3 Chadwick (1958) pp. 79–80; Robinson (2002a) pp. 11–12; Robinson (2002b) pp. 121–2; for further details see Chapter 24.
4 Papazachos et al. (2000). All times are in GMT and latitude/longitude coordinates are specified throughout in degrees and decimal degrees rather than in degrees and minutes. There are minor differences between the data values for earthquake time, location and magnitude cited in this catalogue compared with those provided by an eyewitness geologist: see Grandazzi (1954). These differences affect Grandazzi's estimates of energy content: I have relied on the Papazachos catalogue throughout and recalculated the energy comparisons accordingly.
5 From the discussion at http://www.seismo.unr.edu/ftp/pub/louie/class/100/magnitude.html we can derive the formula: $T = 10^{1.5M-3}$ where T = TNT equivalent (tons) and M = earthquake magnitude.
6 For nuclear test data see http://mt.sopris.net/mpc/military/mike.html
7 Savant (1953) pp. 127–8.
8 Grandazzi (1954) pp. 438, 440.
9 New York Herald Tribune 13 August 1953. Both this account and that of Savant above refer to tidal waves although this is contradicted by Grandazzi (1954) p. 440: for a possible reconciliation see Chapter 33 n. 16.
10 This appeal was broadcast by the BBC Home Service on 16 August 1953 from 9.15 to 9.20 p.m. I am grateful to Peter Hemming for permission to reproduce the text from his website at http://www.thegallerykefalonia.com
11 The answers to these questions are discussed in further detail in Chapter 11.
12 As I soon discovered: I wrote this chapter prior to the Lefkas earthquake of 14 August 2003 and that event is not included in the accompanying calculations. From CNN: 'Earthquake damage on the island of Lefkada, Greece: A powerful earthquake struck islands in western Greece on Thursday, sending panicked residents and tourists into the streets and causing some injuries and damage, officials said. The quake, with a preliminary magnitude of 6.4, occurred at 8:15 a.m. near the Ionian Sea island of Lefkada, about 175 miles northwest of Athens, said the Athens Geodynamic Institute. The U.S. Geological Survey put the magnitude at 6.1.' See www.cnn.com/2003/WORLD/ europe/08/14/greece.earthquake.ap/index.html and EERI (2003).

CHAPTER 2   **Conundrum**

*You will find the scene of the wanderings of Odysseus when you find the cobbler who
sewed up the bag of the winds.*   Eratosthenes, c. 285–194 BC

It is 20 August 1998 and I am standing on the top of a hillside on the mainland of Greece opposite Lefkas island with my daughter Nicola and eldest
son Simon, then aged thirteen and fifteen. It is nearing sunset and we have
scrambled up to see these deserted ruins. They are magnificent: huge walls
reminiscent of those at Mycenae, wonderful arches, the pattern of buried
rooms visible on the soil and terracing stretching across the mountainside. It
is the ancient acropolis of Palairos in Acarnania but sadly we were not the first
to find it: it has been documented since the 1860s.[1]

As the shadows lengthen over Palairos Bay to the south Nicola asks me the
question 'But why did they build it *here*?' She has a point: it is simply too
far distant from the sea to be at a useful location. I think I can answer this
because the previous week I had called on a local expert in Lefkas town, Babis
Katsibas, who had explained to me that in former years he thought that sea
levels in this part of Greece might have been higher. So the flat land that we
can see in the direction of the present bay might have been underwater when
this acropolis was built. If so then it would have been located in a much more
strategically valuable position.

Indeed it would not have taken much of a difference in historical sea levels
to turn the whole Plaghia promontory on which the acropolis stood into an
island, with the sea pushing through northwards from Palairos Bay to Lake
Voulkaria and then westwards out to the bay of Agios Nicolaos (Figure 2.2).[2]
This is thought-provoking because during our holiday we have been reading
The Ulysses Voyage, Tim Severin's delightful recreation of the voyage of Odysseus
home from Troy. Severin proposed the narrow channel between the sand-spit
north-east of Lefkas (also known as Lefkada) and the mainland of Plaghia
as his radical location for the man-eating monster Scylla and the ravenous
whirlpool Charybdis.

Circe, the witch who befriended Odysseus after turning his shipmates into
pigs and back again, had advised him that there were two routes home he could
choose, one which would bring him near the Clashing Rocks and another past
the monster and the whirlpool. We had been to see the cave that Severin had
identified as Scylla's lair but we had found it rather unconvincing. However,
if the whole promontory of Plaghia had once been an island, that might have

FIGURE 2.1
The acropolis of Palairos
(a) Polygonal walls
(b) Well-preserved archway
(c) View south to Palairos Bay
(d) Dry stone walls and foundations

provided an alternative course for Odysseus, one that could have involved caves and former whirlpools that are now on dry land.

We fail to solve this puzzle but it prompts some interesting questions. We drive back to our hotel in Vlicho Bay on the east coast of Lefkas island, still pondering on what we have seen. 'Isn't the *Odyssey* just a work of fiction?' says Simon, 'After all, if Homer can describe man-eating monsters and witches who turn shipmates into pigs, surely it's more likely that the places he describes are imaginary as well?' Perhaps he's right: during his travels Odysseus visits the Land of the Lotus-eaters and also the island of Aiolos that is said to be floating.

So is it all fantasy, an ancient *Lord of the Rings*, in which the people, the events, the objects and the places are unreal? Or is Odysseus more like a Bronze Age James Bond, someone who performs implausible acts that nevertheless take place in real locations? As far as I recall, Ian Fleming's attention to geographical detail was impeccable: indeed part of the enjoyment of the books stems from his juxtaposition of real locations with exaggerated accomplishments.

FIGURE 2.2
Hypothetical island of
Plaghia
*The ancient site of Palairos
stands on a hillside
overlooking Lake Voulkaria to
the north and the modern
town to the south. Colour
interpretation: as Figure 1.3.
Grid: 10 km.*
[Image credits: as
Figure 1.3.]

Although the notion of deploying 'an atomic warhead designed for use with
the Corporal Intermediate Range Guided Missile' in order to steal 'some fifteen
billion dollars' worth of standard mint bars one thousand fine' might sound a
little far-fetched, I wonder whether a historian from the year AD 5200 would
rely on that exaggeration in order to challenge the historical existence of a
place called Fort Knox in America?[3]

To the north of our hotel is the hamlet of Geni and early the next morning I jog past it to the end of the promontory opposite Nidri. A tranquil bay
with moorings, a footpath to a tiny chapel, no other tourists in sight: it is
a place of peace. A dolphin breaks the surface in the bay. I pass a grove of
trees surrounding a gravestone: 'Wilhelm Dörpfeld: 26.12.1853–25.4.1940'.
Dörpfeld! The archaeologist who painstakingly excavated Troy after Heinrich
Schliemann's mismanagement of the site and who then spent the rest of his
life looking for ancient Ithaca. But why is he buried here: Ithaca must be at
least 20 km to the south?

Both Schliemann and Dörpfeld looked for the ruins of ancient Ithaca on the
modern island of the same name.[4] Schliemann visited the island in 1868 but he
failed to unearth anything of significance. After the triumph of his discoveries
of the city and the 'Gold of Troy'[5] in the 1870s he returned to Ithaca to pursue
his quest in 1878, again with no result. He met Dörpfeld in 1881 at Olympia,

FIGURE 2.3
Dörpfeld's grave on Lefkas
*Beyond the promontory
towards the south-west lie
Vlicho Bay and the town
of Nidri.*

close by on the mainland, and their collaboration at Troy began. Schliemann remained obsessed with the quest for Odysseus' city and palace on Ithaca but he died of an ear infection in Naples in 1890, leaving Dörpfeld to keep the exploratory torch alight. Dörpfeld established that there were nine separate layers at Troy and he disagreed with Schliemann's identification of Troy level II as the city described by Homer in the *Iliad*. He identified it instead as Troy level VIIa, a city that he believed showed evidence of a violent invasion around 1200 BC.

In 1897 Dörpfeld visited the modern island of Ithaca for the first time. He too failed to locate any remains of the ancient city and the following year he delivered a lecture about his experiences in Athens. This was read in the Hague by a Homeric enthusiast, A. E. H. Goekoop, who travelled to Athens and offered financial support to Dörpfeld. They returned to Ithaca and started to dig seriously in the north of the island near to a harbour called Polis Bay. They found some walls dating from the sixth century BC but nothing of the Odyssean era which is felt to be some six or seven hundred years earlier.

On 18 March 1900 Dörpfeld was feeling despondent. He had spent three years searching for ancient Ithaca with no result. He looked again at the map of the Ionian Islands and re-read certain sections of the *Odyssey* and he suddenly announced that he had been looking in the wrong place. He was now sure that Homer's descriptions would fit the island of Lefkas much better than that of modern Ithaca. On 1 March the following year he travelled to Lefkas with his team and they started to dig around Vlicho, very near to the hotel at which we are staying (Figure 9.2). They found nothing. Dörpfeld was undeterred. He continued digging there in 1905 but he was also busy at Troy and on Corfu. He returned to Lefkas from time to time and at last he made some significant discoveries, including Mycenaean earthenware, graves and an aqueduct. But still there was no ancient city of Ithaca, no palace of Odysseus.

By 1913 Dörpfeld was living on the Vlicho peninsula and excavating in the area but the following year his work was stopped by the war. In 1921 he returned to Lefkas and continued digging. Although he found impressive artefacts from other periods, there was no significant Late Bronze Age material. In 1927 he published a book announcing that Lefkas was definitely ancient Ithaca[6] but the experts remained unconvinced. By the outbreak of the Second World War Dörpfeld was eighty-five years old, almost blind, the great explorer now living alone on Lefkas. He had achieved international recognition for his work at Troy but ancient Ithaca still eluded him. He died in 1940 and was buried in this beautiful grove of trees on his beloved promontory at Vlicho Bay.

I start jogging back to the hotel. The sun is getting stronger by the minute and soon it will be too hot to run, but I am treading a path that this old man must have trodden hundreds of times, always hoping that this would be the day of the great discovery for which he had yearned all his life. Sir Arthur Evans had achieved global recognition by excavating Knossos on Crete, while Troy unquestionably belonged to Schliemann. Although Dörpfeld's work at Troy was in many ways more valuable than Schliemann's, there is no epitaph to mark it: Dörpfeld's gravestone shows only his dates.

The search for Troy and Ithaca goes back far beyond Schliemann and Dörpfeld. The ancient Greeks themselves had no clear idea where these places might be found. Furthermore, they had no certain knowledge of where and when Homer lived or how much historical reality the *Iliad* and the *Odyssey* reflect. The Homeric poems are a three thousand-year-old enigma that has exerted a magnetic attraction on readers and scholars down the ages.

This enigma is one of tantalising complexity. Imagine a wall that has been covered up by many layers of paint. As one layer is stripped off there is a moment of excitement at the possibility of seeing the original wall itself, but usually this is dashed by the realisation that the next layer is simply another, older layer of paint. For example, the very first page of the *Odyssey* contains a reference to Troy. For years Troy was thought to be a fictitious city until, as we have seen, during the 1870s Schliemann unearthed in the Dardanelles of north-western Turkey a site that resembled Homer's descriptions. Recent geological and archaeological findings[7] appear to support the detailed account of Troy in the *Iliad*, so perhaps Homer was reflecting actual history after all. Indeed the evidence in favour of this location as Homer's Troy has been further reinforced by the publication in 2004 of the English translation of Joachim Latacz' s *Troy and Homer*, which documents the latest excavations.[8] However, these opening lines of the *Odyssey* describing an apparently real town of Troy are then followed by references to Zeus, Poseidon and Circe, two gods and a witch, which brings the reader back to the world of fiction again. That view is sustained for a few more lines until geographical reality intervenes once more in the shape of a reference to Ethiopia.

Turn a few more pages and another deity, Athene, disguises herself as a male mortal called Mentes and visits Odysseus' son Telemachos in his palace on Ithaca. Mentes explains that 'My ship stands here in the country far from town, / In Rheithron bay, below wooded Neïon.' This all sounds plausible again: indeed we are positively itching to consult the map of Ithaca to find the locations of Rheithron and Neïon. The only problem now is that Homer has already implied that Athene is making the whole story up. She is, after all, a goddess: she doesn't need a ship because she can fly straight down from Mount Olympos. She simply needs a cover story to ensure that Mentes sounds credible to Telemachos. Furthermore sophisticated readers such as ourselves know that Athene herself doesn't exist. If there is no Athene, does that also mean that there was no ship, no Rheithron, no Neïon: are we thrown back to viewing the *Odyssey* as a work of fiction again?

But if we listen carefully we can hear Homer whispering gleefully in our ear: 'Not so fast' he murmurs. 'Don't you see that my story is intended to be recited to an audience that already knows where the real Rheithron and Neïon are? They will surely take great delight at my rather sophisticated notion of an imaginary goddess referring to a real location in support of her imaginary excuse to a real prince.' There are echoes here of Shakespeare and Stoppard and it takes a certain effort of concentration to recall that the origin of the story dates from *c.* 1200 BC: the echo is travelling the other way. Within the first few lines of the poem we are forced into the realisation that we are faced with a prehistoric poet of great subtlety and that we cannot expect to interpret the *Odyssey* nor hope to identify its place names without incorporating the performance itself into the framework of our understanding.

These layers of paint make hazardous even the most innocuous of questions. 'When did Odysseus live?' sounds like a reasonable beginning, so let us examine the first coat of paint. As Schliemann and Dörpfeld demonstrated, there is disagreement about the exact date of the Trojan War. The nine successive layers of building at Troy stretch from 2920 BC to 85 BC; the one normally associated with the Trojan War, Troy VII, is dated from 1250 to 1020 BC. Eratosthenes said that this war took place from 1193 to 1184 BC but how wrong might he be?

The alternative estimates arrive in two flavours: conventional and radical. Conventional estimates range anywhere from 1346 to 1127 BC, whereas a recent and more radical view proposes that our entire Mediterranean Dark Age calendar may be up to 250 years too old because of an early error in dating Egyptian dynasties.[9] So '1193–1184 BC' is really just a signpost for the cognoscenti, meaning 'We don't actually know where, whether or when the Trojan War happened, but let's assume for now that it happened where Schliemann found a city, and that it occurred because Homer said it did and let's also assume that it took place when Eratosthenes said it did, because we want to move on to discussing something more interesting about it.'

Any reply to the question 'When did Odysseus live?' therefore contains as its layers of paint assumptions such as (a) the Trojan War actually took place, (b) it was fought over the city that Schliemann identified, (c) it may have been waged from 1193 to 1184 BC but (d) it could instead have been conducted 100 years or more on either side, and also (e) Odysseus was a real person. Now that we are in agreement about the fragility of the underlying structure we are at liberty to paint on top of this edifice an answer to the question of Odysseus' own dates. He was a key figure in the Trojan War so he would probably have been at least twenty years old when it started in 1193. He would therefore have been about thirty when the Trojan War ended.[10] His voyage home took ten years, so he was about forty by the time he returned to Ithaca at the end of the *Odyssey*, perhaps around 1174 BC. We can only guess how long he might have lived afterwards – to die at fifty would be very old by the standards of the time, so perhaps Odysseus' dates are around 1215 BC–1165 BC. Since we can't be at all precise about this, for convenience we will round it to the nearest century and refer to 1200 BC as the nominal date of Odysseus and the *Odyssey*, which makes them about 3,200 years old.

Dates such as this are so far removed from our everyday experiences that they cannot intuitively be related to other prehistory unless one is an expert. As a layman I have found Figure 2.4 useful in providing a perspective on the periods involved. These dates themselves are estimates and, as ever, many of them are also contested.

Conspicuous by its absence from this table is an entry for Homer himself. Why is this? If we can have an entry for Pythagoras and for Aristotle, why not for Homer? We have heard that the Greeks had no certain knowledge of when Homer lived, but our own uncertainty today is yet deeper: we do not even know whether Homer was a single person. What we do know is that whoever he (or they) might have been, the genesis of the *Iliad* and the *Odyssey* took place in a world in which written language as we know it did not yet exist. If you find this notion as intriguing as I do then you should digest James Diggle's Introductory Note at Appendix 1, where you will find a thoughtful discussion of the conundrum.

2800 BC	Stonehenge Phase 1
2100	Bronze Age begins in northern Europe. World population 25 m: Europe 5 m, Americas 2 m
2100	Judaism: naming of God (Yahweh); Abraham moves from Ur to Canaan
1700	Middle Minoan period: height of influence of Crete
1628	Eruption of Thera (Santorini) possibly destroys Minoan civilisation on Crete
1500	Foundation of Hinduism
1450	Book of Exodus: Moses leads the Israelites from Egypt across the Red Sea
1400	Height of influence of Mycenaean civilisation
1360	Tutankhamen becomes King of Egypt
1250–1150	Events of the *Iliad* and the *Odyssey*?
1050	Kingdom of Israel is established; Saul is Israel's first king
1040	Ionian Migration
950	Middle Dark Age – not much is known
776	Coroibos of Elis is first champion at Olympia
6th century	Pythagoras
5th century	Aeschylus, Sophocles, Herodotus, Euripides, Socrates, Thucydides
4th century	Plato, Aristotle, Alexander the Great
c. 0	Jesus Christ
63 BC – AD 24	Strabo

FIGURE 2.4
A Homeric chronology

So if Homer himself is a mysterious figure, then is the *Odyssey* itself true, or was Eratosthenes correct when he said that finding the scenes of Odysseus' voyage is about as likely as finding the cobbler who sewed up the bag of winds?[11] There is clearly considerable disagreement on this subject. On balance the Trojan War itself is generally believed to have taken place: as we have seen, an analysis of Troy VII reveals signs of a conflict and Homer's descriptions of Troy and its surrounding geography appear to be surprisingly accurate. However the wanderings of Odysseus thereafter and incidents such as his battle with Polyphemos the Cyclops exhibit considerable poetical imagination.

Although some of the events that are described in these extraordinary poems are clearly works of exaggeration or fantasy, the locations specified on Ithaca itself are in my view invariably real ones. I believe that this is because Homer wanted his Ithacan listeners to identify with these stories by basing them on actual locations that were personally known to them. By using real locations he achieved a much greater degree of empathy from this audience than if he had invented a wholly imaginary geography. This controversial view presupposes detailed familiarity with Ithacan topography, both by the original composer of the *Odyssey* and also his initial audience. My ambition is to put you on an almost equal footing with them in this regard by the time you have finished reading this book.

Several writers and explorers have attempted to trace Odysseus' actual voyage in considerable detail. In 1858 William Gladstone published a remarkable three-volume work entitled *Studies on Homer and the Homeric Age* and in 1869 he expanded on this research in *Juventus Mundi*. The first publication includes a splendid map representing his perception of Homer's geographical world-view and the second contains some careful navigational calculations:

In a floating or drift passage on the waves, we can trace Homer's idea of what was possible by the supposed transit of Odysseus from a point near Crete to the Thesprotoi [north-western Greece]. It appears to be about half the rate of a ship's motion, or two miles an hour.[12]

One cannot help but be impressed by Gladstone's energies since in 1868 he had become Britain's Prime Minister. Later explorers have followed Odysseus' marine footsteps quite literally. Ernle Bradford spent much of the decade from 1950 to 1960 sailing the Mediterranean, trying to identify locations such as the Land of the Lotus-eaters and the island of Circe, and his 1963 book *Ulysses Found* describes his adventures. The intrepid explorer Tim Severin painstakingly reconstructed a Bronze Age galley which he called the *Argo* and in 1984 he set sail in it, following the route of Jason and the Argonauts in the Black Sea on their quest for the Golden Fleece. The next year he embarked from Troy in an attempt to recreate Odysseus' voyage home to Ithaca.

These and other pioneers have been radical on matters such as the location of Polyphemos' cave and the straits of Scylla and Charybdis, displacing the accumulated wisdom of the millennia in favour of the flicker of a compass needle on an Ionian tack. Their thesis has been that since Homer's account of the voyage involves several real place names, it would be interesting to test the proposition that this was indeed a feasible journey. But when these nautical iconoclasts consider Ithaca itself they have felt obliged to defer to the status quo, following the authorities in identifying the traditional scenes of action and remaining silent on the matter of those revolutionary alternatives that they have elsewhere constructively embraced since they set sail from Troy.

So this present work focuses primarily on the identification of ancient Ithaca and the places that Homer describes upon it. This approach also enables us to avoid the long-established objection that since many of the other locations that Odysseus visits are regarded as being in 'Fantasyland' as opposed to the real world, there is no point in trying to identify them.[13] Where the position of an off-island location is important for identifying an Ithacan puzzle (for example to determine the names of neighbouring islands or the particular Ithacan harbour towards which a ship from such an island might be approaching) then we will of necessity attempt to locate it, but otherwise these mysteries further afield will be left for the consideration of a possible future volume. There are over twenty uncharted place names for us to resolve in or near ancient Ithaca alone and they will keep us quite busy enough.

Notes

1 See www.paleros.net/history.htm

2 Further research on sea level movements in this area is required for this hypothesis to be tested: for more details see Chapter 7 n. 6 and Chapter 34 n. 1. However, a recent research paper suggests that on a number of occasions since 5886 BC the sea has penetrated at least 800 m north of the present southern shoreline in the direction of ancient Palairos. See Vött et al. (2003) p. 124.

3 Fleming (1959) pp. 229, 224.

4 Some of the biographical information in this section is based on the account provided in Goekoop (1990) ch. 2. In English his name can be pronounced 'Hookop'.

5 Antonova et al. (1996).

6 Dörpfeld (1927).

7 Kraft et al. (2003).

8 Latacz (2004).

9 See the discussion in Chapter 24 and also in James (1991).

10 *Iliad* 23.787–92 (Antilochos) 'You know as well as I, my friends, the gods / Still favour older men. For Ajax is / Not much my senior, but *he* [Odysseus] comes from / An altogether earlier generation. / He wears well. None of us except Achilles / Would find it easy to keep pace with him.'

11 Strabo 1.2.15.

12 Gladstone (1869) p. 478.

13 See the notes on Partsch, Hercher and Wolf in Appendix 4. An impeccable example of Fantasyland logic is contained in Heubeck and Hoekstra (1989) p. 44, commenting on *Odyssey* 10.1–4: 'As a floating island [Aiolia] has no fixed location, so there is little point to the attempts, from classical times onwards, to place it on the map.'

CHAPTER 3   **Odyssey**

*At the sources of Western civilisation, themselves its main source, stand two poems on
the grand scale which for sustained beauty and splendour have found no superior,
perhaps no equal, in all the poetry that has followed them. This is the most
remarkable fact in the history of literature.*   J. A. K. Thomson (1963)[1]

The *Odyssey* starts at the end of the Trojan War so it is worth remembering why
this war was fought. We can think of its causes as both commercial and mythological. Commercially Troy stands at the entrance to the channel that links the
Mediterranean Sea with the Black Sea and it is clear that there was significant marine trade via this route in the Bronze Age.[2] Positioned strategically
on this coastline, which has receded several miles since that time,[3] Troy could
command and control all shipping in transit. But this aspect is not discussed
in the *Iliad*: instead the causes of the war originate from a quarrel among the
gods. The story starts some years before the *Iliad* and our information about
these earlier events has come down to us from the work of later poets and
mythographers. In the following account I have highlighted in the text certain descriptions which provide us with geographical clues about Ithaca and
its immediate neighbourhood.[4]

   Much of Greek mythology involves the sexual antics of the gods and the
origin of the Trojan War is no exception. Zeus is characteristically lusting after a
beautiful sea nymph called Thetis, but when the Fates advise him that her son
(the future Achilles) will outshine his father he has second thoughts and offers
her instead to one of her most ardent admirers, Peleus, the King of Phthia.
Thetis is somewhat put out by the prospect of marrying a mere mortal – indeed
for good measure she has also been dating Zeus' brother Poseidon – but by
way of consolation Zeus promises her that all of the royal household of Mount
Olympos will attend her wedding. The marriage feast duly takes place but (in
a scene eerily anticipatory of the pantomime tradition of the Sleeping Beauty)
Eris, the goddess of discord, appears as an uninvited and thereby infuriated
guest. She throws on to the table a golden apple on which are inscribed the
words 'To the fairest' and this prompts a beauty contest at which the finalists
are the three goddesses Hera, Athene and Aphrodite. Hera bases her claim to
the apple on her status as queen of the gods, Athene argues for the award based
on her wisdom, while Aphrodite reminds her fellow contestants that she is
herself the goddess of beauty and therefore the obvious winner. The deadlock

FIGURE 3.1
The location of Troy
Colour interpretation:
mountainous areas → green
ridges; snow cover → white
flecks; lower-lying areas →
sand coloured; water →
dark blue.
[Image credits: NASA
Learning Technologies'
World Wind planetary
visualisation tool and the
global Landsat-7 server
(with special thanks to
Patrick Hogan for priority
access). Websites:
http://onearth.jpl.nasa.gov/,
http://learn.arc.nasa.gov/
worldwind/]

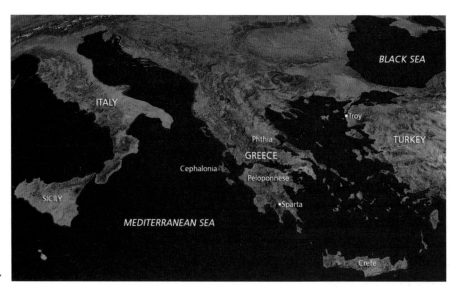

is resolved by Zeus announcing that Paris, the son of Priam and Hecuba of Troy, will be the judge.

The conspiratorial goddesses waylay him on a mountaintop and their bribery for the Judgement of Paris begins. Athene promises him victory in battle, Hera offers him political power but Aphrodite says that she will procure for him a mortal woman as beautiful as herself. This is a prospect that no red-blooded Trojan prince can resist and so Paris awards Aphrodite the prize, thereby earning a lifetime's legacy of resentment from Hera and Athene. The Bronze Age Miss World that year is called Helen and she lives in Sparta, located then as now on the south-east of the Peloponnese (the southern land mass of Greece). Inconveniently for Paris she has recently married King Menelaos but this fails to deter him and he sets sail for her city. The circumstances of Helen's marriage are crucial to the story: she was understandably well regarded by multiple suitors (including Odysseus) and in order to avoid bloodshed among them her stepfather Tyndareos made them all promise not only to respect her choice of husband but also to help him to recover her if she was ever kidnapped.

Menelaos and Helen receive Paris with considerable hospitality and Helen takes her duties particularly seriously when her husband, who is leaving Sparta for a few days to attend a funeral in Crete, rather naïvely suggests that she should continue to entertain Paris. The couple take advantage of the king's absence to elope to Troy and on his return Menelaos discovers that they have also carried off some of the family heirlooms. He is not best pleased: he contacts his brother Agamemnon who lives further north at Mycenae and together they invoke her suitors' promise that they would all help Menelaos to bring her back.

One of the chieftains they call on to enlist is Odysseus, who has married Helen's cousin Penelope and now has an infant son called Telemachos. We hear in the *Iliad* that Odysseus led the gallant Cephallenians from Ithaca and leaf-quivering Neriton, from Crocyleia and rugged Aigilips, men hailing from Zacynthos and from Samos.[5] The suitors are somewhat reluctant to go to war and Odysseus even feigns insanity for a while,[6] but eventually the Greek fleet assembles at Aulis (opposite today's Halkida to the north-west of Athens) and waits for a favourable wind. However the weather forecast is hopeless and Agamemnon is advised to sacrifice his daughter Iphigeneia in order to appease the gods. He does so (or according to some writers, a doe is substituted at the last moment) and a westerly wind obediently arises to blow the Greek navy across to Troy.

The principal Trojan protagonists are King Priam with his many sons, of whom the pre-eminent princes are Paris and Hector. The Achaian (Greek) antagonists include the royal brothers Agamemnon and Menelaos, the warriors Achilles and Ajax, King Nestor of Pylos, Odysseus and many others. Indeed this war is no mere local skirmish: we hear that there are 50,000 men on the Trojan side alone.[7] The first nine years of inconclusive fighting are described by later writers but in the tenth year the main events of the *Iliad* at last begin. The Achaian army captures two beautiful maidens from a neighbouring ally of Troy: Agamemnon takes Chryseis and Achilles claims Briseis. Chryseis' father Chryses is however a priest of Apollo and when Agamemnon ignores his plea to return his daughter, the god punishes the Achaians with a plague. Eventually Agamemnon agrees to give up Chryseis but he then demands Briseis from Achilles instead.

Achilles has by now fallen for Briseis in a big way: he feels he has no alternative other than to give her up to Agamemnon but he is outraged by the king's demand and thereafter refuses to fight for the Achaians – he even prays for a Trojan victory. The tide of battle turns and the Trojans advance beyond the massive trench and wall that the Achaians have built to shield their landed ships. As the first ship is torched the prospects for the Achaians look grim because clearly without a navy they will be unable to return home. Achilles still refuses to join the battle but he lets his friend Patroclos take his place, wearing his armour. Patroclos is promptly killed by Hector and when Achilles discovers this he ends his feud with Agamemnon and rejoins the field of combat in grief-stricken wrath.

Achilles meets Hector outside the Trojan walls and after a furious battle he kills him. He ties Hector's body to his chariot and returns with it to the ranks of the Achaians. Athletic games are then held as part of the rites for Patroclos and on each of the next nine days Achilles drags Hector's body around the funeral bier. Eventually King Priam persuades Achilles to return his son's body and both sides agree to a cease-fire so that Hector's funeral can take place.

Hector's death marks the end of the *Iliad* but still the Greeks have not broken down the walls of Troy. Eventually Odysseus devises the famous plan that is described subsequently in the *Odyssey*: he orders a large hollow wooden horse to be built by the craftsman Epeios.[8] Once it is ready a number of the Greek warriors along with Odysseus climb inside it. The rest of the Greek fleet pretend to sail away but instead they hide behind the nearby island of Tenedos.

The Trojans celebrate what they think is their victory and drag the wooden horse into Troy. That night after most of Troy is asleep or drunk the Greek warriors emerge from the horse and start to slaughter the Trojans, while the Greek fleet sails back into the bay and its soldiers invade the city through its opened gates. Priam is killed beside Zeus' altar and his daughter Cassandra is pulled from the statue of Athene and later carried off to Greece by Agamemnon to be his concubine. In a moment of inconceivable cruelty Hector's little son Astyanax is thrown from the battlements of Troy to prevent any possibility of the dynasty continuing and the city is razed to the ground.

The Trojan War is now over and the victorious Greeks prepare to return to their homeland, so this is the logical starting point for the events of the *Odyssey*. But with his legendary sophistication, Homer begins the poem with the opposite of a flash-back – the first recorded instance of a flash-forward. Instead of starting the *Odyssey* at the beginning of Odysseus' voyage back from Troy and making the story a sequential account of the journey home, the poet plunges into the middle of things (or as the Romans liked to say, *in medias res*). This makes the poem much more interesting to read but also much more difficult to explain, because the various locations are not encountered in the order in which you would expect to find them. The result is a rich and multifaceted combination of plot and place: today we might say that these exist in two separate dimensions and so in Figure 3.2 I have tried to portray them on a spreadsheet.

The narrative of the *Odyssey* is depicted down the rows of Figure 3.2 while the locations that are visited are described in the columns. The shaded area represents locations on Ithaca itself while the unshaded region represents places elsewhere. Odysseus' movements are indicated in purple while those of Telemachos are in blue. Using the diagram as a guide let us unravel the plot and the places of the *Odyssey*.

The poem opens with the gods discussing the plight of Odysseus, held prisoner on the island of Ogygia by the nymph Calypso who has fallen in love with him. We hear that one of these gods is Poseidon who is most irate with Odysseus because earlier in his travels our hero has blinded Poseidon's son,

LOCATION

Odysseus   Telemachos

Location columns (left to right): Troy · Ismaros (Cicones) · Cape Malea & Cythera · Lotus-eaters · Cyclops · Laistrygonians · Aiolia · Aiaia (Circe) · Acheron-Hades · Scylla & Charybdis · Sirens · Thrinacia · Ogygia (Calypso) · Scherie (Phaiacians) · Ithaca coastline · Phorcys Bay · Eumaios pigfarm · Odysseus' platform · Ithaca palace · Ithaca fountain · Telemachos palace · Ithaca meeting place · Laertes farm · Ithaca cove · Ithaca harbour · Pylos · Sparta

ON ITHACA

Book	Line	NARRATIVE	Location
1	11	Odysseus is a prisoner of Calypso on Ogygia	Ogygia (Calypso)
1	96	Telemachos is visited by Athene in Ithaca	Telemachos palace
2	1	Telemachos addresses the Ithacans	Ithaca meeting place
2	413	Telemachos sets sail for Pylos to visit Nestor	Ithaca harbour
3	1	Telemachos arrives at Pylos	Pylos
3	477	Telemachos departs for Sparta to visit Menelaos	Pylos
4	1	Telemachos arrives at Sparta by chariot	Sparta
5	228	Odysseus embarks from Ogygia in a raft	Ogygia (Calypso)
5	451	Odysseus is washed up on the Phaiacians' Scherie	Scherie (Phaiacians)
6	127	Odysseus meets Nausicaa, Alcinoos' daughter	Scherie (Phaiacians)
7	81	Odysseus arrives at Alcinoos' palace	Scherie (Phaiacians)
8	487	Odysseus' Trojan Horse saga is sung by Demodocos	Scherie (Phaiacians)
9	37	*Odysseus recounts his journey from Troy:*	Troy
9	39	*He sacks the Cicones' city of Ismaros*	Ismaros (Cicones)
9	80	*He passes Cape Malea and the island of Cythera*	Cape Malea & Cythera
9	82	*He arrives at the land of the Lotus-eaters*	Lotus-eaters
9	105	*He sails to the land of the Cyclops*	Cyclops
10	1	*He reaches Aiolos' island of Aiolia*	Aiolia
10	28	*He sights Ithaca but his crew open the bag of winds*	Ithaca coastline
10	54	*They are blown back to Aiolia*	Aiolia
10	81	*He reaches Lamos, Telepylos of the Laistrygonians*	Laistrygonians
10	135	*He sails to Circe's island of Aiaia*	Aiaia (Circe)
11	1	*He sails to the mouth of the Acheron to enter Hades*	Acheron-Hades
12	1	*He returns to Circe's island of Aiaia*	Aiaia (Circe)
12	166	*He passes the island of the Sirens lashed to the mast*	Sirens
12	234	*He escapes monstress Scylla and whirlpool Charybdis*	Scylla & Charybdis
12	260	*On Thrinacia his men kill Helios Hyperion's cattle*	Thrinacia
12	426	*He is shipwrecked back to Scylla and Charybdis*	Scylla & Charybdis
12	447	*He floats on mast and keel to Ogygia*	Ogygia (Calypso)
13	93	Odysseus is brought to Ithaca by the Phaiacians	Ithaca coastline
13	221	Odysseus is advised by Athene at Phorcys Bay	Phorcys Bay
14	1	Odysseus in disguise meets Eumaios at the pigfarm	Eumaios pigfarm
15	193	Telemachos departs from Sparta for Pylos	Sparta
15	282	Telemachos sets sail for Ithaca, avoiding an ambush	Pylos
15	495	Telemachos arrives at a cove on the coast of Ithaca	Ithaca cove
16	11	Eumaios recognises Telemachos at the pigfarm	Eumaios pigfarm
16	154	Eumaios is sent by Telemachos to the palace	Eumaios pigfarm
16	186	Odysseus reveals his identity to Telemachos	Eumaios pigfarm
17	26	Telemachos walks to the palace	Ithaca palace
17	204	Odysseus and Eumaios walk down to the fountain	Ithaca fountain
17	336	Odysseus follows Eumaios into the palace	Ithaca palace
18	1	Odysseus beats Iros the beggar in a fight	Ithaca palace
19	103	Odysseus still in disguise is addressed by Penelope	Ithaca palace
20	197	Philoitios the cowherd addresses Odysseus	Ithaca palace
21	118	Telemachos arranges the axes for the contest	Ithaca palace
21	221	Odysseus reveals his identity to Eumaios and Philoitios	Ithaca palace
21	404	Odysseus shoots his arrow through the row of axes	Ithaca palace
22	1	Odysseus kills Antinoos and the massacre begins	Ithaca palace
23	231	Odysseus is reunited with Penelope	Ithaca palace
24	205	Odysseus and Telemachos go down to Laertes' farm	Laertes farm
24	492	Odysseus sees the suitors' relatives approaching	Laertes farm
24	520	Laertes kills Eupeithes, Antinoos' father	Laertes farm
24	541	Odysseus obeys Athene's command for a cease-fire	Laertes farm

FIGURE 3.2 Narrative vs. location in the *Odyssey*

the Cyclops called Polyphemos. Poseidon is the god of the sea and also the god of earthquakes: he reappears throughout the *Odyssey*, continually thwarting Odysseus' attempts to return to Ithaca. Indeed at one level the entire poem can be described as a story about the challenges that beset a mortal who is prevented from returning home because he has offended a god.

This is a most sophisticated opening observation of Homer because he knows that we haven't yet listened to the story of Polyphemos and we won't do so until way down the diagram, at Book 9 line 105. Although this occurs later in the narrative of the *Odyssey* (down the rows) it nevertheless takes place earlier in the journey of Odysseus (along the columns), so this remarkably inventive technique enables the poet to make this reference at the outset. In any case, other gods rally to Odysseus' support and decide that something must be done.

As we have seen, the Trojan War lasted for ten years, but another ten years have now gone by and Odysseus is still absent from his kingdom in Ithaca, which lies low and to the west, the furthest out to sea of a group of neighbouring islands called Ithaca, Same, Doulichion and Zacynthos.[9] Meanwhile his wife Penelope is much in demand from 108 suitors at Odysseus' Palace since whoever marries her will become the new king. Penelope's suitors are not to be confused with those of Helen but apparently these two cousins share the ability to turn Bronze Age manhood weak at the knees. In case you regard this as a somewhat flippant description I should explain at this point that the expression 'weak at the knees' constitutes just another part of our enormous literary debt to Homer: a memorable instance occurs towards the end of the *Odyssey* when Penelope and Odysseus are at last brought together:

> Upon these words her knees and heart went weak –
> She recognised the signs he had disclosed.   23.205–6

Athene decides to help Odysseus and so disguised as a family friend she visits Telemachos at the palace. She pretends to the prince that she has landed on Ithaca at farmlands far from town at Rheithron Bay under Mount Neïon. Her advice is that he should address the Ithacans and warn them that the wining and dining of the suitors at the palace cannot continue for much longer. The suitors are unimpressed by this youthful ultimatum and one of them, Antinoos, devises a plot to assassinate him. Athene also tells Telemachos to search for news of his father from King Nestor in Pylos and King Menelaos in Sparta, who is by now reunited with the errant Helen.

Telemachos embarks for Pylos and Athene sends him a stiff following wind from the west as he leaves Ithaca harbour. When he meets King Nestor he says that he has come from Ithaca that is below Neïon. Nestor lavishes hospitality upon him but sadly he has no news of Odysseus, so Telemachos drives on to Sparta and seeks advice from Menelaos. The king is also delighted to see him and equally hospitable but unfortunately he has no idea where his father is either. Meanwhile back at the palace, Antinoos and the other suitors prepare to kill Telemachos via a marine ambush on his return. They leave Ithaca harbour to sail the straits to the island of Asteris, which is between Ithaca and Samos' rugged cliffs – not large, but it has two harbours where ships can hide and windy heights where lookouts can keep watch.

Back on Ogygia Calypso has at last been persuaded by the gods to allow Odysseus to build a raft and set sail for his homeland. He follows her very specific astronomical advice but at Poseidon's intervention he is shipwrecked off the island of Scherie where the Phaiacians live and eventually washed ashore. King Alcinoos' beautiful daughter Nausicaa is doing the laundry by the seaside when Odysseus crawls stark naked out of the bushes but he manages to calm her concerns while simultaneously arousing her admiration and she leads him off to her father's palace. Nausicaa is a remarkably modern girl: Odysseus tactfully sidelines her hints regarding marriage and remains incognito while endearing himself to her parents and availing himself of their hospitality. Somewhat ironically he finds himself listening to one of the bards of the court singing about the Trojan War and his own role within it. After various athletic contests and more singing and eating he discloses his identity to a rapt audience.

At this point Odysseus recounts the wonderful fables that have caused the *Odyssey* to dwell in our memory down the ages: because they are very well known I shall describe them rather briefly. After he and his crew leave Troy they battle with the Cicones at Ismaros and then they are driven by the winds past Cape Malea and the island of Cythera off to the Land of the Lotus-eaters. Then he visits the land of the Cyclops and is imprisoned and nearly eaten by Polyphemos: he escapes underneath a ram by pretending that his name is 'Nobody'. His next stop is a visit to King Aiolos who gives him a bag of winds. He reaches the coast of his homeland Ithaca only to be swept back to Aiolos because his crewmen open the bag.

After that he narrowly escapes from the Laistrygonian cannibals and has a year-long love affair with the witch-goddess Circe, who has metamorphosed his crewmen into pigs. He sails away from her island Aiaia for a short visit to Hades and then he returns to Circe for a briefing. Following this he is tempted by the deadly Sirens, fights with the sea monster Scylla and escapes from the whirlpool Charybdis, only to find that his crewmen's folly in eating the sacred cattle of Helios on Thrinacia is the cause of a subsequent shipwreck. Washed back to Scylla and Charybdis, he manages to catch hold of the ship's floating mast and is swept away to Calypso's island of Ogygia, which is where the story began.

King Alcinoos is delighted to hear the news of Odysseus' travels and rewards him with treasure. The Phaiacians then embark in a ship to return Odysseus to Ithaca, where they land at Phorcys Bay which has two distinctive jutting headlands overlooked by Mount Neriton. Athene helps Odysseus to bury his treasure in a cave with two entrances near a sacred olive tree at the harbour's head. She then disguises him as a beggar and tells him to seek out his faithful swineherd Eumaios at his Pigfarm, located near Arethousa Spring and Raven's Rock.

Telemachos then returns from Pylos and Sparta and follows Athene's advice to outwit the suitors' ambush by avoiding Asteris completely. Instead he lands near the pigfarm at a bay on the coast of Ithaca, sending on his ship and crewmen to row to Ithaca city harbour.

At the pigfarm Odysseus and Telemachos devise a plan to massacre the suitors and regain control of Ithaca. Eumaios goes down to the palace to tell Penelope secretly that Telemachos has returned. On his way back he passes Hermes' Hill and sees that the suitors in the harbour have returned from their unsuccessful ambush. Eumaios then leads Odysseus, still disguised as a beggar, down from the pigfarm past the distinctive city fountain and he arrives at the palace. The suitors insult him but he gradually increases his authority within the palace while remaining a stranger. Penelope then organises an archery contest and promises to marry any man who can fire an arrow through a line of twelve axes using Odysseus' bow. Needless to say, just as with Cinderella's slipper, none of the suitors can even string the bow but when Odysseus picks it up he deftly fires an arrow through all of the axes.

Odysseus and Telemachos assisted by Eumaios and another faithful servant then kill all the suitors and hang the loose-living maids who have succumbed to their roguish charms. At this point Odysseus announces his identity and effects a romantic reunion with the pensive Penelope. He then goes to visit his elderly father, Laertes, at his remote farmstead with extensive orchards and sloping vineyards. Initially in disguise, he pretends to Laertes that he has landed on Ithaca at farmlands far from town. Laertes reminisces about the time when he was king of the Cephallenians and sacked the city of Nericon, a sturdy fortress out on a headland. The relatives of the dead suitors arrive at the farm intent on reprisals but Laertes kills Antinoos' father and he and Odysseus are just about to continue the bloodshed when there is divine intervention once again.

Zeus despatches Athene to restore peace which she achieves by delivering a memorable and beautiful closing speech. As an injunction against further slaughter she hands down her pacts of peace between both sides for all eternity and with those lines the *Odyssey* concludes.

Homer does not tell us how Odysseus, Penelope and Telemachos spend the rest of their lives. However earlier in the *Odyssey* the blind prophet Teiresias makes an interesting prediction. He says that after killing the suitors Odysseus

Ithaca	Odysseus' island off the west coast of Greece: location disputed
Ithaca city	Its capital
Ithaca harbour	Its harbour, adjacent to the city
Same	The island opposite Ithaca, also known as Samos: location disputed
Doulichion	Another island nearby: location disputed
Zacynthos	An Ionian island to the south: location known
Cephallenians	The people of Ithaca and some other places nearby
Phorcys Bay	The harbour on Ithaca where Odysseus lands
Mount Neriton	The mountain overlooking Phorcys Bay
Asteris	The island between Ithaca and Samos where the suitors try to ambush Telemachos
Arethousa Spring	A spring between Phorcys Bay and Ithaca city
Eumaios' Pigfarm	A farm between Phorcys Bay and Ithaca city
Raven's Rock	A rock outcrop near Arethousa Spring and Eumaios' Pigfarm
Hermes' Hill	A hill between Eumaios' Pigfarm and Odysseus' Palace
Telemachos' Bay	The cove on Ithaca's coast where Telemachos lands
The city fountain	A distinctive fountain on the outskirts of Ithaca city
The city meeting place	A location near the city and palace with seats for a town meeting
Odysseus' Palace	A large palatial building in or near Ithaca city
Crocyleia	A region in or near Ithaca
Aigilips	A region in or near Ithaca
Rheithron Cove	A bay where ships can moor unobserved from Odysseus' Palace
Mount Neïon	A mountain overlooking Rheithron Cove and Ithaca as a whole
Laertes' farm	A farmstead with orchards and vineyards away from the city
Nericon	A fortress within raiding distance of Ithaca out on a headland
Lefkas	It is disputed whether Homer's 'Lefkadian rock' refers to modern Lefkas (Lefkada)
Scherie	The island of the Phaiacians, also known as Phaiacia: probably Corfu

FIGURE 3.3
Key locations in or near Ithaca

will travel to a land whose people know nothing of the sea, where he will make handsome offerings in an attempt to appease Poseidon. He will then return home and make offerings to all the other gods in turn. Teiresias further predicts that when Odysseus is in his old age and his people are in prosperity, death will come to him *ex halos*, which means either 'away from the sea' or 'out of the sea': the Greek expression is ambiguous.[10]

So the highlighted phrases in this summary are the main clues to a Bronze Age detective story, the primary evidence that we have in our quest to identify the whereabouts of ancient Ithaca itself and the principal place names upon it. These correspond to a distinctive list of locations and our task is to identify them all.

Odysseus	King of Ithaca
Laertes	Odysseus' father
Penelope	Odysseus' wife
Telemachos	Odysseus' son
Zeus	King of the gods
Athene	Zeus' daughter, a goddess who favours Odysseus
Poseidon	King of earthquakes and the sea, Polyphemos' father who detests Odysseus
Antinoos	The head suitor and ambush instigator
Eumaios	The keeper of Odysseus' pigs
Philoitios	The keeper of Odysseus' cattle
Nestor	King of Pylos
Menelaos	King of Sparta

FIGURE 3.4
Key personalities
in the *Odyssey*

The plot summary above also provides the names of some of the main personalities in the *Odyssey*. As well as Odysseus' family and his palace retinue there are 108 suitors together with several gods and goddesses, various characters from the *Iliad*, an assortment of individuals from prior Greek myths such as Jason and the Argonauts, local farmers, beggars and resident poets and also the rulers and families of neighbouring kingdoms. A full list of names can at times be bewildering but in fact relatively few of them play a central part in the plot or are involved in the identification of critical place names, so Figure 3.4 presents the key names on a 'need to know' basis rather than as a comprehensive guide.

One of the intriguing aspects of the list of place names in Figure 3.3 is that only one of them can be unambiguously identified on the modern map. This is Zacynthos, an Ionian island off the western coast of Greece (Figure 1.3). Although Cephalonia itself is marked on the modern map, that is just another trap for the unwary since Homer refers to the Cephallenians as a group of people inhabiting Ithaca and some places nearby, rather than a specific island as it is today.

Armed with these clues and cautioned by these warnings it is now time for us to enter the Homeric minefield.

Notes
1 Bowra (1933) p. 9; also quoted in Wace and Stubbings (1962) p. 1.
2 For a discussion of Troy as a trading centre see Latacz (2004) pp. 40–9; for an example of Bronze Age trade via Troy involving stone lamps and vases see Morkot (1996) p. 28. Based on evidence from Hittite cuneiform tablets regarding the vassal state Wilusa and the possible equivalence of the town of (W)ilios with Ilion, the Greek name for Troy, it has been proposed that the causes of the Trojan War may have been founded more on

Mycenaean greed for the wealth and power of Troy than on the romantic rescue of a Spartan queen. See Bryce (1998) pp. 59–63, 397–8.

3 Kraft et al. (2003) p. 165; Latacz (2004) pp. 6–7.

4 I have drawn the subsequent account together with help from several of the standard texts listed in the Bibliography and also from the educational website www.sparknotes.com, as well as from the *Iliad* and the *Odyssey* themselves.

5 *Iliad* 2.631–4.

6 For further details of Odysseus' attempt to fool Agamemnon and Menelaos see Chapter 23.

7 *Iliad* 8.562–3: 'A thousand fires burned in the plain; round each / Illumined by the flames sat fifty men.'

8 *Odyssey* 8.492–520.

9 *Odyssey* 9.21–6. Except where listed in these notes, the references for extracts from the *Odyssey* in this chapter are provided in the first two columns of Figure 3.2.

10 *Odyssey* 11.122–37.

CHAPTER 4　Controversy

When you set out on your journey to Ithaca, pray that the road is long.

Constantine P. Cavafy, *Ithaca* (1911)[1]

Where was Odysseus' Ithaca? This question lies at the core of the Homeric mystery. The present-day island of Ithaca lies to the north-east of Cephalonia and so this is an obvious candidate for Odysseus' birthplace, palace and city. The problem that writers have tackled over many centuries is that the modern island of Ithaca doesn't fit Homer's descriptions very well at all: in fact it contradicts Homer's account in three distinct ways. First, it is in the wrong place relative to the adjacent islands and the sunset. Second, the topography of the island itself is hard to relate to the detailed clues that were listed in the previous chapter. Finally, archaeological excavation has failed to reveal any evidence that the city and palace that Homer describes were once located on this island.

Anyone who wishes to suggest that modern Ithaca might not be the same island as Homer's Ithaca must propose a different modern name for ancient Ithaca and a different ancient name for modern Ithaca, together with a reason why there was a change in both of these islands' names at some point in the intervening period. That presents a significant challenge because there is no well-researched historical record of such a change in island names. It is partly for this reason that the balance of expert opinion today is that ancient and modern Ithaca were the same island and the contradictions that this poses simply reflect Homer's poor grasp of geography.

Nevertheless there has been a plethora of imaginative alternative proposals over the centuries: indeed the challenge appears to have encouraged a streak of geographical radicalism. We have already seen that Dörpfeld resorted to Lefkas in frustration at his inability to relate ancient Ithaca to its modern counterpart, but this was a shift of only a few kilometres and pales into provincial insignificance against some other suggestions. Cambridgeshire, the Baltic, the Ukraine, Scotland and America are among the locations that have been proposed for Odysseus' wanderings, not to mention further possibilities involving volcanic explosion, alien abduction or a related *deus ex machina*.[2] For these reasons I am acutely aware that any suggestion that ancient Ithaca may not have been located on modern Ithaca is for many scholars an admission of intellectual frivolity.

In February 2003 my interest in this controversy was reawakened by the prospect of visiting the Ithaca of today for a summer holiday. In re-reading the *Odyssey* I identified the highlighted passages indicated in the previous plot summary and it became clear that only a few of these would be of immediate assistance in identifying the ancient island of Ithaca. It seemed to me that these four key questions, which I came to regard as the 'Four Key Clues', were as follows:

1 *Does Ithaca lie low and to the west, the furthest out to sea of a group of neighbouring islands called Ithaca, Same, Doulichion and Zacynthos?*
2 *Does Ithaca contain a bay with two distinctive jutting headlands?*
3 *Can a ship leave Ithaca harbour driven by a stiff following wind from the west?*
4 *Is there a two-harboured island called Asteris in the straits between Ithaca and Samos, with windy heights that would enable an ambush to take place?*

There are many other clues but I felt that the best approach would be to start by looking for a solution to these first four and only if this was satisfactory to explore as a subsequent step the more detailed evidence. This approach elevates these four questions to a central position in the detective trail and so it is essential that their English text should be based on a proper analysis of Homer's actual Greek words.

I started with Clue 1 and my first observation was that I could easily locate the islands of Ithaca and Zacynthos on Figure 4.1 but not Same or Doulichion. However there is a town today called Sami on the eastern coast of Cephalonia and Clue 4 spoke about an island between Ithaca and Samos, so perhaps modern Cephalonia was ancient Same. Indeed from time to time Homer refers to Same (pronounced 'sammy') as well as to Samos and scholars seem to be agreed that these two names are synonymous. This tentative identification of the ancient island names is illustrated in Figure 4.1, on which the colour scheme corresponds to altitude.

Doulichion was still nowhere to be found but it was nevertheless abundantly clear that Ithaca was by no means 'low and to the west, the furthest out to sea' of this group of neighbouring islands: instead it looked somewhat mountainous and it was to the east, towards the mainland of Greece. This was such an obvious contradiction that I went back to the *Odyssey* to see if I had misread the text. I hadn't: the version I was reading from the Robert Fagles translation ran as follows:

> I am Odysseus, son of Laertes, known to the world
> for every kind of craft – my fame has reached the skies.
> Sunny Ithaca is my home. Atop her stands our seamark,
> Mount Neriton's leafy ridges shimmering in the wind.

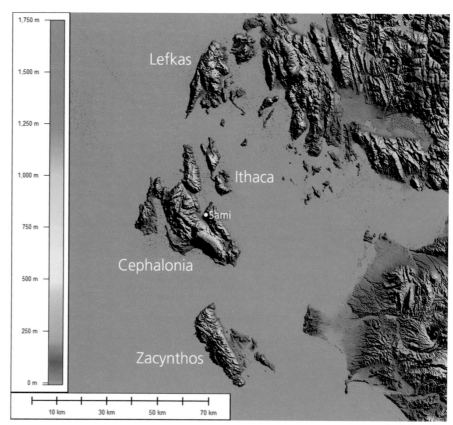

FIGURE 4.1
Elevation map of the southern Ionian Islands
This map has been computer-generated from digital elevation model data obtained from satellite radar altitude scans. Very low-lying areas (less than about 3 m above sea level) may merge into ocean wavetop reflections. [Image credits: DEM data was obtained from the NASA Shuttle Radar Topography Mission (SRTM-90). Horizontal accuracy: 90 m. Processing: Global Mapper – custom elevation shading. Websites: www.mapmart.com, www.globalmapper.com]

> Around her a ring of islands circle side-by-side,
> Doulichion, Same, wooded Zacynthos too, but mine
> lies low and away, the farthest out to sea,
> rearing into the western dusk
> while the others face the east and breaking day.   9.19–26

When I first read this passage I was confused by the apparent contradiction of how Ithaca could be 'the farthest out to sea' while at the same time 'around her a ring of islands circle side-by-side'. The description appeared to defy simple geometry: if these islands lie around Ithaca then surely Ithaca itself cannot be farthest out to sea – one of the others must be instead. Later I consulted a prose translation of the same passage (Murray):

I am Odysseus, son of Laertes, known to all men for my stratagems, and my fame reaches the heavens. I dwell in clear-seen Ithaca; on it is a mountain, Neriton, covered with waving forests, conspicuous from afar; and round it lie many islands close by one another, Dulichium, and Same and wooded Zacynthus. Ithaca itself lies low in the sea, farthest of all toward the dark, but the others lie apart toward the dawn and the sun –

The problem remained: how can Ithaca be 'farthest of all towards the dark' while at the same time 'round it lie many islands'? As far as the identification of Ithaca is concerned, this is perhaps the single most important passage in the *Odyssey* and consequently we are stepping on very well-trodden ground. In the hope of throwing some light on the problem I decided to dust up my rusty memories of ancient Greek, located a Greek version of the *Odyssey* on the Internet[3] and bought a Greek–English dictionary. I looked up the word that Homer uses for 'round' and found the Greek *amphi*, which the dictionary explains as meaning 'on both sides, around, about'. If this text therefore means 'round about lie many islands close by one another' then the geometrical contradiction disappears, so I pressed on to the next issue.

How had others explained away the basic problem that present-day Ithaca does not lie nearest to the 'dark', the westerly direction of dusk, as opposed to the easterly direction of dawn? This problem has caused researchers over the ages to challenge the notion of 'west' that Homer presents here, arguing that the Greek text does not necessarily imply that dark is to the west and dawn to the east. Some of them have argued that the points of the compass were interpreted differently at that time and that the Greek word *zophos* meaning 'darkness' might in this passage instead mean the darkness of the north or north-west.[4] This seemed to me to be a very intricate and somewhat unlikely interpretation of Homer's words, but then I was already guilty of choosing a translation of *amphi* that suited my own purpose so I felt that perhaps I had better withhold judgement for the moment.

As we have seen, there is another well-known difficulty in these lines of the *Odyssey*. Homer describes Ithaca as lying 'low in the sea': the Greek word that he uses is *chthamale*. However, most of the land mass of modern Ithaca is very mountainous, with steep cliffs that drop straight down to the sea, as Figure 4.2 indicates. If you look up this word in the dictionary the translation provided is 'near the ground, on the ground, low, sunken, flat' which seems quite clear, but some scholars have nevertheless grasped the first of these translations with evident relief and suggested that what it might mean instead is that Ithaca was 'near the ground' of the mainland, even though the use of this word in other passages implies a vertical rather than a horizontal proximity.

Several months later James Diggle tackled these problems from first principles and you can read his account in Appendix 1.[5] He reached his solutions with an expert's logic whereas mine were identified via an amateur's intuition, but happily our answers are the same.

So how do the great Homeric authorities interpret this passage? 'As one look at a map shows, these details are not easily reconciled with geographical reality ... The poet cannot have been writing on the basis of first-hand knowledge or even with a map in hand: for information he must have depended on the reports of those who had sailed that way.'[6]

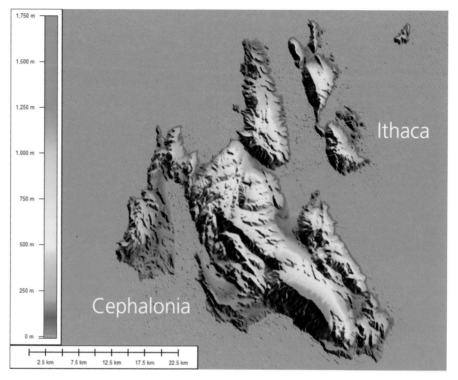

FIGURE 4.2
Elevation map of
Cephalonia and Ithaca
*Colour interpretation: as
Figure 4.1. Note the low
average elevation of the
western peninsula of
Cephalonia compared with
the high average elevation of
today's island of Ithaca.*
[Image credits: as
Figure 4.1.]

How extraordinary! Odysseus is speaking these words to King Alcinoos of
Phaiacia and he is revealing his identity to the court for the first time. Surely
Homer would hardly choose this moment to make a careless mistake? Unless
he was either uninterested in the geography or mischievously committed to
distorting it, there can be little doubt that Homer himself believed that Ithaca
was the farthest of these islands to the west. So either he was right or he
was wrong. If he was right then modern Ithaca cannot be the same as ancient
Ithaca. If he was wrong then I would presumably find the *Odyssey* shot through
with other geographical inconsistencies, but until I found them I resolved to
proceed on the premise that he was right.

However often I read this passage, the message remained obvious and to
interpret it otherwise seemed an act of longitudinal desperation. *Ithaca itself
lies low in the sea, farthest of all towards the dark, but the others lie apart toward the
dawn and the sun.*

Were these the lines that Dörpfeld consulted on 18 March 1900 after three
years of looking on present-day Ithaca with no result, the lines that led him
to spend the rest of his life on Lefkas? He abandoned modern Ithaca and went
to look for ancient Ithaca on another island. But why on earth did he choose
Lefkas? As Figure 4.1 makes abundantly clear, Lefkas is not a satisfactory
solution because it is farthest to the north, not the west. The region that
is obviously the farthest towards the dark is the relatively low-lying western

peninsula of Cephalonia, but that won't work because the island of Cephalonia has already been identified as ancient Same.

Unless . . . unless . . .

I look again at the map of the island. I remember our family holiday five years ago on Lefkas and how we considered the possibility of the adjacent mainland being cut off by the sea as an independent island in ancient times. Somewhere a serendipitous synapse snaps and an unexpected connection is made.

Supposing – just supposing – that the far western peninsula of Cephalonia was once itself cut off by the sea?

Notes

1 Reproduced with permission of Curtis Brown Group Ltd, London, on behalf of the estate of W. H. Auden. Copyright © W. H. Auden, 1961.

2 The list of alternative Homeric venues is a long one: here are some candidates. For Odysseus' sojourn in the Baltic and the identification of Hellas with Estonia see www.jesus1053.com/en/l2-wahl/Abstract-Vinci.htm; for a gripping read of his travels in the Crimea see www.cnw.mk.ua/pushkin/english/homer.htm; for directions on finding Troy at Atlantis see www.atlantis-troja.ch/; for late-breaking news of the Greeks in America and a bulletin on Odysseus held captive by Calypso on Bermuda see http://web.otenet.gr/homers-odyssey/; for his visit to the Cyclops at Thule in Greenland see www.metrum.org/mapping/navigations.htm; for his battle with the Trojans at the Gog Magog hills in Cambridgeshire see www.troy-in-england.co.uk/; and don't miss his visit to the souls of the dead at Culloden Moor in Scotland at http://home-3. tiscali.nl/~meester7/engodyssey.html

3 The most readily accessible Internet source for the *Odyssey* and many other classical texts is www.perseus.tufts.edu/

4 For a 2,000-year old discussion of this point see Strabo 10.2.12; for a more recent treatment see le Noan (2001) ch. 2.

5 See James Diggle's comments on this passage in Appendix 1 Section G.

6 Heubeck and Hoekstra (1989) p. 14 on *Odyssey* 9.21–7.

CHAPTER 5 Schizocephalonia

When you have eliminated the impossible, whatever remains, however improbable, must be the truth. Sir Arthur Conan Doyle, *The Sign of Four* (1890)

The western peninsula of Cephalonia is today called Paliki and on Figure 4.2 it is apparent that much of it is at a low elevation. At the isthmus where Paliki joins the rest of the island there is some low-lying ground at the northern end, but at the southern end the elevation appears to rise. Nevertheless in Figure 5.1 I have drawn the route of a hypothetical former sea channel there that would cut the island in two. When the notion of sea level changes as a possible solution to the location of Homer's Ithaca first occurred to me in February 2003, I didn't know the course of the former marine channel, so I am cheating somewhat with this diagram and superimposing the route that I later came to believe was the correct one.

In subsequent chapters we will be considering the geology behind this proposition and getting to grips with the extraordinary physical changes that have taken place here over the last 3,000 years, but for now I would ask you to suspend your judgement and say to yourself 'Supposing Paliki was once cut off by the sea – how might this fit the four key clues of the previous chapter?'

1 Does Ithaca lie low and to the west, the furthest out to sea of a group of neighbouring islands called Ithaca, Same, Doulichion and Zacynthos?

Under the Schizocephalonia[1] hypothesis the ancient island of Ithaca is clearly to the west and the furthest out to sea. Figure 4.2 also indicates that with the exception of two or three specific peaks, Paliki lies lower than the rest of Cephalonia opposite. The latter becomes ancient Same, which fits with the town of the same name on its eastern coast and also with most other existing theories of Ithaca. These theories generally identify Cephalonia as Same because we are told that the ambush island lies between Ithaca and Samos and therefore they must lie across a strait from each other. Zacynthos remains where it is to the south, but where is Doulichion?

The whereabouts of Doulichion have been a challenge for every Homeric researcher over the ages. Some have located it among a small group of islands towards the mainland which are known as the Echinades, while others have suggested that perhaps it disappeared under the sea in a volcanic eruption. Homer tells us that it is rich in wheat, that it supported more suitors than

Paliki

FIGURE 5.1
Schizocephalonia
*Channel location is indicative
only at this stage. Colour
interpretation: as Figure 1.3.
Grid: 20 km.*
[Image credits: as
Figure 1.3.]

any other island and also that it is close to Ithaca.[2] Doulichion, in short, is an enigma, a name without a place.

The observant reader will note that we have just created an additional problem that also demands a solution. By transferring the name of Ithaca from the modern island of the same name we are left with the challenge of what today's island of Ithaca used to be called in former years. We have generated a second enigma, a place without a name.

Happily an immediate solution suggests itself. Like positive and negative potentials, these two problems could cancel each other out and our theory therefore suggests the possibility that the island now called Ithaca might once have been called Doulichion (Figure 5.2).

I must emphasise that none of this has remotely been proven in the brief discussion of this chapter so far. We are simply exploring the consequences that will arise if it subsequently can be: we are in effect trying to decide whether it would be worth our time and effort to attempt a proof. These mental gymnastics are perfectly familiar to economists but over the years I

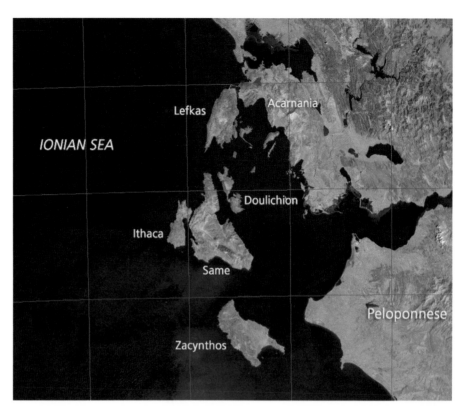

FIGURE 5.2
The ancient identity
of the islands
*Colour interpretation: as
Figure 1.3. Grid: 50 km.*
[Image credits: as
Figure 1.3.]

have learnt that they are regarded with considerable suspicion by those who inhabit the real world. However if the theory of Schizocephalonia could be substantiated then it looked as if it might be capable of meeting the criteria of Question 1.

2 Does Ithaca contain a bay with two distinctive jutting headlands?

> The deep-sea-going ship
> made landfall on the island . . . Ithaca at last.
> There on the coast a haven lies, named for Phorcys,
> the old god of the deep – with two jutting headlands,
> sheared off at the seaward side but shelving towards the bay.
>
> 13.95–8 (transl. Fagles)

The northern coast of the Paliki promontory on the map of Figure 5.1 exhibits two distinctive jutting headlands, but it is not clear from this map whether they are 'sheared off at the seaward side but shelving towards the bay'. There are moments associated with this endeavour that I shall remember for the rest of my life: one of them was the excitement of walking into Blackwell's bookshop

FIGURE 5.3
The jutting headlands of
Northern Paliki
*This detailed tourist map is
based on the Hellenic Military
Geographical Service survey
originals. The village name of
Livadi has been relocated
from west of the harbour to its
present position further south:
see also Figure 16.2.*
[Image credits: Cephalonia
Road Map 1:50000 ©
Freytag–Berndt u. Artaria,
1231 Vienna (with special
thanks to Caroline Pfeiffer
for providing the original
image file).]

in Oxford on 22 February 2003 and buying a detailed map of Cephalonia.[3]
When I opened it the jutting headlands almost sprang off the page (Figure 5.3).
A month later I visited the island and saw them at first hand: we shall consider
these and other photographs on subsequent pages.

I was in Oxford that day on a family outing and also to meet an unusual
and delightful Odyssean enthusiast, Manolis Pantos. A few days earlier I had
spotted on his website[4] a review of a book called *In Search of Ithaca* by C. H.
Goekoop. This book is published only in Dutch but Manolis and two of his
colleagues had apparently translated it into English some years earlier, so I
had sent him an e-mail inquiring about it. When I mentioned that I thought
that relative sea level changes might have had a bearing on the problem he
explained that he had his doubts about such proposals in historical times.
However, he agreed that if the sea level difference was large enough this
might have been sufficient to cut off the Paliki peninsula, thereby making it
accord with Homer's description that ancient Ithaca was towards the west. He

also told me that he had visited the area the previous summer and that the landscape where Paliki joins the main part of Cephalonia involves only a small isthmus.

This was encouraging and after our meeting we continued to correspond. With the author's permission Manolis provided me with access to the English typescript of C. H. Goekoop's book as well as other rare materials and he has been a source of great inspiration and support. I hope that by the time this book appears he and his colleagues will have published their English translation of *In Search of Ithaca*. I have a great admiration for the painstaking research that C. H. Goekoop conducted in putting forward his proposals, even though I do not agree with his conclusions. He is the grandson of the great A. E. H. Goekoop whom I mentioned in Chapter 2 and to whom we will return subsequently.

There is another reason for cautious optimism about the location of these jutting headlands. As we observed in the earlier plot summary of the *Odyssey*, King Alcinoos has sent his Phaiacian sailors to return Odysseus to Ithaca and later we shall review the proposals that equate ancient Phaiacia (also known as Scherie) with Corfu. If that equation is correct then the ship would have been approaching the headlands of Figure 5.3 from the north and hence this bay would have represented their first sighting of ancient Ithaca. When we later turn to the competing theories it will become clear that in most cases their proponents expected the Phaiacians to travel some way past the coastline of their own candidates for Ithaca and to ignore perfectly navigable bays at the unnecessary expense of a longer journey.

The more I looked at Figure 5.3 the more comfortable I became with this answer to Question 2. Although other theories also identify their own Phorcys Bay, none of them as far as I knew involved two headlands of the size and distinctive appearance of these.[5] But once again, nothing in this discussion remotely proves that the hypothesis is correct: there is much evidence yet to be considered, and indeed later I learnt that my excitement about these headlands had been somewhat premature.

3 Can a ship leave Ithaca harbour driven by a stiff following wind from the west?

One of my favourite passages in the *Odyssey* describes the moment when Telemachos sets out on a journey from Ithaca to Sparta via Pylos to consult with King Menelaos regarding the whereabouts of his father Odysseus. The language is so vivid that we can almost imagine ourselves on board as the wind hits the sails and the ship breasts the waves.

> Cables cast off, the crew swung to the oarlocks.
> Bright-eyed Athena sent them a stiff following wind
> rippling out of the west, ruffling over the wine-dark sea

as Telemachos shouted out commands to all his shipmates:
'All lay hands to tackle!' They sprang to orders,
hoisting the pinewood mast, they stepped it firm
in its block amidships, lashed it fast with stays
and with braided rawhide halyards hauled the white sail high.
Suddenly wind hit full and the canvas bellied out
and a dark blue wave, foaming up at the bow,
sang out loud and strong as the ship made way,
skimming the whitecaps, cutting towards her goal.
All running gear secured in the swift black craft,
they set up bowls and brimmed them high with wine
and poured libations out to the everlasting gods
who never die – to Athene first of all,
the daughter of Zeus with flashing sea-gray eyes –
and the ship went plunging all night long and through the dawn.

                                    2.418–34 (transl. Fagles)

It is hard to be unmoved by this beautiful passage and it is impossible not to identify with the proposition that Homer understood the art of sailing in considerable detail: the description is so exact. Let us look at what happens step by step as the ship begins its voyage.

Telemachos is leaving Ithaca harbour en route to Pylos to seek news of his father Odysseus. Pylos is located on the western coast of the Peloponnese[6] which lies to the south-east of Ithaca. The crew start off by rowing but Athene then sends them a following wind from the west. Now a following wind is obviously one that follows a ship, not one that blows against it, so the ship must have been rowed out towards the east in the first place so that a wind blowing up from the west would follow it. There is absolutely no suggestion that the crew rowed out for a period in one direction and then a wind arrived which reversed their course: everything takes place in the same direction.

According to Severin Bronze Age vessels needed a favourable wind to help them sail: they were unable to make progress against the wind by more than a few degrees.[7] So if 'a stiff following wind is rippling out of the west' then the ship must have been rowed out of the harbour in an easterly direction, although not necessarily exactly due east. Therefore the entrance to Ithaca harbour must face in an easterly arc: it certainly cannot face to the west.

At this stage in the discussion we have no evidence at all that Ithaca harbour is where I have marked it: indeed the present hypothesis combined with this passage from the *Odyssey* require only that it is located somewhere along the eastern or southern coast of Homer's Ithaca. But if you look at Figure 5.4 you can see that the area I have suggested would form a wonderful natural harbour

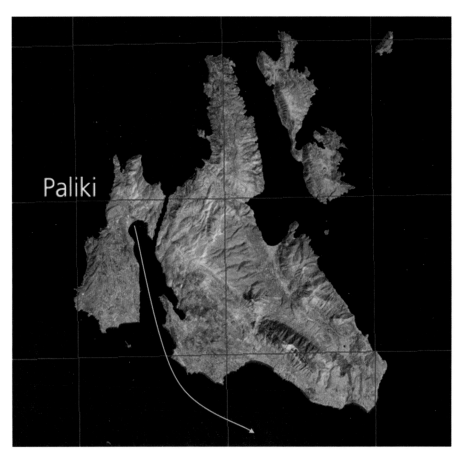

in a bay that is about 2.5 kilometres wide. Furthermore if you consult the same area of Figure 5.3 you can see markings on the map which indicate low-lying irrigation ditches. On later pages we will explore this harbour in more detail, but for now we appear to have the beginnings of a possible answer to Clue 3.

4 Is there a two-harboured island called Asteris in the straits between Ithaca and Samos, with windy heights that would enable an ambush to take place?

No, there is not. There are no islands whatever between Samos/Same and the area called Paliki. The detailed maps show a few barren reefs and an island called Vardianoi, but these lie south of Paliki and so they are not 'between' the two islands. They also lack windy heights. But it would be premature for the reader to abandon the theory of Schizocephalonia at this early stage because, as we shall discover, none of the other locations that have been proposed for ancient Ithaca over the millennia, including the modern island of the same name, comply with this crucial clue either. Almost every proposal regarding the ambush island is unsatisfactory and the fact of the matter is that Asteris has never been properly identified.[8]

So as well as Ithaca itself we now have another mysterious island to pin down. Meanwhile we have met our first problem and it looks insoluble. We shall return to it presently, but before we do so we need to meet some ancient Greeks and that will take another few chapters.

Notes

1 As in 'schizophrenia' which means a split personality, the 'ch' in a Greek word such as this or 'Doulichion' is pronounced as the English 'k'.
2 The references are *Odyssey* 14.335, 16.247 and 9.24 respectively.
3 Freytag-Berndt (2000).
4 See Pantos (2003).
5 But later in the year I encountered some less well-known theories that did: see Appendix 4.
6 See the discussion about Pylos in Chapter 16.
7 '*Argo* had demonstrated that a galley can sail broadside to the wind, and, well handled and shrewdly ballasted, can make a course a few degrees upwind, but little more.' Severin (1987) p. 136.
8 Once again I discovered some unsung kindred spirits in later months: see Appendix 4.

CHAPTER 6 Strabo

The use of travelling is to regulate imagination by reality, and instead of thinking how things may be, to see them as they are. Samuel Johnson (1786)[1]

Strabo was born in a Greek-speaking town called Amaseia (now Amasya, north-east of Ankara in Turkey) probably around 64 BC, and he lived until at least AD 21. His *magnum opus*, appropriately called *Geography*, was written towards the end of his life: it consists of just under 300,000 words and describes in great detail the entire Mediterranean Basin as well as northern Europe and the Middle East.[2]

Although some place names and regions have clearly changed over the last 2,000 years, it is an extraordinary experience to sit down with a copy of *Geography* and a detailed map and to trace Strabo's description around the coastlines of the ancient world. Because of his familiarity with Greece it is particularly rewarding to follow him around a region such as the Peloponnese: a comparison of his Book 6 with today's map reveals an almost exact correspondence. Indeed the accuracy of his findings does not necessarily diminish as he describes places further afield:

Britain is triangular in shape . . . most of the island is flat and overgrown with forests, although many of its districts are hilly. It bears grain, cattle, gold, silver and iron . . . Their weather is more rainy than snowy; and on the days of clear sky fog prevails so long a time that throughout a whole day the sun is to be seen for only three or four hours round about midday. 4.5.1–2

Strabo travelled extensively himself, visiting Rome, Egypt and some of the Greek islands, but he was also dependent on the researches of other explorers and writers in compiling his massive work. However he was careful to warn his readers of possible unreliability or prejudice in his sources, as when describing Ireland:

Concerning this island I have nothing certain to tell, except that its inhabitants are more savage than the Britons, since they are man-eaters as well as heavy eaters,[3] and since further, they count it an honourable thing, when their fathers die, to devour them, and openly to have intercourse, not only with the other women, but also with their mothers and sisters; but I am saying this only with the understanding that I have no trustworthy witnesses for it. 4.5.4

By the time Strabo was writing, Eratosthenes and others such as Zoilus[4] had already sowed the seeds of doubt about the accuracy of Homer's geography and consequently it had become an important mission for Greek writers to re-examine Homer's clues and to compare these with their attempts to document the geography of the ancient world. Strabo was clearly a believer in Homer's commitment to geographical fidelity:

I say this because I am comparing present conditions with those described by Homer;
for we must needs institute this comparison because of the fame of the poet and because
of our familiarity with him from our childhood, since all of us believe that we have not
successfully treated any subject which we may have in hand until there remains in our
treatment nothing that conflicts with what the poet says on the same subject, such
confidence do we have in his words.   8.3.3

It is principally from Strabo that many of our established traditions about the place names in the *Odyssey* have arisen. For example, Strabo locates Scylla and Charybdis in the Straits of Messina between Italy and Sicily and this has become the conventional wisdom ever since. This is in defiance of the fact that Homer says that the channel in question was narrow enough for an arrow to be fired across it,[5] whereas one reads that the main span alone of the proposed new bridge across the Straits of Messina will be 3,300 metres long.[6] We must therefore be careful when reading Strabo to distinguish between the wall and the layers of paint of Chapter 2. He is usually accurate when describing the place names of the ancient world but he is by no means reliable in his attempts to relate these to Homer's work.

Strabo's work is not limited to geographical observation: as we have seen he liked to reflect upon the characteristics of different civilisations as well and he was perhaps the first writer to adopt a linguistically correct attitude to foreigners, rejecting the presumption that they were medically challenged:

Those, therefore, they called barbarians in the special sense of the term, at first
derisively, meaning that they pronounced words thickly or harshly; and then we
misused the word as a general ethnic term, thus making a logical distinction between
the Greeks and all other races. The fact is, however, that through our long
acquaintance and intercourse with the barbarians this effect was at last seen to be the
result, not of a thick pronunciation or any natural defect in the vocal organs, but of the
peculiarities of their several languages.   14.2.28

Earlier in this passage Strabo reflects upon Homer's own use of the word 'barbarian':

But I raise the question, Why does he call them people 'of barbarian speech' but not even once calls them barbarians? 'Because', Apollodorus replies, 'the plural does not fall in with the metre; this is why he does not call them barbarians.'   14.2.28

Apollodorus is reminding Strabo that the metrical structure of epic verse is precise and demanding, so that it frequently obliges the composer to choose a word or an ending to a word that best fits the rhythm of the line rather than that which most literally reflects the underlying meaning. This observation will turn out to be important to us in a later context.

Strabo is one of the ancient writers whom I would most like to have met because he was clearly blessed by an impish sense of humour as well as an insatiable appetite for anecdote. In describing a little-known island on the western coast of Turkey he explains:

Then one comes to Iasus, which lies on an island close to the mainland. It has a harbour; and the people gain most of their livelihood from the sea, for the sea here is well supplied with fish, but the soil of the country is rather poor. Indeed, people fabricate stories of this kind in regard to Iasus: When a citharoede [who played a harp-like instrument] *was giving a recital, the people all listened for a time, but when the bell that announced the sale of fish rang, they all left him and went away to the fish market, except one man who was hard of hearing. The citharoede, therefore, went up to him and said: 'Sir, I am grateful to you for the honour you have done me and for your love of music, for all the others except you went away the moment they heard the sound of the bell.' And the man said, 'What's that you say? Has the bell already rung?' And when the citharoede said 'Yes,' the man said, 'Fare thee well,' and himself arose and went away.*   14.2.21

Further along the coast Strabo's descriptions become even more pointed. Medically qualified readers will recall the condition 'pygalgia' and this was apparently well known to the ancients:

Then comes Pygela,[7] a small town, with a temple of Artemis Munychia, founded by Agamemnon and inhabited by a part of his troops; for it is said that some of his soldiers became afflicted with a disease of the buttocks and were called 'diseased-buttocks', and that, being afflicted with this disease, they stayed there, and that the place thus received this appropriate name.   14.1.20

Pygela is 3 km north of today's tourist resort of Kusadasi and although Agamemnon's soldiers apparently regarded a posting to Pygela as a pain in the ass, we cannot fail to be impressed by Strabo's mastery of detail. This is particularly evident in Book 10 of his *Geography*, where he conducts a long and thoughtful analysis of the geographical descriptions in the *Odyssey* and compares them with his knowledge of the Ionian Islands. He is clearly particularly worried about our first clue, the fact that Homer describes Ithaca as lying to the west of a group of neighbouring islands, and he embarks upon a somewhat tortuous analysis of the meaning of the word *zophos* and its true direction relative to the compass. I referred to this Homeric theory in Chapter 4 and it looks as though Strabo unwittingly created a precedent for centuries of subsequent confusion on this matter.

Strabo also spent a considerable amount of time trying to identify which island was which and his conclusion was that the unknown island of Doulichion lies in the group of small islands towards mainland Greece called the Echinades. This opinion is sharply at odds with Homer's description cited earlier that it is rich in wheat, that it supported more suitors than any other island and also that it is close to Ithaca. However, such is the degree of reverence in which most subsequent scholars have held Strabo that views such as these are to this day frequently regurgitated as established truths.

Nevertheless Strabo usually makes a clear distinction between the way in which he presents topographical facts on the one hand and his theories of Homeric interpretation on the other. His statements about specific locations are presented in an entirely objective manner, whereas when he starts on the detective quest to identify the places to which Homer was referring he deploys a form of courtroom analysis that is quite different from his geographical prose. This distinction becomes of particular importance when he describes Cephalonia:

[15] *Cephallenia lies opposite Acarnania, at a distance of about fifty stadia from Leucatas (some say forty), and about one hundred and eighty from Chelonatas. It has a perimeter of about three hundred stadia, is long, extending towards Euros, and is mountainous. The largest mountain upon it is Ainos, whereon is the temple of Zeus Ainesios; and where the island is narrowest it forms an isthmus so low-lying that it is often submerged from sea to sea. Both Paleis and Cranioi are on the gulf near the narrows.*   10.2.15*

[16] *Between Ithaca and Cephallenia is the small island Asteria (the poet calls it Asteris), which the Scepsian says no longer remains such as the poet describes it, but in it are harbours safe for anchorage with entrances on either side; Apollodorus, however, says that it still remains so to this day, and mentions a town Alalcomenai upon it, situated on the isthmus itself.*   10.2.16*

How much confidence can we have in the description in paragraph 15? The largest mountain on Cephalonia is indeed Mount Ainos; a temple to Zeus has been found on its summit; and Strabo's estimate of 50 stadia to Leucas is accurate (1 stadium is about 185 m and the actual distance is about 9 km).

Although his coastline perimeter value disagrees with today's measurements, this is not unusual given the fractal nature of coastlines.[8] The ancient town of Paleis has been located just north of the modern town of Lixouri and this was the origin of the name Paliki that describes the western region of Cephalonia. The town of Cranioi has also been located: it lies just to the east of the present capital of Argostoli. Both of these towns are on the Gulf of Argostoli where the long bay narrows to a width of about 2.5 km. So Strabo seems to have been very accurately informed about Cephalonian geography.

Where the island is narrowest it forms an isthmus so low-lying that it is often submerged from sea to sea. Both Paleis and Cranioi are on the gulf near the narrows.

When I first read this passage I could hardly believe my luck. Here was Strabo describing the actual existence of the ancient sea channel that I had earlier postulated as a hypothetical solution to the problem of 'furthest to the west'. Furthermore what possible reason could he have to invent this description, since he does not rely on it to reinforce an argument anywhere else within his book? Evidently one of his sources (perhaps Apollodorus, to whom he refers in the next paragraph) was firmly of the view that the sea washed over this isthmus at the narrowest part of the island and so this was just another of the thousands of useful facts that Strabo wished to impart to his readers. But was the narrowest part of the island at the location that I had previously proposed? We know the locations of Paleis and Cranioi, and also of Sami and Pronnoi. The first town is referred to by Herodotus and all four settlements are noted by Thucydides. Both were writing in the fifth century BC and we shall revisit their evidence towards the end of Chapter 21.

I looked back at the map shown in Figure 6.1 where there seems to be the possibility of a slightly narrower cut across the Paliki peninsula in an east–west direction. However, at that point the location is no longer on an isthmus: we are on the peninsula itself. The word 'isthmus' meant in those days the same as it means today (it is of course a Greek word), a narrow neck of land joining two larger land masses, and this description could be applied without difficulty to a former north–south sea channel.

If Strabo's Channel, as I decided to christen it, was 'often submerged' then clearly that implied that it was not always submerged. So by the time Strabo was writing these words around AD 1 the former sea channel was no longer navigable: it had become too shallow. In fact since he relied upon various sources for this geographical briefing it might be that the channel had become closed to marine traffic some time earlier. But what caused the channel to fill in? When did it start to fill in and how long did it take? Was it a gradual or a catastrophic process? How high above sea level is the area now and is the existence of a former sea channel geologically credible? It began to look as

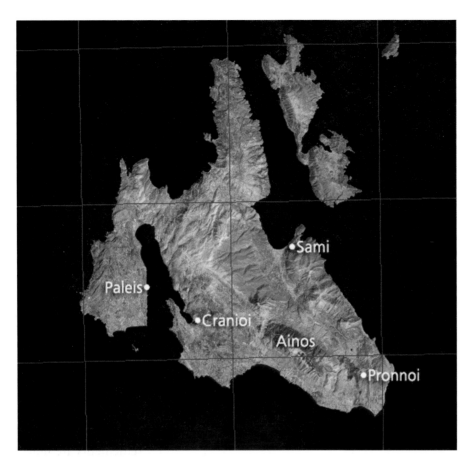

FIGURE 6.1
Interpreting Strabo's
description of Cephalonia
*Colour interpretation: as
Figure 1.3. Grid: 20 km.*
[Image credits: as
Figure 1.3.]

if consulting ancient texts and looking at maps was not going to be enough to solve this problem: some serious geology would be required as well. But before we venture into that field we must do justice to Strabo's subsequent paragraph, which repays some careful reading.

In his paragraph 15 Strabo refers to a frequently submerged isthmus at the narrowest part of the island of Cephalonia. In his paragraph 16 he refers to a small island between Ithaca and Cephalonia called Asteris and he mentions a town Alalcomenai upon it, situated on the isthmus itself. Now clearly this second isthmus cannot be the same as the first isthmus, because the first isthmus is on the narrowest part of Cephalonia whereas the second isthmus is on the small island of Asteris between Ithaca and Cephalonia. So the key question is: how can a small island such as Asteris be large enough to have its own isthmus and also a town thereon?

This is not the only question prompted by paragraph 16. 'The Scepsian' (Demetrius of Scepsis, who was born around 214 BC) says that Asteris 'no longer remains such as the poet describes it, but in it are harbours safe for anchorage with entrances on either side; Apollodorus, however, says that it still remains so to this day'. Apollodorus hailed from Athens and was a generation or so younger than Demetrius. So Strabo's two sources disagreed about Asteris, but nevertheless the description of the harbours is encouraging in relation to Clue 4: 'Is there a two-harboured island called Asteris in the straits between Ithaca and Samos, with windy heights that would enable an ambush to take place?' We will revisit this clue shortly: it is based on Homer's specific descriptions of Asteris which we shall be examining in more detail.

Why did none of the attempts to identify the island of Asteris that I had read to date draw attention to this paragraph 16 of Strabo's? Why did they not emphasise that Apollodorus said that Asteris was large enough to contain an isthmus and a town?[9] One possible explanation is that if these two paragraphs are read with anything other than the obsessive forensic zeal of an amateur detective then the repetition of the word 'isthmus' lulls the reader into thinking that they are references to the same isthmus.

What about Alalcomenai – could that be located with the help of classical texts? Would reading Strabo in the original Greek assist with the interpretation? Could one obtain the works of Apollodorus and Demetrius to see whether Strabo had correctly interpreted them? These two paragraphs of Strabo were about to create the need for some serious classical research, so I decided to park this problem for the time being and to think about it as Apollodorus' Enigma. Meanwhile it was time to start learning something about geology.

Notes

1 Piozzi and Johnson (1786) p. 154.

2 English-speakers usually pronounce Strabo's name with a long 'a' as in 'Straybow'. For a discussion of Strabo's dates see Hornblower and Spawforth (2003) p. 1447. The quotations that follow are taken from Jones (1917–32).

3 In Ireland's defence it should be mentioned that the translator's footnote states that 'Some of the editors read "herb-eaters" instead of "heavy eaters" – perhaps rightly.'

4 Strabo 6.2.4: the translator's footnote says 'Zoilus: (about 400–320 B. C.), the grammarian and rhetorician, of Amphipolis in Macedonia, is chiefly known for the bitterness of his attacks on Homer, which gained him the surname of "Homeromastix" ("scourge of Homer").'

5 *Odyssey* 12.101–2.

6 See data on the proposed Messina Straits Crossing at www.structurae.net/en/structures/data/str04265.php

7 Perhaps Strabo was not being entirely serious about Pygela: see Chapter 33 n. 13.

8 I am not the first to fall out with Strabo on this point: Jacob Spon (of whom we shall hear more in later chapters) disagreed in 1675 with this estimate of Strabo and commented 'But I am not surprised by the errors of ancient geographers, since the modern ones, who by comparison with ancient geography have the advantage of our relations, deviate so grossly in many parts of this land.' See Spon (1678) vol I pp. 79–80. The problem is that the perimeter of a coastline is not an absolute number such as the length of an island: its value depends instead on the precision of the measuring instrument. If you walk very carefully around every small cove you will clearly arrive at

a much larger value for the perimeter than if you stick to the coastal path, whereas if you painstakingly measure the distance with a pair of dividers instead then the result will be greater still. There is no correct answer: the issue is fundamental rather than pragmatic. Its solution is found in fractal geometry: the classic paper is 'How Long Is the Coast of Britain?' in Mandelbrot (1982) ch. 2 paper 5. Strabo himself seemed to be aware of the difficulty: at 14.1.2 he says 'The coasting voyage round Ionia is about three thousand four hundred and thirty stadia, this distance being so great because of the gulfs and the fact that the country forms a peninsula of unusual extent.'

9 During the course of subsequent research for this book I learnt that other researchers have indeed considered these matters: see for example the entries on Gell and Leake in Appendix 4. But most of those who spotted these references have misunderstood where Asteris and Strabo's isthmus actually were.

CHAPTER 7 Geology

The crawling glaciers pierce me with the spears
Of their moon-freezing crystals, the bright chains
Eat with their burning cold into my bones.

Shelley, Prometheus Unbound 1.31 (1819)

Could Strabo have been right? Could there have been an ancient sea channel at the location marked on Figure 5.4 that would have cut off the region known today as Paliki from the rest of Cephalonia and turned it into an island? The most obvious starting point seemed to be to take a closer look at the map. Figure 7.1 is reproduced from the Freytag-Berndt tourist map that I was using at the time and it depicts the region that is now called 'Thinia'. The first encouraging indication was the long streambed running from the northern bay of Agia Kiriaki in a south-westerly direction towards the southern bay of Koumaria, which itself lies in a small corner of the overall Bay of Argostoli. The shading of the contours suggested that this streambed was at a much lower level than the neighbouring terrain. However there was a rather worrying absence of any streambed two-thirds of the way down where the red and yellow roads intersect, so perhaps the former sea channel followed a different course.

Two additional streams and contours on each side also appeared to be feasible on paper and so this resulted in the three candidate locations for Strabo's Channel that are marked on Figure 7.2.

Tracing hypothetical channels on paper was easy: the real issue was the height of the land along these three routes. If this was at or near sea level then I was in with a chance but if there was significant altitude involved then the whole proposition looked doubtful. The best thing to do seemed to be to consult with a local, so I called Alex Matsoukis[1] at our holiday company and asked him if he knew the area. He explained that indeed he did: he was born only a few kilometres away to the north of the island and he frequently drove past Thinia. He said that at Petrikata to the south and at Angonas to the north there are side roads that descend steeply down a sharp valley to a streambed which is almost at sea level. There are lovely bays at each end and the valley extends from coast to coast with abundant wild life: spring flowers, croaking frogs, wild ducks and so on. Indeed spring was a great time to visit Cephalonia: no other tourists, low prices, plenty of accommodation, not too hot – why didn't I come out right away?

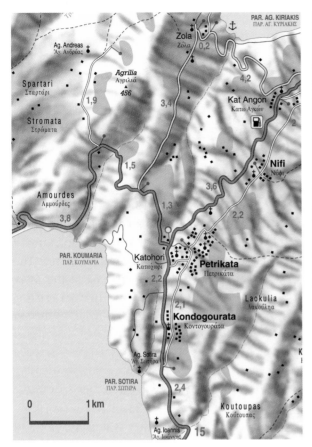

FIGURE 7.1 Freytag-Berndt map of Thinia
Could there have been a marine seaway joining
the north-eastern and south-western bays only
3,200 years ago? [Image credits: as Figure 5.3.]

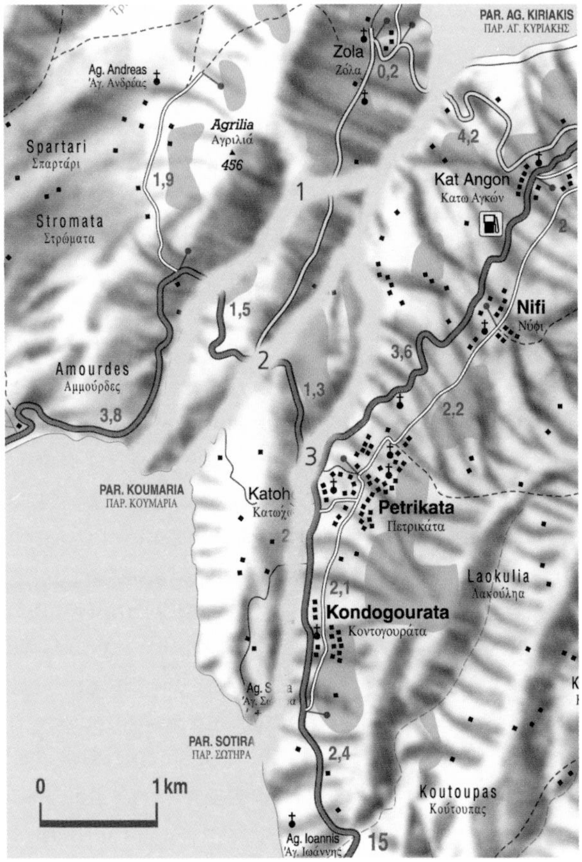

FIGURE 7.2 Three candidates for Strabo's Channel
Based on the shaded contours these three hypothetical
routes seemed to be the only possibilities.
[Image credits: as Figure 5.3.]

March in England has its attractions but this was too good an opportunity to miss. There are no direct charter flights to the island at that time of the year but there is a connecting flight to the island from Athens and I could be out there within a few hours. Why not? But first there was some research to be done. Whatever the current height of the former channel, somehow I had to find out how it had been filled in over a period as recent as the last 3,200 years. That may sound like a long time to the rest of us but to a geologist it is almost yesterday and most of the great changes in the global landscape have taken much longer than that. It was time to visit the Internet.

One of the extraordinary benefits of the Internet is its ability to enable one to acquire some knowledge about an unfamiliar speciality very quickly. There are many traps for the unwary involved in research of this nature but, as Charles Brewer has aptly pointed out, one should 'Be willing to say "I don't know", but strive to decrease the frequency with which you must do so. Samuel Butler observed that "a little knowledge is a dangerous thing, but a little lack of knowledge is also a dangerous thing".'[2] The answer therefore seems to be that it is legitimate to dabble in an area of expertise in which one is not qualified but at the same time it is crucial to regard any finding as tentative until it has been confirmed by an expert. If one adopts these checks and balances then the Internet is intellectually irresistible: it has become 'the thinking man's television', to quote Christopher Hampton who first coined the phrase in a somewhat different context in his play *The Philanthropist*.

My first assault on Google took me to the work of Professor Anastasia Kiratzi at the Department of Geophysics within the University of Thessaloniki and after reading her article[3] I e-mailed her with the question 'Is there any evidence of a general lowering of sea levels relative to the local land mass (i.e. land uprising via tectonic activity) in the Ionian Islands such as Lefkas and Cephalonia over the last 3,000 years? If so, can you point me towards the relevant research articles?' Less than twenty minutes later her reply came back 'I will try to help you with what you want, although I am not an expert in this field. I will ask around.' How extraordinarily thoughtful of her to bother to assist an unknown Internet correspondent whom she would probably never meet or hear from again! So began an international electronic correspondence that has encompassed seismologists, geologists, dendrochronologists, neotectonic experts, classicists, philologists, archaeologists, satellite image specialists, software developers and many other disciplines.

By now I had made arrangements for a preliminary visit to Cephalonia to take place from 20 March to 25 March 2003 and so there was only a week or so available in which to try to assemble some form of understanding of a possible causal mechanism for the infilling of Strabo's Channel. At that time it seemed to me that there were only two possibilities: either the sea level had gone down or the land level had gone up, or perhaps both. I was therefore encouraged to find on the Internet an article with the intriguing title 'Sea Level Variations in the Mediterranean Sea and Black Sea from Satellite Altimetry and Tide Gauges'.[4]

The authors of this study had used satellites to bounce radar pulses off the surface of the Ionian Sea in order to determine its height with great accuracy. If you bear in mind that a satellite essentially orbits around the centre of mass of the earth as a whole without regard to sea level, you can see that this technique can be used to deduce the average height of the sea itself in absolute terms relative to the centre of the earth, rather than by comparison with the local land features. The paper was published in 2002 and it analysed measurements collected for six years from 1993 to 1998.

The surprising result is that it shows that 'while on the average the Mediterranean sea level has been rising, two regions show evidence of sea level fall: the western Mediterranean Sea between the Balearic Islands and Sardinia, and the Ionian basin, between Greece and Sicily. In the Ionian basin, the negative trend reaches -25 mm/year.' In other words, uniquely in these two particular areas the average sea level has fallen by about an inch per year for the period of study, which was the last six years. Could this have been the reason why Strabo's Channel is now no longer underwater?

A reduction in sea levels of 25 mm per year for 3,200 years corresponds to a total decline of 80 m. I didn't yet know how high the land of the channel was today but at first this sounded rather encouraging. However as I started to think about it a number of practical problems presented themselves. First of all, no evidence had been provided in this research article regarding any history of sea level decline prior to 1993 and for all I knew the sea level might have moved up and down in all sorts of ways over the last 3,200 years. Furthermore this movement had been documented as a decline in the sea level specifically in the Ionian basin of Greece and this meant that the sea levels in the adjoining Adriatic, Aegean and most other Mediterranean areas were not declining: in fact they were rising.

Although I could imagine that tidal or gravitational effects could permit a difference of a few centimetres between connected bodies of water, the mind boggled at the notion of the islands of the Ionian Sea looming out of the bottom of a vast oceanic well of water that was 80 m lower than its immediate aquatic surroundings, which were meanwhile heroically resisting the temptation to inundate them via the tsunami of all time. I reluctantly came to the conclusion that although differential sea level changes might have made some minor contribution to the exposure of Strabo's Channel they were unlikely to be a significant factor.

Could the level of the entire volume of water in the Mediterranean Sea have declined significantly over the period prior to these satellite measurements? Unfortunately this radical hypothesis is not borne out by observations either, because in order to avoid a torrent of water cascading through the Straits of Gibraltar this would require a matching decline in sea levels all over the world. An appeal to common sense accompanied by consultation of Tjeerd van Andel's wonderful book *New Views on an Old Planet* made it clear that this was a non-starter.[5] Sea levels have varied enormously over the last 100,000 years and more but over the last 3,000 years the consensus in the Mediterranean Sea is that there have been relatively insignificant changes, although this does not take into account any local effects of land upthrust or subsidence.[6]

So this left what I thought at the time was the only alternative, that the underlying land level had gone up. A few more mouse-clicks identi-fied some of the papers that analyse the impact of the 1953 earthquake in Cephalonia. Two of these were particularly helpful: they were published under the somewhat daunting titles 'Late-Holocene Shoreline Changes related to Paleoseismic Events in the Ionian Islands, Greece'[7] and 'The 1953 Earth-quake in Cephalonia (Western Hellenic Arc): Coastal Uplift and Halotectonic Faulting'.[8] These papers were published in 1994 and they documented the results of extensive interdisciplinary researches on the island involving earthquake experts, geologists, microbiologists and other specialists.

The earthquake experts were understandably interested in identifying the causal factors behind the earthquake itself. I learnt that 'halotectonic' is another good Greek compound word combining *hals*, salt, and *tekton*, builder. Much of the island of Cephalonia is built on a bed of salt and several months later John Underhill, whom we will encounter in Chapter 11, explained to me that this is why the island attracts sea turtles: it turns out that beaches containing grains derived from salt provide exactly the right thermal characteristics to optimise turtle egg incubation.[9]

Meanwhile the geologists were interested in identifying the various rock strata that permeate the island and increasing their understanding of how this land mass has emerged over the millennia. Finally the microbiologists had a very interesting role. I had previously imagined that a fossil was a rather large and distinctive chunk of bone or a visible imprint in an old piece of rock, but I learnt that much research these days involves what are called microfossils: the remains of minute organic creatures that yield their secrets under the microscope and help biologists to understand how things have changed. Some of these organisms survive only in sea water, so if the land level is thrust up then an invisible band of tiny dead fossils is left around the former sea line.

One of the most interesting photographs in these papers is depicted at Figure 7.3. This rock sticks out of the water at Poros, a popular holiday resort on the south-east of Cephalonia: passengers on the Kyllini ferry pass by it every day on their way to the Peloponnese. Various horizontal lines are visible on this rock: let us start by looking at sea level below the largest central boulder. Line 1 is the boundary between the lower region of darker rock near the waterline and the lighter region of rock just above it: it is at a height of about 60 cm above sea level and for scale you may be able to make out a person standing to the right of the indicated number. Then at about the same distance further up there is line 2 in the form of a ledge all around the rock itself. To the right there is line 3 made out of a distinct overhang further up. Finally line 4 is a cleft running through the central boulder a short distance from its summit.

Are these various lines simply accidental or were they the outcome of some underlying cause that affected the rest of the island? The evidence is unambiguous for line 1: sea level prior to the 1953 earthquake was at the top of the lowest band of dark rock. When that terrible quake took place the entire mass of rock in this part of the island was thrust upwards by an average of about 60 cm. The lower band of rock is still dark because fifty years is not enough time for it to have been dried out and bleached by the sun.

The explanation behind the other lines is less clear. Regarding line 2, the geologists say:

FIGURE 7.3
Evidence of uplift in Poros
*Poros is located at the small
finger of land that juts out into
the ocean north of Pronnoi
on Figure 6.1. We shall return
to this distinctive rock
in Chapter 29.*
[Image credits: Stiros et al.
(1994) Figure 2, with
author's numerals
superimposed.]

*Elevations measured for the second, older shoreline reaching +1.2 m near Poros, are
summarised in* [their] *Figure 13. According to the morphology of notches and benches
belonging to this shoreline, its uplift seems to have been relatively rapid, possibly
sudden. Five radiocarbon dates of elevated samples belonging to this second shoreline,
collected from the south-eastern part of the island, have shown ages ranging between
3060–2570 cal. BC and cal. AD 350–710.*[10]

On balance they feel that this second uplift of another 60 cm probably
occurred during the latter of these two date ranges, but they explain that their
evidence is by no means conclusive: in fact it rests on the radiocarbon dating of
a single shell of type *Vermetus triqueter* collected from the walls of an abandoned
sea pool located at this level about 2 km south of Poros.[11] This type of shell is
rather beautiful as Figure 7.4 suggests and the discovery and dating of such a
distinctive specimen at this level on the rock is certainly thought-provoking.
However it is important to put this find into perspective: clearly more than
one sample will be needed to establish a high level of confidence about the
age of this second band.

The geologists do not comment on the identity or age of lines 3 or 4, so
in overall terms their evidence suggests that in addition to the upthrust from
the 1953 event there was at least one other upthrusting earthquake in former
years.

Based on the statistics summarised in Chapter 1 (to be discussed in
more detail in Chapter 11) which indicate that major earthquakes occur on
Cephalonia on average every fifty years, it therefore looks as though events

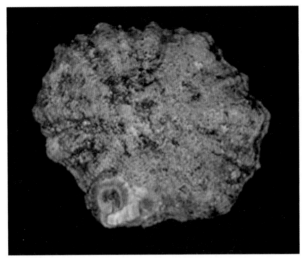

FIGURE 7.4
Vermetus triqueter *shell*
The occupant of the shell can
leave through the hole, which
is typically about 4 mm in
diameter.
[Image credits: Acquario
Comunale Grosseto.
Website:
www.gol.grosseto.it/puam/
comgr/acquario/vermetus_
triquetrus.htm]

that thrust the island upwards are comparatively rare. In case I had misunderstood the papers I managed to contact one of the authors, Professor Stathis Stiros, by mobile phone. While standing on a railway platform near the Gulf of Corinth he was kind enough to confirm to me that the maximum upthrust that has been observed anywhere in Greece over the last few thousand years is about 9 m in western Crete, so he didn't think that an upthrust of land in Cephalonia of many tens of metres in the last few thousand years was remotely possible.

Just how high are the land levels along the three possible routes for Strabo's Channel marked in Figure 7.2? It had become essential to pin these measurements down and so I contacted the Hellenic Military Geographical Service who are responsible for surveying the whole country and who produce very detailed maps on a scale of 1:5000. They had no facilities for despatching them to me by courier but fortunately a long-standing friend of mine, Takis Patrikarakos, was living in Athens and he was kind enough to organise all of this for me.[12] When the maps arrived I pored over them with my son Simon who had selflessly agreed to sacrifice part of his University vacation in rainy England to accompany me out to this sunny island. We drew a deep breath: those contours were not a pretty sight.

The maps told us that the highest point of land along route number 1 is 300 m above sea level. Along route number 2 the figure is 192 m and along route number 3 it is 180 m. In each case the highest point corresponds to the position of the number on the map. This was an absolute disaster. How could Strabo possibly have been right? How could the position of the sea relative to the land in the channel have changed this much in such a geologically short period, especially in view of a presumed maximum change of the order of only a few metres in the level of the surrounding coastline?

Perhaps there was something very strange about the channel. Perhaps there was a very narrow, almost vertical cliffside that didn't show up on the contour map but that would have allowed a sea passage to exist. We needed to find out more about the geology of the isthmus and there was very little time to go before we left for the island. Some further Internet research came up with a research dossier called *The Geological Results of Petroleum Exploration in Western Greece*.[13] It had been written in 1971 jointly by the BP company and the organisation that has subsequently become Greece's IGME, the Institute of Geology and Mineral Exploration. A call to them revealed that the thesis was lengthy and contained large colour maps: it could be consulted in Athens but it was not possible to copy it and courier it to England. But at BP we were luckier: there was one copy still in existence and it could be borrowed from their London library for the princely sum of £7.80. The day before we flew to Greece Simon jumped on a train and within an hour or so we were gazing at the geology of Strabo's Channel. It was the most cost-effective investment that I have ever made.

The section of the map illustrated at Figure 7.5 identifies not the height but the age of the rock in the area we intended to visit. The key diagram alongside it explains how the colours should be interpreted. The green rock is the oldest: it is Cretaceous, anywhere from 144 to 65 million years old. That is just a little younger than the Jurassic rock that has been popularised as the habitat of dinosaurs, so it seemed unlikely that it could have changed its nature significantly in the last 3,200 years. The intermediate colours represent progressively younger rock until we reach the period from 10,000 years ago to today, which is called Holocene. This region is marked on the map in white and in fact it doesn't consist of rock at all: instead it is composed of material such as screes (sandy, ash-like rock fragments), outwash fans (flat or gently sloping surfaces underlain by glacier material), raised beaches and alluvium (stream sediment). What did this map tell us about Strabo's Channel?

If the altitude was marked as high on the Greek Army contour map and if the age of the rock was any colour other than white on the BP/IGME geological map, this meant that we were looking at high altitude ancient terrain, and there was surely no chance that Strabo's Channel could have penetrated such regions as late as 1200 BC. This also ruled out the possibility of the channel cutting through in an east–west direction at the top of Argostoli Bay because the contour map showed significant height there while the geological map also indicated much older rock. A comparison between Figure 7.2 and Figure 7.5 rapidly suggested to us that the only feasible route was the easternmost course marked as option number 3: indeed we drew modest comfort from the fact that the maximum height along this route was a mere 180 m compared to 192 m and 300 m for the others. So there was still a 180 m problem to explain

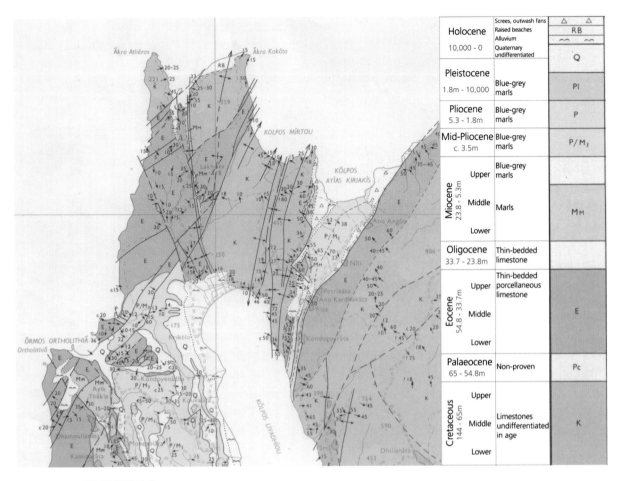

Holocene 10,000 - 0	Screes, outwash fans	△ △
	Raised beaches	R B
	Alluvium	
	Quaternary undifferentiated	Q
Pleistocene 1.8m - 10,000	Blue-grey marls	Pl
Pliocene 5.3 - 1.8m	Blue-grey marls	P
Mid-Pliocene c. 3.5m	Blue-grey marls	P/M₃
Miocene 23.8 - 5.3m Upper	Blue-grey marls	
Middle	Marls	Mм
Lower		
Oligocene 33.7 - 23.8m	Thin-bedded limestone	
Eocene 54.8 - 33.7m Upper	Thin-bedded porcellaneous limestone	E
Middle		
Lower		
Palaeocene 65 - 54.8m	Non-proven	Pc
Cretaceous 144 - 65m Upper	Limestones undifferentiated in age	K
Middle		
Lower		

FIGURE 7.5

BP/IGME 1971 geological map of northern Paliki *The colours indicate the age of the underlying rock, on a scale from green Cretaceous (up to 144 million years old) to white Holocene (within the last 10,000 years).* [Image credits: BP Co. Ltd (1971) Sheet 3.]

but at least the BP/IGME map told us that this problem had been in existence for no more than 10,000 years.

By superimposing the contour map on to the geological map we were able to pin down what we presumed to be the likely course of the channel and the result is illustrated in Figure 7.6. This geological map is actually a later version that IGME updated in 1973, but the principles are the same. If Strabo was right about the channel then this is where we thought it must have been. We knew how long it was – the map showed a distance of about 6 km from coast to coast. We didn't know how wide it was, but both maps indicated that it could be no more than a few hundred metres wide at most and at certain points considerably less – only a few tens of metres.

How bizarre for there to be two islands of this size separated by a narrow channel that was no more than a few tens or hundreds of metres wide! And this channel was unlikely to be particularly deep even in 1200 BC because by Strabo's time it had been more or less filled in: 'where the island is narrowest it forms an isthmus so low-lying that it is often submerged from sea to sea'.

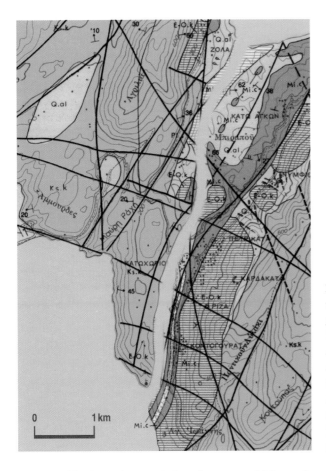

FIGURE 7.6 Channel superimposed on geological map
The channel course marked as number 3 on Figure 7.2 appears to be the only one that corresponds to recent Holocene age rock on this diagram.
[Image credits: IGME (1985).]

Presumably in Odysseus' day there would have been a ferryman available to row travellers across: indeed I hardly think they came on foot to ancient Ithaca.

We flew to Athens on Friday 21 March but before I explain what happened on that first expedition it is time for us to revisit the *Odyssey*.

Notes
1 Alex Matsoukis works with an enterprising travel company at www.ionianislandholi-days.com/
2 We shall meet Samuel Butler again in Chapter 33 ; for the Charles Brewer quote see http://teachpsych.lemoyne.edu/teachpsych/eit/eit2000/eit00-01.rtf
3 Louvari et al. (1999).
4 Cazenave et al. (2002).
5 Van Andel (1994) pp. 77–87.
6 See for example http://maritime.haifa.ac.il/cms/newslett/cms24/cms24_19.htm commenting on the Israeli coast: 'Sea level was lower than −16 m in the middle of the 9th millennium BP, and rose to less than −7 m by the mid 7th millennium BP. It stabilized between −1 m and the present sea level during the Middle Bronze Age. Sea level changes during the historic period fluctuated up to ±0.5 m.' Pirazzoli (1996) says (p. 57) 'Along the coasts of the Tyrrhenian Sea [south-west Italy], for example, such data

demonstrate that 2000 years ago the sea level was about 0.5 m below the present level, but was rising by about 0.75 mm/yr between 50 BC and AD 150'. For the Ionian coast the position is more complex to assess because of uncertainties surrounding the tectonic history: Besonen (1997) states (p. 13) 'Particularly important to note is that during the last 5,000 years, which is the focus of the present study, relative sea level rise along the southwestern Epirote coast has been less than two meters.' A comprehensive review appears in Pirazzoli and Pluet (1991): at p. 92 Graph F depicts sea levels at the Bay of Navarino on the SW Peloponnese and confirms a relatively modest level of increase. The balance of view seems to be that over the last 3,000 years sea levels have not been rising in the Mediterranean very significantly, but this figure takes no account of local tectonic movements. See also Chapter 34 n. 1.

7 Pirazzoli et al. (1994).

8 Stiros et al. (1994).

9 In Wood and Bjorndal (2000) we read that *Caretta Caretta* specialists are at loggerheads over this claim: it appears to have become a hotbed of saline complexity. Those creationists who are momentarily awed that God made sea turtles smart enough to master the equations associated with their own fecundity may like to reach for their copies of Darwin and Dawkins and remind themselves that genes which code for turtles that lay their eggs on the right type of beaches have tended to be passed on to later generations, whereas other turtle genes have not.

10 Pirazzoli et al. (1994) p. 403.

11 Pirazzoli et al. (1994) fig. 8.

12 Since that date a new website has been established at www.gys.gr and some digital maps can now be provided by e-mail: see also the entry for HMGS in the Bibliography.

13 BP Co. Ltd (1971).

CHAPTER 8   Coincidence

Come, answer me precisely – Who are you?
Whose son? Where are your city and your parents?
What ship did you come on? Why did the sailors
Bring you to Ithaca? Who did they claim
To be? For I hardly think you came on foot.[1]   *Odyssey* 1.169–73

In Chapter 2 we heard that at the beginning of the *Odyssey* the goddess Athene, disguised as Mentes, descends from Mount Olympos to advise Telemachos that now that he is coming of age he should assert his authority over the suitors and visit King Menelaos in Sparta in search of news of his father. After offering hospitality to the distinguished visitor Telemachos asks Mentes where he has come from. The most interesting aspect of Telemachos' question is the last line 'For I hardly think you came on foot.' Homer is cracking a joke: not a very good one perhaps, but nevertheless a distinctive attempt at light banter. We know this because the same line appears three more times in the *Odyssey*: when Eumaios greets Odysseus, when Telemachos asks Eumaios where his guest came from and when Telemachos then speaks to his father.[2] So this line is quite deliberate and it must have conveyed some specific meaning to Homer's audience.

The joke is not remotely amusing if the journey to Ithaca involves a significant sea crossing because in that case it would be perfectly obvious that nobody could ever arrive by foot. Homer is not given to gratuitous humour and it is clear that the line must reflect some aspect of the local geography. For this reason these words have been used by those who support Lefkas as Odysseus' Ithaca since at varying times it has been either an island or connected to the mainland via a causeway. Today's holidaymakers on Lefkas drive across this causeway (see Figure 2.2) en route from the airport at Preveza on the mainland of Greece and it is easy to see that, depending on its condition at the time, an ancient visitor to Lefkas could have been either able to walk or alternatively obliged to wade across the narrow crossing. But as we have seen, Lefkas does not lie the furthest to the west of a group of neighbouring islands: it lies strictly to the north and it is not therefore a serious contender.

Meanwhile those who maintain that ancient Ithaca is the same island as modern Ithaca have no credible explanation for these words at all, because the distance from the Greek mainland to modern Ithaca is about 30 km. Even the strait between Cephalonia and modern Ithaca is between 2.5 km and 4 km wide: one could never conceivably come that way on foot.

However, if ancient Ithaca was separated from Same (Cephalonia) by a shallow sea channel that was only a few tens or hundreds of metres wide, Homer's gentle attempts to tease his audience suddenly make a great deal of sense. Mentes (Athene in disguise) and Odysseus could indeed have tried to 'come on foot' but they would undoubtedly have got rather wet in the process. So how did the ancient Ithacans cross Strabo's Channel instead? Homer is thoughtful enough to tell us. In the next passage the suitors are preparing for yet another feast at the expense of the household of Penelope, Odysseus' abandoned wife. Odysseus himself is actually present but he is disguised as a beggar. Philoitios, his faithful cowherd, has arrived at the palace with more food for the suitors, although he is disparaging of their motives and nostalgic for his lord to return:

> Third came that stalwart fellow Philoitios,
> Leading a heifer and fat goats for the suitors.
> They had been brought across by ferrymen,
> Who also ferry people, any who come.
> . . . .
> 'Oh, how I weep for glorious Odysseus.
> He made me his cattle-herd, while still a youngster,
> In the regions where the Cephallenians live.
> Now they have grown past counting, and no man
> Could breed a better crop of broad-browed cattle.
> But others order me to bring them here
> For them to eat.'   20.185–8, 209–15

Philoitios has brought the cattle over by ferry from 'the regions where the Cephallenians live' and so these regions must be separated from Ithaca by water. However in the passage quoted below, the place where these cattle come from is described as the 'mainland' in the phrase 'Twelve mainland herds of cattle'. Where exactly is this 'mainland'?

If you believe that ancient Ithaca and modern Ithaca are the same island then the following problems arise from this passage. Because as we have seen the nearest point of the Greek mainland is about 30 km away from modern Ithaca,[3] you first have to explain the commercial logic associated with this 'no reservation required' Bronze Age ferry service. Personally I find it very hard to imagine that the cattle and goats and 'any who come' would be brought across from the Greek mainland by ferrymen hanging around all day on the off-chance of a speculative fare over this distance, and that is before any consideration of the perils of bad weather and crazed livestock endangering their ships.

Then you must also explain why Philoitios would refer to the mainland of Greece as 'the regions where the Cephallenians live', since that part of Greece was called Acarnania and the Cephallenians did not live there; they inhabited the islands. After you have rationalised that you must then juggle with the following passage from earlier in the *Odyssey*, when Eumaios is describing his master's flocks to his visitor (who is in fact Odysseus, again in disguise):

> His stock was truly vast. No other hero
> Had so much, either on the dark mainland
> Or Ithaca itself. Not even twenty
> Together have such wealth. I'll list it for you:
> Twelve mainland herds of cattle; as many flocks
> Of sheep and droves of pigs and herds of goats
> Are pastured by outsiders and his farmhands.
> And here eleven herds of goats in all
> Graze on the margins, guarded by good men.   14.96–104

In this extract Eumaios explains that his master Odysseus owns twelve herds of cattle, sheep and pigs and goats on the mainland and that outsiders and his own farmhands graze them there: whereas here on Ithaca, eleven goatflocks graze on the margins of the island. So the key question now is: how far away is this mainland? If 'mainland' means the mainland of Greece itself, as the classical authorities have always presumed, then Homer is asking us to believe (a) that Odysseus would keep the bulk of his livestock about 30 km away, (b) that his swineherd here on Ithaca would personally know the exact numbers involved and (c) that he would also know that subcontract labour had been hired.

Odysseus' Palace has been full of suitors (108 in number as we shall later observe) who have been wined and dined for years at his household's expense. The mind boggles at the prospect of a continuous flotilla of ships carrying livestock over this distance: Meals on Keels? Just to hammer home the point, in the famous 'Catalogue of Ships' in the *Iliad* where Homer lists the participants in the Trojan War we read:

> Next Odysseus led his Cephallenian companies,
> gallant-hearted fighters, the island men of Ithaca,
> of Mount Neriton's leafy ridges shimmering in the wind,
> and men who lived in Crocylia and rugged Aegilips
> men who held Zacynthus and men who dwelled near Samos

and mainland men who grazed their flocks across the channel.
That mastermind like Zeus, Odysseus led those fighters on.
In his command sailed twelve ships, prows flashing crimson.

Iliad 2.631–7

That is Fagles' translation but Murray phrases it somewhat differently:

And Odysseus led the great-hearted Cephallenians
who held Ithaca and Neritum, covered with waving forests,
and who dwelt in Crocyleia and rugged Aegilips;
and those who held Zacynthos, and who dwelt about Same,
and held the mainland and dwelt on the shores opposite the isles.
These Odysseus led, the peer of Zeus in counsel.
And with him there followed twelve ships with vermilion prows.

Iliad 2.631–7

This is all rather curious. Fagles' 'mainland men who grazed their flocks across the channel' don't appear to be living in the same place as those of Murray who 'held the mainland and dwelt on the shores opposite the isles', yet these are two alternative translations of the same line of text. Which is the more accurate? When I first encountered these lines I did not have access to James Diggle's expertise and so I tried to translate Homer's words directly. Many people find the Greek alphabet rather beautiful (and if they cannot read it, also rather mysterious) so let us take our courage in our hands and embark upon this modest translation together.

οἳ Σάμον ἀμφενέμοντο,
οἵ τ᾿ ἤπειρον ἔχον ἠδ᾿ ἀντιπέραι᾿ ἐνέμοντο   *Iliad* 2.634–5

If this is all Greek to you then you can pronounce these lines as follows:

Hoi Samon amphenemonto,
Hoi t' êpeiron echon êd' antiperai' enemonto

where ê is pronounced as in 'aim'. I translated this literally via the dictionary as:

Those inhabiting Samos,
Those holding the mainland and living opposite.

How then do the previous two translations compare? Both of them refer to the men on the mainland but Fagles suggests that they 'grazed their flocks across the channel' while Murray proposes that they 'dwelt on the shores opposite the isles'. Meanwhile Homer appears to say nothing of the kind: he simply refers to 'those holding the mainland and living opposite'.

Consider also that all of the people in the above extract are described as 'great-hearted Cephallenians'. The original Greek does not have the equivalent of a semi-colon where Murray has introduced one after 'Aegilips'; after 'Cephallenians' all the following lines are introduced with the phrase 'Those who' right up to the line which starts with 'These Odysseus led'. So Homer regards them all as Cephallenians, which would be a very strange way of describing 'those holding the mainland' if the mainland in question was Acarnania, 30 km away on the mainland of Greece. Just as with the lines of the *Odyssey* from a page or so ago, it simply doesn't make any sense to imagine that the 'mainland' could mean mainland Greece.

The more I thought about this passage, the more I began to suspect that when Homer refers to the 'mainland' he is simply referring to the main land mass of the large island of Same that can be seen by the Ithacans just a few metres away across Strabo's Channel. It was not until several months later that James Diggle analysed these passages professionally: he has tackled the evidence far more rigorously than I can and his exposition and verdict are contained in Appendix 1 Section C. Once again I am happy to say that we find ourselves in agreement, but James has also discovered that line 2.635 of the *Iliad* contains a twist in the tail, one that has been misunderstood by scholars down the ages.

When you consider evidence such as the above you are entitled to say 'Well yes, but perhaps these phrases of Homer just happen to fit with the hypothesis that is being suggested. Maybe Homer was describing imaginary locations all the while, or perhaps he was describing a different location that is as yet unidentified. I agree that this evidence appears broadly supportive of the proposed location of ancient Ithaca, but that may simply be a coincidence.' If that is your sentiment then I don't wish to attempt to argue you out of it at this stage. What I would encourage you to do instead is to make a simple estimate of the chance that it is all coincidental. For example, if you feel that on balance the above argument is only 30% likely to be right and therefore 70% likely to be a chance result, then your assessment that the proposal so far is coincidental is clearly 70%.

Readers who are also statisticians will already have deduced where I am proposing to take this argument but I will spell it out all the same. As we saw earlier, there are somewhat in excess of twenty geographical clues in the *Odyssey* relating to the location of Ithaca itself and I intend to produce evidence to identify them all. If you assess the next argument as also 70% likely to be a pure coincidence then what does that imply for the proposal as a whole? If these geographical clues are independent of each other, in the sense that they can be considered individually rather than in terms of any dependencies, then the probability that there are two entirely coincidental links between the *Odyssey* and the solution proposed in this book is found by multiplying these two figures: in other words it is now only 49%.

So despite the fact that each of these two clues was assessed by you as only 30% likely to be correct, the likelihood that both of them are simultaneous chance correlations is now slightly less than 50%. As more clues are assembled this probability will continue to diminish until by the time we have considered all of the geographical clues I hope to have persuaded you that the probability of all of the places on today's peninsula of Paliki representing a perfect fit to Homer's description of ancient Ithaca entirely by chance is vanishingly low.

If you are trying to fill a particular gap in a jigsaw puzzle and the very first piece you pick up happens to fit it exactly, you will probably consider that this was just a matter of good luck, but if that same experience is then repeated twenty times in succession you must consider the more likely alternative that the pieces in the box have already been placed in order for your benefit. Now it is time for us to see how some of these same pieces have been used in an attempt to create other jigsaw puzzles.

Notes
1 See James Diggle's comments on this passage in Appendix 1 Section J.
2 *Odyssey* 14.190, 16.59 and 16.224.
3 Some writers have suggested that Lefkas was regarded as the mainland, but it is still 9 km away: see the discussion at Strabo 1.3.18.

CHAPTER 9 **Competition**

The facts will eventually test all our theories, and they form, after all, the only
impartial jury to which we can appeal.　　　Agassiz, *Geological Sketches* (1866)[1]

In Chapter 5 we considered the question 'Is there a two-harboured island
called Asteris in the straits between Ithaca and Samos, with windy heights
that would enable an ambush to take place?' (Clue 4). I confessed that my
evolving solution does not yet satisfy this clue but I also suggested that none
of the other locations that have been proposed for ancient Ithaca comply with
it either. If I am to justify this assertion we now need to review the strength
of these existing proposals.

We have already observed that early Greek writers such as Eratosthenes,
Demetrius, Apollodorus and Strabo addressed the mystery of Odysseus' Ithaca.
These writers have been treated with great reverence down the ages: indeed
many of their proposed solutions (particularly those of Strabo) have been
adopted on the basis of their antiquity and general authority rather than as a
result of the inherent logic of their case.

In more recent years there has been a plethora of further proposals. These
theories have been explored in many excellent publications elsewhere[2] and
so I do not propose to embark on another comprehensive discussion of them
in this chapter. Instead I refer readers to Appendix 4 which summarises the
varying views that twenty-three writers down the ages have each held regarding thirty-two Ithacan clues and locations. They remind us that the quest for
Odysseus' birthplace is very familiar ground that one tackles at one's peril.
What I would like to do here instead is to highlight the particular theories that
have most influenced the present enterprise.

In 1806 William Gell visited the island and the following year he published
his findings in *The Geography and Antiquities of Ithaca*. Gell thought that the city
of Ithaca was located on the Aetos isthmus with its harbour to the east, in
or near the present bay of Vathy (Figure 9.1). However any proposals which
place the ancient harbour to the east of this isthmus violate Clue 4, because
if modern Ithaca was also ancient Ithaca then 'the straits between Ithaca and
Same' must lie on the western side of it. Suitors lying in wait in those straits
would never see their victim returning from mainland Greece to a harbour
on the eastern side of Ithaca. Gell's proposal also obviously violates Clue 1,
'Does Ithaca lie low and to the west, the furthest out to sea of a group of
neighbouring islands called Ithaca, Same, Doulichion and Zacynthos?'

FIGURE 9.1
Polis Bay, Aetos isthmus
and Fiscardo harbour
Colour interpretation: as
Figure 1.3. Grid: 5 km.
[Image credits: as
Figure 1.3.]

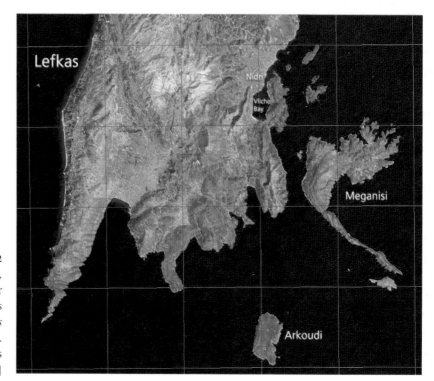

FIGURE 9.2
Nidri and Vlicho Bay,
Dörpfeld's harbour
on Lefkas
Colour interpretation: as
Figure 1.3. Grid: 5 km.
[Image credits: as
Figure 1.3.]

Writing in 1835 William Leake proposed an ingenious alternative: that the city was instead located on the north-western coast of modern Ithaca near the harbour of Polis Bay. However his proposal likewise falls fouls of Clue 1 and it also violates Clue 3, because a ship cannot leave Polis Bay driven by a stiff following wind from the west. As the map indicates, Polis Bay faces to the south-west and we heard in Chapter 5 that a Bronze Age galley can sail only a few degrees into the wind. It would be unable to embark from Polis Bay in such conditions and even if the crew rowed out beyond the headland, the wind would beat the ship back towards the coastline once the crew had hoisted the sail. Instead the poet tells us that 'The canvas billowed in the wind' which strongly suggests an unobstructed easterly course.

In Chapter 2 we heard that by 1900 Dörpfeld had wrestled with the enigma for many years until he came to the conclusion that ancient Ithaca was located on the island of Lefkas. He believed that the city of Ithaca was located in the plain of Nidri alongside its harbour in the bay of Vlicho (Figure 9.2: his grave on the north-eastern promontory is at Figure 2.3). Although Dörpfeld's theory was very controversial at the time and has never been strongly supported, it undoubtedly deserves to be regarded as a contestant so I shall refer to it as the 'Dörpfeld theory'.

Dörpfeld also has difficulty with Clue 1 because the 'island' of Lefkas is furthest to the north rather than to the west. Furthermore in order to keep track of the names of the other islands he is obliged to rechristen Cephalonia as Doulichion and Ithaca as Same, a form of insular musical chairs which would require considerable toponymical research to justify. Dörpfeld faces an additional challenge with his harbour, which is landlocked except for a narrow northern exit. This would be very difficult for a Bronze Age galley to negotiate with a stiff following wind from the west and it also calls for a 270° course reversal, a hazardous manoeuvre with canvas billowing in the wind.

In 1908 Dörpfeld's colleague A. E. H. Goekoop published *Ithaque la Grande* in which he claimed that ancient Ithaca was not on today's island of Ithaca at all but was instead located in south-western Cephalonia. He believed that Odysseus' city was based on the imposing hilltop of St George near the village of Mazarakata (south-east of Argostoli on Figure 1.4) and that the harbour was nearby at Minies, close to the modern airport (see Figure 10.5). In making this proposal he was obliged to put forward the radical suggestion that Ithaca was not itself an island but instead a region of another island. A. E. H. Goekoop's theory attracted relatively little support but it deserves to be mentioned because of its focus on Cephalonia and also because of its influence on his grandson, C. H. Goekoop.

In 1927 Lord Rennell of Rodd published *Homer's Ithaca: A Vindication of Tradition* which reinforced the classical view that Odysseus' island and the modern island of Ithaca were one and the same. As a result the British School of

Archaeology in Athens embarked on investigations in northern Ithaca under the leadership of W. A. Heurtley and Sylvia Benton. Although extensive excavations in the area of Pilikata to the north of Stavros were disappointing, in a cave in the town's harbour of Polis Bay they found evidence of an Odyssean cult together with twelve three-legged cauldrons dating back to the eighth or ninth century BC. This was thought-provoking because Homer says in the *Odyssey* that King Alcinoos and his twelve Phaiacian lords each give Odysseus a tripod and a cauldron before escorting him to Ithaca.[3] We are told that a local land-owner had previously found a thirteenth tripod and so the connection seemed irresistible. We will return to these tripods in Chapter 21: at the time of their excavation it was felt that their later date ruled them out from serious consideration as the actual Odyssean gifts.

Further north of Polis Bay some ruins from a later period have been somewhat imaginatively described as the 'School of Homer'. In his delightful 1842 guidebook William Mure of Caldwell writes:

I was assured at Vathý that the title of School of Homer was invented by the Papa, whose hospitality Gell enjoyed on occasion of his visit, for the purpose of amusing his guest. The old gentleman, I understood, was still alive, and often chuckled with delight over his ingenuity in outwitting the celebrated English antiquary at his own art; and still more at this creation of his fancy having been immortalized with so much pomp and circumstance in the standard work on Ithacan topography. This story seems to be confirmed by the circumstances, that Leake, who visited the place in the same year as Gell, says nothing of any such name. Be this as it may, the title is now become inveterate in 'popular' tradition; and the villagers point out with patriotic pride the platform below as the place of instruction, and the niches in the wall as the book-shelves, asserting that there had once been the remains of tables and benches. The ruined building above, they describe as the 'Schoolmaster's house'.[4]

Work on Ithaca continued sporadically after the Second World War and Gell's location near Vathy for the ancient city and harbour has also been periodically resurrected. A site called 'Odysseus' Castle' is marked at the Aetos isthmus on some tourist maps and boatloads of visitors no doubt descend upon it in the summer.[5] Although the tiny cove of Piso Aetos lies on the western side of this isthmus, by no stretch of the imagination could this be described as a city harbour and it also suffers from the same problem of a countervailing westerly wind.

The balance of expert opinion today favours Polis Bay for the harbour and Pilikata for the site of the city. A recent and very readable account of the proposal appears in J. V. Luce's book *Celebrating Homer's Landscapes* and I shall refer to this tradition as the 'Classical' theory.

In 1987 Tim Severin published *The Ulysses Voyage* which as we have seen described his attempt to locate the entire Odyssean voyage within the Aegean and Ionian basins, albeit with a detour to Libya. Severin sailed in a recreated late Bronze Age galley and one of his most valuable contributions was to focus on small distances and local topography rather than on lengthy international voyages. His book contains striking evidence in support of the location of several other Odyssean place names, but as a marine venture it sheds little light on the specific problem of identifying the island of Ithaca itself.

In 1990 C. H. Goekoop published *Op zoek naar Ithaka* (In search of Ithaca) which provides an exhaustive review of forty-eight passages in the *Iliad* and the *Odyssey* that refer to Ithaca. C. H. Goekoop goes a long way to demonstrating that unless Homer's locations were fictitious, then the present island of Ithaca cannot be Odysseus' birthplace. Like his grandfather he believed that ancient Ithaca was on Cephalonia, but instead of the hilltop of St George he favoured the northern region of Erissos, near the present town of Fiscardo. His proposal that ancient Ithaca is to be found on the northern promontory of Cephalonia was ingenious but once again Clue 1 presents him with a fundamental problem. Furthermore he has to maintain a constant defence of his basic postulate that Ithaca itself is not 'an island' but is instead 'part of an island'. An example of this difficulty occurs in the passage when Telemachos is explaining to King Menelaos of Sparta why he cannot accept his generosity:

Your gift should be a treasure I can store:
Horses I cannot take to Ithaca.
Here they should stay, for you to glory in.
Your kingdom is a broad plain, with much clover,
Galingale, wheat, oats, glistening broad-eared barley.
Ithaca has no meadows or broad horse-runs;
Neither has any of the sea-perched isles.
But there's not one so fair as Ithaca,
Goat-land, more lovely than horse-grazing land.   4.600–8[6]

The penultimate line of this extract is clearly problematic for C. H. Goekoop's theory and there are many other passages which present him with comparable difficulty: for example at 13.95 where the poet says of Ithaca 'Then the seafaring ship approached the island'. However Goekoop fares better than the others with Clue 3: his harbour is located at today's town of Fiscardo and the exit from this is indeed to the south-east, as Figure 9.1 indicates.

I have learnt during the course of this research that a few other writers over the last 100 years have also considered Paliki as a possible solution to Strabo's comment that 'where the island is narrowest it forms an isthmus so low-lying that it is often submerged from sea to sea'.[7] In 1903 the Palikian G. Volterras published a book in Greek entitled *A Critical Study of Homeric Ithaca* which made this proposal, although without evaluating the geological evidence either way.

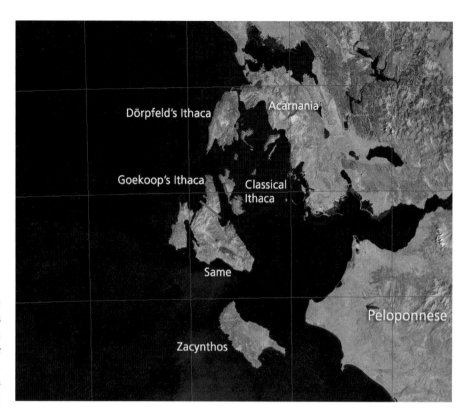

FIGURE 9.3
The three main proposals
for ancient Ithaca
Colour interpretation: as
Figure 1.3. Grid: 50 km.
[Image credits: as
Figure 1.3.]

Another Palikian, the schoolmaster E. S. Tsimaratos who lived from 1874 to 1954, wrote a manuscript which was published posthumously in Greek in 1998. Relying on his local knowledge and on evidence from mediaeval maps, he agreed with Strabo that Paliki might once have been cut off from the rest of Cephalonia, although he also offered no geological explanation for this proposal and he located ancient Ithaca on central Cephalonia rather than on Paliki. Also in 1998 Nikolas Livadas published a book locating Odysseus' Palace in Paliki, but without suggesting that it was once cut off by a former channel.

Writing in French in 2001 and with subsequent publications in 2003 and 2004, Gilles le Noan suggested that Ithaca is located in Paliki but after considering the possibility of a former sea channel he discounted it on the basis of geological advice. Recently Christos Tzakos has regarded Strabo's theory of a channel as feasible, although he continues to identify modern Ithaca as the location of the ancient civilisation. It will be a fitting tribute to Odysseus' heritage if it turns out to be two Palikians from the turn of the century, Volterras and Tsimaratos, who were the first to believe that Strabo might have been right.

The front-runners are generally regarded as the Classical, Dörpfeld and Goekoop theories and their respective claims for Ithaca itself are illustrated in Figure 9.3. The table at Figure 9.4 summarises these proposals and indicates

	Classical	Dörpfeld	Goekoop
Ancient Ithaca (country)	Ithaca	Lefkas	Erissos
Ancient Ithaca (city)	Pilikata (Stavros)	Nidri plain	Fiscardo
Ancient Ithaca (harbour)	Polis Bay	Vlicho Bay	Fiscardo
Doulichion	Echinades	Cephalonia	Cephalonia
Same	Cephalonia	Ithaca	Ithaca
Clue 1: Does Ithaca lie low and to the west, the furthest out to sea of a group of neighbouring islands called Ithaca, Same, Doulichion and Zacynthos?	No: it is mountainous and lies furthest to the east	No: it is furthest to the north	No: it is centrally placed and not an island
Clue 2: Does Ithaca contain a bay with two distinctive jutting headlands?	Possibly: Dexia Bay	Possibly: Syvota Bay	Possibly: Assos Bay
Clue 3: Can a ship leave Ithaca harbour driven by a stiff following wind from the west?	No: the harbour exit faces west	No: the harbour exit faces north	Yes: the harbour exit faces east
Clue 4: Is there a two-harboured island called Asteris in the straits between Ithaca and Samos, with windy heights that would enable an ambush to take place?	Possibly: Dascalion	Possibly: Arkoudi	Possibly: Dascalion

FIGURE 9.4
The theories and the clues

the degree of their compliance with Clues 1, 2, 3 and 4. For a more comprehensive analysis of these and additional theories see Appendix 4.

Since I am stepping on some delicate ground and various closely held beliefs here it may be prudent for me to comment briefly upon this table.

Clue 1 presents a fundamental objection to all three theories: it has either been disregarded or explained away by attempting to redefine the meaning of 'west'.

The whereabouts of Doulichion is still hotly debated. Strabo proposed the Echinades islands between Ithaca and mainland Greece, whereas Luce reminds us of T. W. Allen's suggestion that Doulichion was actually Lefkas. This would leave the Classical supporters with the problem of where Lefkas itself used to be but Luce explains this by saying that 'Readers will probably have noticed that Homer does not mention Lefkas under that name'.[8] This is curious because at the end of the *Odyssey* when the ghosts of the dead suitors are being called down to Hades 'like gibbering bats' Homer tells us at 24.11 that 'They went past Ocean's streams and Leucas rock' and in the Greek it is spelt 'Leukas' just as usual.[9]

As far as Clue 2 is concerned, clearly many islands can claim the existence of a bay with distinctive jutting headlands: in fact this location becomes more important when we start to trace Odysseus' footsteps after he lands there, so we will grant all these theories the benefit of the doubt for the time being.

Clue 3 presents a considerable objection to the Classical and Dörpfeld theories; perhaps unsurprisingly most of those who have chosen to consider this passage have taken refuge in the presumption of poetic licence.

To summarise the evidence so far: both the Classical theory and Dörpfeld's theory are unsatisfactory regarding Clues 1 and 3; Goekoop is unsatisfactory on Clue 1 and he complies with Clue 3 only by introducing the postulate that Ithaca is not an island, in defiance of lines of Homer such as those above. By contrast and as we have already seen in Chapter 5, the hypothesis of Strabo's Channel deals comfortably with all these three clues.

But there is stronger evidence yet to come. Now that we have established the nature and strength of the competition it is time to take a closer look at Clue 4.

Notes

1 Louis Jean Rodolphe Agassiz (1807–73) was the 'Father of Glaciology' and the first proponent of the theory of Ice Ages: see Agassiz and Agassiz (1866).

2 See for example Wace and Stubbings (1962) pp. 398–421 and Goekoop (1990) Chapter 2.

3 *Odyssey* 8.390–1, 13.13–14. Anthony Snodgrass has recently challenged the traditional interpretation of these gift numbers: for a more detailed discussion see Chapter 21.

4 Mure (1842) p. 77. The 'Papa' is described in Gell (1807) p. 109 as the 'Proto Papas, or head priest of the island' and Gell's footnote states 'Called also the Exarchos.'

5 See the entry on *The Odyssey Project* in Appendix 4.

6 See James Diggle's comments on this passage in Appendix 1 Section J.

7 See Pantos' website http://srs.dl.ac.uk/arch/the-ithaca-question/what_do_other_authors_think.htm

8 Luce (1998) p. 172.

9 In Luce's defence the Homeric authorities have been somewhat liberal with the paint-pot here in advising the reader that 'The Leucadian Rock is certainly not Cape Leukatas on the island of Leukas, or indeed any other spot in the real world' (Russo et al. (1992) p. 360). But if that really is the case (which I doubt) then it leaves unanswered the question of why Homer was perverse enough to choose as the name for his imaginary rock that of a real one just a few kilometres away.

CHAPTER 10   **Ambush**

Will all great Neptune's ocean wash this blood
Clean from my hand? No, this my hand will rather
The multitudinous seas incarnadine,
Making the green one red.   Shakespeare, *Macbeth* II.ii.61 (1606)

Antinoos, the main troublemaker of the suitors, has just learnt that Telemachos
is off on a journey to Pylos and Sparta to consult with Kings Nestor and
Menelaos about the whereabouts of his father. He realises that if Telemachos
is allowed to assert his authority as he comes of age then he may become the
hereditary ruler of Ithaca and thereby destroy Antinoos' hopes of gaining the
throne himself.

> Antinoos, Eupeithes' son, addressed them
> In pain. His heart was black and filled to bursting
> With rage, his eyes resembled flashing fire.
> 'God damn it! This journey of Telemachos
> Is too much! What a nerve! "Impossible",
> We said. Without a by-your-leave the boy
> Picked a crack crew and launched and disappeared.
> He's going to be more trouble. I pray that Zeus
> Will clip his wings before he comes of age.
> Just fetch me a fast ship and twenty men:
> I'll lie in wait and catch him on his way
> In the straits between Ithaca and rugged Samos.
> This sea-quest for his father will cost him dear.'   4.660–72[1]

A few pages later the plan is set in motion. Antinoos knows that Telemachos
will be returning from Pylos which is on the Peloponnesian coast to the south-
east of Ithaca and Same, so he chooses an ambush location to surprise him on
his return to Ithaca:

> The suitors climbed in and began their voyage,
> Plotting a merciless death for Telemachos.
> There is a rocky island in mid sea
> Half way between Ithaca and rugged Samos,
> Called Asteris, not large, but with twin bays
> For mooring. Here the Achaian ambush waited.   4.842–7[2]

However, much later we learn that the ambush has been unsuccessful: a herald announces in the palace that Telemachos has returned safely after all. Another of the suitors, Eurymachos, decides to send a ship to recall Antinoos and the other suitors from their failed mission but it then transpires that this won't be necessary:

'Come, let us launch the best black ship we have
And muster seamen who can row, to take them
An urgent order to return at once.'
He was still speaking, when Amphinomos
Turned round and saw a ship in the deep harbour;
The crew were taking down the sail and ready
To row her in. He smiled and said to his comrades:
'No need to send a message: here they are.
Some god has tipped them off, or they themselves
Spotted the ship sail past and couldn't catch her.'   16.348–57

The crewmen disembark and accompany the other suitors to the meeting place where Antinoos gives them a piece of his mind:

Antinoos, Eupeithes' son, addressed them:
'Damn it! The gods have snatched him from our clutches.
By day lookouts stood on the windy heights,
Shift after shift without break; and when the sun set
We never slept the night on land but waited
For dawn at sea on our swift ambush-ship,
Hoping to catch and kill Telemachos.
But meanwhile some god carried him off home.'   16.363–70

In these passages Homer provides some important information about Asteris. It lies in the straits between Ithaca and rocky Samos; its position must enable a surprise ambush to take place; it is not a substantial island but it has twin harbours large enough for ships to moor within; it has windy heights where lookouts can keep watch for Telemachos' ship during the day; and at night the ambush ship can patrol constantly across the straits to try to intercept him. The windy heights must have a good view of the approach to Ithaca that Telemachos is expected to take on his return from Pylos and the lookouts there need to be able to communicate with those on the ship in some way. Our fourth clue is therefore based on these descriptions:

Clue 4: Is there a two-harboured island called Asteris in the straits between Ithaca and Samos, with windy heights that would enable an ambush to take place?

We can now assess some of the existing theories of Ithaca for their compliance with this detailed description. The ambush island candidates are listed in Figure 9.4: the Classical and Goekoop theories favour an island called

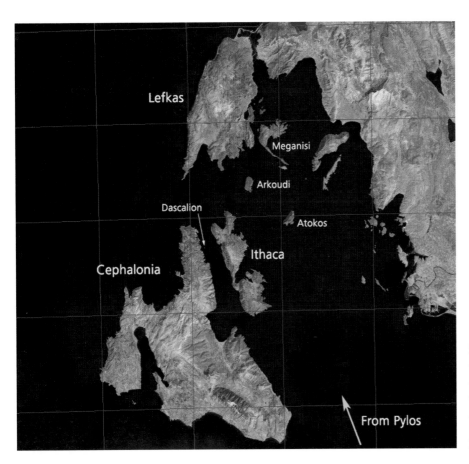

FIGURE 10.1
Candidate islands for
Asteris
*Colour interpretation: as
Figure 1.3. Grid: 20 km.*
[Image credits: as
Figure 1.3.]

Dascalion, while Dörpfeld proposes Arkoudi which we saw on Figure 9.2. The relative location of these islands is depicted in Figure 10.1.

Dörpfeld's choice of Arkoudi lies midway between the northern tip of modern Ithaca and the island of Meganisi. It is relatively small, about 3 km long by 1.5 km wide, with a hilltop of 136 m which could provide windy heights. Today's marine chart shows various inlets which could provide ambush cover, or failing that the ambush vessel could hide around the other side of the island. Although it is somewhat to the west of a direct course from Pylos to Lefkas, it lies on the route that would be followed by a Bronze Age galley that was aiming for the relative safety of the straits between Meganisi and Lefkas.

So why have I suggested that Arkoudi does not comply with Clue 4? Because it does not lie 'in the straits between Ithaca and Samos', for the simple reason that under Dörpfeld's thesis no such straits exist. If we are to follow his radical designation that ancient Ithaca is modern Lefkas and ancient Same is modern Ithaca, then what separates them is about 9 km of open sea. Both of these islands point at each other across this distance with sharp promontories: there is not a strait in sight. Even if there were, Arkoudi lies at least 4 km too far to the east of a line joining these promontories to be capable of being described as 'half way between Ithaca and rugged Samos'. Dörpfeld's theory was already tenuous enough: Arkoudi cannot salvage it.

Dascalion presents a marked contrast to Arkoudi. If you are straining to spot it on Figure 10.1 then that is because it is rather small: about 180 m long and only 30–50 m wide, with its windiest height no more than a few metres above sea level. It is just visible on Figure 9.1 as a tiny dot opposite Polis Bay. This is not a very promising basis for an ambush and Tim Severin, a seasoned sailor, is delightfully disparaging about it:

Unfortunately this little island called Daskalion has not got a single harbour, is barely six feet above water level, and would make a singularly useless observation post. By no stretch of the imagination could it be described as having the 'windy heights' on which the suitors posted their lookouts. The suitors would have found it difficult to moor their boats on this barren reef, let alone mount a watchful guard there.[3]

My own photographs of Dascalion are presented later but I cannot fault Severin's acid prose. The island is far too low for a Bronze Age galley to hide behind, there is no room for one harbour let alone two and there are no windy heights.

C. H. Goekoop recognises these deficiencies. Although he identifies Dascalion as Asteris, he constructs an intricate interpretation involving the windy heights being on the adjacent land above Dolicha Bay[4] on Erissos (the northern Cephalonian cape) and the ships hiding in the bays of this cape rather than on Asteris itself. Unfortunately this explanation does not make for easy reading: once it is finally grasped it becomes clear that Goekoop considers that Asteris itself plays no part at all in the actual ambush. In this interpretation it has to be said that he is singularly at odds with Homer. However, at least Asteris is located in the right place to ambush a ship returning from Pylos to Goekoop's designated port of Fiscardo.

This is not the case for proponents of the Classical theory. As well as having to deal with all the disadvantages of the diminutive size of Dascalion itself, those who believe that ancient Ithaca harbour was located in Polis Bay are faced with the additional challenge of explaining why Antinoos and his crewmen were apparently willing to plan a surprise attack on a vessel that would not only fail to pass by the ambush island but that would studiously avoid it on the other side of the straits nearly 4 km away.

Figure 10.2 illustrates the problem. Any attempt made by the suitors to head in the direction of Telemachos' ship would be spotted by him well before they had a chance of ambush, leaving him with plenty of time either to make safe in Polis Bay harbour or to take evasive action and change his course. Furthermore the entire manoeuvre would have been taking place in the full

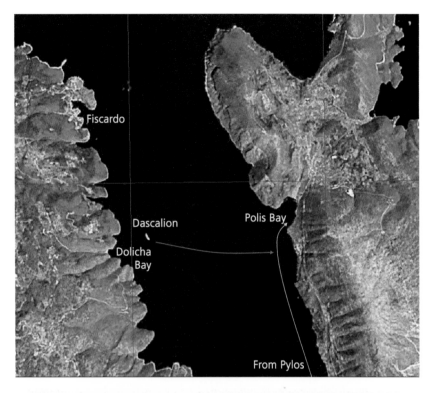

FIGURE 10.2 Dascalion Island and Polis Bay
Colour interpretation: as Figure 1.3. Grid: 5 km.
[Image credits: as Figure 1.3.]

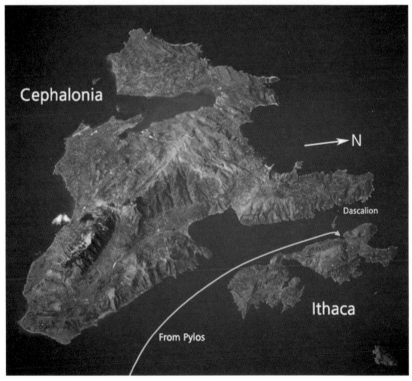

FIGURE 10.3 Space Shuttle view of the classical ambush
Colour interpretation: this is a natural colour positive photograph taken on Kodak ASA 100 film and subsequently digitised.
[Image credits: Earth Sciences and Image Analysis, NASA-Johnson Space Center. 'The Gateway to Astronaut Photography of Earth'. Ref.: STS073-739-33.JPG Website: http://eol.jsc.nasa.gov/scripts/sseop/photo.pl?mission=STS073&roll=739&frame=33]

view of those Ithacans stationed in the harbour at Polis Bay or on the adjacent clifftop, thus making it impossible for Antinoos and his ambush crew to return to the palace under a cloak of assumed innocence.

At 9.29 GMT on 24 October 1995 the Space Shuttle flew over the Ionian Sea in conditions of almost zero cloud cover. Photographs of exceptional clarity ensued and one of these may be helpful to readers in considering this issue. In Figure 10.3 Dascalion is the small dot in the bay at the base of the arrow denoting the suitors' intercept course to Telemachos.

Dascalion has never been remotely credible as the ambush island of Asteris. Over the centuries researchers have simply seized on it because it is the only island in that strait; in most cases they have never visited it or considered the realities of a marine ambush there. As Michael D'Souza has explained to me, in such a manoeuvre the element of surprise was crucial: the preferred tactic would have been to row out suddenly and rapidly from behind a cove or a promontory that the target vessel was passing by just a few tens of metres away. If it was at all possible to ram the victim's boat amidships, so much the better as she sank without trace with all hands drowned. William Murray, the authority on classical naval warfare, provides a gripping account of these tactics in a later marine encounter:

We see from an episode described by Polybius at Chios what strategy was employed by an attacking ship that had successfully holed its opponent. The attacker would back off to a safe position, if possible, and let the attacked ship slowly sink to the waterline. If no one intervened, the attacker could then reapproach the swamped vessel to damage it further by ramming or the attacker could kill the survivors by spear thrust and weapons fire.[5]

None of this would have been possible in the case of Dascalion.

What about Apollodorus' Enigma? So far in this chapter we have taken our texts regarding Asteris only from Homer, but in Chapter 6 we heard that:

Between Ithaca and Cephallenia is the small island Asteria (the poet calls it Asteris), which the Scepsian says no longer remains such as the poet describes it, but in it are harbours safe for anchorage with entrances on either side; Apollodorus, however, says that it still remains so to this day, and mentions a town Alalcomenai upon it, situated on the isthmus itself.

There is no possibility whatever of finding an isthmus, let alone a town, upon Dascalion: indeed the chapel of St Nicholas that is marked on the map is a tiny solitary hut constructed by the grandfather of today's owner of a nearby house.[6] There are only two ways out of this predicament: either we are

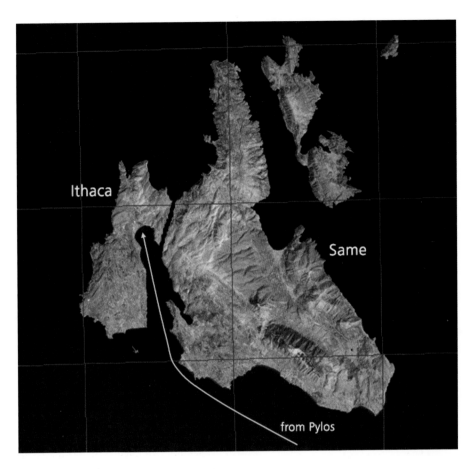

FIGURE 10.4
Telemachos' expected
route home
*Colour interpretation: as
Figure 1.3. Grid: 20 km.*
[Image credits: as
Figure 1.3.]

looking at the wrong straits or Homer was making all this up. Personally I find it more interesting to follow Homer and to look elsewhere for the right straits.

In Chapter 5 we observed at Figure 5.4 the route that Telemachos would take towards Pylos if ancient Ithaca was located on the western promontory of Cephalonia and he was leaving from its harbour at the northern end of Argostoli Bay. Under this hypothesis the suitors would naturally presume that he would be returning the same way, as Figure 10.4 indicates.

If you were Antinoos, the wicked leader of the suitors who are plotting Telemachos' death, where would you choose to hide your ship as you waited for him to return? You need to be sufficiently far from Ithaca city and Odysseus' Palace to avoid being observed in the act of perpetrating your heinous crime. You would like to ambush Telemachos with the maximum of surprise and in conditions in which his opportunity to take evasive action is limited. You also need adjacent windy heights from which your lookouts can spy some distance out to sea so as to give you ample warning of Telemachos' arrival. Finally you must be located between Ithaca and Samos' rugged cliffs, not beyond them. What are your options?

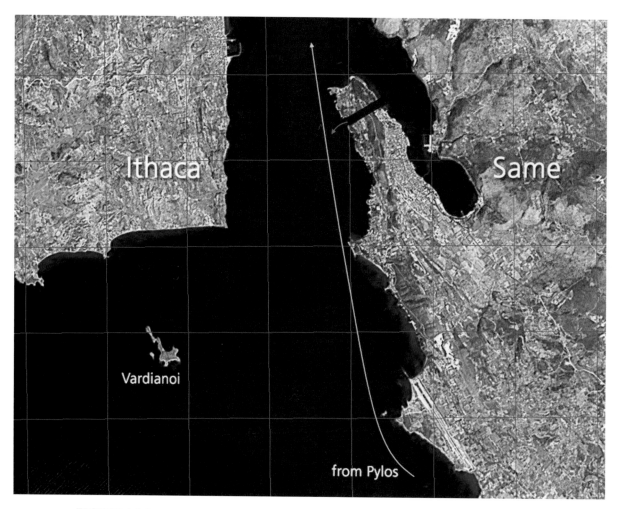

FIGURE 10.5
An ambush island on
Argostoli Point?
*Today's airport runway can
clearly be seen at the bottom of
the satellite image. Colour
interpretation: as Figure 1.3.
Grid: 2 km.*
[Image credits: as
Figure 1.3.]

There is an obvious place to ambush a ship coming into the channel between
Ithaca and Samos: the tip of the Argostoli peninsula. Could there have been an
island there in former years, as suggested by Figure 10.5? If so, how would this
solution compare against the criteria set by Homer? To start with it is undoubtedly between Ithaca and Samos. Although there are other small islands further
south that could be considered, including the island of Vardianoi to the south-
west, none of these are 'between' the two main islands. In fact the coast of
ancient Ithaca turns an unusually sharp right-angle along its southern edge
so this particular issue is quite straightforward.

Would this location be large enough to conceal a Bronze Age galley? Severin
tells us that the length of a twenty-man galley is about 16 m[7] and if this
putative island were sufficiently separated from the promontory there might
be adequate space for the ship to hide. There is also a hill to the south called
Mount Koutsomylos that could have been the location of the windy heights:

the survey map marks its summit as 94 m above sea level. Furthermore at night the ship could patrol across the straits which are about 3 km wide at that point. But could such a small island contain two harbours? And what about Apollodorus, who 'mentions a town Alalcomenai upon it, situated on the isthmus itself'?

I felt somewhat uncomfortable about the idea of proposing two former sea channels, both of which had now disappeared, but there seemed to be no alternative. I managed to locate some photographs of the promontory on the Internet and one of these suggested that there might conceivably be a small island on the promontory's northern tip. If our forthcoming expedition could confirm this then what would be the implications for the outcome of the ambush? How would Telemachos have managed to outwit the suitors and escape?

Telemachos is at the court of King Menelaos in Sparta: he has been trying to get some sleep on the porch but he is kept awake worrying about his father. Athene visits him and tells him it is time for him to come home: his mother is being pressurised to choose one of the suitors and Telemachos needs to return to protect his inheritance. She warns him that the suitors are lying wait in ambush for him and she explains to him how he can outwit them:

> Choice suitors plan to ambush you in the strait
> That lies between Ithaca and rugged Samos,
> Intent on murdering you on your way home.
> It's not to be – the earth will first close over
> Those suitors who eat up your property.
> So keep your sturdy ship far off the islands
> And sail by night and day. Whatever god
> Is guarding you will send a following wind.
> And when you reach the first shore of Ithaca,
> Send on your ship and comrades to the city.
> Yourself, go first to the swineherd, who keeps watch
> Over your pigs and is still loyal to you.
> Spend the night there, and send him to the city
> To give the news to wise Penelope
> That you are now back safely home from Pylos.   15.28–42[8]

Instead of returning to Ithaca harbour straight into the suitor's ambush, Telemachos is to take the long way home and keep well away from the islands. He is to disembark on the coast of Ithaca but send the ship and his shipmates on to the city. He should then go to the pigfarm and stay the night there, but first he must send Eumaios into town to tell his mother Penelope that he is safe and sound.

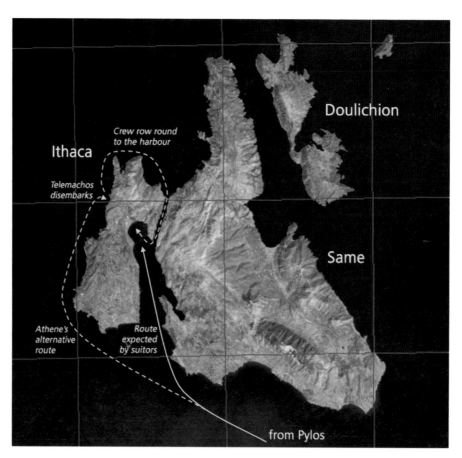

FIGURE 10.6
Athene's advice to
Telemachos
*Colour interpretation: as
Figure 1.3. Grid: 20 km.*
[Image credits: as
Figure 1.3.]

Athene's crafty advice to Telemachos is depicted in Figure 10.6.[9] Readers who are still nostalgic for the Classical theory may like to note that if Telemachos were instead to circumnavigate modern Ithaca anticlockwise his crewmen would gain no advantage, since on returning to Polis Bay from the north they would in fact pass slightly closer to Dascalion than if they had not made that detour in the first place.

Earlier we heard that Amphinomos sees that the unsuccessful suitors have returned to Ithaca harbour and says 'No need to send a message: here they are. / Some god has tipped them off, or they themselves / Spotted the ship sail past and couldn't catch her.' The escape route indicated in Figure 10.6 passes only about 10 km to the south-west of the lookout point on the windy heights and from any likely lookout elevation a Bronze Age galley would be clearly visible. This galley in fact belonged to Noemon, one of the suitors, so it is reasonable to assume that it would also be recognisable to them as a member of the Ithacan home fleet.

However if the same explanation is proposed for the Classical theory or that of Goekoop then the distance involved would instead be about 30 km and the suitors would not be able to see Telemachos' ship heading for the coast at all. Consequently Homer would not have been credible in suggesting to his audience that the suitors might have seen the prince's ship go sailing past: after all, even if we favour his first option 'some god has tipped them off', we must also allow for the contingent credibility of the alternative.

I hope you agree with me that the proposed solution fits in every respect except for that one crucial omission: the map shows no island on the tip of Argostoli peninsula. We did not solve the problem of the missing island until towards the end of our first expedition to Cephalonia and even then our solution was in doubt until we returned home to consult with an expert. I can recall losing hours of sleep agonising about the whereabouts of the island of Asteris so I shall ask you to empathise with our predicament by keeping you in suspense for a chapter or so.

Notes

1 See James Diggle's comments on this passage in Appendix 1 Section J.

2 See James Diggle's comments on this passage in Appendix 1 Section B.

3 Severin (1987) p. 265.

4 Dolicha Bay is attested on both the tourist map (Freytag-Berndt (2000)) and the marine navigation chart (Heikell (2003a)). On the former map it describes a bay just north of Dascalion; on the latter map it is placed just south of it, adjacent to a 301 m summit called (on the former map) Delicho.

5 Murray (1993b) p. 305. Murray's reference is to Polybius 16.6, the Battle of Chios in 201 BC, so unfortunately my reference to his dramatic description of this much later encounter cannot be relied on as a description of Bronze Age warfare. In private correspondence he has kindly advised me that there is no clear evidence of the deliberate use of the ram for offensive purposes before the Battle of Alalia c. 535 BC (Herodotus 1.166.2). In that passage Herodotus tells us that the Phocaeans with a fleet of sixty ships took on twice that number of hostile vessels and although they won the battle 'they lost forty of their ships, and the twenty that remained were useless, their rams being twisted away'. Murray believes that before this period the pointed rams that we see on reliefs, on vases and elsewhere (e.g. on the Assyrian relief in the British Museum and on Dipylon style vases) were primarily used for defensive purposes and as cutwaters. However an intended encounter such as that described by the poet would have been between only two ships with no witnesses and presumably Antinoos and his men would have used whatever practical means were at their disposal.

6 From the holiday website www.sunvil.co.uk we read under Evreti House, Cephalonia 'Just past the tiny hillside hamlet of Evreti, five kilometres south of Fiscardo, Evreti House has a spectacular position to survey the island's coastline with dramatic views over just a few houses on lower hillside terraces and across the sea to Ithaca and the island of Lefkas in the distance. An islet below has a church, built by the grandfather of Stamatis, Evreti House's owner, and dedicated to St Nicholas and those who sail the seas.'

7 Severin (1985) pp. 33, 238–9.

8 See James Diggle's comments on this passage in Appendix 1 Section E.

9 See Chapter 15 for a more detailed discussion of Telemachos' route back from Pylos.

CHAPTER 11 Poseidon

And behold, the veil of the temple was rent in twain from the top to the bottom, and the earth did quake, and the rocks rent.

Matthew 27:51

Close your eyes. Imagine yourself massless, an ethereal cloud of virtual particles able to drift at will through solid matter. Now let yourself float down through the surface of the earth and penetrate the strata below. As you descend you are travelling through time. The first rocks that you meet are clearly the ones that have been deposited most recently, while as you sink deeper and deeper you encounter layers that were formed hundreds of millions of years ago. You do not expect to find these older rocks above the younger rocks: that would be perverse. One of the very first theories that undergraduate geologists learn is the Principle of Superposition: the deeper you go, the older it gets.

At the same time we must also remember that the earth's crust is composed of a small number of large continental plates. Most places on our planet are located well inside the boundary of one or other of these plates, but a few of them are poised on the perimeter. That is a rather uncomfortable place to be because the adjacent plate is constantly pushing up against it or trying to slide past it or underneath it. Sometimes a nearby plate manages to slide right on top of another one and if its rock is from an older era, then the Principle of Superposition is violated. These plates may converge either under the sea, or on land, or between the seabed and the land, as is depicted in Figure 11.1.

As well as this vertical effect, at other times two plates may be moving in opposite horizontal directions and at the boundary a great deal of tension is built up. Try holding your hands beside each other, with one palm facing upwards and the other downwards and with your thumbs just touching. Now start sliding them past each other while simultaneously trying to prevent this motion by aligning the tips of your thumbs. After a while the pressure will simply be too great and your thumbs will snap back to their former position. Continental plates do this all the time: the San Andreas Fault in California is a classic example.

When the plates snap back there is usually an earthquake. If this motion takes place in a horizontal direction then geologists call it a shear or a 'strike-slip' fault, but if the force acts vertically it is called a thrust or a 'compressional' fault. 'Vertically' here may not mean literally at 90 degrees to the earth's surface: the thrust fault may slope diagonally upwards. In that case

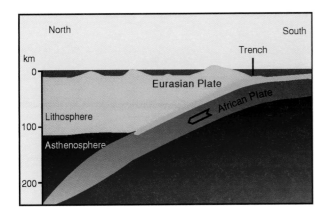

FIGURE 11.1
Oceanic-continental plate
convergence
*'The deepest part of the
subducting plate breaks into
smaller pieces that become
locked in place for long
periods of time before
suddenly moving to generate
large earthquakes . . . often
accompanied by uplift of the
land by as much as a few
metres.'*
[Image credits Cambridge
University Press. Websites:
http://wrgis.wr.usgs.gov/
parks/pltec/converge.html,
http://pubs.usgs.gov/
publications/text/
understanding.html]

when there is a compressional earthquake the earth moves both vertically
and horizontally.

From a tectonic perspective Greece happens to be located in a particularly
critical place: it is at the convergence of Africa and Europe (Figure 11.2).
When we look at a normal map we perceive that Africa starts at the southern shore of the Mediterranean Sea, but if you were to drain the ocean you
would see that the land mass of Africa continues northwards on the seabed
until it slides underneath the land mass of Europe. This African plate is also
moving in a north-easterly direction at a speed of about 1 cm each year. That
may not sound particularly troublesome until one considers that it corresponds to a kilometre of movement over a mere 100,000 years. Meanwhile
this part of Europe (the Aegean plate) is being pushed in a south-westerly
direction at about twice this speed by the relentless pressure of Asia, in the
shape of the North Anatolian Fault. These forces converge at Greece, which
explains why the country is so mountainous and also why it suffers from
earthquakes.

Cephalonia is poised at a particularly delicate location in this interconti-
nental affair. If you sail to the island from Patras on mainland Greece and
watch the echo-sounder as you go, the readout will on average indicate a
seabed depth of less than 100 m, with occasional values of up to about 300 m.
Now continue westwards from Cephalonia and by the time you have sailed
just 10 more kilometres in the direction of Italy something quite extraordinary happens: an extra zero appears on the depth gauge. The 300 metres
has become 3,000 m: you have just sailed over a submarine cliff-edge that is
2 miles high. This island is the last outpost of Europe: it is teetering on the
edge of the continental plate and below it is the abyssal plain of Africa.

Near Cephalonia the boundary between the two continental plates has
folded into a line running from south-west to north-east. The European land
mass lies on the eastern side and it is moving towards the south-west, while

FIGURE 11.2
Continental plate
movement in Eastern
Europe
*Cephalonia is where the
Eurasian/Aegean plate is
colliding with the African
plate at a combined rate of up
to 45 mm per year. That
corresponds to over 2 m of
overlap every fifty years.*
[Image credits:
Skarlatoudis et al. (2004)
Figure 1. Website:
www.cosmos-eq.org/
Projects/Margaris_Paper.
pdf]

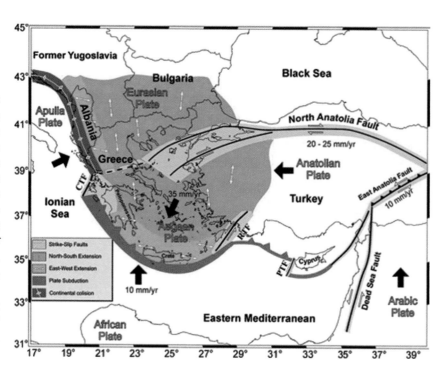

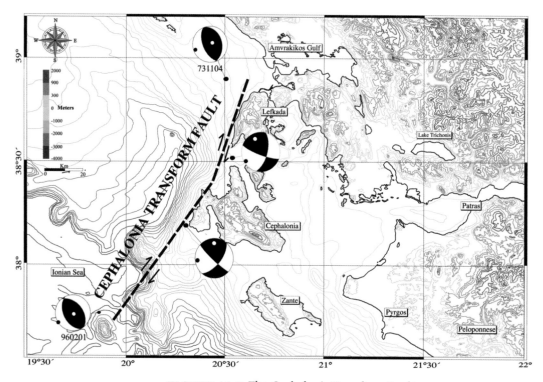

FIGURE 11.3 The Cephalonia Transform Fault
*The dashed line in this diagram corresponds to the segment marked 'CTF' in Figure 11.2. The
African plate is pushing against the European plate while also slipping past it and thrusting
underneath it.* [Image credits: Louvari et al. (1999) Figure 4.]

the African mass is on the western side and it is moving north-east. Figure 11.3 shows us what is going on.

We met Professor Anastasia Kiratzi in Chapter 7 and this diagram is from a paper that she co-authored in 1999. The dashed line is called the 'Cephalonia Transform Fault'. The black and white beach balls are seismologists' indicators of the type of motion along the fault: the depth contours west of Cephalonia are unmistakable. The paper explains that:

The calculated maximum magnitude for the Cephalonia segment is in agreement with the magnitudes of the events of 1767, 1867, and 1953 when the entire segment ruptured . . . These two major fault segments, together with other smaller faults in the Ionian Islands, form the Cephalonia Transform Fault Zone which connects the thrust belt along the Hellenic arc in the south to the thrust belt along north-western Greece and western Albania in the north.[1]

Cephalonia is one of the most seismically active places in the world and research into its earthquakes is therefore a hot topic for experts. In 2002 another paper was published by Mireille Laigle and her colleagues with the following findings:

North of Zakinthos, large earthquakes occur mainly at the western edge of the island of Cephalonia . . . The well-located seismicity extends through Cephalonia Island but not into the marine region east of it . . . For the Cephalonia Island half of this region, a major earthquake of Ms = 7.2 occurred in 1953, and similar magnitude events in 1912 and about twice a century over the three previous centuries are documented. A similar situation is suggested for the Zakinthos half, though with apparently smaller and less frequent events . . . We hence assume a return period of 50 years for the maximum magnitude earthquake in each half of the total 115 km long zone . . . With the parameter values defined above, we find the maximum magnitude of the earthquake that would rupture the entire area to be 7–7.1.[2]

This means that earthquakes of magnitude comparable to that of August 1953 have taken place in Cephalonia about every 50 years over the last 300 years. How far back beyond that is it legitimate to extrapolate these earthquakes? Prior to this paper the established view was that there was no particular reason to assume historical continuity, but the authors' researches suggest that the methodology used by some of these earlier studies may have been inappropriate. Their new findings are that:

The recurrence time and magnitude of major earthquakes are well represented by the available catalogue . . . This result is unexpected with respect to the numerous previous studies.[3]

In other words, an average interval of fifty years between earthquakes of magnitude 7.0 or above can be used as a reasonably reliable guide to the incidence of historical earthquakes in western Cephalonia, stretching back for as long as we are interested. As we have seen, only a very few such earthquakes appear to have elevated the whole land mass but all of them would have 'ruptured the entire area'. So if earthquakes of magnitude 7.0 or above have been happening on average every fifty years since 1200 BC, then there would have been about twenty-four of them between the traditional date ascribed to the events of the *Odyssey* and the period in which Strabo was writing (around AD 1). What was their effect on Strabo's Channel?

Andreas Delaportas was there (from Chapter 1):

And we saw all the stones – big stones, they were loose at the top of the mountain and we saw them just rolling down the mountainside into the ocean. It started on the Sunday with the small earthquakes and then there was the big one.

The journalists were there as well:

From the top of the mountains (because these islands on volcanic ground are very mountainous) blocks of rock detach themselves, start to roll and then hurtle down and crush into pieces the farms in the villages, the public buildings and the pretty low-lying houses in the towns. The quake caused hundreds of huge landslides which blocked the roads and trapped many islanders . . . Landslips sent whole neighbourhoods crumbling into the sea. Some reports said entire inland villages were swallowed up by huge fissures.

Fifty years is the average interval between the largest earthquakes but sizeable tremors are happening all the time. If you go to the website of the Geophysical Laboratory of the University of Thessaloniki you will find a most intriguing 'Catalogue of earthquakes in Greece and surrounding area for the period 550 BC–1999'.[4] Download this into a spreadsheet, specify the latitude, longitude and magnitude of interest and you can see just how much earthquake activity there has been over that period.

In the spring of 2003 I specified the rectangle of Figure 11.4 around Cephalonia from latitude 37.5 to 39.00 N and longitude 19.75 to 21.25 E and arranged for the spreadsheet to identify all tremors of magnitude 4.0 (no major damage but you can certainly feel it) and above. The years in which these earthquakes occurred are listed below: the blue figures correspond to events of magnitude 7.0 or more. Prior to the era of seismographs, qualitative eyewitness descriptions were used as the basis for these numeric estimates.

What does this sequence of years tell us? First we can see that there were ten years in which major earthquakes took place over the period from 1444

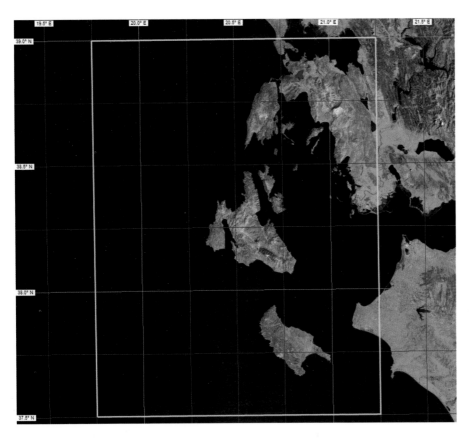

FIGURE 11.4
Cephalonia earthquake zone
Colour interpretation: as Figure 1.3. Grid: 0.25 degrees of latitude and longitude. [Image credits: as Figure 1.3.]

1444 1469 1508 1514 1554 1577 1592 1612 1613 1622 1625 1630 1633 1636 1658 1662 1664 1668 1676 1696 1704 1707 1710 1714 1722 1723 1729 1742 1759 1766 1767 1769 1783 1791 1811 1815 1820 1825 1840 1862 1867 1869 1873 1893 1902 1903 1905 1906 1909 1910 1911 1912 1913 1914 1915 1916 1917 1918 1919 1920 1921 1922 1923 1925 1926 1927 1932 1933 1938 1939 1940 1943 1945 1946 1948 1949 1950 1951 1952 1953 1954 1955 1956 1957 1958 1959 1960 1961 1962 1963 1964 1965 1966 1967 1968 1969 1970 1971 1972 1973 1974 1975 1976 1977 1978 1979 1980 1981 1982 1983 1984 1985 1986 1987 1988 1989 1990 1991 1992 1993 1994 1995 1996 1997 1998 1999

FIGURE 11.5
Years with earthquakes of magnitude 4.0 or above (blue = 7.0 or above)
In several cases there was more than one earthquake of this intensity in the indicated year. [Data source: For earthquake catalogue see Papazachos et al. (2000).]

to 1999. This is an average of one every fifty-five years which ties in closely with the experts' assessment above. Then it is clear that these earthquakes are very irregularly spaced – for example there were no major quakes at all in the sixteenth century, then, just like London buses, three came along in a row in the middle of the seventeenth century. This irregularity makes earthquake prediction very difficult.[5] If you plot these events on a graph over time and calculate a 'best fit line' then the next arithmetical prediction comes up for the year 2048, but this is not really a useful way to think about the matter because they are so sporadic. It is better to think about it in terms of likelihood.

A recent paper by T. M. Tsapanos and colleagues[6] has applied to this problem the powerful statistical technique known as Bayesian theory (conceived in 1763 by the nonconformist Reverend Thomas Bayes in his celebrated 'Essay towards Solving a Problem in the Doctrine of Chances') and their results can be summarised as follows.

The probability of there being an earthquake on Cephalonia of magnitude 6.0 or above from any given date over the following ten-year period is 39.4%. If you double that time horizon to twenty years the probability rises to 62.1%. If you consider a seventy-five-year period then the likelihood rises to 95.7%, which is to all intents and purposes a sure thing. So this means that most of the people who have lived on Cephalonia have experienced an earthquake of magnitude 6.0 or greater in their lifetimes. Although the researchers used data drawn from the period between 1845 and 1999, we have also seen above that 'The recurrence time and magnitude of major earthquakes are well represented by the available catalogue', so this entitles us to presume that the statistics in Odysseus' day were not that dissimilar.

In Chapter 1 we read about the 1953 earthquake, but what was it like to live through some of these other major earthquakes? As part of the EC project *Review of Historical Seismicity in Europe (RHISE) 1989–1993* Paola Albini, Kostas C. Makropoulos and their respective colleagues undertook this historical research in two fascinating papers.[7] Note that the dates mentioned in the following extracts have been adjusted to the Old Style calendar which may give rise to occasional differences as a result of the Gregorian reforms implemented in Greece on 1 March 1923.

28 August 1714
A damaging earthquake in Kefalinia is mentioned in an eighteenth century history of Epirus; it says that after the earthquake in Patras of 27 July:

. . . on 28 August another more dreadful earthquake occurred in Kefalinia, where the Venetian admiral was at anchor with his fleet: the earth opened, hot water flowed out; 280 houses were destroyed, water issued from the earth, and the inhabitants lived two months in the gardens.

9 February 1723
This was a large earthquake in the Ionian Islands that caused serious damage in north Kefalinia. A contemporary note, after describing the effects of the aftershocks of 11 February in Lefkas, adds that

. . . similarly there was an awful earthquake in Zante where a few houses collapsed and many were cracked, and also in Kefalinia it was terrible; there, at Erissos, as well as in Paliki many houses collapsed and some people were killed and very many were

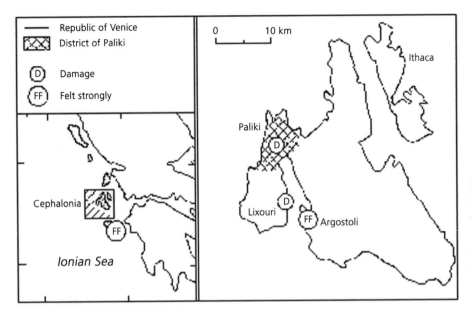

FIGURE 11.6
Effects of the earthquakes
of June 1759
*The northern area of Paliki
around Atheras was severely
affected.*
[Image credits: Albini et al.
(1993).]

injured; also at Lixuri and Argostoli the shock caused great losses as we were told, and the earthquake which caused these losses was the one that occurred on the 9th of February which was great in these parts and which, had it occurred here [in Lefkas] *it would have left nothing standing; and it was the same earthquake that was felt in the Morea* [Peloponnese] *and was perceptible in Korfus and Arta and in all neighbouring regions . . .*

12 June 1741

In the south-west part of the island of Kefalinia all the houses, particularly those in the districts of Lixouri, Argostoli and Borgo (Castro, now Agios Georgios) were shattered. The parish church of Lixouri was totally destroyed as well as a number of public buildings. In the fort of Assos many dwellings collapsed and the rest of the buildings were ruined, apparently without loss of lives.

2 June 1759

There was a series of damaging earthquakes in the western part of Kefalinia (Figure 11.6). According to a contemporary note 'earthquakes began on the 2nd of June and continued until the 5th; the one which happened at noon destroyed many houses and the other on the 3rd caused the collapse of most houses in the villages and in the town . . .' A dispatch from the Venetian authorities in Kefalinia says that 'in the night between June 1 and 2, at about six hours, there was a violent earthquake which was followed by a series of weaker shocks . . . The following morning, at 16 hours, there occurred a much stronger shock . . . that produced great ruin . . .'. The damage caused by the two shocks was concentrated in the district of Paliki and at Lixouri where most of the houses, windmills and churches collapsed and a few lives were lost.

11 July 1766

Preceded by a foreshock before dawn, the main shock occurred one hour after sunrise on 11 July 1766 lasting, with intermissions, three minutes. The earthquake was followed by three other shocks during the same day.

The western part of Kefalinia suffered most. A manuscript note says that most of the houses in the district of Paliki were destroyed and those left standing were damaged. It adds, however, that fifty-two days earlier the south part of Paliki had also suffered from a whirlwind of unprecedented violence which did great damage. Contemporary reports confirm that the damage caused by high winds, which persisted for thirteen minutes, was enormous. The combined damage caused by the earthquake and the wind was such that many families left Paliki and settled in the Morea (Peloponnese). The seriousness of the situation in Kefalinia is testified by a petition to the Venetian *Collegio* produced by Niccolò Salomon, tax-farmer of that island: the *Collegio* recognized the right of his query and asked the Venetian *Senato* to approve the diminution of his debt for the year 1766.

11 July 1767

The research on available sources showed that the time of the mainshock occurrence was '13 hours',[8] and six aftershocks were reported from almost all the Ionian Islands.

The earthquake struck most main towns and villages of Cephalonia. In Lixouri many deaths were reported and almost the whole town suffered great damage. Great damage was also reported from Lixouri fortress and the surrounding villages (people evacuated their houses). In the town of Argostoli and in the fortress very few houses were left inhabitable. Damage was also observed in the walls of the fortress. Further to the north in the Paliki peninsula and in the town and fortress of Assos strong shaking was reported, rocks fell and houses were completely destroyed or evacuated. At least one person died and many were wounded. Piles of stones were seen everywhere. The houses and churches in the fortress of the town were also destroyed.

8–14 March 1862

In addition to the above extracts from the RHISE research, a splendidly Victorian description of Cephalonian earthquakes is to be found in Viscount Kirkwall's memoirs of *Four Years in the Ionian Islands*:

Our house was considered, as regards earthquakes, the most unsafe habitation in the town. It rested partly on the Mole, built by Sir Charles Napier, the ground being formerly under water. Its height of three stories added to the danger. It had been built about twenty years, and there were some splits in the outer wall facing the north, which had been occasioned by shocks fourteen years ago. The shock of the 8th was only the beginning of troubles. Before a week had elapsed we had experienced four earthquakes – one of them more severe than any since 1833.

On Monday 10th, about two p.m., I fancied that my eldest little girl was playing with the handle of the door of my room. This was the first sign of our second earthquake. As in the first case, the weather was fine after a day of wind and storm. The temperature was cold, and the barometer appeared to be wholly unaffected on both occasions. Earthquake No. 3 happened on the 13th at ten p.m. The motion was something like a steamer rolling at sea. My wife was sitting at the time alone in the drawing-room. When the shaking began, she, with great presence of mind, and a laudable eye to economy, seized hold of the moderator lamp to prevent it from falling.

I began to be seriously alarmed. With a wife and two children at the second story of a house reputed unsafe, my position was by no means enviable. It appeared bad, indeed, but worse remained behind.

Few of the English then in Cephalonia will ever forget Friday 14th March 1862. At half-past four that morning occurred the greatest earthquake felt for some years past in the Ionian Islands. In our house every one was fast asleep, in profound darkness; but all were suddenly and startlingly awakened by a tremendous crash. It appeared to me as if the end of all things were at hand, and that I was hastening to eternity! It was as if everything and everybody were falling and crashing together. A violent hurricane of wind, with a noise like the discharge of a huge piece of ordnance, accompanied the shock; whilst the house, rattling, shaking, bounding, completed the terrible sublimity of the moment. There were, I feel sure, few Englishmen who did not pass those seconds, which appeared like minutes – that is, if their minds were sufficiently clear – in recommending themselves to the care of him who 'rides in the whirlwind and directs the storm'. When those ten or twelve seconds of horror had passed away, the sense of relief was beyond the power of description.[9]

In 1989 a comprehensive survey of the Cephalonian seismic zone was performed by John Underhill. His findings include the comments:

Although abrupt cut-off along the whole length of the Cretaceous outcrop led British Petroleum Co. Ltd. (1971) to indicate that a major normal fault downthrown more than 1,500 m bounded the western margin of the Ainos Range, field relations suggest that the fault represents another significant thrust.

Mapping in the Kolpos Agia Kiriaki – Kondogourata area revealed a northeast-dipping Cretaceous-Miocene succession (first described by Bizon, 1967) that was overthrust by cleaved Cretaceous carbonates of the Ainos Range.

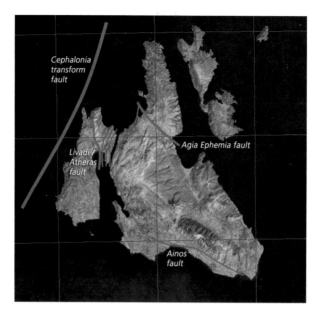

FIGURE 11.7
The seismic picture
of Paliki
*Colour interpretation: as
Figure 1.3. Grid: 20 km.*
[Image credits: after
Underhill (1989)
Figures 5, 6.]

Farther to the east, a zone of intense brecciation occurs bounding the Cretaceous limestones of the Ainos Range. Recent roadcuts to the northwest of Petrikata indicate a northeast dip to the zone of brecciation and locally expose sheared Miocene sediments overthrust by Cretaceous carbonates.[10]

There is no need for the layman's eyes to glaze over at this point: this material is easy to understand and it is also very interesting. We saw in Figure 7.5 that Cretaceous rock is between 65 and 144 million years old. The Ainos Range is the mountainous area in the south-east of the island. A 'major normal fault' acts horizontally whereas a thrust fault acts vertically. The 'Kolpos Agia Kiriaki – Kondogourata area' refers to Strabo's Channel. Miocene rock is between 23.8 and 5.3 million years old. Carbonates are basically limestone.

Brecciation means 'rocks made up out of very angular coarse fragments: may be sedimentary or may be formed by grinding or crushing along faults'. If faults are ground together then this can form breccia, the Italian word for rubble. So north-west of Petrikata, which you can see on Figure 7.1, is an area where the older Cretaceous limestone has thrust itself over the younger Miocene sediment.[11]

The implications of John Underhill's work for the Paliki peninsula are depicted in Figure 11.7. This is a layman's version of a geologist's diagram but it will meet our present purpose. The red lines denote faults where either horizontal or vertical slippage takes place as the rocks are pressed into each other, or try to slide past each other, or are forced up on top of each other by the pressure of Europe bumping into Africa underneath.

So ask yourself: as a Bronze Age Ithacan who just happens to be living in one of the few places in the world in which small earth tremors occur every few weeks, larger ones every few months and colossal ones every few decades – what name would you give to the driving force behind this extraordinary phenomenon? Remember that Odysseus was smart: he was renowned for his cunning. One of the most well-known passages in the *Odyssey* is at 9.408 when Polyphemos replies to his fellow Cyclopes 'My friends, Nobody is killing me with guile or violence'. Anybody who could call himself 'Nobody' in order to confuse his enemy's allies was nobody's fool. So he and his fellow Ithacans were easily intelligent enough to have figured out the physics of Cephalonian seismology. They even had a specific name for it: they called it Poseidon.

Poseidon and his awesome ability to create earthquakes and storms are mentioned throughout both poems – for example:

For now the earth-holder earth-shaker has departed
Into the bright sea.   *Iliad* 15.222–3

The words used for 'earth-holder' and 'earth-shaker' are *gaieochos* and *ennosigaios* and they are regularly applied to Poseidon. The meaning of 'earth-shaker' is clear and a variant of it (*enosichthon*) appears in a passage where Zeus is speaking to Athene at the outset of the *Odyssey*. She asks him why he is punishing Odysseus by delaying his return to Ithaca and he replies that he is not to blame for our hero's misfortunes:

Poseidon the earth-holder is relentless
In anger for the son Odysseus blinded,
The godlike Polyphemos, mightiest
Of Cyclopes. His mother was the nymph
Thoosa, daughter of the sea-god Phorcys,
Who mated with Poseidon in a cave.
The earth-shaker does not wish to kill Odysseus,
But keeps him wandering far away from home.   *Odyssey* 1.68–75

The precise interpretation of 'earth-holder' is disputed by classical scholars but John Underhill may be able to help them, because *gaieochos* can also be translated as 'earth-uplifter'. I think it may be a Bronze Age attempt to describe a compressional thrust fault. If I am right then the inference is that ancient observers witnessed traumatic earth uplifts (comparable to that in Cephalonia in 1953) and associated them with Poseidon.

Exactly where might these uplifts have taken place? There is an important clue in the above passage. Homer's Phorcys Bay is named after the sea-god

Phorcys and father of the nymph Thoosa. Thoosa was ravished by Poseidon in a cave and the result was Polyphemos, the Cyclops whom Odysseus blinded in his travels. So Poseidon is rather personally associated with Phorcys Bay and for very good reason, because on Figure 11.7 it is apparent that a major earthquake fault line passes right through it.

It therefore seems reasonable to propose that the location of ancient Ithaca in an area of such high tectonic activity was the driving force behind the frequent references to Poseidon in the *Odyssey*. This poem and the *Iliad* are, after all, the first works of literature in which the god is mentioned in any detail. There are a few earlier references to Poseidon in the Linear B tablets (which we shall be discussing in Chapter 24), but they tell us nothing about him, so it was quite possibly the Ithacans themselves who developed and refined his identity.

Most interpretations of the *Odyssey* regard Poseidon's antics as a literary device based on occasional natural phenomena, amplified by a liberal dose of Homeric imagination. However we have seen from the geological record that ancient Ithaca is poised directly above the thrust lines of one of the most seismically active places in the world. This recent evidence places the fear of Poseidon and his power to evoke earthquakes and tempests at centre stage in the *Odyssey*. The Ithacans seek an explanation for the savage unpredictability of their immediate environment and the poem provides them with a palaeo-tectonic solution that is both convincing and elegant. Odysseus is the King of Ithaca and Poseidon is punishing him with seismic catastrophes and terrible storms because he has blinded the god's son Polyphemos who was conceived in the island's northernmost bay.

We saw that after the 1766 earthquake many families left Paliki and settled in the Peloponnese. In 1767 rocks fell, houses were completely destroyed or evacuated and piles of stones were seen everywhere. In 1953 Andreas Delaportas 'saw all the stones – big stones, they were loose at the top of the mountain and we saw them just rolling down the mountainside into the ocean' – and after that 90% of the population again left Paliki: at least one family settled in Manhattan.

Earthquakes, rockfalls and emigration . . . So how did Strabo's Channel become dry land?

Notes

1 Louvari et al. (1999) pp. 224, 233, 234. See also Peter (2000) Figure 2.1 and p. 18.
2 Laigle et al. (2002) pp. 248, 250.
3 Laigle et al. (2002) p. 251.
4 Papazachos et al. (2000).
5 See Chapter 1 n.12.
6 Tsapanos et al. (2003) p. 131.
7 For the 1714 to 1766 earthquakes see Albini et al. (1994); for the 1767 earthquake see Makropoulos and Kouskouna (1993).

8 The document explains that the measure '13 hours' is expressed in 'Italian hours'. These are normally reckoned by dividing the day into twenty-four equal intervals, starting at sunset. Thirteen hours at that time of the year would therefore be about 08:00.

9 Kirkwall (1864) vol. II p. 153.

10 Underhill (1989) p. 624. Figure 1 of this paper indicates an offshore setting for the Cephalonia Transform Fault of Figure 11.3 and this has been reproduced in Figure 11.7.

11 Students of Homer will not be intimidated by this geological vocabulary because it was he who invented most of it. 'Miocene' for example originates from the Greek words *meion* meaning 'less' and *kainos* meaning 'new'. Miocene is simply rock that is less new than Oligocene (only a little bit new), Eocene (a new dawn) and Paleocene (oldish but still new). Like much of our language, these words were first recorded by Homer. *Eos* features frequently: 'Rosy-fingered Dawn' is a constant presence in the *Odyssey* (the phrase refers to the weather rather than a wench) and you need look no further than the opening lines of Book 2 to find it (the Homeric phrase is *rhododaktulos Eos*). *Palaios* is there as well: when Telemachos is summoning the nurse Eurycleia from her hiding place after the massacre of the suitors he addresses her as 'old woman, born long ago' and Homer uses the word *palaigenes* (22.395). So it goes: there is hardly an art or a science today whose vocabulary has not been permeated by Homeric expressions.

PART 2 Exploration

Much have I travelled in the realms of gold,
And many goodly states and kingdoms seen;
Round many western islands have I been
Which bards in fealty to Apollo hold.
Oft of one wide expanse had I been told
That deep-browed Homer rules as his demesne;
Yet did I never breathe its pure serene
Till I heard Chapman speak out loud and bold:
Then felt I like some watcher of the skies
When a new planet swims into his ken;
Or like stout Cortez when with eagle eyes
He stared at the Pacific – and all his men
Looked at each other with a wild surmise –
Silent, upon a peak in Darien.

Keats, *On First Looking into Chapman's Homer* (1816)

CHAPTER 12 Thinia

Two voices are there; one is of the Sea,
One of the Mountains; each a mighty Voice.

William Wordsworth, *Thought of a Briton on the Subjugation of Switzerland* (1807)

On Friday 21 March 2003 three of us set out for Cephalonia. Simon and I were accompanied by Chris Goodger, longtime family friend and outstanding professional cameraman. Unfortunately the previous day America and Britain had invaded Iraq and as the holder of the EU's rotating presidency Greece was right in the thick of it. We arrived at Heathrow to find the flight to Athens delayed because of protest action there: it would arrive too late for us to catch our connecting flight to Cephalonia. Chris had to be back in London on Tuesday so every day counted. We managed to get hold of the ferry schedule from Patras to Sami and worked out that we might just make it.

The journey from Athens airport to the west coast of the Peloponnese was memorable. The airport motorway was log-jammed so our Global Positioning Satellite receiver had its baptism of fire, navigating us through the back streets of Athens in the rush hour until at last we found ourselves out on the main road and heading towards the Corinth canal. It was 18:45, the boat left at 20:30 and we had 150 km to drive. The GPS kept us alert to our estimated time of arrival which averaged five minutes after the ferry was due to leave. Somehow we made it to the Patras dockside with ten minutes to go, threw the keys at the waiting car rental man and collapsed in a pool of sweat in the ship's bar.

'So Melis, what do you do outside of the tourist season?' We are being driven over the flank of Mount Ainos by Melis Antoniou, owner of the Greekstones car hire firm who has thoughtfully agreed to meet us close to midnight at Sami dockside. 'I am well boring' he replied, demonstrating what we felt was an impressive grasp of teenage British argot coupled with an unexpected streak of humility previously unremarked in the Greek national persona.

'No but really, there can't be enough tourists to run your business in the winter – how do you keep yourself busy?' He wasn't being modest, he was being literal: he held one of the licences to bore water wells for the villagers on the island. He explained that he had been drilling water wells for many years all over the island and had become very familiar with its geology, although he was not a geologist by training. This was a remarkable coincidence, a strange twist of fate in a sequence of good luck that had started with meeting Babis

FIGURE 12.1 The castle of St George
Before Argostoli became the capital this was the former seat of government of Cephalonia.

FIGURE 12.2
Northern end of Argostoli
Bay
The bay tapers from 3.5 km to
2.5 km wide over a length of
13 km. At its mouth it is
about 20 m deep, reducing to
only a metre or so at its
northern end.

Katsibas on Lefkas several years earlier. In fact we have been blessed by a disproportionate number of such coincidences throughout this endeavour: if I were a superstitious person I might imagine that somebody wants this secret to emerge after all these years.

The next morning on a bright but surprisingly cold day we find that our small villa in Peratata is next to the castle of St George, within a few hundred metres of the location that C. H. Goekoop's grandfather identified as the ancient city of Ithaca (Figure 12.1).

We drive past Argostoli, calibrating the altimeter in the GPS at sea level on the way and stopping to take some photographs of what we hope may be a small island at the tip of the promontory where suitors might hide in ambush. The northern road from the capital passes along the eastern flank of Argostoli Bay with a steep drop down to the sea below us. The view is breathtaking: this is the most magnificent setting imaginable (Figure 12.2).

By 11:30 we are looking down at the tiny chapel of Agia Sotira at the southern exit of what we hope is Strabo's Channel (Figure 12.3). This area of Cephalonia that joins the east of the island to the western peninsula is called Thinia. Later in the year I learn that the road from Argostoli was constructed by Charles James Napier in 1824 while Cephalonia was under British administration. Prior to that the inhabitants of this area were 'obliged to make the steep descent to the landing place at Sotira – the chapel on the Eastern shore of Livadi bay – with the greatest difficulty and from Sotira to

FIGURE 12.3
Agia Sotira Cove (looking
north-west)
*St Sotira's red-roofed chapel
lies beside the sea.*

FIGURE 12.4
Agia Sotira Cove
(looking south-east)
*The cliffs give way to rich
alluvial soil.*

FIGURE 12.5 Crumbling rockface above Agia Sotira
The width of the ravine has shrunk to about 60 m.

FIGURE 12.6 Rising ground above Agia Sotira
The farmhouse is about 160 m above sea level and the infilled gorge there is about 100 m wide.

transport their goods by sea to Argostoli and Lixuri in all weathers and at great expense.'[1]

We descend the narrow winding road and park beside the shore (Figure 12.4). I walk along the seafront to the chapel. This bay is no more than 150 m wide but if we are right it is pivotal to the existence of ancient Ithaca. My mind drifts back 3,200 years and suddenly the beach is no longer there: I am standing on the sea. Past me sail the merchant vessels of the Bronze Age while across the bay boatmen are bringing passengers and cattle over from the mainland, any who come for passage. I imagine Telemachos' crew returning this very way after avoiding the suitors' ambush. Was it on a crisp cool day like this one in the spring?

We don't know, but on the night before he left for Pylos Telemachos slept the night 'wrapped in a fleece of wool' (1.443) so it was probably not midsummer, and when he arrived there the townsfolk were having a sacrificial picnic on the shore (3.4–9) so it may not have been midwinter either.

This location for the southern outlet of Strabo's Channel seems a comfortable fit to the theory. The loose earth is red-tinged and fertile, a marked contrast to the rock walls only a few metres away. However, as we start walking back along the channel towards the north the ground level rises rapidly and the ravine narrows considerably. All around us the walls of the rock face are crumbling and there are piles of loose stone and gravel (Figure 12.5). As we scramble up the banks we start our own rockfalls, small boulders tumbling down into the stream below.

We rapidly find ourselves at a height of 100 m above sea level (Figure 12.6). Although the earth is still loose and arable while the rock formations on each

FIGURE 12.7 The landscape of Katochori
View facing south-east across fields that are 180 m above sea level. The bay of Agia Sotira lies beyond the right of the photograph.

FIGURE 12.8 Valley alongside the road to Zola
View north towards Mount Agrilia. The road here is about 185 m above sea level and at this altitude the gorge is about 160 m wide.

FIGURE 12.9 View of northern channel bay
The view is to the north-north-east. The ground beyond the base of the 'V' is at an altitude of about 80 m above sea level.

FIGURE 12.10 Agia Kiriaki Bay
Zola lies off to the left, while to the east (far right) are the slopes of Mount Imerovigli which reaches an altitude of 993 m.

side are clearly distinct, we cannot help asking ourselves 'Why is this gorge so narrow, and where did all this earth come from?'

The modern road runs a few hundred metres to the east of the ancient seaway and we rejoin the channel at Katochori. Here it is very flat and much wider and there are weatherbeaten limestone rock formations on each side. On the western flank these are not particularly high but on the eastern side the mountains of Kondogourata tower up for hundreds of metres (Figure 12.7).

All around us there is a strange landscape of irregular white limestone sticking up out of the ground, pockmarked with holes and other signs of erosion. We turn off the main road at Petrikata and cross the channel in the direction of Lixouri. Petrikata is a singularly appropriate name: it can be translated as Rockfall. Modern Greek place names can variously help or hinder a quest such as this: some months later in wild excitement I proposed that Kondogourata might mean 'Punt-pole meeting place', from *kontos* and *agora*, but my wise colleague John Bennet (then at the Institute of Archaeology at Oxford University) gently reminded me that *konto* is in fact the modern Greek for 'near'. The fact that just opposite there is a place called Kontagrilias ('near the wild olive trees') and up on a hillside we find a Kontogenada helped me to adjust to toponymical reality: it is rather too steep for punting.

North of this plateau the gradient starts to dip down again and the road branches off to Zola. There is a curious dog-leg in the channel as the road curls round and to our right there is a high tree-covered rock mound stretching along beside us for several hundred metres (Figure 12.8). As we regain height along this road that is cut out of the mountainside we think that the channel used to pass immediately to our right: it is as if we are driving alongside a dried-up canal.

Soon the height of the channel bed drops considerably and now we are within sight of the sea in the northern bay of Agia Kiriaki (Figure 12.9). All around there are strange hillocks and folds beyond the deep drop to the channel course on our right. But the angle of the 'V' at the base of what we presume to be the former channel cliffs is worryingly sharp. Would there have been enough room for a marine channel there if the loose earth was removed from the bottom of the ravine, or would these cliff sides meet each other before reaching sea level? This channel is turning out to be rather trickier than I had hoped.

We enter the village of Zola and take a steep fork to the right, zig-zagging down to the sea. A small harbour with fishing boats nestles in a deserted bay (Figure 12.10): dark clouds scud across the sky as a light rain falls. We gaze out over the grey spring sea. This is better: there is clearly enough room here for a former channel. Once again we imagine ourselves walking on water, looking out across the northern inlet of a sea channel that was last sailed thousands of years ago.

Or was it? There is just so much earth to explain. Assuming that the channel bed was at least a few metres below sea level at that time, and given that it is now 180 m above sea level at its highest point, that represents a maximum rate of infill of about 6 cm every year. Although rockfall along the channel walls looks as if it could explain that amount of debris in the narrower parts of the channel – indeed we had probably added at least another 6 cm here and there ourselves just by walking past – how could it account for the sheer

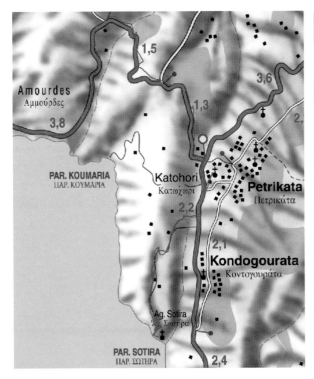

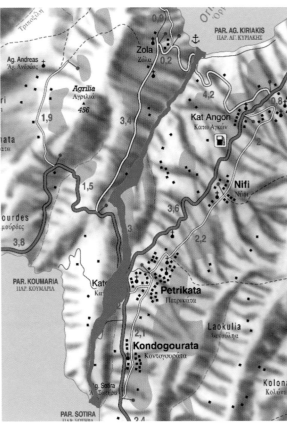

FIGURE 12.11 Exploring the southern exit to the channel
The red track denotes our route, automatically plotted using GPS technology.
[Image credits: as Figure 5.3. Processing: OziExplorer. Track coordinates: Garmin Etrex Vista GPS.]

FIGURE 12.12
First plot of the course of Strabo's Channel
The blue area is an estimate of the course of Strabo's Channel, based on the contours of the ground we had surveyed. [Image credits and processing: as Figure 12.11.]

volume of earth in the central section that is several hundred metres wide? Chris and Simon are looking decidedly sceptical and although they are being too diplomatic to say so, I have to acknowledge that I am a long way from proving that this was once a marine channel. We were clearly going to need advice from a professional geologist.

Back at the villa that evening we connected the GPS receiver to our PC and displayed our route on the survey maps that I had digitised before leaving England. Sailors and outward bound enthusiasts will be familiar with the capabilities of this type of equipment but initially we found it quite uncanny to see every twist and turn of our route displayed on the computer screen. We were using a hand-held gadget that was listening to the signals from orbiting satellites and continually calculating and logging its position and altitude. To our great relief the US military had decided against reducing the accuracy of this global navigational tool during the Iraq invasion and our tracks and waypoints were being recorded to an accuracy of about 6 m (Figure 12.11).

By combining the information from the survey map with our photographs and GPS tracks we came up with our first estimate of the course of Strabo's Channel from north to south (Figure 12.12). We calculated that it ran for a distance of nearly 6 km, varying in width from about 400 m at its widest to only 50 m at its narrowest. It was hard to estimate its depth in ancient times but judging from the slope of its banks there were certainly places where it could not have been more than a few metres deep.

However, plotting a possible course on a computer screen was not the same as proving that it really had been a marine channel in Odysseus' time. What troubled us most were those two questions: why was it so narrow, and where had all the earth come from? It would take nearly six months to find the answers.

Note
1 Cosmetatos (1995) p. 99.

CHAPTER 13   Phorcys

Sleepe after toyle, port after stormie seas,
Ease after warre, death after life doth greatly please.

Edmund Spenser, *The Faerie Queene* I.9.40 (1590)

The next day was 23 March 2003 and we decided to concentrate on the area to the west of the channel in the region where I believed the ancient city of Ithaca to be located. In fact I had been unable to contain my impatience the day before and we had driven round the bay to enjoy our first view of the harbour (Figure 13.1).

This marshy low-lying area looks as if it might previously have been under-water, an encouraging start to the search for the city harbour. We are approaching it from the eastern side, driving round the tall hill called Kastelli, while on the western side the lower hill of Mesovouni is now a large and functioning quarry. But the really striking aspect of this area of northern Paliki is simply how *big* it is. Although we had pored over the maps back in England, we are unprepared for the sheer size of the area to be explored: there seem to be many possible locations for an ancient city and palace.

To my embarrassment I had become over-excited the previous day by hearing some local folklore about 'Odysseus' Palace' and had spent precious expedition time visiting abandoned mediaeval buildings on the opposite hillside (Figure 13.2). My sheepishness at the recollection of calling home from a restaurant that night to say that we had already cracked the problem was only slightly alleviated a few months later when I discovered a book which proposes this same interpretation.[1]

So today we were determined to be disciplined and to follow our cues from the desk research I had performed in England earlier that month. In terms of the overall island geography Homer never actually tells us where to find Ithaca city, so this has to be deduced from other clues and the most obvious one of these is Phorcys Bay. In Chapter 5 we saw that on the map the northern bay of Paliki appears to be an excellent fit to Homer's description, but on this occasion the poet gives us considerably more help:

As soon as that most brilliant star arose
Which is sole herald of the dawning day,
Then the seafaring ship approached the island.
On Ithaca there is a bay of Phorcys,

FIGURE 13.1
Ithaca harbour?
This wetland area is a haven for wildlife. The distance westwards to the tree line is nearly 1 km and the marsh extends to the north by about the same amount.

The old man of the sea: in it, two headlands,
Projecting, sheared off, crouching from the harbour,
Shield it from waves whipped up by blustering winds
Outside. Inside well-timbered ships can ride
Unanchored, when they reach the mooring-place.
There is a leafy olive at its head,
And nearby a delightful misty cave,
Sacred to the nymphs who have the name of Naiads.
Inside are mixing-bowls and double-handled
Jars made of stone, and here the bees store honey.
Inside are long stone looms, at which the nymphs
Weave sea-blue webs, a wondrous sight, and streams
Of ever-flowing water. It has two doors,
One to the north, by which men may descend,
The other to the south, for gods. This way

Men enter not: it is the immortals' path.
They rowed inside: they knew the bay of old.
The ship ran up the beach for half its length
At speed: such strength was in the rowers' arms.   13.93–115

Odysseus is a passenger of the Phaiacians: he has been a guest of their King Alcinoos. Many writers accept the identification of Phaiacia with an island lying to the north of Ithaca (probably Corfu), so we are looking for a harbour in the north of Ithaca with two projecting headlands. Most unusually, it is tranquil enough for boats to be left unmoored. There is an olive tree at its head and nearby is a misty cave with both a north and a south entrance and with flowing water inside. Perhaps there is also some local sea-blue mineral or vegetable material that can be used to stain wool. The shoreline of the harbour is sandy rather than rocky to enable the ship to be beached and there

FIGURE 13.3 Atheras Bay

The view is to the north. The small island of Averonisi stretches slantwise outside the harbour, which is about 250 m wide.

is a relatively unobstructed straight line of access from the sea to enable the oarsmen to pick up speed.

Figure 5.3 provides a map of this part of the island. We drive up the winding hill from the northern end of Argostoli Bay towards Atheras and soon we are passing through the village. In March there are no tourists around and no cafes open: we have the road to ourselves. We start the descent towards the bay but the hillside is thickly wooded and we cannot yet see the view out to sea. At last there is a break in the hedge and we stop the jeep for our first view of Atheras Bay (Figure 13.3).

Nothing has prepared me for this: no amount of research or anticipation, not even a tourist's photograph discovered a few weeks earlier while trawling through the Internet. It is quite simply the most breathtakingly beautiful natural harbour that I have ever seen.

We gaze for a while without saying anything. Atheras Bay is a harbour within a harbour: you can see its western arm in Figure 13.4. The outer contours of both headlands consist of steep cliffs facing towards the open sea; Figure 13.5 shows the skyline of the razor-sharp western face. Later we were to see these cliffs from the seaward side when visiting Telemachos' cove and they are a natural fit to Homer's description 'Projecting, sheared off'.

We return to the jeep and drive down the zigzag road to the beach: it too is deserted. Despite the windy day and the scudding clouds the water is glassy smooth. As we leave the car we walk past the olive tree of Figure 13.6. It is so old that it has grown into some ancient stonework that looks as though it might have been a harbour wall if historical land levels were lower than today. I am clutching a copy of the *Odyssey* and reading out to Chris and Simon the lines 'There is a leafy olive at its head / And nearby a delightful misty cave'. We walk along a path towards the chapel past another ancient olive tree and almost fall into a large sea-cave. We can't see inside it but at the small jetty we meet Spiros the fisherman who agrees to row us over to explore it.

In his boat he explains that he works by day on the fish-farms in Argostoli Bay. We ask him about the wildlife in Atheras Bay: are there by chance any seals? He tells us that not only are there seals but also the occasional shark: in fact the previous summer they had been so abundant they had to be scared away. Why are we interested to hear about the seals? Because the dictionary says that the word for a seal in modern Greek is *phocis* and in ancient Greek *phoce*. Phorcys Bay: the bay of the seals?[2]

Phorcys is a legendary figure from Greek mythology. In Chapter 11 we saw that Homer describes him as a sea-god and father of the nymph Thoosa, who was ravished by Poseidon in a cave and gave birth to Polyphemos. Phorcys was clearly an amorous soul: he is also believed to have had an incestuous relationship with his sister Ceto to become the father of the Graiai and Gorgones, the Hesperian dragon and the Hesperides. Not content with that, he also fathered

FIGURE 13.4
Topography of Atheras Bay
The outer arms of the bay are invisible from the inner harbour.

FIGURE 13.5
The sheer western cliffs of Atheras Bay
Cape Atheras at the tip of the headland is 2.5 km from the bay and its local summit, Mount Kalogiros, is 212 m above sea level.

by either Hecate or Crataïs the female monster Scylla who snatched Odysseus' crewmen from their ship and devoured them as they negotiated the whirlpool of Charybdis. But why was he called Phorcys in the first place? Did the ancient Ithacans believe that he lived in this bay and so named both the old man of the sea and the bay itself after the seals that visited it? The Mediterranean monk-seal is now a protected species but there is evidence that it was much more plentiful in antiquity.[3]

We wade into the cave: the rockface inside has a bluey-green colour from some sort of mineral deposit. We are entering it from the sea, from almost exactly due north. There is no obvious southern exit but perhaps it has been blocked up after all these years.

As well as being protected by the outer and inner headlands, the harbour is also partially shielded by the small island of Averonisi: 'Inside well-timbered ships can ride / Unanchored, when they reach the mooring-place.'

Unusually for this part of Cephalonia the beach is sandy: 'The ship ran up the beach for half its length / At speed: such strength was in the rowers' arms.'

I pinch myself. None of this is possible. Olive trees cannot live for 3,200 years. Caves cannot remain undiscovered for all that time. Sea-blue webs are not spun from aquamarine mineral deposits. The bay cannot meet Homer's description quite so closely. The seals are surely a distraction. Why has Spiros not bothered to anchor his boat as he waits patiently for us to finish exploring the cave? There must be some evidence from the *Odyssey* that disproves this outrageously suitable location.

> And so all things seemed altered to Odysseus –
> The unbroken paths and harbours safe for mooring,
> The beetling crags and the luxuriant trees.   13.194–6

The goddess Athene has brought down a mist so that Odysseus doesn't recognise his homeland. We are looking for unbroken paths, harbours safe for mooring, beetling crags and luxuriant trees. Clearly many locations could meet these rather broad criteria and Atheras Bay is certainly one of them. Athene now tells Odysseus:

> Look how the land lies, then you will believe me –
> The bay of Phorcys, old man of the sea,
> And here a leafy olive at its head
> And nearby a delightful misty cave,
> Sacred to the nymphs who have the name of Naiads.
> This is the spacious vaulted cave where often
> You offered potent hecatombs to the nymphs,
> And this is forest-clad mount Neriton.   13.344–51[4]

As Athene lifts the fog away from Phorcys Bay, Odysseus looks up to see the familiar landmark of Mount Neriton and realises that he has landed on his home shore. The mountain that rears up behind Atheras Bay is today called Mount Lakties: it is to the east of the village of Atheras. In fact as we saw in Chapter 3 there is also an earlier reference to 'leaf-quivering Neriton' in the *Iliad* (2.632).

If the art of great cinema is what Steven Spielberg, quoting Coleridge, calls 'suspension of disbelief', then Atheras Bay is a living movie. This is somehow all too easy: real life cannot be like this. Isn't the *Odyssey* in large part a fable? The next thing we shall see is the glint of gold at the back of the cave where Athene has helped Odysseus to bury it:

FIGURE 13.7
Mount Lakties from
Atheras Bay
*The mountain lies 2.3 km
south-east of the bay and its
summit rises to 518 m.*

Athene, grey-eyed goddess, answered him:
'Cheer up! Don't worry about that. We must
Bury the treasure deep in the hallowed cave
Without delay, to keep it safe for you,
And then consider the best plan of action.'
With that the goddess entered the misty cave,
Feeling for hiding places, while Odysseus
Brought the Phaiacian presents closer up,
Gold, indestructible bronze, and well-made clothes.
He stored them carefully, and Pallas, daughter
Of aigis-bearing Zeus, sealed the mouth with a stone.[5]
Then they sat down by the trunk of the sacred olive
To plot the death of the high and mighty suitors.   13.361–73

Mercifully for our sanity that day there was no gold to be seen.

Notes

1 Livadas (1998) ch. 7.
2 But sadly I later learnt from James Diggle that it is most unlikely that *phoce* and *phorcys* are etymologically related.
3 See www.foi.org.uk/pdf/wildlife/monk_seal.pdf
4 See James Diggle's comments on this passage in Appendix 5 Section J.
5 The aigis is a mythical shield or protective outer garment, generally used by Zeus and Athene. On fifth-century Greek pottery the aigis adorns Athene's shoulders rather like a fashionably minimalist poncho.

CHAPTER 14　Eumaios

It is better to be a human being dissatisfied than a pig satisfied; better to be Socrates dissatisfied than a fool satisfied.　　John Stuart Mill, *Utilitarianism* (1863) ch. 2

After Odysseus has hidden the treasure Athene advises him on what he should do next. We are treated to a vivid description of the location and economics of the palace pigfarm:

> Go first of all to the swineherd, who keeps watch
> Over your pigs and is still loyal to you
> And loves your son and wise Penelope.
> You will find him sitting with the pigs; they feed
> By Raven's Rock and Arethousa Spring,
> Guzzling dark water and munching tasty acorns –
> A diet that builds up healthy fat in pigs.　　　　　13.404–10

The expression 'dark [literally black] water' is found elsewhere in Homer and suggests 'water from deep places where the light cannot reach'.[1] The inference is that the pigs were not drinking from an open stream.

> He climbed a rugged path up from the harbour,
> Along the heights through woods, the way Athene
> Pointed him to the swineherd, of all the servants
> The most faithful steward of his property.
> He found him seated in the porch, on ground
> Exposed to view all round,[2] where he had built
> With his own hands a high surrounding wall,
> A fine big wall, for his absent master's swine,
> Far from his mistress and the old Laertes,
> With quarried stones, topping it with wild pear.
> All round the outside he had driven in stakes,
> Close packed, cut from the black heart of the oak.
> Inside the wall, to house the pigs at night,
> He had built twelve sties, close by each other: in each
> Fifty brood sows slept on the ground. The males
> Slept outside. These were fewer by far, three hundred
> And sixty, and their number was reduced

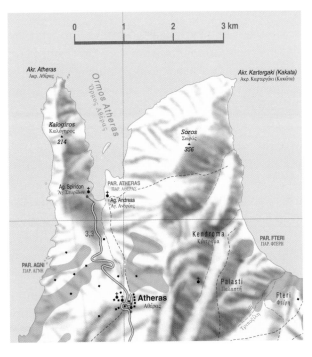

FIGURE 14.1 Atheras /
Arethousa
*The accidental transposition
of syllables in a word is
called* metathesis *and it is
well-established aspect of
language evolution. In Old
English, a bird was a* brid
and dirt was drit; *today's*
flimsy *was formerly* filmsy.
[Image credits: as
Figure 5.3.]

Continuously by the banqueting
Of the noble suitors, since the swineherd always
Sent them the finest of the fatted hogs.   14.1–20

So we are looking for a rugged path through woods up to high ground.
There will be a spring called Arethousa near to Raven's Rock. The pigfarm
has a view all round and it has been walled in personally by the swineherd Eumaios with blocks of stone from a quarry. This farm is hardly a pig
in a poke: there are 600 sows penned in twelve stockades within it, while
360 boars sleep outside – indeed there used to be rather more in the days
before the suitors' feasts. There is a place where the pigs can drink that is not
an open stream; once upon a time there were oak trees that dropped tasty
acorns for them. Earlier that month in England the map had provided three
clues.

The map shows a path to the east of the modern road and it also shows a
stream descending all the way to the bay. However what is particularly striking
is the close relationship between the names Atheras and Arethousa. As we saw
earlier, great care has to be taken in interpreting today's Greek place names but
one cannot help being intrigued by the fact that the transposition of adjacent
syllables makes these names almost identical. So if Arethousa Spring was in
the vicinity of the village of Atheras then Eumaios' Pigfarm and Raven's Rock
should not be far away.

One further clue may help us. Odysseus is in disguise as an old man so Eumaios does not recognise him, but he nevertheless provides him with the traditional hospitality that is afforded to strangers. After they have wined and dined Eumaios lends Odysseus a comfortable cloak to sleep under in the lodge, but he shows his continuing loyalty to his supposedly absent master by going out to sleep outside with the boars to ensure their safety:

> He went to lie down where the white-tusked boars
> Slept, under a hollow rock that broke the north wind.   14.532–3

This hollow rock is clearly close to the pigfarm and it provides protection from the north wind. The wild boars sleep beside it but it is unlikely that they would be unpenned, otherwise they would stray or be attacked by wolves. So presumably Eumaios had created as the farm's outer perimeter 'a high surrounding wall, / A fine big wall, for his absent master's swine' to prevent these boars from escaping, while 'Inside the wall, to house the pigs at night, / He had built twelve sties' for the sows. If that is the case then the 'hollow rock that broke the north wind' must be inside the perimeter wall of the pigfarm.

We have been exploring the open land just south of Atheras for some time but we cannot see anything resembling the old stone walls of a pigfarm. Then Chris looks across to the base of Mount Lakties and suggests that we might wander over towards it. We fight our way through undergrowth and those fiendish metal fences that the Greek farmers of today use to stop their flocks from straying. We turn a corner and catch our breath: we seem to have entered the world of fairytales again (Figure 14.2).

Walls built up of quarried blocks of stone. Ground exposed to a panoramic view. We are talking about events that are supposed to have happened 3,200 years ago and this is like stumbling across a Disneyworld re-creation.

We walk along the side of the stone walls and Chris approaches the hillside (Figure 14.3).

I am reading from the *Odyssey* again and I shout over to him 'Is there any sign of a hollow rock that would break the North Wind?' There is no reply. I follow in his direction but I can't see where he has gone. Then I look towards Mount Lakties and catch sight of him again. The poor fellow is clearly exhausted: he has gone to lie down where the white-tusked boars slept.

What about Arethousa Spring? By the road-sign on the approach to Atheras itself we find a well but it seems to be too modern: or rather it appears to be only a few hundred years old. We don't find a better candidate for the spring that day but on the following day we are blessed by another benign coincidence. We have returned to the area just north of the pigfarm and Chris has strolled up a path to answer the call of nature. 'I think you'd better come and have a

FIGURE 14.2 View south-west from the foothills of Mount Lakties
The mountain is to the left of the photograph. The stone wall enclosure is about 40 m long by 20 m wide.

FIGURE 14.3 Stone wall enclosure below Mount Lakties
The three walls enclose a rectangular space about 40 m long by 20 m wide, with the foothill of Mount Lakties forming the eastern side.

FIGURE 14.4 A hollow rock that breaks the north wind
Chris Goodger is looking out at the camera towards the west: Mount Lakties shelters him from all but a westerly wind.

FIGURE 14.5 A well on the western flank of Mount Lakties
The view is to the south-west and the well is 240 m due north of the stone wall enclosure.

FIGURE 14.6 Detail of the well at Mount Lakties
(a) This well still operates today: we removed its cover and saw the deep notches in the stone made by the bucket rope. (b) The basin is positioned to catch the water from the well runoff: a cool wash for a dusty shepherd; a welcome drink for his sheep.

FIGURE 14.7
The summit of Raven's
Rock?
*This jutting escarpment
resembles the prow of a boat,
with Mount Lakties behind it.
We are 500 m due south of the
enclosure that may be
Eumaios' Pigfarm.*

FIGURE 14.8
View south from the
summit of Raven's Rock
*The mountains to the left
(east) are those of mainland
Cephalonia (Same). To the
south is the summit of Kastelli
and behind it lies the
Argostoli peninsula. The town
of Lixouri and the peninsula
of Paliki, Odysseus' Ithaca, lie
to the west.*

look at this' he says to us. We walk up to where he is standing and look down into a glade of trees on the side of the mountain (Figure 14.5).

There is a stone-capped well and we peer in to see that it is deep and full of water: just below it is a man-made basin (Figure 14.6). The air is completely still: the slanting rays of the late afternoon sun cut lazily across the mountains to the south-west. Everywhere there are wild flowers in bloom: we sense the faint background humming of bees. It is time to suspend disbelief again. Is this the spring that Odysseus passed on his way to the pigfarm?

Later we walk on down the hillside past the pigfarm, still hugging the foothills of Mount Lakties. As we descend towards the valley the profile of the mountain changes dramatically. A steep escarpment juts out above us and as we round its base we glimpse the craggy southern foothills of the mountain that you can see in the top right corner of Figure 14.3. This rock-strewn summit is only about 260 m above sea level and we decide to climb it (Figure 14.7).

Chris is filming and Simon has gone on ahead. It is 5.30 in the afternoon but at this time of the year dusk is only an hour away. As we climb we hear the goatbells echoing from the valley below. The ascent is harder than we expected but at each step the valley opens up beneath us.

A flock of large birds flies past above us, cawing loudly. Chris swears that they are ravens but as he opens up his camera they are gone. Could this be Raven's Rock?

We reach the local summit, a flat plateau before the mountain ascends towards the north. We gaze south across Paliki: between us and the waters of Argostoli Bay rises the steep hill of Kastelli (Figure 14.8). Somewhere down there must be a city and a palace. The area is dauntingly large and we don't know where to find them. But at least we can see the small quarry from which Eumaios may have hewn his blocks of stone.

Notes

1 The actual interpretation of 'dark water' is rather more complex than this: see James Diggle's comments on this passage in Appendix 1 Section J.

2 See James Diggle's comments on this expression in Appendix 1 Section G.

CHAPTER 15   **Asteris**

First of all, though they had eyes to see, they saw to no avail; they had ears, but they did not understand; but, just as shapes in dreams, throughout their length of days, without purpose they wrought all things in confusion. They had neither knowledge of houses built of bricks and turned to face the sun nor yet of work in wood; but dwelt beneath the ground like swarming ants, in sunless caves. They had no sign either of winter or of flowery spring or of fruitful summer on which they could depend but managed everything without judgement, until I taught them to discern the risings of the stars and their settings, which are difficult to distinguish.

Aeschylus, *Prometheus Bound* 447–58 (transl. Smyth)

It is 10 am on Monday 24 March and Chris, Simon and I are looking for something at the tip of the Argostoli promontory. We are searching for a 3,200 year old island and we simply cannot find it. We don't know how much the promontory might have silted up over the period, although it has to be said that the rocks look decidedly ancient, but the problem is rather more profound than that. The difficulty that we are facing is that this particular part of northern Argostoli is rather flat and so there are no windy heights. Even if we were able to persuade ourselves that there might have been a sea channel cutting through a few hundred metres back from the point, it really wouldn't help because there would be no windy heights from which the lookouts could watch. In any case, there is no evidence whatever of a former channel or island and so we are feeling somewhat concerned.

At this point Simon looks up from where we are standing and spots at least three windy heights a few kilometres further south (Figure 15.1). 'I think we're looking in the wrong place' he says. 'The windy heights are over there.'

'But that won't work because there is no chance of finding an island that far down the promontory: it's far too high' I reply with irrelevant logic.

'Didn't you tell me that Goekoop says that Ithaca wasn't an island at all?' he said. 'If Ithaca doesn't have to be an island, then why should Asteris have to be an island either?'

Why should Asteris have to be an island? Well obviously Asteris is an island. For thousands of years everybody has known that Asteris is an island. After all, Homer says that it's an island. Strabo says that it's an island. Even Dörpfeld was looking for an island, otherwise why would he have chosen Arkoudi? Homeric researchers over the centuries have settled on Dascalion as the location of the

FIGURE 15.1
View south from Argostoli
promontory
*The view is from the
lighthouse of St Theodoros,
looking down the peninsula
towards the south-south-east.
The distance to the first radio
aerial tower is 3.5 km.*

ambush precisely because it is the only island between Cephalonia and modern Ithaca. As far as I was aware nobody had ever suggested that Asteris itself was not an island.[1]

Layers of paint . . . I wonder? Did Homer actually say that Asteris was an island? I compare the main English translations of *Odyssey* 4.844–7:

> Off in the middle channel lies a rocky island,
> just between Ithaca and Same's rugged cliffs –
> Asteris – not large, but it has a cove,
> a harbor with two mouths where ships can hide.   (Fagles)

There is a rocky isle in the midst of the sea, midway between Ithaca and rugged Samos, Asteris, of no great size, but in it is a harbour where ships may lie, with an entrance on either side.   (Murray)

> There lies a certain island in the sea,
> 'Twixt rocky Samos and rough Ithaca,
> That cliffy is itself, and nothing great,
> Yet holds convenient havens that two ways let
> Ships in and out, call'd Asteris.   (Chapman)

Fagles says it's an island. Murray says it's an island. Chapman says it's an island. Homer says it's an island. Well, not quite: Homer didn't speak English so he called it a *nesos* instead. We have a kitbag of emergency rations in the jeep and I dig out Liddell and Scott's Greek dictionary:

νῆσος [nêsos]   *an island; also a peninsula when applied to the Peloponnese [the island of Pelops]*

Dear God: can 'nesos' really mean a peninsula? Is that what Homer meant? If so surely this would have been picked up by other researchers earlier. There are many textual traps in the *Odyssey* and it has been combed by philological scholars.

We are in limbo for the rest of the trip but on our return I resolve to consult with an expert. A year or so previously I had met James Diggle of Queens' College Cambridge during a graduate recruitment campaign. Although I am trying to maintain chronological order in this story, James has already been properly introduced earlier in this book so I will fast-forward to a few days after our return to the UK and share our e-mail correspondence of 31 March with you:

Dear Professor Diggle,
I wonder if I might prevail upon your expertise to ask you a question regarding the possible meanings of a particular ancient Greek word? My question is simply whether the word nesos *can refer to a peninsula as well as an island. Liddell and Scott say that it can serve as a description of the entire Peloponnese but I'm unclear whether it is also found in general use for smaller peninsulas.*
With kind regards,
Robert

Dear Robert,
I don't believe that nesos *on its own can be applied to a peninsula, with the exception of (what is a special case) the Peloponnese (as when Sophocles, Oedipus at Colonus 696, refers to it as* nesos Pelopos, *'island of Pelops'). The normal word for 'peninsula' is* chersonesos, *literally 'dry-land island'.*
Kind regards,
James

This was rather what I had initially expected so I felt it only fair to probe a little:

Dear James,
Many thanks for your reply.
Since presumably not even the Corinthians could claim that the Peloponnese was an island, why then I wonder did Sophocles choose to say nesos Pelopos *instead of* chersonesos Pelopos? *I wonder if he was constrained by the metre? Or do you think the words were more or less synonymous at that time – like a colloquial ellipsis of 'omnibus' to 'bus'?*
Best wishes,
Robert

Dear Robert,
Chersonesos *is the ordinary prose word, and Sophocles would not have wanted to use it in high poetry. This is a passage of choral lyric, and the style and diction of such passages are often much more elevated and remote from normal prose usage than the style and diction of passages of tragic dialogue.*

So nesos Pelopos, *'island of Pelops', is simply a poetical alternative for* Peloponnesos, *which means 'Pelops-island'. And I now see that the same expression* Pelopos nesos *had been used at least a century before Sophocles by an unknown epic poet (in a poem, of which we have only a few fragments, called 'Cypria'). So it's not really a case of abbreviation, like bus for omnibus.*

I don't think any prose author would have felt justified in using nesos *for peninsula. I suppose the Greeks outside the Peloponnese (both in Athens, and in Asia Minor or the islands where the epic poet would have been writing) regarded the Peloponnese as so tenuously attached to mainland Greece that it seemed reasonable to call it an island.*
Best wishes,
James

Professor Diggle's reply was becoming more encouraging but I felt that I would be regarded as deeply suspect if I revealed my motives at this stage. He has since forgiven me for the following modest artifice:

Dear James,
It is very kind of you to indulge me in this whimsical question of mine and I mustn't pester you too long on the subject. But I was very interested in the distinction you drew between verse and prose usage and I hope you will permit me a further observation.

I note that Peck describes Cypria as 'a poem in early days ascribed to Homer, but denied to him by Herodotus . . . Later, its author is variously given as Stasinus or Hegesias. It detailed the causes of the Trojan War, and served as a sort of introduction to the Iliad.'

*So with Homer in mind and with the benefit of the word search facility on my PC, I
had a look through the* Odyssey *for instances of 'island' and as an example, I wonder
what your thoughts are on the attached short extract?*
Best wishes
Robert

I enclosed lines 4.844–7 of the *Odyssey* listed above accompanied by the
question:

*In view of the metre I wonder if it is likely that even if Homer had been thinking about
a peninsula here, he would still have opted for* νῆσος [nesos]? *Also, do we know
whether the compound word* χερσόνησος [chersonesos] *had in fact emerged in
Homer's time?*

Back came the reply at 09:48 on 1 April:

Dear Robert,
Homer couldn't have used the word chersonesos *since it cannot be fitted into the
metre of epic verse. The first attestation of the word is Herodotus (2nd half of 5th
century). But Asteris is clearly an island. If Homer had ever wanted to refer to a
peninsula, maybe he would have had to use* nesos. *But (since I don't think he ever
does need to) the issue remains theoretical.*
Best regards,
James

O happy day! I prayed that it was not an April Fool.

Dear James,
Thank you very much indeed for your advice: you have been of very great help.
Every best wish and thank you again,
Robert

You will understand that my state of elation was not affected by James
Diggle's opinion at the time that Asteris was an island: indeed I knew that
nobody would have dreamt of suggesting otherwise and I had not yet paid
him the courtesy of discussing our findings with him. Once I had done so
(at a meeting in May to be described in Chapter 17) James introduced his
own translation of the lines about Asteris and considered the meaning of the
crucial adjective *amphidumoi* which describes the harbours. He then reviewed
Strabo's references to Asteris that we discussed in Chapter 6 and made two
remarkable and encouraging deductions.

The first is that Apollodorus, Strabo's authority, identified Asteris with Argostoli and must therefore have located Alalcomenai on the isthmus of the Argostoli peninsula, while the second is his conclusion that Apollodorus must also have identified ancient Ithaca with Paliki. James' analysis is presented in Appendix 1 Section B and readers are encouraged to consult his expert assessment in parallel with my account of our laymen's adventures on the island.

So let us now assemble the strands of this argument. Homer uses the word *nesos* to describe Asteris. Now *nesos* usually means an island whereas *chersonesos* means a peninsula, but Homer could not have used *chersonesos* when referring to the peninsula of Argostoli for two very good reasons. First, it cannot be fitted into the metre of epic verse and second, the word probably hadn't yet been invented: it doesn't occur in Greek literature until the fifth century BC. So if Homer had wanted to refer to the Argostoli peninsula it appears that he would have had no alternative but to use *nesos*: it was the only word available at the time that would fit the metre.

Homer also mentions 'a harbour with two mouths where ships can hide' (Fagles) or 'a harbour where ships may lie, with an entrance on either side' (Murray). Where might these harbours be? The Argostoli promontory provides an obvious answer: the harbours would be on each side of the promontory itself. Furthermore if the *Odyssey* itself is regarded as Ithaca-centric, in the sense of being written from the viewpoint of those located in Ithaca city and palace, then the usual view of the peninsula would be from Ithaca's harbour at the northern end of the bay from which one can sail directly to an anchorage on either side of the promontory.

Asteris was never an island: it was a promontory all along. How does this affect the suitor's ambush? Let us go back to 24 March and resume our exploration of the Argostoli peninsula. You can see from Figure 15.1 that there are at least two significant hills towards the southern end of the promontory, conveniently identified with radio masts. Later in the summer I photographed them from the east (Figure 15.2). The previous photograph was taken from the northern point of the promontory (the right-hand side of Figure 15.2a) and the close-up shows the two radio masts on their hilltops.

We jump back into the jeep on the tip of the promontory and race up the tracks that run along the central hillside ridge. The first hilltop we encounter lies before the ones with the radio masts and it is clearly not a serious candidate, because if you were a sentry standing on it then your view out to sea would be obscured by the taller hilltops further south, and also there is no obvious place for a Bronze Age galley to wait in ambush. But our next hilltop is a real winner.

(a)

(b)

FIGURE 15.2

Windy heights of Argostoli
from the east

*(a) View south-west over
Argostoli peninsula, with
St Theodoros' lighthouse to
the far right and the southern
tip of Paliki visible behind.
The radio towers are on the
hillside above the cruise liner.
(b) Closeup of Argostoli with
the windy heights on the hill
ridge lying behind. Today's
photograph can be contrasted
with that of late August 1953
(Figure 1.5).*

Mount St Gerasimos is only 148 m high but it provides a breathtaking 360 degree panorama of the whole area with views looking far out to sea. It is also called Mount Spelia, which means 'caves', and there are the tell-tale marks of antiquities indicated on the map. But the most important aspect, as Figure 15.3 indicates, is that it overlooks an inlet called Paliostafida Bay which provides perfect concealment for a Bronze Age galley (Figure 15.4) behind Cape Lardhigos.

In the background of the photograph you can see the long low reef of Vardianoi island which is also marked on the map. However attractive it may be to reconsider this matter of the word 'island', we should remember that Vardianoi could never be the site of the ambush for three reasons: it has no windy heights, it does not lie between Ithaca and Samos and, crucially, it is too far away from Telemachos' supposed course home to be a credible place for an ambush.

Later in the year it was a great pleasure to escort James Diggle up to the hilltop that he had by then legitimised as Homer's windy heights (Figure 15.5).

Once we had satisfied ourselves that the windy heights were credible and the ambush location a realistic one, it was time to visit the bay itself. We drive down the hillside and head for the Mediterranean Hotel whose rooftop looms over the northern end of Paliostafida Bay. After mastering the twists and turns of the narrow lanes we emerge into the bay which is locally called AntoniouBeach (Figure 15.6).

You could hardly ask for a more perfect site for an ambush. The suitors believed that Telemachos would be returning from the south-east, round the point of the headland. Bronze Age sailors generally hugged the coastline if they could and so Telemachos' ship would have passed close to the jutting promontory. Meanwhile the lookouts posted on the hilltop behind would have had ample notice of the ship's arrival, enough to come down from the

FIGURE 15.3 The
ambush at
Paliostafida Bay
*Attempts to derive an
ambush etymology from*
Paliostafida *are thwarted
by its translation: 'ancient
sultanas'*
[Image credits: as
Figure 5.3.]

summit and join the ship's crew on board, or perhaps to reposition themselves
on the adjacent cliffside so as to tell the crew exactly when to start rowing out
for the ambush.

There is a direct line of sight from the hilltop 1,100 m away to the ambush
ship and if necessary a signal could easily be sent by flashing the sun off a
shield. With one of those laser rangefinders used by golfers we measure the
height of the headland at about 42 m above sea level, more than enough to
conceal a Bronze Age galley with or without its mast raised and irrespective of
intervening land level changes.[2] The bay itself is about 220 m wide and there
is ample depth for the shallow draught of the vessel.

Telemachos would never have stood a chance. His crew were weary from the
journey from Pylos since as we saw in Chapter 10 they had been sailing night
and day. By contrast the suitors' crew were fresh: indeed they were probably
bored by the enforced idleness that was punctuated only by their nocturnal
traverse of the 4 km wide mouth of Argostoli Bay to prevent Telemachos
from returning home under cover of darkness. Within seconds of Telemachos
spotting the threat they would have rammed his vessel amidships and he
and his crew would have drowned or have been slain under the sword in a
couple of minutes.[3] The ship would have sunk and all evidence of the terrible
crime would have vanished. Antinoos would have slunk back to the palace

FIGURE 15.4
Cape Lardhigos and
Paliostafida Bay from
St Gerasimos hilltop
*The cape is 1.1 km south-west
from the windy heights and
the island of Vardianoi lies
5 km out to sea. The word
means 'Guardian' in modern
Greek: locally it is also called
Rabbit Island.*

FIGURE 15.5
Panorama from
St Gerasimos hilltop
(a) James Diggle overlooks the
suitors' ambush bay to the
south-west. (b) To the
north-west across the bay is
the low-lying terrain of
Paliki, with its capital town of
Lixouri at the waterline.
(c) North-east of the windy
heights lies Argostoli: the
lagoon of Koutavos separates
it from Same's rugged cliffs.
(d) View to the east. To the left
of the photograph lies the
ancient settlement of Cranioi.

wide-eyed and innocent, disclaiming any knowledge of Telemachos' where-abouts. The prince would simply never have returned and inquiries sent to Pylos would have suggested that he must have been shipwrecked on the way home.

The matter of the two harbours is easily resolved. This ambush location of Paliostafida Bay clearly constitutes one natural harbour while the other is formed by the landlocked inlet on the other side of the Argostoli peninsula that is today called the harbour of Koutavos. As for Apollodorus, who 'mentions a little town on it, Alalcomenai, situated on the isthmus itself':[4] both the isthmus and the town are readily apparent. The modern capital of Argostoli sits on the eastern side of the isthmus and from a strategic viewpoint either it or the windy heights themselves are natural places for an ancient township.

References in the classical literature to Alalcomenai are rare. James Diggle explains in his Appendix that two much later historians refer to it in an Ithacan context but, as he says, this adds nothing to our knowledge. There is an

FIGURE 15.6
Paliostafida Bay
*(a) Looking south from the
beach towards Cape
Lardhigos. (b) View to the
east: the windy heights lie
behind the Mediterranean
Hotel.*

unconnected settlement of that name in Boeotia (eastern Greece) mentioned by Pausanias in the second century AD.[5] In Greek mythology Alalcomeneus raised and taught the goddess Athene and acted as counsellor to Zeus when Hera became angry at her husband. It is also an epithet of Athene meaning 'Repeller of Danger'. In 1984 the name Alalcomenai was adopted to describe the excavations of Professor Sarantis Symeonoglou on modern Ithaca at the Aetos isthmus.[6]

Argostoli has been completely rebuilt since the 1953 earthquake and our inquiries in the museum elicited no Bronze Age history for the settlement itself: indeed the present town dates back only to AD 1650.[7] However, on the other side of the inner bay lies the ancient Bronze Age city of Cranioi with its Cyclopean walls. Given the panoramic view from this hilltop over the approaches to the island and its line of sight communication with Cranioi, it is reasonable to believe that some sort of settlement may have stood on this promontory for many years.

James Diggle favours the windy heights themselves as the site of ancient Alalcomenai: the location is well known for its caves and it is also within direct line of sight of the imposing hilltop of St George to the south-east. There is an ancient well on the summit and there are also fenced-off areas there that may contain an abandoned archaeological site, although our inquiries to date have not confirmed this. Finally, there is another slightly higher hilltop further south (also with a radio mast and visible in Figure 15.2) which is still just in the line of sight from the ambush location and which would provide an even more extensive view out to sea. The saddle of land that lies between these two hilltops would provide ample space for the lost settlement of Alalcomenai.

Asteris lies south-south-east of the northern end of Argostoli Bay and from that viewpoint it actually looks remarkably like an island (Figure 15.7). So even if the word *nesos* tended to imply to the listener that the land was an island rather than a peninsula, this was an understandable misrepresentation.

What about the name Asteris? The word in ancient Greek is quite clear: *aster* means a star and it can also be used to describe a planet (although the Greeks were aware of the distinction: their word *planetes* means 'a wanderer'). So why should the Greeks call this island 'a star'? What on earth is star-like about this peninsula? Neither the view from the land (Figure 15.7) nor the view from the air (Figure 15.3: a luxury afforded at the time only to pioneers such as Daedalus and Icarus) look remotely like a star. So why then was this peninsula called Asteris? Indeed even if you still believe that Asteris is the modern island called Dascalion, then why call that Asteris either, since it also doesn't look at all like a star? Curiously there seems to have been no significant discussion of this point in the scholarly literature.

I must be careful here because I am now moving from exploration to sup-position. In fact I didn't form an opinion about why Asteris has this name

FIGURE 15.7
The 'island' of Asteris from
the northern end of
Argostoli Bay
*View south-south-east from
Akro Samoli: the Argostoli
peninsula looms out of the
haze 7.7 km away.*

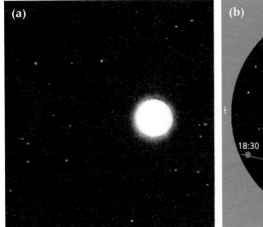
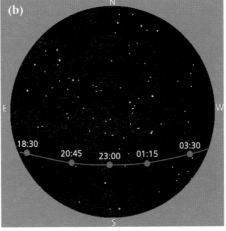

FIGURE 15.8
Mars from Cephalonia

*(a) Photographed on 24
August 2003 near Fiscardo:
compare the relative sizes of
planet and stars.*

*(b) Transit of Mars across the
night sky on that date.*
[Image credits: John
Walker. Website: www.
fourmilab.ch/yoursky/]

until a few months later, and it remains an opinion: I cannot prove it, but let
me share it with you all the same. At that time the newspapers were full of
the fact that the planet Mars was nearer to Earth than it had been for 59,619
years.[8] The date of that closest approach was 27 August, when I happened to
be back in Cephalonia. Mars was indeed very bright: by 24 August it dominated the night sky (Figure 15.8) at a distance of about 0.37 astronomical units

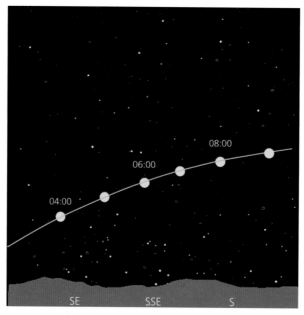

FIGURE 15.9
Transit of Venus from
38°30′N 20°40′E on
1 January 1172 BC
*The centre of the diagram
points south-south-east,
which is the bearing from
Ithaca harbour to Argostoli
promontory.*
[Image credits: John
Walker. Website:
www.fourmilab.ch/
yoursky/]

(an astronomical unit is about 150 million kilometres, the average distance of the earth from the sun).

What was also interesting was its position: it rose in the south-east and it set in the south-west between about 18:30 and 03:30 GMT as the diagram indicates. This and the following analyses were produced by a remarkable Internet-based program created by John Walker in Switzerland: the mind boggles at the challenge of ensuring that such calculations are correctly performed.[9] Note that this star map presents the night sky as it is seen when looking up from the surface of the Earth rather than when looking down as with a normal map, which is why the positions of east and west are reversed.

Although Mars was uniquely visible this year it is a fickle planet: its motion relative to Earth is complex and over its shortest cycle of about sixteen years it wanes from prominence into invisibility. This makes it somewhat unreliable as a basis for peninsular nomenclature, but what about Venus instead, which the Greeks called Hesperos Aster, the evening star that also appears in the morning? In August at this location Venus rises well after sunrise and it is too close to the sun to be visible. But earlier in the year Venus is very distinctive. On 1 January 2003, for example, Venus appeared in the south-east at about 03:00 GMT (05:00 in Cephalonia) and disappeared towards the west after dawn as the sun obscured it from view.

Where then was Venus around dawn in the sky above Cephalonia on, say, Tuesday 1 January 1172 BC (adopting the conventional chronology of Chapter 2)? Figure 15.9 indicates the transit of the planet that day, with the hours stated in GMT (not that the observatory at Greenwich was then functional). This is a view of the horizon for an observer based at the northern end of Argostoli Bay at a location such as 38°30′N 20°40′E. The planet appeared in the east at about 03:00 GMT. Dawn that day was just before 06:00 GMT when Venus was almost exactly due south-south-east of the observer, and as the sun came up it faded from view towards the west. At that time if you were standing at the location that I have proposed as Ithaca's harbour (Figure 5.4) you would have seen the *aster* shining directly above the peninsula of Asteris.

Although Venus was directly above Asteris at dawn on 1 January 1172 BC it is not always in the same position every morning of every month and year. However, when it does appear at dawn above Cephalonia it is almost always in the quadrant between the east and the south. Indeed its appearance at sunrise was noted by Homer. In Chapter 13 we saw the description of Odysseus' arrival at Phorcys Bay and just before that passage there is an account of the Phaiacians' voyage taking him from Scherie to Ithaca.

These are among the most beautiful verses in the *Odyssey* and to celebrate them I would like to introduce you to a new translation by James Diggle. He and I met to discuss this project shortly after our exchange of e-mails and his involvement since then has been of fundamental importance to this quest. As you read his lines below please bear in mind the tripartite difficulty of his task: to achieve a new translation of absolute fidelity to the original; to produce a result in English verse form; and also to create lyrical and lasting poetry.

> As four teamed stallions upon the plain
> Racing as one beneath the lashing whip
> Gallop to goal, their bodies surging high,
> So the ship's stern rose up, and in her wake
> The billows of the thundering ocean seethed.
> Steady she ran, straight on; not even the hawk,
> Fleetest of birds, could have kept pace with her.
> So, running swiftly, she cut through the waves,
> Bearing a man as wise as gods are wise,
> Who after many sufferings endured
> On field of battle and the wearying waves
> Now slept at peace, forgetful of his pains.
> As soon as that most brilliant star arose
> Which is sole herald of the dawning day,
> Then the seafaring ship approached the island.
> On Ithaca there is a bay of Phorcys,
> The old man of the sea: in it, two headlands,
> Projecting, sheared off, crouching from the harbour,
> Shield it from waves whipped up by blustering winds
> Outside.   13.81–100

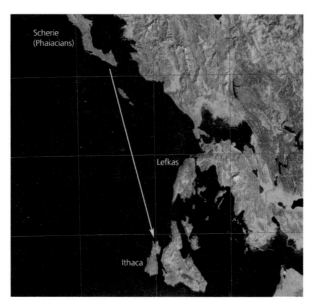

FIGURE 15.10
The guiding star of Asteris
*If the Phaiacians started their
journey from Corfu then their
course to Cephalonia would
be a straight line bearing
south-south-east, in line with
the appearance of Venus.
Grid: 50 km.*
[Image credits: as
Figure 1.3.]

The Phaiacian vessel embarked from Scherie, which most authorities agree was Corfu (see Appendix 4) and 'Steady she ran, straight on' until 'As soon as that most brilliant star arose / Which is sole herald of the dawning day' (Homer uses here the word *aster*) the ship drew near to the headlands of Phorcys Bay. The passage suggests that the star was visible ahead of the ship (although not necessarily directly ahead): there would have been little poetic merit in referring to a star that had appeared astern or hard to port or starboard.

If you consult Figure 15.10 you can see that the helmsman of the Phaiacian vessel maintained a steady course almost exactly south-south-east for the entire journey, so if this journey took place on 1 January 1172 BC then Venus would indeed have been dead ahead of the ship at dawn.[10] If instead the journey was later in the year then Venus would have risen further to the east. Do we know what season of the year it was? Homer doesn't tell us but there are some tantalising clues. In Chapter 12 I suggested that Telemachos' nocturnal attire coupled with the Pylians' religious picnic on the beach indicated that these events probably took place neither in midsummer nor in midwinter. There are many other references to the need for cloaks and tunics in the *Odyssey*: a memorable passage occurs shortly after Odysseus is anonymously reunited with Eumaios:

> He rose, and placed a bed for him by the fire
> And spread upon it skins of sheep and goats.
> Odysseus lay down; over him Eumaios
> Spread out a great thick cloak, which he kept by him
> To put on if a winter storm sprang up.   14.518–22

Later at the pigfarm Odysseus addresses Telemachos, referring to Eumaios:

'Go on your way. He'll guide me, as you order,
As soon as I have warmed myself by the fire.'   17.22–3[11]

One of the co-authors of the *Oxford Commentary on Homer's Odyssey* examines this question of seasons from an astronomical standpoint, referring to a splendid passage which describes our hero navigating with the help of the stars on his voyage from Ogygia to Scherie:[12]

Thrilled by the breeze Odysseus spread the sail,
Then sitting at the rudder steered with skill.
He never closed his eyes in sleep but watched
The Pleiades, Boötes who sets late,
The Great Bear, also called the Wain, which circles
Around and eyes Orion warily:
She and she only never bathes in Ocean.
Divine Calypso had instructed him
To keep her on his left hand as he sailed.   5.269–77

However he concludes that this does not provide enough information to pin down the season and that it is safer to rely upon more conventional evidence, such as when Penelope's maidservants are making her comfortable in the palace:

They raked the embers from the braziers
And fed them with fresh wood for light and warmth.   19.63–4

On the strength of descriptions such as these we can almost certainly rule out the summer, but can we decide whether it was late autumn, winter or early spring? Earlier Odysseus concocts a story to explain to Eumaios how he was cast ashore on Ithaca, since he has by now been disguised by Athene and he needs a convincing alibi to satisfy Eumaios' curiosity:

I wrapped the rags around my head,
Slipped down the landing-plank until the water
Was chest-high, then struck out and started swimming.
Soon I was clear of them and climbed ashore.
Then I crept inland and crouched down in hiding
In a flowery copse.   14.349–54[13]

The Greek word used here for 'flowery' is *poluantheos* which James explains is a rare word that occurs in Homer only once, in this specific passage. Its literal meaning is 'with many flowers' and the horticultural enthusiast will be well acquainted with the eponymous varietal. Its next known occurrence is in the *Hymn to Pan*, where it describes the spring, so perhaps we are entitled to regard it as also suggesting the spring in this context.[14] However there are other suggestions that it may have been closer to winter: when Odysseus is cast ashore on Scherie after his shipwreck at the end of his long voyage from Calypso's island of Ogygia, he says:

> If I spend the night without shelter by the river,
> I fear a hard frost and a heavy dew
> Will be the death of me; and a chill mist
> Can rise up from the river before dawn.   4.466–9

A few lines later we read:

> He quickly scooped up leaves and made himself
> A broad bed – leaves lay scattered on the ground
> In piles, enough to shelter two or three men
> In winter time, however hard the weather.   4.482–5

On balance it therefore looks as if Odysseus landed on Ithaca in the wintertime or early spring: perhaps the Pylian picnickers were hardy souls.

So let us bring together the findings of this chapter. Homer's island of Asteris has never been satisfactorily identified: the tiny island of Dascalion does not stand up to any serious scrutiny. However, in Homer's time the word *nesos* meaning an island was also the only one available to describe a peninsula such as that of Argostoli.[15] Furthermore this peninsula looks very like an island when viewed head-on from the northern end of Argostoli Bay.

Once we have appreciated these points, the promontory of Argostoli passes all Homer's criteria with flying colours. It is certainly two-harboured: the outer harbour provides perfect concealment for a galley while the inner harbour is today in continual use by freighters and cruise liners. It is undoubtedly in the straits between Ithaca and Samos and it has windy heights that would enable an ambush to take place. This location for Asteris also makes complete sense of Athene's advice to Telemachos, as we have seen in Chapter 10 and will be exploring in more depth in Chapter 16. Furthermore we can readily accept Apollodorus' requirement that Asteris should also have an isthmus and a town on it: indeed if James is right about the town being on the hilltop then he has located the lost settlement of Alalcomenai.

These are the substantive points of this chapter and clearly they can be assessed without relying on the additional astronomical and seasonal conjectures that I have proposed above. But there is a certain delight to be had in the possibility that a computer program written in the age of the Internet may help us to solve part of a 3,200 year old mystery and as far as I know there have been no alternative proposals for why the ambush location was named in this very distinctive way.

Night after night the ancient Ithacans saw the star that they called the *aster* rising above the island-like peninsula at the end of their bay. What better name to give to this promontory than Asteris?

Notes

1 But later in this research I learnt that one or two writers had in fact proposed this: see for example the detailed entries under Gell and le Noan in Appendix 4.

2 The top of the mast of a twenty-oar galley is just over 7 m above the waterline: see Severin (1985) p. 239.

3 See Chapter 10 n.5.

4 From this point onwards I have adopted James Diggle's translation (in Appendix 2 Section B) of Strabo's description of Asteris and Alalcomenai at 10.2.16.

5 Pausanias 9.3.4, 9.33.5–7, 9.34.1.

6 See the more detailed entry in Appendix 4.

7 From Kavalieratos (2000): 'Until 1650 the town was located outside the castle, about six miles from the harbour. Due to transportation needs, shops and storehouses were built at Argostoli which became the new capital.'

8 For Mars proximity see www.space.com/spacewatch/where_is_mars.html

9 For orbital calculations see www.fourmilab.ch/yoursky/

10 Livadas suggested that the Phaiacians might have caught sight of Venus on their way to Phorcys Bay, although because his Asteris remained at Dascalion he did not implicate this observation in its nomenclature. He also believed that Odysseus returned to Ithaca in the second fortnight of April when the holm oak was in bloom, but I am not persuaded that we can be that specific about the time of year. See Livadas (1998) pp. 115–18.

11 See James Diggle's comments on this passage in Appendix 1 Section J.

12 See J. B. Hainsworth writing in Heubeck et al. (1988) pp. 277, 320.

13 See James Diggle's comments on this passage in Appendix 1 Section J.

14 See also Livadas (1998) p. 207.

15 The origin of the word Argostoli is unclear: interestingly *argos* means 'shining, bright, glistening', which describes a star rather nicely. Alternatively, and according to the curators of Argostoli Museum, the word Argostoli may derive from *argeo* (to lie waiting) and *stolos* (a fleet) – 'a place where a fleet lies waiting'. Sadly it is too fanciful to think of this in terms of Telemachos' ambush: the name is probably a reference to the function of the inner harbour described above. In 1834 the Reverend Richard Burgess visited the town and in Burgess (1835) vol. I p. 113 he wrote that 'The town of Argostoli is modern, having been built by the Venetians in the course of the last century; but the name is ancient, and taken from that which Strabo gives to the bay – *Argos stolos.*' Curiously there seems to be no trace of this reference anywhere in Strabo's *Geography*, but Burgess was a member of St John's College Cambridge and the author of *The Topography and Antiquities of Rome*, so one presumes that he would hardly have invented this attribution. It is another mystery.

CHAPTER 16   **Telemachos**

A prince should therefore have no other aim or thought, nor take up any other thing for his study, but war and its organisation and discipline, for that is the only art that is necessary to one who commands.   Niccolò Machiavelli, *The Prince* (1532) Ch. 14

In Chapter 10 we learnt that Athene has warned Telemachos about the suitors who are waiting to ambush him at Paliostafida Bay. We considered his route in Figure 10.6 and it is now time to trace his journey home from Pylos to the pigfarm as closely as we can, whether by following the wake of his ship or the imprint of his footsteps. Let us start with a reminder of Athene's sailing directions:

> So keep your sturdy ship far off the islands
> And sail by night and day. Whatever god
> Is guarding you will send a following wind.
> And when you reach the first shore of Ithaca,
> Send on your ship and comrades to the city.
> Yourself, go first to the swineherd, who keeps watch
> Over your pigs and is still loyal to you.
> Spend the night there, and send him to the city
> To give the news to wise Penelope
> That you are now back safely home from Pylos.   15.33–42

Telemachos leaves King Menelaos' palace in Sparta and travels back to Pylos by chariot accompanied by King Nestor's son Peisistratos. He decides against making a courtesy call to the palace because he knows that King Nestor will insist on detaining him with further hospitality. Instead he embarks at once from Pylos and sails towards Ithaca. He is to 'keep your sturdy ship far off the islands' while aiming to 'reach the first shore of Ithaca'. What is his route home and where does he land on Ithaca?

> They went past Crounoi and past fair-streamed Chalcis.
> Then the sun set and all the streets grew dark.
> She made for Pheai, sped by Zeus's wind,
> And passed divine Elis, where the Epeians rule.
> He then aimed for the swift isles, wondering
> Whether he would be caught or escape death.   15.295–300[1]

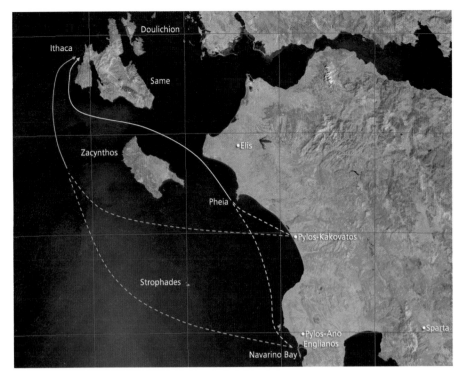

FIGURE 16.1
Telemachos' alternative
courses from Pylos
*At least two sites for Pylos
have been proposed on the
Peloponnese mainland, and
Athene's sailing instructions
also leave us unclear whether
Telemachos sailed north or
south of Zacynthos. Grid:
50 km.* [Image credits: as
Figure 1.3.]

These passages appear to provide us with considerable help but in fact they
contain four distinct difficulties. The first is that the location of ancient Pylos
has been challenged over the ages and at least two places on the western
coast of the Peloponnese have been proposed as the site of Nestor's palace
(Figure 16.1). Although an impressive site has been excavated on a hill ridge
called Ano Englianos in the south-western Peloponnese, even the discoveries
there of Blegen and the decipherment of the Linear B tablets by Ventris and
Chadwick have not settled the matter because the tablets don't contain a
reference to King Nestor.[2] So although this palace to the north of Navarino Bay
is spectacular, it has not been proved that it was Nestor's, which means that we
cannot be absolutely sure of the location of the port from which Telemachos
embarked. Dörpfeld thought that Pylos was further north at Kakovatos and
Strabo devoted over 8,000 words to the puzzle.[3]

The second problem is that many classical authorities believe that lines
15.295–300 quoted above were later additions to the poem and not the work
of its composer, so even if we locate places such as Pheai they may not do us
any good.

Our third challenge is to deal with the rather vague phrase 'the first shore of
Ithaca', which is exacerbated by the fact that the Greek word used for 'shore'
can alternatively carry a meaning such as 'headland' or 'cape'.

Finally we need to remember Amphinomos' comment to his colleagues when he sees the ambush ship returning at 16.355–7: 'No need to send a message: here they are. / Some god has tipped them off, or they themselves / Spotted the ship sail past and couldn't catch her.' If the latter alternative is to be credible to Homer's audience (whether it took place or not) then presumably it requires Telemachos' ship to pass close enough to the Argostoli peninsula to be identifiable, but too far away to be intercepted.

To summarise, we are unsure about where Telemachos started his journey, we cannot rely on the place names that are quoted along his route, we don't know if he was spotted out at sea by the suitors and there is also ambiguity in the description of his destination. When I am faced with a problem such as this I turn to James Diggle and I recommend that you now refer to his analysis of these translations in Appendix 1 Section E. Fortunately all of these routes lead to Ithaca so I shall concentrate on trying to establish where he lands and what he does next.

> Soon fair-throned Dawn arrived. Close by dry land
> The crew struck sail and smartly lowered the mast,
> Then rowed the ship on to its anchorage
> And dropped stone weights and tied the stern with cables,
> Then jumped out of the ship amid the breakers,
> Prepared a meal and mixed the sparkling wine.
> As soon as they had drunk and eaten their fill,
> The shrewd Telemachos began his speech:
> 'Now you must row the black ship to the city,
> While I shall hurry to the fields and herdsmen
> And, when I've seen my farms, go down to town
> Tonight, and in the morning show my thanks
> For the voyage with a feast of meat and wine.'   15.495–507

From the lines above it is clear that Telemachos sails through the night and arrives on Ithaca at dawn to partake in an alcoholic breakfast on the shore. But that same morning we hear something very interesting:

> Back in the hut Odysseus and the swineherd
> Were breakfasting at dawn; the fire was lit
> And the herdsmen had been sent off with the pigs.
> Telemachos approached, and round his heels
> The dogs all wagged their tails but did not bark.   16.1–5

So although Telemachos arrives at 'the first shore of Ithaca' at dawn, he also manages to reach Eumaios' Pigfarm around dawn as well (and we later learn that he enjoys a second breakfast there). This means that the pigfarm must be very close to his landing on Ithaca.

Although Athene hasn't told him exactly where to land, he therefore needs to choose somewhere that will enable him to walk to Eumaios' Pigfarm very quickly. There is further indirect evidence that Athene is prepared to let Telemachos determine his own landing place, because having been instructed by her to go to the pigfarm and 'spend the night there' Telemachos then tells his crewmen that he will instead 'go down to town tonight'. Athene has evidently delegated some of these decisions to Telemachos, perhaps as part of his education in coming of age.

We are also told that the crew 'dropped stone weights and tied the stern with cables, / Then jumped out of the ship amid the breakers' so this hardly sounds like Phorcys Bay, where 'well-timbered ships can ride / Unanchored, when they reach the mooring-place' (13.100–1). Instead it sounds much more like this description of the west coast of Paliki by the veteran Ionian sailor Rod Heikell:

The west coast has little to offer the yachtsman apart from spectacular scenery and delightful coves and beaches that cannot be used because the prevailing NW to W winds send a heavy swell in. Even in the morning before the afternoon breeze has set in there is invariably a considerable ground swell setting onto the coast.[4]

Nautical readers who are suspicious of the precedent involved in using last year's sailing almanac as a basis for determining conditions over 3,000 years ago may take some comfort from William Murray's study of winds in the fourth century BC compared to today, in which he comments that 'we are fully justified in applying modern wind data to the problems of classical antiquity'.[5]

Furthermore we may presume that if Telemachos and his crew had landed at a sandy beach then instead of anchoring they would simply have pulled the ship up on to the shore, as the Phaiacians did when they landed Odysseus, so this is more likely to be a rocky cove. Finally we hear that although they have travelled from Pylos under sail, after breakfast the crew are to row the ship to the city, so there must be a change of direction involved which would prevent them from continuing under sail.

So after he has reached the first shore or headland of Ithaca, Telemachos looks for a rocky cove that is very near to the pigfarm and that will require the crew to switch from sail to oars after he disembarks. Where might this have been?

Before visiting Cephalonia I had seen the bay marked 'Agni Cove' on the tourist map (Figure 16.2) and on paper it looked ideal because it is very close to the pigfarm near Atheras. Petani Beach further to the south is a possibility but it is sandy with fine shingle rather than rocky and it is also a fair way from

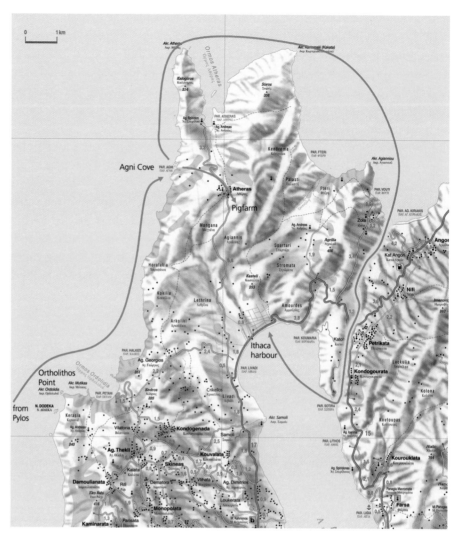

FIGURE 16.2
Telemachos' landing at
Agni Cove
*Three adjustments have been
made to reflect current
nomenclature: Livadi has
been moved to its present
location further south, the
name Akr. (Cape) Louros has
been replaced by Akr. Samoli
and the hillside name of
Crikellos has been added
nearby.*
[Image credits: as
Figure 5.3.]

the pigfarm. Halkes Beach nearby it is also a significant walk. Telemachos must
have known this part of Ithaca like the back of his hand: why give himself an
unnecessary journey?

Shortly after dropping off Telemachos the crew would need to turn hard
to starboard in order to traverse the northern headlands of Phorcys Bay and
then to starboard again to pass through Strabo's Channel, emerging by the
city harbour at the northern end of Argostoli Bay. From Agni Cove this is a
distance of about 23 km and whatever the wind direction, clearly the changes
of course would involve some rowing, especially through the channel. On the
assumption that the city and the palace are somewhere between the pigfarm
and the harbour, Telemachos would easily have had enough time to meet the
crew to give them a feast the next day.

The expedition team woke early on Tuesday 25 March because our return flight was due to leave from Argostoli airport later that morning. Simon volunteers to pack up the villa while Chris and I head off towards Paliki. A crisis emerges as the tank shows we are running out of petrol but eventually we manage to fill up in Argostoli. We take the coast road once again and pass through the sleeping village of Atheras. There has to be a turning off the twisting road down to Atheras Bay to enable us to reach Agni Cove but nothing is signposted.

We choose a track to the left and engage the four-wheel drive. The air is very still: it is not long since dawn. A farmyard, dogs, goats, red earth and stone, a hillside to our left and the sea to our right . . . soon we are forced to stop as the track runs out. We leave the car and walk though an enchanted glade towards the cliff edge. Then we look down.

We are both struck dumb by this view (Figure 16.3). Agni Cove is unreasonably beautiful and impossibly probable. The name means Holy or perhaps Virginal Bay. It is stony, just as it is supposed to be, but there is ample room for a picnic on the shore. The walk to the pigfarm would take less than an hour from here. What does Homer tell us about the distance involved?

Telemachos strapped fine sandals on his feet
And picked up from the deck a sturdy spear
Tipped with sharp bronze. The crew untied the cables,
Then pushed her off and sailed towards the city,
As ordered by the son of godly Odysseus.
He strode on rapidly, until he reached
The yard which housed his countless pigs, near which
The good and faithful swineherd used to sleep.   15.550–7

'He strode on rapidly, until he reached / The yard'. Although it is the striding not the reaching that is described as rapid, these words suggest a brief walk rather than a long march. I turn to my right to look at the path from the cove towards Atheras (Figure 16.4).

To the north we can see the razor-sharp western headland of Atheras Bay (Figure 16.5).

We return to the jeep and find the track down to the sea. The cove is perfect (Figure 16.6). It is so small that as we gaze at it we must be standing very near the spot where the crew took their breakfast over three thousand years ago.

If this is Telemachos' landing on Ithaca, where is the 'first shore' or 'first cape' that constituted his landmark? On Figure 16.2 you can see that there is a very distinctive promontory called Ortholithos Point which marks a sharp right-angle in the coastline half-way up the western coast at the approach to

FIGURE 16.3 Agni Cove from above
The view is to the north-west: the entrance to the cove between the rocks at its mouth is only 70 m wide.

FIGURE 16.4 Telemachos' path to the pigfarm
The path up from the cove crosses the terraces of this narrow (100 m wide) valley.

FIGURE 16.5 The western headland of Atheras Bay
Cape Atheras lies 3.7 km to the north.

FIGURE 16.6 Agni Cove from sea level
Even on a calm day such as this the western swell smashes waves upon the rocks.

Petani Beach. Later in the year James Diggle and I visited it (Figure 16.7): you could hardly wish for a more prominent headland.

So we now have some evidence for Telemachos' landing place on Ithaca; we also have a candidate for the first cape where he sighted land; we know of two possible starting points to his journey from the Peloponnese; and from James Diggle's assessment of the text of the *Odyssey* in Appendix 1 we can form an opinion about whether he sailed to the south or the north of Zacynthos in Figure 16.1. If you favour Athene's admonition to 'keep your sturdy ship far off the islands' then you will opt for the southerly course, whereas if you are influenced by Amphinomos' analysis 'Some god has tipped them off, or they

FIGURE 16.7
Petani Beach and
Ortholithos Point
*View out towards the west
and the landmark of
Ortholithos ('rocks in a
straight line') in the distance.*

themselves / Spotted the ship sail past and couldn't catch her' you may prefer the northerly route.

However this northerly route involves the somewhat awkward observation that if the suitors spotted Telemachos' ship sailing past them towards the west there would presumably be little point in their remaining on duty. If they forthwith abandoned their ambush plans and sailed back to Ithaca harbour they would reach it well before Telemachos' vessel, whereas in fact it is his ship that reaches the harbour first. This is an aspect of the puzzle that we shall address later. Meanwhile the young prince is deposited at Agni Cove so that he can be reunited with his father at the pigfarm after an absence of twenty years.

Chris and I are running late: we have to get back to the villa, pick up Simon and the bags and then race to the airport. We drive back through Atheras and down to Argostoli Bay and on the way we stop to take a few more photographs near the harbour. Chris has been recording everything on tape with a professional camcorder and I have been taking the photographs with a digital still camera, but something seems to have gone wrong with it: each shot is taking far too long to capture. Nevertheless as we drive along the shore past the quarry of Mesovouni and the hill of Kastelli I pause to take a final photograph (Figure 16.8).

We race back to the villa at Peratata and Simon jumps in with the bags. The airport is close by but the side-roads are a nightmare. Eventually we catch sight of the tarmac and our Olympic Airways turboprop to Athens. We throw

FIGURE 16.8
Mesovouni quarry and
Kastelli from Argostoli Bay
*The quarry is about 800 m
away from the camera.*

the keys and our profuse thanks at Melis Antoniou and just then our luck runs out: the flight is overbooked because there is an invalid on board requiring multiple seats so one of us will have to miss it. This is not the best of news because we have been looking forward to a glass of celebratory champagne together.

I say goodbye to Chris and Simon and think about what to do next. Then Maria and her team at the airport are wonderful: they negotiate with the pilot and at last I am out on the runway, waiting to climb aboard, thinking about all the extraordinary good luck that we have had on this trip. But at the aircraft steps the stewardess tells me that the invalid needs yet further space and I am bumped off once again. I walk back to the terminal, waving at the aircraft as it taxies down the runway. This sort of thing is not good for the heart.

The ferry to the mainland is not until the late afternoon. Melis has left with the jeep but I call him up and rebook it for the rest of the day. We chat as he fills in the paperwork again and I ask him idly about those wells that he bores for the villagers. Has he by any chance ever drilled in the area called Thinia, between Agia Sotira and Agia Kiriaki? Yes he has, but it was no good – in fact the villagers were very disappointed with the results because instead of the fresh water that they needed, what they found instead was undrinkable salt water.

Salt water in Strabo's Channel.

How deep was this salt water found? About 250 m below the surface. And where exactly was it discovered? Oh, that was the surprising thing – at least a kilometre inland from the sea. Melis explains more to me but my mind is spinning and I am getting confused with all his dates and depths and place names, so he kindly promises to write out the details and fax them to me in England. He was as good as his word: one week later this fax arrived:

My name is Melis Antoniou, manager of the company Geotritikes Ergasies in Svoronata, Cephalonia. I started working as a driller on Cephalonia in 1985 and created my own business in 1988. During the period 1985–2003 I drilled more than 400 boreholes all over the island. Our main project is the location of underground water. The depths that you can find fresh water on the island vary from area to area (mostly the depth has to do with the altitude of a specific area above sea level). The deepest water-well we have drilled has a depth of 420 meters.

In Cephalonia we use the name 'Thinia' to describe the region that includes the tectonic crack indicated on this map. In that area there are at least 12 boreholes, some drilled by my company and some by others. Borehole B1 [Figure 16.9] was drilled in 1985. It has a total depth of 260 meters and limestone was drilled all the way down the hole. Water with a hypersaline formation was found at a depth of 258 meters and J. Koumantakis, a geologist at the National Technical University of Athens, conducted some research into this at the time.

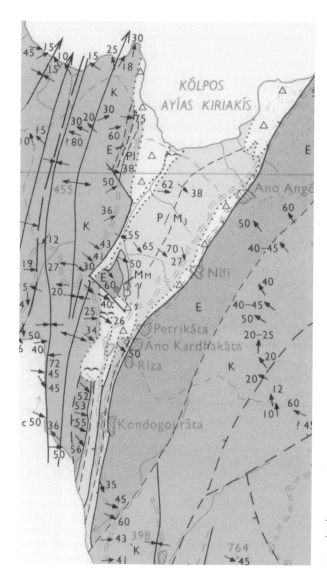

FIGURE 16.9 The salt water borehole
Why did salt water emerge from a drill hole this far from the sea?
[Image credits: as Figure 7.5.]

You ask me how I think this came about. Please remember that I am a driller, not a geologist, and I cannot accept any liability for my views. But in my opinion these unusual drilling samples are the result of a mixture process. In some places soil and rocks have been brought from the surrounding area (because of the winter water-springs, the earthquakes etc.), in some places we have new rock formations as a result of the tectonic pressure and the elevation of the seabed, and in some places we have a combination of both of these causes.

Regarding the white area on the map, I should first point out that the map is not quite up to date. But the fact of finding very new ground and also salt water enclosed at the bottom of the Thinia Area leads me to believe that a large amount of this area was once part of the sea.

FIGURE 16.10
Sunset over the Ionian
Islands
*The view faces the Ionian
Islands. To the right of the
setting sun are the distinctive
north and south peaks of
today's island of Ithaca: to the
left is Cephalonia; and beyond
them lies Paliki, the furthest
to the west.*

What kind of luck was it that bumped me off that flight to Athens? I drive up the hill of the nearby castle of St George and gaze out towards the ocean. These few days have been so compressed: this is all very hard to believe. Melis has just said to me that he thinks that a large amount of this area was once part of the sea. If he is right then Strabo's Channel is real. That means Phorcys Bay is real. Eumaios' Pigfarm is real. Arethousa Spring is real. Asteris is real. Telemachos' cove is real. A great deal of the *Odyssey* must be real as well and it can have been composed only by someone with an intimate familiarity with this island.

Later that day Melis and I drive to Sami harbour and I catch the ferry to Patras. If we want to find Ithaca and also understand how Odysseus and Telemachos felt about their homeland and the islands nearby, then we must observe them the way that they did, from the sea.

The Blue Star ferry sails due east from Sami to Patras: you can see the sun drowning in its western wake in Figure 16.10. As its golden disc sinks towards the horizon there is little room left for doubt about which island 'lies low and to the west, the furthest out to sea of a group of neighbouring islands called Ithaca, Same, Doulichion and Zacynthos'.

Notes

1 See James Diggle's comments on this passage in Appendix 1 Section E.
2 Ventris and Chadwick (1956) p. 137.
3 Strabo's Pylos candidates are discussed from 8.3.1 to 8.3.29. At 8.3.13 he claims to locate Chalcis and Crounoi. The literature on the 'Pylos question' is considerable: there is a particularly interesting discussion at Palmer (1961) pp. 31–89.
4 Heikell (2003b) p. 159.
5 Murray (1993a) p. 33. See also Murray (1982) p. 396: 'The conclusion is unavoidable, that the ancient winds blew at essentially the same times of the year and from the same general directions as they do today. We can now use the full records of local wind data at our disposal with the reasonable assurance that they generally represent ancient conditions – at the very least, the conditions of the fourth and third centuries along the western coast of Akarnania.'

PART 3 Assimilation

There must be a begynnyng of any great matter, but the contenewing unto the end untyll it be thoroughly ffynyshed yeldes the trew glory.
Dispatch from Sir Francis Drake to Sir Francis Walsingham, 17 May 1587

CHAPTER 17 Analysis

*Among European literatures that of ancient Greece has a peculiar place. It is the
earliest of which anything has survived, and it has had the widest influence on
posterity.*

C. M. Bowra (1933)[1]

The coach journey from Patras to Athens provides the traveller with plenty of
time to think. As you cross the Corinth canal you are reminded that by the sixth
century BC the Greeks had already worked out how to avoid circumnavigating
the Peloponnese. Periander constructed a special paved road parallel to today's
canal called the Diolkos, which led from Schinous on the eastern Saronic Gulf
to Poseidonia on the western Gulf of Corinth. The Diolkos was about 3 m
wide and it was paved with blocks of limestone set in a deep layer of sand and
gravel. Along this ran the Olkos, a wheeled vehicle on which ships were borne
overland from one side of the isthmus to the other. Sections of the Diolkos
can still be seen today; the deep parallel ruts in the road are the marks left by
the wheels of the Olkos.[2]

I am in another world for most of this journey. If Paliki really is ancient
Ithaca – and by now I believe that it is – then how can we make it something
more than just another archaeological site? This is the place where Western literature more or less began: surely it has a message for us? On a practical note,
who will believe this amateur adventure? Will any experts take us seriously?
What about the Greek authorities? How many times in the last few hundred
years has some wild-eyed stranger attempted to persuade them that this mystery has been solved? Who is going to dig these secrets out of the ground?
How can we stop Paliki from being destroyed by an influx of tourists? At this
instant America and Britain are invading another ancient civilisation: does
anyone care about this one?

Reality returns on arrival at Athens coach station around midnight. It is
like turning up in Transylvania: disembarking passengers are surrounded by
packs of howling and growling stray dogs, urban warriors with no other place
to go. I find a taxi and head for the airport hotel where my friend Takis
Patrikarakos, the bearer of rare maps, greets me over a late drink. It is impossible to find the words to describe what I believe we have found so I don't
even try.

Air travel is surreal: back in England at lunch the next day it is as if this
whole experience was just a dream. I walk through the Wimbledon woods
with Simon and babble on about how ancient Ithaca could become a symbol

of peace for the world, a place to rejoice and to reflect, a new-found reason for us to take stock of what we have learnt over the last 3,200 years. He listens patiently: his suspicions of my insular obsession are being confirmed by the minute. He prescribes sleep.

Before I retire I remember the camera. Each evening on the island I had transferred the digital photographs taken that day to the hard disk of my computer, but there hadn't yet been time to do that for the final day of the visit. I switch on my PC, plug in the camera and start copying the images over. There is a long delay and my heart sinks. I remember the problem I had on the island: perhaps there will be no photographs on this last day at all. But there are, they are just taking a long time to transfer because half-way through the series each picture has become enormous: 10 Mb instead of the normal 1.5 Mb. I realise what has happened: I had accidentally pressed the button that controls image quality and so the camera has been recording photographs at very high resolution.

When I wake up things have become clearer, as they usually do. There seem to be three tasks ahead of me. The first is to go back to the drawing board and to assemble as much evidence as possible in support of this proposal for ancient Ithaca. The second is to find a way to tell the story about this discovery and its implications. The third is to work out the best thing to do once the story has been told.

I write down the list of locations set out in Figure 3.3 and assess the evidence so far. My proposed location for Ithaca itself and therefore for Same and Doulichion as well is wholly unproven: indeed in the absence of a professional geologist's advice my amateur observations of the channel are of little value. Even if I should turn out to be right in backing Strabo, where is Ithaca city? What proof is there that the low-lying area at the end of the bay is ancient Ithaca harbour? My candidates for Phorcys Bay and Mount Neriton look convincing but that doesn't make them unique: no doubt other researchers have fallen equally in love with quite different locations.

As far as Asteris is concerned, I had not yet conducted my e-mail correspondence with James Diggle so my identification of *nesos* with a peninsula was still purely speculative. My locations for Arethousa Spring, Eumaios' Pigfarm and Raven's Rock are distinctive features, certainly, but so are those claimed by other enthusiasts on other islands, and while Telemachos' bay fits the description, so would another cove near to an alternative pigfarm. Furthermore I have no proposed location for Hermes' Hill, nor the city fountain, nor the city meeting place, nor Crocyleia, Aigilips, Rheithron Cove, Mount Neïon, Laertes' farm or Nericon.

Worst of all I have no clear idea where to find Odysseus' Palace. We had spent some time wandering around the area south of the escarpment that may be Raven's Rock but apart from an abundance of walls and

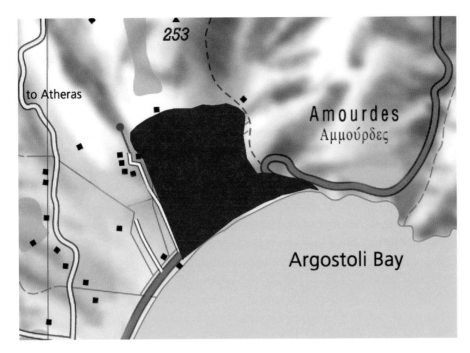

FIGURE 17.1
Boundary of the
lowest-lying harbour area
*The altitude of the coloured
marshland area varies from
0.1 m to 0.8 m its above sea
level. Beyond its western edge
the ground rises slowly,
reaching about 6 m above sea
level beside the Atheras road.*
[Image credits and
processing: as
Figure 12.11.]

enclosures and some curiously cut stones, there seemed to be little of Bronze Age note: sadly no polygonal walls or Mycenaean lion-heads had presented themselves.

The key was surely the harbour, because if I could demonstrate that this meets the clues in the *Odyssey* then the city and palace must lie somewhere between it and the pigfarm. The marshy area of Figure 13.1 extends today for nearly a square kilometre at a depth varying between 0.1 m and 0.8 m above sea level. The adjacent area to the west is a little higher but it is still very low ground. Much of this was therefore immersed before the 1953 upthrust of 60 cm that is depicted in Figure 7.3. If there was an earlier upthrust as suggested by the geologists in Chapter 7 then on the basis of these two land movements alone the depth of the sea in Odysseus' time would have varied between 0.4 m and 1.1 m in the area shown in Figure 17.1. Perhaps there had been more upthrusts and perhaps also the sediment in the harbour had built up over the centuries, but I wanted to work on the basis of known data wherever I could. Would this be enough depth to float a Bronze Age galley?

The best way to answer that question seemed to be to find out from someone who owned one. Fortunately that intrepid explorer Tim Severin had not only built a galley and sailed in it, he had also thoughtfully explained in his book *The Jason Voyage* that the draught of his faithfully reconstructed twenty-seat vessel was only 2 ft and that it consequently needed as little as 2–3 ft of water (0.6 m–0.9 m) in which to float. He had sailed in the same ship in his subsequent voyage in the steps of Odysseus so this seemed to be a fair figure to use.[3]

On the basis of these observations the Ithacan galleys would have been able to float within most of the harbour area outlined in Figure 17.1, although it would have been very shallow. Are there any clues in the *Odyssey* about the harbour's depth? We have already met Antinoos, the leader of the suitors' ambush party, and we hear about the preparations for their departure in Book 4:

> He picked out twenty men, the best there were;
> And off they went to the swift ship on the shore.
> They dragged her first of all into deep water,
> And then they put the mast and sail aboard
> And fixed the oars in leather oarlock straps
> All in due order, and spread out the white sail,
> While proud attendants brought them their equipment.
> They moored her well out in the water, came
> Ashore, had supper, and awaited nightfall.   4.778–86[4]

How deep is 'deep water'? The men are dragging the ship at the time so presumably they remain within wading depth. We don't know how far away from the land 'well out in the water' would have been: perhaps they took her out beyond today's shoreline. On balance this passage didn't therefore seem to be contradicted by the proposed harbour location. What other clues are there? Much later, when Telemachos' crew return to the harbour after depositing him on the west coast, we hear that:

> The sturdy ship which brought Telemachos
> And crew from Pylos put in to Ithaca.
> As soon as they arrived inside the deep harbour
> They dragged the black ship up onto dry land,
> While proud attendants took away their equipment.
> At once they carried off the splendid presents
> To the house of Clytios, and sent a herald
> To Odysseus' palace with the news for wise
> Penelope that her son was in the country.   16.322–30[5]

Here the harbour is again described as 'deep' and this time there is no suggestion of wading, so this passage looks rather more problematical. However to have 'dragged the black ship up onto dry land' is definitely feasible: the terrain along the proposed ancient harbour-line is sand or loose earth rather than rock, particularly along the western and north-western sides. Finally as

we read in Chapter 10, another suitor called Amphinomos observed the return
of the unsuccessful ambush team from his vantage point in the palace, just
after Eurylochos proposed recalling them:

> 'Come, let us launch the best black ship we have
> And muster seamen who can row, to take them
> An urgent order to return at once.'
> He was still speaking, when Amphinomos
> Turned round and saw a ship in the deep harbour;
> The crew were taking down the sail and ready
> To row her in. He smiled and said to his comrades:
> 'No need to send a message: here they are.
> Some god has tipped them off, or they themselves
> Spotted the ship sail past and couldn't catch her.'   16.348–57

So Amphinomos sees the ship 'in the deep harbour', taking down the sail
ready to row her in. Why is there this emphasis on 'deep'? Why did Homer
use the adjective at all if the harbour was shallow? I wondered if 'deep' might
possibly refer to horizontal rather than vertical depth, as in 'deeply indented
from the sea', but it sounded a little thin. Later James Diggle advised me
that it was most unlikely that the Greek words that are used, *benthos* and
polybentheos, could convey anything other than the normal meaning of deep
water. But then how could the men drag the ship along? Could they instead
be pulling it with ropes from the quayside? This was all somewhat puzzling,
so I took some comfort in another piece of evidence describing the harbour.
We reviewed this passage in Chapter 5 when considering the wind direction:
that was Robert Fagles' translation and here is James Diggle's:

> They untied the stern-cables,
> Then went aboard and sat down at the rowlocks.
> Bright-eyed Athene sent them a following wind,
> Strong, westerly, whistling over the wine-dark sea.
> Telemachos bade his shipmates lay all hands
> To the tackle; they obeyed their leader's bidding.
> They raised the pinewood mast and stepped it in
> Its hollow box and made it fast with forestays,
> Then hoist the white sail with ropes of twisted hide.
> The canvas billowed in the wind, and as
> She sped the dark wave thundered round the prow.
> Over the waves she ran pursuing her path.[6]
> The tackle on the swift black ship secured,
> They set out mixing-bowls brim-full with wine

> And poured libations to the immortal gods,
> Above all to the bright-eyed daughter of Zeus.
> All night and through the dawn she sped to her goal.   2.418–34

Athene sends them a following westerly wind: they raise mast and sail, the canvas billows and they are on their way. Crucially, a westerly wind would have supported a south-easterly exit from this harbour and a subsequent bearing of south-south-east down Argostoli Bay.

To summarise: with the exception of a troublesome emphasis on 'deep', this location for Ithaca harbour seems to fit the Odyssean clues. In any case I was confident that no other proposal matches the clues any better and several of them, as we saw previously, flatly contradict them. So on the working assumption that this is the harbour, where might the palace have been? As ever, Homer gives us further hints: indeed we have just read one of them above:

> He was still speaking, when Amphinomos
> Turned round and saw a ship in the deep harbour.   16.351–2

Amphinomos is in the palace at the time, so this passage tells us that the harbour must be visible from it. What else can we find out about the palace? It turns out that there is a considerable amount of intelligence to be gleaned from its relationship with the pigfarm, especially if we work out the over-all timetable, distances and altitudes involved. I had performed some of this research before I left England but now that I had visited the site I realised that the only way to tie down the main locations was to go through the *Odyssey* again with a fine-tooth comb, looking for these topographical clues. Over the next few pages I will set these out and although this analysis is an essential part of the quest, readers who prefer to take the details on trust may fast-forward to Figure 17.2.

In Chapter 14 we read of Odysseus' route to the pigfarm from Phorcys Bay:

> He climbed a rugged path up from the harbour,
> Along the heights through woods, the way Athene
> Pointed him to the swineherd, of all the servants
> The most faithful steward of his property.
> He found him seated in the porch, on ground
> Exposed to view all round, where he had built
> With his own hands a high surrounding wall,
> A fine big wall, for his absent master's swine,
> Far from his mistress and the old Laertes,
> With quarried stones, topping it with wild pear.   14.1–10

So the pigfarm involves an ascent from Phorcys Bay. There is no mention of any subsequent downhill journey: indeed the fact that Odysseus 'climbed a rugged path up from the harbour' until he reached 'ground exposed to view all round' suggests that the ascent was more or less continuous. Clue 1 is therefore that the pigfarm is located on the heights well above Phorcys Bay. Odysseus climbs up the path to the pigfarm some time after his dawn arrival at Phorcys Bay. He has no doubt had a most enjoyable time over the previous weekend, wined and dined by the Phaiacians, and since we will need to keep track of the passage of time over the next few days I will arbitrarily refer to his arrival on Ithaca as a Monday morning.

Odysseus has been disguised by Athene so Eumaios does not recognise him, but in accordance with the established custom of offering hospitality to strangers he provides him with breakfast and various stories are then told. At 14.372–4 Eumaios says 'I live with the pigs, an outcast, never going / To the city, unless wise Penelope / Asks me to come, if news arrives from somewhere.' In the absence of mobile phones Penelope would first have to send a messenger to the pigfarm requesting Eumaios' presence and Clue 2 is therefore that the journey from pigfarm to palace does not appear to be regarded as a particularly significant undertaking. After further food and conversation at 14.457–8 we read 'The night was foul: the moon was hidden, the rain / Lashed down, the west-wind raged relentlessly.' Odysseus contrives the loan of a coat and he goes to sleep in the farmhouse, while as we saw in Chapter 14, loyal Eumaios goes outside to guard the pigs and at 14.532–4 he battles with the rather unpredictable wind: 'He went to lie down where the white-tusked boars / Slept, under a hollow rock that broke the north wind.'

So much for Monday night at the pigfarm. At the outset of Book 15 we hear that Athene goes to Sparta to tell Telemachos to return home promptly. It is night-time when she arrives and unless this scene is a flashback then it is also Monday night in Pylos. On Tuesday morning Telemachos sets off by chariot for Pylos and at 15.185 we hear that he spends Tuesday night at a motel in Pherai owned by Diocles. He leaves Pherai on Wednesday morning at dawn and at 15.193 we hear that he reaches Pylos 'soon afterwards'. As we observed at the outset of Chapter 16, he avoids spending time at Nestor's palace and at 15.292 he sets sail from Pylos on Wednesday evening.

At 15.301 the scene returns to the pigfarm where Odysseus, Eumaios and the herdsmen are spending their own Wednesday evening having a nutritious but perhaps by now somewhat monotonous supper in the farmhouse.[7] At 15.307–11 Odysseus says 'Listen, Eumaios and friends. At dawn I wish / To leave for the city, where I intend to beg, / So as not to be a burden on any of you. / Just give me your advice and a trusty guide / To take me there.' If a stranger who is presumed to be unfamiliar with the route requires a guide then Clue 3 is that the palace is not obviously visible from the pigfarm.

Odysseus and Eumaios talk well into the night and eventually at 15.493–5 we read 'So they conversed with each other, then lay down / To sleep, but only for a little while: / Soon fair-throned Dawn arrived.' The next lines are already familiar: it is Thursday morning and Telemachos is dropped off at Agni Cove at 15.495–7: 'Close by dry land / The crew struck sail and smartly lowered the mast, / Then rowed the ship on to its anchorage'. As we have seen, Book 15 ends with Telemachos walking up to the pigfarm after his breakfast at 15.555–7: 'He strode on rapidly, until he reached / The yard which housed his countless pigs, near which / The good and faithful swineherd used to sleep.'

Book 16 opens with Odysseus (still disguised as a stranger) and Eumaios 'making ready their breakfast at dawn' on Thursday morning when Telemachos arrives at the pigfarm. As we discussed in Chapter 16, this is significant because we have just observed that Telemachos himself does not sail into his cove until dawn, so Clue 4 is that the pigfarm must be relatively close to Telemachos' landfall. Eumaios greets him emotionally and at 16.27–8 he reminds Telemachos that 'You do not often visit the farm and herdsmen, / But stay in town.' This is further support for Clue 2 since it implies that the pigfarm could be visited rather often from the town if Telemachos were so inclined.

At 16.49 Telemachos has a second breakfast with Eumaios and Odysseus. 'When they have satisfied their hunger and thirst' he asks Eumaios at 16.57 where the stranger has come from and there follows another instance of that Homeric rib-splitter 'For I hardly think that he came here on foot' that we discussed in Chapter 8.

Eumaios then says to Telemachos that as the young prince of Ithaca it is up to him to decide what to do with the stranger and at 16.78 Telemachos makes a very interesting reply. He proposes two options: either that he will kit the stranger out with cloak, sword and sandals and send him on his way, or if Eumaios prefers, that he can stay at the pigfarm. But in the latter case Telemachos says at 16.83–4 'I will send you clothes and all the food he needs, / So that he won't be a burden on any of you.' In an era without refrigerated food storage we can deduce from this passage Clue 5, that it would be quite practical for the palace to send regular food parcels to the pigfarm.

Later on Thursday Telemachos mentions to the disguised Odysseus at 16.122–4 'All of the noble lords who rule the islands, / Doulichion and Same and wooded Zacynthos, / And all who rule in rocky Ithaca'. Then at 16.130 Telemachos tells Eumaios to visit Penelope in the palace to inform her that he is safely home from Pylos: Eumaios is to return to the pigfarm after delivering his message. At 16.138 Eumaios asks whether he should 'take a message to Laertes on the same journey' but at 16.150–1 Telemachos replies 'Come back as soon as you have given the message; / Don't wander into the countryside after him.'

Eumaios obeys at once: at 16.154–5 'The swineherd picked his sandals up, then strapped them / Beneath his feet and went towards the city.' Once again there is support for Clue 2, that the journey from pigfarm to palace does not appear to be regarded as a particularly significant undertaking. We also have Clue 6, that Laertes' farmstead lies in the countryside beyond the palace when one is coming from the pigfarm. Notice also that Eumaios sets off in the direction of the city even though he has been instructed to visit Penelope at the palace, so we can now formulate Clue 7: the palace and the city are close to each other.

Once Eumaios has left the pigfarm Athene lifts Odysseus' disguise and he and Telemachos are reunited. They discuss the situation in the palace and Telemachos advises his father that he has 108 suitors to contend with, most of whom apparently come from Doulichion:

> The suitors do not number ten or twenty,
> They are far more, and here is the full tally:
> Fifty-two youths, choice fellows, from Doulichion,
> With six attendants at their beck and call;
> Twenty-four men from Same, from Zacynthos
> Twenty Achaian youths; from Ithaca
> Itself a dozen of the very best.   16.245–51

Still later on Thursday Odysseus tells Telemachos at 16.270–3 what to do on Friday morning: 'At daybreak go back home and mingle with / The insolent suitors. Later in the day / The swineherd will conduct me to the city, / Disguised as some old miserable beggar.' Odysseus then instructs Telemachos on his plan for outwitting the suitors and at 16.322 we encounter the lines listed in the previous discussion which describe the return of Telemachos' crew and vessel to the harbour. The herald who is sent from the ship to the palace meets Eumaios at 16.334–6 'On one and the same errand, to inform / The queen. And when they reached the royal palace, / The herald spoke . . .' so Clue 8 is that a herald from the harbour can meet a messenger from the pigfarm before they arrive at the palace.

As we read earlier, at 16.348 Amphinomos who is seated at the palace catches sight of the suitors' ship returning unsuccessfully from Asteris, so Clue 9 is that the harbour is visible from the palace. At 16.361–2 the conspiring suitors decide to hold a secret meeting to discuss tactics: 'The suitors went to the assembly in a body, / Allowing no one, young or old, to join them.' At 16.396 we learn that Amphinomos comes from 'Doulichion rich in wheat, with grassy meadows'. In the circumstances he proposes to the suitors that they should abandon their plans to assassinate Telemachos and at 16.406–8 'So spoke Amphinomos. They approved the motion, / Then quickly rose and went to the house of Odysseus, / Entered and sat down on the polished seats.' This and the lines at 16.361–2 suggest Clue 10, that the place of assembly is close to the palace.

Penelope then gives Antinoos a piece of her mind and at 16.452–4 we hear 'The worthy swineherd came back in the evening / To Odysseus and his son. They had just killed / A year-old pig and were preparing dinner.' Athene reapplies Odysseus' disguise just in time to keep Eumaios in the dark about his identity and so this provides us with Clue 11, that one can arrive back at the pigfarm in the evening having set out for the palace some time during the day. The fact that at 16.270 Odysseus is already referring to daybreak of the next day when talking to Telemachos suggests that Eumaios probably left for the palace on Thursday afternoon: in any case we know he returned in the evening. When Eumaios returns to the pigfarm from the palace at the end of Book 16 Telemachos asks him whether the suitors have yet returned from Asteris. Eumaios replies:

> I did not think of going down to town[8]
> To inquire of that: I wanted to deliver
> The message and return here with all speed.
> I fell in with a messenger sent by
> Your shipmates: he was first to address your mother.
> One thing I know: I saw it for myself.
> By now I had walked up above the city
> To the Hill of Hermes, when I saw a ship
> Entering our harbour. It was fully manned
> And heavy with shields and double-bladed spears.
> I took it to be them, but can't be sure.   16.465–475

This passage provides us with four important pieces of information. Eumaios 'did not think of going down to town' on the round trip between the pigfarm and the palace, so Clue 12 is that the city lies below the palace. On his way back he 'walked up above the city / To the Hill of Hermes' so Clue 13 is that Hermes' Hill lies above the city. Since he had not yet reached the pigfarm Clue 14 is that Hermes' Hill lies between the city and the pigfarm. At the hill 'I saw a ship / Entering our harbour. It was fully manned / And heavy with shields and double-bladed spears' so Clue 15 is that from Hermes' Hill the harbour is clearly visible.

After another sustaining meal, no doubt involving further fatalities for the porcine population, Odysseus, Telemachos and Eumaios fall asleep. Book 17 starts at dawn on Friday morning. Telemachos has been reunited with Odysseus: he now leaves the pigfarm en route to the palace and his journey is described as follows:

Telemachos strode quickly through the farm,
His mind full of dark thoughts against the suitors.
As soon as he had reached the stately palace
He leaned his spear against a lofty pillar,
Crossed the stone threshold, and then went inside.   17.26–30

He strides quickly through the farm and by implication (it is not stated explicitly) he reaches the palace fairly soon: it certainly doesn't sound like a journey of several hours. But what is particularly interesting here is what is *not* mentioned: the city, because if Telemachos had to walk all the way through the city in order to reach the palace, we would rather expect to have read something about it. This is perhaps the first historically recorded observation of the case of 'The dog that didn't bark', from Sir Arthur Conan Doyle's famous story 'The Adventure of Silver Blaze':

Inspector Gregory:
'Is there any other point to which you would wish to draw my attention?'
Holmes:
'To the curious incident of the dog in the night-time.'
'The dog did nothing in the night-time.'
'That was the curious incident', remarked Sherlock Holmes.[9]

To develop this point further, we should note that after Telemachos arrives at the palace and partakes in a tearful reunion with his old nurse Eurycleia (who was 'by far the first to see him') and his mother Penelope, Homer then says:

Telemachos, spear in hand, strode from the hall,
A pair of nimble hounds about his heels.
Athene shed on him a heavenly grace,
And all watched him with wonder as he approached.
The haughty suitors flocked around him, mouthing
Kind words, but brewing black thoughts in their hearts.
He steered clear of the general throng and went
To sit where old friends from his father's time,
Mentes and Antiphos and Halitherses,
Were sitting. They demanded all his news.
Up came Peiraios the spearman with a stranger,
Whom he had brought through the city to the assembly.
Telemachos turned at once to face the stranger.   17.61–73

A few lines later at 17.84 we hear that 'So saying he took the care-worn stranger home.' The stranger is Theoclymenos, a rather mysterious prophet who has been given free passage by Telemachos from Pylos to Ithaca. On the basis of this elaborate greeting by 'the general throng' it seems safe to assume that Telemachos had not already passed through the city when he reached the palace, so Clue 16 is that the palace can be reached from the pigfarm without passing through the city. This deduction is supported by Clue 7 above: Eumaios also reaches the palace from the pigfarm without going down to the city. The narrative also provides further support for the proximity of the place of assembly to both the city and the palace, already identified above as Clue 10: the implication is that Telemachos walked out of the palace and rather soon reached the place of assembly.

At 17.167–9 we hear that 'Before the hall the high and mighty suitors / Amused themselves with javelin and discus, / On a levelled sports-ground, where they often played.' The current world record for javelin throwing is about 100 m and for the discus the distance is about 75 m, but the achievements of today's Olympic athletes are probably unrepresentative of conditions 3,200 years ago.[10] Furthermore the suitors were not especially fit: they had been gorging themselves on roast pork for several years. Even after a generous allowance of space at each end and at the sides to avoid the unintentional manslaughter of passers-by, this suggests as Clue 17 that there is a levelled sportsground about 100 m long in front of the palace.

Immediately afterwards at 16.170–1 we read 'When it was time for dinner and the sheep / Came in from the fields all round', so Clue 18 is that the palace and city are surrounded by fields suitable for livestock. At 17.190–1 Eumaios says to the still-disguised Odysseus 'Let's go. The best part of the day is gone, / And it can get quite chilly towards evening', which provides us with further support for the previous proposition that all this activity is certainly not taking place in the summer.

When Eumaios leads Odysseus still in disguise from the pigfarm to the city late on Friday afternoon we read:

'Let's go; but you must lead me all the way.
Just give me a stick to lean on, if you have one
Cut ready, because you said the ground is slippery.'

Advancing down the rocky road they neared
The town and reached the fountain where the townsfolk
Drew water – well-built, flowing fair, the work
Of Ithacos, Neritos, and Polyctor.
Around it was a circling grove of poplars

Fed by the moist earth, and cool water flowed
Down from a rock. Above was built an altar
To the nymphs, on which all travellers made an offering.

                                        17.194–6, 204–11

This passage tells us that there is an elaborate fountain on the outskirts of the town on a path that leads to it from the pigfarm. The townsfolk draw water from it, so clearly there must also be a path to it from the city. This fountain has an altar 'on which all travellers made an offering'. Where do these travellers come from? Presumably only a minority would arrive at Phorcys Bay and pass by the pigfarm. Most travellers by land would be ferried across Strabo's Channel; travellers by sea would sail into the harbour. So several paths must converge at this fountain, linking the pigfarm, the city, Strabo's Channel and the harbour.

Around the fountain is 'a circling grove of poplars' and mature poplars are tall trees. On the assumption that the project's landscape gardener was Ithacos, Neritos or Polyctor and that he had seen fully grown poplars before, we can deduce that these trees would have been spaced out accordingly, implying a fairly substantial diameter for the grove. But the really interesting question about these poplars is this: how were they watered? Poplars are notoriously thirsty trees, so much so that they are today used to draw contaminated water from landfill sites: 'With roots that extend to 10 feet deep or more, rapidly growing poplars draw large amounts of water and nutrients from the soil.'[11]

Clearly the fountain must be drawing its water from a stream, and to cultivate a row of poplars alongside this stream would be quite achievable. However, to grow a *circle* of poplars poses a very special challenge in a country as dry and as hot as Greece. How does one create a circular irrigation channel? Somehow the design or location of this fountain must be contributing to a solution. Clue 19 is that several paths converge at an elaborate fountain, linking the pigfarm, the city, Strabo's Channel and the harbour, and somehow a circular grove of poplars is irrigated.

At this fountain Odysseus has an altercation with Melanthios the goatherd and after that at 17.255 Melanthios 'Went on, and very quickly reached the palace', so Clue 20 is that the palace is not far from the fountain.

Odysseus and Eumaios follow and at 17.264–8 Odysseus, pretending not to recognise his own palace, says 'Eumaios, this palace of Odysseus is / A fine one, easily picked out from any number: / One building after another, courtyard walled / And crenellated, sturdy double-gates – / no man could possibly equip it better.' So Clue 21 is that the palace consists of multiple buildings and Clue 22 is that the palace has a walled courtyard with double gates. There are many more hints in the *Odyssey* about the layout of the palace and indeed some scholars have attempted an architectural reconstruction,[12] but this present attempt to formulate a list of clues does not require us to be specific about its interior design.

There is also a very important additional clue concealed within this passage. Odysseus is not blind: he looks up and sees his fine palace with one building after another and a walled courtyard with double gates. Clearly these would be visible only in the daytime, so it must still be light. But we saw at 17.190–1 above that when Odysseus and Eumaios were still at the pigfarm, Eumaios said 'Let's go. The best part of the day is gone, / And it can get quite chilly towards evening.' So we now have a much more precise calibration of the distance from the pigfarm to the palace: Clue 23 is that one can leave the pigfarm when the best part of the day is gone and still arrive at the palace before nightfall. To remove any doubt that it is still light, after a considerable amount of further action at the palace Odysseus says at 17.569–70 'So tell Penelope to wait in the hall, / Impatient though she is, until the sun sets.'

At the conclusion of Book 17 we learn at 17.603–6 that Eumaios returns to the pigfarm to guard the swine on Friday evening: 'When he had satisfied his thirst and hunger, / He made for the swine, leaving the courts and hall / Still full of banqueters, now making merry / With song and dance, as evening had drawn on.'

In Book 18 Odysseus progressively increases his personal authority among the suitors and, still in disguise, meets his wife Penelope after a lapse of twenty years. At the end of the Book we read of the suitors at 18.427–8 that 'When they had poured and drunk all that they wished, / They went off, each to his own home, to sleep', so Clue 24 is that there are at least 108 houses available to the suitors in the city of Ithaca before making allowances for the resident population.

At 19.47–50 we hear that 'Telemachos then strode out through the hall, / By the light of blazing torches, to the bedroom / Where he always used to sleep. There he lay down / And waited for the arrival of bright dawn.' After a long discussion with the disguised Odysseus in Book 19 Penelope falls asleep at 19.603–4: 'Then she shed tears for Odysseus, her dear husband, / Till Athene cast sweet sleep upon her eyelids.' Eventually Odysseus himself falls asleep at 20.54–5 with some help from Athene: 'So spoke the noble goddess, then cast sleep / Upon his eyelids, and returned to Olympos.'

On Saturday morning Penelope wakes early and prays to the goddess Artemis at 20.91: 'Close on her words came Dawn enthroned in gold.' Odysseus also wakes up: he walks outside, holds up his hands and asks Zeus to send him a sign. His prayers are promptly answered by a thunderbolt that is appreciated over at the mill at 20.105–8: 'A miller-woman voiced words of good omen / From a nearby room where the royal handmills stood, / At which twelve women ground out barley-meal / And wheat-flour, foods that put the marrow in men.' So Clue 25 is that there is a substantial mill in or near the palace.

At 20.153–4 Penelope instructs the palace staff 'Other women, go / To the spring for water and quickly bring it here' and at 158 'Twenty went off to the dark-water spring'. The unusual phrase 'dark-water' that is used here has the same specific meaning as in Chapter 14: water in deep places where the light cannot reach it. So Clue 26 is that the palace is supplied from a source of deep water that the light cannot reach. The women return from the spring and at 20.162–3 we hear that 'After them came the swineherd / Bringing three fatted hogs, the best he had.' So Eumaios is now back at the palace having spent the night at the pigfarm and Clue 27 is that the distance from the pigfarm to the palace is appropriate for driving live boars.

At 20.185 we meet Philoitios again, the cowherd of Chapter 8 who keeps his flock on the mainland:

> Third came that stalwart fellow Philoitios,
> Leading a heifer and fat goats for the suitors.
> They had been brought across by ferrymen,
> Who also ferry people, any who come.   20.185–8

Clue 28 is therefore that the palace is located close enough to Strabo's Channel for cows and goats to be walked towards it along the path from the mainland. In the remainder of Book 20 a strong sense of foreboding develops among the suitors and in Book 21 the scene is set for the famous competition to shoot an arrow through the twelve axes.[13] At 21.221 Odysseus reveals his identity to Eumaios and Philoitios and at the end of Book 21 he wins the contest.

The massacre of the suitors begins at Book 22 and the treacherous goatherd Melanthios is strung up alive to wait for the dawn:

> 'Now you'll keep watch all night, Melanthios,
> In the comfortable bed that you deserve.
> You won't miss Dawn arriving throned in gold
> From Ocean's streams – the time you usually
> Bring goats for the suitors' banquets in the palace.'   22.195–9

Clue 29 is therefore that the sun's rays strike the palace at dawn. The bloodshed continues all day and into the night until every suitor is dead:

> Odysseus cast a sharp eye round his palace,
> In case a lone survivor lurked in hiding,
> Still fearing for his life. He saw the heaps

Of bodies lying in blood and dust, like fish
Drawn from the grey sea in a net of mesh
And spilled by fishers on the curving beach.   22.381–6

Later in Book 22 the women clean up the mess and then the disloyal ones who have slept with the suitors are summarily hanged by Telemachos. Melanthios fares only marginally better: after letting him down from the rafters at 22.474–7 'They dragged Melanthios through the porch and courtyard, / Sliced off his nose and ears with merciless sword, / Ripped off his testicles, raw meat for dogs, / And lopped his hands and feet, flushed full with rage.'

In Book 23 Odysseus is reunited at last with Penelope: at 23.207–8 'The tears burst forth, she ran towards him, flung / Her arms about his neck and kissed his head'. Although it is by now nearing dawn on Sunday morning, at 23.243 Athene makes special arrangements for the exhausted but elated couple: 'She made Night linger when its course was finished' so that 'When they had taken their pleasure in the joys of love' at 23.300 they still have enough time to tell each other what they have been up to for the last twenty years. Eventually at 23.342 they fall asleep and Athene thoughtfully invokes daylight saving time again, prolonging the advent of dawn so that they are fully refreshed by the time they wake up.

At 23.359 Odysseus announces 'Now I will go to the farm with its many trees, / To see my noble father'. He rouses Telemachos, Eumaios and Philoitios and they arm themselves in anticipation of meeting the relatives of the dead suitors, but Athene has another trick up her sleeve: at 23.369–72 'They donned bronze armour, opened the doors and left, / Odysseus in the lead. By now the earth / Was lit by daylight. But Athene hid them / In night and quickly led them from the city.' The final events of the *Odyssey* take place at Laertes' farm for which we will look in a subsequent chapter.

The preceding clues were based on Odysseus' return to Ithaca from Chapter 14 onwards, but some useful further observations can also be made from earlier chapters. At 1.303–4 Athene says to Telemachos at the palace 'But now I shall go down to my swift ship / And comrades', so this provides us with Clue 30, that the palace is located above sea level.[14] Then at 1.330 we hear that Penelope 'descended the tall staircase from her chamber' and at 1.362 she 'went upstairs to her chamber with her handmaids', so Clue 31 is that the palace must have an upper floor as well as a ground floor.

At 1.424 there is further confirmation of the destination of the suitors as they leave the palace 'each to his own home' and then at 1.425–7 there is a rather thought-provoking passage: 'With much on his mind Telemachos made for bed. / His bedroom was a lofty chamber off / The fair courtyard, in a place with a view all round.' James Diggle explains in Appendix 1 Section I that there are some textual dilemmas here but on balance we are entitled to propose Clue 32, that Telemachos' high bedroom in the palace commands a surrounding view.

At the beginning of Book 2 Telemachos asks the heralds to call an assembly:

As soon as rosy-fingered Dawn appeared,
Odysseus' son sprang from his bed and dressed,
Then slung a sharp sword from his shoulder, strapped
Fine sandals on his glistening feet, and strode
Out of his bedroom, every inch a god.
Without delay he bade the clear-voiced criers
Call the long-haired Achaians to the assembly.
They called, and the Achaians quickly came.
When all were gathered in the meeting place,
Telemachos set out, bronze spear in hand,
A pair of nimble hounds about his heels.
Athene shed on him a heavenly grace,
And all watched him with wonder as he approached.
The elders yielded him his father's seat.   2.1–14

The suitors 'quickly came' so this supports our existing Clue 10, that the place of assembly is close to the palace. What might Odysseus' seat be made of? There is no suggestion that the meeting place is other than outdoors, where wooden seats would clearly be impractical. At a comparable place of assembly in Scherie we are told at 8.6 that the Phaiacians 'Sat side by side on seats of polished stone' so it seems reasonable to propose Clue 33, that the meeting place of the city of Ithaca is probably equipped with stone seats. Then at 2.146 there is some fascinating indirect guidance about the layout of the city:

So spoke Telemachos. In answer Zeus
Despatched two eagles from a mountain peak.
They flew a while upon the gusting breezes,
Close to each other, pinions at full stretch.
But when they reached the middle of the assembly,
They wheeled about, wings beating rapidly,
Stared at the heads of all, death in their eyes,
Clawed with their talons at their cheeks and necks,
And sped off to the right through houses and city.   2.146–54[15]

In terms of Greek divination 'to the right' means 'to the east': in order to avoid confusion the Greeks always interpreted their omens by looking to the north. In another augury involving Theoclymenos at 15.525 we hear that 'Upon these words a bird flew by on the right' and in the *Iliad* there is an interesting observation on the matter from a Trojan warrior called Polydamas:

> This is the way a soothsayer would interpret,
> Who knew his signs and had the people's trust.   *Iliad* 12.228–9

Hector replies:

> You tell me I should put my trust in birds
> Flapping their wings. I could not care a damn
> Whether they fly to right towards dawn and sun
> Or whether they fly left towards darkening dusk.   *Iliad* 12.237–40

Although Hector describes himself as unconvinced by the art of divination he is clearly familiar with its protocols. The flightpath of these eagles is therefore significant for the local geography of Ithaca. Zeus despatched them 'from a mountain peak', then they 'flew a while upon the gusting breezes' until 'they reached the middle of the assembly', 'wheeled about', 'looked at the heads of all' and finally 'sped off to the right through houses and city'. From the comments above we can conclude that 'to the right' means 'to the east', so the houses and city of Ithaca must be to the east of the meeting place. However there is a textual complication here; James Diggle warns us in Appendix 1 Section J that the last three lines are suspect, so we shall have to change 'must be' to 'may be'.

But where is the mountain peak relative to this meeting place? It clearly cannot itself be to the east because the eagles 'sped off to the right': they did not retrace their flight. If the viewpoint of the poet's description is north-facing, as traditional divination suggests, then the mountain could also hardly be to the south because that would result in the descent of the eagles being unseen until the last moment when they 'wheeled about'.

So the mountain peak must be either to the north or to the west of the meeting place. The fact that these eagles are evidently in full view throughout their flight makes it more likely that the townfolk held them in their forward gaze throughout their descent, without initially turning their heads to the west. This is support for Clue 34, that there is a mountain peak near the city, visible from the place of assembly and probably to its north. Furthermore we can also derive Clue 35, that the houses and city of Ithaca may be to the east of the meeting place.

After the assembly has broken up we read at 2.260–1 that 'Telemachos went to the shore, apart from the others, / And, washing his hands in the grey sea, prayed to Athene.' He goes off on his own to the shore: there is no mention of him passing through the city nor reaching the deep harbour. The Greek word for 'shore' that is used here (in the accusative) is *thina*, pronounced as in our name 'Tina': it describes a sandy beach and is not at all the same as the word for a harbour, which is usually *limen*.[16] After Athene has appeared to Telemachos on the shore and volunteered to organise a ship and crew for his journey to Pylos, we hear at 2.297–8 that he 'Did not wait long, when he had heard her voice, / But made for home, oppressed by anxious thoughts' – again no mention of the city or the harbour. So this suggests Clue 36, that there may be a stretch of the seashore accessible from the meeting place and the palace without having to traverse the city or visit the harbour.

At 2.389–92 Athene 'Dragged the swift ship to the sea, and stored in her / All the equipment that good vessels carry, / And moored her by the far edge of the harbour. / Then all his worthy comrades gathered round.' But why did Athene go to the trouble of mooring the swift ship at the 'far edge' of the harbour: why could the vessel not have sailed from the end of the harbour nearest to the city where the ships would normally be drawn up? We gain the impression that Athene doesn't want the suitors to know about Telemachos' imminent departure because at 2.394–8 'She went off to the palace of noble Odysseus, / And shed sweet sleep upon the drinking suitors, / Fuddled their minds and made them drop their cups. / They soon got up and went off through the city / To rest, for sleep was falling on their eyelids.' A few lines later at 2.411–12 Telemachos says 'My mother and the maids know nothing of this; / There is one woman only whom I told', so this looks like a somewhat covert embarkation.

But surely at least one of the 108 sleepy suitors would have seen Telemachos and his crew leave, or indeed Penelope herself might have caught sight of him, since we know from Clue 9 that the harbour is visible from the palace? However, if the far edge of the harbour is not visible from the palace then Athene might well decide to moor the ship there so that their departure will be unobserved. This yields us Clue 37, that the far edge of the harbour may be invisible from the palace.[17]

So by the end of this analysis the thirty-seven clues of Figure 17.2 have emerged and this table brings together some essential information. For example, it is clear from Clues 2, 5, 11, 23 and 27 that the pigfarm cannot be far from the palace. However, those who believe that ancient Ithaca is modern Ithaca locate the pigfarm at the south of that island, near Marathia, and the palace at the north, near Polis Bay. J. V. Luce in his *Celebrating Homer's Land-scapes* calculates that the distance involved is about fourteen miles. Happily he reminds us that 'the round-trip would be less than thirty miles, a long but far from impossible day's walk for a hardy Greek herdsman'.[18] I mention this point not out of any unkindness to Luce but to demonstrate that the classical hypothesis is not only a non-starter in regard to its external geography (modern Ithaca is not the furthest to the west) but that it also fails the test of internal topography (Eumaios and others can clearly travel quite quickly between the pigfarm and the palace).

1	The pigfarm is located on the heights well above Phorcys Bay.
2	The journey from pigfarm to palace is not regarded as a particularly significant undertaking.
3	The palace is not obviously visible from the pigfarm.
4	The pigfarm must be relatively close to Telemachos' landfall.
5	It would be quite practical for the palace to send regular food parcels to the pigfarm.
6	Laertes' farmstead lies in the countryside beyond the palace when one is coming from the pigfarm.
7	The palace and the city are close to each other.
8	A herald from the harbour can meet a messenger from the pigfarm before they arrive at the palace.
9	The harbour is visible from the palace.
10	The place of assembly is close to the palace.
11	One can arrive back at the pigfarm in the evening having set out for the palace some time during the day.
12	The city lies below the palace.
13	Hermes' Hill lies above the city.
14	Hermes' Hill lies between the city and the pigfarm.
15	From Hermes' Hill the harbour is clearly visible.
16	The palace can be reached from the pigfarm without passing through the city.
17	There is a levelled sportsground about 100 m long in front of the palace.
18	The palace and city are surrounded by fields suitable for livestock.
19	Several paths converge at an elaborate fountain, linking the pigfarm, the city, Strabo's Channel and the harbour, and somehow a circular grove of poplars is irrigated.
20	The palace is not far from the fountain.
21	The palace consists of multiple buildings.
22	The palace has a walled courtyard with double gates.
23	One can leave the pigfarm when the best part of the day is gone and still arrive at the palace before night fall.
24	There are at least 108 houses available to the suitors in the city of Ithaca before making allowances for the resident population.
25	There is a substantial mill near the palace.
26	The palace is supplied from a source of deep water that the light cannot reach.
27	The distance from the pigfarm to the palace is appropriate for driving live boars.
28	The palace is located close enough to Strabo's Channel for cows and goats to be walked towards it along the path from the mainland.
29	The sun's rays strike the palace at dawn.
30	The palace is located above sea level.
31	The palace must have an upper floor as well as a ground floor.
32	Telemachos' high bedroom in the palace commands a surrounding view.
33	The meeting place of the city of Ithaca is probably equipped with stone seats.
34	There is a mountain peak near the city, visible from the place of assembly and probably to its north.
35	The houses and city of Ithaca may be to the east of the meeting place.
36	There may be a stretch of the seashore accessible from the meeting place and the palace without having to traverse the city or visit the harbour.
37	The far edge of the harbour may be invisible from the palace.

FIGURE 17.2 The palace clues

Which of these clues provides us with the best place to start looking for the palace? As these findings emerge in April 2003 after my return to England I focus on Clue 9: *The harbour is visible from the palace*. Yes, but by now I know that there are many potential sites for the palace from which the harbour is visible, so that doesn't help me much. Then I am struck by the blindingly obvious proposition that if the harbour is visible from the palace then the palace must also be visible from the harbour.

I am confident about the location of the harbour but have I taken any photographs from it looking up to the hillside? One of the delights but also the tyrannies of modern digital cameras with capacious memory cards is that you tend to take a very large number of photographs because there is no film to change: I have come back with over 750 images after only a few days. I browse through them and Figure 16.8 catches my eye: it was taken from today's shoreline near the centre of the harbour.

Where would Odysseus have built his palace? Clue 30 tells us that *The palace is located above sea level*, Clue 7 that *The palace and the city are close to each other* and Clue 12 that *The city lies below the palace*. Odysseus would have constructed his palace where almost every palace at the time was constructed: on a hillside. Lawrence Durrell puts it precisely:

What would be the basic requirements for a sea-dog's lair – the central citadel where the faithful Penelope might spend so many years yawning at her loom? An eminence, first of all, to give as good a view as possible of the surrounding country. The command of one or more harbours. Lastly a place with a bit of green land nearby or round about it where, in times of peace, one could farm a little, pasturing cattle or goats.[19]

There are two obvious hillsides in Figure 16.8: Mesovouni on the left, which is about 90 m high and has been turned into a modern quarry, and the 250 m tall hilltop of Kastelli on the right. For a terrible moment I wonder whether Odysseus' Palace has inadvertently been crushed by machinery within living memory. Then I remember that before the 1953 earthquake elevated the island by about 60 cm, the ancient harbour line was nearly a kilometre further inland, indented between these two hills. Furthermore the straight edge that I have marked on Figure 17.1 as the western edge of the lowest ground in the harbour is quite arbitrary: the ground further west of that line is only slightly less low-lying, so it would also have been either submerged or at least very marshy. This means that during the Bronze Age there would have been either sea or at least very wet marshland in front of both Mesovouni and Kastelli.

Clue 17 tells us that *There is a levelled sportsground about 100 m long in front of the palace*. If either Mesovouni or Kastelli were the palace location then presumably the suitors would have been throwing their javelins and discus about on an underwater sportsground. That seems most unlikely, so perhaps

FIGURE 17.3
Optical zoom of hillside
above harbour
*The distance from the coast
road to the northern hilltop
(with the distinctive two trees)
is 2.4 km.*

FIGURE 17.4
Digital zoom of hillside
above harbour
*The modern road to Atheras
runs along the tree line
half-way up the hillside.*

the palace hilltop was further back from the sea. I look at Figure 16.8 and notice the green hill-ridge along the skyline. I click the zoom button and again there is that infuriating delay while the picture loads. Then I realise why: it is one of the last photographs that I took before racing to the airport and it has been accidentally recorded in very high resolution. This means that I can now zoom in much further without losing image quality. The next photograph on the disk is also high resolution and better still, I had used the camera's telescopic lens. I click the mouse and look at the screen of my PC. At first nothing happens: then an image slowly loads (Figure 17.3).

I click the mouse again (Figure 17.4). There is a road running across the base of the hill that I have driven along several times but I had never thought of looking up above it: we had spent our time wandering around further to the north-east.

What are all those stone walls and patterns on the top of this twin hillside? What view does it have of the harbour? How does Asteris appear from its summit? How far away is the pigfarm? Is there a levelled sportsground in front of it? What about the meeting place? Is there a fountain nearby at which all travellers make an offering?

Could this stone-strewn double hilltop be the ancient site of Odysseus' Palace?

Notes

1 Bowra (1933) Introduction.
2 www.city-of-loutraki.gr/history-culture/the-diolkos-corinth-canal.htm
3 Severin (1985) pp. 177, 215; Severin (1987) p. 35.
4 See James Diggle's comments on this passage in Appendix 1 Section J.
5 See James Diggle's comments on this passage in Appendix 1 Section J.
6 See James Diggle's comments on this line in Appendix 1 Section J.
7 Although it is Wednesday for Telemachos, the last mention of Odysseus was at the end of Book 14 on Monday night, so it ought to be Tuesday for him. For an interesting discussion of this see Page (1955) pp. 66–8: '[the poet] leaves Odysseus, *asleep at night*, in Ithaca, and passes at once to Telemachos, *asleep at night*, in Sparta . . . You are not allowed to comment that Telemachos must have spent an unconscionable time at Sparta . . . To the Epic poet the question "How long is it since we last saw Telemachos?" is nonsensical: there were no events concerning Telemachos in the interval; and time, with reference to Telemachos, exists only as a measure of the duration of events in which Telemachos is engaged.' If this perception is applied instead to Odysseus it allows us to ignore his rather boring Tuesday. However Page continues somewhat disapprovingly: 'If you now consult your calendar you will find that you have been hoodwinked. For in the interval between the beginning of the Fifteenth Book and the arrival of Telemachos at Ithaca you will see, if you look closely, that for Telemachos two days have passed, for Odysseus only one. Our poet has advanced greatly in technique: but it is now apparent that he has strained to breaking-point the convention that one series of events in time is not to be related to another within the same time.'
8 See James Diggle's comments on this line in Appendix 1 Section J.
9 Conan Doyle (1892).

10 At www.iaaf.org/statistics/records/ we read that the current world record for throwing the discus is 74.08 m by Jürgen Schult at Neubrandenburg on 6 June 1986. In Harris (1964) pp. 90–2 we learn that this sport has advanced considerably over the last century: in 1896 the winning throw was only 29.15 m but by 1964 it had improved to over 61 m. The ancient records are enigmatic: Harris explains that an athlete named Phayllus 'jumped five over fifty feet, but threw the discus five short of a hundred (28.96 m)' and he interprets this epigram as reflecting a comparatively poor discus performance. He identifies a separate reference to a throw of 100 cubits (45.72 m) but warns us that there is some doubt about its reliability as it was apparently achieved with a double-weight discus on the headlands of the Gallipoli peninsula by the 4.57 m high ghost of Protesilaus, the first Greek to be killed in the Trojan war. Turning to the javelin, the current world record is 98.48 m by Jan Zelezný at Jena on 25 May 1996 and Harris explains at pp. 95–7: 'Of Greek standards of performance with the javelin we know even less than of their achievements in the jump and discus throwing . . . In the whole of ancient literature there appears to be only one passage which throws any light at all on the subject, and it is a very oblique light. Statius, describing in the *Thebaid* the course for the chariot race, says that in length it was three times a bow shot and four times a javelin throw.' After taking into account the fact that the ancient elder-wood javelin shaft is lighter than its modern equivalent and based on a hippodrome length of 400 yd (366 m), Harris concludes that 'We are probably justified in assuming that the best Greek throwers could achieve well over 300 feet (91 m).'

11 See www.ch2m.com/phyto/Poplar.htm

12 See Figure 26.5.

13 The challenge of shooting an arrow through twelve axes is not thought to imply a Superman-like penetration of solid metal. Various interpretations have been suggested: a credible proposal (Wace and Stubbings (1962) pp. 534–5) is that the wooden hafts of doubleheaded axes were removed and the blades stood up in a long mound of earth so that the socket-holes in the axe-heads were aligned. This would present a succession of twelve holes each of a few centimetres in diameter, through which a crack marksman would attempt to shoot the arrow.

14 Anthony Snodgrass has pointed out that the Greek preposition *kata* does not always mean 'down' in the sense of altitude: in fact it is often used by the ancient Greeks to describe a journey from inland to coast. Indeed this usage recurs in modern English: as recently as 1902 John Masefield could open his poem *Sea Fever* with the line 'I must down to the seas again, to the lonely sea and the sky'. But I think we are nevertheless entitled (and with Durrell, see n. 19) to assume that no Bronze Age chieftain would choose to construct his palace at sea level if an adjacent hillside was available instead.

15 See James Diggle's comments on this passage in Appendix 1 Section J.

16 In Chapter 7 we saw that the name 'Thinia' is used today to describe the Strabo's Channel isthmus. It might be attractive to the amateur but it is a source of apoplexy for the expert to speculate on a possible connection between this word and Homer's word 'Thina', which describes a sandy beach. In Greek (in the accusative) this is θῖνα (*thîna*), whereas the name of the region is actually Θηνηα (*thênêa*) with two 'etas' (long 'e's). The coincidence occurs simply because when transcribed into the Latin alphabet the modern custom is to represent eta with 'i'. Regarding the derivation of the name Thinia itself, Elias Toumasatos of the Corgialenios Library in Argostoli has explained to me that the local scholar Tsitselis links this to 'Athenian' and notes that 'In some writers one encounters, out of ignorance, Tinea, and Phinaia'. See Tsitselis (1877) p. 845.

17 This is one of several original observations of C. H. Goekoop: see Goekoop (1990) ch. III p. 66 (fragment 7).

18 Luce (1998) p. 218; map p. 177.

19 Durrell (1978) p. 45.

CHAPTER 18 Inquiry

Where there is much desire to learn, there of necessity will be much arguing, much writing, many opinions; for opinion in good men is but knowledge in the making.

Milton, *Areopagitica* (1644) para. 89

On returning to England at the end of March 2003 I make contact with James Diggle at Cambridge and the correspondence of Chapter 15 is the immediate result. He becomes interested in the motive behind my questions and agrees to a confidential meeting, so I arrange to visit him in his rooms at Queens' College Cambridge on 12 May. He is an authority on Greek and Latin, a Fellow of the British Academy and a Corresponding Member of the Academy of Athens, which is regarded as the continuation of Plato's Academy and the highest scientific institution in Greece. He is currently actively involved as Chairman of the Advisory Committee of the Greek Lexicon Project, a major undertaking aimed at producing an entirely new Greek–English dictionary.

He is also a former Orator of Cambridge University, a role dating back to 1521 which requires the incumbent 'to write addresses for presentation to the Sovereign and formal letters for presentation to other universities and institutions. He shall present to the Chancellor and University persons on whom the titles of degrees are conferred *honoris causa*.' In *Cambridge Orations 1982–1993: A Selection*, the elegant volume which he published on retiring from the office, the list of those for whom he has composed such Latin orations reads like an international Who's Who: Jorge Luis Borges, Ted Hughes, Stephen Hawking, Paul Erdös, Sir Alec Guinness, Iris Murdoch . . . I particularly like his tribute to James Watson: indeed Pliny himself might have been taken aback by the news that 'the model revealed the chemical structure of DNA':

qua fabricatione omnis patefacta est acidi deoxyribonucleici conformatio.

A natural scientist such as Pliny would also have enjoyed the gentle alphabetic pun at the end: 'a Jason who once sailed the Cam in quest of the golden molecule, an Oedipus who once solved the riddle of life in the Cavendish':

Iasona alterum aureae praedae petitorem, alterum Oedipum Sphingis domitorem CauenDishiaNAe.[1]

I have given some thought to how to present this proposal to James Diggle so as to avoid a response of total incredulity and disbelief, but to my great relief he does not dismiss my findings out of hand. He is instead intrigued by the realisation that the theory of Schizocephalonia and Asteris makes sense out of the observations of Strabo and Apollodorus.

As James gets to grips with their observations I see that he is becoming attracted to the idea that this radical proposition may just be correct. Furthermore he explains to me that the problem of ancient Ithaca being described as 'farthest to the west' has been a fundamental challenge for every Homeric theory for thousands of years: by cutting Cephalonia in two that problem is immediately solved. We talk on into the evening and he invites me to join him at High Table, a great honour for me since I had spent the period from 1970 to 1973 as an undergraduate up the road at Christ's College gazing longingly at the vintage claret passing by. It is nearly midnight by the time I have shown him most of my evidence and I ask him what he thinks. He gives me a supportive response and promises to write to me with his considered view. I retire happily for the night and two days later he sends me an e-mail that lifts my spirits:

It was a great delight for me to listen to your exposition, and a great privilege to be entrusted with it. The two pillars of your case are the identification of (i) Strabo's channel and (ii) the 'island'. For the former, you have, so it appeared, an exceptionally strong case, backed by the experts, and capable, I assume, of being demonstrated as true. On the latter, you convinced me, because you put me in possession of the necessary facts and let me draw my own conclusion.

I saw, before we met, that there was a serious problem of interpretation in Strabo's text, connected with what you had described as Apollodorus' Enigma. But when you reminded me of the conclusion which I had reached earlier about the possible use of the word 'nesos' as peninsula, the solution to the enigma was immediately apparent. The way to make sense of Strabo is to recognise that when he speaks of 'the isthmus itself' he is referring back to his word 'nesion' (little island) and not to the isthmus he has mentioned before that (your 'channel'). Unless the text is hopelessly corrupt, this is the natural interpretation of his words (that innocent-looking 'itself' is the telling word).

Further, it gives us a way of making sense of the controversy between Apollodorus and Demetrius. Possibly Demetrius, when he said that Asteris 'no longer remains such as the poet describes it', assumed (reasonably enough, since everyone else has) that Homer was describing an island, and couldn't find a suitable island in the channel between (modern) Ithaca and Cephallenia. But Apollodorus recognised that Homer must have been referring to a peninsula; and he believed that he could identify this peninsula.[2]

This is the first time that I have tried to explain this proposal to an expert with so much specialist knowledge of the subject and it is wonderful news that he is now on board. Not only is he persuaded but he also offers to help me to pursue the theory professionally, an opportunity that I had hardly dared even to dream about. Since that date James has guided the project unerringly and he has given tirelessly of his time in identifying ancient sources and advising me of their reliability, in translating the many crucial passages from the *Odyssey* and also in constructively criticising my successive drafts of this book.

Earlier that day in Cambridge I also meet Professor Tjeerd van Andel. He is a living geological legend, the discoverer of geothermal vents and the author of that inspiring owner's manual *New Views on an Old Planet*. He is a global authority on the impact of human habitation on the landscape, especially in Greece. I show him my pictures of Strabo's Channel and ask him for his advice and opinion. His verdict contains both good and bad news. The good news is that 'I cannot think that any mechanism other than an ancient seabed and the erosion of surface "terra rossa" could be responsible for this.' The bad news is that 'I am very concerned about the required rates of uplift or infill.'

'Terra rossa' is the characteristic red earth that is ubiquitous in Greece: it is formed by the erosion of limestone mountaintops which contain iron oxide impurities. These are washed down to the valleys and in the process they stain the earth orange-brown. Tjeerd is gently telling me: yes, there probably was an ancient seabed in the area of Strabo's Channel, but in the absence of any mechanism other than the natural processes of erosion and tectonic upthrust, substantially more than 3,000 years of geological time would be required to infill the previous void to its present maximum depth of around 180 m. Tjeerd also explains that erosion of the mountaintops can be accelerated by human intervention: apparently Bronze Age sailors who strip the mountainside of trees for their navies are among the culprits. Later I find a passage in the *Iliad* describing the death of the Trojan warrior Asios at the hands of Idomeneus that supports this observation:

> He fell, like oak or poplar or tall pine,
> Which woodmen chop down on the mountainside
> With whetted axes for ship-building timber.   *Iliad* 13.389–91

Other environmental offenders apparently include goats, because unlike sheep which nibble away at the shoots, goats tend to rip an entire shrub out of the soil and on a slope this can seriously affect surface stability.

Meanwhile Melis Antoniou has sent me his geological observations about Thinia, the area of Strabo's Channel, and I track down the geologist who made the findings of salt water in the channel, Professor Ioannis Koumantakis. He is now Professor of Hydrogeology and Technical Geology at the School of Mining and Metallurgical Engineering at the National Technical University of Athens. He sends me his paper *Hypersaline Waters in an Enclosed Limestone*

Body of Kefalonia and it arrives on 2 May. It looks very thought-provoking but unfortunately it is quite incomprehensible because it is written in Greek and apparently no English translation is available.

The Google translator cannot help me with Greek but fortunately I have acquired two indispensable Odyssean research tools. One is an Optical Character Recognition program for the Greek alphabet: if you present it with a scanned page of Greek text it will convert this into a text-based document. The other is a language translation package which converts modern Greek into English. I click with the mouse on the appropriate buttons and look eagerly at the screen for geological enlightenment:

The limestones in which were found the brines they is regionally egjnwvjsme'noj from neogenej's marls. their surface spread. It amounts in 20.000 m roughly and, as it was realised, they do not have hydraulic epjkojgwnj'a neither with the sea neither with the neighbouring limestones.

Belatedly I realise that the present-day competence of machine translation from typescript Greek to English is still at the level that Samuel Johnson would have recognised when he articulated that profoundly incorrect utterance 'Sir, a woman preaching is like a dog's walking on his hind legs. It is not done well; but you are surprised to find it done at all.' Only a woman could help me now and via the Internet once again I found her: Karen Rich womanfully volunteered to translate Professor Koumantakis' paper properly and the preceding lines at last swam into view:[3]

The limestone in which the brine was found is peripherally enclosed by neogene marl. Its surface area amounts to approximately 20,000 m^2 and, as was established, it has no hydraulic connection, either with the sea or with the neighbouring limestone. This is evidenced, on the one hand by the existing geological conditions, and on the other by the correlation of the chemical constitution of the hypersaline waters, sea water and the underground waters of the neighbouring environment. The absence of free oxygen and the existence of a large quantity of H_2S show that no communication exists either with the surface of the ground and that consequently, 'feeding' from the penetration of rainwater is non-existent. That is to say, this is limestone with a penetration factor of zero.

From the comparison of the ionic constitution of the brine with that of sea water, sea water carrying salts because of evaporation, the water of salt mines and water from sedimentation, it is established that here we have hypersaline underground waters from sedimentation Na-Cl, enriched with Ca and Mg, which were created in the initial stages of the evaporation of sea water.

Enclosed in the area of development of the practically waterproof marly formations, is a small oblong limestone mass, length 1 km. and average width 200 m [north of

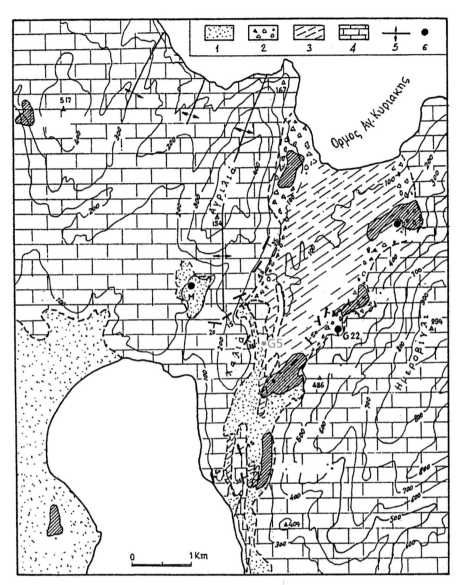

FIGURE 18.1
Thinia borehole G5 in
1985 (Koumantakis)
*This map is directly
comparable to Figure 16.9.
Key – 1: alluvium; 2: screes; 3:
miocene (mainly marls); 4:
limestones (upper cretaceous –
eocene); 5: anticline axis; 6:
boreholes (G5: boreholes with
brines, M: Metaxatos
borehole).*
[Koumantakis and
Minides (1989) p. 64, after
IGME (1985), BP Co. Ltd
(1971) with their own
observations.]

G5 on Figure 18.1]. *Its extent is approximately 20,000 m², with an altitude of 213
m at its highest point and 120 m at its lowest, at the northern edge of its perimeter . . .*

Conclusions:
*The Thinia brine in enclosed Eocene limestone came into contact with the atmosphere
on 8.11.85 for the first time in millions of years. Here we have hypersaline water of
sedimentation enriched by Na and Cl and secondarily by Ca and Mg, which was
created in the initial stages of evaporation of sea water. Moderate temperatures and
strong convertive properties are dominant.*

So having at last translated scientific Greek into scientific English, let us now turn scientific English into ordinary English. On 8 November 1985 a borehole is drilled in Strabo's Channel at the location marked as G5 on Figure 18.1, which is located at about 192 m above sea level. The drillers bore down past sea level until they reach a depth of 230 m, about 38 m below the surface of the sea, when water emerges. But there are two disappointing aspects associated with this water. One is that the volume is only 2 cubic metres per hour, which would be woefully inadequate for a thirsty village. The other is that the water is not fresh: in fact it is salty. Subsequently at a drilling depth of about 258 m the drill-bit meets another layer of water that provides a pressure of 30 cubic metres per hour, but it is also salty. How salty? Koumantakis goes on to explain:

In clear crystal NaCl the ratio Na/Cl is equal to 0.65. Moreover, Johnson (1981), showed that for oilfield brines the above ratio has a value of 0.55 and this falls continuously as the total dissolved salts of a brine increase. For the brine from the Thinia borehole G5, the ratio Na/Cl has a value of 0.58. This value does not completely agree with that of 0.65 (dissolution of crystals NaCl), because our sample does not clearly represent that of the hypersaline waters at 260 metres, because it has suffered 10–20% rarefaction, due to its mixing with the clearer water at 230 metres.

So the water of low pressure at 230 m depth is much less salty than that encountered at about 260 m. Koumantakis tells us that the deeper layer of water has been cut off from the atmosphere for 'millions of years'. That phrase sounds less than exact, so I contact him and he kindly e-mails me back (I am translating from his French):

Our term 'millions of years' is my qualitative expression of an estimate and does not represent an absolute date. Unfortunately we were unable to perform an exact dating. The response to your second question is: yes, it is possible that the less salty water encountered at 230 m is of a more recent age than the very salty water at 260 m.

This is very interesting. To summarise: at about 40 m below today's sea level at location G5 on the map about 3 km away from the sea there is some fairly salty trapped water of relatively low pressure and indeterminate age, while at another 30 m below that there is some much saltier water of higher pressure that is believed to be very old. Furthermore the block of limestone in which this water has been found is about 1 km by 200 m long, contains Eocene *Nummulites* and is unconnected with the local neogene marly strata on which it rests.

Eocene rock is from 54 million to 34 million years old and *Nummulites* are a type of fossil with a thin flat round shell containing many small spiral chambers. Neogene marly strata, by contrast, means clay, dating anywhere from 24 million years ago to the present day. So what are two distinct layers of salty water doing well inland in Strabo's Channel, caught up within or underneath a block of limestone that is about 40 million years old? And what is a block of this size doing sitting on its own on top of more recent clay? I have no idea but it all sounds rather significant. I decide to make contact with John Underhill of Edinburgh University, whose thesis on Cephalonian geology we encountered in Chapter 11. He is busy advising oil companies about how to understand what is coming up in their drilling samples but happily he is able to see me on 17 June.

The Grant Institute is a somewhat forbidding looking building on the University campus but there is a cheerful atmosphere within. John comes to greet me and we find an empty room in which to discuss the enigma of Strabo's Channel. He is the Professor of Stratigraphy there and he explains to me that he has been visiting Cephalonia and sending students to it for most summers over the last eighteen years. It is obvious that his experience, combined with his PhD thesis on the geology of the island, makes him an international expert on this topic. I unfold the geological and survey maps on the floor and wonder how best to explain my amateur theory about Cephalonian geology to the man who probably knows more about this region than anyone else on the planet. But in his spare time John is a football referee of serious calibre: he is used to putting the players of the Scottish Premier League at their ease and he does a wonderful job of helping me to relax. 'Why don't you start by showing me the photographs?' he says, and so off we go.

I had already forwarded him Professor Koumantakis' paper and he is clearly intrigued by what this might mean. He is concerned about the sheer amount of landfill but open-minded about possible causes. He tells me about the great Alaskan rockslide of 10 July 1958 and later I look it up on the Internet:[4]

Violent ground motion along the Fairweather fault caused a huge landslide in the upper part of Lituya Bay. Forty million cubic yards of dirt and rocks cascaded down a 3,000 foot slope near the head of the bay. The landslide clipped off the front of the Lituya glacier as it fell into the bay. A huge splash wave surged up the opposite slope to the unbelievable height of 1740 feet (535 meters). The surging water denuded the slope of trees and soils. Even above the 1700-foot level trees were uprooted and thrown uphill by the force of the water. This is by far the biggest splash wave recorded anywhere in the world. In 1936 a landslide into Leon Lake, Norway, created a splash wave 230 feet high, and at Cape Lopatka on the Kamchatka Peninsula, a tsunami wave 210 feet high broke on the coast in 1737.

An hour or so later we are discussing dates because he is now so intrigued by the possibility that this channel might once have existed that he knows that he has to fly out to see the terrain for himself. This is magnificent news: there is simply nobody else better qualified to assess the geology of Strabo's Channel than John and he is now proposing to come out to see it with me in August. I take the shuttle back to Heathrow in a state of high excitement.

Tjeerd van Andel has encouraged me to meet Professor James Jackson and on 19 June I am back in Cambridge again at the Bullard Laboratories, a converted stately home on the outskirts of the city surrounded by fields of sheep. James Jackson is regarded as one of the most brilliant neotectonic experts in the world: he has rewritten the rulebook about the way earthquakes and faulting take place. As he explains in his website:

My work exploits techniques in earthquake source seismology, geomorphology, space geodesy and remote sensing to examine how the continents are deforming today on all scales: from the details of the fault rupture in single earthquakes, to how that faulting has created the local geomorphology and structure, to how regional fault patterns and motions can accommodate deformation of vast continental areas. I thus address problems in structural geology and tectonics by focusing on places that are active now, rather than on older, inactive, basins and mountain belts.

We look at the photographs of Strabo's Channel and his view is similar to Tjeerd's: there is simply too much infill for the normal processes of erosion and occasional earthquakes to have contributed this amount of height within only 3,000 years. If this channel was once under the sea the critical question is therefore: when? For Strabo to have been right, the geologists require some kind of catastrophic event, like the sudden detachment of an adjacent mountainside or a comparable major landslide which would have infilled the central area at a stroke.

He shows me some fascinating photographs of massive landslides in Iran and his message is clear: unless we can find evidence of this nature then the entire theory remains mere speculation. If we can find comparable events in Cephalonia then we are in with a chance, otherwise this is all fantasy. As I am preparing to leave he says 'Try Quickbird or Ikonos.' I ask him what he means and he explains that they are the best of the new range of commercial geomapping satellites: they may be able to help us find what we are looking for.

At lunch I join James Diggle and meet Professor Anthony Snodgrass, Laurence Professor Emeritus of Classical Archaeology at the University of Cambridge. Professor Snodgrass is one of the world's most distinguished archaeologists. His fieldwork includes directing the Cambridge/Bradford

Boeotian Expedition, an archaeological survey begun in 1979. He was Sather Professor of Classical Literature at the University of California at Berkeley in 1984/5 and is a Fellow of the Society of Antiquaries of London, Fellow of the British Academy and a Senior Fellow of the Centre for Hellenic Studies of Harvard University. He is also the Chairman of The British Committee for the Reunification of the Parthenon Marbles.

He listens patiently to an ex-economist explaining his theory of Odyssean archaeology as we overlook the banks of the River Cam. Later we move on to James Diggle's rooms and I show him the photographic evidence. There is a great deal of it and he is very patient. Finally I am silent and so is he. At last he speaks:

I think the case you make is a very attractive one. I would strongly advise you to wait until the geologists have done their work later this year but you should then approach the new Director of the British School at Athens, Dr. James Whitley. He is my own former pupil and he is himself a seasoned field archaeologist who has been conducting his own surface survey project in Eastern Crete. I think he might be open to suggestions for the School to become involved in coordinating a 'synergasia' between the Greek Archaeological Service Ephorate for Cephalonia and an appropriate British institution. But there are also other well-known British explorers of Bronze Age sites (as we hope this will turn out to be) and I can certainly suggest some names for you to approach there as well.

It takes me a minute or so to realise that in the last hour Anthony Snodgrass has moved from scepticism to pragmatism: he hopes that Paliki will turn out to be a Bronze Age site of significant importance and he is already considering the practicalities of excavation. His own time is already committed to a lecture series in Australia and many other engagements but a few days later he introduces me via e-mail to Dr John Bennet, Sinclair and Rachel Hood Lecturer in Aegean Prehistory at the Institute of Archaeology of the University of Oxford (now Professor of Archaeology at Sheffield University).

I visit John Bennet in Oxford on 25 June. His own interests include prehistoric and early historic Aegean, the archaeology and history of Crete, early writing and administrative systems such as Linear B and the integration of archaeological and textual evidence. He has taken part in and supervised many fieldwork projects, including PRAP: the Pylos Regional Archaeology Project. Pylos! So John already knows a great deal about Homer and Telemachos. This makes him a veritable expert and as the photographs and maps emerge he becomes sympathetic to the central thrust of this new proposal. He explains that archaeologists cannot visit sites in a professional capacity without first obtaining fieldwork permits and that the application process takes a substantial amount of time, but he is nevertheless happy to provide background advice and to become more involved as events unfold.

John is very busy at present on Knossos but he finds this proposal interesting. He feels that it is essential to get the geology clear first: the theory of Schizocephalonia is a plausible model but the archaeology should follow the geology. We should try to obtain aerial photographs if we can and we should do our best to photograph *in situ* as much pottery as we can. Once a credible case can be made he agrees with Anthony Snodgrass that we should then approach the Director of the British School at Athens.

By the end of June I sit back and consider the experts' views. Professor James Diggle believes the theory meets the evidence of Homer and Strabo. Professor Tjeerd van Andel thinks that the channel was once a seabed but he is very concerned about the required rates of uplift or infill. Professor John Underhill is intrigued and wants to come out to see the area with me in August. Professor James Jackson says that we need to find evidence of catastrophic landslides to account for the amount of earth in the channel: natural processes are too slow. Professor Anthony Snodgrass thinks that the case is an attractive one but he advises me to wait until the geology is clearer before approaching the proper authorities. Finally Dr John Bennet is also sympathetic and he agrees with Anthony Snodgrass regarding tactics.

Something is missing from this list. I have been to each of these meetings expecting to listen to an overwhelming counter-argument, but six experts have now listened patiently to this proposal for the prior existence of Strabo's Channel and although each of them has outlined certain reservations, not one of them has declared that the theory is impossible.

But there is a seventh expert who jolts me back to reality. I have been thinking about that old olive tree in Atheras Bay. How old do olive trees grow? How can one determine their age? Do they re-seed themselves nearby when they die? In April I contact Daniel Miles, who runs the Dendrochronology Laboratory, part of the Oxford Research Laboratory for Archaeology and the History of Art. These are once again splendid Homeric terms: *dendron* is a tree (because of Athene's fog Odysseus fails to recognise the *dendrea telethoonta*, the 'luxuriant trees' in Phorcys Bay at 13.196) while *chronos* means time. Daniel refers me to a database of the world's oldest trees: the statistics are shown in Figure 18.2.

The Greeks are more confident: at a website[5] run by their Ministry of Foreign Affairs we read that: 'Many people claim that the oldest olive tree, 5,000 years old, is in Pano Vouves, in Kolymvari, Chania [Crete]. The average life expectancy of an olive tree is 300–600 years.'

If the oldest olive tree really is 5,000 years old then 3,200 years is a mere stripling. Daniel also suggests that I contact Professor Peter Kuniholm, who

Species	Age	Location
4,000 + years		
Pinus longaeva	4,844	Wheeler Pk, Nevada
Pinus longaeva	4,789	Methusela Walk, California
3,000 + years		
Fitzroya cupressoides	3,622	Chile
Sequoiadendron giganteum	3,266	Sierra Nevada, California
Sequoiadendron giganteum	3,220	Sierra Nevada, California
Sequoiadendron giganteum	3,075	Sierra Nevada, California
Sequoiadendron giganteum	3,033	Sierra Nevada, California
2,000 + years		
Juniperus occidentalis	2,675	Sierra Nevada, California
Pinus aristata	2,435	Central Colorado
Ficus religiosa	2,217	Sri Lanka
Sequoia sempervirens	2,200	Northern California
Juniperus occidentalis	2,200	Sierra Nevada, California
Pinus balfouriana	2,110	Sierra Nevada, California

FIGURE 18.2
The world's oldest trees Pinus longaeva *is the bristlecone pine;* Fitzroya cupressoides *is the (Spanish) Alerce;* Sequoiadendron giganteum *is the Sierra redwood. But where is the Greek olive tree?*
[Source: Rocky Mountain Tree Ring Research Website: www.rmtrr.org/oldlist.htm]

runs The Malcolm and Carolyn Wiener Laboratory for Aegean and Near Eastern Dendrochronology at Cornell University, appropriately located in Ithaca (NY). His reply is kind but realistic:

If I had five quid for every 'ancient' olive tree I have been told about, I would be able to go for a serious night out on the town in the swankiest part of the West End of London. I might have seen one with about 300 annual rings, but the segments of the tree were split apart by rot. Moreover, olives rot out from the centre, so one is usually faced with a big hole in the middle. Counting and measuring the rings, indeed deciding whether a little wiggly line is a 'ring' at all, is a very chancy affair at best. Two adjacent radii will often produce a different ring-count (so the 'rings' are not annual rings at all). And if one has a really large ring, all that one learns is that the gardener must have been unusually assiduous that year . . .

I suspect that I have the (formerly) oldest tree in Greece in my lab. It was born in 1255 and was cut down in 1981 by mistake on the part of the foresters at Grevena. They said that if they had known it was so old, they would have made it into a national monument. It is a Greybark Pine (Pinus leukodermis). I think we are way ahead of the olives here. There is no scientific evidence whatever that olives last so long . . . anywhere. Sorry if this is a disappointment. Do let me know if you ever see a really old tree.

'There is no scientific evidence whatever that olives last so long . . . any-where'. Peter Kuniholm is an authority on this matter but in that great Popperian tradition, 'absence of evidence is not evidence of absence'. We used to think there were no black swans either until they were located in Australia. I resolve to keep an open mind on the subject while acknowledging that the balance of probability indicates that the tree that I saw is most unlikely to be the same as the one that shaded Odysseus. Meanwhile I am being tormented by those hilltops in the photograph of Figure 17.4 and eventually I can no longer resist the temptation of slipping back to the island.

Notes

1 Diggle (1994) p. 98.
2 James Diggle's matured views on these issues are explained in more detail in Appendix 1 Section B.
3 Koumantakis and Mimides (1989).
4 www.gi.alaska.edu/ScienceForum/ASF1/109.html
5 www.mfa.gr/english/greece/living/symbols/olive.html

CHAPTER 19

Landscape

In the spring of the year 1806 I set out in a Zantiote boat, in company with two
English gentlemen, Mr. Raikes and Mr. Dodwell, from the coast of the Morea, for the
purpose of visiting Ithaca, and of satisfying ourselves, if possible, by a very particular
examination, of the veracity or falsehood of the relations of Homer on the localities of
the island.   William Gell, *The Geography and Antiquities of Ithaca* (1807)[1]

It is 23 May 2003 and I am back in Cephalonia, standing on the double hilltop
of Chapter 17 with my friend Dr Michael D'Souza who is waiting for me to
say that we have completed a full circle. He is holding on to the base of a 10 m
fibreglass mast on the top of which is perched a semi-professional camcorder
(Figure 19.1). As we rotate the mast we are hoping that what will emerge
from the resulting film footage is a panoramic view of the site.

By now we have spent several hours walking about this hillside and it is
safe to say that we are thoroughly confused. The landscape is covered with dry
stone walls of varying heights running off in directions that seem to us to be
quite arbitrary. The vegetation varies from thin scrub that we can easily walk
through to dense packed foliage that defies penetration. We have brought
with us a pair of walkie-talkies and every few minutes one of us calls to the
other to come over and take a look at an unusually cut rock, or a marking that
doesn't appear natural to the amateur eye. Mike thinks he has found a series of
small rectangular enclosed areas that could perhaps have been storerooms. We
walk round them, then we ask each other why such storerooms would still be
exposed to the eye some 3,000 years after they were constructed, as opposed
to being buried many metres below the surface and requiring excavation to
reveal their secrets. Probably all that we are seeing on the surface are the
relatively recent efforts of mediaeval shepherds to create enclosures for their
flocks of sheep.

My wife Jean and I have taken a week's spring break to explore some of the
places that these Odyssean clues are suggesting. By now you will appreciate
that my family is deeply concerned about my behaviour: this is clearly the
male menopause cutting in with a vengeance and so for safety's sake they feel
the need to escort me. Our conversations are greatly enriched by Mike: he
is a delightful travelling companion, a latter-day polymath whose domains
of expertise range from diagnosing the medical provenance of Polyphemos' eye via the migratory traditions of the Dorians to the morphology of
Linear B. Usually he is found administering to the sick and the needy of

FIGURE 19.1
Aerial photography
on a budget
*The telescopic mast has been
acquired from a German
manufacturer specialising in
amateur radio aerials: the
camera is controlled from the
ground via its infra-red
keypad.*

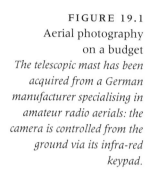

Kingston-upon-Thames but having been sworn to secrecy he was unable to resist the opportunity of joining us to walk about this hilltop in the knowledge of what may lie beneath.

Our thirteen-year old son Matthew has been granted a week's school leave to further his study of ancient Greek and it is he who takes this photograph as we struggle with the mast. A few moments later the fibreglass sections suddenly slip and camera and mast concertina themselves down on to my hands in a split second. Remarkably neither my fingers nor the camera are damaged and we also have some interesting action footage to watch that evening in the villa, but sadly the panoramic views that emerge simply show us more stone walls and brush foliage. Where is the evidence of a palace?

Earlier that week we park the jeep at a convenient spot off the road to Atheras just behind the hilltop of Figure 17.4 and start to climb towards the summit. In fact this hill has a double summit: it is shaped in the form of a saddle with two peaks of almost the same height, one to the north on the right of the photograph and the other to the south nearest the bay. We walk up the back of the hill towards the northern summit and as we reach the brow of the hill we have our first view of the harbour (Figure 19.2).

For a moment we are puzzled by the island that is visible in the distance but then we remember: it is not an island, it is the Argostoli peninsula, the *nesos* of Asteris where the suitors tried to ambush Telemachos. But in this light it looks just like an island in the middle of the bay. To our left rises Kastelli and in the centre is the quarry hill of Mesovouni. To its right and much closer to us is the southern peak of this double hilltop. We sit on the rocks and try to absorb this overwhelming view. It is warm but not yet too hot: it will be another few months before the fierce heat of August will have burnt the landscape to copper bronze.

We collect our bags and start walking towards the southern hilltop and almost at once there is a vista of strangely shaped rocks and stone walls (Figure 19.3). Some of the rocks have indentations and holes in them that look as if they might be artificial but then again perhaps it is just weathering: three millennia is a long time for a rock to age on an exposed hilltop. Clearly these walls have been constructed by somebody and this puzzling layout must meet some original purpose, but we just cannot figure out the geometry at all. If there is a palace on this hilltop, is it buried under our feet or are we looking at the ruins of it all around us? We begin to see why there is rather more to archaeology than meets the eye.

As we approach the southern hilltop the stonework is equally mysterious (Figure 19.4).

At the summit of the southern hilltop we set down our bags again and take in the breathtaking view across the bay (Figure 19.5).

Once again the peninsula of Argostoli appears island-like on the horizon, while in front of us lies a fertile valley between the hills of Kastelli on our left and Mesovouni to our right, behind which is the large quarry. In the foreground below the road are orchards: the marshy plain of the ancient harbour lies beyond them by the sea. Across the water to the left we can just about make out the white edge of the Agia Sotira inlet where we believe Strabo's Channel used to join the bay.

It is 3 pm local time on Sunday May 18 2003. Are we at last standing where Homer locates Athene in Book 1 of the *Odyssey* while she is pretending to be Mentes and addressing Telemachos at the palace?

'I am the son of wise Anchialos,
Mentes, king of the Taphians, rowing men.
I am here with ship and shipmates, bound abroad
Over the wine-dark main for Temese,
In search of bronze. I carry glinting iron.
My ship stands here in the country far from town,
In Rheithron bay, below wooded Neïon.
The ties between our families go back
To early times – if you will go and ask
Old King Laertes, who they say no longer
Visits the town but lives a life of misery
Away in the countryside with one old woman,
Who serves him food and drink when his limbs grow weary,
As he crawls along his hilly vineyard's slopes.
I come this time because they said your father
Was home.'

1.180–95[2]

FIGURE 19.2 Argostoli Bay from the northern hilltop
To the east (left) lie the mountains of central Cephalonia; to the west are the low-lying plains of Paliki.

FIGURE 19.3 View between the two hilltops *(a) View to the south: the landscape is strewn with stone walls and foundations (b) Holes for rotating gate-shafts – or simply water erosion? (c) Why are these rocks arranged in rectangular patterns? (d) View to the north: why was a stone wall built here?*

FIGURE 19.4
View of the southern hilltop
Ruined stone terraces stretch around the southern slope of this hilltop. In the background to the far left is the start of the Crikellos hill.

FIGURE 19.5
View south-south-east
from the southern hilltop
*In the far distance looms the
peninsula of Argostoli: 'There
is a rocky island in mid
sea/Half way between Ithaca
and rugged Samos' (4.842–5).*

There are some complexities associated with this passage that James Diggle explains to us in Appendix 1. His conclusion throws light on Athene's statement 'My ship stands here in the country far from town, / In Rheithron bay, below wooded Neïon.' Since the word for 'here' implies an act of pointing by the speaker, Athene will be pointing down the bay when she explains to Telemachos where her ship is standing.

This view in front of us may be the one that the poet describes the two of them as seeing some 3,200 years ago. Can Telemachos see her ship? No he cannot, otherwise he would not have just asked her where it is, using a now familiar refrain:

> Come, answer me precisely – Who are you?
> Whose son? Where are your city and your parents?
> What ship did you come on? Why did the sailors
> Bring you to Ithaca? Who did they claim
> To be? For I hardly think you came on foot.   1.169–73

Athene is pointing down the bay towards a ship that Telemachos cannot see. In fact as we discussed in Chapter 2, there are two reasons why he cannot see it. The first reason is that Athene has explained that her ship is hidden from view somewhere down the bay. The second is that the ship doesn't actually exist because Athene is not Mentes: she is a goddess who has just winged her way down from Mount Olympos and so Homer's audience knows that she doesn't really have a ship at all. Here then is the crucial point.

Homer's audience knows that Athene wants Telemachos to believe that she is a mortal, Mentes, the king of the Taphians, who would obviously have needed a real ship on which to sail to Ithaca. So as far as Telemachos is concerned she therefore has to pretend that she does indeed have a real ship. But at the same time it is essential that the audience appreciates that Telemachos cannot actually see a ship, since if he says he can then the whole story will fall apart because they know that there isn't one. The poet's description 'far from town' is by no means arbitrary: the logic of the situation combined with the topographical knowledge of his audience absolutely oblige Homer to arrange for Athene to state that her imaginary ship cannot be seen from the palace.

From this part of the island there are only three places on the bay where an imaginary ship can be hidden. You can see these in Figure 19.5, and Figure 19.2 may also be helpful. It could be concealed either in the harbour beyond the Mesovouni quarry or along the bay to the east (on the left of the photograph) or along the bay to the west. We can immediately rule out the harbour because that is not 'far from town'. We can also rule out the eastern shoreline for two reasons: the phrase 'in the country' implies open fields whereas the eastern shoreline is formed of steep cliffs going down to the sea, and also that part of it which is 'far from town' is not in Ithaca at all: it is on the far side of Strabo's Channel in Same.

So Athene must be pretending that her ship is moored on the western shore of Argostoli Bay, and for it to be out of sight from the hilltop it must be presumed to lie somewhere beyond the spit of land that you can see jutting out into the bay on the right hand side of the photograph. It could in theory be moored arbitrarily far down that shoreline, indeed as far as modern day Lixouri at the south-west end of the bay, but that would stretch the credulity of the audience to breaking point, because in that case why on earth would Athene propose to Telemachos that (disguised as Mentes) she has moored about 12 km away and walked to the palace to meet him on foot?

This point is so fundamental that Homer knows that Athene had better explain to Telemachos why she hasn't moored in the harbour like everyone else – and so he arranges for her to do just that. As we read a few pages earlier, in a masterpiece of elliptical discourse she says at 1.187–95 that 'The ties between our families go back / To early times – if you will go and ask / Old King Laertes, who they say no longer / Visits the town but lives a life of misery / Away in the countryside with one old woman, / Who serves him food and drink when his limbs grow weary, / As he crawls along his hilly vineyard's slopes. / I come this time because they said your father / Was home.' In other words without actually saying so, she creates the impression that she may have visited Laertes prior to coming up to the palace to look for Odysseus and that is therefore why she moored her ship 'In Rheithron bay, below wooded Neïon'.

Telemachos has no difficulty with this explanation: indeed they move on together to discussing the whereabouts of Odysseus. This has four important implications which I will bring together later in some new clues for Laertes: (1) there is a suitable place to moor a ship beyond the spit of land at the north-west of Argostoli Bay, (2) the mooring is called Rheithron Bay, (3) it lies under wooded Mount Neïon and (4) Laertes' farm is nearby. We should also note in passing that (5) Athene does not say that Laertes' farm is invisible from the palace, only that her ship is.

I stand on the highest rock on the summit and begin to turn clockwise. To the south-west in the distance (Figure 19.6) there is the long ridge of a mountain range that runs parallel to the coast along most of Paliki: nearby is the village of Kontogenada where the great archaeologist Spyridon Marinatos found tholos tombs in 1933.[3] Today the highest point of this mountain range is called Mount Milo: it has transmitter towers on it and it lies just beyond the village of Kaminarata.

Although the mountain's peak is only 435 m high it dominates the west of Cephalonia. Mount Ainos towards the east is much higher at 1,627 m but when Paliki was itself an island called Ithaca it could not claim Mount Ainos as its own: that privilege belonged to its neighbour Same.

I believe the ancient Ithacans had their own name for this mountain: they called it Mount Neïon (Figure 19.7). That is why Telemachos says to King Nestor at 3.81 'We come from Ithaca beneath mount Neïon': much of the island of ancient Ithaca lies beneath its wooded flanks.[4]

I keep turning. To the north-west (Figure 19.8) there is a rolling hillside studded with stone walls for keeping in flocks of goats or sheep, so Clue 18: *The palace and city are surrounded by fields suitable for livestock* applies on this side of the hilltop anyway.

To the north (Figure 19.9) the town of Atheras is perched up on the hillside at the foot of Mount Lakties.

Further north-east the 518 m peak of Mount Lakties stands out against the skyline (Figure 19.10) and from here it is a perfect candidate for Homer's Mount Neriton.

To the east (Figure 19.11) there is a lush valley bordering the slopes of Kastelli: later we will visit the ruins that lie there. In the distance are the mountains that lie on the far side of Strabo's Channel.

FIGURE 19.6 View south-west from the hilltop
The western coast lies beyond the mountain ridge in the distance.

FIGURE 19.7 Mount Neïon from the Petani road
It is early evening on 20 May 2003. There is no more beautiful time nor month on this island.

FIGURE 19.8 View north-west from the hilltop
The hillsides are on the cusp between the winter's verdant greens and the summer's burnt browns.

FIGURE 19.9 View north from the hilltop
Atheras is a village of modern red-roofed dwellings: we need look no further than Figure 11.6 for the reason.

The summit on which we are standing enjoys a panoramic view of the countryside and I am reminded of Clue 32: *Telemachos' high bedroom in the palace commands a surrounding view.*

During the March expedition I had photographed Simon climbing up Raven's Rock (Figure 19.12). Our double hilltop is marked in the middle distance, together with Mesovouni, the large quarry and Kastelli on the east side of the harbour. Eumaios' Pigfarm is not shown on this photograph: it is to the north, off to the right-hand side of the photograph.

What is rather striking is the long hill ridge in the foreground: anyone ascending from the hilltop behind or from the harbour area in the direction of

FIGURE 19.10
View of Mount Lakties
north-east from the hilltop
The demands of a 360°
panorama have masked the
mountain's summit behind a
bush. For an unobstructed
view see Figure 23.12.

the pigfarm would have to cross it. Chris Goodger and I had climbed up over it when were exploring there in March: it is a strange hill, rather like a long wide wave breaking over the hillside (Figure 19.13). It seems a possible candidate for the Hill of Hermes that Eumaios crosses on his return to the pigfarm from the palace, when he sees the suitors' ship returning unsuccessfully from the ambush to the harbour, because from the brow of this hill the harbour is clearly visible.

As I walk down the valley there is ample evidence of a substantial former streambed. Beside it to the north-east of the palace hilltop there is a distinctive structure that for a moment looks as if it could have been the city fountain described at Clue 19: *Several paths converge at an elaborate fountain, linking the pigfarm, the city, Strabo's Channel and the harbour, and somehow a circular grove of poplars is irrigated* (Figure 19.14).

Later in Oxford John Bennet looks at this photograph and tells me that it is probably just a mediaeval lime kiln,[5] but he is interested to hear that in the undergrowth beside this kiln there seems to be some kind of buried stonework. Could this be an artificial channel that once conveyed water from the river? It is intriguing but I am out of my depth: we need an archaeologist on site to interpret all this.

A few hundred metres further down the valley the streambed descends into a ravine that provides a thought-provoking possible solution for Clue 26: *The palace is supplied from a source of deep water that the light cannot reach* (Figure 19.15).

FIGURE 19.11 View east of Kastelli from the hilltop
The summit of Kastelli is 250 m above sea level while that of Imerovigli in the distance is just short of a kilometre at 993 m.

FIGURE 19.12
View south-west from
Raven's Rock
*These hills are harder to climb
than Simon's stance suggests:
the ground is not flat but is
inundated with rocks of up to
a metre or more: every step
must be carefully judged.*

FIGURE 19.13
Hermes' Hill from
Raven's Rock?
*Eumaios' Pigfarm lies off to
the right of the photograph.*

FIGURE 19.14
A strange construction at
the city stream
*A shaped stonework channel
appears to emerge at the rear
left of the construction.*

FIGURE 19.15 A source of deep water that the light cannot reach
*Although the stream runs across the surface of the valley for most of its length, half-way towards the
sea it drops down into this deep ravine where it collects into cascading pools during the rainy season.*

FIGURE 19.16
Olive grove in downtown Ithaca
This entire valley is peppered with the incongruous juxtaposition of vegetation invading abandoned habitation – but when was it inhabited?

FIGURE 19.17 Unusual rocks above the double hilltop *(a) This rock exhibits surprisingly uniform vertical and horizontal markings. (b) The length and precision of this straight edge seems unnatural. (c) The rectangular notch is neatly recessed in this stone. (d) Another neatly chiselled recess is evident in the centre of this large rounded rock.*

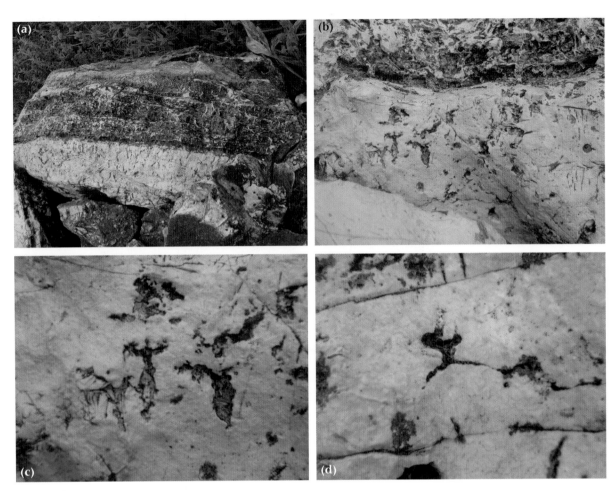

FIGURE 19.18
Strange rock markings
near the double hilltop
*(a) The white area below that
is divided from the rougher
stone above seems to have
some form of coating on it.
(b) To the left centre are some
intriguing shapes that look
like cartoon figures. (c) Is this
a man fighting an eagle, or
are these just random natural
marks? (d) Is this a suitor
exercising on the sportsground
(Clue 17 on Figure 17.2) or is
it just the wear and tear of the
passing millennia?*

As the stream emerges into the flat marshland I find myself alongside a rectangular area of distinctive stonework near a group of unreasonably old olive trees (Figure 19.16). As I reach the marshland there is a another larger area with old stonework: could this have been the ancient quayside of Ithaca harbour?

The problem I am finding is that whereas the type of archaeology that is depicted in the movies involves Harrison Ford-like figures brushing through exotic undergrowth to unveil long-lost temples, what we are seeing today consists only of a series of tantalising hints: enigmatic stone markings and enclosures scattered all over the valley and hillside, but nothing that we can really point to and say 'Aha!'.

Here are some examples (Figure 19.17): one of them looks rather like the kind of milling wheel that you might find at Clue 25: *There is a substantial mill near the palace.*[6] Another one contains a strikingly rectangular hole, a third one shows a suspiciously straight edge while a fourth looks rather like a tortoise

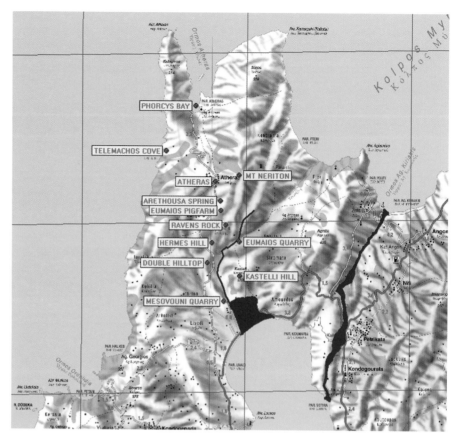

FIGURE 19.19
The initial plan of ancient
Ithaca and Strabo's
Channel
*The locations have been
derived from GPS coordinates.
The blue line denotes the
course of the main stream.
Grid: 5 km.*
[Image credits and
processing: as
Figure 12.11.]

with a strangely marked back. What can be made of these rocks? Are they man-made or formed naturally by some process of erosion? If they have been worked by man, what age might they be? I simply have no idea.

Also enigmatic is a marked rock that we found cast aside from the construction of the modern road on the putative palace hillside (Figure 19.18). Is this simply a natural formation that has been eroded into these unusual shapes through weathering or is someone trying to tell us a story? I am uncomfortably aware that I lack any kind of expertise to assess this material.

Slowly the geography of ancient Ithaca is starting to come together. In Figure 19.19 the principal place names are marked on the survey map: they were originally recorded on the GPS receiver and then uploaded to the computer. Also marked on the map is the streambed that descends from the mountain and runs down to the harbour.

It is all very confusing. What I need is some way of relating the individual details I can see as I wander around the site to this bigger picture of northern Paliki as a whole: a way of seeing the wood as well as the trees. I rack my brains for a way to bring together both large and small scale visualisation but in June the problem is unexpectedly solved for me.

Notes

1 Gell (1807) p. 15.
2 See James Diggle's comments on this passage in Appendix 1 Section F.
3 A tholos tomb is a beehive-shaped grave covered with earth: see for example Souyoudzoglou-Haywood (1999) p. 43.
4 See James Diggle's comments on this passage in Appendix 1 Section J.
5 A lime kiln is a furnace built in the open air near a source of limestone which is burnt to produce quicklime (a component of builder's mortar, fluxes, disinfectants and other compounds): see www.seaham.i12.com/sos/lime.html
6 Did Homeric mills employ circular millstones? From Moritz (1958) pp. 4–6: 'In the Homeric poems "mills" occur only in two passages of the *Odyssey* [7.104 and 20.106–11] . . . From these passages it has been inferred that rotary mills must be meant . . . Homer says that one of Odysseus' maids "halted her mill and spoke a word, a sign to her lord", his language has been thought to compel the inference that a rotating type of mill is meant . . . [but] there is no mill – rotary or non-rotary – worked by human power which, with grain between the stones, would require a positive effort to bring it to a halt.'

CHAPTER 20 Quickbird

I'll put a girdle round about the earth
In forty minutes.   Shakespeare, *A Midsummer-Night's Dream* (1596) II. i.175

Launched on 18 October 2001 and orbiting 450 km above the surface of the earth is a commercial satellite called Quickbird. Its owners, Digital Globe, claim that it collects photographic images of the Earth that have the highest resolution, largest footprint (area coverage) and highest accuracy of any commercially available satellite imagery in the world. A single digital photograph from its cameras can resolve ground details as small as 60 cm. That is precise enough to make out an individual person lying on a beach: a car stands out easily. We have long since suspected that military satellites can do all this: indeed it is rumoured that the best spy satellites can now resolve newspaper headlines. What is however remarkable is that commercial imagery of this resolution can now be purchased over the Internet by anyone who wants it.

There are two ways in which you can use Quickbird to acquire satellite images of a chosen area of the Earth's surface. If you are a company and expense is no object, you submit your order to point the satellite's camera in a particular direction on its next suitable flyover and to take your chosen photographs at the appointed moment. If your area of interest is obscured by clouds you may have to request repeat shots from multiple angles. Your photographs are then transmitted by the satellite to its base station and once you have settled your bill you can download them across the Internet.

That approach is outside the scope of an amateur exploration budget so the alternative is to wait until the satellite photographs your area of interest at the behest of its owners, to add to the growing stock of their archive photography that can then be ordered from stock at much lower cost. The problem here is that it could take years for a particular part of the earth's surface to be added to this archive; even when it is, your area of interest may be affected by cloud cover.

But in another of those wonderful coincidences that have blessed this project, at 09:28:24 GMT on 30 May 2003 the shutter of the Quickbird camera opens over western Cephalonia on a perfect, cloudless summer day and captures high resolution colour images for archive stock in multiple colour bands: red, green, blue and near infra-red. The combination of the red, green and blue images delivers a stunning series of photographs in natural colour, while the near infra-red band causes areas of well-watered vegetation to show up in red. This is because lush foliage contains significant quantities of chlorophyll, which reflects light at this wavelength.[1] Broadly speaking, the

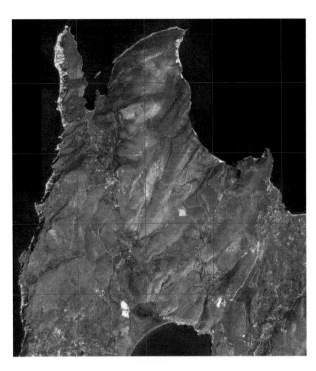

FIGURE 20.1
Quickbird image of
northern Paliki
*Colour interpretation:
near infra-red → red;
red → green; green → blue;
blue → none. This means
that chlorophyll-rich
well-watered vegetation
appears red; a red roof
appears green; a green roof
appears blue; a blue roof is
lost. Grid: 2 km.* [Image
credits: Digital Globe
Quickbird 60 cm
resolution false colour
satellite image.
Processing: OziExplorer.
Websites:
www.digitalglobe.com,
www.eurimage.com,
www.oziexplorer.com/]

damper and more verdant the vegetation, the brighter the shade of red that results.

Figure 20.1 is a visual spreadsheet: it contains 21,163 rows and 14,378 columns and each of these 304,281,614 cells identifies an area on the ground about 60 cm square and can differentiate between multiple values of colour and intensity. This single image file occupies nearly 1 gigabyte of computer memory and that is why (as we shall shortly discover) we can zoom in to identify every individual shrub in northern Paliki. Meanwhile you can clearly make out the shape of Atheras Bay in the north, and just above the curve of Argostoli Bay you can see the reflection of the Mesovouni quarry.

At this very low level of magnification the images from Quickbird are little different from those from Landsat-7 that I have used as maps of Cephalonia and the Ionian region, but the advantages of high resolution emerge as we start to zoom in to inspect a detail on the ground.

I click on the map and Figure 20.2 appears on the screen. I have chosen the near infra-red option and on these images the colour code is different from the Landsat convention: as we have heard, the reddish hue now indicates vegetation. The roads of northen Paliki appear in precise definition and the white scar of the Mesovouni quarry is clearly visible.

I click again (Figure 20.3): now I can make out individual buildings and the patchwork quilt of field boundaries.

Another click (Figure 20.4) and the view is almost vertiginous: we are hovering over the northern curve of Argostoli Bay and even details such as a tiny jetty stand out clearly.

FIGURE 20.2 Ithaca harbour from Quickbird (low resolution)
Colour interpretation: as Figure 20.1. Grid: 1 km.
[Image credits: as Figure 20.1.]

FIGURE 20.3 Ithaca harbour from Quickbird (medium resolution)
Colour interpretation: as Figure 20.1. Grid: 1 km.
[Image credits: as Figure 20.1.]

FIGURE 20.4 Ithaca harbour from Quickbird (high resolution)
Colour interpretation: as Figure 20.1. Grid: 200 m.
[Image credits: as Figure 20.1.]

FIGURE 20.5 Ithaca harbour from Quickbird (extreme resolution)
Colour interpretation: as Figure 20.1. Grid: 50 m.
[Image credits: as Figure 20.1.]

With one more click I can distinguish individual vehicles on the road and each tree and shrub in the fields (Figure 20.5). It is staggering that this image was captured from a satellite orbiting the planet 450 km away. It is quite simply a visual revolution: it changes everything. I can now continue the search for Odysseus back in England: indeed from anywhere in the world.

I decide to hunt down Eumaios. We saw the photographs of the location that I surmised might be his pigfarm in Chapter 14: what does it look like from space (Figure 20.6)?

The area marked to the north of the image is the stone-walled enclosure shown in Figure 14.2: it is about 40 m long by 15 m wide. Along its eastern

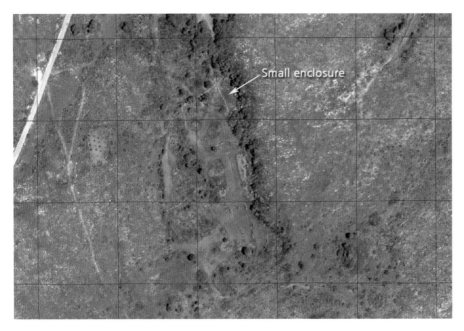

FIGURE 20.6
Eumaios' Pigfarm from
Quickbird (high
resolution)
*Colour interpretation: as
Figure 20.1. Grid: 100 m.*
[Image credits: as
Figure 20.1.]

flank and continuing southwards is the base of Mount Lakties. The green
colour to the west of the mountain is soil: its area forms a stockade of about
235 m by 100 m containing further stone wall enclosures. We saw in Chapter
14 that there were 600 sows confined in twelve pens, while 360 boars slept
outside. The numbers of pigs had been depleted by the voracious suitors and
Eumaios bemoaned the fact that he used to have more. If this meant about
1,500 livestock then each would have enjoyed up to 15 square m of land,
more than enough space to flourish.

What is particularly striking is the bright red area of damp and lush vegetation in the centre of the photograph. It is about 60 m long and it is positioned
centrally along the eastern border of the stockade at the foot of Mount Lakties.
But what is it doing here? Recall these lines from Chapter 14:

> Go first of all to the swineherd, who keeps watch
> Over your pigs and is still loyal to you
> And loves your son and wise Penelope.
> You will find him sitting with the pigs; they feed
> By Raven's Rock and Arethousa Spring,
> Guzzling dark water and munching tasty acorns –
> A diet that builds up healthy fat in pigs.   13.404–10

We have seen that 'dark water' means water in deep places, where the light
cannot reach it. I click the mouse to zoom out the Quickbird satellite imagery
(Figure 20.7).

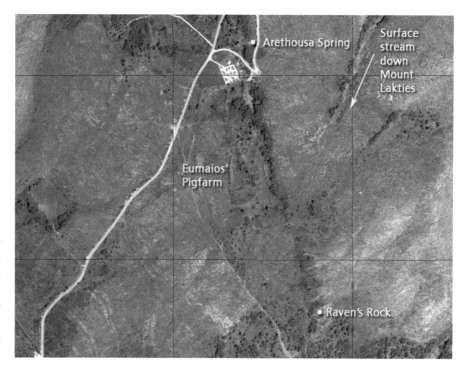

There is a stream that courses down Mount Lakties (Neriton) and disappears into the porous limestone about 150 m to the north-east of the red area of damp vegetation. It surfaces again at the red area, which is why there is 'dark water' there. Today the area is overgrown with thick ferns (Figure 20.8) and as you walk through it your boots become sodden. Water oozes out of clefts in the rock and trickles down the rockface. Furthermore John Underhill later explained to me that the Livadi (or Atheras) Thrust, one of the fault lines of Figure 11.7, runs up through the valley of ancient Ithaca, past the pigfarm and Arethousa Spring and then down to Phorcys Bay. Fault lines of this nature tend to represent a natural contour for underground springs; if you wanted to establish a large pigfarm full of thirsty pigs somewhere up above the palace this would undoubtedly be a good place to choose.

Although I had walked past these ferns before, without the satellite imagery I would never have made the connection between them and the submerged spring from the flanks of Mount Lakties.

In the months ahead I spend hours looking at these Quickbird images, zooming in for content and zooming back out again for context. This technology is truly awesome: in our search for the destructive wake of Poseidon we have been vested with the eyesight of Zeus.

On 7 July I download the first of these enormous image files and with mounting excitement I zoom in on the double hilltop (Figure 20.9).

FIGURE 20.8
Pigs guzzle dark water
*The high chlorophyll content
of the damp ferns shows up
clearly as a bright red area on
Figure 20.6.*

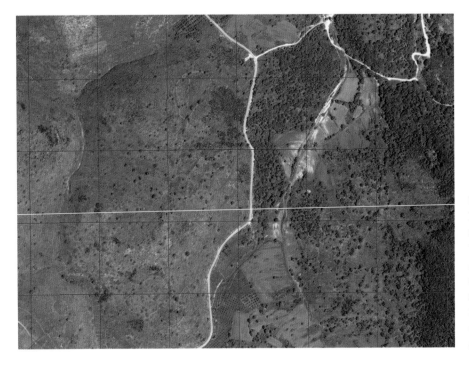

FIGURE 20.9
Double hilltop (medium
resolution)
*The double hilltop lies to the
left of the road: on both sides
of it a dense network of dry
stone walls is visible. Colour
interpretation: as Figure 20.1.
Grid: 200 m.* [Image credits:
as Figure 20.1.]

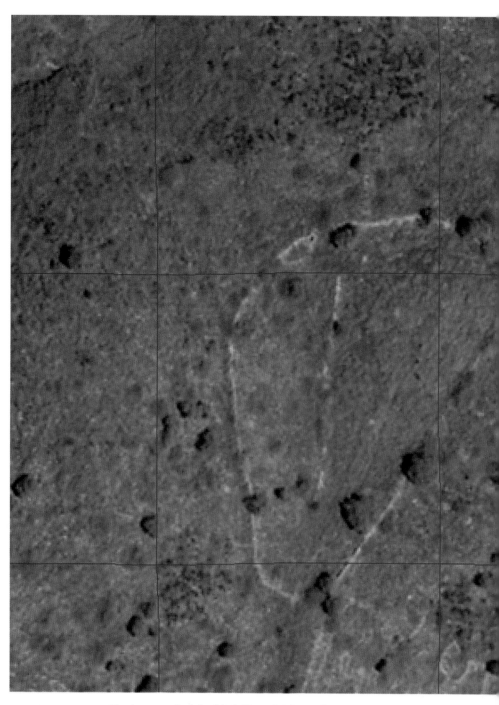

FIGURE 20.10 Northern end of double hilltop (high resolution)
The road is modern: the stone walls and terraces cross over it descending down the hillside on the right. But how old are they and who built them? Colour interpretation: as Figure 20.1. Grid: 100 m. [Image credits: as Figure 20.1.]

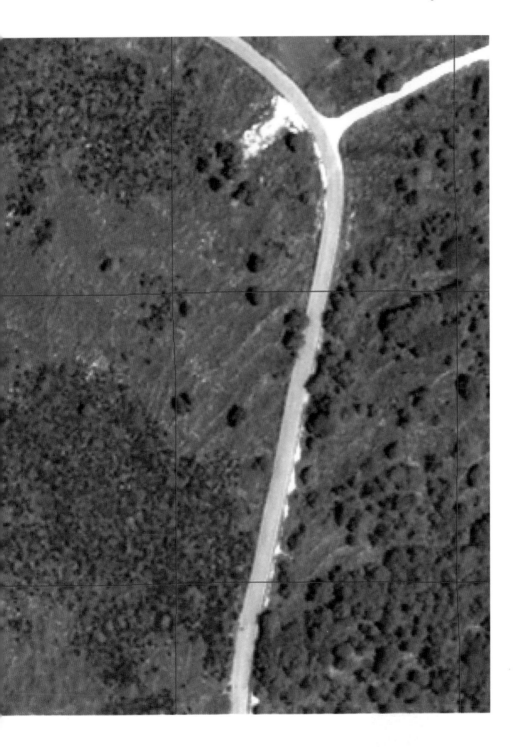

The hilltop is to the left of the road that snakes up from the south. In May we had parked the jeep at the west-facing cul-de-sac towards the top of the picture but we had missed the markings that I could now make out on the ground, especially after a further zoom.

The white lines that you can see on the photograph are dry stone walls. The pink blobs are individual trees and the dark circles beside them are their shadows. We should not get too excited about these walls: there are dry stone walls all over Cephalonia dating back to the mediaeval period when the islanders lived in communities scattered across the countryside. But perhaps a mediaeval stone wall might be built along the lines of a previous and now buried fortification: after all, if the foundations are already in place why not re-use them? Furthermore a dense network of stone walls along a particular hillside is clear evidence of previous occupation, and this occupation might go back for a long time. Communities tend to stay in the places where they were founded because this was usually in a place that was sensible to occupy: close to running water, close to food, perhaps also close to the sea.

We will return to the double hilltop before long but now I would like to take you on a visit to the Ithacan suburbs. One of the most striking Quickbird images is a settlement on the eastern side of the island, adjacent to the former marine channel. If you refer back to Figure 20.2 then in the north-eastern corner of Argostoli Bay you can see the distinctive zig-zag of a track that descends to the secluded beach of Koumaria. In Figure 20.11 we can see this in greater detail. The proposed course of Strabo's Channel is close to the modern road from Argostoli, which is grey-coloured on the photograph and runs from south to north-east. The track down to Koumaria Beach branches off westwards and crosses a hillside that overlooks the channel. On this hillside there is a very unusual pattern of stone walls. It is hard to make out their details in this photograph but all we now need to do is to press the zoom button a few times (Figure 20.12).

I had driven along the road from Argostoli to Lixouri many times but I had not thought to climb up above it and look across to the west (Figure 20.13).

When I did so the view was extraordinary: I could even match the trees on the hilltop with those in the satellite view. I am not competent to judge the date of an ancient settlement such as this: that will have to wait for professional archaeologists. But the location of this area of walls and enclosures is significant: it is precisely where the ancient Ithacans would have built a frontier town. It is the Bronze Age Checkpoint Charlie for all those who crossed over to Ithaca from Sami 3,200 years ago and I think we may have a clue about its name: I believe that it could have been called Aigilips.

I have to admit that this is a long-shot. We saw in Chapter 3 that Homer describes Ithaca and its neighbourhood in the *Iliad*:

FIGURE 20.11
Northern Argostoli Bay
(low resolution)
*The Argostoli–Fiscardo road
runs from south to north
along the right-most vertical
grid line. Further to the east is
the old road that winds
through the villages of Thinia.
Grid: 500 m.* [Image credits:
as Figure 20.1.]

FIGURE 20.12 Settlement at southern end of channel (medium resolution)
*The density of these stone walls seems far too high for animal enclosures: are they the ruined
foundations of dwellings? Grid: 100 m.* [Image credits: as Figure 20.1.]

FIGURE 20.13
Settlement at southern
end of channel (from
above road)
*The remarkably flat surface of
the fields in the foreground is
an abrupt contrast to this
dense stone-walled hillside: on
its western side it slopes down
steeply to the sea.*

> Odysseus led the gallant Cephallenians,
> From Ithaca and leaf-quivering Neriton,
> From Crocyleia and rugged Aigilips,
> Men hailing from Zacynthos and from Samos,
> From the mainland and the region opposite.
> Odysseus, equal in resource to Zeus,
> Led these, together with twelve red-cheeked ships.   *Iliad* 2.631–7

By now we have candidate locations for Ithaca city and leaf-quivering Neriton mountain. Zacynthos is the island to the south of Ithaca and Samos (i.e. Same) is the island of eastern Cephalonia which is called 'the mainland'. 'The region opposite' is an interesting phrase: in Appendix 1 James Diggle argues that this can only mean 'the region opposite the mainland', in other words the southern part of Paliki across Argostoli Bay, towards present-day Lixouri. The problem lies with the phrase 'From Crocyleia and rugged Aigilips' since these two locations are mentioned only in this one line of the *Iliad*: they do not even recur in the *Odyssey* so this is our only clue. Expert opinion divides rather sharply on their identification and the following diagnosis explains why:

> From Ithaca (island/city) and leaf-quivering Neriton (mountain),
> From Crocyleia (?) and rugged Aigilips (?),
> Men hailing from Zacynthos (island) and from Samos (island/city),
> From the mainland (area) and the region opposite (area).

If we are to take a stab at locating two places that are mentioned only once in about 270,000 words of epic verse and with the sole description 'rugged' applied to one of them, then it would clearly help to have an idea about what sort of feature they might represent. The problem is that this description is sandwiched between references to Ithaca island/city and Neriton mountain on the one hand, and to Zacynthos island and Samos island/city on the other. Consequently some researchers take their cue from the first line and regard Crocyleia and Aigilips as representing regions of the island of ancient Ithaca, whereas others give priority to the textual proximity of Zacynthos and Samos and declare that Crocyleia and rugged Aigilips must themselves be islands.

The insular enthusiasts usually interpret Crocyleia as today's island of Arkoudi and Aigilips as today's Atokos. We saw where these islands are located at Figure 10.1: Arkoudi lies north-north-east of modern Ithaca and Dörpfeld thought that it must have been the ambush island of Asteris. It has an overall area of about 420 hectares, a hilltop 136 m high and as I write it is up

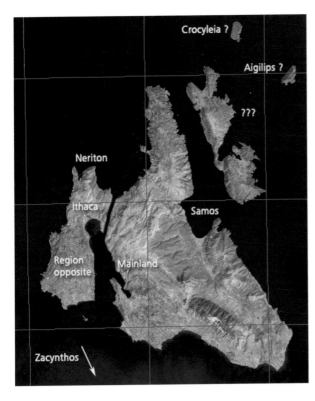

FIGURE 20.14
Crocyleia and Aigilips as islands
If Paliki is ancient Ithaca then why would Homer refer to Arkoudi (supposedly Crocyleia) and Atokos (supposedly Aigilips) without mentioning the much larger island in between? Colour interpretation: as Figure 1.3. Grid: 20 km. [Image credits: as Figure 1.3.]

for sale with a glowing agent's description: '420 hectares, own groundwater, small natural harbour. The island is suitable for the structure of a large tourist complex. In view of the soil morphology an 18-hole golf course would be easy to realise.'[2]

Atokos is of similar size: it lies about 9 km south-east of Arkoudi, to the north-east of modern Ithaca: it has a spectacular 333 m high cliff that slopes steeply down to the sea and it deserves the description 'rugged'. It is now deserted but it boasts a cove called 'One House Bay'. The fact that these two distinct small islands exist off the coast of modern Ithaca is obviously of interest and at first sight it seems perfectly reasonable to suggest that it may be these islands to which Homer was referring in the *Iliad*.

However, if that is the case then there is a very interesting omission in the above lines – another glaring case of 'The dog that didn't bark.' The poet is extolling Odysseus, leader of the gallant Cephallenians: he refers to his native Ithaca and to the leaf-quivering mountain of Neriton – and then he apparently does something very strange indeed. He skips straight over the modern island of Ithaca (in Chapter 34 we shall examine the suggestion made in Chapter 5 that it was called Doulichion) and he then alights upon two tiny islands of about 2 square km in size that he has never referred to before and will never refer to again (Figure 20.14).

Why on earth would Homer do that? Why would he entirely omit a large island that is comparable in size to the whole of ancient Ithaca in the interests of referring to two nondescript small islands beyond it that may not even have provided an adequate supply of running water, let alone food for their putative inhabitants? Once it is clear that ancient Ithaca is not the same as modern Ithaca, this selective identification of Crocyleia and Aigilips as islands makes no sense at all. So we are then left with the alternative interpretation, that they are not islands but are instead regions. If that is so then on which island might they be?

There is a clue, albeit a very tenuous one, in the construction of the lines above. The poet says 'Odysseus led the gallant Cephallenians, / From Ithaca and leaf-quivering Neriton, / From Crocyleia and rugged Aigilips', and in his description of Neriton, Crocyleia and Aigilips all three places are introduced with the word 'and'. The word-for-word translation is 'and Neriton leaf-quivering, / and Crocyleia inhabiting and Aigilips rugged'. However although the next line continues to describe the gallant Cephallenians, its construction is different: 'those holding Zacynthos'. James Diggle warns us in his Appendix that the choice of verbs in this passage is dictated by the metre rather than their precise meaning and so we can hardly depend upon the absence of 'and' to indicate a shift of emphasis. But the fact that Crocyleia and Aigilips are described in this way immediately after Ithaca and its mountain of Neriton may indicate that they are also regions of Ithaca.

The settlement on the hillside at Figure 20.13 is at the entrance to Strabo's Channel and it constitutes the southern end of the extreme eastern extent of ancient Ithaca. If we draw a radius at this distance from Ithaca palace and city we arrive at the circle depicted in Figure 20.15. Almost exactly opposite the proposed site of Aigilips is a very distinctive hillside that might be the ancient location of Crocyleia. Today it bears a rather interesting name: it is called Crikellos.[3]

I have not been able to find out for how long the Crikellos hillside has had this name and furthermore the etymology of the name itself is not very helpful: Crikellos and Crocyleia may both stem from the word for a crocus, but then again they may not. However what is interesting about this hillside is that there are polygonal stone walls on its summit: indeed an ancient stone wall surrounds most of the summit itself. For that reason at least one recent Homeric theorist[4] has proposed that this hillside is in fact the site of Odysseus' Palace, and the local folklore reinforces the suggestion. There is also an abandoned church nearby and some other tumble-down buildings deserted after the 1953 earthquake: these were the self-same ruins that distracted me during our first trip to the island at Figure 13.2.

In the valley to the west of Crikellos hillside is the excavation site of Oikopeda. It lies close to the village of Kontogenada where Marinatos

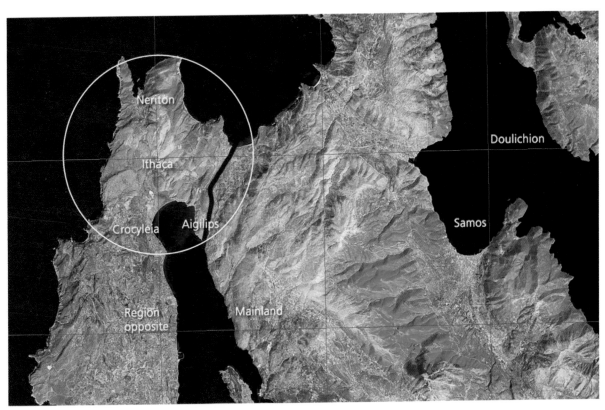

FIGURE 20.15
Crocyleia and Aigilips as regions
If our identification of 'Ithaca and leaf-quivering Neriton' is correct then 'Crocyleia and rugged Aigilips' are more likely to be nearby. Colour interpretation: as Figure 1.3. Grid: 10 km. [Image credits: as Figure 1.3.]

discovered the tholos tombs in 1933: he also explored this site from 1921 onwards. He found 'the earliest Late Bronze Age pottery from Kefalonia, datable to LH II-IIIA1 [c. 1400–1350] . . . The rest of the pottery dates from LH IIIA2-IIIB [c. 1350–1200]'.[5]

As well as the archaeological sites of Kontogenada and Oikopeda there is another small site about 1 km to the north of Crikellos hill called Helleniko, located in 1996: 'The square tower is situated on rather flat rich agricultural land and probably belongs to a farmstead (rather than being a watchtower). It measures a little more than 5 m [square] . . . the walls are 1 m thick and double.'[6] This location is near the Petani road less than 1 km south-west of the double hilltop and once again supports Clue 18: *The palace and city are surrounded by fields suitable for livestock.*

We may never be able to prove the identity of Crocyleia and Aigilips but there doesn't seem to be a logical flaw with this proposal and the connection between the names Crikellos and Crocyleia remains rather striking. Other proposals exist: C. H. Goekoop points out that the name Krokylia is still used to identify a barren area of southern Erissos between Myrtos Beach and the peak of Kalon Oros to its west.[7] This location is north of the deep rift of the Pylaros valley on the upper right of Figure 20.15 and it would place Crocyleia

FIGURE 20.16
Jim's sheep on Crikellos
hillside
*The view is to the south: the
bay of Argostoli is just visible
at the top left. This hill is a
narrow saddle that separates
the coastal plain from the
Oikopeda valley to the west.*

in Same rather than in Ithaca: so far I have not been able to identify this place name on the island. But I have no doubt that speculation about the identity of Crocyleia and Aigilips will continue: indeed I was earlier impressed by the observation that Figure 5.3 shows a 'Kokilia' and an 'Arkoliki' to the west of Ithaca harbour until James Diggle gently disabused me of that etymology.

When I visit the Crikellos hillside again later in the year I meet Jim, a shepherd from Kontogenada looking after his sheep among the ruins. He identifies the ancient walls for me and he explains how excited visiting archaeologists become when they see them. He tells me the names of the local hills and he identifies the site of Oikopeda across the valley to the west. As I listen to him I wonder how it is that he speaks such excellent English. I ask him and he says that he emigrated from Cephalonia when he was young and lived for thirty years in New Jersey. Now he has returned to the land of his birthplace and he is living once again in the simple village where he grew up.

I think about Jim from time to time now that I am back in England. How can one explain the attraction of rural Cephalonia to the people of New Jersey? How can one do the reverse? Which of these lifestyles is best, or is that a meaningless question? As Jim's sheep bask in the autumn sun on the Crikellos hillside (Figure 20.16) it seems as if the centuries are suspended: there is very little difference between what he is doing now and what his ancestors were doing 3,200 years ago.

I wonder whether those ancestors were more or less content than we are today. I wonder whether their sheep looked much the same.

Notes

1 For a non-technical explanation see http://imagers.gsfc.nasa.gov/ems/infrared.html; further complexities are described in Carter and Spiering (2002).
2 www.topsite-hellas.com/insel1.htm
3 This name is in local use in the adjacent village of Livadi and is also confirmed by the author of an alternative theory, the autochthonous Livadas (1998) p. 95. It is correctly located on the BP/IGME 1971 geological map at Figure 7.5 where it is spelled Krikélo.
4 Livadas (1998) ch. 7.
5 Souyoudzoglou-Haywood (1999) p. 43.
6 Randsborg (2002) p. 105.
7 Goekoop (1990) p. 116.

CHAPTER 21

Doulichion

We shall defend our island, whatever the cost may be.

Sir Winston Spencer Churchill (4 June 1940)

On 17 May 2003 I arrive in Cephalonia with family volunteers to stay in Villa Rowena for a week in a village called Matsoukata, near Fiscardo on the north-east coast. This part of the island is to the north of the Agia Ephemia fault line that you can see in Figure 11.7 and consequently the area escaped most of the destruction of the 1953 earthquake. The region is called Erissos and we saw in Chapter 9 that it is where C. H. Goekoop believes ancient Ithaca to be located. In another of those unexpected coincidences which have strangely associated themselves with this venture, we look out of the balcony when we arrive to see a large island across the bay and a small but rather distinctive island near to our coastline (Figure 21.1).

The large island across the strait is today called Ithaca and the small island is called Dascalion. I had researched Dascalion back in England and we have discussed it in earlier chapters but it is nevertheless a strange feeling to see it from my bedroom window. In the dip of the mountains towards the left of the Ithacan skyline is an inlet called Polis Bay which is believed by most authorities to be the site of ancient Ithaca harbour. At the head of the bay is a small town called Stavros and further up that valley is a region called Pilikata that is regarded by the majority of experts as the site of ancient Ithaca city. It appears that we have booked ourselves into the lion's den.

We leave the villa and take the jeep along some tracks and find ourselves emerging above a cove almost immediately opposite Dascalion (Figure 21.2). On the nautical map the name of the place where we are now standing is Ormos Doulicha – Doulicha Bay.[1] I am perhaps prejudiced but somehow Dascalion isn't looking any bigger, nor its heights more windswept.

There are motorboats for hire in Fiscardo and on Monday 19 May we decide to take a boat trip. The straits are about 4 km wide and it takes us around twenty minutes to reach Ithaca with our outboard motor at two-thirds throttle. The coastline adjacent to Polis Bay drops sheer to the sea: this is the only harbour on the north-west of the island.

Polis Bay is a small and pretty inlet and there is evidence of previous archaeological activity as soon as we arrive. A signboard relates the discovery in the 1930s of the Loizos Cave by the archaeologist Sylvia Benton. Although it explains that the cave is no longer visible because of erosion and earthquakes,

FIGURE 21.1
Dascalion from Villa
Rowena
The steep cliffs of modern
Ithaca rise abruptly across the
strait: the valley to the left is
Polis Bay and Dascalion is the
tiny island in the foreground.
See Figure 10.2 for location
details.

it displays a rather alarming photograph of a member of the exploration crew emerging like a disturbed troglodyte from the cave into the sunlight (Figure 21.4).[2]

The poster explains that some remnants of the enigmatic and beautiful tripods that were found in the cave are on display at the Stavros Museum so we wind our way up the track to the small town. Dascalion is now no longer visible but by climbing up the southern slopes of the inlet we think we can just about make it out as a tiny white streak on the far right of the strait (Figure 21.5).

Using the camera's telephoto lens I confirm that it is still there on the horizon (Figure 21.6).

We reach Stavros and observe the statue of Odysseus exhibited with pride in the town square (Figure 21.7(b)).

Sadly the museum is shut (never visit Greek archaeological sites on a Monday) which is a pity because the cauldrons and the tripods are felt by many Homeric researchers to be important. Here are the relevant passages: we are in Phaiacia at the court of King Alcinoos and Odysseus has not yet revealed his identity. The first discussion takes place in Book 8 just after Odysseus has praised the king on the excellence of his dancers. Alcinoos is delighted by the compliment and announces to the assembled company:

> Captains and leaders of Phaiacia, hear me.
> I think the stranger is a man of good sense:
> So let us make him an appropriate gift.
> Twelve noble princes hold authority
> Throughout the land – including me, thirteen.
> Bring him, each one of you, a laundered robe
> And tunic and a talent of precious gold.
> Let's quickly stack them here, so that our guest,
> Possessed of these, may go to dinner happy.   8.387–95

The twelve noble princes agree with the king's proposal and they send off heralds to assemble these gifts. The champion wrestler Euryalos, who has earlier slighted Odysseus by saying that he is no athlete, makes amends by giving him a silver-studded sword and an ivory scabbard. Alcinoos himself also gives Odysseus a cloak and tunic and he adds to this already copious pile of presents his own gold libation cup. All of these gifts are placed inside a beautiful chest from the palace's treasure chamber and Odysseus then fastens a cord around its lid with a special knot that Circe has taught him.

At the start of Book 9 Odysseus tells the court who he really is and he embarks upon the tale of his journey home from Troy. We hear no more of this chest full of riches until Book 13, when Odysseus has finished relating the spell-binding story of his adventures and is now making ready to leave Phaiacia for Ithaca. Alcinoos confirms that the previous gifts are still intact but he then proposes yet further donations, to be financed via the local exchequer:

> Our guest will find packed in a polished chest
> The clothes, wrought gold, and all the other gifts
> Which the Phaiacian counsellors brought here.
> But let us each now give him a large tripod
> And cauldron. We'll recoup the cost from taxes:
> It's too much for one man to foot the bill.   13.10–15

Everyone agrees to this effortless extravagance and they go off to bed.

> As soon as rosy-fingered Dawn appeared
> They hastened to the ship with the gifts of bronze.   13.18–19

FIGURE 21.2 Dascalion from Doulicha Bay
'There is a rocky island in mid sea / Half way between Ithaca and rugged Samos, / Called Asteris, not large, but with twin bays / For mooring. Here the Achaian ambush waited' (4.844–7) But can we seriously imagine that it was here?

FIGURE 21.3
The sheer north-west
coastline of modern Ithaca
*If this was also ancient Ithaca
then why did the poet say
'Ithaca itself lies low, furthest
to sea'?*

These passages have sometimes been interpreted as implying a total of thirteen bronze tripods and cauldrons. The following day when Odysseus wakes
up on ancient Ithaca we read:

> Athene, grey-eyed goddess, answered him:
> 'Cheer up! Don't worry about that. We must
> Bury the treasure deep in the hallowed cave
> Without delay, to keep it safe for you,
> And then consider the best plan of action.'
> With that the goddess entered the misty cave,
> Feeling for hiding places, while Odysseus
> Brought the Phaiacian presents closer up,
> Gold, indestructible bronze, and well-made clothes.
> He stored them carefully, and Pallas, daughter
> Of aigis-bearing Zeus, sealed the mouth with a stone.
> Then they sat down by the trunk of the sacred olive
> To plot the death of the high and mighty suitors.
>   13.361–73

FIGURE 21.4
The exploration of Loizos Cave
Sylvia Benton coordinates activity from the chair above the cave while an intrepid worker emerges from within.
[Image credits: reproduced with the permission of Mrs Fotini Couvaras, Curator of the Stavros Museum, Ithaca, and with the kind consent of the folklore writer Mrs Olympia Megalogenis–Lecatsas who provided the photograph from her personal archive.]

FIGURE 21.5
Looking for Dascalion from Polis Bay
Dascalion is 4 km away from us and it is well-nigh invisible.

FIGURE 21.6 Zoom lens focusing on Dascalion

With a 280 mm zoom lens the barren flat island materialises in the distance.

FIGURE 21.7
Looking for Odysseus'
Palace on Ithaca island
*(a) The valley above Polis
Bay. (b) The head of Odysseus
in the Stavros town square.
(c) The inland valley is flat
and agricultural. (d) An
enterprising Bronze Age
identification.*

Odysseus and Athene hide the Phaiacian tripods and the cauldrons in the Cave of the Nymphs by the olive tree at the head of the harbour of Phorcys Bay. We hear no more of them for several thousand years until Sylvia Benton excavates twelve cauldrons and tripods from the Polis Bay cave in the 1930s.[3] Helen Waterhouse advises us that a thirteenth set is believed to have been melted down in 1873 by Loizos, the landowner.[4] The tripods were originally dated to somewhere between 1000 and 800 BC but their date was subsequently revised to the later end of this range. In view of the presumed date of the Trojan War around 1200 BC it is therefore felt that these cannot be the actual gifts of the Phaiacians but instead they are perhaps votive offerings at a subsequent shrine to Odysseus. The reconstructed workmanship is quite remarkable (Figure 21.8)[5] and the whole affair has attracted considerable speculation.

Could they have been the 'actual' tripods given to Odysseus? Perhaps because of a 2,000-year long history of false hopes on the identification of

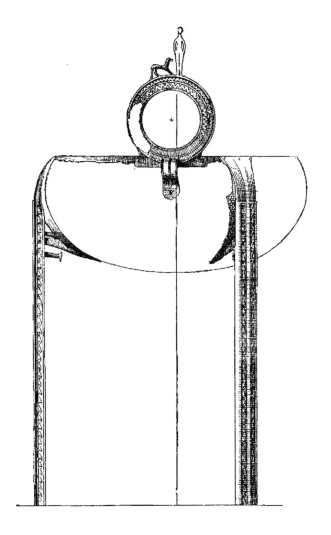

FIGURE 21.8
Reconstruction of a
Polis Bay tripod
*The tripod is described as of
height c. 3 ft (about 0.9 m).
The third leg is presumably
hidden behind that on the
right while the vertical
centreline is a draftsman's
artefact.*
[Image credits: Wace and
Stubbings (1962) Plate 33
pp. xvii, 420; *British School
at Athens Archaeological
Reports* (1988–9), 35 p. 67
figure 17. Reproduced
with the permission of
Palgrave Macmillan.]

Ithaca, in some archaeological circles the mere suggestion of an association between an object and the Odyssean text is today treated with great suspicion. The opening remarks of Helen Waterhouse in her 1996 paper 'From Ithaca to the *Odyssey*' for the British School at Athens make apparent her concern regarding this professional sensitivity and potential stigma: 'I will make no apology for a title linking archaeology to the epic.'[6] But in his paper on Ithaca in the 1962 *A Companion to Homer* F. H. Stubbings felt less exposed to the basilisk-like glare of his colleagues:

The sea has risen in level since ancient times[7] and invaded the floor of the cave, and the roof has at some period collapsed, but in spite of these obstacles it was possible to excavate a rich stratified deposit of pottery and votive offerings ranging from the Bronze Age to the first century A.D. A number of inscribed sherds prove that the cave was sacred to the Nymphs, and a fragment of a terracotta mask of the first or second century B.C. inscribed ΕΥΧΗΝ ΟΔΥΣΣΕΙ – *'a votive offering to Odysseus' – shows that it was associated also with Odysseus . . .*

The most remarkable of all the votive objects found are twelve bronze tripod-cauldrons of the ninth to eighth centuries B.C. These, though imperfectly preserved, are of very beautiful workmanship, and indicate that the shrine was of considerable importance at that period. It seems certain that this shrine helped to inspire the description of the Cave of the Nymphs in the Odyssey. Possibly the cave of Marmarospilia, above Vathy, was also in the poet's mind; we have seen that it suits the story well in position and form.

But as the Polis cave is proved to have been connected in historical times with the legend of Odysseus, it is even possible to see in the bronze tripods the 'originals' of those which Odysseus in the poem brings home from Phaiacia. They are not of the Mycenaean period, but probably older than the writing of the Odyssey, and sufficiently remarkable as works of art to have acquired a traditional association with the local hero. Even their number fits. Alcinoos and his twelve fellow-rulers each gave Odysseus 'a great tripod and a cauldron'. In the Polis cave were remains of twelve tripods: the thirteenth had been found previously by Loizos.[8]

Intriguingly Stubbings turns the poet's chain of cause and effect around: instead of suggesting that these are the actual tripods that a real Odysseus brought to Ithaca, he asks us to consider instead that the tripods were well known before the *Odyssey* was written and that this part of the poem was phrased to suit their existing description and quantity.

Sylvia Benton's researches on the Polis Bay cave and other areas on today's island of Ithaca are at present being documented and extended by C. Morgan of King's College London and A. Soteriou of the Greek Archaeological Service. Progress reports have appeared in several publications[9] and it will be of significant interest to learn of their further findings. Meanwhile we should perhaps keep an open mind about the number and the provenance of these tripods.[10]

We ask for the way to the Pilikata archaeological site of ancient Ithaca but apart from some sections of stone wall documented by Christina Souyoudzoglou-Haywood[11] there is nowhere particularly striking for the Odyssean tourist in search of an ancient city and palace to visit. In her article Helen Waterhouse explains that:

This broad eminence, commanding as it does the three bays of Aphales, Polis and Phrikes, has always seemed a likely site for the palace of Odysseus. Mainly perhaps because of heavy occupation in subsequent periods, its excavation proved disappointing. Besides a good range of EH [Early Helladic: 3000–2000 BC] *pottery, nothing was recovered but a few kylix* [large open cup] *stems, in poor preservation, and scattered blocks, few in situ from a possible Cyclopean enceinte* [enclosure].

FIGURE 21.9
'School of Homer'
In 1807 Gell wrote 'the villagers point out with patriotic pride the platform below as the place of instruction, and the niches in the wall as the book-shelves'.

After further inquiries and a rather long walk through the dusty roads we reach a location enterprisingly signposted as 'School of Homer' (Agios Athanassios). There are signs of current excavation in progress, although not today, and the uncovered stonework is impressive (Figure 21.9). However, this particular site dates from a much later period; it has never been seriously proposed as the location of Odysseus' Palace or Ithaca city and only small quantities of pottery have been found. Souyoudzoglou-Haywood explains that 'In a spring chamber (originally mistaken for a tholos tomb) about 200 m down the slope, some Mycenaean pottery was recovered (the stem of two kylikes and of one stemmed bowl).'[12]

Earlier in Chapter 9 we read of the enterprising invention of this name by William Gell's Greek host in 1842 and apparently this tradition has been preserved in the locality. As J. V. Luce explains in *Celebrating Homer's Landscapes*:

The site is known as Pilikata, and W. A. Heurtley, the director of the excavations, argued for it as the likeliest site for a palace, though admittedly no remains of buildings answering to such a description were found. One would not expect anything on the scale of Mycenae or Pylos, but as one stands at Pilikata at the highest point of the ridge, it is easy to imagine an Odysseus lording it here in a well-timbered hall that has vanished without trace.[13]

FIGURE 21.10
Dascalion from our
motorboat
*We aborted the search for
Apollodorus' 'town
Alalcomenai upon it, situated
on the isthmus itself':
Dascalion's only occupants
are its seagulls.*

Fortunately one's Mycenaean expectations are not affronted because no hint of a palatial building has been found. Indeed not only is it delightfully easy to imagine an Odysseus lording it here in Pilikata, with only a modicum of additional effort we can conjure him up almost anywhere else in Greece in some other well-timbered hall that has also tiresomely vanished without trace.

An alternative palace site on present-day Ithaca is proposed by some researchers at the central isthmus of Aetos but this then runs into the critical difficulty of lacking any form of ambush island. Dascalion is the only candidate island for the classical hypothesis and since Telemachos was returning from Pylos in the south-east it would be nonsensical to propose a home port for his destination that he would reach without any prospect of sailing past the ambush island. This effectively rules out the Aetos hypothesis and we were soon to find further arguments against the Polis Bay proposal as well, when we discovered (as surmised in Chapter 10) that from Dascalion it is not practical to ambush anyone who is heading for that bay from the south-east.

It is late afternoon as we embark from Polis Bay back over the strait to Cephalonia. We aim towards Dascalion and about twenty minutes later we draw up beside it (Figure 21.10). There are flocks of seagulls nesting on this reef: we drift past an abandoned hut and a tiny ruined chapel. The land in the centre is a few metres above today's sea level but the colour of the rocks suggests that before 1953 it was about 60 cm lower and the history of tectonic upthrust makes it likely that in Odysseus' day even more of the reef was submerged. There is nowhere for a galley to conceal itself; there is no possibility of a harbour, let alone two; there are no windy heights and there is certainly no isthmus on Dascalion nor the remotest hint of Apollodorus' town of Alalcomenai.

Furthermore as James Diggle has pointed out in Appendix 1, the word that is used at 16.367 when Antinoos says 'We never slept the night on land' is *epeiros* which suggests something much more substantial than a rock.[14] Indeed Schliemann himself was on our side in this matter:

'Its length is 586 feet; its breadth varies between 108 feet and 176 feet. On account of these small dimensions it cannot possibly be identified with the Homeric Asteris which, as the poet says, had two ports, each of them with two entrances.'[15]

Even if all of this evidence is discounted and we imagine, as did Schliemann himself perhaps in desperation, some larger foundations of Dascalion slipping Atlantis-like under the waves (perchance to vanish without trace in a direction contrary to the prevailing seismic upthrust), nobody hiding on or near Dascalion could ever ambush anybody heading from Pylos for Polis Bay. This is because it would take the best part of an hour for a Bronze Age galley to cross over to the far coastline, during which time the villains would be in full view of their intended victims who would have ample opportunity to escape. This point seems to have eluded those such as C. H. Goekoop and others who have proposed that the 'windy heights' might have been on the adjacent coast of Cephalonia.[16] The fact remains that Dascalion is simply far too distant from Polis Bay to represent any conceivable form of maritime threat.

If Dascalion was not the ambush island of Asteris then the argument for modern Ithaca being the site of ancient Ithaca completely disappears. Remember Homer's description of the ambush island:

The suitors climbed in and began their voyage,
Plotting a merciless death for Telemachos.
There is a rocky island in mid sea
Half way between Ithaca and rugged Samos,
Called Asteris, not large, but with twin bays
For mooring. Here the Achaian ambush waited.   4.842–7

The implications of this are profound. Asteris is in the sea between Ithaca and Samos, and Samos/Same is unquestionably the main land mass of Cephalonia. However, we now know that Dascalion cannot have been Asteris, also that there is no other island in this stretch of the sea and there is no seismic evidence for an insular submersion. It follows that the modern island of Ithaca that you can see right across the straits in Figure 21.1 cannot have been ancient Ithaca.

In view of its size and prominence this island of modern Ithaca could hardly have been ignored by the poet, so if it was not once ancient Ithaca then what was it called instead at that time? In Chapter 5 we saw that Doulichion has

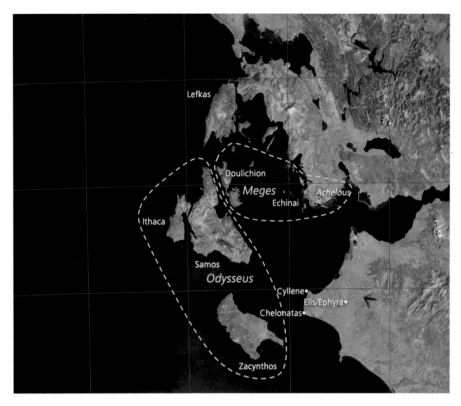

FIGURE 21.11
The domains of Meges
and Odysseus
Colour interpretation: as
Figure 1.3. Grid: 50 km.
[Image credits: as
Figure 1.3.]

for centuries represented a name without a corresponding place, whereas by relocating ancient Ithaca, modern Ithaca has now become a place without a corresponding name. The temptation to solve the puzzle by assigning the Homeric name Doulichion to the island that is today called Ithaca is therefore very strong, but is there any independent support for this solution? Earlier we heard that Doulichion is rich in wheat, that it supported more suitors than any other island and also that it is close to Ithaca. We need to assemble these and other clues: this time there are rather fewer than there were in the quest for Odysseus' Palace. The first relevant passage occurs in the *Iliad*:

> Men from Doulichion and the sacred isles
> Of Echinai, across the sea from Elis,
> Were led by Meges, warrior son of Phyleus,
> The horseman loved by Zeus, who quarrelled with
> His father and migrated to Doulichion.
> Forty black ships sailed under his command.   *Iliad* 2.625–30[17]

This provides us with Doulichion Clue 1: Men from Doulichion and the sacred isles of Echinai are under the leadership of Meges, not Odysseus. The

Echinai are also known as the Echinades and they are located near the mouth of the Achelous river (Figure 21.11).

Strabo explains to us that these islands are 'several in number, poor-soiled and rugged' and that they lie between 5–15 stades off the estuary (about 1–3 km). Interestingly he also says that 'in earlier times they lay out to the high sea, but the silt brought down by the Achelous has already joined some of them to the mainland and will do the same to others' (10.2.19). Apparently by Strabo's time the river outflow had changed the topology considerably. There is further support for this description from Thucydides writing around 400 BC:

Opposite to Oeniadae lie most of the islands called Echinades, so close to the mouths of the Achelous that that powerful stream is constantly forming deposits against them, and has already joined some of the islands to the continent, and seems likely in no long while to do the same with the rest. For the current is strong, deep, and turbid, and the islands are so thick together that they serve to imprison the alluvial deposit and prevent its dispersing, lying, as they do, not in one line, but irregularly, so as to leave no direct passage for the water into the open sea. The islands in question are uninhabited and of no great size. (2.102.3–5)

However, in Odysseus' time we know that these islands were inhabited and led by Meges, so perhaps as Thucydides describes there were formerly some larger inhabited islands that have now become a part of the mainland of Acarnania, leaving only the smaller uninhabited ones behind.

James Diggle points out in his Appendix that the lines 'Men from Doulichion and the sacred isles / Of Echinai, across the sea from Elis' are geographically ambiguous: it is unclear whether 'across the sea from Elis' refers only to the Echinai or also to Doulichion. So Clue 2 is that the Echinai are across the sea from Elis, and Doulichion may be also. From this passage we can in addition glean Clue 3, that Doulichion and the Echinai together provide forty ships for Troy. These greatly outnumber those of Odysseus, who musters only twelve:

Odysseus led the gallant Cephallenians,
From Ithaca and leaf-quivering Neriton,
From Crocyleia and rugged Aigilips,
Men hailing from Zacynthos and from Same,
From the mainland and the region opposite.
Odysseus, equal in resource to Zeus,
Led these, together with twelve red-cheeked ships.   *Iliad* 2.631–7

This provides us with a clear distinction of the respective territories of Meges and Odysseus.[18] It is highly unlikely that either of these leaders would have tolerated the existence of a Gibraltar-like dependency of the other within their own sphere of influence, so Clue 4 is that Doulichion and the Echinai are geographically distinct from Ithaca, Neriton, Crocyleia, Aigilips, Zacynthos and Same. The remaining Homeric clues are in the *Odyssey*:

> All of the noble lords who rule the islands,
> Doulichion and Same and wooded Zacynthos,
> And all who rule in rocky Ithaca.   1.245–7

This yields Clue 5, that Doulichion has its own noble lords.

> I am Odysseus, Laertes' son, world-famed
> For stratagems: my name has reached the heavens.
> Bright Ithaca is my home: it has a mountain,
> Leaf-quivering Neriton, far visible.
> Around are many islands, close to each other,
> Doulichion and Same and wooded Zacynthos.
> Ithaca itself lies low, furthest to sea
> Towards dusk; the rest, apart, face dawn and sun.   9.19–26[19]

This passage provides us with Clue 6, that Doulichion, Same and Zacynthos are nearby Ithaca.

> It happened that a ship owned by Thesprotians
> Was going to Doulichion rich in wheat.
> He told the crew to treat me well and take me
> To king Acastos. But they hatched a plot
> To plunge me deeper into misery.
> When the ship had sailed a good way from the land,
> They set about their scheme to make me a slave.
> They stripped me of my cloak and shirt and gave me
> A nasty set of rags, the very ones
> You see me wearing now. When, in the evening,
> They reached the farmlands of bright Ithaca,
> They bound me tight with plaited ropes and left me
> On board the vessel, while they disembarked
> And took a hasty supper by the shore.   14.334–47[20]

This passage precedes Odysseus' discovery of the 'flowery copse' in Chapter 15 and it provides us with Clue 7, that Doulichion is rich in wheat. The text is another of Odysseus' fabrications but it nevertheless needs to be geographically consistent so we shall pursue it for a little longer. In the ensuing lines the crew turn out to be pirates: Odysseus tells Eumaios that instead of taking him to Doulichion, they decide to land him on Ithaca. Because Thesprotia lies to the north of Lefkas some commentators have proposed that if the pirates detoured to Ithaca while en route to Doulichion, Doulichion itself must lie to the south of Ithaca.[21]

I don't think that follows: at line 14.339 Odysseus says 'When the ship had sailed a good way from the land / They set about their scheme to make me a slave.' This suggests that the Thesprotian crew were looking for a slave market. An obvious one was Ithaca and so they rapidly discarded the instruction to sail to Doulichion. Indeed having concocted this dastardly plot they would have wanted to 'sail a good way from the land' and remain as far away from Doulichion as possible, otherwise they might have bumped into one of King Acastos' pilots who would have scuppered their chances of making a few obols on the sly. Instead Odysseus pretends to Eumaios that they simply keep to the open sea west of Lefkas and sail due south to Ithaca instead of south-east to Doulichion.

The passage therefore provides us with Clue 8, that pirates embarking from Thesprotia could sail a good way from land and divert to Ithaca instead of Doulichion, but that does not require Ithaca to be on a direct route from Thesprotia to Doulichion. It also gives us Clue 9, that Acastos is the king of Doulichion. In the *Iliad* we heard that Meges was the leader of the Doulichians but that was some years earlier, so no contradiction is implied. A page or so later there is another brief mention of Doulichion when Odysseus is still spinning his yarn to Eumaios:

And if your master comes back to this house,
Give me a cloak and tunic and I'll make for
Doulichion, my intended destination.   14.395–7

So this provides us with Clue 10, that Doulichion is a desirable destination not far from Ithaca. Then there are these lines:

The suitors do not number ten or twenty,
They are far more, and here is the full tally:
Fifty-two youths, choice fellows, from Doulichion,
With six attendants at their beck and call;
Twenty-four men from Same, from Zacynthos
Twenty Achaian youths; from Ithaca
Itself a dozen of the very best.   16.245–51

So Clue 11 is that Doulichion provides fifty-two suitors and six attendants, whereas Same provides twenty-four, Zacynthos twenty and Ithaca only twelve. At first sight this is puzzling because Same is a larger island than our candidate for Doulichion, but clearly what matters here is population density rather than land area and that is influenced by other factors such as habitable area, agricultural potential and proximity to civilisation. Although modern Ithaca rises steeply from the sea, there are flat inland areas that are eminently habitable and cultivable. By contrast, although ancient Ithaca slopes gently down to the sea on its southern and south-eastern sides, there is relatively little flat agricultural land elsewhere in its interior.

Another important factor pointed out to me by Lawrence Cartier[22] is that when a Bronze Age colonist decides to embark from mainland Greece to start a new life in the Ionian Islands, this Doulichion is the first significant island to be encountered, so why bother to travel further? Meges' father Phyleus opted for Doulichion so as to put a suitable distance between him and his own father: 'Meges, warrior son of Phyleus, / The horseman loved by Zeus, who quarrelled with / His father and migrated to Doulichion.' Phyleus appears to have lived near Ephyra (see below) so this looks like a short north-westerly migration for him.

> Amphinomos, famous son of princely Nisos,
> Aretes' son, addressed the assembled suitors.
> He was chief suitor from the verdant isle
> Doulichion, rich in wheat. Penelope
> Approved his talk, for he was well intentioned.   16.394–8

This provides us with Clue 12, that Amphinomos, son of Nisos, son of Aretes, leads the suitors from Doulichion, and Clue 13, that Doulichion is not only rich in wheat (which we knew already) but it is also verdant with grassy meadows. Sadly we learn later in the *Odyssey* that Amphinomos is insufficiently well intentioned to avoid a grisly fate at the hands of Telemachos when the suitors are massacred:

> Telemachos was quick, and from behind
> He struck him with his bronze-tipped spear between
> The shoulder-blades and drove it through his chest.
> He crashed to earth and hit the ground full-face.   22.91–4

The remaining references add little to our understanding of this island: apparently Amphinomos inherited his positive qualities from his father, also from Doulichion:

> 'Amphinomos', replied resourceful Odysseus,
> 'You seem to me to be a man of sense,
> Just like your father – men speak well of him,
> The good and wealthy Nisos of Doulichion.'   18.124–7

So Clue 14 is that Amphinomos' father Nisos of Doulichion was a good and wealthy man. At 18.394–6 we hear 'That said, Eurymachos picked up a stool. / Odysseus, in alarm, crouched by the knees / Of Amphinomos from Doulichion', and at 18.423–4 'The noble Moulios from Doulichion, / Amphinomos' squire, mixed them a bowl of wine', so Clue 15 is that the herald Moulios comes from Doulichion. The remaining direct references at 19.130 and 19.291 confirm what we already know. Then at 21.343 there is an interesting indirect hint when Telemachos is speaking to Penelope:[23]

The shrewd Telemachos replied to her:
'Mother, none of the Achaians has more right
Than I to give or to refuse the bow –
Not those who rule in rocky Ithaca
Or on the islands off horse-grazing Elis.'   21.343–7

Telemachos categorises the suitors in two sets: they dwell either in Ithaca or on the islands off Elis. Since we already know from 16.245 above that Doulichion, Same, Zacynthos and Ithaca are the only homes of the suitors, it follows that the poet must regard the description 'the islands off horse-grazing Elis' as an appropriate geographical reference to Doulichion, Same and Zacynthos, giving rise to Clue 16: Doulichion, Same and Zacynthos are islands off horse-grazing Elis.

Figure 21.12 summarises the clues about Doulichion. How well does modern Ithaca fit these clues? They fall into three categories: geographical (2, 4, 6, 8, 10, 16), personal (1, 3, 5, 9, 11, 12, 14, 15) and agricultural (7, 13). The relevant locations are depicted in Figure 21.11. Taking the geographical clues first, Clue 2 in conjunction with Clue 4 clearly supports an interpretation that both Doulichion and the Echinai are 'across the sea from Elis', although not in exactly the same direction. Since we already know that Ithaca is to the west, the furthest out to sea, it follows from Clue 4 that Doulichion and the Echinai must be to the east of Ithaca and its nearby islands, which on the map they are. Clues 6 and 10 are easily satisfied: our Doulichion is only about 4 km from Same. Clue 8 is also complied with: as we have seen the pirates could veer west of Lefkas and head straight for Ithaca without sailing close to Doulichion at all. Finally a glance at Figure 21.11 comfortably confirms Clue 16. It therefore looks as if our candidate island for Doulichion fits all of these geographical clues.

The personal clues require more detailed investigation. Starting with Clue 1, at *Iliad* 13.691–2 we hear that 'Meges, the son of Phyleus, and Amphion / And Dracios commanded the Epeians' while in Chapter 16 we saw that at *Odyssey* 15.298 Telemachos 'passed divine Elis, where the Epeians rule'. At *Iliad* 15.518–19 'Polydamas slew Otos of Cyllene, / Comrade of Phyleus'

1	In the *Iliad* men from Doulichion and the sacred isles of Echinai are under the leadership of Meges, not Odysseus.
2	The Echinai are across the sea from Elis, and Doulichion may be also.
3	Doulichion and the Echinai together provide forty ships for Troy.
4	Doulichion and the Echinai are geographically distinct from Ithaca, Neriton, Crocyleia, Aigilips, Zacynthos and Same.
5	Doulichion has its own noble lords.
6	Doulichion, Same and Zacynthos are nearby Ithaca.
7	Doulichion is rich in wheat.
8	Pirates embarking from Thesprotia could sail a good way from land and divert to Ithaca instead of Doulichion, but that does not require Ithaca to be on a direct route from Thesprotia to Doulichion.
9	In the *Odyssey* Acastos is the king of Doulichion.
10	Doulichion is a desirable destination not far from Ithaca.
11	Doulichion provides fifty-two suitors and six attendants, whereas Same provides twenty-four, Zacynthos twenty and Ithaca only twelve.
12	Amphinomos, son of Nisos, son of Aretes, leads the suitors from Doulichion.
13	As well as being rich in wheat, Doulichion has verdant grassy meadows.
14	Amphinomos' father Nisos of Doulichion was a good and wealthy man.
15	The herald Moulios comes from Doulichion.
16	Doulichion, Same and Zacynthos are islands off horse-grazing Elis.

FIGURE 21.12
Doulichion clues

son, and ruler of / The great-hearted Epeians.' Cyllene is marked just to the north of the western tip of the Peloponnese, so Otos and Meges were presumably friends at the time when Meges was living there when he was younger and his father and grandfather had not yet fallen out.

At *Iliad* 15.529–31 Meges' 'thick corslet saved his life, / Fitted with plates of mail: Phyleus had brought it / From Ephyre, by the river Selleeis'[24] and Strabo tells us in his Book 8.3.5 that 'It is between Chelonatas and Cyllene that the River Peneios empties; as also the river Selleeis, which is mentioned by the poet and flows out of Pholoe. On the Selleeis is situated a city Ephyra, which is to be distinguished from the Thesprotian, Thessalian and Corinthian Ephyras.'[25]

On Figure 21.11 we can see the area around Elis where Meges grew up and also the proposed location of the island of Doulichion to which he emigrated. All of this points to a consistent easterly locus of political and military power for Meges, compared to a westerly orbit for Odysseus. Furthermore this clearly shows that the islands of Atokos and Arkoudi must have also been in Meges' domain, not that of Odysseus, supporting the proposal of Chapter 20 that Crocyleia and Aigilips are nothing to do with these islands.

FIGURE 21.13
The verdant northern
valley of modern Ithaca
*'He was chief suitor from the
verdant isle / Doulichion rich
in wheat' (16.396–8).*

As these references show, the Homeric descriptions of Meges support this identification of Doulichion. So far I have not found any comparable evidence for Acastos, Amphinomos, Nisos, Aretes or Moulios in the *Iliad* or the *Odyssey* or in other sources in relation to clues 9, 12, 14 and 15 but perhaps a reader will rise to this challenge. Meanwhile clues 3, 5 and 11 appear to be mutually consistent in their emphasis on Doulichion as a significant Bronze Age presence: Doulichion and the Echinai together provide forty ships for Troy, Doulichion has its own noble lords and Doulichion provides fifty-two suitors and six attendants; whereas Same provides twenty-four, Zacynthos twenty and Ithaca only twelve. If you accept the argument proposed above that an island's population depends on factors such as habitable area, agricultural potential and proximity to civilisation rather than simply on its surface area then there is no contradiction here.

Finally the agricultural clues at 7 and 13 state that Doulichion has grassy meadows and is rich in wheat. The pattern of agricultural activity has doubtless changed over the millennia but Figure 21.13 indicates that the northern valley near Anogi (on the way to the 'School of Homer') is a lush agricultural bowl that would certainly support wheat fields and grassy meadows. As Mark Bittlestone has pointed out, these valleys represent a natural collection basin for the rainfall from the surrounding mountains.

My own summary of the match between these Homeric clues for Doulichion and modern Ithaca is that there is no dismaying contradiction but there is also no decisive confirmation. Is there any evidence elsewhere that can help us? Strabo says at his Book 10.2.19 'To the east of Zacynthos and Cephallenia are situated the Echinades Islands, among which is Doulichion, now called Dolicha.' We must be wary here because although at 10.2.15 Strabo memorably explained to us that 'Where the island is narrowest it forms a low isthmus, so that it is often submerged from sea to sea'[26] ironically he failed to realise the implications of this seaway that I have christened Strabo's Channel. As we have seen, he identifies ancient Ithaca as modern Ithaca although he is puzzled about why it is not to the west, the furthest out to sea and also by its mismatch with other descriptions. He quotes a circumference for Ithaca that disagrees with today's value, but as with Cephalonia itself in Chapter 6 he is often at odds with modern measures of perimeter. So he is more or less obliged to locate Doulichion with the Echinades because he has no other island available and we should not therefore rely on this identification.

But what about his statement that Doulichion is 'now called Dolicha'? Figure 21.2 depicts Dascalion from Doulicha Bay and it is photographed from the Cephalonian side, from ancient Same. So why is there a bay on Cephalonia called Doulicha Bay exactly opposite the northern harbour of ancient Dolicha? Might it have been thus named because it was the embarkation harbour for Dolicha? In other words, if you are situated on Same and you want to get to Dolicha, you would need to take the ferry from Dolicha Bay. It is intriguing but perhaps circumstantial.

Another interesting observation is that by the eighth century BC when the Olympic Games were instituted on the mainland near Elis, one of the events was the *dolichos*, an endurance race of 3,800 m.[27] Perhaps it is just a coincidence that the distance from Doulicha Bay to Doulichion is exactly 1 *dolichos*, although it would be fascinating to know if the flow of cause and effect was actually reversed: that the event was named after the length of the crossing from Same to Doulichion. But this is probably too whimsical a speculation because the Greek word simply means 'long': indeed this usage predates New York's Long Island by several millennia.

The suggestion that modern Ithaca was formerly Doulichion is not an original one: the name is used to describe the island on several historical maps. Figure 21.14 is a detail from a map of the Ionian Islands produced by the Parisian cartographer Jean-Baptiste Bourguignon d'Anville in 1768.[28] On today's island of Ithaca you can see the inscription 'ITHACA, forte et Dulichium' ('Ithaca, perhaps also Dulichium'). Just to be on the safe side (and no doubt following Strabo) he has also applied the name 'Dolicha' to an island of the Echinades to the east.

The difficulty with this material is one of knowing whether the map-maker was following an established tradition of local nomenclature or whether it was more a case of wishful thinking based on the Homeric texts. Indeed d'Anville

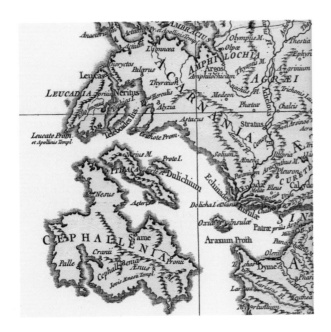

FIGURE 21.14
D'Anville's
eighteenth-century map of
Cephalonia
*The cartographer indicates
that today's Ithaca might
have been ancient Doulichion.*
[Image credits: d'Anville
(1768), published in le
Noan (2001).]

himself has conveniently drawn an island called Asteris where no such land
mass exists. However in his 2001 interactive publication *A la recherche d'Ithaque*
Gilles le Noan devotes a chapter[29] to this question and he identifies a history
of this usage dating back to the Romans. When I received his CD-ROM in
June 2003 I was delighted to find that he has unearthed some unique and
persuasive material.

Working backwards through the centuries, Gilles le Noan points out that
the intrepid explorer Jacob Spon, accompanying Sir George Wheler, says in
his *Travels in Italy, Dalmatia, Greece and the Levant in 1675–1676*:

Regarding [Thiaki], *I think that it is the island of Dulichium, because there is in front
a large Port with the hovels of a town still called Dolicha, as Strabo remarked that it
was called in his time; that seems to me to be convincing enough.*[30]

Spon somewhat heretically located ancient Ithaca on the tiny island of
Atokos by appealing to Strabo's perimeter estimates, but we have already
noted the ancient muddle on this matter. However the most interesting detail
that le Noan has identified here is that on 1 August 1675 when Spon and
Wheler visited modern Ithaca (Thiaki) there were apparently still the ruins of
a town there called Dolicha. In his own subsequent account of their voyage
(largely a translation of Spon's French publication) Wheler confirms that this
port was on the eastern side, which was probably therefore today's capital of
Vathy.[31]

Le Noan then cites two descriptions of Ithaca from a book about celebrated islands published in Venice in 1576 by Thomaso Porcacchi:

Subordinate to the island of Cefalonia is the Island of Théachi, formerly known as Ithace, which is also called Dulichio and Island of Compare, the fatherland of Ulysses.
One finds Dulichio, which was formerly called Ithaca and is today known as the Island of Compare and Théachi, the homeland of Ulysses, mountainous with great cliffs and a small plain in the centre.[32]

From a 1575 'Universal Cosmography' le Noan has tracked down the line:

It appears that Dulichia and Ithaca are still known today under the name Val de Compare.[33]

He also cites Cristoforo Buondelmonti, writing (in Latin) probably in the 1420s:

We have discussed Leucas [Lefkas]. We now move to Dulichia, which was once Ithaca and is now called Val di Compare.[34]

The Orsini family of Naples occupied the islands from the beginning of the thirteenth century and they were followed by the Venetians until 1797. Le Noan believes that during this period of nearly 600 years the ancient Greek name of Dulichia lapsed and was replaced by the Italian 'Val di Compare'. He suggests that during this period travellers and geographers looking for the homeland of Odysseus continued to refer to the Island of Compare by what they believed to be its ancient name of Ithaca. After the Venetian occupation there was an obvious need to christen the island with a Greek name and the natural (and also popular) choice would therefore have been Thiaki/Ithaca.

Support for le Noan's hypothesis comes from the splendid William Mure whom we first encountered in Chapter 9 as he giggled over Gell's gullibility. I was delighted to discover that on 21 February 1838 as he sailed into modern Ithaca he informed his readers that:

In the year 1504 Ithaca was uninhabited, and record is extant of privileges offered by the Venetian government to the settlers by whom it was repeopled.[35]

Mure acknowledged in a footnote that he had gleaned this invaluable intelligence from his compatriot William Leake who travelled to Ithaca on 15 September 1806. Leake stayed with the English vice-consul Constantine Zavó whose father held the same office for fifty years and who 'has lately excited considerable discontent by disarming the Ithacans and taking away from them even the small knives which they wore in their girdles'. Zavó would therefore appear to be a law-abiding and reliable source for Leake's statement that:

In a decree of the senate of Venice, dated in the year 1504, of which a copy still exists at Vathy, lands are offered gratia, and an exemption from all imposts for ten years in the uninhabited island lying on the eastern side of Cefalonia called Val di Compare, or Val di Compagne: in consequence of this decree the island was occupied, and 25 years afterwards it was governed by a Venetian styled Il Capitano.[36]

If today's island of Ithaca was described in 1504 by the senate of Venice as uninhabited then presumably its last Greek occupant had left it some years previously. Given that it was then resettled over the next twenty-five years by immigrants attracted by tax exemptions (who were also prepared to submit to the governorship of a Venetian styled Il Capitano) it seems to me not implausible that its original Greek name of Dulichia might have been mislaid in the process.

We now return to le Noan who has researched the island nomenclature further back in time: he quotes from a 'Maritime Itinerary' of the second to third centuries AD:

The islands Cephalenia, Zacinthos and Dulichia: here is mount Ithacus, where the homeland of Ulysses is.

This description lists only three islands: Ithaca is not mentioned as an island at all and its name has been transferred to a mountain on Doulichion. In Appendix 1 Section D James Diggle has revisited this and other classical references to Doulichion and he presents us with some additional findings. Writing in the first century BC, Virgil describes Odysseus' ships as Dulichian not Ithacan, and Propertius refers to Odysseus returning to Dulichia rather than to Ithaca. James concludes his analysis by explaining that by the first century BC it appears that today's island of Ithaca was then called Dulichia.

We already have two anchor points for our subsequent discussion of the timescale of infill in Strabo's Channel: (a) it was open for navigation in the time of Odysseus and (b) it had become harder or impossible to navigate by the time of Strabo's sources (second century BC). We can now add (c): by the first century BC ancient Ithaca so little resembled an island that its name had been transferred to a real island nearby, even though that island already had a name of its own, and by the second to third century AD the former two islands had fused together into the single island of Cephalonia.

Just how solid was the channel infill in Strabo's time? Writing about the battle of Plataia between the Greeks and the Persians in 479 BC Herodotus says:

Next to the men of Hermione were six hundred Eretrians and Styreans; next to them, four hundred Chalcidians; next again, five hundred Ampraciots. After these stood eight hundred Leucadians and Anactorians, and next to them two hundred from Pale in Cephallenia.

(9.28.5)

This tells us that by the fifth century BC Herodotus regards Pale as part of Cephallenia, not Ithaca. A little later Thucydides is writing about the Peloponnesian War (431–404 BC) and he says of the Athenians:

Next they sailed to the island of Cephallenia and brought it over without using force. Cephallenia lies off Acarnania and Leucas, and consists of four states, the Paleans, Cranians, Samaeans, and Pronaeans.

(2.30.2)

So by the end of the fifth century BC it is clear that Thucydides also thinks of Cephallenia as a single island. We can therefore draw back our third anchor from the first to the fifth century BC: it appears that the former marine channel had already been bridged by then. But the land-bridge at that time must have been little higher than a sandbank to enable Strabo to have written 'Where the island is narrowest it forms an isthmus, so that it is often submerged from sea to sea.' Today's 180 m high central infill must therefore have resulted from one or more subsequent – and very substantial – landslips.

On our way back from Dascalion to Fiscardo we meet the search launch that has come out to find us: I am contrite because we are late returning the boat. This town was named after the Norman Roberto Guiscardo who landed on Cephalonia in AD 1082 but it dates back much earlier than that: a short tour reveals Roman ruins by the seafront. Further to the north there is the shell of a sixth- to ninth-century Byzantine monastery on the promontory amidst an area of extensive and strangely distorted ancient stonework. As we walk up from the harbour I look down to see a sloping stone with some unusual markings on it (Figure 21.15).

Is it just coincidental that these indentations look rather like fish? Did they arise from natural weathering or did somebody patiently produce them? If they are man-made, then who carved these simple fish designs upon this rock and when were they created? The one at the bottom right looks surprisingly like a lobster: was it a local fisherman a few years ago who chiselled away idly at this stone? Could it instead have been a Venetian or one of Orsini's earlier Neapolitans? Might it have been one of Roberto Guiscardo's men, gazing out at this beautiful harbour not long after his compatriot invaded England, or instead a Byzantine monk many years before that? Was it a Roman centurion, chipping away as he waited for a ship to take him home across the Adriatic? Or were these shapes carved in Odysseus' time around 1200 BC?

FIGURE 21.15
Strange rock carvings at
Fiscardo
*Are these random natural
shapes or artificial images of
marine life?*

Perhaps sailors used this harbour even earlier. This is the northernmost point of Cephalonia: from here the *Captain Aristides* ferry departs for Lefkas and other destinations. It is a natural place for an ancient settlement and in 1984 the archaeologist George Kavvadias published findings in his book *Paleolithic Cephalonia*[37] claiming that the presence of 'Fiscardo man' can be identified as far back as 50,000 BC. That is sufficiently long ago for the sea level to have been at least 100 m lower than it is today and for Cephalonia to have been joined to mainland Greece via a land bridge. These global sea level changes have nothing to do with the local upthrusting earthquakes that act in the opposite direction in Cephalonia: instead they reflect the advance and decline of glaciers at the north and south poles.

As I watch the tourists filling the restaurants on the seafront it is almost impossible to imagine a town's history stretching out along a chronological scale of this magnitude. How many warriors over how many millennia have arrived from land or sea to invade this natural haven? Could one of them have been Odysseus' father?

Notes
1 Heikell (2003a). This place name is also reported in Gell (1807) p. 74.
2 The photograph is reproduced with the kind permission of Mrs Fotini Kouvara, curator of the Stavros Museum. It is also reproduced in Souyoudzoglou-Haywood (1999) plate 23A, where the caption reads 'Sylvia Benton emerging from the cave of Polis during her investigations.' I am however indebted to Dr Catherine Morgan for advising me that

the person emerging from the cave is not in fact Sylvia Benton herself; instead it is she who is supervising the proceedings from the chair above.

3 I later learnt that this cave was explored by Vollgraff in 1907; see Appendix 4.
4 Waterhouse (1996).
5 Wace and Stubbings (1962) p. 420.
6 Waterhouse (1996).
7 This observation is consistent with the average rise of 1 m per 1,000 years documented in Chapter 7 n.6 but it does not take account of any local tectonic movements on modern Ithaca itself.
8 Wace and Stubbings (1962) p. 418.
9 Morgan (2003) pp. 218–20; Whitley (2003) pp. 42–4; Whitley (2002–3) p. 31.
10 Anthony Snodgrass points out that the 'Twelve noble princes [who] / hold authority throughout the land – including me, thirteen' at 8.390–1 are probably not the same group (either in composition or in number) as those referred to much later at 13.13–14 in the words 'But let us each now give him a large tripod / And cauldron.' He suggests that although the first set of gifts (robes, tunics and gold talents) was donated by Alcinoos and the twelve noble princes, the second set (tripods and cauldrons) involved an unspecifed number of donors. His reasoning runs as follows.

At 7.186 Alcinoos addresses the 'Captains and leaders of Phaiacia'. He tells them to enjoy their dinner and then go home to bed. At 7.189 he then says to them 'Tomorrow we shall summon more of the elders' so that they can entertain the stranger again and make provision for his return home. The next day the party resumes in the palace after an assembly and at 8.387 Alcinoos once more addresses the 'Captains and leaders', proposing that he and the twelve 'noble princes' should donate clothes and gold. The twelve comply and their presents, together with Euryalos' silver-studded sword and ivory scabbard and Alcinoos' cloak, tunic and gold libation cup, are placed inside the treasure chest which Odysseus then fastens using Circe's knot.

Much later on, when Odysseus has finished telling his tales, Alcinoos addresses the whole company, whom he describes at 13.8–9 as the 'regular drinkers of his wine', and calls for gifts of a tripod and cauldron from each one (13.13–15). These habitual alcoholics are presumably those referred to as the 'elders' of 7.189 and they are clearly distinct from the earlier group of Alcinoos and his twelve 'noble princes'.

Anthony also regards as noteworthy the use of the third person plural *eneikan* at 13.12 in reference to the first group ('gifts which *they* brought here'), compared with the first person plural *domen* for the second group at 13.13 ('*we* must give him'). It is indeed curious that Alcinoos should expect the same twelve princes who have already produced and packed their gifts for Odysseus to go and fetch some more, even if (to use Anthony's apt expression) they can claim them on expenses.

During a visit to the Stavros Museum on 11 August 2004 Anthony formed the opinion that of the fifteen individual tripod-legs on display, only two pairs were from the same tripod. This means that there are at least thirteen tripods at the museum rather than the twelve that have previously been documented. The inclusion of the 'missing' tripod allegedly discovered by the landowner Loizos then brings us to the unexpected position of accounting for at least fourteen tripods. However if Anthony's interpretation is correct there is no reason why there should ever have been exactly thirteen tripods in the first place, so the rather convenient total of thirteen tripods that are alleged to have been found may represent a combination of overactive imagination with underactive analysis.

11 Souyoudzoglou-Haywood (1999) plates 64b, 64c.
12 Souyoudzoglou-Haywood (1999) p. 95.
13 Luce (1998) pp. 178–9.
14 The same observation was made by C. H. Goekoop: see Goekoop (1990) ch. 3 p. 92 (fragment 37).

15 Schliemann (1880) p. 46; Schliemann (1869) p. 75; quoted in Schuchhardt and Schliemann (1891) p. 304.

16 Goekoop (1990) ch. 3. p. 92 (fragment 37).

17 See James Diggle's comments on this passage in Appendix 1 Section J.

18 On the basis of these boundaries Meges would appear to have contributed to the Trojan War a dramatically greater ratio of ships per acre of land than Odysseus. Others have considered the possibility that Meges' dominion may have extended to the mainland area of Acarnania: see for example le Noan (2004) pp. 25–32.

19 See James Diggle's comments on this passage in Appendix 1 Section G.

20 See James Diggle's comments on this passage in Appendix 1 Section J.

21 See for example Goekoop (1990) ch. 3 p. 86 (fragment 27).

22 Lawrence Cartier is my solicitor: I must be particularly scrupulous in recognising his contribution.

23 This observation is due to C. H. Goekoop: see Goekoop (1990) ch. 3 p. 95 (fragment 42).

24 For a remarkable photograph and description of a late fifteenth-century BC corslet found in 1960 at Dendra near Mycenae see Snodgrass (1967) p. 24 and fig. 9.

25 Strabo may not have located these river estuaries correctly because today's maps show the river Peneios joining the sea to the south-east of Chelonatas. Even taking into account known changes in the shoreline in this area, an estuary between Chelonatas and Cyllene would seem to require water to climb up through the hilly countryside of that promontory to a height of about 100 m above sea level. Perhaps we can allow the great geographer the odd slip. This geographical anomaly was noted by Leake who wrote 'for that the Peneius was the Selleeis of the poet, there can be little doubt, as it is the only considerable river in this part of the country.' He also felt that 'the probability is, that the town of Elis was at that time named Ephyra, and that it assumed under Oxylus [the Aetolian, on the return of the Heraclidae], who enlarged it, the name which had before been applied to the district [of Elis]' (Leake (1830) vol. I pp. 6–7).

26 From this point onwards I have adopted James Diggle's translation (in Appendix 2 Section B) of Strabo's description of the semi-submerged isthmus at 10.2.15.

27 See http://www.georama.gr/eng/world/06.html

28 D'Anville (1768), published in le Noan (2001).

29 Le Noan (2001) ch. 5.

30 Spon (1678) vol. I, pp. 77–80.

31 Wheler (1682) Book 1 p. 36.

32 Porcacchi (1576) pp. 75, 96.

33 Münster and de Belleforest (1575) vol. II, p. 85.

34 Buondelmonti (c. 1385–1430) p. 57.

35 Mure (1842) vol. I p. 39.

36 Leake (1835) vol. III p. 25.

37 Kavvadias (1984) p. 14.

CHAPTER 22 Laertes

> *'If only,*
> *By father Zeus, Athene, and Apollo,*
> *I were the man I was when I took the city*
> *Of well-built Nericon, the mainland cape,*
> *As ruler of the Cephallenians.'*
>
>

Odyssey 24.375–9

Laertes is speaking to his son just after their reunion towards the end of the *Odyssey*. All the suitors have been slaughtered and Odysseus has left the palace in search of his father. Once again there is a unique place name reference: the word 'Nericon' occurs only in this one passage of the *Odyssey* and never in the *Iliad*. Scholars have pointed out that the place names Nericon, Neriton and Neïon are strangely similar, but we are clearly dealing with three quite distinct locations. Nericon is described here as a well-built city: it cannot possibly be confused with leaf-quivering Mount Neriton which looms above Phorcys Bay. Meanwhile Mount Neïon, as we saw in Chapter 19, is distinct from Mount Neriton and lies along the western coast of Paliki.[1]

What else do we know about Laertes? He married Anticleia, who died of grief when Odysseus was on his travels. Her father was Autolycos of whom a brief but effective character assassination is provided at 19.395: 'he excelled all men in thievery and in oaths'. Her mother was Amphithea and as a youth Odysseus used to visit his maternal grandparents near Parnassos, a voyage of about 180 km along the northern coast of the Gulf of Corinth. During a hunting expedition there a white-tusked boar scarred his leg and it is this mark that identifies him to Philoitios the cowherd and to Eumaios at 21.220, to Eurycleia his nursemaid at 19.394 and to Laertes himself at 24.330. It must have been a traumatic injury and I shudder to think of the language that filled the air when his grandfather heard about the incident.

We learn from Telemachos at 16.118 that Laertes' father was Arceisios. His mother was Chalcomedousa and we also read at 15.363 that Odysseus had a sister, Ctimene, who was sent to Same to be married.[2] We are not sure whom she married but the Byzantine scholar Eustathius in his commentary on the *Odyssey* suggests that her husband was Eurylochos, who accompanied Odysseus on his return from Troy and provided wise advice to him regarding Circe. Unfortunately Eurylochos' appetite triumphed over his judgement on the island of Helios where he encouraged the crew to partake of rump steak, a feast that greatly displeased the sungod so that all except Odysseus perished

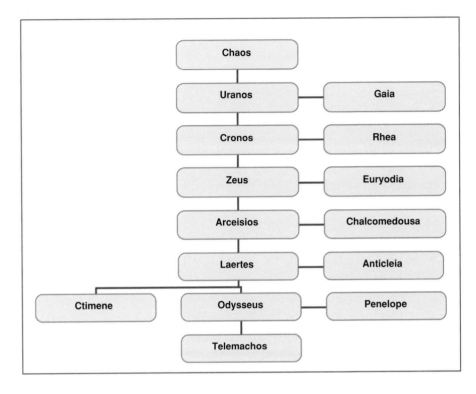

FIGURE 22.1
Odysseus' family tree
[Data source: Newman
and Newman (2003)
p. 5c.]

in the ensuing shipwreck. We do not hear whether Odysseus subsequently apologised to his sister about his culpable negligence over the drowning of his brother-in-law.

Odysseus' wife Penelope was the daughter of Icarios and Periboia (or maybe Polycaste: Icarios had roving eyes). It is perhaps time to take a look at the Odyssean family tree (Figure 22.1) where for clarity I have focused on the paternal line. From a reproductive standpoint this simple diagram is massively incomplete: indeed most of the Greeks at that time were notorious philanderers and the extent of their dalliances with nymphs, mortals and assorted goddesses is described in a remarkable recent publication called *A Genealogical Chart of Greek Mythology* which traces the ancestors of Odysseus as well as 3,672 other figures of Greek mythology interrelated over twenty generations.[3]

Homer does not refer to Telemachos' possible marriage and progeny although others do, but I have resisted the temptation to speculate on that in the diagram. What is however rather striking from the chart is the observation that Zeus was felt to be Odysseus' great-grandfather, albeit not through any labour of Hera but via a rather briefer confinement in a Bronze Age broom cupboard with a wench called Euryodia. By this account our hero's blood is distinctly blue: on Ithaca he is indeed a living legend.

As well as the challenge of identifying Nericon we also need to work out the location of Laertes' farm. In Chapter 19 we deduced from Telemachos' conversation with Athene five important clues: (1) there is a suitable place to moor a ship beyond the spit of land at the north-west of Argostoli Bay, (2) the mooring is called Rheithron Bay, (3) it lies under wooded Mount Neïon, (4) Laertes' farm is nearby and (5) Athene does not say that Laertes' farm is invisible from the palace, only that her ship is. From the palace clue list of Chapter 17 we also have Clue 6: Laertes' farmstead lies in the countryside beyond the palace when one is coming from the pigfarm. We also saw that Athene refers to Laertes at line at 1.193 as crawling 'along his hilly vineyard's slopes' so Clue 7 is that there is a steep vineyard at Laertes' farm.

At 23.359–60 Odysseus announces 'Now I will go to the farm with its many trees, / To see my noble father' so Clue 8 is that the farm has many trees. At 24.205–6, 12 we hear that 'They went down from the town and quickly reached / Laertes' fine, well-built estate . . . in the country far from town' so Clue 9 is that from the palace one can reach Laertes' estate quickly, even though it is far from town and Clue 10 is that the farm is lower than the town. At 24.223–5 we hear that 'They had gone off / To gather stones for a protecting wall / For the orchard',[4] so Clue 11 is that the farm has an orchard.

Then at 24.299–301 Laertes asks Odysseus (whom he does not yet recognise) a very interesting question:

> Where is the ship which brought you and your godly
> Companions here? Or were you a passenger
> On another's ship, which landed you and left?

This provides us with Clue 12, that Laertes cannot see Odysseus' ship from his farmstead, and also Clue 13, that Laertes can see the sea from his farmland. Odysseus replies at 24.306–8:

> Some god drove me hither
> Off course from Sicily, against my wish.
> My ship stands here in the country far from town.

This is of considerable help for two reasons. First, if you had set sail from Sicily and been blown off course so as to end up in ancient Ithaca then it is clear from Figure 22.2 that you would be far more likely to enter the wide mouth of Argostoli Bay in the south than the narrow inlet of Strabo's Channel from the north. There are no feasible locations for a farmstead on the steep western coast of Ithaca so this provides us with Clue 14, that Odysseus' supposed ship is moored somewhere in Argostoli Bay.

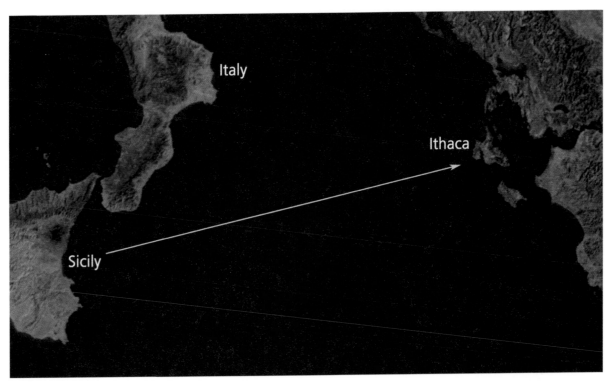

FIGURE 22.2
Odysseus' supposed
course from Sicily
*Colour interpretation: as
Figure 3.1.*
[Image credits: as
Figure 3.1.]

Second, if the line 'My ship stands *here* in the country far from town' sounds familiar then that is because it is. We first encountered it in Chapter 2 when Athene disguised as Mentes describes her imaginary ship to Telemachos at the beginning of the *Odyssey* (1.185–6):

My ship stands here in the country far from town,
In Rheithron bay, below wooded Neïon.

This passage was then discussed in more detail in Chapter 19 where we identified the spit of land in Figure 19.5 as the geographical feature that would maintain the credibility of Athene's description to an Ithacan audience. Now we fast-forward to the closing lines of the poem and this time it is Odysseus in disguise who says to Laertes at 24.308:

My ship stands here in the country far from town.

This line that Odysseus delivers is exactly the same as the first line that Athene uttered earlier: he even uses the same word to mean 'over here'. However, in this case he does not follow up these words with Athene's second line:

In Rheithron bay, below wooded Neïon.

We saw earlier that Athene was pointing down the bay towards a ship that Telemachos cannot see. This time it is Odysseus who is pointing down the bay towards a ship that Laertes cannot see. We know Laertes cannot see it because he has just asked Odysseus where it is:

> Where is the ship which brought you and your godly
> Companions here?

And again there are two good reasons why Laertes cannot see Odysseus' ship. The first is that Odysseus says that his ship stands 'over here' in the country far from town – in other words it is not far from where Laertes is standing but it is nevertheless hidden from his view. The second is that, as before, the ship doesn't actually exist because Odysseus is only kidding his father when he says that he has sailed in from Sicily – in fact he has just walked down from the palace: 'They went down from the town and quickly reached / Laertes' fine, well-built estate.' So once more we are obliged to recognise a crucial point.

Homer's audience knows that Odysseus wants Laertes to believe that he is a visitor from Sicily who would obviously have needed a real ship on which to sail to Ithaca. So as far as Laertes is concerned Odysseus therefore has to pretend that he does indeed have a real ship. But at the same time it is essential that the audience appreciates that Laertes cannot actually see a ship, since if he says he can then the whole story will fall apart because they know that there isn't one. Just as at the outset of the *Odyssey*, the poet's description 'far from town' is by no means arbitrary: the logic of the situation combined with the topographical knowledge of his audience obliges Homer to have Odysseus state that his imaginary ship cannot be seen from Laertes' farmstead.

We concluded previously that Athene must be pretending that her ship is moored on the western shore of Argostoli Bay and for it to be out of sight from the palace hilltop it must be presumed to lie somewhere beyond the spit of land jutting out into the bay in Figure 19.5. Although this analysis does not prove that these two imaginary ships were moored in exactly the same place, the requirement for marine concealment combined with reasonable proximity and the repetition of the same opening line of description makes this seem likely. So this diagnosis provides us with Clue 15, that Odysseus can moor an imaginary ship close to Laertes' farm but nevertheless out of view, and also Clue 16, that it is likely that Athene's imaginary ship and that of Odysseus were moored in the same place. Furthermore the fact that Odysseus says to Laertes that his ship is 'in the country far from town' whereas one can 'quickly walk down from the town' to reach the farm supports Clue 17, that one reaches the farm before the mooring when walking down from the town. At 24.353–5 Laertes says:

I am terrified that all the Ithacans
May rush to fight us here and send round news
To the cities of the Cephallenians.

This provides us with Clue 18, that all the Ithacans can reach Laertes' farm quite rapidly, and also Clue 19, that the cities of the Cephallenians are not identical to those of Ithaca even though in the *Iliad* we read (at 2.631) that Odysseus led the gallant Cephallenians. At 24.375–9 we encounter the lines that opened this chapter:

The shrewd Laertes answered him: 'If only,
By father Zeus, Athene, and Apollo,
I were the man I was when I took the city
Of well-built Nericon, the mainland cape,
As ruler of the Cephallenians.'

So from this we deduce Clue 20 that well-built Nericon is on a mainland cape, Clue 21 that Laertes was once the ruler of the Cephallenians and Clue 22 that Nericon can meaningfully be captured by a ruler of the Cephallenians, so prior to that it was presumably not regarded as part of the Cephallenian empire.

We also note the use of the word 'mainland' again (the Greek word is *epeiros*) and you will recall the detailed discussion of its meaning in Chapter 8 and Appendix 1. The outcome of that analysis was that when the word 'mainland' is used on Ithaca, it refers to the main land mass of Same (i.e. eastern Cephalonia) rather than to Greece itself, but otherwise the conventional meaning of mainland Greece generally applies. However we should also remember that the 'island' of Lefkas has at varying times been connected to the mainland of Greece via a causeway, so it too may be referred to as 'mainland'. This gives us three logical possibilities and Clue 23 is therefore that the cape of Nericon could be on Same or on Lefkas or even on the mainland of Greece itself.

Finally we should note Clue 24, that when Athene says 'In Rheithron Bay' the Greek place name 'Rheithron' also means a river or stream, and Clue 25, that the word used for 'bay' (*limen*) can also mean a creek, harbour or haven.

So once again, by the end of this analysis twenty-five clues have emerged (see Figure 22.3).

Clues 4, 7, 8 and 11 indicate that Laertes' farm is nearby and it has a steep vineyard with many trees and an orchard. We hear quite a lot more about the farm's arboriculture: at 24.221 it is described as having a 'fruitful vineyard'; at 24.222 a 'great orchard'; at 24.226 a 'well-made vineyard'; and at 24.234 Laertes stands beside a 'tall pear tree'. At 24.245–7 Odysseus says 'All things in the garden, / Each plant, each fig, each vine, each pear, each olive, / Each

1	There is a suitable place to moor a ship beyond the spit of land at the north-west of Argostoli Bay.
2	The mooring is called Rheithron Bay.
3	It lies under wooded Mount Neïon.
4	Laertes' farm is nearby.
5	Athene does not say that Laertes' farm is invisible from the palace, only that her ship is.
6	Laertes' farmstead lies in the countryside beyond the palace when one is coming from the pigfarm.
7	There is a steep vineyard at Laertes' farm.
8	The farm has many trees.
9	From the palace one can reach Laertes' estate quickly, even though it is far from town.
10	The farm is lower than the town.
11	The farm has an orchard.
12	Laertes cannot see Odysseus' ship from his farmstead.
13	Laertes can see the sea from his farmland.
14	Odysseus' supposed ship is moored somewhere in Argostoli Bay.
15	Odysseus can moor an imaginary ship close to Laertes' farm but nevertheless out of view.
16	It is likely that Athene's imaginary ship and that of Odysseus were moored in the same place.
17	One reaches the farm before the mooring when walking down from the town.
18	All the Ithacans can reach Laertes' farm quite rapidly.
19	The cities of the Cephallenians are not identical to those of Ithaca even though in the *Iliad* we read (at 2.631) that 'Odysseus led the gallant Cephallenians'.
20	Well-built Nericon is on a mainland cape.
21	Laertes was once the ruler of the Cephallenians.
22	Nericon can meaningfully be captured by a ruler of the Cephallenians, so prior to that it was not regarded as part of the Cephallenian empire.
23	The cape of Nericon could be on Same or on Lefkas or even on the mainland of Greece itself.
24	When Athene says 'In Rheithron bay' the Greek place name Rheithron also means a river or stream.
25	The word used for 'bay' (*limen*) can also mean a creek, harbour or haven.

FIGURE 22.3
Laertes' clues

flower-bed is tended carefully.' After he reveals his identity to his father with the story of the wound from the white-tusked boar he says:

> 'Once, when I was a boy, I followed you
> Around the orchard, begging you for trees.
> You gave me what I asked, and as we passed them
> You named each one: let me describe them now.
> You gave me thirteen pear-trees, ten of apple,
> And forty figs, and promised you would add
> As many as fifty vine-rows, with all kinds
> Of clustering grapes, and each row ripening
> In turn, whatever season pressed upon them.'

24.336–44

Once again there is a dog that doesn't bark. What do all these vines and trees need in order to flourish? Water, clearly, and plenty of it. It is inconceivable that an orchard on this scale could be watered by bringing buckets from afar: it must lie on the course of a significant stream. Could that stream be the Rheithron? Not if the farm is by the sea, because Clues 2, 24 and 25 tell us that the Rheithron stream is at or near the mooring of the imaginary ships, while at the same time Clue 12 tells us that Laertes cannot see Odysseus' ship from his farmstead. Could his farm instead lie on the Rheithron brook but some way upstream from the sea, well inland so that he cannot see Odysseus' ship? No, because Clue 10 tells us that the farm is lower than the town and Clue 13 indicates that Laertes can see the sea from his farmland. So this means that Laertes' farm must lie near the sea on a different stream to Rheithron and Clue 17 enables us to deduce that this stream is reached first when walking down from the town.

We are therefore looking for two streams on the north-west of Argostoli Bay, one of them discharging into the sea near the spit of land that juts out into the bay (and thereby naming an adjacent bay for the mooring that is concealed from both the palace and the farm), and the other running out closer to the town and capable of watering a very significant orchard. It is time to consult Quickbird again.

The only significant watercourses near the spit of land are readily apparent from the infra-red imagery and I have highlighted them on Figure 22.4.[5]

The southernmost stream joins the bay at a point (Figure 22.5) that is today called Cape Samoli.

A few more clicks on the mouse reveals a small jetty to the south of the point (Figure 22.6). I am curious about this jetty: could it have been there during the Bronze Age? What does all this look like on the ground?

The Rheithron stream is now a modest outflow meandering through the fields and discharging into Argostoli Bay through waving reeds and pebbled banks (Figure 22.7). Although the Crikellos hill lies behind it and generally obscures the view to Mount Neïon in the far west, there is a 'V'-shaped cleft in the middle of it that enables one to see through to the mountains behind – but only if one is standing within a few hundred metres of this particular point.

This stream crosses the modern road to Lixouri at the ancient village just a short distance inland called Samoli. There is something timeless about the way that its watercourse cuts through the valley and the fields above the bay (Figure 22.8).

The jetty to the south that I could see on the satellite image is undoubtedly old, but I cannot tell how old. However the adjacent stonework above the present shoreline identifies a time when the sea levels here were higher and the water clearly lapped at these rocks (Figure 22.9). Even the 60 cm upthrust in 1953 would have made a significant difference to the local sea level at this location.

northern
stream

southern
stream

FIGURE 22.4
Low resolution image of
NW Argostoli Bay with
streams
Colour interpretation: as
Figure 20.1. Grid: 1 km.
[Image credits: as
Figure 20.1.]

FIGURE 22.5
Medium resolution image
of Rheithron stream
Colour interpretation: as
Figure 20.1. Grid: 500 m.
[Image credits: as
Figure 20.1.]

FIGURE 22.6
High resolution image of
Rheithron stream
*Colour interpretation: as
Figure 20.1. Grid: 200 m.*
[Image credits: as
Figure 20.1.]

FIGURE 22.7
Rheithron stream
at Cape Samoli
*'My ship stands here in the
country far from town, / In
Rheithron bay, below wooded
Neïon' (1.185–6). Only along
this short stretch of the
coastline can one actually see
the distant mountain behind
the nearby hills.*

FIGURE 22.8
The Rheithron stream in
the Samoli countryside
*The photograph was taken
looking westwards from the
junction of the stream and the
Lixouri road on Figure 22.5.*

Meanwhile there is Laertes' farm to consider further to the north. As we saw this must also be based on a watercourse and Figure 22.4 shows us that there is only one significant stream available. In Figure 22.10 this area has been magnified: it lies on the Atheras road just north of the turning to Petani Beach. The stream shows bright pink in this false infra-red image as it descends the hillside from the left. In the centre of the photograph you can see it curving past a plantation of regularly spaced trees.

In Figure 22.11 the magnification is increased again. There are extensive signs of agriculture across the terrain and a distinctive geometrical pattern within the orchard. The northernmost track off the main road winds up the steep slopes of a hillside to a farmhouse.

The view from the top of the hill is spectacular: in the distance I can just make out the Argostoli peninsula shimmering in the heat-haze, for all the world like an island rising up from the sea (Figure 22.12).

FIGURE 22.9 The jetty in Rheithron Bay
(a) From this jetty the view to Ithaca harbour is obscured by Cape Samoli. (b) The jetty wall was clearly constructed at a time when land levels were lower than today.

FIGURE 22.10
Medium resolution image of Laertes' farm
Colour interpretation: as Figure 20.1. Grid: 500 m.
[Image credits: as Figure 20.1.]

I look down at the orchards of Laertes' farm, still under cultivation. After twenty years of absence Odysseus has at last returned to meet his father, the former great King of the Cephallenians. At 24.217–18 he wonders 'if he will recognise me when he sees me, / Or fail to know me, absent for so long.' He passes through 'the great orchard' and eventually at 24.226–7 'he found his father alone in the well-made vineyard, / Digging about a plant'.

FIGURE 22.11
High resolution image of
Laertes' farm
Colour interpretation: as
Figure 20.1. Grid: 200 m.
[Image credits: as
Figure 20.1.]

Horticulture is entwined with pathos here (24.227–8): 'he was clothed in a dirty tunic, patched and wretched', he wears oxhide on his shins to guard against scratches and gloves to protect himself from the thorns, and 'on his head a goatskin-cap, nursing his sorrow'(24.230–1).

Odysseus 'stood still beneath a tall pear tree, and shed tears' and decided that he must introduce himself elliptically, perhaps to lessen the shock. So he pretends to be a visitor and as we have heard, Laertes asks him

> Where is the ship which brought you and your godly
> Companions here? Or were you a passenger
> On another's ship, which landed you and left?   24.299–301

As I listen to his reply I look out at the view of Figure 22.12 towards the spit of Cape Samoli. Odysseus was reunited with his father many years ago but I can still see him pointing out today:

> My ship stands *here* in the country far from town.

The steep banks of the vineyard are now populated mainly by olive trees but Athene was accurate in describing Laertes as crawling 'along his hilly vineyard's slopes'. At 24.223–5 we can picture Laertes' faithful servant Dolios, when 'They had gone off / To gather stones for a protecting wall / For the orchard, and the old man led the way.' In Figure 22.13 the vineyard slope is

FIGURE 22.12
Laertes' Farm – view of
orchards from farmhouse
*From this location Cape
Samoli protrudes prominently
into Argostoli Bay.*

in the foreground while the distinctive peak of Kastelli is to the far right and
Mount Lakties (Neriton) is on the horizon. If you trace back from it leftwards
along the skyline, the small tree-topped summit that just protrudes in the
middle distance is the double hilltop which we have been exploring for traces
of Odysseus' Palace. Although it is a local landmark I must confess that from
this view it is curiously unimpressive compared with these other hills.

When you look back at Figure 22.3 I hope you will agree that these locations
for the Rheithron stream and Laertes' farm meet all the relevant clues without
any difficulty. Rheithron Bay is the broad curve to the south of the point of
Cape Samoli and the Rheithron stream emerges at the point itself. You can see
from Figure 19.2 that a (hypothetical) ship can be hidden beyond this point
so that it is invisible from the palace and it is clear from Figure 22.12 that it
would also be invisible from the location of Laertes' farm.

As the day wears on and dusk sets in on this fertile plot of land near the sea,
old King Laertes gazes out from his 'fine house' at 24.361 and sees the lights
blazing out from the palace. A visit to his daughter-in-law and young grandson
is easy to organise: it is little more than half an hour's walk. I wonder what
he thinks about the suitors' dissolute occupation of their home for so many

FIGURE 22.13
Laertes' Farm – steep
slopes of the vineyard
*Cephalonia continues to be
famous for its wines: the dry
white Robola is particularly
well regarded.*

years and the resulting tension for all the citizens of Ithaca. Why does he not intervene? No doubt he would do so 'If only, / By father Zeus, Athene, and Apollo, / I were the man I was when I took the city / Of well-built Nericon, the mainland cape, / As ruler of the Cephallenians.'

So where then was Nericon? Clue 23 provides the tantalising possibility that it was located at the headland of Fiscardo since that would have indeed represented 'the mainland cape' of Same. It is also possible that prior to its capture the people dwelling in that part of Same (now called Erissos) were not regarded as Cephallenians as Clue 22 requires, although that argument may sound like special pleading.

However, the likeliest answer seems to be that Nericon was instead situated on the island of Lefkas to the north. In his description of the 'Revolt of Mytilene' in 428 BC Thucydides describes the battle fleet of the Athenians and its assault on Oeniadae, a town at the mouth of the Achelous river that we heard about in Chapter 21. He writes of their commander Asopius:

As, however, the inhabitants would not come over to him, he dismissed his army but himself sailed to Leucas and made a descent upon Nericus. On his way back from Nericus he and part of his army were slain by the people of that place, who rallied to its defence, and by a few guards. The Athenians first stood out to sea and then later recovered their dead from the Leucadians under a truce. (3.7)

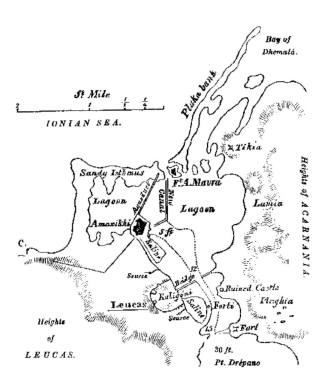

FIGURE 22.14
Leake's map of the ancient
settlement of Leucas
*Leake's travels in Greece were
far too comprehensive to
constitute nineteenth-century
tourism: while following the
footsteps of Pausanias he
succeeded in collecting a great
deal of intelligence for the
British about the Turkish
occupation.*
[Image credits: Leake
(1835) vol. III p. 11.]

On 11 September 1806 the indefatigable William Leake lands at the walls of the Russian garrison at the fortress of Agia Mavra on the north-east promontory of Lefkas. He and his companions walk 'along the narrow summit of an aqueduct which crosses the lagoon and conveys water to the fort. It is supported by about 260 arches and is 1300 yards in length.' It ends at 'the modern capital of Leucas, named Amaxíkhi'. The next day 'we proceed to the paleókastro, or remains of the city of Leucas, a mile and a half to the south east of Amaxíkhi. The site is called Kaligóni, and consists of irregular heights, forming the last falls of the central ridge of the island, at the foot of which is a narrow plain between the heights and the lagoon.' This hillside 'is probably a part of the Nericus mentioned in the *Odyssey*, which Laertes boasts to have taken, and which, even in the Peloponnesian war, had not yet assumed the name of Leucas'.[6]

Leake drew for his readers the map that you can see at Figure 22.14 (which can be compared directly with the satellite image at Figure 2.2) and on 25 August 2003 Mike D'Souza and I decide to pay Nericon a visit. Amaxíkhi is today called Lefkas town: the hillside of Leucas on Leake's map is marked as 'Nirikos' in the local guidebooks, which repeat the view that this is the settlement that Laertes conquered. It is an eminently acceptable candidate: it consists of some quite extensive polygonal stone ruins on a hilltop overlooking the causeway to the mainland of Acarnania (Figure 22.15). I still retain an affection

FIGURE 22.15 Nericon on Lefkas

(a) The ruins are more impressive than one expects but surprisingly hard to locate: the tourists on Lefkas are perhaps more interested in the beaches than the Bronze Age. (b) The capital town of Lefkas and Leake's sandy isthmus beyond are visible in the distance.

FIGURE 22.16 Dörpfeld's tumuli at Nidri

By contrast with Nericon the tombs are less impressive than one expects but surprisingly easy to locate.

FIGURE 22.17 Low-lying Ithaca?

'Ithaca itself lies low': was Homer describing this island?

for that paleolithic headland of Fiscardo but it is time to be pragmatic: if Thucydides was happy with Leucas as ancient Nericon then so am I.

On the way back past Nidri we visit the Bronze Age tumuli that Dörpfeld laboured so long to uncover in the belief that Lefkas was ancient Ithaca (Figure 22.16).

As we take the ferry back to Cephalonia modern Ithaca looms on our left with its high cliffs stretching down steeply to the ocean. From here it is very difficult to see how anyone could ever have regarded this island as meeting

FIGURE 22.18
Low-lying Paliki
*Or was Homer instead
describing this island?*

the description that we first encountered in Chapter 4, in which Ithaca is said to be *chthamale* – lying low in the sea (Figure 22.17).

By contrast this photograph of Paliki viewed from the northern end of Argostoli Bay leaves us in no such difficulty (Figure 22.18).

Notes

1 The city of Nericon and the mountains of Neriton and Neïon are not to be confused with the hydraulic engineer named Neritos who co-designed the Ithaca city fountain with his colleagues Ithacos and Polyctor (17.207). But perhaps Ithacos and Neritos won the vote in the first settlers' ballot for the name of their island and its distinctive northern peak.

2 Sadly this *entente cordiale* between noble Ithacan and Samian families was to last for no longer than 2,800 years. On 1 August 1675 (AD) the explorer Jacob Spon, travelling with Sir George Wheler, visited Argostoli and observed that 'It is fertile, with oil, red wine, excellent muscats and raisins of the type that we call Corinthian, from which it reaps a tidy income. The location of the fortress and the residence of the Governor is called Argostoli. There is a large port that is enclosed all around, but anchors do not hold well there. At the mouth of this port there is a large village called Luxuri inhabited by wealthy Corinthian raisin merchants. Civil war has broken out between them

recently because of a quarrel between two families. They form into gangs of fifty or sixty who fight each other as cruelly as the Turks fight the Christians.' See Spon (1678) vol. I pp. 77–8. For details of the port see Chapter 15 n.7. The rivalry between Argostolians and Lixourians may well have pre-dated Spon's visit and it certainly continued thereafter: in 1825 the British Military Governor Charles Napier wrote: 'There is a mortal hatred between the inhabitants of Argostoli and Lixuri' (Cosmetatos (1995) p. 121).

3 Newman and Newman (2003) p. 5c.

4 See James Diggle's comments on this passage in Appendix 1 Section J.

5 I am grateful to Tjeerd van Andel for pointing out that springs were historically more numerous in these geological settings and that they can cease to flow by becoming naturally blocked via the deposition of travertine (a massive form of calcium carbonate that corresponds to onyx) or via the establishment of modern wells. There is also a very marked disparity between rainfall on Cephalonia in summer versus winter, which is often described by the islanders as the 'rainy season'. A visit in the summer to the town of Lixouri a few kilometres to the south reveals a substantial dried-up riverbed which in recent winters has been known to flood the adjacent streets. Although it therefore seems likely that there were more streams in this area in Laertes' day than there are now, those that are identified on the satellite image would probably have been among the more substantial at that time because they descend directly from the catchment areas in the mountains to the west.

6 Leake (1835) vol. III pp. 10–16.

CHAPTER 23　**Network**

But still they lead me back to the long winding road.
You left me standing here a long long time ago.
John Lennon and Paul McCartney, The Long and Winding Road (1970)[1]

Tucked away behind the main street in Argostoli is an imposing building called the Corgialenios Museum and Library. It is a focal point for cultural activities within the island and during our visit in May 2003 I call in there to acquire *The Roads of Cefalonia*, a beautifully researched book by Helen Cosmetatos that describes how the roads into the interior and around the vertiginous coastline were constructed. I want to buy rather than borrow a copy and this creates a problem because the bookshop in the museum is shut, but when the librarian Elias Toumasatos hears that I am about to return to London he volunteers to retrieve one for me. That is the essence of this island and its people: they are justly proud of their Cephalonia and they care that you care about it.

Cosmetatos explains that the long-standing Venetian rule over the island was replaced by that of the French in 1797 and then by the Russians a year later. Sovereignty over the island follows the course of the Napoleonic War: the French return triumphant in 1807 but the British then blockade the Ionian Islands and in 1809 they become a British protectorate until reunification with Greece in 1864. One of the first curiosities that the British discover is that there are very few serviceable roads, so in 1809 they build their first one on the Argostoli peninsula. The following year the new Commandant of the island is a man with the distinctly un-English name of Charles-Philippe de Bosset, an Anglophile of Swiss descent who has served in the British army. His energy in building new roads through the rugged countryside is formidable and this is followed from 1822 onwards by even more spectacular efforts from his successor, Charles James Napier. A third Commandant, Charles Sebright, Baron d'Everton, continued the improvements and the result is essentially the road network of today.

These roads open up the previously almost inaccessible interior of the island and launch a process of economic transformation. What especially interests me are the roads that are built in Northern Paliki. Figure 23.1 is reproduced from the chapter describing the construction of the road from Argostoli to Lixouri:[2] the dotted lines indicate the existing tracks while the solid lines depict the proposed new roads. Clearly in some locations the new roads are

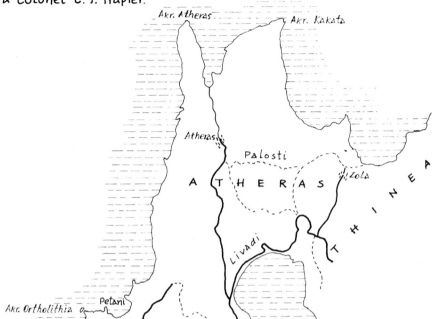

PALLI — Lixouri
Planned and built by Major C.P. de Bosset
& Colonel C.T. Napier.

FIGURE 23.1
Nineteenth-century road
construction in Paliki
*Today's coastal road from
Thinia to Lixouri was not
built until 1823.*
[Image credits: Cosmetatos
(1995) p. 120. Reproduced
with the permission of the
Corgialenios Museum,
Argostoli.]

built over the existing tracks but in other sites they are entirely new. For example, the road to Atheras that you can see snaking up towards you from the sea in Figure 22.18 is part of the Paliki section started on 1 February 1823 and completed by the British occupying forces for a total cost of £3,085 18s 4d. Furthermore the road at sea level along the northern curve of Argostoli Bay depicted in Figure 13.1 is also new: its eastern section has to be blasted into the sheer rock face of the coastal cliffs.[3]

If these are some of the new roads, where are the old ones? Figure 23.2 is an attempt to recreate the former network of major paths and cart-tracks from the satellite imagery and also from the indications on Figure 23.1. In most cases these routes are still negotiable but some of them are based on rather faint ground indications that indicate abandonment in favour of the new highways. This satellite picture deploys true colour processing rather than highlighting the infra-red band, so this is how Paliki appears from space. The diagram also marks the course of the main streams in the area.

There are three prominent tracks running from the eastern area of Strabo's Channel towards the north-western part of the island. Of these the central path is the most obvious route from the channel, so on 23 May we decide to follow the footsteps of Philoitios, the cowherd of Chapter 17:

FIGURE 23.2
Former roads and streams
of northern Paliki
*Colour interpretation: natural
colour.*
[Image credits: Digital
Globe Quickbird 60 cm
resolution natural colour
satellite image. Processing:
OziExplorer. Websites:
www.digitalglobe.com,
www.eurimage.com,
www.oziexplorer.com/]

Third came that stalwart fellow Philoitios,
Leading a heifer and fat goats for the suitors.
They had been brought across by ferrymen,
Who also ferry people, any who come.   20.185–8

We are not sure where Philoitios kept his cattle on Same but it seems likely that they have been ferried across the channel so as to connect with one of the two paths that meet at the junction towards the east of the diagram, close to a modern quarry that is memorably marked on the roadside today with the sign 'Danger – Cory Exit'. From there he presumably proceeds with his cows around the horseshoe-shaped area that is today called Kritonou, branching off towards the north and then taking the junction west in the direction of the tall hill of Kastelli. That area is lush and agricultural: indeed later in the year on a return visit I bump into some of Eumaios' retinue still rooting about (Figure 23.3).

FIGURE 23.3
Descendants of
Eumaios' herd
They were wandering by the
roadside, near the 'R' of
ATHERAS in
Figure 23.1.

After driving across the plateau and walking over the saddle of land between Kastelli and the hilltop to its north the view down into the valley is spectacular (Figure 23.4).

In this photograph there are abundant dry stone walls in the valley. Could these be the ruins of Ithaca city? The double hilltop that is my candidate for the palace hill rises above the modern road in the distance. We drive the jeep down as far as we can but the track rapidly deteriorates into a rutted path so we disembark to explore on foot.

As we walk along the track we see beside us in the woodland the remains of an old stone-walled track (Figure 23.5). We make our way over to it through the woodland foliage and we try to follow it down into the valley. Here and there it disappears into dense shrubbery but then the path resumes before long. Ancient masonry is a magnet for wind-borne seeds: water washes them down into the cracks between the rocks and this creates a protected environment in which plant roots can flourish undisturbed.

This is the first time we have visited this part of the valley and it is easy to become lost, so I press the 'Find' button on the GPS receiver and ask for the nearest waypoint (a previously stored latitude/longitude coordinate). The closest one is marked 'Fountain' and a click on the 'Go To' option instructs the gadget to display a compass bearing to the chosen location.

I wait for a second as the instrument locates the bearing, then look down at the screen. The direction arrow is pointing dead ahead: this ancient track is

FIGURE 23.4
View west from Kastelli
*There was obviously a
settlement at one time in this
valley – but when?*

FIGURE 23.5
The ancient road
north-west of Kastelli
*Not shown in the photograph
are the numerous goats who
have the benefit of this
beautiful scenery.*

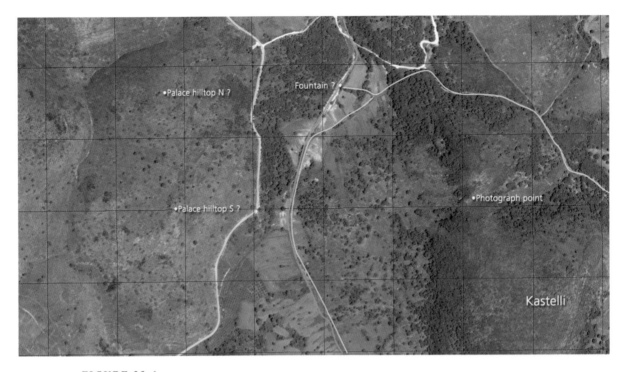

FIGURE 23.6
West of Kastelli (medium resolution)
The hilltops are as marked, but was Odysseus' Palace there? Colour interpretation: as Figure 20.1. Grid: 200 m.
[Image credits: as Figure 20.1.]

taking us directly to the structure of Figure 19.14 beside the stream that I had visited from the west a few days earlier.

If this was the site of Polyctor's fountain then it has to be located in the right place to slake the thirst of travellers to Ithaca city. They did not approach it from the same direction as Odysseus and Eumaios because the pigfarm lies to the north and relatively few travellers would have arrived via Phorcys Bay. Most travellers would have crossed Strabo's Channel and arrived from the east as we did (Figure 23.6). But there was another way to travel to Ithaca city: by sea from the south.

In Chapter 3 we heard that two distinguished visitors did so as part of their conscription campaign for the Trojan War: Agamemnon, King of Mycenae, and his brother Menelaos, King of Sparta. If you believe, as I do, that Odysseus was living in northern Paliki at the time then they would have sailed up Argostoli Bay and anchored their ships in Ithaca harbour. What happened next? The northern end of the marsh-filled area is about 1.3 km distant from the double hilltop and there is a continual upward gradient towards the southern summit at 127 m above sea level and the northern summit at 148 m. Did Odysseus come down and greet them at the harbour or did they visit him on this hilltop?

There is a tradition that Odysseus didn't want to go to war at all so he feigned madness in a very unusual way. The kings found him pretending to furrow the sands of the seashore with an ox and a horse yoked to his plough.[4] One of their advisers, Palamedes, outwitted him by having his baby Telemachos placed in

FIGURE 23.7
The road up from Ithaca
harbour
*Did Agamemnon and
Menelaos reach Odysseus'
Palace via this road?*

the plough's path, thus forcing Odysseus to divert the path of the plough so as
to save his son and thereby reveal his sanity. Later Odysseus allegedly took his
revenge on Palamedes by having him drowned. Whether this story is true or
not (it is not part of the *Iliad* or the *Odyssey*) we can presume that Agamemnon
and Menelaos returned to the palace with Odysseus for a customary bout of
Bronze Age hospitality, no doubt involving the usual lunchtime special of roast
pork. So how did they get to the palace? Did these three great leaders walk all
the way there?

The ruins in the valley occupy an extensive area of about 1 square kilometre
in total and so it was not until a visit later in the year that a possible answer
became clear. There is an ancient paved road ascending from the harbour
through the valley (Figure 23.7) and it is well suited for conveying cargo and
people by wagons or chariots of some kind.

This road is a candidate for the route along which Odysseus escorted
Agamemnon and Menelaos up to his palace, but even to my untrained eye
it appears to be in remarkably good condition. Indeed some time later when
I showed this photograph to Tjeerd van Andel he described it as a Turkish
mule-path. That was a disappointment, but perhaps there are the foundations
of a much older road underneath.

What did Odysseus' Palace look like when the Mycenaean kings arrived?
Here are the relevant clues, repeated from Figure 17.2:

7   *The palace and the city are close to each other.*

10   *The place of assembly is close to the palace.*

12   *The city lies below the palace.*

17   *There is a levelled sportsground about 100 m long in front of the palace.*

19   *Several paths converge at an elaborate fountain, linking the pigfarm, the city, Strabo's Channel and the harbour, and somehow a circular grove of poplars is irrigated.*

20   *The palace is not far from the fountain.*

21   *The palace consists of multiple buildings.*

22   *The palace has a walled courtyard with double gates.*

29   *The sun's rays strike the palace at dawn.*

30   *The palace is located above sea level.*

31   *The palace must have an upper floor as well as a ground floor.*

32   *Telemachos' high bedroom in the palace commands a surrounding view.*

33   *The meeting place of the city of Ithaca is probably equipped with stone seats.*

35   *The houses and city of Ithaca may be to the east of the meeting place.*

We saw in Chapter 19 that the southernmost of the two hilltops affords the best view out over the harbour and the bay and so this is a candidate for the palace location. However the actual summit itself is too small an area to accommodate the multiple buildings of Clue 21, although it would be well suited for Telemachos' high bedroom with a surrounding view. It seemed to me that an obvious place to build an extensive complex of buildings would be between the two hilltops, on the flank of the hill facing east towards Kastelli, and this direction also complies with Clue 29: it catches the rays of the early morning sun.

This location for the palace is certainly close to the stream that would have fed the fountain, and at least three paths meet there as we have just seen. We dealt with the requirement for proximity to a stream earlier: indeed on this hillside the serving girls have two streams to choose from, one on the east coursing down through Ithaca city and a second private watercourse in the valley to the west. We will return to consider the location of the meeting place and the sportsground shortly, but what was intriguing me was the satellite imagery of this area (Figure 23.8).

I had to keep reminding myself that satellites can see through space but not through time, and so what it was showing on the ground is the composite effect of many years of inhabitation of the area. It would be unwise to jump to the conclusion that the strange pattern of dry-stone walls on this hilltop is an indication of any arrangement that was extant during the Late Bronze Age: if a shepherd decided to build an enclosure for his flock there in the nineteenth century AD then that is what the satellite will photograph. The

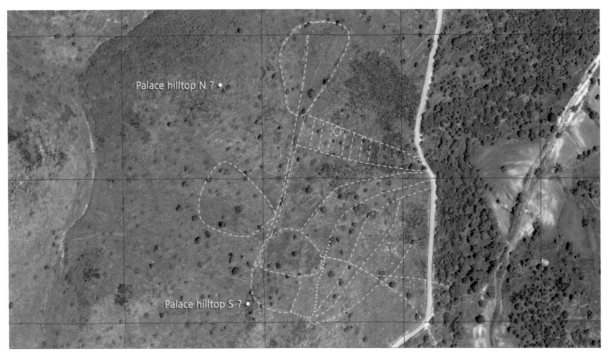

Palace hilltop N ? •

Palace hilltop S ? •

FIGURE 23.8
Pattern of stone walls on
the palace hilltop
The distinctive twin trees of
Figure 19.3d are clearly
visible at the northern
summit. A stream runs down
the valley to the west as well
as to the east. Colour
interpretation: as Figure 20.1.
Grid: 200 m.
[Image credits: as
Figure 20.1.]

natural processes of mountaintop erosion and wind-blown soil infill usually
cause ancient structures to become buried over time: indeed Schliemann had
to excavate at Troy to an initial depth of around 5 m to uncover its topless
towers.[5] Nevertheless from time to time some parts of ancient structures can
remain exposed, particularly if they are situated on hilltops where wind and
rain can dissolve the sediment of centuries rather than in valleys where these
deposits tend to accumulate.

So when I looked at this photograph the question that I kept asking myself
was: is this pattern simply the geometry of animal enclosures that have been
created by shepherds over the intervening period, or do these patterns reflect
(at least in part) the layout of an ancient civilisation?

At the southern end of Figure 23.8 where the lower of the two stone walls
crosses the corner of the modern road I thought that there might be a possible
meeting place involving banked rows of stone terraces continuing down the
hillside (Figure 23.9).

It may be just a trick of the light but there is an indentation on one of
those rocks that looks just about the right size for a Bronze Age bottom
(Figure 23.10).

In Chapters 10 and 17 we heard of the suitors' plot to ambush Telemachos
and we may now like to consider some relevant clues from that discussion.

FIGURE 23.9
Location of the meeting
place?
*(a) 'When all were gathered
in the meeting place, /
Telemachos set out, bronze
spear in hand, / A pair of
nimble hounds about his
heels' (2.9–11) (b) 'Athene
shed on him a heavenly
grace, / And all watched
him with wonder as he
approached' (2.12–13).*

FIGURE 23.10
Stone seat carved into the
rock?
*'The elders yielded him his
father's seat' (2.14).*

> Before the hall the high and mighty suitors
> Amused themselves with javelin and discus,
> On a levelled sportsground, where they often played.   4.625–7

The suitors' leaders Antinoos and Eurymachos hear that Telemachos has borrowed a ship from Noemon and gone to Pylos. The news appals them and they
put an end to these frolics:

They made them stop their games and sit down together   4.659

Antinoos addresses the suitors:

His heart was black and filled to bursting
With rage, his eyes resembled flashing fire.   4.661–2

He announces his plan to ambush Telemachos at Asteris:

They all approved, and told him to proceed,
Then quickly rose and went to the house of Odysseus.   4.673–4

These passages suggest that all this action is taking place at locations that are very near to each other. The sportsground is 'before the hall' – right in front of the palace: it is not some way away. It is levelled rather than merely level, which implies some artificial intervention in the landscape. They are made to 'stop their games and sit down together' – they don't wander off to some other location to meet, they sit down there and then. Antinoos is clearly very put out by this news and gives them a major bollocking. Finally they 'quickly rose and went to the house of Odysseus' and the implication is that the palace is adjacent as we heard before.

You can see from Figure 23.9 that the ground in front of this area is flat and currently planted with crops. A hedge runs across the centre of the area: on the western side there are rows of orchards and on the eastern side there are fields (Figure 23.11).

In the distance on the left you can make out the harbour and the mountains of Same rising from the sea, while on the right is the hilltop of Mesovouni, the rear of the modern quarry. This flat region is about 300 m long by 130 m wide, more than enough for the world record javelin throw of about 100 m that we reviewed in Chapter 17, let alone for the more modest achievements of overfed Bronze Age suitors.

34 *There is a mountain peak near the city, visible from the place of assembly and probably to its north.*
35 *The houses and city of Ithaca may be to the east of the meeting place.*
36 *There may be a stretch of the seashore accessible from the meeting place and the palace without having to traverse the city or visit the harbour.*
37 *The far edge of the harbour may be invisible from the palace.*

What of the remaining palace clues? Mount Lakties is indeed located to the north of the place of assembly: the relative bearing is shown at Figure 23.2. The houses and city of Ithaca are located to the east of the meeting place as

FIGURE 23.11
The levelled sportsground?
'Before the hall the high and mighty suitors / Amused themselves with javelin and discus, / On a levelled sportsground, where they often played' (4.625–7).

Figure 23.4 confirms. Figure 23.2 also shows us that from the double hilltop one can reach the sea via two alternative routes: either by walking through the city and down the paved road to the harbour, or by diverting to the west of the Mesovouni quarry hill and reaching the western shoreline, which is in the form of a long curve. It may be fanciful to attach any significance to the words 'curving beach' at 22.386 but in view of the shape of this beach it is nevertheless interesting to consider why this particular simile surfaced in the poet's mind at that precise time:

> He saw the heaps
> Of bodies lying in blood and dust, like fish
> Drawn from the grey sea in a net of mesh
> And spilled by fishers on the curving beach.   22.383–6

FIGURE 23.12
Atheras, Mount Neriton
and Raven's Rock
*'You will find him sitting
with the pigs; they feed /
By Raven's Rock and Arethousa
Spring' (13.407–8).*

Finally as far as Clue 37 is concerned, a brief look at Figure 19.5 is enough to confirm that one reason why Athene at 2.389–91 'Dragged the swift ship to the sea, and stored in her / All the equipment that good vessels carry, / And moored her by the far edge of the harbour' could have been so as to hide the ship from the view of the palace and the suitors prior to Telemachos' departure to Pylos. Another benefit would have been a more rapid embarkation.

So on the face of it this double hilltop seemed to represent a good fit to the clues for the location of Odysseus' Palace. But some nagging doubts remained. First, the kind of dry stone wall enclosures that are revealed in Figure 23.8 exist everywhere in Cephalonia, and they cannot all be the site of Odysseus' Palace. Then I had heard from John Bennet that the construction by the stream of Figure 19.14 was probably not the site of an ancient fountain but simply a mediaeval lime kiln. Tjeerd van Andel regarded my candidate for Agamemnon's Avenue as a Turkish mule path, while James Diggle had

FIGURE 23.13 The tenants of Raven's Rock

'Ravens nest in single pairs (pairs which stay away from other nesting pairs). Evidence suggests that, o~~n~~ paired, ravens will remain mated for life. They build their nests on cliff ledges and cavities, or in trees.' [www.shades-of-night.com/aviary/ravendoc.html]

diplomatically intimated that he found Figure 19.13 less than impressive as the site of Hermes' Hill. Furthermore the view from Laertes' farm to my proposed palace hilltop was hardly distinctive and when James had visited the latter he had seen no traces of pottery on the ground. Somehow I needed to find some solid evidence about the palace one way or the other.

Another unanswered question was how Raven's Rock earned its name. I mentioned in Chapter 14 that in March 2003 Chris Goodger narrowly missed photographing some ravens flying above the unusual escarpment south of Atheras that we had identified as Raven's Rock. On our return in May there is no sign of them. I return again to the island in August: still no ravens.

On 14 November 2003 I climb Mount Lakties, the mountain that fits with Homer's description of ancient Neriton (Figure 23.12). After admiring the stunning view I descend towards the east via a track that you can see winding down the valley on the skyline at the far right of the picture. The candidate for Raven's Rock that we saw at Figure 14.7 is the platform-like promontory almost exactly at the centre of the photograph.

As I look west across the mountain towards the summit of Raven's Rock an unexpected movement catches my eye. My heart misses a beat and Figure 23.13 explains why.

For the next half-hour I watch these birds arcing through the sky above their eponymous Rock and cawing to each other as they settle on its boulders. Somehow I hardly think they flew this way by chance.

Notes

1 Reproduced with the permission of Sony/ATV Music Publishing Ltd.
2 Cosmetatos (1995) p. 120.
3 I have traversed most of these tracks but I am not convinced that the path that snakes down to Zola at the north-eastern corner of the Cosmetatos map is feasible: it appears to be descending down the sheer flank of Mount Agrilia.
4 The earliest version of the story appears in Evelyn-White (1914) pp. 493, 505; see also later writers e.g. Luce (1998) p. 16.
5 Schuchhardt and Schliemann (1891) p. 7.

CHAPTER 24   **Pottery**

For millions of years mankind lived just like the animals. Then something happened
which unleashed the power of our imagination. We learned to talk.
    Stephen Hawking, *Keep Talking* (British Telecom 1993, Pink Floyd 1994)[1]

Archaeology is not about ravens: it is about pots, because unlike ravens, fragments of pottery are almost indestructible. Many of the great archaeological sites were first identified by finding ceramic material and any respectable
course in archaeology today regards this aspect as fundamental. Pottery is
therefore almost synonymous with archaeology and if you cannot find any of
it then you probably don't have anything very interesting to discuss with an
archaeologist.

There is by now a meticulous taxonomy of pottery design which enables
archaeologists to date a site by reference to the known date of examples of the
same style elsewhere. These comparisons are made not only between different
sites in the same country but also on an international basis, because pottery
was traded by land and sea during the Bronze Age.

This description may make archaeological dating sound rather routine but
in fact it is nothing of the kind. Controversies abound and I want to introduce
one at the outset of this chapter. I should add that I am by no means qualified
to assess its merits either way but it is important that we should be aware
that the debate exists, because its eventual resolution will have considerable
implications for our understanding of ancient Ithaca.

First let us share some background. The Early Bronze Age runs from 3000 to
2100 BC, the Middle Bronze Age from 2100 to 1550 BC and the Late Bronze
Age from 1550 to 1050 BC. The styles of Greek pottery associated with these
periods are by now well understood and documented,[2] but unfortunately
there is nothing about a Greek vase *per se* which tells you its age: unaccountably
the potters of the day did not think of inscribing the date of its manufacture
on the base. However, because vases, jugs and other objects of Greek design
from this period have also been found during the excavation of Egyptian
tombs, archaeologists have established what they call a synchronism between
these locations. This means that the discovery of the same design of pottery
at two different places is felt to imply that those two sites (or more specifically,
the depths at which the items were found on those sites) are of the same
period.

This observation applies to pottery of all ages, not just the Bronze Age, but the Late Bronze Age is the period of our present interest. In other words, if you think that you already know the date of the Egyptian tomb in which you found pottery of a particular design, and if pottery of a very similar design is then found 3 m below ground level somewhere in Cephalonia, then it is felt reasonable to propose that this Greek find is of about the same date as the Egyptian one. However, in order for this approach to work one clearly has to be comfortable about the age of the comparative site that is being used as a reference.

The chronology of the Egyptian Pharaonic dynasties was the first significant series of historical reference dates to be established in the field of archaeology and these dates have been an essential part of the archaeologist's toolkit ever since. They were initially calculated from astronomical observations in the Egyptian literature and also by making some assumptions about the average length of a typical Pharaonic dynasty.[3] Some of the details originated from descriptions by Manetho, an Egyptian priest of the third century BC, and in the 1880s they were converted into a coherent framework by Victorian scholars. This now represents a temporal tape measure that runs through thirty dynasties of Egyptian rulers, stretching from 2920 BC to 343 BC. These Egyptian dynasties are divided into four epochs preceded by an Archaic period and separated by three Intermediate periods, of which the Third Intermediate Period (Twenty-first to Twenty-fifth Dynasties, 1070–665 BC) is of particular interest to us.[4]

Wherever possible, archaeological finds elsewhere are related to this Egyptian dynastic template and this relationship is then used to determine a date for the newly discovered site. However, a direct comparison of this nature is not always possible because the design of the vase from Cephalonia that you would like to date may not have turned up in Egypt at all: perhaps the nearest comparison is from a site in eastern Italy. In these circumstances the best you can then do is to adopt the date that has already been assessed for this Italian site, which also may not have been linked directly to Egypt but instead indirectly via one or more other intermediate sites. Consequently most archaeological dating of ceramics is established via a series of indirect synchronisms back to the Egyptian dynasties, which themselves depend on evidence that includes the writings of a third-century BC priest.

Not surprisingly many archaeologists would like to find a more direct approach and they have looked to objective tests as an alternative.[5] Scientific techniques such as radiocarbon dating rely on the intrinsic physical properties of the object under scrutiny, but they are subject to statistical error and they also require calibration and correction for historical atmospheric variation and other factors. Radiocarbon tests themselves can nevertheless provide reasonably precise dating of Bronze Age objects (e.g. accurate to $+/-$ fifty years within specified confidence limits) but they are applicable only to material that was once living in close association with ceramics, such as animal or vegetable matter. This helps us with the dating of pottery only if there is an organic residue, such as an uneaten breakfast. More recent techniques such as optically stimulated luminescence can date some inorganic materials directly, but they are not yet in widespread use because the background radiation near the sample must first be measured with delicate equipment and the sample then removed and transported in absolute darkness.

There is another dating technique available which is in principle capable of great accuracy and that is dendrochronology, the examination of tree rings. If you cut across the trunk of a tree you will usually see a pattern of concentric rings, each of which normally reflects a year of growth. By counting the rings you can determine how old the tree was when it fell or was cut down and ceased growing. It would be delightful if you could determine the age of a building by counting the tree rings in its timber beams, but unfortunately that doesn't work because if you count the number of rings in a wooden beam you simply learn how old that piece of wood was when it died. Clearly the tree might have been only fifty years of age when it was cut down to form part of a dwelling that was built in the year 1500 BC.

It is not enough to count the rings: we need to be able to identify a distinctive pattern of rings and prove that these date from particular years. In principle this is possible because trees do not grow uniformly: there are growth spurts in good years with the right rainfall and sunshine, and vice versa for years of drought. Ideally all we therefore need to do in order to date buildings back to the Late Bronze Age is to find a convenient 3,500 year old tree, cut through it and count all its growth rings and then match their distinctive pattern against the core of a particular tree found in the construction of our building. As we compare the two growth rings we should be able to find a point where the pattern of thick and thin rings is the same on both trees and that ought to tell us the absolute age of the timber in our building.

Unfortunately events once again conspire to complicate matters. Trees of that age are not generally available outside of the Californian sequoia or bristle cone populations[6] so instead one has to assemble a series of reference trees of overlapping ages. You start with a live tree that is say 300 years old and then you match the growth rings in that against a dead tree that lived over the period from perhaps 200 to 500 years ago, and then you do the same for another overlapping period earlier in time. The idea is to build up an established sequence of patterns of dated growth rings and then to compare this with a newly found piece of ancient timber and try to match them up. The complications continue: it is not much use trying to compare the rings of an oak tree with those of an olive because their growth patterns are very different.

FIGURE 24.1
Growth rings from an
olive tree in Atheras Bay
This example is from a large
bough of a felled tree. The
olive is a less reliable
candidate for
dendrochronology than other
trees: see Peter Kuniholm's
comments at the end of
Chapter 18.

Furthermore a tree could be cut down and stored for many years before its wood was incorporated into a particular building, or it could be salvaged for reuse from a much older construction. Difficulties also arise when trimming the outer tree rings for a squared beam. These factors can distort the assessment of a building's age by several centuries.[7] For these reasons it would be a mistake to regard dendrochronology as an exact science.[8]

My intention in introducing this discussion of dating techniques is to focus on the rather surprising fact (surprising at least to a layman) that even today the most routine source of archaeological dating continues to be that of establishing a comparison with the Egyptian dynasties by means of pottery. The answers which emerge are therefore crucially dependent on the accuracy with which those Egyptian dynasties themselves have been dated. The analogy of a temporal tape measure is appropriate: if you want to make reliable measurements of a building then it is essential to use an accurate measure.

So let us now turn to the controversy. What do you think the reaction of architects would be if somebody published research one day which proposed that all the tape measures they have been using were incorrectly calibrated? That all the lengths and widths and heights of all the buildings in the world are inaccurate by some very significant amount: that a 100 m high building is actually only 95 m high because the measures are wrong? I think we can safely assume that, irrespective of the quality of the research, its reception would be less than rapturous because there would simply be too many professional reputations at stake.

That is to some extent indicative of the response to recent research which has challenged the authenticity of the dating of the Egyptian dynasties.[9] Part of the researchers' purpose has been to provide an explanation of why the period from about 1050 to 800 BC represents a cultural void across many loosely related civilisations. This period is called the 'Dark Age' and the evidence provided indicates that whether you look in Cyprus, Greece, Syria, the Hittite region (northern Turkey), Mesopotamia (Iraq) or Egypt itself, you tend to find that nothing of any significance happened at that time and there is no news to report. It is as if the lights went off all over the ancient world in 1050 BC; everyone was put into a state of suspended animation and then reawakened in 800 BC. Why might this have been the case?[10]

Various conventional explanations have been provided, such as a change in the global climate or the outbreak of disease, but this phenomenon stretches across multiple climatic zones and continents and it is difficult to find a single cause that could credibly affect so many different locations and cultures. The radical solution proposed by these researchers is that the problem is an artificial one introduced by a faulty Egyptian tape measure. To correct this they propose that you have to subtract up to 250 years from the Egyptian Third Intermediate Period of 1070–665 BC. In other words, any published dates that appear prior to about 1070 BC have to be reduced by up to 250 years: not just in Egypt but in any country whose archaeological dates have been established by reference to the Egyptian dynasties. This includes Greece.

Many criticisms have been levelled at these proposals but at least nobody can accuse their originators of being unimaginative. Their assimilation requires a great deal of careful study and that is perhaps one of the principal problems for their proponents, because for the amateur the subject matter is dauntingly complex while for the professional the conclusions are deeply disturbing. Furthermore the authors of these theories live for the most part outside of the conventional world of archaeology and the popularisation of one of these hypotheses in the media has not endeared it to experts in the field.

At this point I must repeat my caveat that I am not competent to judge the merits of this complex case and I also have no personal bias either way, but if it turns out to be true then it means that the Trojan War did not take place around 1200 BC but was instead waged around 950 BC, and that the events of the *Odyssey* therefore took place somewhere around 950–900 BC. So as you can see, archaeology today is by no means an exact science. Dating is only a part of it, but nevertheless it will be fascinating to follow this debate as it unfolds.

Cephalonia itself has been the subject of professional archaeological activity for many years. We heard in Chapter 19 and Chapter 20 that the great classical

FIGURE 24.2
Mycenaean sarcophagus
found in Tomb A at
Kontogenada
This stone coffin or larnax
was discovered only 2 km
upstream from the brook
identified as Homer's
Rheithron.
[Image credits:
photographed in Argostoli
Museum with the kind
permission of Dr Andreas
Soteriou, Greek
Archaeological Service.]

archaeologist Marinatos excavated tholos tombs in Kontogenada. You can see the location of this village on Figure 16.2: it is only a few kilometres away from the harbour that I have proposed as that of ancient Ithaca. Marinatos was himself born in Paliki and the results of these and many other finds from all over the island are now displayed in the beautifully appointed Archaeological Museum in Argostoli.

Significant Bronze Age finds have been made at multiple locations across Cephalonia. A Mycenaean sarcophagus was found also at Kontogenada (Figure 24.2) and in 1992 the largest tholos tomb in western Greece was discovered by Lazaros Kolonas at Tzanata–Borzi, near Poros, dating from the fourteenth century BC.

In 2002 a Danish team published a painstaking review of all the known archaeological sites on the island.[11] Another splendid new book devoted to the archaeology of the Ionian Islands during this period has recently brought together many previously undocumented or relatively unknown sites.[12] So there have already been many Bronze Age discoveries on the island, but actually what everyone would like to find on Cephalonia and indeed elsewhere in Greece are clay tablets, because we want to read what the Greeks of 1200 BC (or perhaps 950 BC) were writing.

Given the length of the *Iliad* and the *Odyssey* we might expect to find multiple references to writing in these poems, but there is only one and that is somewhat indirect.[13] Anteia 'lusts madly' after a warrior called Bellerophon but she is unable to seduce him 'since his mind was upright' (the original lacks innuendo). Then as now, hell has no fury like a woman scorned: she complains of Bellerophon's non-existent advances to her husband Proitos and suggests that he might like to choose between eliminating either Bellerophon in revenge or himself in cuckolded shame. Proitos does not want blood on his hands but he also values his own existence, so he now faces a dilemma. His wife's family are drawn from Mafia stock and so he decides to have Bellerophon terminated via a contract killing organised through a murder note:

> He shrank from killing him. Instead he sent him
> To Lycia with a lethal introduction,
> Sinister signs etched on a folding tablet,
> To show his father-in-law – to ensure his death.

> When the tenth rosy-fingered dawn appeared,
> He asked what token he had brought from Proitos
> His son-in-law and begged to examine it.   *Iliad* 6. 167–70, 174–6

The phrase 'folding tablet' indicates that the words were inscribed on a writing board called a *diptych*. Until recently such boards were believed to date from no earlier than the seventh century BC, but between 1984 and 1994 the contents of a remarkable Bronze Age shipwreck at Uluburun near Kas in south-west Turkey were brought to the surface. One of the finds included a thirteenth-century BC diptych, reassembled from a depth of 50 m (Figure 24.3). This was used by covering the recessed inner face of each side with wax which was then marked with the message. Once the board was folded shut the wax surface was protected from accidental indentations.

Unless Proitos' message was written in a secret family code, this passage from the *Iliad* also tells us that reading and writing were hardly universal at the time, since clearly Bellerophon himself was unable to interpret the deadly message that he innocently conveyed. So what kind of writing might have been used? The Greek alphabet had not yet been devised and so the chances are that Proitos was writing in a script called Linear B.

One of the greatest archaeological events of the last century was the discovery and later decipherment of ancient writing on tablets found at Knossos, Pylos, Mycenae and Thebes. The story is by now well known and I will summarise it rather briefly. In 1878 a Heraklion merchant and amateur archaeologist aptly named Minos Kalokairinos started excavating at Knossos in Crete, where he unearthed painted walls and also items of pottery. Some of these he

sent to international museums and in 1894 he met Arthur (later Sir Arthur) Evans, whose interests had been aroused by inscriptions that he had seen on sealstones.

After extensive negotiations Evans took over the Knossos excavations and on 30 March 1900 he found clay tablets inscribed with an unknown script. Although some fragments of these tablets had surfaced previously, this was the first time that a significant collection had been found *in situ*. Partial publication of his findings took place a few years later, but the combination of the 1914–18 war and Sir Arthur's somewhat proprietorial attitude to Knossos meant that it was difficult for others to access the original material. Despite many attempts to crack its code the ancient language, by then called Linear B, remained undeciphered.

In 1939 similar tablets were discovered by Carl Blegen at Ano Englianos in the south-western Peloponnese. A town today named Pylos lies close by and the excavation of a magnificent palace in the area was a catalyst for the suggestion that this could have been the site of King Nestor's citadel of Pylos which Telemachos visited. At the time there was by no means universal agreement on this proposal: several different places in Greece share this name and *Pulos* is related to the word that means 'gateway'. However the discovery of the Pylos tablets revealed the revolutionary fact that Linear B was not confined to Crete, as Evans had expected, but was in use on the Greek mainland as well.

FIGURE 24.4 A pithos jar excavated by Kalokairinos at Knossos *'Minoan, about 1450–1400 BC. The rope decoration may reflect the way such huge jars were transported. Height: 113 cm.'* [Image credits: © Copyright The Trustees of The British Museum. Website: www.thebritishmuseum. ac.uk/compass/ixbin/ goto?id=OBJ3360]

In 1952 A. J. B. Wace found similar inscribed tablets at Mycenae and additional finds at Thebes brought the total of Linear B material to several thousand specimens. An example from Pylos is shown in Figure 24.5. They were and they are quite magnificent, but there was one enormous problem: nobody could decipher the language in which they were written.

In October 1936 Michael Ventris, then a fourteen-year old schoolboy, visited a Minoan exhibition at Burlington House in London where he met the eighty-five-year old Evans who offered to show his group around.[14] The news that nobody could read the Linear B tablets captured Ventris' imagination and four years later he published his first contribution to the problem. Although he became an architect he continued to wrestle with the enigma until on 1 July 1952 he announced on BBC radio that he had deciphered the language and that contrary to expectations it was an archaic form of Greek. On 25 June the following year *The Times* devoted a leader to his achievement alongside an article on Edmund Hillary's recent conquest of Everest.[15]

Ventris continued to work on the script with John Chadwick, a Cambridge Greek scholar, and together they produced the manuscript of *Documents in Mycenaean Greek*. This was sent to Cambridge University Press in the summer of 1955 and published in autumn 1956, just a few weeks after Ventris' tragic death in a road accident. The solution to this extraordinary puzzle has added enormously to our knowledge of Bronze Age Greece and two very accessible accounts of it are available: Chadwick's 1958 book *The Decipherment of Linear B* and Andrew Robinson's 2002 biography *The Man Who Deciphered Linear B: The Story of Michael Ventris*.

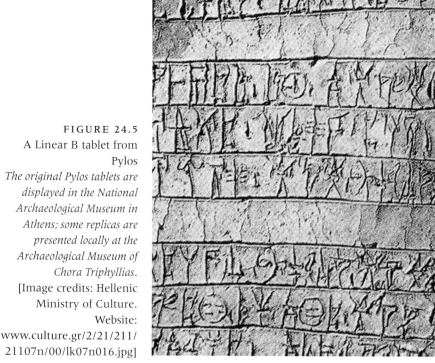

FIGURE 24.5
A Linear B tablet from
Pylos
*The original Pylos tablets are
displayed in the National
Archaeological Museum in
Athens; some replicas are
presented locally at the
Archaeological Museum of
Chora Triphyllias.*
[Image credits: Hellenic
Ministry of Culture.
Website:
www.culture.gr/2/21/211/
21107n/00/lk07n016.jpg]

Linear B is a syllabic script: instead of having a relatively small set of consonants and vowels as in English, the Linear B alphabet has a much larger set of signs arranged in three groups. In the first group are about ninety signs which represent either a vowel or a consonant followed by a vowel: this large number is required because of the need to assign an individual symbol to each viable consonant–vowel combination. For example, in Linear B the following symbols each represent a different syllable starting with the sound 'p':

‡ *pa*   ‍ *po*   ▷ *pe*

If you want to order an Italian beer in Linear B you might ask for a:

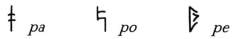

pe-ro-ni

A second group of these signs are ideograms, representations of objects such as 'man' ⋔ or 'deer' ⋈ which stand for the whole name rather than for only a syllable, while a third group of signs indicate numerals, weights and measures.

The first major surprise was Ventris' revelation that the language represented by the writing of Linear B was an early version of ancient Greek. One of the great triumphs of the decipherment took place in 1953 when Carl Blegen applied this 'experimental syllabary' to a newly discovered tablet from Pylos which dealt with catalogues of pots of varying kinds. The tablet contained the symbol ⊟ for a tripod-based vessel and this had already been identified within the second group of ideograms. However, this tripod ideogram was accompanied by some Linear B syllables from the first group: transliterated into English one of these words read 'ti-ri-po-de'.[16] The ideogram matched the syllabic description only if these syllables were interpreted as Greek; furthermore the noun ending was a Greek 'dual' form indicating a quantity of two, and a quantity of two tripods was indeed noted on the tablet. An adjacent set of syllables read 'a-pu ke-ka-u-me-no ke-re-a' which in Homeric Greek can be written *apokekaumenos skelea* meaning 'with its legs burnt off'. Many more examples clinched the matter and the conclusion is that in Knossos, Pylos, Thebes and Mycenae the scribes wrote an early form of Greek.

Another rather less welcome surprise was that when the tablets were deciphered the secrets they yielded were not, as we might have hoped, poems, letters, descriptions of battles, migrations or other historical events. Instead they were accounting records set out in the form of lists: agricultural production, local place names, infantry locations, palace assets such as chariots, the names of individuals, trade indebtedness and so on. It is a sobering observation that the practice of accountancy turns out to be at least this old: here are some examples of Bronze Age creditor accounts and inventory records:

Kokalos repaid the following quantity of olive oil to Eumedes: 648 litres of oil.
One footstool inlaid with a man and a horse and an octopus and a griffin (or a palm tree) in ivory.
One pair of wheels, bound with bronze, unfit for service.[17]

Given that these tablets are felt to pre-date Homeric Troy and Ithaca, what if anything does the decipherment of Linear B tell us about Ithaca? The first curious point is that all four of the civilisations at Knossos, Pylos, Thebes and Mycenae show clear evidence of destruction by fire. It was only by this means that the contents of the tablets were preserved: their soft clay surface was baked in the resulting inferno. The date of these conflagrations can only be estimated: significantly Chadwick says 'In prehistoric periods we can only work from synchronisms with other cultures which have a recorded history and for prehistoric Greece this means chiefly Egypt. Datable Egyptian objects were found at Knossos and it is from these and similar finds that the date of 1400 BC for the destruction of the palace is obtained.'[18]

A few paragraphs previously he explains that the destruction of the palace at Pylos is regarded by archaeologists as having taken place about 200 years later in 1200 BC: in the light of our previous discussion about chronologies he also states rather revealingly 'but the similarities between the two sets of records are such that many have wondered if this difference in time were not illusory'.[19] Although the complexities of the archaeological strata at Knossos are better understood now than they were in 1958 it is nevertheless thought-provoking that Chadwick regarded this as a 200-year discontinuity.

Some familiar Homeric personalities are identified in the Linear B tablets: Zeus, Hera, Poseidon, Hermes, Athene and Artemis are all present.[20] When Odysseus meets Penelope in the *Odyssey*, still in disguise, his reply to her question about his ancestry involves a fabricated account of his origins as the brother of Idomeneus of Crete whom we encountered in Chapter 18. In this passage Odysseus mentions place names such as Knossos and Amnisos on Crete and these are also present in the Linear B tablets.[21]

Ventris and Chadwick suggested that the Linear B word 'ko-ro-ku-ra-i-jo' found on a tablet from Pylos may correspond to the Ithacan place name Crocyleia although it might instead implicate Corcyra (Corfu).[22] Another Linear B expert, L. R. Palmer, favoured the Crocyleia interpretation.[23] In the following two extracts the symbol ⚤ is the ideogram we encountered above for a man, while the syllable 'pu$_2$' indicates a second version of the 'pu' syllable:

ne-wo-ki-to wo-wi-ja ko-ro-ku-ra-i-jo
⚤ 20 me-ta-qe pe-i e-qe-ta
di-wi-je-u

On the borders of Newokito:
Twenty men of Krokula
(and with them the Follower Diwieus)

a-ke-re-wa ko-ro-ku-ra-i-jo ⚤ 50
me-ta-qe pe-i e-qe-ta ka-e-sa-me-no
a-pu$_2$-ka

Fifty men of Krokula at Akerewa
(and with them the Follower
Kaesamenos of Apuka)

There is something quite magnificent about the accomplishment of these two brilliant scholars in reconstructing this lost language from the application of sheer logic to strange marks on clay tablets. These sonorous syllables also have a hypnotic, almost Hiawathan quality about them: indeed the articulation of a lengthy Linear B passage might constitute an imaginative method of sending infants to sleep.

Also appearing in the Pylos tablets is the name *Ne-ri-to*, identified as the owner or guardian of thirty rams,[24] although it is impossible to say whether he was related to Neritos, co-architect of the city fountain alongside Ithacos and Polyctor whom we encountered in Chapter 17.

The name *Do-ri-ka-o* occurs both at Knossos and at Pylos and is thought to mean Dolikhaon. Chadwick suggests that this may be a man's name:[25] presumably it might also be a reference to the island of Doulichion. But etymological appearances can be deceptive: in the fourth century BC Aristotle's pupil Theophrastus used *dolichos* (which we encountered in Chapter 21) as a name for *Vigna sinensis*, the cowpea or black-eyed pea.[26]

If Linear B was used in Pylos around 1200 BC then at what point was the Greek alphabet and the framework of classical literacy adopted? The later Greeks recorded that in 776 BC the first Olympic games took place at Olympia near Elis in the Peloponnese, which is only about 55 km south-east of Cephalonia. Chadwick observes of that period that 'it marks and symbolises the adoption in Greece of the Phoenician alphabet, from which ultimately all other alphabets are descended; from the eighth century BC onwards the Greeks were a literate people, able to record their own history'.[27]

Writing in the fifth century BC Herodotus tells us:

These Phoenicians who came with Cadmus and of whom the Gephyraeans were a part brought with them to Hellas, among many other kinds of learning, the alphabet, which had been unknown before this, I think, to the Greeks. As time went on the sound and the form of the letters were changed. At this time the Greeks who were settled around them were for the most part Ionians, and after being taught the letters by the Phoenicians, they used them with a few changes of form. In so doing, they gave to these characters the name of Phoenician, as was quite fair seeing that the Phoenicians had brought them into Greece. The Ionians have also from ancient times called sheets of papyrus skins, since they formerly used the skins of sheep and goats due to the lack of papyrus. Even to this day there are many foreigners who write on such skins.   5.58

Hellas is an ancient name for Greece and the Phoenicians came from Lebanon, so Herodotus is telling us that the Greek alphabet was derived from an early western Semitic script, probably between the ninth and eighth centuries BC. Some writers have suggested that one of the catalysts for the introduction of this new alphabet might have been the desire to transcribe the *Iliad* and the *Odyssey* from their oral form into a more permanent record, as Linear B would have been a hopelessly clumsy vehicle for poetry of this subtlety. Whether or not this was the case, it is intriguing to learn that after the flourishing period of the Linear B tablets, there is a gap of over 400 years from about 1200 to 770 BC during which we have found no further examples of writing in Greece at all.

To summarise, the best evidence that we have is that at the time of Odysseus the form of writing available to the Ithacans was Linear B. It would have been

gratifying to have found some examples of this script strewn around the double hilltop and the valley below it, but, as Figure 19.17 and Figure 19.18 indicate, by summer 2003 the only surface finds involved some cut stones and unusual rock markings which may simply be the result of weathering. In any case the Linear B material found at other locations has been on clay tablets and vases rather than engraved on stones. However, at this very early stage of the proposed identification of ancient Ithaca we should not rule out the possibility that subsurface Linear B material could exist on Cephalonia because the tablets found elsewhere have generally been discovered only after site excavation and provided they were baked in a fire.

By the end of 2003 I had visited the island four times and it would also have been encouraging to have observed a treasure-trove of thought-provoking sherds of pottery that could be dated back to the appropriate period, but that had not happened either. However John Underhill's researches had turned up one rather interesting item exposed to the surface.

Figure 24.6 is not an example of pottery at all: it is a fossil embedded in the rock wall of Paliostafida Bay which we visited at Figure 15.6. John spotted it as he was striding towards the suitors' ambush anchorage and he explains that these are pecten shells in plioquaternary rock that is about 1–3 million years old. However old we may regard the era of Odysseus, it is rather humbling to think that a few million years ago inside this very shell was a clam which had long since evolved a defensive mobile home in which to dwell in this bay, if indeed it was a bay at that time.

So why were no significant traces of pottery encountered? Indeed how much pottery might we expect to find if the double hilltop was a real Bronze Age site? Could it be that we simply did not have the trained eye of archaeologists? Did repetitive earthquakes over a period of about three thousand years tend to shatter pottery and cause its fragments to percolate deep into the soil? Or were we looking in the wrong place? Once again it was time to consult an expert.

In Chapter 18 we heard of the Cambridge/Bradford Boeotian Expedition, a major archaeological survey co-directed by Anthony Snodgrass and his colleague John Bintliff of Bradford University. This project was launched in 1979 and it has amassed a wealth of painstakingly researched material about the normal dispersion of pottery in the vicinity of Bronze Age sites in Boeotia, a region of ancient Greece to the north-west of Athens.

In their 1988 paper[28] Bintliff and Snodgrass wanted to account for the uniformly high volume of ancient pottery sherds that appear to be strewn across uninhabited agricultural fields. What could be the cause of this counter-intuitive outcome? First they eliminated a standard explanation:

One model for off-site scatters, a feature of archaeological folklore, is the mythical donkey off whose back pots are supposed to have fallen, leaving trails of sherds in otherwise unimportant zones of the landscape. Given the sheer quantity of off-site pottery and its carpet-like distribution, as well as the clear correlation of its density with proximity to occupation sites, this model must be ruled out as a major causal explanation.

Next they considered and dispensed with the possibility of multiple zones of less intensive habitation: as they explain, this could not give rise to a 'virtually continuous spread of artefacts'. Then they looked at a third possibility, that an explanation might be found in the effects of the weather and of ploughing. But as they point out, 'pottery eroding from a site should have minimum upslope distribution' whereas in fact 'The off-site carpet stretches across the landscape, ignoring natural barriers to movement from known sites, there is plentiful material found upslope from existing sites and beyond the reasonable scope of ploughing smears.'

So having considered and eliminated these alternatives and on the basis of their very considerable collective field experience they then offered a most remarkable (and uncannily prescient) alternative proposal:

The model to be introduced here appears at present to offer the most satisfactory explanation for the carpet-like distribution we have described. Put simply, it proposes that prehistoric, ancient, medieval and early modern farmers in Boeotia systematically collected animal and human excrement, together with household rubbish, and regularly spread it across the cultivated landscape as fertiliser. Leavening this mainly organic material was some ceramic debris – broken pots, house tiles – which thus found its way continuously into those sectors of the landscape most assiduously cultivated.

That ancient populations stored fertilising manure on their farms and spread it over their fields is well attested in the historical sources (perhaps the best-known reference being the description of the manure heap beside the palace in Ithaka in Book 17 of the Odyssey).

How appropriate that the authors should have chosen this particular reference! It forms a part of the poet's very moving description of the death of Odysseus' old dog Argos after he is reunited at last with his master:

> In days of old the young men used to take him
> To chase after wild goats and deer and hares.
> But now, his master gone, he lay abandoned
> In the deep dung of mules and cattle, heaped
> Outside the gates for slaves to take away,
> Manure for the mighty holdings of Odysseus.   17.294–9

So we now have it on Homeric authority that animal dung from the palace was used as manure to spread over the land of ancient Ithaca; and we have it on archaeological authority that household debris, including broken pots and tiles, was mixed in with this manure. The implications are irrefutable: if there is no carpet of Bronze Age pottery in the fields near to the proposed palace of Odysseus then I have probably identified the wrong hilltop.

Some of the objects discovered in these expeditions continue to haunt me and one of them is the rock depicted in Figure 19.17. A closeup of these strange markings is shown in Figure 24.7 and from time to time I find myself turning back to the Linear B example of Figure 24.5 and idly comparing the two of them. No doubt this rock simply shows the effects of erosion: the markings are not very clear and it has presumably been exposed to the elements for countless centuries. As we heard previously, Linear B is found on clay not on stone anyway, although a still undeciphered antecedent of it called Linear A has been found engraved on stone objects in Crete.[29]

I really should pull myself together and cease from speculating on the matter but there is one aspect that still puzzles and intrigues me. I can understand that the natural processes of weathering might create the vertical indentations and inverted 'U' shapes on this rock. But I do not understand how rainwater or other forms of erosion can create those parallel horizontal lines, spaced

just as if they were intended to delineate writing. Perhaps it is a trick of the light.

FIGURE 24.7
Detail of rock markings
from Figure 19.18
*Is this just natural erosion or
is some other factor at work?*

Notes

1 From the 'Stephen Hawking' British Telecom commercial 1 May 1993, by courtesy of BT Archives.
2 See for example Lacy (1967); Dickinson (1994).
3 See Kitchen (1987).
4 James (1991) p. 223.
5 For a discussion of dating techniques and difficulties see Aitken (1990) and Manning (1992).
6 See Figure 18.2.
7 James (1991) p. 323.
8 But its precision is increasing each year: see for example Kuniholm et al. (2002). An interesting bibliography is provided at www.arts.cornell.edu/dendro/pikbib.html#biblio
9 The best-known publications on this topic are James (1991) and Rohl (1995). For an academic discussion see the findings of the colloquium presented in Åström (1987). A recent re-appraisal, albeit with more modest chronological corrections, appears at Wiener (2003). A comprehensive list of the major subsequent developments in this proposal and its reception and debate by experts is provided at www.centuries.co.uk

10 There are many independent accounts of this surprising phenomenon: see for example Snodgrass (1967) pp. 35–6: 'the lack of sound information about this first Dark Age is so acute that we can hardly obtain a true picture of it . . . There are no traces of the art of writing in Greece from about 1200 to 750 BC . . . Illumination of the Dark Age, therefore, still rests almost entirely with archaeology, but at this period its lantern is a dim one. For, together with the art of writing, most of the forms of representational art known to the Mycenaeans now appear to be lost. Frescoes, relief and inlaid metalwork, carved stones and figured scenes on vases all vanish for a time at least. Weapons and other artefacts are left to tell their somewhat arid tale.'

11 Randsborg (2002).

12 Souyoudzoglou-Haywood (1999).

13 It has sometimes been suggested that other references ought to be considered, such as *Iliad* 7.175–6 'Each marked his lot / And cast it in the helmet of Agamemnon'. However there is no need to write on one's lot even if one is literate. You may simply make your mark, as any illiterate person is still allowed to do. The idea that the warriors on the battlefield wrote their names in Linear B is a needless flight of fancy. See Lorimer (1950) pp. 474–5 and Kirk et al. (1985–93) vol. II p. 258.

14 Contrary to former accounts Ventris did not attend Evans' scheduled lecture on 16 October 1936: see Robinson (2002b) pp. 21–3.

15 Robinson (2002b) pp. 121–2.

16 Robinson (2002b) p. 119.

17 Chadwick (1958) Appendix paras. 6, 7, 9.

18 Chadwick (1958) p. 107.

19 Chadwick (1958) p. 106.

20 Ventris and Chadwick (1956) pp. 125–9. My researches were based on this first edition of *Documents in Mycenaean Greek*; a second edition was published in 1973.

21 *Odyssey* 19.164–202; Chadwick (1958) p. 125.

22 Ventris and Chadwick (1956) pp. 145, 192, 398.

23 Palmer (1963) p. 156.

24 Ventris and Chadwick (1956) p. 199 [61]; Webster (1958) p. 124.

25 Chadwick (1958) quoted in Kirk (1964) p. 122.

26 Shipp (1961) quoted in Kirk (1964) p. 129. The reference is to Theophrastus, *Historia Plantarum* 8.3.2. In my efforts to make botanical history by establishing that this pea grows uniquely on modern Ithaca I thought I had struck gold when Google returned the headline 'The history of the black-eyed pea: like most folks in the south, Athenians have been eating black-eyed peas longer than anyone can remember' but on closer inspection this turns out to refer to the daily diet of the denizens of Athens, Texas; see www.athenstx.org/History.htm

27 Chadwick (1958) p. 5.

28 Bintliff and Snodgrass (1988); the subsequent extracts are quoted from pp. 507–8.

29 Chadwick (1958) p. 129.

CHAPTER 25 Drama

God takes on many forms;
God often does the unexpected.
He foils what was imagined
And makes the unimaginable happen.
That is what happened here today.

Euripides (epilogue to The Bacchae and other plays)

It is 24 May 2003 and once again there is a plane to catch in a few hours and too little time left to explore this wonderful island. Michael D'Souza and my son Matthew are driving with me along the road from Strabo's Channel towards ancient Ithaca and we have just traversed the inverted horseshoe to the right of centre on Figure 23.2. That diagram shows the layout of the ancient roads, but the modern road continues down to the coast and then westwards along the northern shore of Argostoli Bay. I stop the car for a natural break and wander a short way up an old track. At that time I have not yet pieced together the layout of the old road network and I don't realise that this path is one of the ancient routes from the channel to Ithaca harbour. But something about the scenery catches my eye and I walk past a gate into a clearing surrounded by an unusual terraced hillside.

The hillside is sculpted into a series of rock ledges and later in the summer John Underhill explains that this is a natural geological formation called a 'well-bedded limestone of the upper Cretaceous era': there is another example of it further north in the same valley. I walk up over the rock ledges and arrive at the summit where the open fields are criss-crossed by a dense network of dry stone walls. In the distance is the hill of Kastelli: it would be good to walk across to it but time is running out and Mike and Matthew will be wondering where I am. After retracing my steps to the crest of the hillside I stop in sheer disbelief (Figure 25.1).

As I walk down past tier after tier of stone ledges I cannot dispel the feeling that I am descending from the dress circle down to the more expensive circle seats and finally reaching the stalls (Figure 25.2).

Mike and Matthew join me and pose obligingly at a location where a stone construction, probably another lime kiln, doubles as a podium (Figure 25.3).

I walk down towards the focus of this extraordinary natural theatre and reach the stage. Mike and Matthew are sitting in the circle seats and I photograph them with a telephoto lens in Figure 25.4.

FIGURE 25.1
Terraced rock formation at
the northern end of
the bay
*The view is north-east
towards the Agrilia
mountainside: on Figure 5.3
the area is named Amourdes.*

FIGURE 25.2
Detail of terraced rock
formation
*These terraces are clearly
naturally formed: but have
they also been artificially
smoothed for spectators?*

FIGURE 25.3
Lime kiln in front of
terraced ledges
*For a lime kiln description see
the notes to Chapter 19.*

FIGURE 25.4
Close-up of central rock ledges
The photograph was taken with a 280 mm zoom lens.

The unmagnified view from where I am standing is that of Figure 25.5. They are talking normally to each other over 100 m away from me but I can hear every word that they are saying. It is the same for them: if I speak at normal volume on this stage they can hear me quite distinctly. This natural theatre is blessed with perfect acoustics.

You can see the overall shape of the theatre from Figure 25.6, which was taken later in the year from the other side of the valley looking due west. The old road snakes up the hillside towards the top left of the photograph, but what is not visible from this image is that the natural stone seating also extends along the hillside to the left of the old road, so that the seats form an arc enclosing two sides of the central stage.

The existence of this natural theatre on the road to Ithaca city with its geologically formed rows of seating and its wonderful acoustics does not prove that it has ever been used for meetings or performances. Although some of the rock ledges look suspiciously smooth, professional examination of the stonework will be required to determine whether it has been chiselled to facilitate audience accommodation. New techniques for dating the age of stone based on its first exposure to the atmosphere have recently become available[1] and if these can be applied to this site it should be possible to confirm whether and when there has been man-made abrasion of these rock ledges.

FIGURE 25.5
Unmagnified view of
central rock ledges
*View westwards from the
'stage' of the natural theatre.*

FIGURE 25.6
The theatrical terraced
rock formation
*View across the valley from
the quarry west of the Zola
road junction.*

FIGURE 25.7
Aerial photograph of the
Argostoli peninsula
*The bay in which the suitors
waited to ambush Telemachos
is at the centre of the
photograph: the windy
heights where the lookouts
waited lie on the ridge behind
the white hotel building.*

If it can be shown that this natural theatre was modified for actual performances then we will be left with some fascinating open questions. When did these take place? Could dramatic performances have been taking place in an Ithacan theatre several hundred years before the emergence of classical drama in the fifth century at Athens? If so, what kind of production was enacted at the time? Who composed it? Who acted in it? Who came to see these performances? How many people were in the audience? We can take a stab at that: the length of the auditorium along the western terrace alone is about 300 m and there are about twenty such terraces, so a generous spacing of one spectator per metre could accommodate up to 6,000 people. If an audience of this size assembled there, where did they all come from? Why did the theatre fall into disuse? Why was it not continually used over many centuries as were other theatres in places such as Epidauros? At this stage there can be no firm answers to these questions, indeed there can be no real answers at all. But I think we are entitled to use our imagination (provided we realise that

FIGURE 25.8
Aerial photograph of
Argostoli Bay
Agrilia is the mountain to the
left of centre and Imerovigli
lies to the right. A former
harbour shoreline (to be
discussed in Chapter 30) is
readily apparent from the
photograph.

to do so is not the same as to research) and in Chapter 33 I will consider some
speculative possibilities.

We reach the airport and in no time at all the plane is taxiing along the
runway. In May the charter flights to Cephalonia begin so we have the luxury
of a direct route to Gatwick. The flight path takes us straight over Paliki and
fortunately I am sitting on a window seat on the right hand side of the aircraft.
That represents two more benign coincidences to add to our growing list.

Figure 25.7 is an aerial photograph of the southern end of the Argostoli
peninsula. Closest to the camera is Cape Lardhigos and behind it is Paliostafida
Bay where the suitors tried to ambush Telemachos. This bay is one of the twin
harbours mentioned by Homer and the other harbour is on the far side of the
promontory. The lookout hillside with the windy heights, Mount St Gerasimos,
lies behind the hotel building at the far end of the beach.

As the plane gains altitude over Paliki we reach the northern end of Argostoli
Bay. In Figure 25.8 you can see the spit of the Rheithron estuary jutting out
into the bay and providing a natural hiding place for the imaginary vessels

of Athene and Odysseus. At the northern end of the bay to the left of the picture you can distinguish the low-lying contours of the former harbour. The tiny cove of Agia Sotira lies on the far right of the image while the bay of Agia Kiriaki lies at the other end of the isthmus at the top centre of the photograph. A comparison with Figure 20.2 may be helpful.

It is a magnificent, beautiful and seductive island. Each time that I return to it there are more questions to research, new places to visit and additional hypotheses to test, but I can hardly emigrate: much of the work must be performed back in England. That distance also reinforces a necessary degree of detachment. When one is on Paliki it is all too easy to imagine a real Odysseus and his tangible fellow citizens going about their business, but in Kingston-upon-Thames the vision is not quite the same. There one's thoughts are percolated by the knowledge that for nearly three thousand years this poem has been regarded as the brilliant creation of a fertile imagination. How can these views be reconciled?

Note

1 For a sympathetic introduction to cosmogenic nuclide surface exposure dating see
   http://www.geos.ed.ac.uk/facilities/cosmolab/sgj_final.PDF

CHAPTER 26 **Exodus**

'Beauty is truth, truth beauty,' – that is all
Ye know on earth, and all ye need to know.   Keats, *Ode on a Grecian Urn* (1819)

Our goals in this chapter are twofold: to acquaint ourselves with the origin and migration of the Ionians and also to build a framework that may help us to distinguish between myth and truth in the narrative of the *Odyssey*. The link between these two objectives is less tenuous than one might suppose because the various accounts of the origin of the Ionians include a liberal dose of the most beautiful myths. We also need to lay some groundwork for a question to be tackled in Chapter 33: since most experts believe that Homer lived several centuries after the events of the *Odyssey* on the western coast of what is now called Turkey but was then called Ionia, how did he learn so much about the local geography of Ithaca?

Let us start by considering the Ionian Migration, which is depicted in Figure 26.1 by the red arrows. What prompted this exodus? There is a considerable scholarly debate on this issue. Until a few decades ago it was widely believed that at some time in the latter half of the twelfth century BC a barbaric race called the Dorians invaded southern Greece. A leader of the Dorians called Hyllus was said to be a son of Heracles[1] and for this reason the Dorian Invasion is also referred to by the ancient historians as 'The Return of the Heraclidae'. One account[2] of this traditional view describes an invasion route depicted by the yellow arrows on Figure 26.1. However, the long-standing belief in a Dorian invasion has in recent years been challenged by archaeologists, who point out that the evidence of such an invasion seems thin on the ground and also that this was a period of fundamental collapse of the Late Bronze Age civilisation. James Whitley puts the matter in perspective: 'This is not to deny that there may well have been movements of people in the less settled conditions which followed the fall of the Mycenaean palaces. It is rather to assert that we cannot necessarily "track" these movements by looking at changes in fashion, burial or dress.'[3]

If the Dorian Invasion is in doubt, what alternative causes might have prompted what has been called the 'Bronze Age Catastrophe' and triggered the Ionian Migration? In a thoughtful review of the prevailing theories Robert Drews considers alternative proposals such as earthquakes, other migrations, the introduction of ironworking, drought, endemic collapse and the advent of raiders before suggesting that 'the Catastrophe was the result of a new style

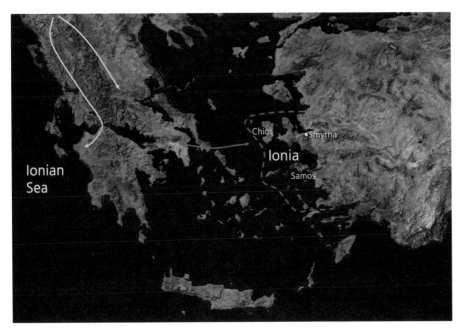

FIGURE 26.1
The Ionian Migration
*Archaeologists question the
evidence for the Dorian
Invasion; by contrast the
Ionian Migration is not in
doubt. Something triggered
this exodus, but its cause has
not yet been established.
Colour interpretation: as
Figure 3.1.* [Image credits:
as Figure 3.1.]

of warfare that appeared toward the end of the thirteenth century B.C.'.[4] This view has also been challenged but, for whatever reason, it appears that at about this time southern Greece became a less attractive place in which to live and many of its residents decided – or were forced – to leave.

Some of these emigrants are called Ionians: we hear from Strabo that 'the Attic people of ancient times were called Ionians, and from that stock sprang those Ionians who colonised Asia' (8.1.2). Homer himself refers to 'the Ionians with trailing robes' (*Iliad* 13.685) fighting at Troy alongside Boiotians, Locrians, Phthians, Epeians and Athenians. The name *i-ja-wo-ne* appears on the Linear B tablets from Knossos and is thought to refer to 'Ionians', which would make the name Mycenaean or pre-Mycenaean and therefore very ancient indeed.[5] So the dispossessed Ionians of the Peloponnese decide to travel east, taking their name to these new settlements on the coast of Asia Minor and the outlying islands, a geographical area which then becomes known as Ionia.[6]

Whether mythical or real, the Dorian Invasion is traditionally dated to about eighty years after the Trojan War and the Ionian Migration to some sixty years after that, which on the conventional chronology corresponds to around 1060 BC.[7] The emigrants probably travel via Athens where they meet with other colonists. Their destination is the region around today's city of Izmir which was then called Smyrna. There they colonise the strip of land together with some of the offshore islands that you can see in Figure 26.1: the mainland area is only about 150 km long and 50 km wide.

To the south of Izmir you can see an island with the familiar name of Samos and this is not a coincidence. Strabo says that the island was called Samos 'after some native hero or after someone who colonised it from Ithaca or Cephallenia' (14.1.15). Iamblichus (who lived from AD 240 to 325 and wrote a *Life of Pythagoras*) provides further details:

It is said that Ancaios who lived in Same in Cephallenia was a son of Zeus (a title which he owed either to his physical prowess or to some greatness of soul) and surpassed the rest of the Cephallenians in wisdom and reputation. He received an oracle from the Pythia, instructing him to form a colony from Cephallenia and Arcadia and Thessaly and to take in addition colonists from the Athenians and the Epidaurians and the Chalcidians and, as leader of all these, to colonize an island that was called Melamphyllos because of its soil and land, and to call the city Samos, in place of Same in Cephallenia. The oracle went as follows:
　'Ancaios, I order you to colonize an island in the sea, Samos, in place of Same. At present its name is Phyllis.'[8]

The Pythia was the priestess of the Delphic oracle and *melamphyllos* means 'black-leaved'. Pythagoras himself was born on Samos in the mid-sixth century BC.

Now Cephalonia is one of the so-called 'Ionian' islands and it lies in the 'Ionian' Sea, so how did this name come to be attached to this sea and these islands? The modern explanation is that 'the name would seem to originate from early Ionian seafaring to the west'.[9] This description presumably refers to the Ionians of the Peloponnese rather than to the subsequent colonists of Asia Minor: the notion that the Ionian Sea might have earned its name because descendants of the east-bound colonists chose to revisit their old haunts is distinctly unappealing. But if we can believe the tradition of Ancaios reported above then at least some of these Ionian emigrants came from the Ionian island of Same.

Assembling this information we may therefore propose the following summary as material for the reconstruction to be presented in Chapter 33:

1 *There is general archaeological and linguistic agreement that the people called Ionians originally lived in the Peloponnese.*
2 *Around 1060 BC a number of the Ionians migrated eastwards and colonised part of the western coast of Asia Minor, giving it the name Ionia.*
3 *One group of these Ionian emigrants originally lived on Same where they were ruled by Ancaios.*
4 *Ancaios led colonists from Same and from other places in Greece to an island off the coast of Asia Minor called Phyllis or Melamphyllos, which they renamed Samos.*

By contrast with the sketchy evidence in support of the Dorian Invasion, the Ionian Migration is extensively documented and the reality of this exodus is not in serious doubt. But we will now depart from the world of historical evidence and enter the realm of myth. To date I have tried to resist this temptation but there is a reason for this imaginative indulgence which I will develop in this chapter.

The Greeks themselves were unsure about the origin of the name 'Ionian' so they invented a myth to account for it: in fact for good measure they invented three. The first myth was concocted by the Athenians, who liked to believe that the name originated from Ion, son of King Xouthos of Athens.[10] This sounds like a rather blatant case of Atheno-centrism and so we can hardly be expected to rely on it.

The second myth is recorded by Strabo. When comparing the names Ionian and Adriatic, he says that 'According to Theopompus, the first name came from a man, a native of Issa, who once ruled over the region, whereas the Adrias was named after a river' (7.5.9). In the footnote on that page of the Loeb edition of Strabo we read that the man's name was Ionios.[11] Ancient Issa turns up a few pages earlier at 7.5.5 where we learn that it is the island of Lissa, now called Vis, off the coast of Croatia.

The third myth is just as imaginary but far more beautiful: it has no direct relevance to our case but let us enjoy it all the same. The tragic dramatist Aeschylus, who was born in 525 BC, wrote over seventy plays but only seven of these have survived, one of which is *Prometheus Bound*. This is the first in a trilogy; the other two are *Prometheus Unbound* and *Prometheus the Fire-Bringer*, but these are lost. The version of *Prometheus Unbound* that is familiar to us today is a very different work composed by Shelley and it is to this that I refer in the Prologue. Here are the lines from Aeschylus, *Prometheus Bound* in which Prometheus is addressing Io:

> On reaching the Molossian plains, and the rock-wall
> Which towers above Dodona, where Thesprotian Zeus
> Has his oracular seat, where grow the speaking oaks –
> A marvel past belief – by which you were addressed
> Plainly and unambiguously as the destined bride
> Of Zeus – does that truth touch you? – from that place you rushed,
> Plagued by the gadfly's sting, along the sea-shore path
> To the wide Adriatic, whence back yet again
> The storm of frenzy drove you on your wild flight here.
> And that bay of the sea shall for all future time –
> Mark this – be called Ionian, to perpetuate
> For all mankind the story of Io's wanderings.
>
> Aeschylus, *Prometheus Bound* 830–41 (transl. Vellacott)[12]

Io is a rather unlucky personality in Greek mythology: the story according to Ovid[13] runs as follows. Zeus fancies Inachus' beautiful daughter Io and before long he has his wicked way with her in the fields, shielded from his wife Hera via a convenient cloud. However, Hera becomes suspicious and so Zeus turns Io into a cow, hoping that Hera will imagine that he is instead pursuing an innocuous hobby of animal husbandry (a dangerously ambiguous phrase as Ovid tells us that 'even as a cow she was lovely').

Hera is unimpressed and confiscates the cow, entrusting it to the hundred-eyed Argos to guard for her. Argos' zeal as a watchman provides no opportunity for Io to escape to enable Zeus to arrange their next tryst so he despatches Hermes to sort Argos out. Hermes eventually manages to behead Argos after sending him to sleep by telling him some spectacularly boring stories and Argos' hundred eyes are thereafter immortalised as the decorative motif on the peacock's tail.

Hera is furious and banishes Io: plagued by gadflies she moos interminably around Greece until she reaches Dodona, which is an oracle in the form of a sacred oak about 8 km south-west of present-day Ioannina in north-west Greece. Aeschylus tells us that she then wanders frenziedly along the western coast until she reaches the present-day Adriatic[14] which thereafter bears her name as the Ionian Sea. However there is a happy ending for Io: she ends up in Egypt, is restored to human form by Zeus and bears Epaphus (Apis) to be the first king of Memphis.

We can hardly treat a maiden called Io who metamorphoses into a cow as a real person, but this interplay of myth and reality in Aeschylus' explanation of the etymology of the Ionian Sea reminds us that the definition of what counts as 'true' in poems such as this and the *Odyssey* is far from straightforward.

In Chapter 2 I used the phrase 'layers of paint' to describe the Homeric controversy and I asked whether Odysseus was a James Bond-like figure performing implausible acts in real locations on Ithaca. Actually my comparison is an unfortunate one because James Bond himself did not exist. Even though he and other characters in Fleming's novels were modelled on some of the author's acquaintances, that does not make them real. Furthermore the action from time to time involves objects and technologies (invented by the immortal Q) that also do not exist. What kind of framework can we adopt to describe such situations?

I must tread carefully here because it would be unwise to stray into an area such as literary theory about which I am uninformed. But I think we can nevertheless develop a common-sense classification which may help us with the question 'Is the *Odyssey* true?' The following framework has helped my own understanding of these issues but I am not suggesting that it is anything other than what C. H. Waddington describes as an optional 'Tool for Thought' in his eponymous book, so if you find it unhelpful you can simply ignore it.

	People	Objects	Locations	Events
Odyssey - off Ithaca				
Actual	Menelaos	Ship	Cape Malea	Visit to Sparta
Exaggerated	Polyphemos	Whirlpool	Phaiacia (Scherie)	Voyage by raft
Imaginary	Zeus	Bag of winds	Floating Aiolia	Turned into pigs

FIGURE 26.2
Reality Matrix examples
for the *Odyssey* (off Ithaca)

When reflecting on the truth of the *Odyssey* I tend to consider four principal elements: People, Objects, Locations and Events; the acronym forms a useful mnemonic, the pole of the debate. As we saw above, an author can insert imaginary people into actual locations, or actual objects can play a part in imaginary events. And as well as being actual or imaginary, they can also be half-and-half: they can be exaggerated. These various elements can therefore each be categorised as either Actual, Exaggerated or Imaginary and I use this simple framework to provide a rigorous method of classifying the truth or falsehood of the narrative.

For convenience I call this a Reality Matrix and in Figure 26.2 I have drawn up such a table using as examples some of the activities of the *Odyssey* that take place away from the island of Ithaca. I emphasise that these are simply arbitrary examples that I have chosen; they are clearly not an exhaustive list.

To start with the first column of the matrix, Menelaos lived in Sparta and as far as we are aware he was an actual person rather than a figment of Homer's imagination. By contrast, Polyphemos lived in the land of the Cyclopses and although large people existed at the time, as undoubtedly did cannibals, he is clearly an exaggerated personality. But that is not the same as to be wholly imaginary, in the sense that we regard Zeus as imaginary.

Likewise we can consider some of the objects that contribute to the action away from Ithaca. The ships that are described are clearly real ones: Homer did not have to invent the concept of a ship or describe it as five times as large as it really was. By contrast, whirlpools certainly exist, but the whirlpool of Charybdis sounds implausibly dangerous:

> Quaking with fear we sailed into the strait.
> On that side Scylla lay, on this Charybdis
> Sucked in the salt sea terrifyingly;
> And when she spewed it out, she seethed and boiled
> Just like a cauldron on a fire; the spray
> Shot high and drenched the cliff tops on both sides.   12.234–9

This is superheated spray indeed, especially since a few pages earlier at 12.73 we learn that one of these cliffs 'Reached the broad heaven with its pointed peak' and half-way up it there is the lair of Scylla, itself so high that at 12.83–4 we are told that 'No bowman firing from the hollow ship, / However strong his arm, could reach that cave.' Nevertheless Charybdis is recognisably a whirlpool, whereas a sealed bag of winds that can blow a ship back from Ithaca to Aiolia is surely the stuff of poetic imagination.

The same simple taxonomy readily applies to Odyssean locations. Cape Malea is passed by Odysseus at 9.80 on his wind-blown journey from Ismaros to the land of the Lotus-eaters : it continues to exist today beside Cythera at the south-eastern tip of the Peloponnese on Figure 26.1. But although Scherie, the island of the Phaiacians, is believed to be the ancient name for Corfu, its palace is notoriously described at 7.114–18 as containing an orchard in which 'grow tall leafy trees, / Pear-trees and pomegranates, apple trees / With glossy fruits, sweet figs, luxuriant olives. / Their fruit grows all year round and does not die / Or fail in either summer or winter time.' This fecundity seems somewhat far-fetched unless King Alcinoos was the early pioneer of a biodome such as the Eden Project in Cornwall, and we have no historical evidence for that hypothesis.

As a different example, the island of Aiolia where Odysseus is given the bag of winds is described in some translations at 10.1 as 'floating' which places it fairly and squarely in our Imaginary category. As James Diggle has told me, even Herodotus had some difficulty with the geophysics involved: in relation to another such island called Chemmis he says that 'It lies in a deep broad lake . . . and the Egyptians says that it is a floating island. I myself never saw it float or move, and I wondered, when I heard about it, if there really is such a thing as a floating island.'[15] Those imaginative commentators who have equated floating islands with icebergs have yet to explain their formation and longevity in a lake in the temperate latitudes of Egypt.

Turning to the last column of Figure 26.2, an event such as Telemachos' visit to Sparta can clearly be regarded as Actual: there is nothing intrinsically fanciful about such a journey (although that does not prove that it happened in the way that Homer describes). By contrast Odysseus' journey by raft from Ogygia to Scherie is described at 5.278 as taking seventeen days, which sounds like an exaggeration. Finally Circe's conversion of his shipmates into pigs at 10.241 suggests a mastery of genetic engineering that today's DNA specialists can only dream about (indeed one sincerely hopes that they do not).

What seems to emerge from these examples is that in the off-Ithaca passages of the *Odyssey*, Homer incorporates all the available shades of truth, exaggeration and imagination in his description of people, objects, locations and events. What is the comparable position for his narrative on Ithaca itself? Figure 26.3 is my attempt to quote some examples based on the description of Ithaca that I have presented in this book so far. If you are uncomfortable with the latter then you will not be reassured by this second table, but at least it has the virtue of consistency.

	People	Objects	Locations	Events
Odyssey - on Ithaca				
Actual	Eumaios	Marital bed	Pigfarm	Suitors' feasts
Exaggerated	-	-	-	-
Imaginary	Athene	-	-	Divine intervention

FIGURE 26.3
Reality Matrix examples
for the *Odyssey* (on Ithaca)

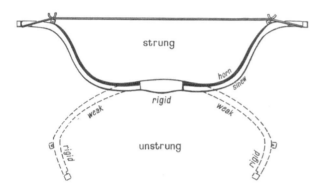

FIGURE 26.4
The probable construction
of Odysseus' Bow
*'Such bows . . . are more
powerful than the ordinary
bow: to string them is difficult,
and it cannot be accomplished
by one pair of hands unless
the stringer sits or squats and
braces the bow under one
thigh and over the other
knee.'* [Image credits: Wace
and Stubbings (1962)
p. 519. Reproduced with
the permission of Palgrave
Macmillan.]

On the island of Ithaca itself the descriptions of people seem to fall into only the Actual and Imaginary categories, corresponding to mortals and gods: I cannot find any obvious examples of exaggerated personalities such as Polyphemos. Regarding objects, the majority of those described seem perfectly reasonable – even the bed of Odysseus and Penelope that is described at 23.181 as hewn by him out of an olive tree is hardly implausible.

The description of Odysseus' bow at first appears to involve some exaggeration since only Odysseus can string it (as opposed to draw it). However, in a fascinating discussion about its construction we hear from Wace and Stubbings in their *Companion to Homer* that this difficulty was probably the result of lack of familiarity rather than inadequate strength:

What is presumably intended is what is usually called a 'composite bow', made partly of wood, partly of sinews and horn, the latter acting in effect as powerful springs. Such bows, known both in antiquity and in modern times, are readily recognizable when represented in art from the characteristic reverse curvature of the tips. They are more powerful than the ordinary bow: to string them is difficult, and it cannot be accomplished by one pair of hands unless the stringer sits or squats and braces the bow under one thigh and over the other knee . . . An early form of the composite bow must have been known to the Mycenaean Greeks.[16]

As far as Ithacan locations are concerned it is the purpose of this present volume to suggest that all of these are accurately described by Homer. Finally, I find most of the events that are described on the island perfectly credible,

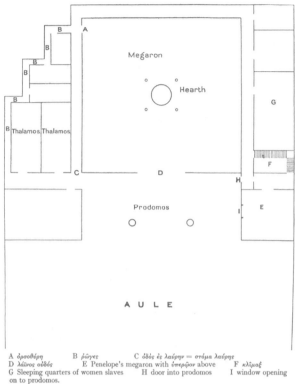

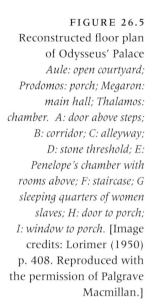

FIGURE 26.5
Reconstructed floor plan
of Odysseus' Palace
Aule: open courtyard;
Prodomos: porch; Megaron:
main hall; Thalamos:
chamber. A: door above steps;
B: corridor; C: alleyway;
D: stone threshold; E:
Penelope's chamber with
rooms above; F: staircase; G
sleeping quarters of women
slaves; H: door to porch;
I: window to porch. [Image
credits: Lorimer (1950)
p. 408. Reproduced with
the permission of Palgrave
Macmillan.]

with the possible exception of the odds associated with Odysseus, Telemachos, Eumaios and Philoitios (the loyal cowherd) triumphing against 108 suitors. But here again Homer is at pains to point out that Odysseus was equipped with the element of surprise and long-range weaponry with which to tackle the suitors who were trapped in the dining hall. A detailed study of the relationship between the description of the massacre and the layout of the palace is presented in Lorimer's *Homer and the Monuments* and her resulting floor plan is depicted in Figure 26.5.

Using this palace plan for guidance Lorimer suggests that one of the key elements of the battle fits into place. During the massacre the poet tells us:

> There was an opening in the sturdy wall
> Close by the threshold. It led to an alley
> And was secured by snugly-fitting doors.
> Odysseus told the swineherd to stand guard
> Beside it: there was only one approach.
> Ageleos shouted out for all to hear –
> 'Friends, can't somebody climb up to the opening,
> Raise the alarm and call for help at once?
> This fellow's shooting days will soon be over.' 22.126–34

Lorimer relates this description to her floor plan as follows:

The episode can now be clearly reconstructed. The Suitors, huddling at the inner end of the hall, propose to Melanthios to slip out by the orsothyre [A – the rear side door] *(which he has every chance of doing unobserved, since the crowd of suitors masks his movements) and by way of the laure* [C – narrow passageway] *try to gain the courtyard. Melanthios points out that as the laure has its exit in the prodomos* [porch], *that will bring him too near to Odysseus and his party; and we know that in fact Eumaios, though he forgets his job in the excitement of watching events in the hall, had been told to watch this very spot . . .*[17]

The telling point about Lorimer's explanation is not that it is necessarily the right one: indeed we may never know what the right one is. It is simply that it is credible and consistent with the notion that a carefully planned coup carried out by four individuals led by a master of ingenuity with detailed knowledge of his own palace could succeed against opposition of this magnitude. If the event is exaggerated then this exaggeration is certainly not in a league with that which converted an unusually large meat-eater into a Polyphemos.

The events on Ithaca which are clearly imaginary from a modern perspective are those which involve the intervention of the gods. However, the dividing line between gods and mortals at the time of Homer was much less solid than it is today: so much so that, as we have seen, Zeus himself chose frequently to consort with mortal maidens. In an era that pre-dated scientific inquiry and on an island that was regularly shaken by inexplicable natural phenomena such as thunderstorms and earthquakes, we should not be surprised to hear that there was a continuity of belief rather than a bronze curtain between superstition and reality.

Listening to the gods was perhaps like listening to the voice of your con-science and perhaps also to your conscious thought processes. Indeed at least one brave psychologist has advanced the theory that human beings existed before the development of consciousness itself, intriguingly proposing that at the time of the *Odyssey* they were pre-conscious, guided by auditory hallucinations which they interpreted as the voices of the gods.[18]

Whatever personal construct of the gods an individual Ithacan held, it seems to me that in his many references to the intervention of Zeus, Athene and other deities, Homer was not deliberately injecting imaginary figures, any more than in his references to earthquakes he was describing an imaginary phenomenon. Today we believe that earthquakes are caused by continental plate tectonics, but at that time the geological explanation was called Poseidon. Lightning for us is an electrical phenomenon associated with a voltage gradient between two clouds or between a cloud and the ground, but for the Ithacans the physics involved Zeus' thunderbolts. We may regard a feat of

	Score

Actual	*1*
Exaggerated	*2*
Imaginary	*4*

FIGURE 26.6
Reality Index scores

extraordinary bravery as driven by an adrenaline surge, but in those days the biochemistry was called Athene: indeed we still refer to 'superhuman' courage. Today we regard such gods as imaginary but for Homer and Odysseus they were real.

Clearly the few examples above are hardly exhaustive, but my own belief is that Homer intended his descriptions of people, objects, locations and events on Ithaca itself to be actual: it is only our modern attitude to passages describing the actions of the gods that obliges us to categorise them as imaginary. By contrast, I believe that Homer deliberately intended to inject some exaggerated and imaginary material into his account of Odysseus' activities away from Ithaca.

It would be useful to have a way of describing these patterns of truth, exaggeration and imagination more concisely and to achieve this we can amuse ourselves by borrowing a simple approach from binary arithmetic (Figure 26.6).

We can use this table as follows. If the people are actual then we can score this as a 1, if they are exaggerated this counts as a 2 and if they are imaginary the score is a 4. If there are some actual people and also some imaginary people in a given narrative then we can add their scores together to make 5; if there are some people of all three types then the overall score is 7. If we can do this for people we can clearly also score the remaining elements (objects, locations and events) in the same way, and the combination of these scores gives us a 4-digit result that I call a Reality Index. If there are no instances at all of an element (we have all had the misfortune of reading a very dull story in which no memorable events occur) then it scores a 0. The outcome of this procedure is that the higher the Reality Index, the less real is the corresponding subject matter.

The Reality Matrix for the plot of the *Odyssey* away from the island of Ithaca in Figure 26.2 contains examples of all three categories for all four elements, so its Reality Index is 7777. By contrast, the Reality Index for activity on Ithaca itself Figure 26.3 is quite different: 5115, and this much lower value identifies an essential difference in the respective narratives. Furthermore if divine intervention is reinterpreted as Bronze Age science then its score drops to 1111: it appears to be real in every respect.

	Score	People	Objects	Locations	Events
Odyssey - off Ithaca					
Actual	1	Menelaos	Ship	Cape Malea	Visit to Sparta
Exaggerated	2	Polyphemos	Whirlpool	Phaiacia (Scherie)	Voyage by raft
Imaginary	4	Zeus	Bag of winds	Floating Aiolia	Turned into pigs
Odyssey - on Ithaca					
Actual	1	Eumaios	Marital bed	Pigfarm	Suitors' feasts
Exaggerated	2	-	-	-	-
Imaginary	4	Athene	-	-	Divine intervention
Reality Index					
Odyssey - Off Ithaca		7	7	7	7
Odyssey - On Ithaca		5	1	1	5
Biography		1	1	1	1
Bible (fundamentalist)		1	1	1	1
Bible (anthropologist)		5	5	1	5
J. R. Tolkien		4	5	4	4
Ian Fleming		2	1	3	6
J. G. Ballard		5	1	1	5

FIGURE 26.7
Reality Index examples

I have no illusions that this attempt to create a Gödelian form of reference scheme[19] for literature will catch on like proverbial wildfire, but Figure 26.7 presents my personal assessment of the reality index of some other published works. My chosen examples are biographies, the Bible, J. R. Tolkien, Ian Fleming and J. G. Ballard. Your own scores for these works may differ from mine, but curiously I discovered that my figure of 5115 for the *Odyssey* on Ithaca turns out to be the same as the value that I have given to Ballard's novels. Perhaps the dream-like quality of his visions of the near future bears some comparison with the trance-like experience of a conversation with a god from the distant past.

We heard earlier that Hyllus was said to be the son of Heracles whose name conjures up the eponymous Labours. Are we also expected to believe that Heracles cleaned the Augean stables by diverting the rivers Alpheios and Peneios through them, along with his eleven other implausible accomplishments? I don't think that this need worry us too much. The Labours of Heracles involve exaggerated and imaginary people, objects and events that take place in both real and imaginary locations: their score is a fanciful 6656. By contrast, there is copious archaeological and linguistic evidence for the migration of the Ionians: their score is a clear 1111.

The fact that the ancient Greeks liked to amuse themselves with elegant stories does not make their entire lives a poetic fiction. What we would very much like to know is just how many of the locations described in the *Odyssey* might be real. My present observation is that the closer we get to Ithaca itself, the more reliable Homer's topographical evidence becomes. Why might this be the case? In Chapter 33 I will offer a possible explanation.

Not included in the table is a reality index for Ovid's enchanting story of Io, the gadfly-tormented cow. When she is a human she is actual, which counts as a 1, but as a cow I tend to regard her as imaginary, with a score of 4. By contrast the hundred-eyed Argos is exaggerated because he presumably had only two eyes in reality, so the composite score for Io's people is 7. Turning to the story's objects, Zeus' tactical cloud sounds exaggerated, which gives us a 2, whereas the geographical locations appear to be real, with a score of 1. Finally the event associated with the creation of the peacock's tail decoration certainly sounds imaginary, with a score of 4, and none of the other events sound real either. Bringing these scores together results in a reality index of 7214 for the tale of Io: it is a delightful myth based around real locations.

Does any of this analysis actually tell us anything? Computer-literate readers will recognise that we have constructed a schema capable of representing distinctions between 4,096 shades of reality, which is probably far more than we will ever need. I find that this provides me with a useful perspective from which to consider the question 'Is the *Odyssey* true?', but I appreciate that others may regard it as digital sophistry. Indeed I feel sure that it would have been of little help to Zeus when cross-questioned by Hera about his conjugal fidelity. I think that she might have accused him of being uneconomical with the truth.

Notes
1 Newman and Newman (2003) p. 60a.
2 Lacy (1967) p. 284.
3 Whitley (2001) p. 80.
4 Drews (1993) p. 33.
5 Ventris and Chadwick (1956) p. 419; see also Kirk et al. (1985–93) on 13.685–8.
6 Emlyn-Jones (1980) ch. 2; Huxley (1966) ch. 2.
7 Thucydides 1.12.3; Pausanias 7.2.1–4.
8 See also Sakellariou (1958) p. 96.
9 Hornblower and Spawforth (2003) p. 764.
10 Herodotus 7.94, 8.44; Euripides, *Ion* 1581–8; Strabo 9.1.18.
11 'Ionios, an Illyrian according to the Scholiasts (quoting Theopompus) on Apollonius (*Argonautica* 4.308) and Pindar (*Pythian Odes* 3.120).'
12 Reproduced with the permission of The Society of Authors as the Literary Representative of the Estate of Philip Vellacott.
13 Ovid *Metamorphoses* Book 1.
14 Aeschylus refers to the Gulf of Rhea which is the present-day Adriatic.

15 Herodotus 2.156. However if we admit of islands composed of dense mats of floating vegetation then such a phenomenon exists today only 70 km NNE of Paliki in the Lake Voulkaria of Chapter 2, where it is described by botanists using Homer's word for floating, *plote*. See Bousinos et al. (2001).

16 Lorimer (1950) pp. 289–300; Wace and Stubbings (1962) pp. 518–20; see also Lorimer (1950) pp. 289–300.

17 Lorimer (1950) pp. 408, 423–4.

18 Jaynes (1979).

19 In one of the most famous theorems of mathematics Kurt Gödel demonstrated in 1931 that in every formal mathematical system there are undecidable arithmetical propositions that cannot be proved either true or false within that system. His proof made use of a technique in which textual axioms in the system were replaced by combinations of prime numbers and the resulting 'Incompleteness Theorem' showed that the structure of mathematics itself contains inherent contradictions that cannot be resolved. See Gödel (1931).

PART 4 Revelation

When the facts change, I change my mind. What do you do, sir?

John Maynard Keynes (1883–1946)

CHAPTER 27   **Rockfall**

It was a work of genius, and at the same time a lonely and potentially soul-destroying
project. It was the work of one man, with one idea, bent upon the all-encompassing
mission of making a geological map of England and Wales. It was unimaginably
difficult, physically as well as intellectually. It required tens of thousands of miles of
solitary travel, the close study of more than 50,000 square miles of territory that
extended from the tip of Devon to the borders of Scotland, from the Welsh Marches to
the coast of Kent.   Simon Winchester, *The Map that Changed the World* (2001)[1]

Tuesday 26 August 2003: the alarm goes off at 5.00 am and soon I am driving
through the darkened roads of Erissos towards Argostoli airport. John Underhill has spent the night travelling from Edinburgh via Athens and his flight is
due in at 06:55. A single point of light shines ahead of me: as the first rays of
dawn brighten the sky alongside Argostoli Bay it is still clearly visible towards
the west. It is Mars and as we saw in Figure 15.8, tomorrow night it will reach
its brightest intensity for nearly sixty thousand years.

It is worth staying awake while driving along these roads of Cephalonia because they involve some of the most hair-raising drops imaginable.
Figure 27.1 depicts the fate that awaits a sleepy driver whose concentration
lapses momentarily on the approach to Angonas above Agia Kiriaki Bay, the
northern exit of Strabo's Channel. If your vehicle veers off the road at the top
left of the photograph you will be launched down a 40° slope that will plunge
you straight into the sea. No amount of braking or four-wheel drive grip will
help because the surface of the incline is populated by loose rubble that will
accompany you like an avalanche.

These loose rocks have clearly come down from the mountains above and
this process is taking place almost continuously. As well as free-form rubble,
sometimes whole sections of the rockface detach themselves and slide down
the mountainside: in Figure 27.2 you can see that a massive oval-shaped
segment has slipped down a nearby cliff and is poised perilously above the
sea, waiting for the next earthquake to bring about its baptism.

If there is a deep enough area of the sea below the rockfall then much of
this rubble will eventually dissipate as a result of wave action, but if the sea is
shallow then this may take some time. Figure 27.3 shows a major slide further
south on this stretch of coast that came within just a metre or so of demolishing
the cliff-hugging road. Much of this fallen material has been washed away by
the sea but you can still see a pile of debris on the beach. If however the rockfall

FIGURE 27.1
South-facing view
towards Agia Kiriaki
*The village of Zola lies at the
far side of the bay under
Mount Agrilia.*

FIGURE 27.2
Detached rock segment
above Myrtos Bay
*In the summer the bay is
packed with tourists: the
beach is claimed to win
regular votes as one of the ten
most beautiful in the world.*

FIGURE 27.3
Major rockfall north of
Agia Kiriaki
*The road from Fiscardo passes
within a few metres of the top
of this massive rockfall.*

takes place in an inland area then there is no sea to wash away the rubble and it simply stays in place, waiting for the next rockslide to hurtle down and cover it over. Even to a layman it is clear that this process of mountainous erosion has been going on for thousands of years.

John's arrival on Cephalonia is of fundamental importance. However striking the correlation between Homer's descriptions and the island's geography, if John tells us that Strabo's Channel could not have existed then this will create a massive and potentially fatal problem for the theory. He has been visiting the island professionally for eighteen years and earlier in Scotland he asked me what I would do if the outcome turned out to be negative. My instinctive reply was the remark of a true obsessive: that I'd be disappointed but that I'd offer to work with him instead to develop some new geology. Notwithstanding my convictions, John is not a man to be persuaded of something against his professional experience: when you have 60,000 football fans shouting down at you from the stands it has the effect of stiffening the sinews.

The Olympic Airways island shuttle lands precisely on time and John strides through the airport with his geologist's knapsack on his back. For a man who hasn't slept for twenty-four hours he looks decidedly dapper. He changes and we breakfast at the Mediterranean Hotel where we contemplate before us the scene of the world's oldest attempted marine ambush.

The next three days are as busy as any that I can remember: from 8 am to 8 pm I follow John around Strabo's Channel with my notebook in hand, listening, trying to learn some geology and occasionally interjecting with a layman's 'But why?' We start by visiting the Agia Sotira southern channel exit of Figure 12.4 and I wince as John draws in his breath at how narrow it is. Somehow all my photographs and evidence such as the finding of seawater inland and the anomalous block of Eocene limestone now seem rather thin. We drive north and when he sees the valley of Figure 12.8 he starts to sketch on his notepad the angle of the 'V' compared with its height above sea level. It looks ominous: whichever way you draw it, the sides of the valley seem to intersect at its base well above sea level.

This time we are staying in Villa Aquarius at Markandonata in north-west Erissos: each morning John and I drive south along the stunning cliff road and each evening we are reunited with my abandoned family over dinner in Fiscardo. These journeys provide us with forty minutes to plan the events of the day and in the evening to reflect on what we have just learnt. As we drive home after the second day he asks me whether I want him to start with the good news or the bad news. I opt for the latter:

'The bad news is that there is no possibility that a former marine channel used to exist along the course that you have proposed. It is too narrow and the geometry just doesn't work. Well before reaching sea level, the valley walls would have closed up to block any inlet. I'm sorry, but as a professional geologist I have to tell you that your candidate route for Strabo's Channel simply did not exist.'

So that's it: end of project. I am driving and I dare not look round at him, partly because we may go off the road if I do and partly because I don't think he's bluffing. After all, what kind of good news could there possibly be after this? That he's discovered some new kind of fossil? I am silent. John remorselessly continues:

'The good news however is that it's quite clear to me a channel could have existed: it's just that you have located it too far to the west. As far as I can see, if there was a channel, its course would have been a few hundred metres further to the east.'

The most precipitous part of this road involves the circumnavigation of the cliffside of Myrtos Beach. At that precise moment we are several hundred metres above it in the pitch darkness and its pristine pebbles narrowly avoid high-altitude indentation from the front half of our trusty Suzuki Jimny:

'John, this is encouraging news but nevertheless quite extraordinary. Surely all that exists several hundred metres to the east of where I imagined the ancient channel to have flowed is the base of a mountain. Have I heard you right?'
'Yes. What you thought was the channel was actually the outflow from a lake: let me explain . . .'

Over the rest of his stay with us in August John patiently elucidated for me the underlying geology. There were some subsequent modifications and refinements and we returned to the island in November 2003 and in July and August 2004 to test these assumptions. Further visits will be needed to calibrate the geological timescale accurately: the latest news of this may be contained within the Postscript to this book.

At this point professional geologists will prefer to digest John's Appendix 2 and this will tell them concisely all that they need to know. But I have learnt through this experience that theirs is a most unusual and interesting profession: indeed the rest of us mere mortals may describe it by paraphrasing Scott Fitzgerald's perceptive observation and Hemingway's laconic reply: 'The geologists are not like us.' – 'Yes, they have more imagination.' Most of us regard the landscape as fixed, as something immutable, the most solid aspect of our existence. If you live in London or Surrey or in New York City or Westchester County then you do not expect to walk out of your front door one morning to find the ground before you at a wholly new gradient and altitude.

However the imagination of a geologist can easily stretch to this possibility: indeed it can be likened to a grotesquely speeded-up movie in which each frame corresponds to a year rather than about 1/25 of a second. For these terrestrial visionaries twenty-five years themselves pass in a second and a minute corresponds to a millennium and a half, while the passage of an hour approaches 100,000 years. In fact I suspect that by this time a geologist's brain goes logarithmic because timespans of the order of a billion years can clearly be contemplated without controversy. They are the globe's plastic surgeons: our solid earth is but their melted fondue.

The alternative explanation is that everyone else finds this sort of thing really easy to understand and the problem lies only with me. Either way I am going to attempt to compress into a few pages and diagrams the mental gymnastics to which John sadistically subjected me over several months because I really do think that this is one of the most extraordinary stories that I have ever heard. I hope you will be equally captivated. I should add that at the date of this writing a scientific timescale had not yet been established for the phenomena I am about to explain and so the dates mentioned below are at present only informed estimates.

The Holocene period runs from 10,000 years ago to today and during that time the indications are that the western peninsula of present-day Cephalonia was separated from its eastern mainland by a narrow channel that defined two distinct islands. How can we be reasonably sure about this? Let us turn to the geologist's view of the age of these rocks.

Figure 27.4 shows the extension of Figure 7.5 and Figure 7.6 to the whole of northern Paliki. This map was produced in 1973 as an update to the previous

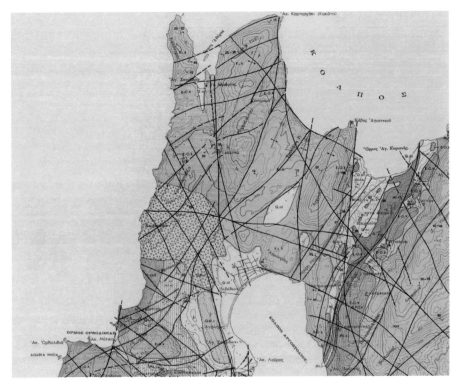

FIGURE 27.4
IGME 1973 geological map
of NW Cephalonia
*The black lines on the
diagram indicate proposed
faults of various kinds. This
aspect was updated by John
Underhill's 1989 paper: see
Figure 11.7 and Appendix 2.*
[Image credits: IGME
(1985).]

joint BP/IGME survey. The different colours correspond to the age of the rocks and for the avoidance of too much complexity I will refer only to the main distinctions.

The light cream colour is Holocene alluvium: it is fresh sediment no more than 10,000 years old. This includes the north-western part of Argostoli Bay and the ancient harbour of Ithaca: it also describes some of the ground in between Agia Kiriaki to the north and Argostoli Bay itself. The bright green adjacent area is Cretaceous, between 144 and 65 million years old. The other colours lie in between: the light pink is Paleogene (65–24 m years old), the brown is Miocene (24–5 m years old), the yellow is Pliocene (5–2 m years old) and the brown spotted region is Pleistocene (2 m – 10,000 years old).

If you look back at Figure 7.6 you can see that to the east of what I then thought to be the course of Strabo's Channel there is some very ancient rock. In Figure 27.4 this is the dark brown Miocene segment that stretches from shore to shore. John's diagnosis therefore puts the channel slap bang on top of rock that is between 24 and 5 million years old. How can this possibly make any sense? The answer is to lift the picture off the page.

Impressive though satellite technology is, the images lack a crucial ingredient: we don't know the height of the photographed features above sea level. By contrast, the old-fashioned paper-based surveyors' plans that I received from Athens in March 2003 incorporate the usual contours that tell us how high above sea level any point on the map happens to be. What we really need is a way to combine this information with a 2-dimensional map or photograph and in the last decade or so that has become possible: it is called a Digital Elevation Model (DEM).

In a DEM there is a digital value that represents the height above sea level of each point in a rectangular grid spread across the area of interest. There are two principal ways of obtaining these height values. The first is to examine the surveyors' maps and convert these into a table of digital altitudes. Although this process can be computer-assisted it remains labour-intensive and prone to errors because of indistinct contour lines, smudges on the paper and differences in the style and reliability of the surveyors involved.

The other technique is to perform stereoscopic photography, either from satellites or from aircraft. By overflying the target area and taking matched pairs of photographs from a known distance apart, the two images can be compared and the altitude information automatically extracted, using the same principles that the human eye exploits in our binocular vision. If you look out of the window at a landscape for a minute or two and then shut one eye, you realise that you have now lost your normal perception of distance, but with both your eyes open again the distance information is preserved.

That is the theory, but the likelihood of obtaining DEM data for Cephalonia seemed remote until September 2003 when I logged into the Hellenic Military Geographical Service website[2] and discovered to my delight that DEM altitude data for the whole of Greece had just become available at a horizontal grid resolution of 30 m. Furthermore in November the US Mapmart service announced the availability of 90 m resolution DEM data across the whole of Europe.[3] By combining the HMGS data with the Quickbird satellite images I could now fly around the island while sitting at home.

Returning to Figure 27.4, the Digital Elevation Model was now programmed with the height of this area to a horizontal accuracy of 30 m square and a vertical accuracy of a few metres. That enabled me to elevate this IGME geological diagram and also to turn the picture round so as to look towards Argostoli from the northern exit of the channel.

In Figure 27.5 you can see the result of doing just that and it is now evident that the channel area is what John with a geologist's precision refers to as 'a mess'. The world does not evolve organically like this, with a patchwork quilt of rocks of quite different ages *in situ* on the ground (i.e. connected to the bedrock as opposed to simply resting on top if it). The only credible explanation for this kind of geological formation is that some of it slid down from the mountains above.

FIGURE 27.5

Digital elevation version of IGME geological map

In a Digital Elevation Model (DEM) a computer program is used to elevate the surface of a map or aerial photograph according to the corresponding altitude data values.
[Image credits: IGME (1985). Data source: DEM data from Hellenic Military Geographical Service. Processing: OziExplorer 3D. Websites: www.gys.gr, www.oziexplorer.com/]

Once it became clear that this is what had happened then John decided to return with me in November 2003 to re-survey the channel geology accompanied by Morgan Jones, an outstanding postgraduate student of his. The 1973 IGME map was only a part of an overall Ionian Islands survey and this in turn formed just one component of an extensive search for oil. At that time there was no particular merit in concentrating excessively on the geomorphology of this small valley and so it was inevitable that some details would need to be reassessed. John's updated diagram is at Figure 27.6 on which the colour scheme and age ranges are different: here is the explanation of the main areas.

The green colour continues to be Cretaceous, 144–65 million years old; the dark pink area is now Paleogene, 65–24 million years old and the light pink is Miocene, 24–5 million years old. Ignoring some of the other details for the moment, the most important addition is the dark blue area which is described as 'Landslipped'. John e-mailed me this diagram on 2 December 2003 and one of the benefits of modern technology is that within an hour or so I had plugged it into the digital elevation model and sent it back to him.

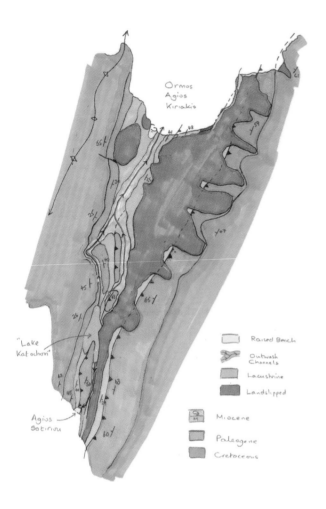

Raised Beach

Outwash Channels

Lacustrine

Landslipped

Miocene

Palaeogene

Cretaceous

FIGURE 27.6
John Underhill's survey of
the channel geology
*This beautiful manuscript
diagram is an accurately
scaled representation of the
Thinia isthmus. The dark
blue area represents landslip
material that has descended
from the mountains above.*
[Image credits: Underhill –
on-site survey November
2003.]

The resulting perspective view is displayed at Figure 27.7. The technique
is actually quite simple: first one geo-references the diagram by specifying the latitude and longitude of some known locations and then the digital elevation information is used to add the correct height to the resulting
landscape.

There is a great deal of information that we can discern from this diagram
and as ever it is best to start at the beginning. First of all, the purple-blue
area represents loose landfill that has detached itself from Mount Imerovigli
(993 m) to the east and hurtled down the slope: the smaller dark blue ovals
to the right have likewise descended from Mount Agrilia (456 m) to the west
(the right of the diagram). This is a remarkable observation when we consider
the overall size of the blue area: its total length is about 8 km and its maximum
width up the slope is about 600 m in extent. This prompts us to ask at least four
new questions: what was at sea level beforehand, why did so much landfill
material descend, where did it come from and when did all this happen? We
do not have complete answers to these questions yet, so what follows is my

FIGURE 27.7
Digital Elevation Model of
John Underhill's survey
*John Underhill observed that
his scaled 2D mapping of the
landslip aligned almost
perfectly with the 3D elevation
values from the scalloped
areas of the mountainside.*
[Image credits: as Figure
27.6. Data source and
processing: as Figure 27.5.]

layman's interpretation of John's present understanding as he has described it in geological language in Appendix 2.

What was at sea level beforehand? If you imagine all the dark blue material removed from Figure 27.7 then you can see that Mount Imerovigli previously sloped steeply down towards the sea. You can identify this more clearly on Figure 27.8 which is a close-up of the northern channel approach. On it is marked the former entrance to Strabo's Channel, which is here only about 230 m wide. If you were a Bronze Age sailor approaching the channel then to your left you would look up at the steep cliffside of Same, with Mount Imerovigli looming nearly a kilometre up above you, while to your right you would look out across the undulating hillocks of Ithaca which rise up in the background towards the lower peak of Mount Agrilia.

For now you can ignore the crimson stream in its small valley to the right of centre since we will be discussing that in a page or so, but I will nevertheless freely admit to my former ignorance since that is where I previously imagined the northern channel entrance to be.

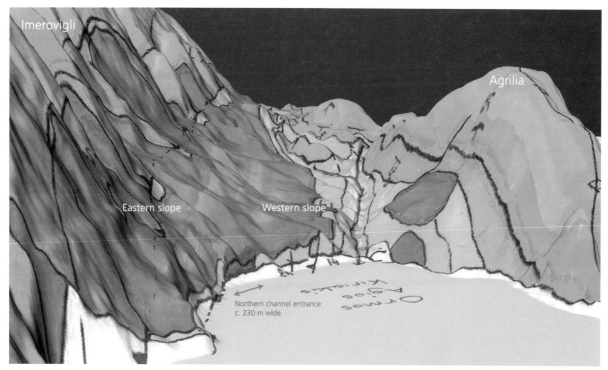

FIGURE 27.8
Digital elevation close-up
of northern channel
entrance
*It is now obvious that this
landslipped material has
descended from the
mountainside. But when did
it fall? Was it a single event or
a succession? And what was
the nature of the terrain there
beforehand?*
[Image credits: as Figure
27.6. Data source and
processing: as Figure 27.5.]

The length of the channel itself is about 6.5 km and because it is so narrow we will certainly have to row all the way. Tim Severin, captain of the Jason and Ulysses voyages, advises us that 'oared ships averaged something in the region of two knots on long journeys as the constant grind of rowing day after day sapped the energy of the rowers'.[4] One knot is 1.85 km per hour: even if our rowers are fresh we are unlikely to exceed 5 km per hour and so it will take us well over an hour to traverse Strabo's Channel.

As we make headway through the channel, the steep slope on our left stays more or less the same throughout but the previously gentle slope of the hillside of Ithaca to our right becomes progressively more severe. By the time we have rowed half-way through the coastline of Ithaca rises almost sheer on our right. The feeling is decidedly claustrophobic: we are rowing through a narrow channel with cliffs on each side, but whereas the Samian cliffs keep going on up and up, on the Ithacan side there is an elevated plateau and we are at the mercy of whoever might be standing up there armed with rocks or bows and arrows.

As we reach the three-quarter mark the cliffs to our west open up into a bowl-shaped valley with a distinctive hill ridge about 400 m away from us. On its crest there is the settlement of Aigilips and we know what it looks like: we have seen it in Figure 20.13. Although this area is coloured in as a light blue lake on John's diagram at Figure 27.7, as far as we are aware at the time of

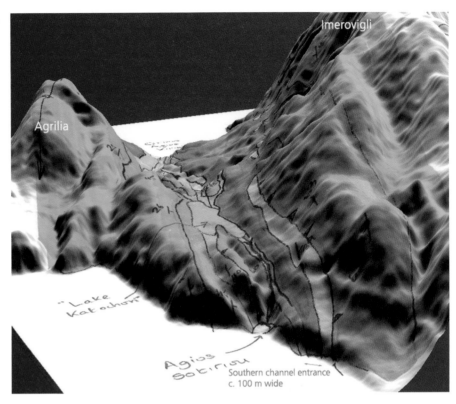

FIGURE 27.9
Digital elevation closeup of
southern channel entrance
For a comparison with the
corresponding satellite image
see Figure 32.23.
[Image credits: as Figure
20.1. Data source and
processing: as Figure 27.5.]

our Bronze Age transit that lake did not exist, and nor did the adjacent dark blue landfill: the coast of Ithaca simply sloped down to sea level to meet the channel.

We row on past it and now we are at last approaching the southern exit of the channel. Its width is little more than about 100 m and we are greatly relieved to leave this narrow natural chasm and to hoist our sail in the sunny reaches of Argostoli Bay (Figure 27.9). In this image you can see that the southern entrance to the channel is not located at Agia Sotira as I previously believed: instead it emerges into the bay about 500 m further south.

It is an extraordinary geological outcome but even non-geologists will find it hard to believe in this diagnosis without some solid evidence. We can make a start on this with further help from satellites. An excellent source of Landsat medium resolution satellite images is available on the Internet and even better, at the time of writing it is free.[5] Figure 27.10 shows the result of downloading an image of the island of Cephalonia and combining it with altitude data from the digital elevation model. The left hand side of this image can be compared directly with Figure 27.8. The false colour coding on Landsat imagery is different from that of Quickbird. Trees, bushes, crops and wetland vegetation are coloured green; bare soil and urban areas are lavender; water is black or dark

FIGURE 27.10
Landsat digital elevation
of northern Paliki
*The landslipped material in
the Thinia isthmus is readily
apparent. The steep slope of
the adjacent mountainsides
down to the sea is of major
relevance to the case for
Strabo's Channel.*
[Image credits: as Figure
1.3. Data source: as Figure
4.1. Processing: as Figure
27.5.]

blue. Even to my untrained eye it was becoming obvious that this part of the island had slid down from the mountains above.

Shortly we will look at the mechanism that caused all this landfill to occur but before we do so you may like to inspect the contours of the ancient channel itself. This is not as easy as it sounds because it has been covered all along its length by up to 180 m of landfill and there has been ample time for vegetation to grow over it and for houses, villages and roads to take root. In short, the possibility of detecting the former channel sounds pretty remote.

But to our surprise and delight it turns out that infrared satellite photography can tell the difference between vegetation that is growing on loose rubble compared with vegetation that is based on *in-situ* bedrock. Over a short distance you cannot see the distinction but over a long enough segment you can, and we have a length of 6.5 km as a reference. Better still, this particular imagery is also in the public domain, courtesy of the NASA Web Map Viewer.[6] You do not need to harbour suspicions of my digital manipulation: you can download and assess this photograph for yourself.

The image on the left is a raw view of the available satellite imagery: I have simply adjusted the contrast and brightness to bring out the whiter false-colour area along the channel contours. The right hand image is a duplicate with the channel superimposed. Its course is where John has defined it but I have taken some modest liberties by adding small-scale indentations along its

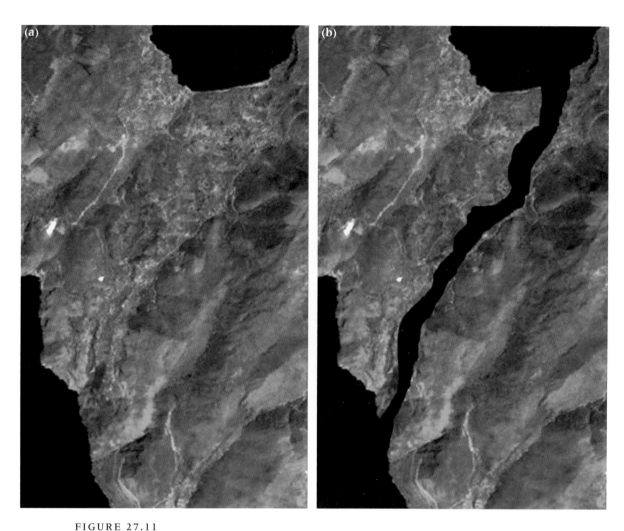

FIGURE 27.11
NASA infra-red imagery
of Strabo's Channel
*(a) Raw satellite image
(contrast and brightness
optimised). Colour
interpretation: as Figure 20.1.
(b) Cutaway section
corresponding to lighter areas
of imagery.*
[Image credits: JPL World
Map Service: World
Topography layer – WMS
Global Mosaic. Websites:
http://viewer.digitalearth.
gov/viewer.cgi,
http://wms.jpl.nasa.gov/]

banks so as to follow the white borderline of the infrared image. Subsequent research will be required to confirm the exact contours of this buried coastline but its essential nature is not likely to change.

It is remarkable that from space we can still see the outline of Strabo's Channel today. The explanation may be that the landslipped material is more porous than bedrock and so its water retention characteristics differ from the neighbouring terrain, which is why the Landsat image there is whiter. If that is so then we must be cautious because it means that the white area denotes only a significant depth of landslipped material rather than a subterranean sea channel. But if subsequent tests prove that there was once a marine seaway separating the two islands, then this is undoubtedly where it used to be.

What about that mysterious lake? As the landfall material progressively fills up the channel, eventually the light blue area that you can see in Figure 27.9 becomes land-locked: the accumulating debris encloses its northern, southern

FIGURE 27.12
Lake Katochori
*The hillside ruins identified as
Aigilips in Figure 20.13 lie to
the right.*

and eastern extent, with the hillside which I have proposed for the settlement of Aigilips on its west. Rainwater from the mountainsides collects within it because it is a 'closed drainage system' and the result is the formation of a large irregularly shaped lake, about 1 km long and 250 m at its widest. When a lake such as this forms it has the effect of flattening its own bed and that is why this area today is still so flat and fertile.

In Figure 27.12 you can see the southern end of the ancient lakebed that John Underhill has discovered. In the distance is the bay of Argostoli and to the right is the presumed site of Aigilips. The area is today called Katochori which means 'place below' – in fact almost 'under the hill'. Personally I think we should therefore christen it Lake Underhill but I am told that acts of auto-toponymy are frowned upon in geological circles. Perhaps we should adopt John's apt proposal and call it Lake Katochori instead.

Lake Katochori flourishes for a considerable period of time – we do not know for how long but we will be addressing the issue of timescales later. As we walk up over the hillside in that era we are greeted by the stunningly beautiful sight of this land-locked natural reservoir. It is hard to estimate its average depth with any precision but since the ancient lakebed level was essentially where we see it today (although subsequent mountaintop erosion will have added some further layers of soil) and in view of the height of the surrounding hillsides, somewhere around 10–20 metres of depth seems a reasonable estimate.

By now the surface area of the lake has expanded to about 250,000 square metres and if we assume an average depth of around 15 metres then this corresponds to a volume approaching 4 million cubic metres of water. At some point the lake breaches its northern or southern earth dam, flowing out along one of the outwash streams marked on Figure 27.7 and Figure 27.9. Several such stream ravines are shown on John's diagram and these probably existed well before the lake was formed, since they represent natural catchment routes for the rainwater coming off the mountains. Over geological time these streams have carved those V-shaped notches into the landscape, creating the ravines which I mistook for the course of Strabo's Channel. To this day a gentle stream continues to run through the northern valley into the bay of Agia Kiriaki, but that is not where the ancient channel emerged.

That, in a rather copious nutshell, is what John believes has happened to Strabo's Channel and the extraordinary thing about it is this: there is absolutely no surface indication of a former marine seaway at all. It has taken his painstaking geomorphological analysis to identify the hidden evidence and that is why this secret has eluded us over so many centuries.

It is 4.30 pm on 28 August 2003: John's visit is nearly ended and we have not yet seen the southern entrance to the channel, because the only vantage point from which one might see such an opening is a boat. We are running out of time and on the offchance that we might find a fisherman we drive down to the tiny cove of Lithos Beach, about a kilometre to the south of Agia Sotira. Once again the gods are smiling on us – not only is there a boat in sight but its engine is running at the tiny jetty, almost as if this were planned. We jump in and our boatman, who works at the nearby fish-farm, asks us where we want to go. Argostoli? Lixouri? Perhaps Livadi, across the bay? Well no actually: we want you to take us to a completely featureless section of the coastline about 500 m to the north, wait for a few minutes for us to take some photographs and then bring us back again.

Fortunately the Cephalonians became acclimatised to British eccentricity many years ago and after the surprise wears off our request seems to present no real difficulty. We edge along the coastline until John asks the boatman to stop. He stares at the hillside and so do I. The boatman looks at us enigmatically: I photograph it and the result is depicted at Figure 27.13. But as you can see, this image shows no sign of a channel opening at all, so why were we so elated? It is easier to follow the course of the former channel if we back away from the shoreline.

In August 2004 I returned to Cephalonia with my family and spent a week learning to sail from the Sea-Trek base in Lixouri. That also enabled me to gain a marine perspective on these locations by sailing around them at leisure. Figure 27.14 was taken from the deck of our Atlantic 31 yacht as we were struggling to furl the genoa (and to remember what all these new nautical

FIGURE 27.13
The buried southern
entrance to the channel
*The colour of the landslipped
material in the foreground
contrasts sharply with that of
the mountain behind.*

terms mean). The small white flash of rock just above the shoreline in the centre of this photograph corresponds to the triangular section of exposed rock in Figure 27.13. This photograph holds the key to a most remarkable geological phenomenon.

Let me start by admitting again to my naïveté of March 2003. The tiny bay of Agia Sotira to the left of the photograph is the scene of Figure 12.3 through to Figure 12.6 and I now know that this area has no bearing whatever on the course of Strabo's Channel. It is simply an outwash ravine that is a naturally eroded exit for the rainwaters that have collected over the millennia in the valley above.

The road that traverses the mountainside on the right marks what geologists call a 'contact': it indicates the boundary between the bedrock above and the rockfall below. It is no accident that this road follows the demarcation of the geology because it was cut through the rockface during the British occupation in the mid-nineteenth century. If you were a Victorian engineer

FIGURE 27.14
A marine perspective on
the southern channel exit
*The bay of Agia Sotira lies
towards the left.*

aiming to build a lasting road network, would you construct your new highway on solid bedrock or on mobile landfill? And would you build it any higher up the mountain than was necessary? In Figure 27.15 you can see that the road follows a treeline about one third of the way down from the top of the photograph. The crucial point to appreciate about this photograph is that *everything you can see below the treeline has slid down the mountain.*

If you allow your imagination to remove all of this rockfall material then you will see in front of you the ancient channel. What I would now like to do is to remove the rockfall from Figure 27.14. That is hard to achieve on a photograph without making the bedrock of the mountainside beneath appear artificial, so in Figure 27.16 I have focused only on the opening of the channel itself. Try to imagine as well that on each side of the channel the lighter brown landslip material is no longer there: beneath it is a darker grey/brown surface of solid limestone, matching the colour of the mountainside above the road.

We do not yet know if there was a line of sight all the way through from south to north or whether the narrowness and the contours of the passage obscured the view. But we do now know why Homer wrote:

Third came that stalwart fellow Philoitios,
Leading a heifer and fat goats for the suitors.
They had been brought across by ferrymen,
Who also ferry people, any who come.   20.185–8

We are at the channel's south-eastern exit so this is where the entre-preneurial Samian ferrymen would have been based. On the hillside of Figure 27.15 are visible the dry stone walls of an abandoned settlement, but this must be of more recent origin since it has been built on the rockfall itself. Perhaps there is a more ancient village buried underneath.

Later in November I make my way back to the northern bay of Agia Kiriaki to see if I can photograph from the sea that other hidden channel entrance as well. Once again my luck is in: the taverna owner offers to take me out in his boat to look at the bay and soon I am looking at the buried northern entrance (Figure 27.17).

On a return visit John and I scramble up that hillside and we are encouraged to discover that this cleft that you can see at the eastern end (left) of the photograph in the cliff above the beach is much more distinctive than we had imagined (Figure 27.18).

The ridge line across the back of the ravine is composed of rockfall mate-rial, whereas the bedrock itself is exposed close to the foreground. When the rockfall happened this area was initially uniformly covered, but subsequently the runoff from the winter rains has eroded its way into this loose material and cut away the small valley that we see in this photograph.

Further to the west along Agia Kiriaki Beach there is a rather dramatic sea cliff that is composed entirely of landslip material. You can see John Underhill beside this in Figure 27.19, a photograph taken in August 2003. This beach cliff has been successively eroded by the winter waves and it reveals an inter-esting form of layering: at its lower face it has been 'reworked' by the sea. This means that this part of the cliff, which is today about 2 m above sea level, was once underwater: the sea has smoothed its layers of conglomerated rock.

There can be only two reasons why it is now above the ground: either sea levels have declined or land levels have thrust upwards. We shall revisit this evidence in Chapter 29.

If you still find these channel entrances somewhat unconvincing then I am not surprised. Even after the preceding explanation it takes a considerable effort of the imagination to push the rockfall back up the mountains and to see instead a former channel opening. From a personal perspective this difficulty

FIGURE 27.15
Dry stone walls at the
southern channel entrance
*Everything below the tree line
towards the top of the
photograph is landslip
material.*

FIGURE 27.16
Reconstruction of the
southern channel exit
*This simulation has involved
simply the removal of material
from Figure 27.14. In reality
the remaining surfaces would
not exhibit landslip material
and the sides of Strabo's
Channel would be visible
beyond the gap.*

has been a blessing in disguise, because if the channel was more obvious then it would have been discovered many years ago. Strabo's description of the isthmus has naturally been noted by others but the existence of an apparently solid mountainside has acted as a formidable deterrent to its acceptance. Writing in 1879 about his words 'Where the island is narrowest it forms a low isthmus, so that it is often submerged from sea to sea' the French archaeologist Riemann said:

This last suggestion seems quite extraordinary: there is not a single place on the island where this could be true: the isthmus that Strabo apparently describes would be that of Agia Kiriaki which joins the peninsula of Paliki to the main bulk of the island; but this isthmus is more than 500 feet above sea level.[7]

In his 2001 publication Gilles le Noan explained that he consulted with geologists regarding the possibility of earthquakes infilling the channel but

FIGURE 27.17
The buried northern
entrance to the channel
*The former entrance to the
channel is in the centre of the
photograph, buried under an
avalanche of rock.*

FIGURE 27.18
Northern channel ravine
at Agia Kiriaki
The view is to the south-west.

FIGURE 27.19
John Underhill at the Agia
Kiriaki beach wall (August
2003)
*Imerovigli towers up to nearly
a kilometre in the
background. The vertical
beach cliff in the foreground
has been eroded by the winter
waves.*

the advice he received was that Strabo's description of a partially submerged isthmus appears impossible wherever on Paliki one attempts to locate it.[8] However, he also reported that in 1903 the Palikian Gerasimos Volterras had taken Strabo's description seriously. Le Noan's and Volterras' theories are discussed in more detail in Appendix 4.

We have been exploring the question 'What was at sea level beforehand?' and the answer that has been put forward in this chapter is this: a narrow marine channel between the two islands of Same and ancient Ithaca. But this is still a proposal, not yet a proof. You are perfectly entitled to say that even though John Underhill has determined that there have been massive landslides all along this valley, that does not prove that the sea used to penetrate from the northern end of Argostoli Bay right through to the bay of Agia Kiriaki. How do we know that there is not a solid bridge of bedrock underneath the rockfall?

If we set aside the historical evidence of Homer's descriptions of the 'island' of Ithaca and also Strabo's account of the sea-washed low-lying isthmus, then probably the only way that this point can be proved beyond possible doubt is to conduct large-scale seismographic tests all along the valley of Thinia. That will demonstrate whether (fatally) there is a buried layer of bedrock crossing from east to west above sea level, or whether all of the material down to sea level has landslipped. That will be a worth-while endeavour but it is clearly outside the scope of the preliminary researches that have been conducted to date. Comprehensive scientific dating tests will then need to be applied to the successive layers of rockfall all along the isthmus (see Figure A2.24). That will be a major project which will require substantial time and resources. However, two further sets of observations provide us with provisional support for the proposition that Strabo was right.

Crucially, John has been able to determine that below the rockfall material, the extrapolated contours of the underlying bedrock enable a channel to have reached all the way from north to south: as he says in Appendix 2:

Significantly, since the bedrock profile projects to a level at or below sea-level irrespective of where it is constructed along the length of the Thinia valley, the intriguing possibility exists that this palaeovalley formed a narrow marine channel connecting Kolpos Agia Kiriaki with Kolpos Livadhiou, with the present Paliki peninsula therefore having once been an island.

If you look at Figure 27.16 and take yourself back to an era before any rock-fall, the question that John is addressing here is as follows: did the mountains on each side drop down to the sea and leave a marine channel in between, or was there a region where the two hillsides met to form a land valley instead? John's survey of the entire length of Thinia demonstrates that the natural continuation of the observable bedrock slope on each side does indeed leave enough room for the sea to have penetrated throughout. Of course even this does not prove that the sea really did go through: there might still be that unusual subterranean bedrock outcrop that does not follow the existing hillside contours. The diagrams in John's Appendix 2 are supportive rather than a proof, but he has at least eliminated an important objection.

Another area of study that may in time support the former existence of Strabo's Channel has the virtue of being quite independent of these current researches. Marine sedimentology is the study of the size and chemical composition of the particles suspended in sea water and it can provide a great deal of information about their provenance. Shallow water particles have a diameter and a chemistry that is different from those in deep water, and the characteristics of a particular area can cause the particles from there to be distinctive and therefore traceable. This may provide us with a fascinating opportunity to test whether Strabo's Channel was once a marine seaway.

In this part of the Mediterranean a major current called the Ionian Surface Water travels southwards from the northern Adriatic down the centre of the Ionian Sea. In doing so it creates an anticlockwise eddy that results in a north-westerly current past Cephalonia.[9] If similar conditions prevailed in the Late Bronze Age then a northbound current would have passed through Strabo's Channel, transporting sediments through it. Can we therefore determine whether there is anything distinctive about the sedimentary particles in Argostoli Bay and if so, whether the same type of particles have been (unexpectedly) found in the bay of Agia Kiriaki? If so there would be a strong suggestion that they had reached the bay via Strabo's Channel.

The shallow northern waters of Argostoli Bay were studied via just such a project between 1966 and 1968 by the Ionian geologist Karl Braune, who identified what he described as aberrant deep-water samples there. He also analysed micro-fossils such as *Foraminifera* and claimed that there were unexpected deep-water varieties of these as well. In both cases he was puzzled by the fact that these aberrant samples existed only at the shallow northern end of the landlocked bay, not at its southern exit. Although he did not study the bay of Agia Kiriaki nor propose the former existence of Strabo's Channel, he felt that these results were consistent with (what was for him a most puzzling) 'inwash from the open sea'.[10]

Marine sedimentology has matured very considerably since that time and Tjeerd van Andel has pointed out that Braune's work would need to be replaced by a modern study if the results are to be relied upon, but for now the interesting idea that emerges is that a new study of the characteristics of these two bays might enable us to determine if there has ever been a direct marine connection between them.

But it is time now to leave the issue of what was at sea level beforehand and consider instead those other three questions. Why did so much landfill material descend, where did it come from and when did all this happen?

Notes

1 Winchester (2001) p. 195. Reproduced with the permission of Penguin Books Ltd.
2 See www.gys.gr/ENGLISH/EN1.htm
3 Mapmart is located at www.mapmart.com. Other useful guides to satellite and DEM data are located at www.globalmapper.com and www.oziexplorer.com (in the Maps and OziExplorer 3D sections); these sites also provide programs for visualising and manipulating this data.
4 Severin (1987) p. 145.
5 As of this writing Landsat satellite imagery can be downloaded from https://zulu.ssc.nasa.gov/mrsid/mrsid.pl and DEM data from http://edc.usgs.gov/srtm/data/obtainingdata.html
6 This image was obtained from http://viewer.digitalearth.gov/viewer.cgi by specifying the World Topography layer. This consists of pan-sharpened false colour Landsat imagery from the WMS Global Mosaic provided by JPL World Map Service at http://wms.jpl.nasa.gov/
7 Riemann (1879) p. 9.
8 Le Noan (2001) ch. 10.
9 Robinson et al. (2001) p. 16; Heikell (2003b) p. 23.
10 Braune (1973) pp. 109, 118.

CHAPTER 28 Earthquake

EARTH is rocking in space!
And the thunders crash up with a roar upon roar,
* And the eddying lightnings flash fire in my face,*
And the whirlwinds are whirling the dust round and round, –
* And the blasts of the winds universal leap free*
And blow each upon each, with a passion of sound,
* And æther goes mingling in storm with the sea!*
Such a curse on my head, in a manifest dread,
* From the hand of your Zeus has been hurtled along!*
O my mother's fair glory! O Æther, enringing
All eyes with the sweet common light of thy bringing,
* Dost see how I suffer this wrong?*

1083–93

Prometheus Amid Hurricane and Earthquake Utters his Last Words,
from *Aeschylus: Prometheus Bound* (transl. Elizabeth Barrett Browning) (1833)

It is 9.20 local time on Sunday 16 November 2003 and John Underhill, Morgan Jones and I are standing above Lake Katochori enjoying the view of Figure 27.12. We are just a few hundred metres west of the Oasis residence in Petrikata where we have been staying with Nick and Nancy Kalogiratos. I have taken John to this escarpment because I want to photograph Figure 27.12 and also to record a short film of him explaining the landscape beyond. I am attaching the camcorder to the tripodabout a metre away from the adjacent precipice when suddenly a fast freight train passes underground.

Instinctively we draw back from the drop and a few seconds later I curse the fact that the camera was not running. We have just experienced a significant earthquake but I have no record of it. Later we retrieve the Internet log and learn that it was a strike-slip type of magnitude 5.3.[1] You will recall from Chapter 11 that strike-slip earthquakes propagate horizontally whereas thrust or compressional earthquakes also have a vertical component. This tremor was fascinating rather than terrifying: let me tell you how it felt.

Imagine that some eccentric decides to build a long train tunnel in the middle of the countryside for no good reason and also without telling anybody else about it.[2] Unknown to you the tunnel is just a metre or so below your feet. Suddenly a very loud, very fast train rushes through the tunnel without any warning. The ground trembles, the noise is strange and deafening and then after a few seconds it is gone: silence reigns once more. That is the closest

FIGURE 28.1
Digital elevation view of
Ainos fault line
*The fault runs all along the
foothill of Imerovigli
mountain*
[Image credits: As Figures
27.6. Data source and
processing: As Figure
27.5.]

I can get to an explanation: that is how it felt and I have borrowed this metaphor from the observer of a far more severe earthquake; we will read his own description before long.

Now we must ask the question: why? Why did so much landfill material descend into this seagirt valley so catastrophically that it not only blocked the channel but also erased all visible traces of its former existence? The answer is contained in Figure 28.1.

The location marked 'Viewpoint' on this image is where we experienced the earthquake: it is about 270 m above sea level and by comparison Late Kato-chori is itself about 190 m above sea level. If you walk about half a kilometre back up the slope you reach a level at which John has drawn a black line on the map all the way along the isthmus: at this point its height is about 340 m. It is the northern segment of the Ainos fault that we saw in Figure 11.7 and it runs all the way from the south-east tip of Cephalonia up past Argostoli Bay and through the Thinia isthmus until it eventually disappears into the sea in Assos Bay. It is indeed just like a train track through the mountains: the noise that we heard and the rumbling that we felt originated from a ghost train running along it from south to north at incredible speed.

The mountains through which it runs are not a homogeneous mass of rock: they have a layered internal structure consisting of sloping beds of rock interspersed by 'bedding planes' that resemble a giant pack of cards. Millions of years ago these cards were flat but the eastern end of them has been pushed up by the collision of Africa with Europe so that by now they are tilted here at an average angle of 60°. As a result they slope precipitously down towards sea level in the ancient channel.

These layers of rock are on average only about 50–60 cm thick and they are separated by thin boundaries (the 'bedding planes') consisting of less than a centimetre of compressed particles of earth and rock. Water seeps down into these boundaries, lubricating them like a Teflon coating and increasing the chance that one day a layer will start to slip. The first layer to slip may not necessarily be the top one: whichever it is, it will carry down with it all the layers that lie above.

Although the boundary material between the layers is relatively slippery there is a counter-influence that acts so as to glue the cards together. It is, surprisingly, the simple fact of the penetration of plant and tree roots from the surface soil down into the upper layers, as if the top few cards in the pack were stitched together here and there with cotton thread. This vegetable material not only stabilises the bedding planes, it also holds the surface soil together and acts as a natural barrier to halt the fall of loose rocks and boulders.

In Chapter 18 Tjeerd van Andel explained that mountaintop erosion can be accelerated by Bronze Age sailors who strip the trees for their navies and also by the overcropping of goats. The *Iliad* passage that I quoted there refers to the 'oak or poplar or tall pine, / Which woodmen chop down on the mountainside / With whetted axes for ship-building timber' so this practice was clearly prevalent at that time. We also know from the work of Marinatos that the devastation of the mountainsides accelerated during the last millennium. Writing about Mount Ainos he says:

The felling of trees by the Venetians, to furnish timber for their shipyards, was the prime cause of the destruction of the forest in the more accessible parts. The greatest devastations were effected by savage fires which recurred frequently and which were nearly always deliberately kindled in order to provide arable land whose virgin fertility was amazing. The two worst fires occurred just before 1600 and in 1797. During the first, two thirds of the forest, which was then 14 km long by 5 km wide, were destroyed. The second one, though smaller in extent, lasted for several weeks and destroyed half of the remaining forest. The climate of the island is said to have changed since then.[3]

The evidence suggests that the Venetians were not the first perpetrators of ecological vandalism in Cephalonia. In the introduction to their comprehensive review of Cephalonian archaeological sites the Danish team writing in 2002 says:

By the time of the early Holocene, Greece was covered by woodland dominated by oak, maple, elm, hazel and lime at lower and intermediate altitudes. At higher altitudes (1000–1600 m) coniferous trees dominated . . . Around 4000 BP [c. 2000 BC[4]] the humidity level and the climatic conditions were much like today and after 3500 BP any vegetational changes detectable in pollen sequences are the effects of human exploitation.[5]

As we have seen, limestone usually contains irregularly spaced pockets of iron oxide and as these minerals dissolve through erosion there are two major effects: the remaining limestone becomes inter-penetrated by randomly shaped holes, like a Swiss cheese; and the iron oxides that wash down the mountainside create the reddy-brown soil that is a distinctive characteristic of much of the Greek countryside. Writing on this subject of *terra rossa* van Andel compares the effects of human intervention with slower-moving natural causes:

Since the early Neolithic (c. 9000 BP) however, farming, deforestation, soil erosion and other human injuries to the landscape have become a new and often the main cause of landscape disruption, one that operates on a much shorter timescale than the others.[6]

In her 1999 study of the Ionian Islands from 3000 to 800 BC Christina Souyoudzoglou-Haywood summarises the position:

Recent studies of the Greek landscape have shown that the processes of erosion and alluviation display great local and temporal variability, and that they are to a large extent anthropogenic . . . Human activity, in particular land clearance and deforestation, is now seen as the major cause of soil erosion and deposition during the Holocene.[7]

So those Teflon-like bedding planes of Mount Imerovigli probably became unstable during the Bronze Age period as a result of the deforestation of its summit and slopes by the Samians. That in itself would have been enough to create a serious volume of rockfall, but as it happens the Ainos fault line passes along the western side of this mountain and when a high magnitude earthquake triggered it the effects would have been catastrophic.

The detailed geometry of this fault line is complex and expert readers should refer to John's Appendix 2 for a proper understanding of its structure and dynamics, but it is nevertheless worthwhile for the rest of us to persevere with his Figure A2.21. This is a cross-sectional view at the northern end of the channel (its exact location is indicated in his Figure A2.3), with the high peak of Imerovigli to our right (east) and Agrilia to our left (west). These peaks are defined by the red line which indicates the altitude of the surface (vertical scale) at varying distances across the channel (horizontal scale). An altitude of 0 corresponds to sea level and the small grey area in the centre denotes the contour of Strabo's Channel. Although the diagram reflects John's detailed on-site observations and measurements, the extent of this dip below sea level is at present a supposition.

The brick-like patterns coming up from underground denote the slope of the bedding planes of the mountains. Their angles are accurate but the bricks themselves are purely illustrative of the very thin planes. The lighter shaded area above the red line is today empty space: it represents the projected height of the mountains in the absence of erosion. In the discussion of the Cephalonia Transform Fault in Chapter 11 we learnt that the African continental ridge lies only a few kilometres out to sea and it is pushing eastwards against Europe. In fact it is pushing sufficiently hard that it has wedged itself underneath Europe, and this has created an upthrust along the diagonal black line marked as the compressional Ainos fault. At the base of Imerovigli the bedding planes are tilted as we heard above at an average angle of about 60°. This value is the specific angle at this location but it varies elsewhere because the bedding plane itself is actually curved as you can see: it is as if we bent the whole pack of cards between our fingers.

In Chapter 11 I described the simple experiment of trying to slide your hands past each other while preventing this motion via the opposing tips of your thumbs. As the pressure becomes too great your thumbs snap back to their former position and this is what happens as Africa pushes itself under Europe. For a while there is no surface motion but within the rocks the tension is built up until it suddenly releases all its pent-up energy in a single snap. When that happens the effect is like having one end of the pack of cards struck by an upward-bouncing springboard. Because this Ainos Thrust springboard is angled at about 30° to the horizontal this means that for every 1 metre that the land is thrust upwards, it simultaneously moves about 2 metres westwards.

To complicate matters, this thrust-like compressional motion of Europe is not the only force that is acting on the Thinia isthmus. As the lateral arrows on Figure 11.3 show, Africa is also moving towards the north-east while Europe is sliding past it to the south-west: you have to think of its motion in three dimensions rather than two. This effect causes the continental plates to slip past each other horizontally without any significant vertical impact. Although this second mechanism also involves a periodic buildup and sudden release of tension, the frequency and amplitude (i.e. timing and severity) of the strike-slip earthquakes is not the same as that of the thrust events. Of the two, the thrust earthquakes are the most dangerous: fortunately they are also much less frequent.

This means that there are two types of earthquake in Cephalonia: frequent horizontal strike-slip events of medium severity and infrequent vertical thrust events of grave severity. It appears that the reliable raconteur Viscount Kirkwall may have experienced two different types of earthquake in 1867, although there is no record of a permanent uplift of the island at that time. His house was built in Argostoli on land reclaimed from the sea which placed it virtually on top of the Ainos fault:

I may here observe that the two great earthquakes of 14th March and 11th May were very dissimilar. The first came in a violent storm, the second in a perfect calm. The motion of the first was rapid and saltatory, that of the second slow, undulating and oscillatory. The one came accompanied by fearful noises; the other was comparatively silent, except the creaking of the walls and the furniture as the house swayed slowly to and fro for many seconds, that seemed like minutes. The first had suggested to my mind some monstrous giant seizing and shaking our house in a paroxysm of fury. The second was more suggestive of a rolling vessel, insufficiently ballasted.[8]

What happens to the rocks on Mount Imerovigli when these earthquakes occur? There are four possible effects. The first effect is that both types of earthquake will naturally dislodge free-standing boulders and create major surface rockslides. These hurtle down the slope as we have heard and come to rest on the land or in the sea beneath. That in itself is enough to create a significant volume of landfill, but it is dwarfed by the second effect, which is that both types of earthquake can also cause these bedding planes to detach and slide in their entirety down the mountainside, depositing far more massive volumes of rubble at its base.

Words alone are an inadequate basis for understanding a bedding plane failure of this magnitude. In Figure 28.2 you can see Mount Imerovigli, the highest point of the eastern channel flank. We have heard that its summit is just under 1 km high and the photograph demonstrates that the adjacent peaks are only a little lower: the mountaintop is almost horizontal here. Once again there is a road that runs along the treeline at the foot of the mountain and we have to remember that *everything we can see below the treeline has slid down the mountain.*

Now look at the very distinctive 'V'-shaped scallops that have formed into the mountainside. The central one is above the village of Nifi, about two-thirds of the way towards the northern end of Thinia: in Figure 28.3 you can see this in more detail. This is the area from where all the rock below had fallen: you can see the sharp edges at the top of the scallop where the bedding planes have failed. So it is not just a matter of surface boulders being shaken down by earthquakes: instead massive segments of the mountain have themselves detached and thundered down into the valley below.

FIGURE 28.2
Landslip below Mount Imerovigli
The line of the Ainos fault coincides with the tree line and the old road at the eastern edge of the villages. Everything that is visible below it has slipped down the mountain.

FIGURE 28.3
The mountainside village of Nifi
This village and the others on the eastern side of Thinia are sitting on the remains of a massive rock avalanche.

FIGURE 28.4
Computer simulation of
active mountain formation
*This distinctive pattern
emerges from the interplay of
factors such as
earthquake-induced uplift
and rockfall, stream
formation and erosion.*
[Image credits: Willett
et al. (2001) p. 465.]

These unusually shaped mountainsides are symptomatic of a long-term balance of tectonic and erosional forces. Geologists are only recently beginning to understand the causal mechanisms involved and in Figure 28.4 you can see a striking comparison with Figure 28.2. This computer-generated landscape is from a geological paper written in 2001 in which a theoretical model is used to create artificial mountainsides that are then compared with real locations. Comparisons are made in the paper with sites in New Zealand, Taiwan and Washington state and it will be very interesting to learn whether the mountains of Paliki can be modelled by the same approach.[9]

As well as bedding plane failure the thrust fault alone can add two more deadly ingredients. The third effect is that, like a springboard, it is capable of bodily displacing a massive slab of the mountain both upwards and westwards at a ratio of 1 metre up for every 2 metres to the west. When this occurs the outer edge of the displaced slab may find itself completely unsupported by any rocks below – literally projected into thin air. Within a split second the whole section starts to drop, but a part of it is not simply sliding down the mountainside: it is now almost in free fall through the air. We heard about the 1958 Alaskan earthquake in Chapter 18 and here is a description of the accompanying rockfall:

The giant wave runup of 1720 feet at the head of the Bay and the subsequent huge wave along the main body of Lituya Bay were caused primarily by the enormous subaerial rockfall into Gilbert Inlet. The triggering mechanism of this rockfall and the effects that it produced were significantly different from those of subaerial or submarine landslides. This was not a gradual process as with a landslide, but a very sudden event. The giant rockfall was triggered impulsively. Thus, the term rockfall rather than rockslide or landslide, is used to distinguish this particular type of phenomenon and to explain the subsequent effects of its impulsive impact. In some respects, corrected for scale factors of mass, terminal velocity and angle of entry, the impact of this rockfall into Gilbert Inlet could be considered analogous to that of an asteroid falling on earth. To explain the impulsive mechanism of wave generation from such impact we must first examine the time history of events immediately following the onset of the earthquake and the intense ground motions and accelerations that triggered the rockfall.[10]

This phenomenon of almost vertical rockfall was also observed during the 1953 earthquake on the western coast of Cephalonia:

During a lull we saw in the extreme south of the peninsula of Paliki the summit of a promontory slip down almost vertically and crash into the sea, while an enormous column of yellow dust climbed up very high into the sky.[11]

Millions of tons of rock descending in almost free fall into Strabo's Channel would have been a truly awesome sight. The first such rockfall would have splashed at high velocity into the channel and forced a very large volume of water up across the Ithacan coastline towards the Agrilia mountainside, which is about 1,500 feet high. We should not assume that this wave would have been as high as the 1,720-foot monster of Gilbert Inlet because the horizontal reach of the water in the channel is much smaller, but nevertheless I would not have liked to be standing on the western side of the channel at the time. In view of the width of the channel and the slope of the mountainside the debris from this first rockfall may not have blocked it completely, but it would certainly have narrowed it and extended the foot of the mountain across from the east.

When the next such earthquake occurred the falling debris would roll down over these new foundations and penetrate further across the channel. Think of a child building a sandcastle: every time another bucket of dry sand is poured over the top it slides down the sides and extends the base of the castle further outwards.

After a few more earthquakes of this nature it starts to become difficult to navigate through the channel around these rockfalls. Perhaps dredging parties are organised to keep a narrow route clear through it but after further earthquakes even this becomes impossible.

The centuries pass by and the rocks keep crashing down. Now the isthmus is so shallow that it has become unnavigable, but in stormy weather the waves still break over the sandbanks and mudflats from time to time. At some point during the first or second centuries BC one of Strabo's scouts was there: after all why else would he write 'Where the island is narrowest it forms a low isthmus, so that it is often submerged from sea to sea'? His word 'often' can hardly refer to anything other than the effect of winter storms, so this observation must have been made at the northern end of the former channel since that is the only place where the full force of the sea impacts it. If you turn to John Underhill's Appendix 2 and refer to his Figure A2.24, then the infill by then would be as if all of the landslips marked 1 and 2 had descended, but only part of landslip 3.

More centuries, more earthquakes, more rockfall, more debris accumulating in what was once Strabo's Channel . . . By the second or third century AD the author of the 'Maritime Itinerary' (as we heard in Chapter 21) referred only to 'the islands Cephalenia, Zacinthos and Dulichia'. He did not refer to a fourth island called Ithaca because it was no longer an island at all.

These effects on their own are enough to explain the landscape that we see in Thinia today. But there is a monstrous fourth effect yet to be considered; and we also need to answer that final question: when did this devastating activity take place?

Notes

1 http://lemnos.geo.auth.gr/the_seisnet/WEB_PANAS/777.htm
2 Less implausible than you might imagine: see for example the splendid story of the agoraphobic fifth Duke of Portland in Jackson (1997) and summarised at www.historic-uk.com/CultureUK/briteccentrics.htm; also of note are the subterranean exploits of the eccentic Victorian millionaire Joseph Williamson at Edge Hill near Liverpool at http://news.bbc.co.uk/1/hi/england/2342183.stm
3 Marinatos (1962) p. 54.
4 BP dates normally refer to the number of years 'Before Present', which means before the radiocarbon standard reference date of 1950, on the assumption that the half-life of radiocarbon is 5,568 years and the amount of radiocarbon in the atmosphere has been constant. In fact the proportion of radiocarbon in the atmosphere has varied over time and also the true half-life of radiocarbon is 5,730 years, not the original measured value of 5,568 years. In the absence of a calibrated date it is therefore not possible to translate BP into conventional dates directly, but subtracting 2,000 years provides a rough approximation. For further details refer to websites such as www.rlaha.ox.ac.uk
5 Randsborg (2002) p. 136.
6 Van Andel (1994) p. 370.
7 Souyoudzoglou-Haywood (1999) p. 5.
8 Kirkwall (1864) p. 161.
9 Willett et al. (2001) p. 465; see also Densmore et al. (1998).
10 www.drgeorgepc.com/Tsunami1958LituyaB.html
11 Grandazzi (1954) p. 435.

CHAPTER 29   **Uplift**

The sacred streams
Flow back uphill:
Right turns to wrong.
Men plan deceit,
And what they pledged
No longer holds.

Euripides, *Medea* 410–14

The earthquake of 12 August 1953 did not merely shake Cephalonia: it also uplifted most of the island by an average of 60 cm. We saw the watermarked stone in Figure 1.5, while Figure 11.7 indicates that the Agia Ephemia fault that runs along the Pylaros valley sometimes insulates the Erissos peninsula to the north from the worst of these seismic effects. We also read reports of a tidal wave inundating the coastal plain shortly afterwards. The magnitude of this earthquake was 7.2 and here is an eyewitness account provided the following year by Maurice Grandazzi, then a young geographer who later became the deputy Secretary General of the French Geographical Society. He called it *The Last Days of Argostoli*:

It was the unexpected outcome of a trip to Greece which resulted in me experiencing the August 1953 earthquake in the Ionian Islands. Together with about sixty other French colleagues we had arrived on Friday August 7th on the island of Cephalonia. We were based in a comfortable campsite situated on the ridge of the Argostoli peninsula, annexed to a hotel called Pharaoh which on one side overlooked the beach and open sea and on the other provided a view of the town and bay. We were due to stay there for a whole week before continuing our voyage towards mainland Greece and Crete. In the event we remained there for only a little over five days during which we were subjected to a total of 114 seismic shocks.

I was in my tent on Sunday August 9th at about 09:40 when the first shock occurred. I had the sudden sensation of wobbling, as if overcome by vertigo, while at the same time I heard an abnormal sound that I could not identify. Instinctively I threw myself outside where I saw the perplexed faces of those who had simultaneously abandoned their own tents. I scarcely had time to focus on my colleagues, to hear the cries of distress which rose up from Argostoli and to see below us in the streets people who were fleeing in all directions, when the rumbling grew louder, as if an enormous train was emerging from the ground. The earth was shaken sideways, vibrating more and more quickly. The phantom express train passed below us with a thunderous noise, as if it were crossing a gigantic subterranean iron bridge, or as if it were propelling a giant sawblade ahead of it, splitting the rocks at high speed.

I was standing on the grass, facing the bay of Argostoli, my legs spread wide apart as I tried to keep my balance, my eyes drawn to the clouds of dust which rose from the city and the mountains across the bay. Suddenly, as if the train had disappeared over the horizon, the world became calm again. Then I saw on looking over to Pharaoh at the other end of the campsite that my wife, who had been writing a letter outdoors beside the hotel, had hurriedly moved to the open ground when she saw the walls of the terrace shaking above her head. Later she realised that if the building had collapsed at that moment she would not have been far enough away to avoid being buried.

With the immediate disturbance over we walked down to the town. Almost everywhere the sides of the houses had cracked and the old dry-stone walls of the town had fallen apart. In the port, the collapse of a cornice and a balcony located below it had destroyed a car parked underneath.

From that time on the ground continued to tremble, but neither on that Sunday nor on the following Monday were there any further catastrophic shocks. The second large tremor did not take place until the morning of Tuesday August 11th but there were numerous foreshocks. During Monday night and early Tuesday morning the ground vibrated strongly under our tents and a violent and unusual wind seemed to spring up from the sea and assail us on our plateau. One after another the dogs started to howl, the donkeys began to bray and the cocks crowed in the night, and this grew into an uninterrupted cacophony of animals in distress. A deeply troubled atmosphere prevented almost everyone in the campsite from sleeping. Suddenly at 05:30 in the morning a terrible jolt, much worse that the first one, threw everyone outside. The ground vibrated at tremendous speed. Clamours of despair rose from Argostoli. In a split second 70% of the houses of the city became uninhabitable: some were deeply cracked and others simply collapsed.

On the evening of Tuesday August 11th a night of absolute darkness presided among us. Beneath the stars of this moonless sky there was not a light to be seen. We had eaten out in the open with our only source of illumination being a candle brought by a priest: its flickering flame kept dying out because of the wind. Everyone slept on the grass, both as a precaution and also because of emergency orders prohibiting people from returning to their houses.

The ground became more and more disturbed. During the day, anybody standing still could feel the land moving underfoot: the sensation was more distinct when sitting down and even more so when reclining. That night our campbeds were continually jolted by earth tremors. It was like trying to sleep on the seats of a train, with side-to-side rolling and abrupt jolts, followed by brief lulls and then suddenly repeated movements which woke us up with a start. Sometimes it felt like the gentle ripple of a wave passing by, at other times like the pandemonium of a shunting engine whose wheels had stuck. Our courage and our nerves were frayed by these sudden shocks.

The night of August 11th was disturbed by these continuous tremors. But on the morning of Wednesday 12th August the earth appeared to be calm. My French colleagues took advantage of this to head off in various directions. My wife and I went down to the beach. The sea was beautiful and the sun shone brilliantly in a clear sky. After a while I suggested to my wife that we might return to Pharaoh by climbing straight up over the rocky hillside. We started our ascent but while we were talking to each other we lost sight of the main route up and we found ourselves instead following a small path across to the right which led us away from the slope towards a level plateau. This moment of inattention turned out to be our salvation. We had been following this path for only a few minutes (it was by then 11:25) when the ground began to shake violently. It was the third major quake that had started, the strongest of those that afflicted the islands.

The trembling became stronger and stronger so that we were thrown about on this path more violently than if we had been in a ship cast adrift on a surging sea. The whole island was vibrating on its foundations just like a dog that shakes itself when coming out of the water. The landscape, perfectly solid a few seconds earlier, now started to flow as if it was the surface of a liquid that was being agitated. The earth burst open like a fruit, shattering like a broken glass. Cracks opened under our feet in a flash with a noise like thunder. We jumped like goats to avoid them and to try to keep our balance. From the top of this ridge that was wobbling like gelatine and which seemed to be folding up on itself we saw 10-ton rocks hurtling down and crushing the olive trees to bits. The noise was terrifying, combining underground rumbling and cracking of the surface with the crash of falling rocks and the cries of humanity. We felt ourselves caught up in some infernal dance, in an incredible vision of the end of the world. We wondered whether we were going to be absorbed into the ground or drowned in the sea or crushed by rockfall.

During a lull we saw in the extreme south of the peninsula of Paliki the summit of a promontory slip down almost vertically and crash into the sea, while an enormous column of yellow dust climbed up very high in the sky. Another such cloud billowed out of Argostoli, which was cut down like a house of cards; and the smoke and dust reduced the visibility between us to only three metres.

The shuddering of the earth was followed by convulsions so intense that each time they stopped, we ran in all directions to find a flat, clay-based surface, something stabilised by the roots of the olive trees and above all far away from the falling rocks and the mountainside. When we finally regained the path to the summit we found our route cut off along much of its length by wide and deep fissures and also by fallen rocks lying transversely across the path. The Pharaoh hotel had been razed to the ground. Argostoli did not exist any more and the whole of Cephalonia had become an island of disaster.

In the middle of the night of August 12th we were evacuated by the warship Alpheios of the Hellenic Royal Navy. The fire raging in the ruins of Argostoli and the red sky above the shattered city was our last sight of this murderous land in which we had left a piece of our hearts.[1]

FIGURE 29.1
Raised beach north of Agia
Kiriaki
*The sea once covered this
raised beach, but as with
Figure 1.5 that was because
the entire island has been
thrust upwards by about 6 m
over a period of time, rather
than as a result of sea level
changes.*

That is what it felt like to be near the fault line of an earthquake that thrust the island up by only 60 cm. Now imagine instead being a bystander at an earthquake that raised it by a full 4 m. It is literally unimaginable, but here is why we should do our best to try.

By the end of his August 2003 visit John Underhill had accumulated considerable evidence of 'raised beaches'. These are precisely what they sound like: a beach that is now up on the land rather than under the water. You can see an example in Figure 29.1 and although this may look like just another section of flat rock, a geologist can tell from its surface that it was formerly submerged. These raised beaches exist at multiple locations across Cephalonia and they are generally at a height of about 6 m above the current sea level. Their existence has been noted previously: the 1971 BP/IGME joint survey pointed out that 'Raised beaches, of loosely cemented sandstones and sandy clays, are found along the south coasts of the island and on the Lixourion peninsula [Paliki]',[2] but what does not yet seem to have been considered is their historical significance.

The interesting questions to ask about these raised beaches are: when were they last submerged and how did the change happen? The evidence that we need comes from the rock near Poros that we saw at Figure 7.3. John has investigated this and other rocks on the island in terms of the eroded marine notches that they exhibit. The underlying mechanism here is that the longer a rock is at a particular level relative to the sea, the deeper will be the eroded notch at that level. In fact there is rather more to it than this simple summary suggests and as a way of visualising these interactions I have found the following analogy useful.

What would happen if an iceberg was floating in a warm-surfaced sea – one that was cold everywhere except for its surface? Clearly the warmth of the surface water would melt into the iceberg at that point, but not below nor above, and so the effect would be to create a notch in the iceberg at surface level. Can we predict how deep into the iceberg that notch would penetrate? For a given temperature of water, the longer the iceberg is immersed, the deeper the notch that will be cut into the ice. To turn the argument around, if we were looking at an existing notch on an iceberg then the depth to which it was indented would give us an indication of how long the surface of the sea has been at that level.

Suppose that for some reason the iceberg is suddenly pushed upwards: perhaps a whale makes its home underneath. Now the previously formed notch will be above the warm water level and it will not be eroded there any further: instead a new notch will start to form at sea level lower down the ice. So the depth of each of a series of notches on the iceberg tells us about the amount of time for which the warm water was at that level. This argument assumes that all other factors remain constant: no change in the surface water temperature, consistency of texture of the iceberg and so on. The idea is illustrated in Figure 29.2.

Supposing now that instead of a sudden movement of the iceberg, the level of the sea itself declines slowly and uniformly over a long period. Then the warm surface water will cut a short distance into the iceberg all along this intermediate vertical distance (Figure 29.3). From a logical perspective the formation of these iceberg notches is perfectly obvious, but from a visual and intuitive viewpoint these diagrams repay some effort of familiarisation.

This iceberg comparison relates directly to the much slower effects of erosion of limestone or organic material by surface wave action. Rocks that are exposed to the waves become eroded over time by the constant agitation at the surface and so a notch appears. If the sea level itself changes over a long period this will give rise to the type of continuous indentation depicted in Figure 29.3.

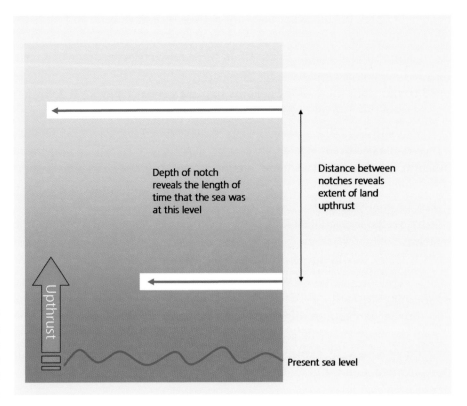

Depth of notch
reveals the length of
time that the sea was
at this level

Distance between
notches reveals
extent of land
upthrust

Upthrust

Present sea level

FIGURE 29.2
Marine erosion with
sudden uplifts
*For simplicity a grey rectangle
has been used to represent the
rock surface.*

However, if there is a sudden upthrust of the land from one level to another –
a phenomenon that geologists call a 'coseismic uplift' when it accompanies an
earthquake – then there will be an intermediate uneroded zone and a new
notch will then start to be eroded lower down the rockface.

To summarise, the central observations are (a) the horizontal depth of
the notch is proportional to the period of time that the sea was at that
level, (b) the vertical interval between notches reflects the extent of land
upthrust or sea level change and (c) the less indentation there is between
successive notches, the more catastrophic and sudden was the upthrust. Furthermore there is a correlation between (b) and (c) in the form of (d):
sea level changes do not happen catastrophically, whereas land upthrusts
can.

Let us now apply this marine notch model to the Poros rock. Figure 29.4
is comparable to Figure 7.3 but the notches and benches are rather clearer.
Simon is wading back from the rock after measuring the heights involved: a
critical area is enlarged at Figure 29.5.

This phenomenon of a wave-eroded notch is by no means unique to Poros.
Another example can be seen at the delightful beach of Lepeda, south of
Lixouri on Paliki, where Matthew provides scale (Figure 29.6(b)).

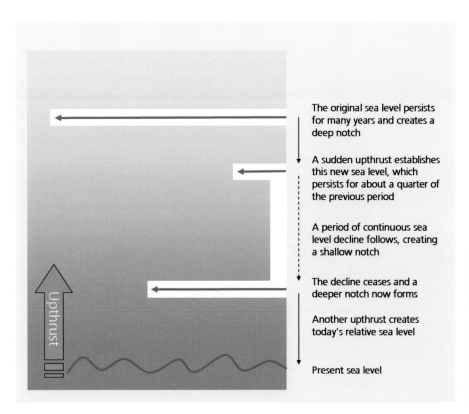

The original sea level persists for many years and creates a deep notch

A sudden upthrust establishes this new sea level, which persists for about a quarter of the previous period

A period of continuous sea level decline follows, creating a shallow notch

The decline ceases and a deeper notch now forms

Another upthrust creates today's relative sea level

Present sea level

Upthrust

FIGURE 29.3
Marine erosion with both sudden uplifts and sea level decline
Further complications ensue in the real world because rocks are not rectangular, nor are erosion rates constant over time even in the absence of tectonic uplift.

These and more extensive observations made by John and his students have enabled him to make the following preliminary diagnosis of the cause of the raised beaches on the island. Four separate earthquakes may each have contributed to their present 6 m elevation above today's sea level. Under this hypothesis earthquake 1 (E1) would have raised the island by 4 m, earthquake 2 (E2) by 0.8 m, earthquake 3 (E3) by 0.6 m and earthquake 4 (E4) we know to have raised it by another 0.6 m. With the exception of E4 these provisional estimates are likely to be revised as further evidence is assembled regarding sea level changes: if sea levels have also been rising then some of these coseismic uplifts will have been even greater.

As far as their timing is concerned, we know that E4 was in 1953 but we have very little information about the dates of the others. However, the depth of the notches tells us something about the relative amount of time between them and for the Poros rock alone, a preliminary assessment indicates a retrospective ratio of about 1:1:7. We do not yet know how long 1 of these units lasted so for convenience I will refer to it as an 'eon'. The ratio therefore means that the sea level prior to earthquake 4 in 1953 lasted for 1 eon, the level prior to earthquake 3 also lasted for about 1 eon and the level prior to earthquake 2 lasted for about 7 eons. The usual caveats apply: marine erosion is not a uniform process so there is a very wide margin of error in these estimates. What

FIGURE 29.4
The Poros rock revisited
The rock can be inspected less strenuously from the comfortable confines of a nearby cafe on the Poros waterfront while waiting for the Kyllini ferry.

we would now like to determine is how long an eon is because that may give us very approximate dates for the earthquakes themselves.

If you wish to relate these statistics to the erosion of notches on the Poros rock then Figure 29.7 is a schematic version of what John has observed. Seismic upthrust has caused the rock to move upwards, which means that the relative position of sea level on the rock has moved downwards. Prior to E1, the first earthquake, the sea level on the rockface was at the top blue line in the diagram, which corresponds to the top-most cleft in Figure 29.4, and it had eroded into the rock there quite considerably. In this case we need not worry about the depth of that erosion because we are not trying to go back to an earthquake date before E1.

At time E1 the rock is raised by a shocking 4 m, creating a new sea level line on it at the 'Pre-E2' mark (the height of Simon's head in Figure 29.5). The sea erodes the rock there about seven times deeper than at the lower two marks, so this gives us a relative period of about 7 eons. Then E2 occurs, thrusting the

FIGURE 29.5
Detail of the Poros rock
*Compare (a) the level of the
brown rock band, (b) the
black rock level that Simon is
standing on and (c) the
prominent notch at the level of
his head, with the uplift
diagram at Figure 29.3*

rock upwards by 0.8 m and creating a new 'Pre-E3' sea level (at the height of Simon's feet). That lasts for 1 eon, then E3 thrusts the rock upwards by 0.6 m to the 'Pre-E4' level (the brown/black rock boundary). Another eon goes by until E4 takes place in 1953 with an uplift of 0.6 m.

In terms of the cumulative heights at which we can see these ancient raised beaches today, a beach that dates to the pre-E1 period is now 6 m above today's sea level; a pre-E2 beach is 2 m above today's sea level; a pre-E3 beach is 1.2 m above today's sea level and, as we know, a pre-E4 beach is 60 cm above today's sea level.

Can we identify any of these earthquakes in the Cephalonian tectonic record? So far I have failed to find any reference to the island's land mass being thrust upwards prior to 1953. Perhaps the inhabitants at the time were too stunned to register the phenomenon, but alternatively it may be that its omission in the documents available to us during the last few centuries is significant: another case of the 'dog that didn't bark'. For example, Viscount Kirkwall was clearly an urbane and perceptive individual: he minutely observed two distinct types of earthquake and if his house had suddenly elevated itself by 60 cm relative to the adjacent sea level then I feel sure that he would have reported it. Indeed anyone who had the presence of mind to compliment his wife during an earthquake on her frugality in rescuing the moderator lamp clearly had his wits about him. However, as far as the 1860s

FIGURE 29.6
Erosion notches elsewhere
on Cephalonia
*(a) Lepeda Beach. The view is
to the east from about 2 km
south of Lixouri. The
low-lying Argostoli
promontory is visible on the
right.*

*(b) This closeup of a section of
the Lepeda Beach rock shows
the evidence of two upthrusts:
the dark band corresponds to
the pre-1953 sea level, while
the eroded notch above it
indicates an earlier sea level
contour.*

(c) Limenia Beach. This striking, almost circular rock lies in a bay about 1.5 km south of Poros. The erosional effects of the former sea level are clearly visible around its circumference.

(d) Closeup of the Limenia Beach rock. Its distinctive hour-glass like shape exhibits the 'solution notches' which are a characteristic of uplifting coastlines. Comparable examples exist elsewhere in Greece, such as at Psatha, north-east of Corinth. [www.esc.cam.ac.uk/~simon00/photos_greece.html]

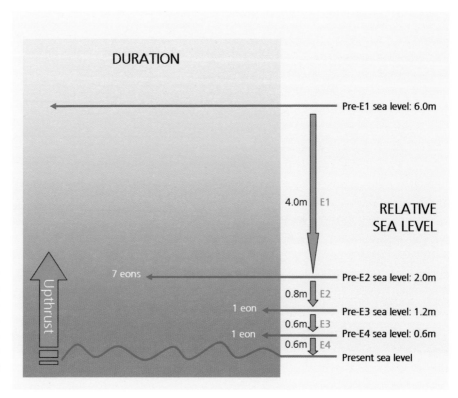

FIGURE 29.7
Notch erosion in Poros Bay
*Although specific values have
been assigned here to the
upthrust heights and relative
time periods, these are at
present provisional and
subject to a wide margin of
error.*

are concerned I can find no mention of any upthrust in land levels throughout
the 339 pages of his *Four Years in the Ionian Islands*.

There is some further evidence to assist us in the shape of our Figure 11.5:
'Years with earthquakes of magnitude 4.0 or above', because these upthrusts
can hardly have been associated with earthquakes of lesser potency. Having
excluded Kirkwall's period of the 1860s the shortlist from that catalogue identifies the years 1444, 1469, 1633, 1636, 1658, 1766 and 1767. The margin of
estimation error on these marine notches does not allow for fine distinctions
so in terms of fifty-year intervals we might as well round these dates to *c.* 1450,
c. 1650 and *c.* 1750. In which of these periods might an uplifting earthquake
have occurred?

In Chapter 11 we saw several quite detailed accounts of the earthquakes
of the eighteenth century. On 28 August 1714 *280 houses were destroyed, water
issued from the earth, and the inhabitants lived two months in the gardens*; on 9
February 1723 *at Erissos as well as in Paliki many houses collapsed and some people
were killed*; on 12 June 1741 *the parish church of Lixouri was totally destroyed as
well as a number of public buildings*; on 2 June 1759 *earthquakes continued until
the 5th . . . in the district of Paliki and at Lixouri where most of the houses, windmills
and churches collapsed and a few lives were lost*; on 11 July 1766 *The western part*

of Kefalinia suffered most. A manuscript note says most of the houses in the district of Paliki were destroyed and those left standing were damaged; on 11 July 1767 *In Lixouri many deaths were reported and almost the whole town suffered great damage.* But nowhere do we read in these contemporary descriptions about something far more significant: the whole island being pushed up by about two feet. It may be only circumstantial evidence but the presumption is that an uplift is not mentioned because it didn't happen in that century.

The records for the mid-seventeenth century are somewhat thinner. The 1633 earthquake is described as being of sufficient power to have separated the islet of Agios Sostis on Zacynthos from the adjacent coast.[3] Three years later 'The earthquake of September 30, 1636 – *a mezza ora di notte* – at midnight, was devastating. Trees were uprooted on Aenos and the capital of Kefallonia, the Castle of St. George, suffered great damages. 150 houses crumbled and the powder magazine caught fire, burning people and animals alive . . . Petros Sarlos, a Notary of the time, (1630–1652) writes ". . . great earthquake and the houses fell in all the island and in the castle and in the original palaces".'[4] So if E3 took place *c.* 1650 then the 300-odd years to E4 in 1953 would represent 1 eon. Using the 1:1:7 ratio, that would give us a date of around AD 1350 for E2 and 750 BC for E1, but with a very wide margin of error.

The 1469 earthquake is estimated as being of magnitude 7.2 and centred around Argostoli, which makes it similar in strength to that of 1953.[5] There were many tremors on Cephalonia with great destruction of buildings and loss of life: Lefkas was also affected.[6] It is also reported that boulders on the south-eastern coast of Italy were transported by a tsunami travelling from the south that may have resulted from an earthquake during this period. The largest rock of about 80 tons in weight 'slid for about 40 m from the m.s.l. [mean sea level] to about 1.8 m above sea level' where it split into four pieces.[7] Using radiocarbon tests the authors date this event to between 1421 and 1568. Although they provisionally attribute the tsunami to the large earthquake of 5 December 1456 that affected all of southern Italy, that is believed to have been centred north-east of Naples, an unlikely epicentre for a north-travelling tsunami that impacted the Ionian coast of Apulia.[8] By contrast, this part of Italy is about 250 km across the unobstructed open sea from the north-west of Cephalonia.

Further research will be needed to assess whether the 1469 earthquake in Argostoli could have been the cause of this tsunami, but if we consider *c.* 1450 as a possible date for E3 then 1 eon would now last for 500 years, in which case E2 would have taken place in AD 950 and E1 around 2550 BC. But once again we must remind ourselves that these ratio-derived dates are hardly precise: they are simply order-of-magnitude estimates.

On AD 21 July 365 a very large earthquake is believed to have occurred off the south-western coast of Crete, tilting the island upwards by up to 9 m and damaging buildings as far away as Libya and Cyprus. The size of this event has been estimated as comparable to the 1964 Alaskan earthquake of magnitude 8.4 and it caused a tsunami that impacted many areas of the Mediterranean, inundating the Nile Delta at Alexandria. This date is of especial interest to us because in Chapter 7 we heard that the geologists who surveyed the coastline of Cephalonia identified not only the 60 cm uplifted coastline of the 1953 earthquake but also an earlier uplift of the same height, albeit based on the evidence of a single shell. Together these correspond to a 1.2 m older shoreline near Poros whose 'uplift seems to have been relatively rapid, possibly sudden'. The radiocarbon evidence collected at the time showed ages ranging between 3060–2570 BC and AD 350–710: the latter date range includes the AD 365 earthquake, which is thought-provoking.

In his historical review of the Cretan earthquake Professor Stiros refers to Socrates Scholasticus, a fifth-century AD writer, who reported that 'the sea changed its familiar boundaries; for in some places the quaking was so severe that places where previously people walked they could now sail. In other places the sea retreated so far that the bottom of the sea was found to be dry. And this happened in AD 365 ("in the first year of administration of the two rulers Valens and Valentinian").' He points out 'This is the only near-contemporary report for a permanent marine regression accompanying the earthquake. It is loosely confirmed by later sources, for instance the ninth century historian Georgius Monachus, who specifies that this phenomenon happened in the Adriatic and the Aegean.'

Stiros and other authors have proposed that a cluster of geologically related earthquakes took place in this period which they describe as the 'Early Byzantine Tectonic Paroxysm'.[9] The proposal is interesting but controversial: indeed in commenting on evidence from the fourth to sixth centuries AD Stiros warns us 'However, the western Greece mainland and the Ionian Islands represent a real "terra incognita" for historical seismology during the critical period.' Subsequent researchers have proposed that the major Cretan uplift instead took place between AD 480 and 500.[10]

In 373 BC a massive earthquake in the Corinthian Gulf destroyed the city of Bura and sank the city of Helice.[11] It has been suggested that this earthquake was also responsible for the shattering of a building and its contents on (modern) Ithaca at the Aetos isthmus.[12] The distance between Helice and Aetos is about 130 km and if this was the same event that raised the island of Cephalonia by 4 m then it would presumably have uplifted much of the northern Peloponnese as well, unless there was independent causation.

There is evidence of an earthquake in the twelfth century BC at Midea near Mycenae in the Peloponnese. Reporting on the excavation from 1983 to 1994 the archaeologists say that 'The collapse of the West Gate and the buildings inside the Acropolis cannot have been the result of war . . . Signs of a possible earthquake are seen everywhere inside the Citadel of Midea in collapsed, distorted, curved and tilted walls . . . In one of the rooms in the East Gate area the skeleton of a young girl was found, whose skull and backbone were smashed under fallen stones: it seems to belong to an earthquake victim.'[13] A date in the twelfth century BC is clearly of interest to us as a Cephalonian earthquake candidate but the distance from Mycenae to Argostoli is about 210 km and once again, if this same earthquake impacted Cephalonia it would presumably also have had a very considerable effect on the entire northern Peloponnese. It is fascinating to learn that these diagnoses can emerge from archaeological excavation.

The suggestion that earthquakes may have destroyed the Bronze Age civilisation is not a new one: it was first proposed by the archaeologist Claude Schaeffer in 1948.[14] This was well before the modern theory of plate tectonics emerged and his proposal was not widely accepted. However the possibility of earthquake-based destruction was considered in an article by Elizabeth French of the British School at Athens. Rather tellingly her paper opens with the words:

Archaeologists of my generation, who attended university in the immediate aftermath of Schaeffer's great work (1948), were brought up to view earthquakes, like religion, as an explanation of archaeological phenomena to be avoided if at all possible. Thus it is only recently that the presence of an earthquake at Mycenae has begun to be a serious hypothesis.[15]

However as Amos Nur has pithily pointed out: 'People do not intentionally bury their dead in the rubble of collapsed buildings.'[16] Nur is a seismologist rather than an archaeologist and he has proposed that a series of major seismic events called an 'earthquake storm' may have occurred near the end of the Late Bronze Age in the period *c.* 1225–1175 BC[17] and precipitated major changes in society at that time:

It appears therefore that, in general, large earthquakes in the Eastern Mediterranean tend to occur in episodic 'storms' that unzip the main plate boundaries during short, 30–100 year, periods separated by 300–500 years of relative quiescence. The implication of this for archaeology is that a great deal of physical damage over a large area and the resulting societal effects are expected to have happened during relatively short periods of time.[18]

That is another controversial proposal and this book is not the place to debate the argument either way. Nevertheless, since earthquakes normally occur as a result of the buildup of tension between two surfaces, once the earthquake has taken place then this tension is relieved and so it is normal for this to be followed by a period of relative quiescence. However, we do not need to rely upon earthquakes across the whole of Greece to support the present argument, because the seismic fault lines on Cephalonia and its adjacent islands are unique: as we have heard they are the frontline where Africa collides with Europe.

I must be careful here to avoid the accusation of choosing convenient dates simply so as to fit the proposals of this book. That is not the purpose of this discussion: indeed the only way to determine these dates will be to perform the appropriate scientific tests. The present objective is simply to see if the available historical evidence contradicts the theory. If it did that might present a problem, but of course the fact that it doesn't by no means proves the hypothesis. However part of my purpose is to make the case for such tests to be conducted and so it is interesting to see that the historical evidence is not inconsistent with John Underhill's diagnosis of a series of very substantial uplifting earthquakes having occurred in Cephalonia over the last few thousand years.

What would have been the impact of such earthquakes on ancient Ithaca? If a major uplift happened at the time of Odysseus then either there would have been no *Odyssey* at all or at the very least one would imagine that some reference to the catastrophe would have been handed down in the poem. Although there are many references to the antics of Poseidon the earthshaker, including several violent storms and a memorable account at 13.162 of the Phaiacians' ship being turned by him to stone as it approached its home port of Scherie, there are no descriptions of the eschatological catastrophe that would have resulted from the whole island being uplifted by a colossal earthquake.

If however a massive earthquake happened not long after the events of the *Odyssey* then it could have coincided with the collapse of the Bronze Age that we heard about in Chapter 26 and the Ionian Migration of the mid-eleventh century. If so, might it have preceded or followed it? The possibility that a major earthquake on Cephalonia acted as a spur to migration from the island is intriguing. What was it that Andreas Delaportas said in Chapter 1?

And everyone was so frightened: nearly everyone left. The population of Cephalonia was 125,000 before the earthquake and about 90% of the people left. Even now it is still only about 25,000 people.

This hypothesis is tempting but the difficulty with it is that if the earthquake preceded the migration then one would expect some record of it to have been handed down via the colonists who fled to Ionia. By contrast, if the Ionian Migration took place first and the earthquake happened subsequently it would explain why we simply have no information whatever about the once-thriving metropolis of Ithaca in the period after Homer's descriptions in the *Odyssey*.

Ithaca was a flourishing Bronze Age city: a gateway to Italy and points west. Homer's descriptions in the *Odyssey* convey the impression of a busy metropolis with a large palace and an active agricultural economy. There was also a constant flux of trade: ships arrive there from Sicily to the west and from Thesprotia to the north, voyages are made to Pylos on the east and the place names of Crete further south are familiar to those in Odysseus' palace. It was a well-respected provincial military power as well: why else would Agamemnon and Menelaos visit Odysseus to conscript him with his men and their 'twelve red-cheeked ships' into the Trojan War?

So why is it that after the *Odyssey* we never hear another word from ancient Ithaca?[19]

Notes

1 Grandazzi (1968). This is a summary of the eyewitness account provided by Grandazzi on 20 February 1954 to the Geographical Society of Paris, which was also published in *Geographia*, vol. 33 (June 1954) and elsewhere. Time of day references are based on the local clock, two hours later than GMT. The extract from Grandazzi quoted in Chapter 27 is from his subsequent publication which specifies that the rockslide was on Paliki; for consistency I have retained that detail here.

2 BP Co Ltd (1971) p. 55.

3 www.zanteweb.gr/resorts/Agios%20Sostis

4 Livada-Duca (2000) p. 49.

5 Makropoulos and Kouskouna (1993).

6 Galanopoulos (1955) p. 94.

7 Mastronuzzi and Sansò (2000) pp. 96, 101.

8 Boschi et al. (1995).

9 Pirazzoli et al. (1996).

10 Stiros (2001) pp. 545, 556, 558; see also Stiros and Papageorgiou (2001). The Cretan uplift was re-examined in a subsequent paper which identified several raised beaches at 6 m above present sea level and used Bayesian techniques to reach the conclusion that 'the highest probability for the date of this critical event is associated with a later date (around AD 480–500) rather than AD 365, as most previous scholars have suggested'. Price et al. (2002) pp. 195–200.

11 Drews (1993) p. 38.

12 Tomlinson (1995–6) p. 16.

13 Åström and Demakopoulou (1996) p. 39.

14 Schaeffer (1948) quoted in Nur (2002) p. 772.

15 French (1996) p. 51.

16 Nur (2002) p. 789.

17 Nur (2000) p. 61. For an opposing view see Drews (1993) ch. 3.
18 Nur (2002) p. 771.
19 'The Cephallenian Islands: Under this name, following the example of the Alexandrian grammarians, we comprise those islands which in Homer form the empire of Odysseus, namely, Ithaca, Cephallenia or Same, and Zacynthos; I have already intimated that I have nothing to say about Dulichion. This empire of Odysseus entirely disappears in our history . . . After the time of the *Odyssey* those islands are scarcely mentioned at all . . . the empire was broken up, and the dynasty of Odysseus disappeared'. Niebuhr (1853) vol. I pp. 153–4.

CHAPTER 30

Shoreline

Considering the unanimity of ancient testimony on the location of Ithaka, it is surprising that any alternative should ever have been seriously considered.

Hope Simpson and Lazenby, *The Catalogue of the Ships in Homer's* Iliad (1970)[1]

The shoreline around Cephalonia today is about 60 cm higher than it was prior to 12 August 1953. How much higher than this was it in Odysseus' time? That depends upon the dates of the uplifting earthquakes compared to the date on which our hero awakened in Phorcys Bay. In the previous chapter we saw that there is considerable uncertainty about the former and in Chapter 2 we observed that there are wide-ranging estimates for the latter, so any answer to this question will at best be only indicative. Nevertheless it is instructive to review the possibilities.

We have four earthquakes to consider and we know that E4 took place in 1953. The earliest proposed date for E3 is AD 350 and it may have been much later. So that leaves us with E2 and E1 to think about, and there are only three cases: either they both occurred before the time of Odysseus, or E1 was before and E2 after, or both were after. If John's estimate of the uplift magnitudes are correct (and ignoring any sea level changes for the time being) then these three scenarios correspond to former shorelines that were respectively either 1.2 m, 2 m or 6 m higher than they are today. How would these higher shorelines have changed the layout of Ithaca city harbour, Telemachos' cove, Rheithron cove, Asteris and Phorcys Bay. How would they have affected Strabo's Channel?

Starting with the harbour, we could use the digital elevation model to form a rough idea of the position of the former coastline but actually this is a classic case in which the oldest technology is the most accurate. On Figure 30.1 these contours from the hand-drawn maps of the Greek Army geographic service have been superimposed on the corresponding satellite image. The blue line is the 6 m contour; the green line is the 2 m contour and the yellow line is 1.2 m. The result is thought-provoking: under every scenario the former harbour was nearly 1 km further inland than the curving bay of today.

What are the implications of this for the Homeric narrative? Does it solve any problems or does it instead create new ones? The ancient shoreline considerably extends the area of northern Argostoli Bay and furthermore its contours reinforce the identification of this location as the obvious place within the bay for the harbour of Ithaca. The sea now passes closer to the farmstead that

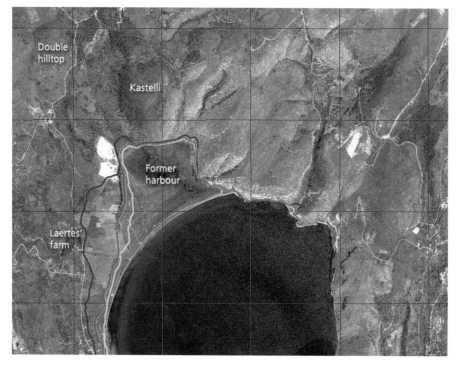

FIGURE 30.1
Northern end of Argostoli
Bay with 6, 2 and 1.2 m
contours
Compare this with the aerial
photograph of Figure 25.8.
Colour interpretation: blue
line = 6 m contour; green
line = 2 m contour; yellow
line = 1.2 m contour.
Remainder: as Figure 20.1.
Grid: 1 km.
[Image credits: as Figure
20.1.]

once belonged to Laertes and this helps us to appreciate a father's words to his disguised son:

> Where is the ship which brought you and your godly
> Companions here? Or were you a passenger
> On another's ship, which landed you and left?   24.299–301

The fact that the ancient shoreline now penetrates almost 1 km further to the north also helps us to understand why Eumaios did not need to use binoculars when he said:

> One thing I know: I saw it for myself.
> By now I had walked up above the city
> To the Hill of Hermes, when I saw a ship
> Entering our harbour. It was fully manned
> And heavy with shields and double-bladed spears.
> I took it to be them, but can't be sure.   16.470–5

As we saw in Chapter 17, the flat marshy area of Figure 13.1 today varies between about 0.1 m and 0.8 m in depth: our three earthquake uplift scenarios therefore correspond to an average harbour depth in Odysseus' day of either

FIGURE 30.2
Close-up satellite image of the former harbour inlet
Colour interpretation: blue line = 6 m contour.
Remainder: as Figure 20.1.
Grid: 100 m.
[Image credits: as Figure 20.1.]

0.7, 1.5 or 5.5 metres. The first of these would, as we have seen, be very shallow indeed for Bronze Age galleys but either of the latter two would be perfectly adequate. Indeed the second scenario corresponds to a progressive deepening of the main harbour from 1.2 m to 1.9 m, which is precisely appropriate for a description such as that at 4.780 'They dragged her first of all into deep water' since it would enable the crew to stay within their depth while pulling the vessel out. If the 5.5 m value applied at that time instead then the main part of the harbour would have been very deep indeed and the dragging of ships would presumably have taken place down the shallower slope of its northern inlet.

So it looks as though we may be able to resolve those troubling observations about the 'deep harbour' from Chapter 17 and I regard this as an outcome of major significance. Homer was right and I was wrong: the harbour of Ithaca was deep all along.

Thus far a higher shoreline in Odysseus' day seems to help us considerably with the poem's interpretation, but is there any actual evidence that the sea was once there? Figure 30.2 is a close-up of the inlet between Mesovouni, the quarry hill, and Kastelli to the east: it is the northern inlet of the ancient harbour and on it you can see some distinctive white lines. Once John had explained his raised beach observations I became fascinated by these

FIGURE 30.3
The 6 m contour at Ithaca
harbour
*The trees in the foreground
correspond to those in the top
right corner of the inlet of
Figure 30.2.*

marks and so on 15 November 2003 I walked down the valley to see them
(Figure 30.3).

This is a view from east to west: in the background you can see the quarry.
As I crossed this field it suddenly became obvious that I was on an ancient
beach: the curving earth bank is exactly the right shape to constitute a former
shoreline. As Figure 30.2 indicates, there are similar terraces lower down the
valley that correspond to lower harbour depths.

What is particularly interesting is the stone wall which you can see on
the far right and which resumes at intervals along the sweep of the earth
bank. When you walk along this it is clear that it used to run the whole way
across the shoreline, but over the centuries some of the stones have been
removed for other uses. The wall has no doubt been rebuilt and reused as a
field boundary, but it and the curving earth bank reinforce John Underhill's
hypothesis that there was once a shoreline here about 6 m higher than the

FIGURE 30.4
Satellite image of Agni
Cove shoreline
Colour interpretation: blue
line = 6 m contour.
Remainder: as Figure 20.1.
Grid: 100 m.
[Image credits: as
Figure 20.1.]

present sea level, although the proof of this will depend on borehole sampling and other scientific tests.

An uplift of this magnitude elsewhere in ancient Ithaca is equally thought-provoking. What would Telemachos' cove have looked like? Figure 30.4 shows the 6 m contour there: the 2 m and 1.2 m contours obviously shrink back from it towards the shoreline. You can see these curving terraces at the centre of Figure 16.4. On 25 March 2003 I turned around from photographing the cove and captured the beautiful meadow behind us (Figure 30.5). Now I understand why today it is so flat: when Telemachos landed there the forward part of it was under the sea.

What about Rheithron Bay? Figure 30.1 shows that the north-western side of Argostoli Bay was set back from where it is today, but this would have made no difference to its suitability as a hiding place for Athene's and Odysseus' imaginary ships.

As far as Asteris is concerned the depth difference has no effect on the suitors' ambush cove of Paliostafida Bay: even with land levels up to 6 m lower there is still plenty of room to conceal the galley. However this constitutes the *coup de grace* for any lingering Dascalion supporters because that barren reef would then have been even more submerged.

The shoreline change has important implications at the northern channel exit of Agia Kiriaki. You will recall from Figure 27.19 that the lower face of the beach cliff about 2 m above present sea level has been reworked by the sea: it was once underwater and the sea has smoothed the layers of conglomerated rock. This meant that either sea levels had declined or land levels had thrust

FIGURE 30.5
The former beach
of Agni Cove
*'Close by dry land / The crew
struck sail and smartly
lowered the mast, / Then
rowed the ship on to its
anchorage / And dropped
stone weights and tied the
stern with cables' (15.495–8).*

upwards. As it happens the former explanation would have run counter to the Holocene sea level history (to be discussed in the next chapter): in any case we now know that the underlying cause was the uplift. So this confirms that the coastline of Cephalonia was at one time 2 m lower there than it is today, although it does not tell us when.

We also need to consider the effect of a higher shoreline on Phorcys Bay, which is indicated in Figure 30.6. This is where I have to eat particularly humble pie because the position of the former coastline would cause the cave that I proposed in Chapter 13 to be underwater. Even in the absence of an upthrust I should have realised this earlier, since the cave that I located is already partially submerged and the poet's detailed description makes no mention of the sea passing through it. If the uplift was as much as 6 m then I will also have to explain how in Odysseus' time my beloved ancient olive tree was growing out of the sea. Perhaps the experts are right and it isn't 3,200 years old after all.

But where then is the Cave of the Nymphs? Let us read those lines once again:

There is a leafy olive at its head,
And nearby a delightful misty cave,
Sacred to the nymphs who have the name of Naiads.
Inside are mixing-bowls and double-handled

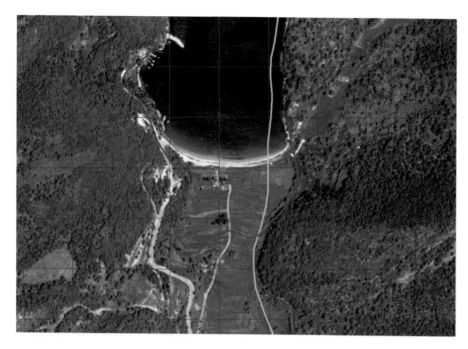

FIGURE 30.6
Satellite image of Phorcys
Bay shoreline with 6 m
contour
*Colour interpretation: blue
line = 6 m contour; light blue
line = Livadi/Atheras Thrust.
Remainder: as Figure 20.1.
Grid: 100 m.*
[Image credits: as
Figure 20.1.]

> Jars made of stone, and here the bees store honey.
> Inside are long stone looms, at which the nymphs
> Weave sea-blue webs, a wondrous sight, and streams
> Of ever-flowing water. It has two doors,
> One to the north, by which men may descend,
> The other to the south, for gods. This way
> Men enter not: it is the immortals' path.   13.102–12

James is adamant about his translation: the 'streams / Of ever-flowing water' are fresh not salty, they flow through the cave and the poet is not referring to the runoff of winter rainfall from the mountains: his streams last all the year round. When we inspected the pigfarm at Figure 20.6 I related that John Underhill had explained to me that the Livadi/Atheras Thrust runs up through the valley of ancient Ithaca, past the pigfarm and Arethousa Spring and then down to Phorcys Bay and that fault lines of this nature tend to represent a natural contour for underground springs.

You can see its course in Figure 30.6: the stream is only just below the surface: indeed the surrounding earth is permanently damp. There is a shallow well where it emerges on the present-day beach and it then flows out into the sea, hugging the eastern shore until it dissipates in the ocean. If you swim during the summer in that part of Atheras Bay (a delightful experience) you can sense the cooler temperature of the fresh spring water and on the millpond-like surface you can see its distinctive trail gliding out to sea.

FIGURE 30.7
The 6 m harbour head and
the underground spring
*The grey-green foliage of the
olive trees on the hillside
stands out against the brighter
green of the other shrubs.*

We know that the olive tree stood at the harbour's head: how near to it was the cave? We saw the answer in Chapter 13:

> With that the goddess entered the misty cave,
> Feeling for hiding places, while Odysseus
> Brought the Phaiacian presents closer up,
> Gold, indestructible bronze, and well-made clothes.
> He stored them carefully, and Pallas, daughter
> Of aigis-bearing Zeus, sealed the mouth with a stone.
> Then they sat down by the trunk of the sacred olive
> To plot the death of the high and mighty suitors.   13.366–73

This suggests that the two were virtually adjacent:[2] both the cave and the olive tree would have been close to the intersection of the spring and the former coastline, near to where the two blue lines meet on Figure 30.6. This is on the opposite side of the bay to where I thought the cave was located on my first visit to Atheras Bay in March 2003. A good beach together with a hunt for treasure in a cave represents a legitimate family outing and ever since John pointed us in the right direction we have been embarked upon a speleological safari.

Figure 30.7 is photographed facing east: you can see the raised bank of the old harbour and the familiar flat expanse of a field that was then under the sea.

FIGURE 30.8
Olive tree at the 6 m
harbour head
*This specimen has wrapped its
lower trunk and roots around
the rocks.*

Off to the right of this image the harbour wall curves away from the hillside
towards the south.

You can also see the distinctive foliage of several olive trees in the wood and
they are not exactly spring chickens (Figure 30.8): by contrast the specimen of
Figure 13.6 is a mere sapling. Can we finally lay to rest that oleanderic ghost
concerning their age? Professor Kuniholm warned me that the 5,000-year old
claim is mere fantasy and in *Remarkable Trees of the World* Thomas Pakenham
explains why:

*The trunks of olive trees, bowed under the weight of 600 or 700 years, become
gradually perforated like a colander. Then they die or are blown down, or are cut
down by an invading army – only to leap up, young trees again, from their ancient
roots. If only we could imitate the olive!*[3]

So sadly none of these olives can be the actual tree behind which the
Phaiacians placed Odysseus's treasure for safe-keeping while he was sleeping soundly on Phorcys' beach. But I think they might just be its great-great
grandchildren.

What about the Cave of the Nymphs? John explains that this hillside is of
a type known as karstified limestone. Acidic groundwater has passed through
it, dissolving the calcium carbonate, and this often results in the formation
of natural caves. Other characteristics of karst hillsides include swallow holes

FIGURE 30.9
Cross-section of a doline
(swallow hole)
*'Formation of a doline
(sinkhole) by roof collapse or
dissolution in a subterranean
drainage system. The doline
shown here has a subaqueous
exit in a lake or sea, but
subareal [above water]
outlets are also common.'*
[Image credits: Curtis N.
Runnels and Tjeerd van
Andel writing in Wiseman
and Zachos (2003) p. 58.]

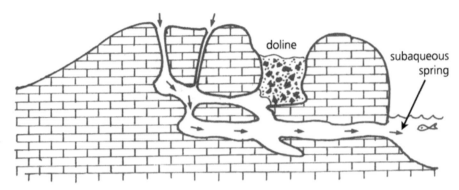

(also termed sink-holes), which are exposed limestone joints down which a surface stream or river disappears. There are spectacular examples of this process in many other parts of the world including the famous caves at Malham[4] in Yorkshire, inspiration for Charles Kingsley's novel *The Water Babies*. The geological term is a 'doline' and the mechanism is illustrated in Figure 30.9.[5]

In August 2003 we looked in this corner of Atheras Bay for a cave but without success. If the cave was as significant in size as Homer tells us then it may be that a whole expanse of the hillside photographed in Figure 30.7 has collapsed. There is a similar karst hillside on the opposite side of the bay but with no evidence of a permanent stream. The poet is clearly describing a large cave and we also know that it is literally on top of an earthquake fault line. That year I came to the conclusion that it had fallen in but I hoped that one day it might be discovered, complete with its crushed mixing-bowls and double-handled jars made of stone.

In that same month James Diggle made an important literary breakthrough just a few metres away while standing on the beach of Atheras Bay. When I first identified this as Homer's Phorcys Bay I assumed that the 'two headlands' that the poet describes were its massive outer promontories. However when James looked at the map he was sceptical about my identification. He pointed out that Homer's text describes the headlands quite unambiguously. They are not at the far edges of the harbour as we might expect: instead they are described most unusually as 'in it'.

> Then the seafaring ship approached the island.
> On Ithaca there is a bay of Phorcys,
> The old man of the sea: in it, two headlands,
> Projecting, sheared off, crouching from the harbour,
> Shield it from waves whipped up by blustering winds
> Outside.   13.95–100

That description, James explained, did not fit the outer headlands of Atheras Bay. At the same time he confessed that he did not understand how any

FIGURE 30.10
The crouching headlands
in Phorcys Bay
*The view from above is at
Figure 13.3. It is these inner
headlands that Homer refers
to in describing Odysseus'
return to Ithaca, not the great
outer arms of Figure 5.3.*

headlands could be described as being 'in' a harbour, or in what sense these or any other headlands might be described as 'crouching from the harbour'. One of the most delightful moments of the entire project took place when we stood together on the beach of Phorcys Bay and digested the view of Figure 30.10.

Suddenly James exclaimed: 'Good heavens! Don't you see? It's unbelievable! There they are: the two headlands really are *in* the harbour'. To the bewilderment of the bystanding bathers he then declaimed from the *Odyssey* the lines starting at 'two headlands' above: *Duo de probletes en auto aktai aporroges, limenos poti pepteuiai*!

What James had observed is that from the beach one's view is restricted by the two inner headlands which enclose the harbour. These are the ones that you can see in Figure 30.10 (and also in Figure 13.3), with the island of Averonisi just beyond. These inner headlands create a natural break for the wind and waves in a bay that is already protected by its massive outer promontories. After recovering from the shock of philological enlightenment

James wrote the more measured report that you can read in Appendix 1 Section H.

So the excitement that I described in Chapter 5 on opening the map of Cephalonia in Blackwell's bookshop was premature: I had identified the wrong headlands. The original composer of the *Odyssey* was equipped with neither a digital elevation model nor a light aircraft. Even if he sailed out to sea far enough to observe the two outer promontories of the bay, the fact that these are 3.2 km apart makes it impossible for him then to have described them as located 'in the bay'. By contrast, the view of the inner headlands of Phorcys Bay that one sees when descending from Atheras at Figure 13.3 or from the beach at Figure 30.10 makes such a description entirely natural. And although this formation of double headlands is rather unusual, if you walk down to the bay or you stand on its shore then Homer's lines are an elegant and immediate way of describing exactly what you see.

As John Underhill has pointed out, the streams that the poet describes as Arethousa Spring follow the Livadi/Atheras Thrust both to the north and to the south of Mount Lakties. You can see the southern rivulet on Figure 23.2: it flows down the western side of the double hilltop and out into Argostoli Bay, keeping a course that is separate to that of the former main torrent through the city. The northern stream descends down Atheras valley and past the cave location into Atheras Bay. There as we have seen it mixes with the salt water along the eastern shore, shimmering like a ribbon in the glassy sea. If you let your imagination wander for a moment you might think that this stream had been pursued all the way down the mountain until it managed to escape its assailant by swimming far out into the ocean.

The Latin poet Ovid, born in 43 BC, relates a wonderful legend along these lines.[6] The river-god Alpheios falls in love with a huntress nymph from Achaia and pursues her across the Peloponnese all the way to Elis. There she prays for help to the goddess of archery who sends down a white cloud to conceal her, but she is trapped inside it and the drops of her perspiration rapidly turn her into a stream herself. Her seducer turns himself back into a river so as to have his wicked watery way with her but just in time the goddess 'splits open the earth and she plunges into its gloomy caverns'.

Via this unusual underground route she somewhat surprisingly reaches Ortygia, the eastern headland of the harbour of Syracuse in Sicily. Ovid leaves us in suspense as far as Alpheios' unrequited love is concerned but Pausanias, writing in the second century AD, completes the myth by explaining 'But that the Alpheios passes through the sea and mingles his waters with the spring at this place I cannot disbelieve, as I know that the god at Delphi confirms the story.'[7]

It is just another myth, of no real importance, but there is one curious aspect that continues to intrigue me: the name of Ovid's nymph was Arethousa. No doubt it is just a coincidence: after all several different Arethousas are listed in the classical dictionaries. But perhaps there are not too many other places with a spring called Arethousa which plunges through the gloomy caverns of the earth to mingle with a river that passes through the sea.

Notes

1 Hope Simpson and Lazenby (1970) p. 103.
2 By contrast, at www.showcaves.com/english/gr/showcaves/Marmarospilia.html we read that one of the alleged sites for the Cave of the Nymphs at the Aetos isthmus on today's island of Ithaca is 2.5 km away from the shoreline and at an altitude of 180 m above sea level. A photograph is provided at http://web.quick.cz/polasekj/images/phorcy_2.jpg
3 Pakenham (2002) p. 162.
4 www.yorkshire-dales.com/malham/index.html
5 Runnels and van Andel (2003) p. 58.
6 Ovid, *Metamorphoses* Book 5.572–641.
7 Pausanias 5.7.2.

CHAPTER 31   **Epiphany**

Was this the face that launch'd a thousand ships,
And burnt the topless towers of Ilium?

Christopher Marlowe,
The Tragical History of Doctor Faustus (1604)

During July and August 2004 a group of experts met on the island to put this book's hypothesis to the test. The primary focus was geological research, conducted within the framework of John Underhill's permit from IGME, the Athens-based Institute of Geology and Mineral Exploration. Per Wikstroem of Radarteam flew in from northern Sweden with a ground-penetrating radar antenna capable of scanning down to a depth of 30 m. John's geology students Murphy Shayne, James Sterry and Ruth Anderson spent several weeks on the island conducting detailed mapping surveys and they also mastered the art of drilling shallow boreholes with a handheld auger.

Christopher Bronk Ramsey and Jean-Luc Schwenninger of the Oxford Research Laboratory for Archaeology and the History of Art (RLAHA) identified locations for radiocarbon (C14) and optically stimulated luminescence (OSL) dating and supervised the collection of samples. These processes require a large amount of laboratory time and the outcome is awaited with considerable anticipation: depending on the publication timetable for this book it is hoped that preliminary results may be presented at Appendix 5. John, James Diggle and I overlapped for a week or so at a time and Simon spent five weeks on-site looking after the project logistics. Finally, by great good fortune Anthony Snodgrass and his wife Annemarie were also able to visit the island for a few days and lend their expert eyes to some of the challenges that emerged.

The first scientific finding emerged when Per Wikstroem's radar antenna traversed the raised harbour between Kastelli and Mesovouni (Figure 30.2 and Figure 30.3). The scan was started two terraces uphill from the 6 m terrace marked on Figure 30.2 and it proceeded down the valley towards the sea, ending at the point where the harbour widens. Initially the radar beam penetrated comfortably through several metres of soil but as the antenna descended towards the former shoreline, the beam penetration broke up below the surface. Per explained that in his experience the reason for this was that the soil layer at this location was electrically conductive and this was preventing the radar trace from penetrating deeper. One of the factors that can cause soil to

become more conductive is when it is mixed with salt and Per regards this
result as consistent with the soil's former immersion in salt water.

So this evidence provides support for the proposal that the area that I have
diagnosed as the inlet of ancient Ithaca harbour in Figure 30.2 was once under
the sea. In case this result was simply coincidental he then repeated the same
test at Agni Cove, the beach on the north-west coast where Telemachos is
believed to have landed.

At Agni Cove (Figure 31.1) radar scans were conducted in directions both
parallel and orthogonal to the shoreline. The first scan was the long one
(266 m) marked in red in the direction of the sea. At the intersection with
the terrace between the green and yellow lines the beam penetration dropped
suddenly from 7.5 m to 2.5 m below ground level. The green and yellow scans
were then performed parallel to the sea: the higher one (green) penetrated
consistently down to 7.5 m all along its length while the lower one (yellow)
was limited to a depth of 2.5 m. Once again these readings suggested that the
ground below the terrace between these two scans was formerly under the
sea.

Although Per was unable to say when these marine immersions happened,
John Underhill explained that there are realistically only two possibilities:
either during the late Holocene period (the last few thousand years), or alternatively during the last inter-glacial period around 120,000 years ago. This is
because at other intermediate periods the sea level was much lower than it is
today, so the sea could not have reached this far up the island at those times.

FIGURE 31.2
Agia Kiriaki exposed wall
under Mount Imerovigli
*This wall was not visible the
previous autumn and must
have been exposed as a result
of the winter waves. The
following week an estimate of
its age was made by Anthony
Snodgrass.*

This observation therefore narrows the range of possible dates down to these two alternatives, but can we make any further deductions about which of the two periods is the more likely?

As it happens we can, because during the earlier inter-glacial period the sea actually reached a maximum level considerably higher than it has so far regained during the recent Holocene. This is why it is called inter-glacial: the glaciers had melted, raising the sea. So if these traces of salt were the result of an inter-glacial marine immersion that had remained in the soil for about 120,000 years, then the regions above the terraces of Figure 30.3 and Figure 31.1 would also be conductive. Since they are not, the implication is that any inter-glacial salt deposits must have leached out of the soil over that length of time. The interruption to the radar beam that Per was picking up nearer to the sea must therefore correspond to the conductive effects of a later salt water inundation. This suggests that these beaches were covered by the sea during the Holocene period – at some point during the last 10,000 years.

This was excellent news: the first independent corroboration of John's diagnosis of a Holocene era tectonic uplift. But then on 27 July 2004 he made a sensational discovery (Figure 31.2). The photograph is from Agia Kiriaki Beach, taken at almost exactly the same location as Figure 27.19 the previous year. It shows the face of a man-made wall and John was adamant that it was not visible during our last visit in November 2003. So it must have been exposed as a result of erosion since then, probably by the force of the winter

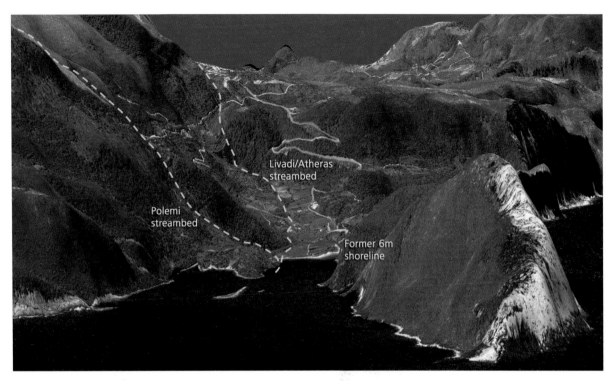

Livadi/Atheras
streambed

Polemi
streambed

Former 6m
shoreline

FIGURE 31.3
Intersecting spring lines at
Atheras Bay
*The intersection of the Polemi
spring with the former
harbour is at its eastern
extremity in Figure 30.6 and
about 120 metres north-east
of where we were looking for
the cave previously.*
[Image credits: Digital
Globe Quickbird 60 cm
resolution false colour
satellite image. Data
source: DEM data from
Hellenic Military
Geographical Service.
Processing: OziExplorer
3D.]

waves. The visible region of the wall at that time was 1.45 m high and the exposed base of the wall was measured (with some difficulty and imprecision) as about 2 m above present sea level and about 4 m below the top of the beach cliff.

Would anyone attempt to build a wall beneath an existing landslide? Presumably not, so this means that the rockfall must have come down after this wall was built. That in itself demonstrates that one or more rockfalls in this region did take place and also that they must have occurred at a date after the human habitation of this area. But it also demonstrates another crucial point.

This is the precise location at which John had previously observed the layers of material that have been reworked by the sea at a height of about 2 m above today's sea level. We discussed these in Chapter 27 and in Chapter 30; they were once underwater and they consist of at least two bands: a 9 cm band of 'grey clast supported conglomerate' towards the top of the exposed apex of the wall and above that a 35 cm region of 'bedded aqueous deposits'. So this tells us that someone built a wall here with its foundations underwater at a time when this part of the island was formerly 2 m lower in the sea.[1] If we can find out when the wall was built it will provide us with an earliest date for earthquake 2.

What else can we deduce about these rockslides? Strabo observed 'Where the island is narrowest it forms a low isthmus, so that it is often submerged

FIGURE 31.4
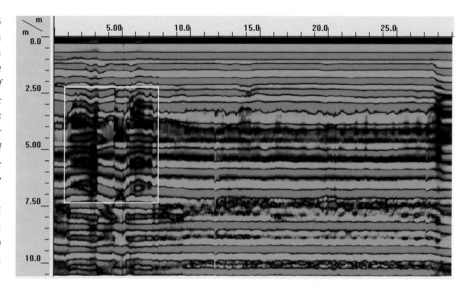

FIGURE 31.4
Anomalous echo in
Atheras Bay radar scan
Vertical scale is an
approximate calibration of
subterranean depth;
horizontal scale shows
distance travelled. Regular
alternating green and red
bands denote uniform terrain;
grey shadow indicates possible
cavities or boulder reflections.
[Image credits: GSSI
Radan 6.0. Data source:
GSSI SIR-3000 and 2000
control units; Radarteam
100 MHz antenna.]

from sea to sea' and from this it follows that the sea must still have been able to penetrate through the isthmus from time to time around the first century BC. That means that the central part of the isthmus cannot then have been at its present height of 180 m above sea level. Furthermore, given our observations about winter waves in Chapter 28, the first rockfall to have blocked the channel intermittently must have occurred at its northern end, because at any other location along the channel (including its southern exit in the protected bay of Argostoli) the winter waves would not have affected it.

Presumably it must also have been a less drastic landslide than the one in the photograph, because that one must have blocked the channel permanently. As suggested in Chapter 28 and at Figure A2.24 of John's Appendix 2, it therefore looks as if there has been a series of successive landslips over the centuries that have extended the base of Mount Imerovigli across from the east. Each new rockslide thundered down over the surface of the previous one and reached further across the bay towards the west.

Two days after the discovery of this wall Per's radar antenna proved itself invaluable again at Atheras Bay. It had become clear that the spring line of Figure 30.6 was not the only source of fresh water in that corner of the bay: there appears to be another one that descends from Mount Polemi to the north-east, joining the bay at the same place (Figure 31.3). This image was produced by superimposing the Quickbird satellite imagery on to the height framework from the digital elevation model. At that location Per's radar antenna picked up the traces of a subterranean void. This was analysed using GSSI Radan software and the results are shown in Figure 31.4.

Per's interpretation of the area enclosed by the white rectangle is that the echoes are consistent with a subterranean air void, while the vertical

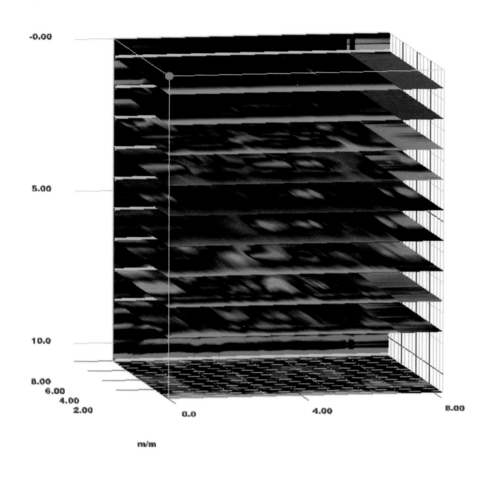

FIGURE 31.5
3D recreation of Atheras
Bay subterranean void
*Colour interpretation: as for
Figure 31.4.*
[Image credits and data
source: as for Figure 31.4.]

features at 4 m and 6 m from the left hand edge of the image may represent
faults.

The surface area was traversed via multiple scans in a rectangular pattern and the resulting three-dimensional reconstruction is displayed in
Figure 31.5. This indicates that there may be a subterranean air cavity at
this location of cross-sectional area approximately 3 m × 7 m and at a depth
varying between 2.5 m and 7.5 m.[2] If this analysis is subsequently confirmed
by excavation then we may at last have discovered the Cave of the Nymphs.
This is clearly something to be determined by a future phase of the project
rather than now but I am restless with excitement to hear of the result.

At noon on Saturday 7 August 2004 I greet James Diggle, Anthony
Snodgrass and his wife Annemarie at Argostoli airport. After collecting the
bags from the conveyor belt we drive the few miles to the Mediterranean
Hotel which provides the tripartite benefit of a cool drink, a view of the suitors' ambush bay and a cloakroom in which to change from English travellers'
clothing into Greek exploratory attire.

FIGURE 31.6
Ithaca revealed behind
Asteris
*The lighthouse is at the
northern end of the Argostoli
peninsula, Homer's ambush
'island' of Asteris.*

We drive into Argostoli and catch the car ferry to Lixouri. As we pass the lighthouse of Agios Theodoros on the *nesos* of Asteris (Figure 31.6) we see that beyond it to the west:

Ithaca itself lies low, furthest to sea
Towards dusk; the rest, apart, face dawn and sun.   9.25–6

John Underhill is drawing to the end of his own stay on the island and after a reunion lunch at the northern end of Argostoli Bay we aim for Agia Kiriaki Beach, passing on the way the putative theatre where Anthony inspects the terraces. His verdict there is open: as a prehistoric place of performance it is neither ruled in nor ruled out.

At the beach John shows us his newly discovered wall with its adjacent layers reworked by the sea 2 m above today's sea level. There is evidence that it may continue eastwards and one possibility is that it encloses an ancient harbour at the mouth of Strabo's Channel. But how ancient? Anthony has considerable experience of excavating walls of many different types of construction and his opinion is as follows.

This wall was built by creating a raft of small stones and then embedding the larger ones on top. Red conglomerate has been used from time to time as an alternative to limestone. The technique is like Mycenaean and the wall was probably constructed some time from c. 1500 BC onwards.

So John has found a Mycenaean-like wall buried below a rockslide that can only have come down from the V-shaped gullies in the mountainside behind. That is an observation of great significance to this project because it provides us with four separate items of information.

The first implication is that the rockslide that covered this wall could not have occurred before 1500 BC since walls of this construction are not known prior to that date, although it could have taken place at any time thereafter.

The second is that the dating of this wall provides us with an earliest date for the 1.2 m uplift of earthquake 2. That uplift could not have taken place before 1500 BC either, otherwise this wall would not have been partially underwater. We should note in passing that there is no reason why the landslip that covered this wall should have occurred at the same time as earthquake 2: the two events are not necessarily related.

The third is that the existence of a once semi-submerged wall of this style and date at an elevation of about 2 m above today's sea level is supportive of the proposal that this was a sea wall built to protect a shoreline 2 m higher than it is today. If this Mycenaean-like wall was contemporaneous with Odysseus then this answers the question of the previous chapter: E1 happened before the time of Odysseus and E2 some time afterwards. However Anthony Snodgrass adds that the date range for the wall is 'between 1500 BC and AD 500 as the outermost limits, but with a strong inclination towards the upper end of that bracket', so it could instead have been built after the time of Odysseus. In that case E1 might have been experienced by the Bronze Age Ithacans at a time when the island was 6 m lower in the sea.

The fourth implication is that at that time the seabed of Strabo's Channel was 2 m lower then than it is today and the channel was also 4 m shallower than before the first earthquake. John's cross-sectional diagrams in Appendix 2 indicate that it can never have been very deep originally, so these progressive uplifts have been making it shallower and shallower. We can now empathise with Homer's repeated and hitherto rather puzzling description of the journey to ancient Ithaca: 'For I hardly think you came on foot.'

The next day is spent in exploring Strabo's Channel and revisiting the Agia Kiriaki beach wall. Our lunch at Zola harbour is an exuberant celebration, a fitting farewell for John whose flight home leaves later that afternoon. Then on 9 August we visit the valley between Kastelli and the Mesovouni quarry to embark on an investigation of major importance.

In Chapter 24 we heard about Homer's description of manure-spreading and its implications for the dispersion of Bronze Age pottery. If we are now in the ancient city of the Ithacans we should expect the ground to yield copious quantities of sherds. Anthony, Annemarie, James and I spread out in a line and we walk slowly up from the harbour, looking down at our feet for fragments. We stay in touch via the walkie-talkies and at any moment I expect to hear that there has been a find. But after two hours of walking we have discovered nothing of any value. I am uncomfortably reminded that when James visited the double hilltop with me the previous summer he saw no sherds on the ground there either. How can these locations be so right and yet so wrong?

We are staying in Villa Arozza outside Fiscardo, very close to the Villa Rowena that I had rented the year before and that evening over dinner we discuss this paradox. By now Anthony has also visited Atheras Bay and the pigfarm with us and he is not unsympathetic to the proposal as a whole, but he explains that over the centuries an island such as Cephalonia will have experienced many waves of invasion, destruction and rebuilding. He agrees with me that the road of Figure 23.7 shows the effects of human habitation in this valley but he also agrees with Tjeerd van Andel's diagnosis that it is a Turkish mule path. He readily accepts that Figure 19.17 shows a millstone that has been cut by a man's hand and that Figure 20.13 depicts walls that have been artificially constructed, but he also explains that there is no reason to assume that these are ancient artefacts: in fact they are probably only mediaeval.

On my first visit to Cephalonia back in March 2003 I had stumbled across the ruins of an old building on a hillside not far from Raven's Rock, but I had impatiently dismissed it as irrelevant: just another trap for the unwary like the soi-disant 'Odysseus' Palace' of Figure 13.2. But when Anthony visited it he christened it the 'Catalan castle' from his experiences in Boeotia (Figure 31.7). In that region from AD 1311 onwards the Duchy of Athens was ruled by the kings of Aragon and Sicily who were the lords of Catalonia. Their 'Catalan Company' remained in control of much of the central Greek mainland until 1388 when they were replaced by the Florentines, who were themselves conquered by the Ottoman Turks in 1456.

The mediaeval history of Cephalonia itself dates from around 1082 with the arrival of the Guiscardo family whom we encountered in Chapter 21. The Normans of Sicily took power in 1185 and they were followed by the Orsini family from 1194. A Venetian, Roberto of Taranto, administered Cephalonia from 1351 but in 1357 he gave it to the Tocchi family who were cousins of the Orsinis. The Tocchi ruled over the island until the first Turkish occupation in 1479 and the eventual surrender of the island to the Ottoman Empire in 1485. On Christmas Eve 1500 the Venetians and Spaniards stormed the Castle

FIGURE 31.7
The 'Catalan castle' near
Raven's Rock
In view of the island's
occupation the castle is
probably Venetian but
Anthony Snodgrass was
reminded of his experiences in
Boeotia, where the Catalan
Company held sway from
1311 to 1388.

of St George at the end of a fifty-day siege and recaptured the island. After the Spaniards departed the Venetians ruled it for nearly 300 years, sparring with the Turks who occupied the Peloponnese until 1716 and with their erstwhile allies the Spaniards who attempted to invade it again in 1532. As we heard in Chapter 23, the Venetians finally succumbed to the French in 1797.[3]

From a defensive standpoint the main stronghold on the island was indeed the Castle of St George, to the south of present-day Argostoli. North of Paliki the Castle of Assos was another military asset: it overlooks the bay of Agia Kiriaki and could act as a base from which to defend the island against a naval invasion. The eastern coastline is protected by the narrow strait between Cephalonia and Ithaca whose entrances could be patrolled, but that left the whole western expanse of Paliki vulnerable. Fortunately for the Cephalonians (and as we have also appreciated in considering Telemachos' return from Pylos) there are very few places on that sheer western coastline that permit ships to land. Agni Cove itself is much too small to accommodate an invasion fleet and although Petani Beach is larger, there is no harbour there and the ascent up the adjacent cliffs is precipitous, even via the modern road.

But Atheras Bay would have been perfect: 'in it, two headlands, / Projecting, sheared off, crouching from the harbour, / Shield it from waves whipped up by blustering winds / Outside. Inside well-timbered ships can ride / Unanchored, when they reach the mooring-place' (13.97–101) A mediaeval invasion force landing here could occupy Paliki rapidly, counting on the difficult terrain between it and the main body of Cephalonia to deter

FIGURE 31.8
Kastelli from the eastern
plateau
*Mount Milo (Neïon) is visible
in the distance beyond the bay.*

land-based opposition. Once the invaders had captured Paliki they could reinforce themselves at their leisure until they were ready to mount an assault on the territory across the bay. No governor of Cephalonia could ignore such a threat: no wonder a castle was built in this strategic position to keep a constant watch over the northern headlands and out to sea. So the presence of a mediaeval castle at this location may help to explain why there are so many dry stone walls and enclosures in this valley. They are old and they are abandoned, but they were not built by Odysseus.

So is my prized double hilltop merely a similar site of mediaeval activity? James had found no sherds there and indeed when Anthony and Annemarie inspected the adjacent olive groves with us later that same week, no sherds were found either in those well-furrowed fields. But you will understand that on 10 August I was not yet ready to abandon the site for Odysseus' Palace that I had been cherishing for over a year and with only a few days left before our flight home I was hoping for a miracle.

I am silently praying that Anthony will find something special on the double hilltop after all while I drive the four of us towards it along the track that follows in the footsteps of Philoitios. It is the same route that I had taken the previous year (described in Chapter 23) and by now we are approaching the eastern side of Kastelli (Figure 31.8) where our path is at an elevation of about 180 m above sea level.

As we near the hillside Anthony asks me a crucial question:

FIGURE 31.9
Kastelli from the raised harbour to the south-west
If John Underhill's diagnosis of raised shorelines is confirmed by dating, then in Odysseus' day the sea washed at the foot of Kastelli and Homer was accurate in describing a 'deep harbour'.

Remind me why you discounted the possibility that the palace itself might have been located on the summit of Kastelli?

Kastelli? It sounds like the name of just another mediaeval castle. I reply that I had initially identified Kastelli as a possible site for the palace but I had subsequently ruled it out because I felt that otherwise the sportsground in front of the palace would have been positioned right in the middle of the harbour. After all, Palace Clue 17 from Chapter 17 enables us to be fairly categorical about this: 'There is a levelled sportsground about 100 m long in front of the palace.'

Might not the sportsground itself be located somewhere on Kastelli hillside?

Well no, obviously not. A sportsground is like an Olympic stadium, isn't it? Surely you cannot create one right up on a hillside? After all, look how high it is (Figure 31.9: we are approaching from the plateau to the right).

Anthony tactfully perseveres:

I wonder if you have read the accounts of other early acropolis sites that we know of? Panopeus, for example, which 'towers above the hamlet of Agios Vlasis on the southern edge of a broad valley bounded on the west by the foothills of Mount Parnassos'? Or Arene, a settlement mentioned by Homer that is usually identified with Samikon, a high hilltop south of the river Alpheios? Or Dorion? Or Orchomenos in Arcadia, which 'occupied the summit of a high conical hill'? Or the Menelaion, which is believed to be the palace of King Menelaos of Sparta and is located 'in a conspicuous position on a narrow plateau high above the east bank of the Eurotas'? As far as Bronze Age citadels are concerned, it seems to have been a question of the higher the better.[4]

That description hits home. Simon and I had visited Samikon in the western Peloponnese the previous month and we had been very struck by its altitude of around 250 m above sea level, about the same elevation as this. That in turn triggers a memory of a rare reference to Kastelli in the archaeological literature of 1995:

Paliki area. The surface survey carried out by the Danish Archaeological Institute and the 6th EPCA in the E part of Kefalonia was continued for a third year. Work focussed on the Erissos peninsula, which constitutes the NE part of the island. Only a few sites were located. Furthermore, more topographical studies and plotting of architectural entities were carried out, as well as plans and photography of the most interesting portable finds.   (ADelt 245–6)

In the location of Kastelli, on the top of the hill with a panoramic view of the Argostoli bay, flint flakes and very few handmade potsherds of PR [prehistoric] date were collected.   (ADelt 246).[5]

I explain to Anthony that I had climbed across the north-western slope of Kastelli the previous November on a dull winter's day and had found it overgrown with maquis and rather hard going. He gently points out to me the saddle of land on the hilltop straight in front of us and also the flat intermediate hilltop to our right. We leave the jeep and begin to walk up the saddle, spreading out to maximise the chances of spotting sherds of pottery.

The four of us stay in touch via the walkie-talkies again as we climb the slope. Almost immediately Annemarie radios that there is a high density of sherds to be seen at her feet. As we reach the summit of the saddle (Figure 31.10) Anthony and James confirm that they are also seeing a significant volume of pottery. There is an art to spotting these pieces and I rapidly find that my own eyes are not adept at the task. But within a short period of time Anthony is able to identify a considerable number of these fragments as of Bronze Age date: and some of them are Mycenaean.

FIGURE 31.10
Kastelli – the
south-eastern saddle
*The area is at the other side of
the earth-covered ridge at the
centre of Figure 31.8.*

FIGURE 31.11
Terrace below Kastelli
summit
*View from the eastern slope of
Kastelli looking north towards
Mount Lakties (Neriton).*

FIGURE 31.12
View south from Kastelli
hilltop
The evidence suggests that this
is the view from Odysseus'
Palace towards the peninsula
that Homer calls Asteris.

We ascend from there to the intermediate hilltop and then on towards the summit itself. Several of these areas are large enough to make excellent sportsgrounds; and all the while Mycenaean sherds remain visible on the surface as we walk.

As we near the top of the hill Anthony identifies ancient terraces and their retaining walls (Figure 31.11). At last we reach the summit where there is a trigonometric pedestal: the Hellenic Military Geographic Service survey map marks this point as 251.69 m above sea level. Then we turn southwards to face the sea (Figure 31.12).

Sometimes the spirit tells us what the intellect cannot. This is a view that defies description and resists photography. To see it once is to realise that you could never walk away to make your home on a lower contour. To awaken here at the start of each day is to experience a sensation so sublime that it renders you immortal. On this hilltop you will sup at the table of the gods: a palace built here is a passport to Olympos. From this summit you will plan the takeover of Troy; from these mountains you will fell the trees for your galleys; from this harbour you will sail with your fleet to rescue Helen. On this hilltop you are truly Odysseus: and however far you travel, you will always return.

Notes

1 There is a logical alternative: that the wall was built much earlier when the island was 6 m lower than today, but this appears implausible because its foundations would then have been about 5 m below the sea's surface.

2 These depth figures depend upon the estimated dielectric constant of limestone: on the basis of Per Wikstroem's experience a figure of 8.0 was used.

3 Livada-Duca (2000) pp. 9–53.

4 While we were in the field Anthony Snodgrass summarised these descriptions from memory but on his return he furnished me with the appropriate references from which I have quoted here: Hope Simpson and Lazenby (1970) pp. 42, 76, 85, 91 and Catling (1976–7) p. 24. I learnt that these acropolis sites are hardly unique: in summarising his experiences after an extensive tour of the Peloponnese, Leake comments 'for we find in every part of Greece, that the most remarkable summits, with the exception perhaps of the highest and most inaccessible of all, have been fortified, or have had fortresses near them, being generally the same name as the mountains themselves' (Leake (1830) vol. II p. 13).

5 Blackman (2001) p. 44, translating from Soteriou (1995). It is unclear from these sources whether the finds on Kastelli were made by the Danish Archaeological Institute or via an unrelated survey; the site is not listed in Randsborg (2002) nor in Souyoudzoglou-Haywood (1999). But I am happy to record that Dr Andreas Soteriou of the Greek Archaeological Service has confirmed that it was he who climbed Kastelli and found those prehistoric sherds upon its summit.

CHAPTER 32 **Ithaca**

Always keep Ithaca in your mind.
To arrive there is your ultimate goal.
But do not hurry the voyage at all.
It is better to let it last for many years;
and to anchor at the island when you are old,
rich with all you have gained on the way,
not expecting that Ithaca will offer you riches.   Constantine P. Cavafy, *Ithaca* (1911)[1]

The beach of Agia Sotira that I thought was the southern exit of Strabo's Channel is 400 m north of the real exit that John Underhill identified. The western outer headland of Atheras Bay that I thought was the one described by Homer is 1,700 m north of the real inner headland that James Diggle identified. And the double hilltop that I thought was the site of Odysseus' Palace is 1,000 metres due west of the real palace site that Anthony Snodgrass identified. It is all a matter of metres, but those metres mark the difference between theory and reality.

In this chapter we can at last embark on a guided tour of ancient Ithaca, but I must first issue a caveat concerning the computer-generated maps that we shall be using. If you compare the digitally produced image of Figure 32.1 with the aerial photograph of Figure 25.8 you will see some important differences.

The most obvious distinction is that these are false colour images, with red signifying chlorophyll-rich lush vegetation. Also of immediate note is the abrupt cutoff around the borders of the digital image, which simply represents the limits of the elevation and satellite data that I obtained. A more dramatic sensation of height may be apparent because the vertical scale that links real-world metres to centimetres on the page is up to us to define: we can shrink or expand it as we like, flattening or growing these mountains (while maintaining their relative proportion) at the click of a mouse.

A careful look at the landscape also reveals that this computer-generated terrain is somewhat smoother here than it is in reality: that is because a 30 m horizontal grid for altitude data has been superimposed on a 60 cm grid for photographic detail and so the finer-grained undulations have been averaged out. But the most important aspect of a digital elevation model is simply this: we can now fly to wherever we want at the touch of a button, because the software can immediately generate a view of anywhere in the target area from any vantage point and at any magnification.

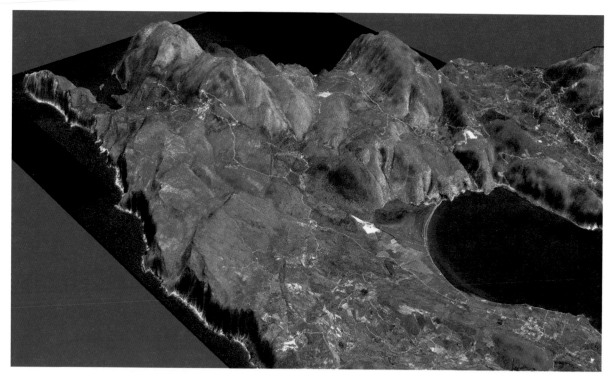

FIGURE 32.1
Digital elevation image of
northern Paliki
*Colour interpretation: as
Figure 20.1.*
[Image credits: Digital
Globe Quickbird 60 cm
resolution false colour
satellite image. Data
source: DEM data from
Hellenic Military
Geographical Service.
Processing: OziExplorer
3D.]

So where in ancient Ithaca shall we go to today? The temptation to trace the return of Odysseus is irresistible: indeed after 3,200 years it is high time that we celebrated his homecoming.

We are crewmen on the Phaiacian ship escorting the sleeping Odysseus, approaching Phorcys Bay in Figure 32.2. After passing the outer headlands we drop our sails and row past the small island of Averonisi. Homer does not mention this island in the *Odyssey* but even today it is only 270 m long, 50 m wide and a maximum of 13 m high: at that time it was probably between 2 m and 6 m lower in the water.

> They rowed inside: they knew the bay of old.
> The ship ran up the beach for half its length
> At speed: such strength was in the rowers' arms.   13.113–15

The beach of Figure 32.3 was then further inland but there is no exposed bedrock there so our ship easily runs up for half its length. Odysseus is put ashore still sleeping and his treasure is stashed beside him. In the morning he awakens and meets Athene, who helps him hide it in a cave near the harbour's head:

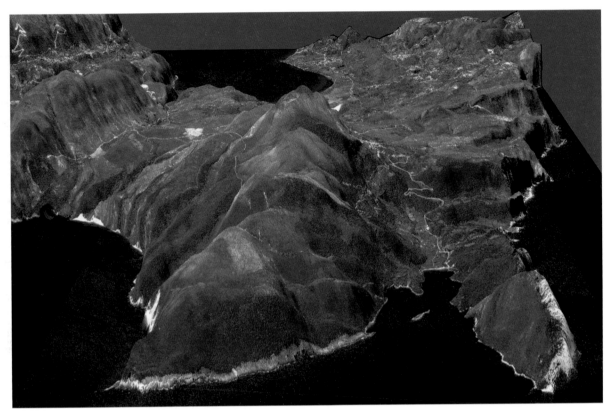

FIGURE 32.2
Digital elevation image of
Phorcys Bay
*Colour interpretation: as
Figure 20.1.*
[Image credits, data and
processing: as Figure 32.1.]

There is a leafy olive at its head,
And nearby a delightful misty cave,
Sacred to the nymphs who have the name of Naiads.
Inside are mixing-bowls and double-handled
Jars made of stone, and here the bees store honey.
Inside are long stone looms, at which the nymphs
Weave sea-blue webs, a wondrous sight, and streams
Of ever-flowing water. It has two doors,
One to the north, by which men may descend,
The other to the south, for gods. This way
Men enter not: it is the immortals' path.   13.102–12

All you can see of the cave location today are some large limestone boulders
(Figure 32.4), but given the uplift they are precisely where the poet describes.
Olive trees still grow nearby, there are permanent streams passing through
the area and as we saw in Figure 31.5, ground-penetrating radar has picked
up the echo of an anomalous subterranean void there.

Athene then disguises Odysseus and he makes his way to the pigfarm:

He climbed a rugged path up from the harbour,
Along the heights through woods, the way Athene
Pointed him to the swineherd, of all the servants
The most faithful steward of his property.   14.1–4

Two paths up from Phorcys Bay to the town of Atheras are visible in
Figure 32.5. The modern road lies nearer to us on the western flank of the
hillside but there is also an ancient path that hugs the base of Mount Neriton
to the east. Meanwhile the small V-shaped cove at the bottom of the picture
should by now be familiar: it is the site of Telemachos' landfall after his journey
from Pylos and it is one of the few places along that savage western coastline
where a ship can safely disembark a royal passenger.

I doubt that the present road up from Atheras Bay existed 3,000 years ago. I
think that Odysseus took the ancient path up from the sea, leaving the beach
from the cave on its eastern side. Because he is in disguise there is no risk that
he will be recognised by other Ithacans on the way. The distance from the
shore to the pigfarm is little more than 3 km, less than an hour's walk.

A question that has puzzled Odyssean experts over the years is why Telemachos did not also land at Phorcys Bay; or if he did, why doesn't the poet say so?
I had no good answer to this puzzle until my son Mark explained it to me, and
like all good explanations from a ten-year-old it is obvious once you hear it:

Telemachos strapped fine sandals on his feet
And picked up from the deck a sturdy spear
Tipped with sharp bronze. The crew untied the cables,
Then pushed her off and sailed towards the city,
As ordered by the son of godly Odysseus.
He strode on rapidly, until he reached
The yard which housed his countless pigs, near which
The good and faithful swineherd used to sleep.   15.550–7

The distance from Telemachos' cove to the pigfarm is also about 3 km and
unlike his father, Telemachos has no disguise: indeed he is instantly recognisable as the young prince:

Even as he spoke, his dear son suddenly
Stood in the porch. The swineherd sprang to his feet
Amazed; the bowls in which he had been busy
Mixing the sparkling wine dropped from his grasp.
He went to meet his master, kissed his head,
His eyes and both his hands, and wept for joy.   16.11–16

FIGURE 32.3
Atheras Bay from the sea
*Photograph taken from the
end of the harbour wall
shown at Figure 30.6.*

FIGURE 32.4
Phorcys Bay – location of
the subterranean void
*Prior to the uplift the former
shoreline was closer to these
rocks.*

FIGURE 32.5 Digital elevation view of Telemachos' cove
Colour interpretation: as Figure 20.1.
[Image credits, data and processing: as Figure 32.1.]

Mount Neriton

Arethousa Spring(s)

Eumaios' Pigfarm

Raven's Rock

Telemachos has been briefed about the plotting suitors by Athene: she has warned him at 15.30 that they are 'Intent on murdering you on your way home'. Mark realised that he therefore decides to drop anchor at the remote Agni Cove deliberately: he must choose a route up to the pigfarm that will avoid the risk of being recognised and the murderous suitors thereby informed about his return from Pylos and his precise whereabouts.

On the way to the pigfarm Odysseus passes Arethousa Spring and in August 2003 Mark spotted another well that is perhaps more credible than that of Figure 14.5. Just a few metres to the south (the right-most arrow on Figure 32.6) this beautiful and surprisingly elaborate well is built up on to a circular stone podium (Figure 32.7); to date it has narrowly escaped destruction from adjacent road works. Whether or not this construction is the actual Bronze Age spring of Arethousa is perhaps less important than the observation that a water-bearing fault line runs just below the surface in exactly the right place for a spring to emerge or a well to be built here.

Go first of all to the swineherd, who keeps watch
Over your pigs and is still loyal to you
And loves your son and wise Penelope.
You will find him sitting with the pigs; they feed
By Raven's Rock and Arethousa Spring,
Guzzling dark water and munching tasty acorns –
A diet that builds up healthy fat in pigs.

13.404–10

FIGURE 32.6
Digital elevation view of the pigfarm
Colour interpretation: as Figure 20.1.
[Image credits, data and processing: as Figure 32.1.]

FIGURE 32.7
A fitting candidate for
Arethousa Spring
*The Livadi/Atheras fault line
ensures an abundance of
spring water along the
western side of Mount
Neriton.*

Eumaios' Pigfarm is portrayed again at Figure 32.8. There is also a deep gully a few hundred metres further to the north (at the left of Figure 32.6) which benefits from the moist fault line as well and it may be that Eumaios had extended his pigfarm to include it: if so then his agricultural holdings would have been very substantial.

At the summit of the distinctive hill sloping towards the left in the background is Raven's Rock, but a serious problem has now emerged: with the palace located on Kastelli my argument that the low long ridge of Figure 19.13 is Hermes' Hill has disappeared, because it is in entirely the wrong place. Although that creates momentary relief for James, who was never comfortable with my identification of that location in the first place, any sense of elation soon evaporates as we realise that we are now missing a vital element of the story.

On 11 August 2004 James and I return to Kastelli with the intention of resolving this deficiency but first we remind each other of the relevant clues from Chapter 17. We recall that after being given his instructions by Telemachos, Eumaios sets off in the direction of the city even though he has actually been asked to visit Penelope at the palace, which gave us Clue 7, that the palace and the city must be close to each other. Clue 11 told us that he arrives back at the pigfarm that same evening and when Telemachos asks him whether the suitors have yet returned from Asteris, Eumaios replies that:

FIGURE 32.8
Eumaios' pigfarm revisited
Over a 3,000 year interval the walls have been rebuilt many times, but this site for the pigfarm matches Homer's description exactly.

I did not think of going down to town
To inquire of that: I wanted to deliver
The message and return here with all speed.
I fell in with a messenger sent by
Your shipmates: he was first to address your mother.
One thing I know: I saw it for myself.
By now I had walked up above the city
To the Hill of Hermes, when I saw a ship
Entering our harbour. It was fully manned
And heavy with shields and double-bladed spears.
I took it to be them, but can't be sure.   16.465–75

This passage yielded Clue 12, the city lies below the palace; Clue 13, Hermes' Hill lies above the city; Clue 14, Hermes' Hill lies between the city and the pigfarm and Clue 15, from Hermes' Hill the harbour is clearly visible. So to summarise, we are looking for a hill that lies between the palace and the pigfarm; it is up above the city and when you reach it on the path from the palace there is a clear view of the harbour of ancient Ithaca.

James and I are now standing once again on the summit of Kastelli, looking northwards towards Mount Neriton which you can see in the distance in Figure 32.9. If Eumaios was walking back from here to the pigfarm then the route he would have taken is the diagonal one that stretches from bottom

FIGURE 32.9
Raven's Rock and Mount
Neriton from Kastelli
*If Eumaios was returning
from the palace here to his
pigfarm on the far side of
Raven's Rock, where does he
pass by Hermes' Hill?*

right to top left in the photograph. Because the pigfarm is built up against
the foothills on the other side of Raven's Rock, his path must turn there from
north-west to due north.

So where on earth is this Hermes' Hill? After accounting for Mount
Neriton and Raven's Rock, all that are left are rather two modest hillocks and
a larger hillside that is much too far away to the east to be passed by Eumaios.
The hillock that is covered by trees is the site of the Catalan castle that Anthony
had identified but it hardly seems distinctive enough to count as that of
Hermes.

James is silent. As the August sun beats down he looks up at Mount Neriton
on the skyline and back to the diagonal path before us. Then he points straight
ahead:

There it is. That is Hermes' Hill.

I look at where he is pointing. I see the majestic mountain, I see the avian
rock, but I see no Hill of Hermes. I ask him where he is looking.

Do you see that long ridge line that runs east from the summit of Raven's Rock?

Well yes of course I can see it, but that, I reply, is surely Raven's Rock itself.
How can it also be Hermes' Hill?

I think Hermes' Hill is the name of that entire lower hillside on the southern foothills of Mount Neriton. Raven's Rock is simply the name that the Ithacans gave to the distinct escarpment at its western end. They are not separate entities: the Rock is a part of the Hill.

I am intrigued by his explanation but at first it sounds to me like special pleading. Raven's Rock has always been regarded as a distinct Odyssean feature in its own right: as far as I was aware nobody had ever suggested that it was a part of Hermes' Hill.

There is another reason why your former ridge would never do, because when Eumaios crossed it he would have his back to the harbour, so why should he turn around 180 degrees to look at it? He is surely more likely to be concentrating on the view ahead of him. But if Hermes' Hill is at the new location I am proposing then what we need to discover is whether Eumaios' gaze is automatically drawn to the harbour on his left as he reaches the turning point on the path. Do you think he would be able to see it from there?

My reply is: yes, almost certainly, because by then Kastelli will no longer be blocking his view to the south.

Let's go and check. Because if the first moment when the harbour becomes visible is at the foot of Hermes' Hill then Eumaios' account of his journey falls beautifully into place. 'By now I had walked up above the city / To the Hill of Hermes, when I saw a ship / Entering our harbour.' Why should he mention the Hill of Hermes at all? Because that may be precisely where and when he first catches sight of the harbour as he is emerging from the woodlands lower down the path. If that is the case then it would be entirely natural for him to look left and enjoy the open view down to the bay.

We walk back down Kastelli and regain the jeep. Around us the air is still: a heat-haze shimmers over the valley. It is another cloudless day in Cephalonia but in summer that is no surprise. We follow the route that you can see in Figure 32.10. It emerges above the small quarry of Figure 14.8 and we zig-zag around it. If we are right then Eumaios must have passed this quarry every time he visited the palace: no wonder at 14.6–10 'he had built / With his own hands a high surrounding wall, / A fine big wall, for his absent master's swine, / Far from his mistress and the old Laertes, / With quarried stones'.

We bump up the track and as we emerge from the woodland into the open expanse above it the steep slope of Raven's Rock looms up to our right. Beyond it the curve of Hermes' Hill stretches far to the east, well away from this local escarpment. I park the jeep at the crest of the path. As we turn to look south the view is all that James could have hoped for (Figure 32.11).

Turning point   Raven's Rock

Hermes' Hill

FIGURE 32.10
Hermes' Hill and the
turning point
James Diggle realised that
Hermes' Hill is the name of
the separate hillside to the
south of Mount Neriton:
Raven's Rock is the cliff-like
formation on its western edge.

Mount Neriton

FIGURE 32.11
Ithaca harbour from the
turning point at Hermes'
Hill
*The distinctive point of Cape
Samoli reaches out into the
bay: it is behind this spit of
land that Homer has Athene
pretending to Telemachos that
her ship is concealed.*

It is an instinctive reaction to look down the valley towards the sea as you arrive at this point in the path, and at that time the head of the harbour was about 1 km further inland: the suitors and their ship would have been clearly visible.

So Hermes' Hill, instead of being merely a place encountered somewhere on the journey between palace and pigfarm, becomes somewhere of pivotal importance in the *Odyssey*. It is introduced into the narrative here precisely because it marks the point where the harbour becomes visible on the path from palace to pigfarm. By contrast Raven's Rock, which is a part of the Hill, plays a different role in the poem: it marks the point alongside Arethousa Spring where the palatial porkers eat and drink.

The next day, 12 August, Anthony and Annemarie return with us to Kastelli to explore its slopes and neighbourhood. We resume the *Odyssey* at Book 17: Eumaios has returned to the pigfarm and Telemachos himself now goes to the palace:

Telemachos strode quickly through the farm,
His mind full of dark thoughts against the suitors.
As soon as he had reached the stately palace
He leaned his spear against a lofty pillar,
Crossed the stone threshold and then went inside.   17.26–30

FIGURE 32.12
The route from pigfarm
to palace
*Colour interpretation: as
Figure 20.1.*
[Image credits, data and
processing: as Figure 32.1.]

You can see his route past Hermes' Hill in Figure 32.12: the total distance from the pigfarm to the palace is only about 1.5 km.

Later that day Eumaios accompanies the disguised Odysseus down to the city:

> Advancing down the rocky road they neared
> The town and reached the fountain where the townsfolk
> Drew water – well-built, flowing fair, the work
> Of Ithacos, Neritos, and Polyctor.
> Around it was a circling grove of poplars
> Fed by the moist earth, and cool water flowed
> Down from a rock. Above was built an altar
> To the nymphs, on which all travellers made an offering.   17.204–11

The rocky road is still there but what about the fountain? Clue 19 from Chapter 17 tells us that 'several paths converge at an elaborate fountain, linking the pigfarm, the city, Strabo's Channel and the harbour, and somehow a circular grove of poplars is irrigated'. In Figure 32.13 I have drawn in the path of the main stream that descends from Hermes' Hill: you can see where it is crossed by our path from the pigfarm. The bright white area just beyond is

To palace

Stream

From pigfarm

Eumaios' small quarry and the path leading off this to the right (southwards) leads through the valley to the harbour.

At the intersection of the rocky road and the stream there is an area of light pink on the false-colour satellite image. As at Eumaios' Pigfarm itself, this corresponds to moist vegetation and because the image was captured on 30 May 2003 rather than in the wintertime, the moisture must be coming from an underground spring rather than from standing rainwater. Figure 32.14 is the two-dimensional satellite image of this from directly above.

It is a most unusual phenomenon. Running down from the adjacent hillside is the stream, but jutting out at right angles to it is the Livadi/Atheras fault line that we first encountered in Figure 11.7. A more detailed map of this geological anomaly is presented at Figure 27.4 and there you can see that in the region north of the harbour where three different coloured ages of rock meet there is a network of criss-crossing fault lines. That is why the bright pink-coded vegetation captured by the satellite's camera stays damp all summer long.

In Figure 32.15 you can see Hermes' Hill in the distance with Raven's Rock as its western hilltop and the rocky road coming down towards us. The stream runs across the centre of the picture from right to left and lush ferns surround the field containing the olive tree. The diameter of this field is 58 m. That is ample space in which to plant a grove of shady poplars.

Rocky road from pigfarm

Circular grove

Stream descends to harbour

Path to palace

FIGURE 32.14
Satellite image of the
circular grove
*Colour interpretation: as
Figure 20.1. Diameter of the
grove: 58 m.*
[Image credits: as
Figure 20.1.]

What then of the fountain? The word conjures up an image of a ornate carved structure such as the Trevi in Rome, but the Greek word *krene* can also refer to a cascade of water fed by the stream itself: 'cool water flowed / Down from a rock. Above was built an altar' (17.209–10). Furthermore the phrase 'Around it was a circling grove of poplars / Fed by the moist earth' (17.208–9) does not require the fountain to be at the grove's centre: it could instead be on its periphery. The word used here for 'around' is our familiar friend *amphi* from Chapter 4: in Appendix 1 Section G James Diggle points out that '*amphi* regularly means "near", with proximity its sole implication and no possible implication of encirclement'. In this case it is therefore the grove itself that is described as circling rather than the fountain as encircled.

At 5 pm James and I scramble down the streambed to the left of Figure 32.15 and at the intersection of the two stream lines marked on Figure 32.14 our efforts are rewarded by the arresting sight of a natural cascade (Figure 32.16). At this location the stream sits on bedrock and John Underhill's opinion is that this is probably the route of a fault line. Above it is a man-made wall that suggests that historically this has been a good place to seek refreshment from the natural watercourse.

Did Ithacos, Neritos and Polyctor construct their altar here on the periphery of their grove of poplars? Did they divert the flow of water so that it emerged out from a rock topped by the altarstones? Or did they succeed instead in

FIGURE 32.15
The circular
stream-moistened grove
*View to the north: Hermes'
Hill is in the background and
Raven's Rock at its western
limit.*

FIGURE 32.16
The cascade in the
streambed
The sharply eroded walls of
the streambed indicate that a
considerable volume of water
still descends during the
island's rainy season: see
Chapter 22 n. 5 for details.

routing part of the stream through to a more conventional form of fountain within the grove itself? This remarkable geological formation is an apt location about which the poet might write 'Around it was a circling grove of poplars / Fed by the moist earth' (17.208–9) and it just happens to be situated on the rocky road that leads from pigfarm to palace. However Anthony reminds us that the distance from the northern plateau of Kastelli to 'the fountain where the townsfolk / Drew water' (17.205–6) is about 700 m, an unusually long way if this was the city's only water supply.

After Odysseus has suffered the indignity of being kicked in the hip by Melanthios the goatherd (who as we saw in Chapter 17 will later pay a high price for his impudence) he and Eumaios stride on to the palace. We recall at 17.255 that Melanthios 'Went on, and very quickly reached the palace' and hence our Clue 20 that the palace is not far from the fountain.

From it they ascend the path that emerges to the right of Figure 32.17 and Odysseus then sets eye on his palace hilltop for the first time in twenty years (Figure 32.18).

At 17.266–8 he remarks on 'One building after another, courtyard walled / And crenellated, sturdy double-gates – ', our Clues 21 and 22.

There are several distinctive features about Kastelli. It contains three extensive plateaus facing north, north-east and east; any one of these is large enough to have accommodated the sportsground of Clue 17. The north-eastern

Kastelli summit : 252m
Terrace – inner: 245m
Terrace – outer: 237m
Plateau – north-eastern: 220m
Plateau – northern: 180m
Plateau – eastern: 190m
Kastelli lakebed: 150m

FIGURE 32.17
Kastelli from the east
*Measurements: elevation
above sea level. Colour
interpretation: as Figure 20.1.*
[Image credits, data and
processing: as Figure 32.1.]

terrace, for example, is about 110 m across. There are also both outer and inner terraces on the way to the summit and at 80 m diameter the outer one could also have been the suitors' recreation area.

Where was Ithaca city itself? Anthony Snodgrass favours the eastern plateau of Figure 32.17: it lies close to the palace, it could be defended if necessary and, most importantly, it represents an area that even today yields Bronze Age sherds. If we seek alternative locations or sprawling suburbs, both the valley to the west of Kastelli and also the dried-up lakebed marked on the photograph remain intriguing, although to date neither of them has yielded convincing fragments of pottery.

At the latter location there are karst limestone formations on the slope of Kastelli which probably contained further spring lines at that time. Clearly visible in the digital image of Figure 32.19 is a crescent-shaped damp area of the lakebed, hinting at further fault lines beneath. Today there is damp soil there and wells are still in use at that precise location: could these have been an alternative source of water for the city? As well as 'the fountain where the townsfolk / Drew water' (17.205–6) by the grove of poplars, we recall that at 20.158 after Penelope's bidding 'Twenty went off to the dark-water spring' which sounds like a different supply. Or was the city fountain itself here rather than at the location below Raven's Rock? The crescent-shaped damp area lies on the circumference of a circle about 200 m across: could this instead have been the 'circling grove of poplars / Fed by the moist earth'

FIGURE 32.18
Kastelli from the south
'Before the hall the high and mighty suitors / Amused themselves with javelin and discus, / On a levelled sportsground, where they often played' (17.167–9). Anthony Snodgrass saw that Kastelli contains plateaus large enough for such a sportsground.

FIGURE 32.19
The dried up lakebed east of Kastelli
Could terra rossa from the hillside have covered over Mycenaean sherds here? What is the significance of the pattern of buried stonework that shows up on this image? Colour interpretation: as Figure 20.1. Grid: 100 m. [Image credits: as Figure 20.1.]

(17.208–9)? Although there is no stream there to feed a fountain today there might well have been one 3,000 or more years ago.

Also visible on the former lakebed is a network of stone walls and enclosures buried below the surface and contrasting with the green-coloured soil above: are these more mediaeval remains or are they associated in some way with ancient Ithaca? Could some part of the city even be buried below the deep *terra rossa* on the surface? It would, after all, be a fitting location for those eagles at 2.154 who 'sped off to the right through houses and city' thereby providing us with Clue 35 of Chapter 17: 'the houses and city of Ithaca may be to the east of the meeting place.'

What of the meeting place itself? We know from Clue 10 that 'the place of assembly is close to the palace'; from Clue 33 that it was 'probably equipped with stone seats'; from Clue 34 that 'there is a mountain peak near the city, visible from the place of assembly and probably to its north'; from Clue 35 above that 'the houses and city of Ithaca may be to the east of the meeting place'; and from Clue 36 that 'there may be a stretch of the seashore accessible from the meeting place and the palace without having to traverse the city or visit the harbour'.

If we rely on Clue 34 then the best location for the meeting place would be the slope leading down to the northern plateau, since there is a good view of Mount Neriton from there. Today that area is replete with impressive terrace walls, although Anthony Snodgrass has also identified the remains of mediaeval roads and conduits in this area so we should not interpret the photograph at Figure 32.20 too literally.

In effect we are now spoilt for choice: there are several different sites at which the city, sportsground and meeting place could be located on or around Kastelli in such a way as to comply with the list of thirty-seven clues summarised at Figure 17.2. In fact the only one which is at all problematical for some layouts is Clue 35 above, but James has in any case advised us that the lines on which this interpretation is based are regarded as suspect.

The crucial points are simply these. Kastelli is a prehistoric location identified in the archaeological literature of 1995; Mycenaean sherds are visible on the ground here; its location on the island fits precisely with the manifold clues presented in the *Odyssey*; and the island itself, separated from Same by Strabo's Channel, lies furthest to the west.

In Chapter 10 we read of the unsuccessful ambush by the suitors who return to the meeting place to plan their next steps. You will recall Antinoos' devious words on the subject:

Antinoos, Eupeithes' son, addressed them:
'Damn it! The gods have snatched him from our clutches.
By day lookouts stood on the windy heights,

FIGURE 32.20
Terraced walls on northern
slope of Kastelli
*The hilltop shows evidence of
mediaeval as well as
Mycenaean occupation*

> Shift after shift without break; and when the sun set
> We never slept the night on land but waited
> For dawn at sea on our swift ambush-ship,
> Hoping to catch and kill Telemachos.
> But meanwhile some god carried him off home.'   16.363–70

While sailing with my family on the Sea-Trek boat in August 2004 I had the opportunity of following Telemachos' presumed course from a south-easterly direction, as if returning from Pylos towards Cape Lardhigos, the point of land illustrated in Figure 15.4.

The suitors anticipate that Telemachos and his crew will be tired after their voyage from Pylos and they are also presumed to be off their guard because they have just come in sight of their destination. Above Cape Lardhigos in Figure 32.21 you can see through the haze the peak of Mount Neriton, and to the left there is the white scar of the quarry that marks the western limit of Ithaca harbour. In between them the palace on the summit of Kastelli beckons the young prince home. As they round the cape the suitors intend to ambush them: for scale you can see a speedboat conveniently emerging in precisely the right position.

But Telemachos never goes anywhere near this ambush cape. He follows Athene's advice and sails up the far western coast of Ithaca, putting in at Agni Cove. After breakfast he sends his men round to Agia Kiriaki while he

FIGURE 32.21
The approach from Pylos
to Cape Lardhigos
*The aerial view is at Figure
25.7. Mount Neriton looms in
the distance and the palace on
Kastelli summit is directly
behind the point.*

walks up alone to the pigfarm. As his crew enter that bay they do not see the view that greets us today (Figure 32.22). Instead they row past a harbour wall of Mycenaean-like design that is only now emerging after being buried for centuries under a rockfall. It marks the entrance to a narrow channel that separates Same from Ithaca and enables them to row all the way through to Argostoli Bay.

As Telemachos' crewmen reach the southern opening of the channel they emerge through twin cliffs that are so well defined that even after catastrophic landslips, their abrupt boundaries can clearly be seen in the centre of the Quickbird satellite imagery (Figure 32.23).

How can we be sure that Strabo's Channel was actually navigable in Odysseus' time? A scientific proof of this will require the application of more advanced techniques than have so far been available and these will take some time. Meanwhile we may remind ourselves of Koumantakis' diagnosis of inland pockets of salt water at Figure 18.1. But now that we have come this

FIGURE 32.22 Digital elevation view of northern channel exit
Colour interpretation: as Figure 20.1 with brightness and contrast enhanced.
[Image credits, data and processing: as Figure 32.1.]

FIGURE 32.23 Digital elevation view of southern channel exit
The ragged former coastline proceeds from the shoreline on the right towards the centre of the image, where it then veers northwards through the isthmus, following the sides of the mountain.
[Colour interpretation, image credits, data and processing: as Figure 32.1.]

far, is a former channel still strictly necessary to the plot of the *Odyssey*? While the hypotheses of this book were being developed, several collaborators considered the idea that Paliki might have been connected to eastern Cephalonia during the Bronze Age after all. If *nesos* can mean a peninsula rather than an island in the case of Asteris, then why not for the whole of Ithaca as well? The possibility that Ithaca itself was not an island was also proposed by both A. E. H. and C. H. Goekoop and it now needs to be laid to rest.

There are at least three good reasons why we can be confident that ancient Ithaca was surrounded by the sea. First, as we saw in Chapter 9, the poet consistently refers to Ithaca as a *nesos*. James Diggle has considered the usage of this word carefully and as he explains at the end of Appendix 1 Section B, Asteris must be regarded as a special case because it actually *looks* like an island from the northern end of the bay. The notion that *nesos* can indiscriminately signify an island or a peninsula is a Homeric hare that we may not let loose in the fertile fields of our imagination. When we read at 13.95 'Then the seafaring ship approached the island' that is exactly what is meant. Furthermore if Ithaca were a peninsula connected to Same we could make little sense of the poet's description at 9.23–6 'Around are many islands, close to each other, / Doulichion and Same and wooded Zacynthos. / Ithaca itself lies low, furthest to sea / Towards dusk; the rest, apart, face dawn and sun.'

Second, we have the evidence about the ferry between Ithaca and Same in Chapter 8. At 20.185–8 we recall the lines 'Third came that stalwart fellow Philoitios, / Leading a heifer and fat goats for the suitors. / They had been brought across by ferrymen, / Who also ferry people, any who come.' Note that both animals and people are conveyed. If a land-based crossing were available it would clearly be far easier to use it (even if it meant a longer walk) than to go to all the bother of designing and building a bovine transportation vessel.

Third, if Strabo's Channel does not exist, how can Telemachos' crewmen reach the harbour from Agni Cove? They will have to sail around the combined island of ancient Ithaca and Same, which is today's Cephalonia. If they continue on their northwards course, encircling Cephalonia clockwise, the total distance of their voyage will be about 126 km. If instead they reverse course and proceed anticlockwise, the distance will be about 43 km. During either of these detours they will find themselves sailing far away from the city, in defiance of lines 15.552–3: 'The crew untied the cables, / Then pushed her off and sailed towards the city'.

These voyages will also take considerably longer than the route via Strabo's Channel, which as we have seen is only about 23 km in length. This is important because in Chapter 17 we learnt that the crewmen leave Telemachos after breakfast at dawn and later that same day at 16.322–3 'The sturdy ship which brought Telemachos / And crew from Pylos put in to Ithaca.' Their return must be well before nightfall because the ambush party reaches the harbour after them and it is still daylight then: Amphinomos spots the suitors from the palace and Eumaios sees them from the turning point of Hermes' Hill. On this basis we can rule out a clockwise route: it could not possibly be completed within a day.

Can an anticlockwise course bring Telemachos' crewmen to the harbour in time? We know that they arrive at Agni Cove under sail, since at 15.495–7 we read 'Close by dry land / The crew struck sail and smartly lowered the mast, / Then rowed the ship on to its anchorage'. A course reversal therefore requires them to row against the wind all the way down the western coast of Paliki, averaging no more than the 5 km per hour of Chapter 27. With Herculean effort they might just make it to the harbour in time: but unfortunately there is a fatal obstacle in their way.

Crucially, if Strabo's Channel is a low-lying land bridge rather than a marine seaway, then Telemachos' crew have no alternative but to enter Argostoli Bay from the south. So after all their hard work to avoid the suitors they are eventually spotted at the mouth of the bay anyway, making a nonsense of Athene's warning. Instead nothing of the sort happens: they adopt this cunning back-door route to the harbour, bypassing the suitors entirely.

When Amphinomos sees that the suitors have later returned of their own accord, no wonder he says at 16.355–7 'No need to send a message: here they are. / Some god has tipped them off, or they themselves / Spotted the ship sail past and couldn't catch her.' Failing divine warning (a clever reference to Athene, of whose intervention he was unaware) Amphinomos presumes that Telemachos' crewmen somehow escape the suitors and outsail them as they are pursued up the bay. But any Ithacan listening to the *Odyssey* knows that actually the suitors recognise their own ship (it belongs to one of them, Noemon) emerging from the southern entrance of Strabo's Channel. That is a distance of about 12 km but a Bronze Age galley there is clearly visible from the windy heights of Mount Gerasimos, as you can see from Figure 15.5.

After guarding the mouth of the bay so patiently, night after night and day after day, the suitors must have been flabbergasted and then infuriated to see Telemachos' crewmen appearing unexpectedly at its northern end. But to an audience who knows the local geography it is a superb tactical ruse: a perfect example of Odyssean brain over brawn. Furthermore since this is the first time that the suitors see the returning vessel we can lend weight to James Diggle's proposal in Chapter 16 that 'keep your sturdy ship far off the islands' (15.33) implies a southerly route home from Pylos. We no longer need to allow for the possibility that the suitors might have seen the ship sailing westwards on its way home, which enables us to dispense with that awkward observation that if they had done so they would then have had ample time to reach Ithaca harbour before the return of the young prince's crew.

Meanwhile Telemachos himself is safe and sound at the pigfarm. A shiver runs down my spine as I consider what would have happened to him if he had failed to heed Athene's advice to take the long way home around ancient Ithaca and had instead chosen the direct route back from Pylos.

A shiver of a different kind runs down my spine when I consider: *How could the poet have described this ambush location so exactly? How did he know the layout of those headlands of Phorcys Bay so well? Who told him about the route to the pigfarm via Agni Cove? How did he know that on your way back to the pigfarm from the palace you catch sight of the harbour precisely as you pass Hermes' Hill? And where did he learn about the permanently moist earth circle that feeds the poplars at the fountain?*

How could a composer who allegedly lived on the other side of the Aegean Sea over 450 km away and who was believed to have committed this epic poem to writing hundreds of years later possibly have known ancient Ithaca so intimately? Was the entire poem a colossal feat of coincidental imagination? Or did Homer have inside knowledge of Ithaca itself?

Note

1 Reproduced with the permission of Curtis Brown Group Ltd, London, on behalf of the estate of W. H. Auden. Copyright © W. H. Auden, 1961.

CHAPTER 33 **Intuition**

Our suspicion that Homer does not know in detail the geography of western Greece can be confirmed elsewhere. When he describes the location of Odysseus' home, Ithaca, his geography is so palpably faulty that scholars have tried to argue that it was not modern Itháki at all. John Chadwick, *The Mycenaean World* (1976)[1]

On 27 September 1897 Samuel Butler, author of the utopian satire *Erewhon*, completes a radical thesis on the identity of the author of the *Odyssey* and the location of ancient Ithaca. He has spent a considerable amount of time on his researches, some of which have already been published as individual papers, and his Preface indicates that he is somewhat aggrieved by the deafening silence that has so far greeted his proposals. Although he is confident of the merits of his case he is also conscious that no single proposition in it can necessarily be proved beyond doubt: it will always be possible to explain it away as a coincidence. He therefore claims that the relationship between his own identifications and the poet's descriptions in the *Odyssey* involve too many such coincidences for it to be plausible that the overall resemblance is itself a matter of chance. Warming to the underlying statistics he argues:

Let us suppose that a policeman is told to look out for an elderly gentleman of about sixty; he is a foreigner, speaks a little English but not much, is lame in his left foot, has blue eyes, a bottle nose, and is about 5ft. 10in. high. How many of these features will the policeman require before he feels pretty sure that he has found his man? If he sees any foreigner he will look at him. If he sees one who is about 5ft. 10in. high he will note his age, if this proves to be about sixty years, and further, if the man limps on his left foot, he will probably feel safe in stopping him. If, as he is sure to do, he finds he has a bottle nose, he will leave the blue eyes and broken English alone, and will bring the man before the magistrate.

If it is then found that the man's eyes are hazel, and that he either speaks English fluently or does not speak it at all – is the magistrate likely to discharge the prisoner on account of these small discrepancies between him and the description given of him, when so many other of the required characteristics are found present? Will he not rather require the prisoner to bring forward very convincing proof that it is a case of mistaken identity?[2]

Butler takes it for granted that the readers of his day will be aware that a bottle nose indicates a history of alcoholism. He continues by explaining that his example involves only a few points of close comparison, whereas by the time he has demonstrated the 'much more numerous and weightier points of agreement' between his solution to the Homeric puzzle and the descriptions in the *Odyssey*, it would beggar belief for any reasonable readers to disagree with him. However, sadly for Butler they do:

Eminent Homeric scholars have told me, not once nor twice – and not meekly, but with an air as though they were crushing me – that my case rests in the main on geographical features that are not unknown to other parts of the coast, and upon legends which also belong to other places.

He complains bitterly about this persistent and wilful disbelief ('It is a line which eminent Homeric scholars almost invariably take when discussing my Odyssean theory') and he dies a few years later on 18 June 1902. I discovered this story some time after proposing an almost identical statistical argument at the end of Chapter 8 and in the circumstances I think it would be unwise to rely upon it, even though Samuel Butler's thesis was that Homer was a woman and that ancient Ithaca was located on the island of Marettimo near Trapani on the north-western coast of Sicily.[3]

The difficulty with Butler's approach to deploying statistics in support of his case is that he is asking his readers to rely upon probability theory so as to justify the adoption of a counterintuitive solution, at least in regard to the geography of his proposals. After all, if I tell you that I can prove beyond reasonable doubt that all adult herrings speak fluent Lithuanian then it really doesn't matter how advanced a mathematical theory I then deploy: you are not going to believe me. My own view of the appropriate use of statistics in such circumstances differs from that of Butler: let me explain.

If you remain uncomfortable with the observations and their interpretation that I have presented in this volume then it is probably time to put the book down because I have run out of further evidence with which to try to convince you. What is important to you at this stage is your intuition, not my statistical calculations, and if your intuition tells you that something is wrong then sadly we will now do best to part company. You are unpersuaded by what has been discussed hitherto and I respect your view even though I disagree with it: I hope that you have enjoyed at least some part of the journey.

I want to draw the attention of those who have decided to stay the course to a different statistical interpretation of the correspondence of Ithacan geography with the Homeric plot and narrative. We started in Chapter 4 with four major clues on the basis of which I proposed that we should reject various prior Ithacan theories. After that we amassed at Figure 17.2 a further thirty-seven Palace Clues, at Figure 21.12 we brought together sixteen clues about Doulichion and then at Figure 22.3 there were twenty-five more clues about

Laertes. That amounts to eighty-two points of resemblance between Paliki (as cut off by Strabo's Channel) and Homer's description of ancient Ithaca. Admittedly a few of these similarities concern people rather than places but the majority involve local topography. Consider a few examples, as if one were reading from a Bronze Age Michelin guide:

On approaching Ithaca from Scherie you will catch sight of the bay of Phorcys. Notice the two rather unusual projecting headlands located right inside the bay: they 'crouch' from the harbour so as to shield it from waves whipped up by blustering winds outside. If you look further afield you will discover a two-harboured island-like peninsula called Asteris: this lies in the straits between Ithaca and Samos and it has windy heights that enable lookouts to signal to a raiding party planning an ambush in the cove below.

A herald from Ithaca harbour can meet a messenger from the pigfarm before they arrive at the palace: on the way back the messenger will round the Hill of Hermes. There is a direct route from this pigfarm to the palace that bypasses the city. There is also a substantial levelled sportsground in front of the palace and several paths meet at an elaborate fountain outside the city, linking the pigfarm, Strabo's Channel, the city and the harbour.

Doulichion and the Echinai are geographically distinct from Ithaca, Neriton, Crocyleia, Aigilips, Zacynthos and Same. Pirates embarking from Thesprotia can sail far from land and divert to Ithaca instead of Doulichion. There is a suitable place to moor a ship beyond the spit of land at the north-west of Argostoli Bay. This location is invisible from the palace and from Laertes' farm, and one arrives at this farm before reaching the mooring when walking down from the town.

The question at which I believe we should point our statistical searchlight is this: could the original composer of the *Odyssey* have described ancient Ithaca this accurately and consistently based only on an oral account that was handed down to him over several centuries and delivered to him several hundred kilometres away? Or do we think it more likely that the essence of these verses was composed by a poet who walked the paths of ancient Ithaca himself?

It is not, after all, a mere matter of memorising the descriptions above and those of the other clues: it concerns instead the challenge of recreating this entire geography in one's head from an orally conveyed account and then not making a single spatial error when describing it in a narrative that extends to over 100,000 words of verse. This is not simply a question of faithfully reproducing all the specific clues that have been listed so far: it is also about a consistent interpretation of their manifold geographical interrelationships and implications.

When we live in a place ourselves we automatically build a vivid internal representation of its layout within our brains and we can then consult that mental model directly without needing to visit the actual sites. If you are a Londoner and I ask you the way from Embankment underground to Victoria Station, you can quickly visualise a stroll up to Charing Cross, past Trafalgar Square, down The Mall, around Buckingham Palace and on to the station. The fact that nobody has specifically taught you this particular route and that you may never have walked it yourself is irrelevant: your innate capability does not require you to have memorised the walk beforehand because you can deduce it from your mental map.

In any case it would be pointless to try to remember all such routes by rote because once there are more than a few places involved the number of possible journeys becomes enormous: indeed the resultant challenge has been immortalised in mathematical conundra such as the Travelling Salesman problem that regularly brings even large computers to their knees. Given this neurophysiological reality I find it very hard to believe that Homer could have described the geography of Ithaca so consistently without spending some considerable time on the island himself.

That is a heretical suggestion for eminent Homeric scholars because, as with Chadwick, the brilliant co-decipherer of Linear B, the disguise of Strabo's Channel has caused most experts to regard Homer's geography as 'palpably faulty'. But we now know that their premise was mistaken. Homer's Ithacan geography was precise and he relates it with that precision in every description of Ithaca in the *Odyssey*. If he says a harbour was deep, then deep it was.

Readers who are not Homeric experts may be wondering what all the fuss is about: indeed it is surely easier to tell a long and consistent story about a place that you know rather than about one that is relayed to you second-hand. But as we have seen, the conventional wisdom is that the *Odyssey* was composed several hundred years after the Trojan War by a poet living on the western coast of what is now Turkey. How then could this Homer possibly have walked on ancient Ithaca and described what he saw in the poem?

The controversy surrounding the identity, date and place of birth of Homer is at least as old as that surrounding the location of ancient Ithaca and it would be far too ambitious to embark on a full-scale exploration of this issue now. But it may nevertheless be useful to summarise some of the main proposals.

Ancient writers could not agree on Homer's dates. According to Hecataeus and Eratosthenes he lived near to the time of the people and events that he described, around 1200 BC. Thucydides (1.3.3) dated him much later: 'long after the Trojan war'. Herodotus (2.53.2) was more precise: not more than 400 years before his own time, about 850 BC. Theopompus dated him later still, in the time of Archilochus of Paros, around 700–650 BC.[4] As we observed in Figure 2.4, we are used to some uncertainty in the dates of those who lived

FIGURE 33.1
The seven contenders for
Homer's birthplace

Smyr-	na	Chi-	os	Col-	oph-	on	Sa-	la-	mis	Rho-	dos	Arg-	os	Ath-	en-	ae
–	˘	˘	–	˘	˘	–	˘	˘	–	˘	˘	–	˘	˘	–	–

so long ago but a range of estimates differing by 500 years is unusual to say the least: it is almost as if these historians were describing different people.

As for the place where Homer lived, there are seven primary contenders and they happen to fit into a perfect hexameter (Figure 33.1). Smyrna and Colophon are on the mainland of Asia Minor in Ionia (see Figure 26.1) and Chios is the large island on the north-west of the Ionian region. Salamis is on Cyprus, Rhodos is the island to the extreme south-east of the Aegean Sea, Argos is located in the north-east of the Peloponnese and Athens is the final contender. Once again there is an extraordinary variation in these claims, this time a distance of about 1,000 km between the two that are furthest apart (Argos and Salamis). The favourite is generally regarded as Chios because a guild of performers called the Homeridae lived there and they preserved and recited Homer's verses.

A further complication concerns the age-old question of whether the *Iliad* and the *Odyssey* were composed by the same poet. There are many arguments in both directions but one of the most impressive continues to be a magnificent analysis of the language of the two poems published in 1955 by Denys Page, Regius Professor of Greek at Cambridge. His conclusion on this point runs as follows:

Thus the evidence strongly suggests not only that these two poems were largely created by persons possessed of two divergent stocks of phrases, but also that they were transmitted to posterity by persons whose own language developed differently or at different paces, or who differed at least in respect of what was deemed admissible in Epic verse. The Odyssey *has so much that the* Iliad *must have used if it was known; the* Iliad *has so much that the* Odyssey *must have used if it was known. The differences cannot be explained in terms of the priority in time of the one poem over the other: they point clearly enough to the conclusion that the two poems were composed and transmitted in separate regions of Hellas.*[5]

Page believes that the *Iliad* was probably composed in Ionia and 'that the Odyssean poet lived in a region isolated from that in which the *Iliad* was composed'. He speculates on whether this could have been mainland Greece but he then discards this hypothesis without explaining why in favour of 'some other centre of Ionian life in the eastern Aegean'. We will return shortly to the question of where else this 'other centre of Ionian life' might have been: for now the core idea that emerges from Page's analysis is that the *Iliad* and the *Odyssey* were composed by different people and that those people lived in different regions of Greece.

Page's analysis revolves around linguistic style and vocabulary and to this day Homer continues to surprise us by the novelty of his poetic innovation. For example, you may have noticed that from time to time I address you as the reader directly: indeed I am doing so now. As a modern reader you are probably so used to this device that you hardly give it a second thought, but if you think about it for a moment it is really rather curious. By definition I am writing this typescript many months prior to the publication of the book, whereas you are reading it rather later. So 'you' do not yet exist for me, but I am hoping that you will materialise in due course and because I am more interested in your perceptions than in mine I am attempting to transport the locus of my consciousness forwards into your own predicted time and space. The word for this literary device is (inevitably) a Greek one: it is called 'apostrophe' and there are no prizes for guessing who thought of it first:

> Swineherd Eumaios, you replied to him
> 14.55, 14.165, 14.360, 14.442, 14.507, 16.60, 16.135, 16.464,
> 17.272, 17.311, 17.380, 17.512
> Swineherd Eumaios, you replied with feeling   15.325
> Swineherd Eumaios, you replied to her   17.579
> Swineherd Eumaios, you said, mocking him   22.194

You may imagine that I have been over-zealous in reproducing these particular fifteen examples of apostrophe in the poem but actually they are not merely examples: they are the exhaustive list. The instances above represent the only occasions in which Homer addresses one of his characters personally in this way in the *Odyssey* and they are confined uniquely to Eumaios. This is really very strange. A modern commentator remarks:

In the Iliad *several persons are addressed by the poet himself, esp. Patroclus, and sometimes this apostrophe serves to heighten the pathos of the scene . . . In the case of Eumaios, however, it is difficult to see why this should be the case in the 15 places where the phrase occurs.*[6]

In a recent thought-provoking analysis of this phenomenon Bruce Louden comments:

Only the narrator and members of Odysseus' immediate family address Eumaios by his proper name, while other characters address him generically as 'subota', swineherd. Such restricted use of the name suggests an affinity between the narrator and those characters sympathetic to Eumaios . . . For an oral, listening audience, the apostrophes would have a considerably greater impact than for our reading audience. The bard would appear to address his listeners, individually. I suggest that the bard's direct address to Eumaios embodies direct address to the external audience in performance.[7]

The *Odyssey* is an endless mine of such curiosities, innovations and delights and it delivers them in verses that have intrigued, entranced and inspired the architects of civilisation for well over 2,500 years. Homer's powers of imagination will always remain supreme, but now that we know that ancient Ithaca was a real place rather than another of his inventions it is perhaps time to draw together some of our recent evidence and to attempt to reconstruct what really happened there.

A reconstruction such as that which follows is not the same as the evidence-based reasoning that was presented in earlier chapters. The aim is to bring together the principal observations discussed to date into a coherent historical explanation. There are many gaps in our present knowledge, particularly in relation to geological dates, and so some components of this reconstruction are at present stitched together by informed guesses. Be warned therefore that more than one reconstruction can be devised to fit today's facts, let alone tomorrow's: indeed I shall be surprised if new evidence does not modify this proposal very soon after its composition. We must aspire with Keynes to have the courage to change our minds when the facts change.

Let us start this reconstruction by returning to Page's view of the place where the original composer of the *Odyssey* lived. As we have just seen, having determined that the *Odyssey* was developed in 'a region isolated from that in which the *Iliad* was composed' he then considers whether this could have been mainland Greece, but almost immediately he opts instead for 'some other centre of Ionian life in the eastern Aegean'. Where might this be? Page states most of his arguments with impressive force but he is uncharacteristically diffident on this point.

The new evidence that we have assembled enables us to propose a quite different location for the 'other centre of Ionian life' that Page is seeking: the Ionian Islands themselves off the western coast of Greece. They are clearly linguistically isolated from the Ionia to the east but as we saw in Chapter 26 there are crucial links between them: Ancaios of Same colonised Samos in Ionia and a contingent of Ithacan and Cephalonian emigrants accompanied him. So the detailed and precise topographical knowledge of Ithaca that is exhibited in the *Odyssey* could have travelled with the colonists to reach Ionia.

Page also says that the *Iliad* and the *Odyssey* 'were transmitted to posterity by persons whose own language developed differently or at different paces' and interestingly Herodotus tells us that the settlers of the twelve distinct Ionian regions 'use not all the same speech but four different dialects'. The

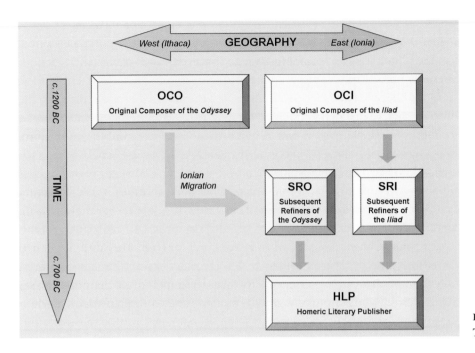

FIGURE 33.2
The Homeric Commission

first dialect is spoken by three of the regions, the second by six, the third by two 'but the Samians have a language which is their own and none other's' (1.141). On the issue of geographical and linguistic separation we therefore have the beginnings of a credible thesis.

What of the time discrepancies? Earlier we saw that there is a gap of 500 years between the various estimates of Homer's dates, so Figure 33.2 is an attempt to reconcile these geographical and temporal gulfs in terms of five distinct roles.

If we adopt Page's view then the Original Composer of the *Odyssey* (OCO) lived in a different part of Greece from the Original Composer of the *Iliad* (OCI). They may have been unaware of each other's respective compositions although clearly both were well informed about historical events such as the Trojan War. The remarkable familiarity with Ithacan topography that is displayed by the OCO and the extraordinary vividness of the events that he describes suggest that he lived on Ithaca at or around the time of the events of the *Odyssey*, in accordance with the verdict of Hecataeus and Eratosthenes. By the same argument, since comparable geographical and descriptive fidelity is displayed in the *Iliad*, the Original Composer of the *Iliad* (OCI) almost certainly visited the plain of Troy and may also have fought in the Trojan War.

The oral tradition established by the OCO then passed to one or more Subsequent Refiners of the *Odyssey* (SRO). These refiners took the core of the poem to Ionia during the Migration and its development continued there. The same process of refinement took place for the *Iliad*. Eventually, as the

Greek written language evolved using the Phoenician alphabet as opposed to Linear B, it became possible to set the poems down in writing in the essential form in which we know them today, and this project was undertaken for both poems by one or more entrepreneurial Ionians whom we may describe as the Homeric Literary Publisher (HLP). Although these activities are depicted in the diagram as five distinct roles, once the poems reached Ionia the Subsequent Refiners of both the *Odyssey* and the *Iliad* might have involved the same group of people.

So who then was the 'original' Homer? He was clearly a supremely gifted representative of the ancient tradition of *aoidoi* and there is evidence that these composers go back to the Mycenaean era.[8] However under this analysis there were at least two such gifted *aoidoi*: the OCO and the OCI. The OCO lived in Ithaca at or around the time of Odysseus' return from Troy and he turned the events that he saw and those that were described to him into the most magnificent lines of epic verse. But how was this momentous result achieved? Surely the OCO did not come down one morning for breakfast and begin a long recital? In Chapter 25 we heard about the remarkable natural theatre and it will be fascinating to learn more about its history as scientific dating tests are applied. It should be possible to determine whether the stone terraces have been worked on in some way. It may count as long odds but it would be extraordinarily exciting if it turns out that this was the arena in which the Original Composer of the *Odyssey* developed, rehearsed and presented his poetry.

Could the OCO have recited the *Odyssey* here to the members of the palace and also to the citizens of Ithaca? The theatre is less than 2 km from Kastelli: it is on the ancient road from Strabo's Channel to Ithaca Palace and city; it has almost perfect acoustics and its geologically formed stone terraces could accommodate thousands of spectators from Ithaca and also from Same. There would have been a special resonance for this audience in the descriptions of nearby geographical locations since they would have naturally been familiar with their own island and with some of the neighbouring lands as well. Repeated lines such as 'For I hardly think you came on foot' would have brought the house down: the developing *Odyssey* would have been a popular Saturday night's entertainment.

If performances of some kind did take place here then they must have happened before the Ionian Migration and also before the uplifting earthquake of that period: as Matthew Bittlestone suggested when we discovered it, there would be no point in staging productions for the inhabitants of a deserted city. Matthew also considered the implications of the fact that Odysseus, Penelope, Telemachos, Laertes and Eumaios are the only witnesses to much of the action described in the *Odyssey*. If the poem is based on a true sequence of events – albeit with some of the exaggeration that we have discussed – then it could not have been composed without the poet asking each of these five major participants to explain to him what happened to them at various points in the story.

So the Original Composer of the *Odyssey* must have not only been intimately familiar with the local geography, he also needed personal access to the principal characters or their near descendants. What did Bruce Louden suggest to us a few pages ago? 'The bard would appear to address his listeners, individually. I suggest that the bard's direct address to Eumaios embodies direct address to the external audience in performance.' Eumaios survived the massacre of the suitors: was he then an honoured guest at the theatre? Did the Original Composer of the *Odyssey* turn around and look at Eumaios as he said 'Swineherd Eumaios, you replied to him'? As James Diggle has confirmed, the use of 'you' here is anomalous and has never been adequately explained.

The suggestion that the OCO might have lived on Ithaca is supported by the fact that the *Odyssey* itself contains references to two such bards, Phemios and Demodocos,[9] so they were clearly a feature of Ithacan and Phaiacian society at the time. But if the OCO lived on Ithaca and had personal access to the principal people involved or their near descendants, who might he have been? One of the many romantic accounts of the identity of Homer appears in a work published in its current form around the time of Hadrian (Roman Emperor from AD 117 to 138) but based on an earlier account by Alcidamas (*c.* 400 BC). In these lines the Delphic oracle is referred to by the name of its priestess Pythia, and Epicaste is another name for Polycaste of Pylos:

We will set down, however, what we have heard to have been said by the Pythia concerning Homer in the time of the most sacred Emperor Hadrian. When the monarch inquired from what city Homer came, and whose son he was, the priestess delivered a response in hexameters after this fashion:

> *'Do you ask me of the obscure race and country of the heavenly siren? Ithaca is his country, Telemachos his father, and Epicaste, Nestor's daughter, the mother that bare him, a man by far the wisest of mortal kind.'*

This we must most implicitly believe, the inquirer and the answerer being who they are – especially since the poet has so greatly glorified his grandfather in his works.[10]

As the translator Hugh Evelyn-White remarked in 1914 'The whole tract is of course mere romance; its only values are the insight it gives into ancient speculations about Homer.'[11] But what a splendid romance, and how interesting those ancient speculations, to imagine that Homer might have learnt the story from Odysseus himself while sitting on his grandfather's knee!

Leaving aside this delightful but historically unreliable suggestion, the name 'Homer' may refer to any of these five personalities: to the OCO, the OCI, the SRO, the SRI or even the HLP himself. We may never know the answer to this question but we should perhaps keep an open mind on the matter of those Egyptian chronologies that were discussed in Chapter 24. If some of these alternative interpretations turn out to be true then it means, as we saw, that the Trojan War might have been waged as late as the tenth century BC rather than the twelfth century and this would have the effect of compressing the time dimension on Figure 33.2 very considerably.

To summarise, in the absence of any new developments or discoveries that might back-date the development of the Greek written language or forward-date the Trojan War we can assume that these roles were carried out by different individuals. It also seems clear that the OCO composed in a different place from the OCI and it is also quite possible that all except the OCO lived in Ionia. This would make the OCO a rather special figure, almost a folk-memory, from the viewpoint of the others.

We now need to interleave the classical evidence with the geological background so as to create a coherent history of ancient Ithaca. In the following attempt to reconstruct a plausible sequence of events I have tried to avoid the trap of relying on the more fanciful historical proposals.

1 For convenience we will date the Trojan War as 1193–1184 BC although there is substantial uncertainty about this estimate. Homer's descriptions of Ithaca in the *Odyssey* ten years after the war *c.* 1174 BC indicate that at that time Same and ancient Ithaca were two separate islands.

2 Same was the main part of today's island of Cephalonia and ancient Ithaca was its western peninsula, now called Paliki. They were separated by 'Strabo's Channel', a narrow seaway located at the isthmus now called Thinia.

3 The island to the east of Cephalonia that is today called Ithaca was then known as Doulichion: it was a 'verdant isle . . . rich in wheat' and well populated. Although Odysseus was the overall commander of all the soldiers from these islands during the Trojan War, Doulichion came under the jurisdiction of Meges rather than Odysseus.

4 The land mass of ancient Ithaca was from 2 m to 6 m lower in the sea than it is now and that is why Homer repeatedly describes Ithaca harbour as 'deep': today it is a low-lying marsh.

5 Almost all the locations on Ithaca that are described in the *Odyssey* can be identified today in northern Paliki. At present the only reference in the poem to a place on Ithaca itself that does not yet match an actual site on Paliki is the Nymphs' Cave at Phorcys Bay. Ground-penetrating radar indicates that

this may be buried below karst limestone features which are themselves at the right place.

6 It is proposed that the principal people who are described in the *Odyssey* as living on Ithaca itself existed in reality around the time of the Trojan War: in particular Odysseus, Penelope, Telemachos, Laertes and Eumaios. The events and the objects that are associated in the story with the island of Ithaca are also regarded as essentially accurate.

7 By contrast, the people, objects, locations and events that are described in the *Odyssey* away from Ithaca itself are of three types: actual, exaggerated and imaginary. Under this interpretation Odysseus actually fought at Troy and he actually returned home to Ithaca and combated the suitors, but his return may not have taken a full ten years, he probably failed to locate a genuinely floating island and he did not see his compatriots turned into real pigs on the way.

8 On Ithaca at that time there is an outstandingly creative poet who progressively composes a series of related ballads about the exploits of Odysseus: we will refer to him as the Original Composer of the *Odyssey* (OCO). The case for the OCO residing on Ithaca itself rests on the detail and accuracy with which he describes the island. There is a very close correspondence involving well over fifty descriptions and the chances of all of these being conveyed to the poet so accurately over a gulf of many centuries and kilometres are regarded as very small.

9 The OCO may have used the natural theatre to the east of Ithaca city as a forum in which to develop, refine and present his poetry. Eumaios may have been a member of this audience from time to time because the OCO addresses him directly in his poems.

10 The Ionian Migration takes place around 1040 BC and it involves several groups of colonists from all over southern Greece.

11 The name 'Ionian', as in the Ionian Islands and the Ionian Sea of today, was associated with this western area of Greece at that time. Many of the islanders leave Ithaca and emigrate to Asia Minor, where they and other Ionians give this name to the new settlement of Smyrna and its surroundings, centred around today's Izmir in Turkey.

12 Ancaios of Same leaves with a group of Ithacans and Cephallenians to found the island of Samos to the south of Smyrna.

13 Twelve distinct regions are settled in Asia Minor; eleven of them share three regional dialects but the dialect of Samos is unique.

14 By now the cultural descendants of the OCO on Ithaca have become the Subsequent Refiners of the *Odyssey* (SRO). Some of them also leave for Ionia as well and they take their oral version(s) of the *Odyssey* with them, where it flourishes on Samos and also on the island of Chios.

15 In Ionia the SRO meet other poets who have been developing a different poem describing the story of the *Iliad*. They are the Subsequent Refiners of the *Iliad* (SRI) which was created in or near Troy itself by the Original Composer(s) of the *Iliad* (OCI). The OCI had access to the town and region of Troy and may also have taken part in the war and met some of the personalities involved.

16 By the seventh or sixth century BC the Greek alphabet has developed to the extent that the *Iliad* and the *Odyssey* can now be written down. We can refer to the supervisor of this project as the Homeric Literary Publisher (HLP) because by now the task is one of fidelity rather than creativity.

17 At some date between the events of the *Odyssey* and the end of the sixth century BC (see paragraph 24 below) there is a massive earthquake in ancient Ithaca which elevates the island by at least 0.8 m (and perhaps as much as 4 m) relative to the local sea level and causes enormous destruction. The shorelines are drastically altered, the dwellings are destroyed and many people are killed by the sheer force of the quake or by rocks, falling masonry, fire, tsunami or subsequent destitution.

18 Catastrophic rockfall into Strabo's Channel causes it to become partially obstructed and a huge wave rears up on to the western shore of the channel and across the Ithacan coastline. As the rockfall settles, pockets of salt-laden sea water are trapped underground. The two former islands now resemble a single land mass with a low-lying isthmus that still permits the sea to penetrate from time to time.

19 The Ainos thrust line associated with this earthquake passes west of Argostoli along the eastern side of the bay: it then continues through the sidewall of the sheer eastern slopes of Strabo's Channel and enters the seabed of Agia Kiriaki. The Livadi/Atheras spur branches off at the northern end of the bay and passes up alongside Kastelli, through Eumaios' Pigfarm, Arethousa Spring and the foothills of Mount Neriton: it then continues down past the location described by Homer for the Nymphs' Cave and enters the seabed at Phorcys Bay. The effects of the earthquake were particularly severe along these two fault lines, and the city, palace and cave were reduced to rubble.

20 If the ancient settlement of Alalcomenai existed at that time on the ridge of the hillside above Argostoli then it would also have been destroyed.

21 The earthquake relieves much of the stress energy stored in the underlying fault system and so the average incidence of seismic events is reduced for many centuries thereafter. Although there are frequent rockslides there are no more massive rockfalls in Strabo's Channel over that period and so its shape does not change very much.

22 Meanwhile the scale of the destruction, the continuing tremors and superstitious awe cause the terrified surviving Ithacans to leave the island that is

today called Cephalonia and to cross over to the adjacent island of Doulichion (today's Ithaca). This has also been badly affected by the earthquake but less so than Ithaca because the fault lines are further away. They adopt the name Ithaca for their new home, but since the name Doulichion also describes the main settlement at or near present-day Vathy, this usage is retained for the town and it coexists with Ithaca as the name of the whole island.

23 After a period of desertion Cephalonia starts to be repopulated, centred on Cranioi, Same, Pronnoi and Pale. Alalcomenai is also reoccupied or occupied for the first time. No significant attempt is made to reinhabit ancient Ithaca city or the Kastelli palace, perhaps because of the wrath of Poseidon. Same and former Ithaca are now a single land mass and because the occupants were already called the Cephallenians, this name is adopted for the enlarged island.

24 In the fifth century BC Herodotus regards the settlement of Pale on today's Paliki as being part of Cephallenia, not Ithaca.

25 By the end of the fifth century BC Thucydides also treats Cephallenia as a single island.

26 At or around the time of Apollodorus in *c.* 150 BC the status of Strabo's Channel is such that it is still capable of being flooded by the sea. Nevertheless the visual impression is that this is a single island with a low flooded isthmus, rather than two islands with a partially infilled channel between them.

27 The evidence for this is reported *c.* AD 1 by Strabo, who is probably reflecting the lost writings of Apollodorus: 'Where the island is narrowest it forms a low isthmus, so that it is often submerged from sea to sea. Near the narrows, on the gulf, are Paleis and Cranioi' (10.2.15).

28 Strabo says in his next paragraph: 'Between Ithaca and Cephallenia is the small island Asteria, which is called Asteris by the poet. The Scepsian says that it does not remain such as the poet describes it, "with twin bays for mooring". But Apollodorus says that it does remain so to this day, and he mentions a little town on it, Alalcomenai, situated on the isthmus itself' (10.2.16).

29 The fact that Strabo uses the name Asteria rather than Asteris indicates that Asteria must have been a name in local use on the island, since it is not mentioned elsewhere in the literature in this context. The name could have been obtained by Strabo from either the work of the Scepsian (Demetrius) or more probably from Apollodorus.

30 We do not know if Apollodorus visited the island personally but either he or his source evidently saw the 'low isthmus where the island is narrowest'. To reach the isthmus he sails up the bay of Argostoli past Paleis and Cranioi and moors on the north-eastern corner of the bay. He then inspects the

channel area and notices that the sea is still cutting through it, but the scale of rockfall is so enormous that he is unaware or unsure about the former geology.

31 As he sails back down the bay he sees that there are harbours on each side of the island-like Argostoli peninsula and a small town called Alalcomenai on its hill-ridge. He enquires about the name of this peninsula and is told that it is called Asteria.

32 When Apollodorus hears the word Asteria he identifies this with Homer's Asteris. He deduces that this must mean that Argostoli Gulf was once the 'strait between Ithaca and Same' and that Paliki was formerly the separate island of ancient Ithaca, the 'furthest to the west' as the OCO describes it.

33 Strabo says that Apollodorus disagreed with Demetrius, who did not find 'twin bays for mooring' on Asteris, presumably because he had located it elsewhere (perhaps at Dascalion like others after him).

34 Around AD 1 Strabo is assembling the evidence for his *Geography* and he reads the descriptions of Demetrius and Apollodorus. He notes the discrepancy in their respective accounts but he does not use their evidence to work out the location of ancient Ithaca. This is not surprising: without an accurate map of the coastline and orientation of Cephalonia (and such maps that did exist remained very unreliable right up to the eighteenth century AD) one would not connect an observation about the semi-submerged isthmus with Homer's description that 'Ithaca is to the west, the farthest out to sea.'

35 If it was obvious on inspection that there had been a major rockfall joining up what had hitherto been two separate islands then other observers would have deduced the location of ancient Ithaca, because there was a great deal of interest in this subject among Homeric scholars in antiquity. The implication is therefore that the combination of the uplift and the rockfall created a landscape which resembled a partially submerged isthmus on a single island, as opposed to a partially covered channel between two separate islands.

36 As the seismic stresses start to build up again there are further earthquakes and rockfalls at an average interval of fifty years. These earthquakes do not elevate the island but the rockfall progressively spreads out over the existing debris and eventually completely buries the channel, creating an elevated landscape.

37 The independent island of Ithaca has by now completely disappeared. Virgil and Propertius refer to Odysseus' homeland as Dulichia and the 'Maritime Itinerary' speaks only of the islands of Cephalenia, Zacinthos and Dulichia, which now contains a mountain called Ithacus.

38 Once Strabo's Channel is completely infilled a land-locked basin is created. Rainwater from the mountainside collects within it because it has nowhere

to drain out to and the result is the formation of a large irregularly shaped lake, about 1 km long and 250 m at its widest. When a lake such as this forms it has the effect of flattening its own bed and that is why this area today is still so flat and fertile.

39 'Lake Katochori' flourishes for a considerable period of time but it eventually overflows its earth dam, draining out via one of the existing outwash ravines which have carved V-shaped notches into the soft limestone walls of their valleys.

40 Meanwhile at some point probably after about AD 350 another uplifting earthquake occurs and the land mass of Cephalonia is elevated by a further 0.6 m relative to local sea levels.

41 Around 1420 Cristoforo Buondelmonti states that 'Dulichia was once Ithaca and is now called Val di Compare.' By 1504 Doulichion has become uninhabited but the inducement of free land and a tax holiday causes it to be repopulated by 1529 when it is governed by the Venetians. The departure of the former Greek islanders combined with mass immigration under Venetian rule causes the original Greek name of Doulichion to be abandoned.

42 Both the 1575 *Universal Cosmography* of Münster and Belleforest and the 1576 Venice *Insulario* of Thomaso Porcacchi state that the island previously known as Doulichion and Ithaca is now called 'Val de Compare'.

43 From Jacob Spon's visit to the island in 1675–6 and his account in his *Travels in Italy, Dalmatia, Greece and the Levant* we observe that 'Doulichion' and 'Val de Compare' have now lapsed as that island's names: it is called Ithaca again but its principal port is still called 'Dolicha'.

44 Other non-uplifting earthquakes continue to occur throughout this period with an average interval of around fifty years.

45 On Wednesday 12 August 1953 another uplifting earthquake raises the island of Cephalonia relative to sea level by a further 0.6 m. There is terrible death and destruction and the combination of this disaster and the preceding world war and civil war causes about 90% of the population of Cephalonia to emigrate.

As with any process of reconstruction I have had to make some intuitive leaps here and there and it is to be expected that new findings may change this sequence of events quite considerably. The date estimates for the earthquakes are by no means robust and revisions are to be expected as scientific results are assembled. It might also be determined, for example, that the natural theatre is simply that and its terraced seats have never been shaped or smoothed for an audience. From a dramatic perspective that would be a pity but such aspects are not essential to this diagnosis. Nevertheless there remain various loose ends and I refer to some of these below rather than in the preceding analysis since they probably reside at the far end of that bell-shaped curve that we call the normal distribution. If you wish to criticise this theory please therefore refrain from regarding the following reflections as its core components: they are but whimsical speculation.

First I must confess that I continue to be puzzled by those tripods from the Cave of the Nymphs. Perhaps they are not related to their namesakes from the poem, but let's just suppose for a moment that they are: when and where might they have originated? I am not qualified to comment on their dates, other than to say that in view of the discussion in Chapter 24 regarding the possibility of synchronisms with Egyptian dynasties that could be up to 250 years adrift, it might just be worth taking another look at the gap between Odysseus' conventional dates in the twelfth century BC and that upper estimate of around 1000 BC for the tripods.

As far as the place of their discovery is concerned, Polis Bay is precisely the destination on Doulichion that a group of earthquake-crazed Ithacans fleeing from their island across the ruins of Same would aim for: indeed it is one of the very few harbours on its sheer western coastline. As we saw in the same chapter, the embarkation cove of Doulicha Bay still exists opposite Polis Bay in Erissos. If the tripods were valuable enough to be given to Odysseus by King Alcinoos and his colleagues then they were presumably also valuable enough to be snatched from the devastation of Ithaca as its citizens fled.

On arrival at Polis Bay the Loizos Cave location would have been a good place to hide them were it not for the continuing tremors that may have caused the cave to collapse before they could be recovered.[12] So although the claims that 'exactly the right number' of thirteen were found are probably illusory, it would make a fascinating research project for their age to be pinned down more precisely and their movements to be traced in more detail. I suppose I find myself recklessly returning to the company of Samuel Butler here: how many tripods do we have to identify before we arrest the foreigner with the bottle nose?

There are many other thought-provoking surprises and puzzles left to answer in marrying the reconstruction above to the poem and the place. Is it coincidental that both around Smyrna (Izmir) and in the emigrants' island of Samos there are elongated horseshoe-shaped bays of similar appearance to the Bay of Argostoli? Did that geography influence the choice of settlement of the Ithacans? Is it of relevance that both ancient Ithaca and the island of Samos are very close to the same parallel of 38° North, so that the view of the stars from each island is almost identical? Indeed we have come full circle from Chapter 6: just opposite Samos on the Asia Minor mainland lies ancient Pygela, that proverbial pain in the ass.[13]

But there is a further possibility, albeit entirely speculative, that we have not yet considered at all. In Chapter 1 we heard that at 9:24 GMT on Wednesday

12 August 1953 an earthquake of magnitude 7.2 elevated most of Cephalonia by 60 cm and caused a tsunami:

And simultaneously, the sea stirs. A tidal wave submerges the interior of Cephalonia over a distance of three hundred meters inland. In Ithaca and in Zante, the spectacle is the same. The reckless sudden advance of the sea makes the islanders believe that their island is being swallowed up by the ocean . . . Tidal waves swept the port of Vathy, capital of Ithaca.

How do tsunamis happen? Professor Mark Cramer of the Virginia Polytechnic Institute and State University provides an explanation on his website:

Although tsunamis are only a meter or so high as they propagate in the deep ocean, they can grow to several meters by the time they reach shore. Tsunamis are typically generated by earthquakes or underwater landslides.

Tsunamis are just ordinary water waves and comply with the same physics as waves in your coffee cup or bathtub. However, because they are generated by geophysical forces, they also carry geophysical energy and momentum levels which can be devastating to mere humans.

One of the interesting characteristics of tsunamis is that they can travel at speeds approaching 500 mph while in the deep ocean. When the tsunami approaches the shore it amplifies due to the decrease in depth. The general idea that waves amplify or attenuate in spatially varying media (in this case, it is the depth which is varying in the direction of wave propagation) is a well known fact in the general theory of waves and can be found in most fields of mechanics and applied physics.[14]

The epicentre of the 1953 earthquake is listed in the catalogues as located under the seabed to the south-west of Paliki but those coordinates are only approximate: John Underhill's researches suggest that it was probably triggered under the land in the south-east of the island near Skala, where the abandoned village of Palaeo-Skala was destroyed.[15] If the epicentre was land-based then although some unusual waves might be generated, they would be relatively minor and this corresponds to the reported observation in 1953 of a sea disturbance on 12 August 1953 in Lourdha Bay to the south-west of Skala.[16] However, earthquakes can equally well have their epicentre under the seabed – the major tremor north-west of Lefkas on 14 August 2003 is a good example.[17]

What can we then say about the likelihood of a tsunami accompanying the uplift referred to at point 17 above, that took place at some time between the events of the *Odyssey* and the end of the sixth century BC? Statistically speaking we are on safe ground. In his 2002 publication Dale Dominey-Howes

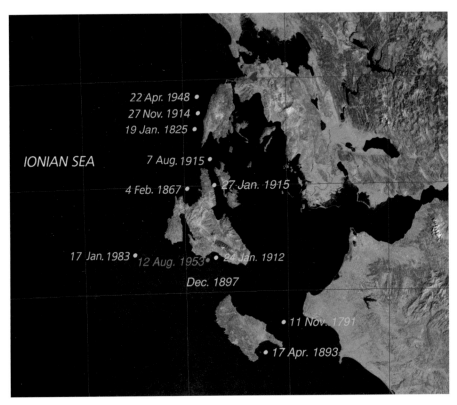

FIGURE 33.3
Tsunamis off Cephalonia,
1791–1983
Colour interpretation: as
Figure 1.3. Grid: 50 km.
[Image credits: as Figure
1.3. Data source:
Papadopoulos (2001).]

of Macquarie University in Sydney identifies the western coast of Greece as a region of high historical tsunamic activity and points out that:

The Aegean region is susceptible to the occurrence of tsunamis because of its tectonic
setting . . . Many large and destructive earthquakes, volcanic eruptions and associated
tsunamis have occurred from antiquity to the present in the eastern Mediterranean
Sea . . . A total of 159 tsunami events occurring between 1628 BC and AD 1996 are
included [in the 1998 Tsunami Catalogue].[18]

The Tsunami Catalogue itself lists a total of twelve events in the region of Cephalonia between 1791 and 1983. As well as the 1953 sea disturbance these include in 1791 'Sea-wave in Zante', in 1825 'Inundation in Lefkada', in 1897 'Sea withdrawal in Kephalonia' and somewhat ominously in 1912 'Ship attacked by a big wave'. The dates and locations of these tsunamis are indicated on Figure 33.3.[19] So it is hardly special pleading to suggest that an earlier earthquake could have been accompanied by a tsunami. We do not know where it might have originated but in this part of the book we are permitted to indulge our imagination and ask 'What if its epicentre was in the sea due south of Argostoli Bay?' If that was the case then there would have been five crucial differences compared with 1953.

The first difference concerns horizontal compression. Because the 1953 event radiates outwards from the region of Skala, any waves that are generated are travelling in the unconfined ocean. However, a tsunami wavefront travelling northwards up Argostoli Bay is compressed by the narrowing surface area and is also affected by a complex set of wavefront reflections and interference patterns from the sides of the bay.

Secondly, the bay becomes very shallow towards the north: one can wade outwards from the present beach for some distance, whereas the depth of the sea south of Argostoli is about 300 m. Cramer provides the underlying equations which enable one to compute wave speed and relative wave height as a tsunami approaches a progressively shallowing shoreline.[20] The results in this case are that a 300 m seabed depth at the ocean epicentre creates a tsunami initially travelling at about 120 mph. By the time it is half-way up Argostoli Bay with a depth today of about 20 m its speed has reduced to around 30 mph but its height has doubled. By the time it reaches a wading depth of 30 cm, assuming that the wavefront has not yet broken, the tsunami has slowed to about 4 mph but its height is now ten times higher than at the epicentre.

The third difference between the tsunami of 1953 and one occurring between 1200 and 500 BC is that prior to the earthquake the island (or at least the part that is south of Erissos) was at least 2 m lower in the water than it is today. If the uplift happens simultaneously with the earthquake then an enormous volume of water is draining out of the ancient harbour at about the same time as the tsunami arrives, creating massive turbulence. If instead the earthquake and the uplift are spread out over a number of days (as in 1953) then as the tsunami reaches the 2.5 km wide semicircular northern end of Argostoli Bay it is funnelled towards the north-west into the 1.5 km wide entrance of the harbour depicted in Figure 30.1.

As it surges into the mouth of the harbour it is focused towards the harbour's head in Figure 30.2, which is only about 150 m wide. Even allowing for overspill beyond the harbour extent, the width of that valley is constricted by the hillsides of Mesovouni to the west and Kastelli to the east and is no more than about 350 m wide. The result is an appalling amplification and focusing of the tsunami into this narrow space and a very substantial increase in wave height as it surges up the valley.

The fourth point is that the infill of rockfall into Strabo's Channel a few minutes earlier has expelled a large volume of sea water into Agia Kiriaki bay to the north and Argostoli Bay to the south. A torrent of water is pouring out of the southern channel entrance and causing sea levels in the northern end of the bay to be chaotic and more voluminous than usual.

Finally, the fifth factor is that an earthquake which can uplift an island by 0.8 metres is even more powerful than one that lifts it by 0.6 metres and so it must have had a magnitude considerably greater than the figure of 7.2 for

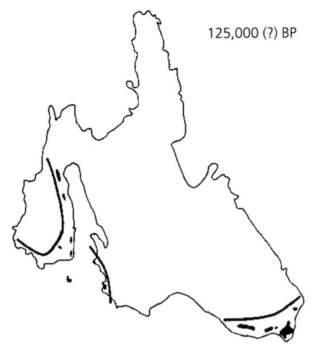

125,000 (?) BP

FIGURE 33.4
Former Cephalonian
shoreline
*The previous occasion when
sea levels were known to be
this high was during the last
inter-glacial period about
125,000 years ago. But why
then was the fossil that
characterises that period not
found?*
[Image credits: Stiros et al.
(1994) p. 839.]

12 August 1953. If the uplift at this time was as much as 4 m then its power would have been simply unimaginable. We heard above that 'tsunamis are only a meter or so high as they propagate in the deep ocean' but an earthquake of this magnitude propagating on the relatively shallow shelf south of Argostoli would be likely to give rise to an initial wave height at or beyond the top end of this range. Based only on vertical amplification, a 2 m initial wave height would today translate into a 20 m wave at a wading depth of 30 cm: if we add to that the effect of horizontal constriction and amplification by the ancient harbour topography, the tsunami's height as it reached the harbour head of ancient Ithaca could have been very much greater.

Did this ancient tsunami happen? We do not know and it will take a concerted scientific enquiry to determine the answer. But there is one intriguing piece of information that has been puzzling me since Chapter 7 that might contain a clue. Figure 33.4 appears in the multidisciplinary paper on the 1953 earthquake by Professor Stiros and his colleagues that I cited there.[21] On it the bold lines indicate the contour of a shoreline that has been provisionally dated to the interglacial period 125,000 years ago by examining the local sediments.

Commenting on this diagram the authors say:

In the literature there is also evidence of fossil Pleistocene shorelines. At different sites along the southern coast of the island [Figure 33.4], at heights varying between 6.5 m and 21.6 m, Braune (1973) and BP Co. et al (1985) reported marine sediments, locally forming terraces, which were assigned a Tyrrhenian age (c. 125,000 years). Although the characteristic fossil Strombus bubonius was not found, a Tyrrhenian age may be assumed for those sediments, in analogy with those of the opposite Peloponnesian coast (Keraudren 1971).

This is rather curious. These former publications apparently reported that marine sediments were found at heights varying between 6.5 m and 21.6 m on the Paliki shoreline and also on the south-east of Cephalonia (at the solid inshore lines on the diagram). In attempting to date these sediments the earlier researchers looked for the characteristic fossil associated with the Tyrrhenian period 125,000 years ago called *Strombus bubonius* but it was unexpectedly absent. In search of an explanation we are then invited to consider instead a Tyrrhenian shoreline on the Peloponnesian coast opposite, where this fossil presumably does appear. The fact that the Peloponnesian coast is about 30 km away to the south-east and that its tectonic setting is different is not discussed.

Perhaps it is just a coincidence, but when I look at Figure 33.4 and I read that marine sediments were found on ancient Ithaca at heights from 6.5 m–21.6 m above sea level; and when I hear that there is unexpectedly no local evidence that they were 125,000 years old as they ought to be; and when I remember John Underhill's discovery of an uplift; and when I calculate that a 2 m initial tsunami wave height would translate into a 20 m wave at the northern end of this bay: somehow I am unable to shake off the ghost of that bottle-nosed foreigner again. What if the former shoreline on Figure 33.4 is not 125,000 years old at all, but is instead the trace of a tsunami that engulfed ancient Ithaca?

We cannot begin to imagine the horror of this. After the initial tremors there is the most devastating earthquake: the earth splits open, the houses are razed to the ground and falling rocks hurtle down from the mountainside to crush the civilians who have survived the initial shock. The air is thick with the cries of the wounded, the trapped and the dying. A dense fog of dust rises up to turn day into night, or perhaps it is already night-time. Strabo's Channel implodes and a huge wave washes up from it on to the north-eastern coast of Ithaca.

The terrified citizens who are still alive peer out from the rubble of this once glorious city towards their beloved Asteris. Through the dark cloud of suspended debris they catch sight of something that cannot be believed. A massive wall of water is advancing up the gulf towards them. As its width is compressed by the narrowing bottleneck of the newly enclosed bay it meets a flood of seawater expelled southwards from Strabo's Channel.

In the tumult of collision the tsunami grows yet taller and advances towards the mouth of the harbour. In the last kilometre of its passage it is channelled into the even narrower confines of the ancient harbour-head of the Ithacans. The monstrous wave rears up higher and higher and at its crest they see the triumphant figure of Poseidon, surfing into Ithaca to seek his revenge upon Odysseus at last.

As the sea water races up the valley those who have not been crushed by the rocks and falling masonry draw their final gasps of breath beneath those deceptively gentle waves. Only one man foresaw this and he was blind:

> I give you a sign that you will recognise:
> When some wayfarer meets you and claims that
> You carry on your shoulder a winnowing-fan,
> Then plant the slim oar in the ground and make
> A handsome sacrifice to lord Poseidon,
> A sheep, a bull, a boar that mounts the sows,
> And then go home and offer hecatombs
> To the immortal gods who hold broad heaven,
> To all in turn. For you a gentle death,
> Death ever so gentle shall come from the sea
> In sleek old age. The people round about you
> Shall prosper. What I tell you shall come true.   11.126–37

Did Odysseus drown in Ithaca and the survivors leave to prosper in Ionia?

Notes

1 Chadwick (1976) p. 186.
2 Butler (1897) p. 160: the author uses this argument in support of his identification of the island of Trapani with that of the Phaiacians' island of Scherie.
3 'The lofty and rugged island of Marettimo did duty in the writer's mind for Ithaca' (Butler (1897) p. 177).
4 'In the historical part of his *Geography* where he dealt seriously with Homeric problems, Eratosthenes fixed Homer's *floruit* a hundred years after the Trojan war, but before the Ionic migration' (Pfeiffer (1968) p. 164). See also Graziosi (2002) ch. 3 ('The Date of Homer'), where the quotation at p. 124 from the *Lives of Homer* is of particular interest: 'Some say that he lived at the time of the Trojan War and that he was a direct witness of it: others that he lived one hundred years after the war; others still one hundred and fifty after it' (*Vita Plutarchea* 1.95–8).
5 Page (1955) p. 157; the subsequent two references are from p. 149 and p. 159.
6 Heubeck and Hoekstra (1989) pp. 195–6.
7 Louden (1999) p. 62.
8 See James Diggle's comments on *aoidoi* in Appendix 1 Section A. For a recent analysis of the possible transmission of the *Iliad* see Latacz (2004) pp. 250–77.
9 Demodocos appears throughout *Odyssey* Book 8 and also at 13.28; Phemios at *Odyssey* 1.154, 337; 17.263; 22.331.
10 Evelyn-White (1914) line 328.
11 Evelyn-White (1914) Introduction p. xliii.

12 As this book was going to press I received a vivid reminder of Keynes' admonition to be flexible in the face of new facts. Catherine Morgan's latest bulletin from Ithaca at Whitley (2004) p. 38 reports that 'In the Polis cave, final observations were plotted onto the first full map of the site and re-checked against observations of geology and geomorphology. The geological features of the area and their impact on the evolution of the landscape around this location are now understood. This in turn has provided valuable information with which to interpret the evolution of the site in terms of cliff collapse and erosion, and hence to make better-informed judgements about the form and function of the site during antiquity. The conclusion drawn in 2002, that it is unlikely that any major cave-like structure could have existed at the site of the Polis "cave", is confirmed. Instead, a preliminary reconstruction suggests a small, mostly open, sheltered area, protected from the sea by a large collapsed section of the S. cliff face. Contrary to Benton's assumption that this was the roof of the cave, collapsed since antiquity, it has fallen from the cliff wall and was almost certainly in its present position throughout the life of the "shrine".'

13 The Barrington Atlas marks the location as P(h)ygela and I am beginning to suspect that it may instead have been named after the ancient settlement of Phigaleia in Arcadia (central Peloponnese). If that speculation turns out to be correct then it looks as though Strabo was either teasing his readers or had fallen victim to a most entertaining yarn. See Talbert (2000) p. 56; also of interest is www.kusadasi.net/historical/phygale.htm

14 www.eng.vt.edu/fluids/msc/my_pages/ocean/tsunami.htm

15 Papazachos et al. (2000) list the epicentre as south-west of Paliki at 38.10N 20.35E. This differs from the value of 38.10N 20.80E quoted in Grandazzi (1954) p. 451, which is to the south-east of Cephalonia near Skala, the location favoured by John Underhill. This is also close to that specified by Stiros et al. (1994) p. 836, who however state only that it is 'expected to be accurate to within 50 km'.

16 Papadopoulos (2001). The 12 August 1953 event is recorded at 09:24 GMT at the location indicated on Figure 33.3 in Lourdha Bay (38.10N 20.60E) as a 'Sea disturbance in Kefalonia'. However, an eyewitness account (Grandazzi (1954) p. 440) states 'Contrary to what has been published, the earthquake of the Ionian Islands was not accompanied by any tidal waves.' In support of this Grandazzi quotes the experience of observers on a west-facing beach of the Argostoli peninsula and also private correspondence from A. Galanopoulos. Grandazzi reports that in the bay of Argostoli his companions 'saw a fitful sea with short, hard, ragged waves; they described it as "bubbling" but they were unanimous in declaring that there was no change in its height nor inundation of the beach'. This corresponds to the catalogue description above but it does not explain other eyewitness accounts reported in the newspapers: perhaps these were influenced by the general hysteria.

17 See Chapter 1 n.12.

18 Dominey-Howes (2002).

19 Papadopoulos (2001). For the 1897 tsunami no day in the month is provided in the catalogue nor any position apart from 'Sea withdrawal in Kefalinia'.

20 See also Synolakis (1991).

21 See Chapter 7 n.8.

CHAPTER 34 **Vision**

Vision is the art of seeing things invisible. Jonathan Swift, *Miscellanies* (1726)

Looking back through my correspondence I see that it was on 9 February 2003 that our family decided to book a summer holiday on Cephalonia. It appears that it was a near thing: I had forgotten that we had been considering Corsica, Tuscany or Turkey as alternatives. Seven weeks later I returned from a short exploration of the island and wrote down the three tasks mentioned in Chapter 17. The first was to assemble the evidence, the second was to tell the story and the third was to work out the best thing to do once the story had been told. That sequence seemed logical at the time but actually these three objectives turn out to be interdependent, because as the story unfolds it forces the search for new evidence, and as that evidence emerges it affects the best thing to do next.

The issue of sea level verification[1] is just one of the many areas in which an amateur can rapidly get out of his depth; in fact the need for comprehensive further research is becoming increasingly apparent in almost every specialist area on which I have drawn for these findings. It has been an extraordinary experience and an enormous privilege to have worked with James Diggle, John Underhill and those other experts listed in the Acknowledgements, but I think that the activity that I shall call the Phase A project is now drawing to a close. It represents only a beginning: its purpose has been to demonstrate that there is something both very new and very old to be found in Cephalonia and that we should now treat the existence of ancient Ithaca rather seriously.

Before any Phase B activity can be considered the Greek authorities must be informed of these researches so that they can evaluate the credibility of the proposals and orchestrate what follows. The typescript of this book is intended as both a prelude and a stimulus to that discussion. If they find the case convincing then by the time the book is published a plan for Phase B will have been drawn up. It will be for them to decide how the next steps should be conducted: all I can do here is to sketch some possibilities.

When Heinrich Schliemann started on his excavation of Troy there were no infra-red satellite cameras, no global positioning systems, no ground-penetrating radar: in fact all that he really had was his intuition and a gang of workmen with spades. So he started to dig and as is well known, he was incredibly lucky (or perhaps amazingly intuitive):

Next year he began the great work of his life, the excavation of Troy. The first sod was turned on Hissarlik in April 1870. It was only a preliminary cutting, to decide how deep was the accumulation of debris on the hill. When the first ancient wall came to light, at a depth of sixteen feet, it was clear that extensive operations would be necessary before the ancient city could be laid bare.[2]

To locate one of the ancient walls of Troy from a preliminary cutting without any technology to guide him was an extraordinary achievement. However, in the years that followed Schliemann dug trenches right through ancient fortifications, mixed up different layers, failed to document his findings rigorously, purloined treasures and perpetrated what some archaeologists today would regard as acts of historical vandalism. There have been great scientific strides since then and so today it is possible to design an introductory Phase B project that does not need to disturb the sites below the surface at all. Instead of creating a gaping wound in the landscape of Cephalonia, its purpose will be to provide the intelligence that will permit selective excavation in Phase C.

What kind of activities will Phase B involve? As I have suggested, advice will be needed from experts on sea level who can conduct a detailed analysis of the marine history of the Cephalonian shoreline. Microbiologists will be in demand to examine the fossil traces comprehensively and identify the various species for dating. Further work with carbon-14 and other scientific dating techniques will be required for the assessment of many samples, and dendrochronologists will be of great value as well. Sedimentologists will be encouraged to compare the marine particles at each end of Strabo's Channel. Experts in bedding plane collapse and the resultant rockfall dynamics will have a major contribution to make. John Underhill has already made enormous strides but he will soon need a resident team to expand upon his detailed study of the geomorphology of the relevant parts of the island. Satellite imagery experts will be essential so that every inch of the terrain can be studied in depth. Specialists in harbour borehole sampling will be required to analyse the ancient raised beaches.

The project team will need to make extensive use of ground-penetrating radar and other non-destructive imaging techniques such as gravimetric and seismic analysis in order to map the contours of Strabo's Channel. Seismologists will be in demand to recreate the tectonic history. Tsunami specialists will need to assess the ancient marine sediment contours and to consider feasible wavefront trajectories. Techniques that have not yet been considered such as lichenometry may turn out to be valuable. Speleologists will be required to guide in the identification of the Cave of the Nymphs. Computer experts with geographical information system expertise will be needed to integrate all of this imagery. A mobile communications network will have to be established to link the team members and their data together. Photographers will be required to capture the findings at each stage.

The reaction of Homeric experts to these proposals is eagerly awaited. Irrespective of whether this is critical or supportive – and there is likely to be a wide spectrum of response – some form of secretariat will be required to ensure that existing information and new developments can be effectively shared.

Meanwhile we have not yet addressed the archaeological aspects: indeed it is a symptom of the progress that has been made since Schliemann's day that so much can be done in an interdisciplinary manner before embarking on detailed surface surveys or actual excavation. This project will be uniquely demanding because there are multiple interrelated sites: the palace, the city, the harbour, Eumaios' Pigfarm, Arethousa Spring, Phorcys Bay and Alalcomenai, to name just some of the more obvious locations. It seems likely that each of these will require a dedicated team of archaeologists to survey the surface for pottery and other artefacts, and they will need to draw upon the scientific resources listed above as well as on their own specific expertise.

Documentation, archiving, transport, accommodation, food and logistics support will be required for all of these participants. On-site security will be needed, access control to prevent the sites from being overrun, website establishment and maintenance, e-mail management, progress publications, briefing conferences, tourist liaison, volunteer coordination, VIP visit arrangements, administration, accounting, overall project management, fund-raising, sponsorship . . . and all of this represents only Phase B: professional evaluation prior to excavation.

What will be the result? We should not set ourselves unrealistic expectations, especially in this particular part of the world. The special problems of Cephalonian archaeology have been clearly expressed by Dr Klaus Randsborg of Copenhagen University, leader of the recent comprehensive survey.[3] Reporting on his earlier work on the island in 1991–2 he commented:

Devastating earthquakes are also known from earlier periods [than the latter half of the eighth century BC] *and are no doubt largely responsible for the poor state of preservation of the antique stone architecture. Earthquakes like that of 1953 can destroy even field terraces and start substantial erosion, a fact which is of great importance for the evaluation of archaeological survey data.*[4]

But if the technology is adequate and we are armed with good luck, we may see through the rubble that has smothered Strabo's Channel and identify the ancient coastline beneath. The wall that has been partially uncovered at the northern exit of the channel may yet reveal an ancient harbour. As at

Pompeii, there is a chance that the terrible suddenness of the earthquake and the tsunami, if there was one, literally froze a civilisation in its tracks.

We may be able to prove the location of the Cave of the Nymphs, which will complete our quest for the Ithacan clues from the *Odyssey*. We may also pinpoint the precise sites of the city, the meeting place and the sportsground and thereby discover how ancient Ithaca was organised and how its Bronze Age population ran their daily lives.

With a carefully conducted programme we will then be able to propose a detailed plan for the keyhole surgery that may uncover the actual buildings themselves, if some parts of them are still preserved deep below the surface of Paliki. Indeed who knows what other artefacts may be found buried beneath the soil? As we saw in Chapter 29, after the events of the *Odyssey* we never hear another word from ancient Ithaca. Against this historical vacuum the incomparable riches of Troy stand in stark but beguiling contrast.

Are there priceless archaeological treasures to be found in Cephalonia? Could there be Linear B tablets? Might the Gold of Homer's Troy be complemented by the Gold of Homer's Ithaca? We shall learn only if we have the courage and the confidence to look.

And as well as applying this technology to the past, we may also think of focusing it on the future. With a concentration of expertise such as this on the island, can we find a way of warning the people of the Ionian Islands about the risks of another earthquake or tsunami, and can we help them to minimise the loss of life and livelihood when it occurs?

These investigations will clearly represent a major commitment. But whatever the results of this interdisciplinary activity, we shall also have the chance of discovering something unique and irreplaceable about our cultural ancestors.

We shall know for the first time whether Odysseus, Penelope, Telemachos, Laertes and the rest of the Ithacans were real people who lived and breathed over 3,000 years ago on Paliki. We shall stand where they stood and see the same landscape that they saw. We shall gaze out at the ocean from those same cliffs from which they viewed the wine-dark sea.

We shall drink from the waters of Arethousa Spring and watch the ravens gliding effortlessly above their eponymous rock. We shall follow the footpaths over the hills where those ancient heroes walked and the timeless sounds of Greece shall sound in our ears as they did in theirs.

As we look down the bay we shall see Asteris as they saw it, half-island half-peninsula, shimmering in the sea. As night falls we shall see the constellations from where Odysseus saw them: and if we are patient we may catch sight of the morning star suspended above its namesake, fading into rosy-fingered dawn.

FIGURE 34.1
Rosy-fingered night sky
*Photographed above Agni
Cove.*

Notes

1 Several apparently conflicting pieces of sea level evidence have yet to be reconciled; these include a comparison of former sea levels at Lefkas and Palairos with those on Cephalonia and also within the Polis Bay cave. I am grateful to William Murray of the University of South Florida and to Kurt Lambeck of the Australian National University at Canberra for their advice on this topic. There are three interrelated factors involved: eustatic sea level changes (mainly glacier melting), isostatic sea level changes (elastic deformation of the land mass under the changing glacial load) and tectonic land level changes (local land upthrust or subsidence). Because of its very active tectonic history it is not possible to import results from other areas of the Mediterranean for direct comparison with this region of the Ionian Sea and so further local studies will be required. Meanwhile there is thought-provoking material in Murray (1983), Murray (1986), Lambeck (1995), Lambeck and Bard (2000), Lambeck and Chappell (2001) and Pirazzoli (1996).

2 Schuchhardt and Schliemann (1891) p. 7.

3 Randsborg (2002).

4 French (1992–3) p. 25.

Epilogue But, soon or late, it is ideas, not vested interests, which are dangerous for good or evil.

John Maynard Keynes,
The General Theory of Employment, Interest and Money (1936)

25 March 2003, the road from Patras to Athens . . . In the darkness of the night coach near Corinth I am haunted by a waking dream. I am walking on these ancient Ithacan hillsides and I now know that this place is so beautiful and unspoiled that it would be a sin against humanity to reveal it. But I also know that it contains a message for us that is so powerful and compelling that it would also be a sin against humanity not to reveal it. I would like to protect Paliki but even if I choose to forget what I have seen then in time others will find it: there is no way back from this discovery.

Three thousand years is a geological instant and an anthropological eternity. Once you have read the *Odyssey* and you have trod the paths of ancient Ithaca there is a fundamental question that remains: What will the people of AD 5000 think of *us*?

The ending of the poem is disputed: there are those who regard it as a later addition. No matter: it is still sublime. Odysseus has fought for ten years in the battles at Troy, he has attacked the Cicones, he has blinded Polyphemos, he has massacred the suitors, he has killed the disloyal maidservants: and now he is fighting once again outside Laertes' home. He stands beside his son and his father and with only a few servants to help them they face the combined wrath of the dead suitors' families. They are locked into this conflict forever: the eye that was for an eye has become a deadly trade of honour that can never slacken, never rest. There can be no end to this affair: the blood that they shed today will be shed by their children for all eternity. And then suddenly Athene intervenes:

Then on the foremost fighters fell Odysseus and his glorious son and thrust at them with swords and double-edged spears. And now they would have killed them all, and cut them off from returning, had not Athene, daughter of Zeus, who bears the aegis, shouted aloud, and held back all the fighters, saying:

   'Cease from painful war, men of Ithaca, so that without bloodshed you may speedily be parted.'

So spoke Athene, and pale fear seized them. Then in their terror the arms flew from their hands and fell one and all to the ground, as the goddess uttered her voice, and they turned towards the city, eager to save their lives. Terribly then shouted the much-enduring, noble Odysseus, and gathering himself together he swooped upon them like an eagle of lofty flight, and at that moment the son of Cronos let go a flaming thunderbolt, and down it fell before the flashing-eyed daughter of the mighty sire. Then flashing-eyed Athene spoke to Odysseus saying:

'Son of Laertes, sprung from Zeus, Odysseus of many devices, hold your hand, and stop the strife of war, common to all, for fear Zeus whose voice is borne afar may perhaps become angry with you.'

So spoke Athene, and he obeyed, and was glad at heart. Then for the future a solemn truce between the two sides was made by Pallas Athene, daughter of Zeus, who bears the aegis, in the likeness of Mentor both in form and in voice.

24.526–548 (transl. Murray)

The Ithacans gave us two priceless gifts: they gave us poetry and they gave us peace. We have kept their art of poetry alive but we have lost their promise of peace. Now that we know where they lived there is something that we must do. We must find a route to peace again so that the people of AD 5000 will have something to remember us by. I do not know where we shall find it but there is no time to lose.

The coach is still hot but my waking dream takes me to a large pavilion: in it are fountains of water that are kept deliciously cool. I hear the sound of laughter and a little girl takes me by the hand. As I step outside into the sunlight with her I see something extraordinary. I cannot explain it, I cannot understand it, so I ask her what it means:

It is the Day of the Children's Walk. Every year for one week in the spring, all the Presidents of all the different countries in the world come here to ancient Ithaca to be together. And every autumn, the Ministers of all the different religions come for a week as well. And one child from every country in the world is chosen to join them: we live in this Peace Pavilion with our parents. The visitors have no conferences, agendas, bodyguards or staff: this place is protected and we are all quite safe. By the end of the week we are all good friends. That is today, so we celebrate with the Children's Walk.

She scampers off to join the others. Each child takes a President's hand and leads the way up the rocky path from the palace. Around Hermes' Hill they go, through Eumaios' Pigfarm and past Arethousa Spring, alongside the foothills of Mount Neriton and on down the hillside past the Cave of the Nymphs to Phorcys Bay. There they stand on the seashore as the glassy-smooth surface mirrors the sun and the ribbon of fresh spring water meanders out into the ocean. They look out at the crouching headlands and the island lying beyond. There is nothing left to say. This place and this planet are too beautiful to fight over: they do not need Athene to pledge their truce of peace.

Into the bay sails a galley, but this time it is not the Phaiacians bearing the sleeping Odysseus: it is the first of a convoy that has come to take them home. At its prow is the only television camera allowed on the island this week and it is sending the Presidents' pledge of peace to the six billion people of the world who depend upon them.

I awoke as the coach entered Athens but I cannot forget the dream.

APPENDIX 1 James Diggle: a philologist reflects

The chief part of this Appendix is Section B, in which I discuss Strabo and his sources and what they say about the channel and about Asteris. There follow several shorter sections in which I comment on some important issues which have been raised in this book or draw attention to problems in the Greek text and in its interpretation. For the reader who would like more detailed discussion on specific points I recommend *A Commentary on Homer's Odyssey* published by Oxford University Press (3 volumes (1988–92), by M. Fernández-Galiano, J. B. Hainsworth, A. Heubeck, A. Hoekstra, J. Russo, S. West.

I begin with an 'Introductory note' (Section A), in which I say what is distinctive about the text of the *Odyssey* and why it poses difficult and unusual problems for its interpreter.

Section A Introductory note

The *Odyssey* is a very different kind of text from (to take two other familiar epic poems) Virgil's *Aeneid* and Milton's *Paradise Lost*. Virgil and Milton composed their poems for a reading public, and we know precisely when and in what circumstances they composed them. The Greeks attributed the *Iliad* and the *Odyssey* to a poet whom they called Homer. But they knew no more about 'Homer' than we do. We do not know when and in what circumstances the *Odyssey* was composed. We do know that, to begin with, it was not designed for reading.

The poems could not have been written down much before 700 BC (the Greeks did not acquire their written alphabet, which is adapted from the Phoenician script, until the eighth century), and it is possible that they were not written down until as much as a century or more after that. But they have their origins much earlier, in a pre-literate society, where poetry was composed and performed orally by highly trained bards (*aoidoi*, 'singers', like Phemios at the court of Odysseus, and Demodocos at the Phaiacian court). We can be fairly confident that a tradition of oral poetry existed in Mycenaean times, that is, at the time of the events which are described in the poems.

The most obvious stylistic feature of the *Iliad* and the *Odyssey* is the use of repeated 'formulaic' phrases. Rarely, for example, are ships simply ships: they are usually 'swift' ships or 'black' ships or 'well-built' ships, and the like. And the epithet which a ship is given on a particular occasion is dictated not by sense (that is, not by deliberate selection) but by the needs of grammar and metre (each of these phrases has a different metrical or grammatical function). These are examples of the very simplest formulaic phrases. There are countless others, longer and more complex. They provide the building-blocks from which the poet composes his verses. He has in his repertoire a vast stock of expressions which will cover many of his needs, and from this stock he can take, with no conscious effort, as he composes, the expression which metre and grammar require. And this not only helps in the creation of new poetry. It helps in the preservation of older poetry. For example, once an object or a place or an activity has been aptly described in one or in several lines of verse, there is no reason to change that description. It becomes part of the poetical heritage, easily memorised, available for use by poets of the next generation.

The *Odyssey* has its origins in orally composed poetry of this kind. But there is still much room for dispute over precisely when, and how, the poem achieved its present form. Did an oral poet compose the poem several centuries before writing became available? If so, how much might it have been altered or adapted before it was written down? Or did the poet come later in the tradition, and use writing to create, or at least to record, his poem? Or did he dictate it to a scribe? Or was his poem preserved at first by professional reciters (the so-called 'rhapsodes', who succeeded the creative oral poets)?

These questions admit no certain answer. It was necessary that they should be asked, so that the reader should be aware that there are some territories into which we have entered in this book where much remains speculative and certainty is unattainable. But one thing is certain and of first importance: although the *Odyssey* was written down several centuries after the events which it describes, it has its origin in a poetical tradition which continued unbroken during those intervening centuries.

Our difficulties and uncertainties do not end here. The *Odyssey* was available in written form by, at the latest, the end of the sixth century BC. But how many versions of it were available? We must not think in terms of a single authoritative version, accurately copied by scribe after scribe. Some of the copies that were available in antiquity showed considerable differences from each other. In the third and second centuries BC scholars associated with the Library at Alexandria in Egypt collected and compared available manuscripts of the poem, and attempted to establish the most authentic text. Two of these scholars, Aristophanes of Byzantium and Aristarchus, I shall mention in the sections which follow. What we know of their judgements on the text comes from the so-called 'scholia', or ancient commentaries, begun by other early scholars in Alexandria and added to by later scholars. We know, in particular, that they pronounced a substantial number of verses in the poems to be inauthentic. Sometimes (we are explicitly told) they did so because the verses were absent from some of the manuscripts which they were using. Sometimes we have to conjecture their reasons: reasons perhaps of language, sense and style. These were learned men, who knew far more about the poems and their language and the texts in which they had been transmitted than we can hope to know. And we must take their judgements seriously.

For the most part, we are obliged to base our text of the *Odyssey* on manuscripts which date from about AD 1000 onwards. But, in addition to these, we have a fair number of fragments of ancient texts, written on papyrus, preserved in the sands of Egypt. Sometimes these papyri differ from our mediaeval manuscripts; sometimes they confirm the judgements of the Alexandrian scholars. Again, I shall mention the evidence of these papyri where it becomes relevant.

Section B   Strabo and his sources

Strabo, who wrote his *Geography* in the early years of the first century AD, is by far the most important source of ancient geographical knowledge that we have, not least because he relies heavily on earlier and more knowledgeable authors now lost to us.

In a long section of his tenth book (10.2.8–26) he discusses the geography of the Ionian Islands, and in particular the attempts of earlier writers to identify the places to which Homer refers. He cites his sources haphazardly and with tantalising allusiveness, and sometimes we may doubt whether he has fully taken in the points which they were making. But some things of value emerge. Here are the two most valuable.

(i) In §15 Strabo says of Cephallenia:

Where the island is narrowest it forms a low isthmus, so that it [the island] is often submerged from sea to sea. Near the narrows, on the gulf, are Paleis and Cranioi.

He cites no source. But source he must have had: he did not learn this from personal observation.

(ii) His next words, in §16, are these:

Between Ithaca and Cephallenia is the small island Asteria, which is called Asteris by the poet. The Scepsian says that it does not remain such as the poet describes it, 'with twin bays for mooring'. But Apollodorus says that it does remain so to this day, and he mentions a little town on it, Alalcomenai, situated on the isthmus itself.

The two authors to whom Strabo refers are Demetrius of Scepsis (near Troy) and Apollodorus of Athens, both writing in the middle of the second century BC. Demetrius wrote a long work on a brief passage in the second Book of the *Iliad* listing the Trojan forces. For what we know about this work (rather little) see R. Pfeiffer, *History of Classical Scholarship: From the Beginnings to the End of the Hellenistic Age* (Oxford 1968) pp. 249–51. Apollodorus (who used Demetrius' work) collaborated for a time with the great Homeric scholar Aristarchus (see the 'Introductory note' above). Among his works was a book *On the Catalogue of the Ships*, the passage describing the Greek forces which takes up a large part of the second Book of the *Iliad*. Much of what we know of this work is derived from references (like this one) in Strabo. Surviving quotations and paraphrases from the work are collected by F. Jacoby, *Die Fragmente der griechischen Historiker* II B (Berlin 1929) 244, F 154–207. The passage cited above is F 202. For more on Apollodorus see Pfeiffer, *History of Classical Scholarship* pp. 252–66.

We have no idea where Demetrius looked for Asteris and failed to find it. Equally, we do not know for sure where Apollodorus found it. But he did find it, and just as Homer describes it, 'with twin bays for mooring'. Moreover it had a little town 'on the isthmus itself'. He gives us the name of that little town, Alalcomenai. This is a name which crops up in two much later sources (Plutarch and Stephanus of Byzantium). Unfortunately they add nothing to our knowledge. They designate Alalcomenai, vaguely, as 'city of the Ithacans' or 'city on Ithaca'. That is no surprise. Any city which tradition placed in the domain of Odysseus would be placed on Ithaca by later writers, who knew much less than Apollodorus.

The town was 'on the isthmus itself'. That is a puzzling expression. The puzzle lies not in the word 'isthmus' but in the word 'itself'. Islands do occasionally have isthmuses, narrow strips of land connecting two otherwise separate parts. But would we say, of such an island, 'The island of X has a town on the isthmus itself'? No. We would say 'The island of X has a town on the isthmus'. So why does Strabo add the word 'itself'?

An island *may* have, but usually does not have, an isthmus. What usually does have an isthmus is a peninsula. The isthmus is a narrow neck of land linking the 'island' to the mainland. And it is the isthmus which turns the island into an 'almost-island' (the literal meaning of 'peninsula'). Therefore the mention of an isthmus in connection with a peninsula comes as no surprise. So let us consider the possibility that Apollodorus, when he refers to Asteris and its isthmus, is describing not an island but a peninsula. In this case he will be saying that the peninsula of Asteris has a little town 'on the isthmus itself', 'on the actual isthmus'. That is a natural thing to say. We are no longer puzzled by 'itself'.

Strabo refers to Asteris again, near the beginning of his work. In his first Book he has a long discussion of places which have suffered physical change or have disappeared because of earthquakes, eruptions and similar cataclysms. In the course of this discussion (at 1.3.18) he says that in the neighbourhood of the Ionian Islands are several peninsulas which were once islands. After listing these he mentions Asteris, which, he says, 'has undergone change'. And he relates this change to the disappearance of the two harbours mentioned by Homer.

One of the Echinades islands, the one formerly called Artemita, has become mainland. And they say that others of the little islands around the river Acheloos have suffered the same from the silting up of the sea by the river; and the rest of them too, as Herodotus says, are in the process of being silted up. And there are certain Aitolian promontories which were formerly islands. And Asteria, which the poet calls Asteris, has undergone change:

There is a rocky island in mid sea,
Called Asteris, not large, but with twin bays
For mooring.

But at the present day it does not even afford a decent place to drop anchor.

Strabo cites no sources for these statements. But he is clearly reflecting what he has read in earlier writers. He has no personal knowledge of Asteris. We can see this from the passage which we have already examined. There he could cite only the contradictory opinions of Demetrius and Apollodorus. He cited the opinion of Demetrius that Asteris no longer has the appearance that it once had ('with twin bays for mooring'). Here he cites much the same view: Asteris, so far from having those bays, does not even afford a decent anchorage. Presumably he is echoing Demetrius here too. Indeed, at the opening of the previous section (1.3.17) he makes a general acknowledgement that Demetrius is his source hereabouts. As before, we have no idea what island Demetrius has in mind, and how precisely (apart from losing its two harbours) it has changed. But let us observe the curious fact that Strabo (or Demetrius) appends this mention of Asteris to a list of islands which are now joined to the mainland.

Let us look more closely at those lines of Homer which Strabo quoted (or rather, partially quoted, for he left one out):

> There is a rocky island in mid sea,
> Half way between Ithaca and rugged Samos,
> Called Asteris, not large, but with twin bays
> For mooring.   4.844–7

In line 846 'twin' translates an adjective (*amphidumos*) which appears only here in Homer and does not appear again for many centuries. It is derived from *amphi* ('around', 'on each side') and *-dumos* (as in *didumos*, 'twin'). So it must mean 'twin', with the more specific sense 'with one on each side'. In the third century BC the recondite poet Callimachus, borrowing the word from this passage, has the expression 'the *amphidumos* Phaiacian harbour' (fr. 15 Pfeiffer), by which he means the two harbours which stand one on each side of the main town of the island of Corfu (traditionally identified with Phaiacia). According to the *Odyssey* (6.263) the Phaiacians had a harbour 'on each side of the city'.

Now I add a further piece to the jigsaw: a passage in which the word 'island' indisputably describes a peninsula. It comes from Apollonius of Rhodes (third century BC), author of an epic poem about the adventures of the Argonauts. Apollonius is a learned and allusive poet, who is for ever showing how cleverly he can adapt the language of Homer to new contexts and uses. In Book 1, lines 936–40, he describes the peninsula of Cyzicus in the Propontis (Sea of Marmara).

There is a steep island inside the Propontis, sloping down into the sea, just offshore from the rich grainfields of the Phrygian mainland, from which it is separated only by a low sea-washed isthmus. Its shores are amphidumoi.

This description is based on the Homeric description of Asteris, as two linguistic details prove. First, the shores (or possibly headlands) are *amphidumoi*. Whether Apollonius means simply 'twin', or 'with twin harbours', is unclear. But that is not important. What is of decisive importance is that this adjective appears only once in Homer, in the description of Asteris, and does not appear again until it is borrowed from Homer by Apollonius (in this passage) and by his contemporary, the equally learned and allusive poet Callimachus (as I mentioned above). Second, the opening of his description, 'There is a steep island', echoes Homer's 'There is a rocky island'.

So Apollonius, while using language which recalls Homeric Asteris, describes the peninsula of Cyzicus as an island. That he really does regard Cyzicus as a peninsula, and not an island, is not in doubt, because he refers to its 'isthmus'. Actually, Apollonius is playing a game with his readers, as he often does. There is a long-standing dispute (from antiquity to modern times) whether the peninsula of Cyzicus was ever originally an island. Apollonius is having it both ways, or, rather, his use of language reflects the controversy. Perhaps it was because he knew of a current controversy about the nature of Asteris (island or peninsula or island turned peninsula?) that he chose to model his description of Cyzicus on Asteris. At all events, one thing is beyond dispute: a poet echoing Homer's description of Asteris used the word 'island' to describe a peninsula.

We return to Apollodorus. I have suggested that he may have imagined Asteris to be a peninsula. If he did, what peninsula might he have had in mind?

Let us consider the possibility that it was the Argostoli peninsula. If it was, then what follows? It follows that he must have identified Ithaca with W. Cephallenia (modern Paliki). For, if Asteris is the Argostoli peninsula, then the strait in which it lies ('between Ithaca and rugged Samos') is the strait between E. and W. Cephallenia.

But Apollodorus' reasoning will have taken the reverse direction. He will not have reasoned 'Asteris is the Argostoli peninsula: therefore Ithaca is W. Cephallenia', but rather 'Ithaca is W. Cephallenia: therefore Asteris is the Argostoli peninsula'; for the former proposition is not obviously true, while the second is all but inescapable.

Is there any reason why Apollodorus should not have identified Ithaca with W. Cephallenia? None at all. He may have understood the implications of Strabo's Channel, and inferred that W. Cephallenia was once an island. Indeed, there is every possibility that Apollodorus himself was the source for Strabo's description of the channel. And he may have interpreted *Iliad* 2.635, 'the mainland and the region opposite', in the way that I shall argue that it must be interpreted, as referring to E. and W. Cephallenia (see Section C).

Enough of speculation. I end with hard fact. If you stand on the high ground at the northern end of Argostoli Bay and you look directly down towards the ocean, you see a remarkable sight. In the middle of the bay, some 10 km distant, silhouetted against the higher ground of Cephallenia behind it, stands a small island. It has a low ridge curving gently down to the sea on its western side; and at the western tip, where land meets sea, a small strip of water is visible between that tip and the land behind, hinting at the existence of a narrow strait between island and mainland. But it is not an island. It is the Argostoli peninsula, which, seen head on, from this direction, is for all the world an island.

Section C   The mainland (*Iliad* 2.631–7)

Odysseus led the gallant Cephallenians,
From Ithaca and leaf-quivering Neriton,
From Crocyleia and rugged Aigilips,
Men hailing from Zacynthos and from Samos,
From the mainland and the region opposite.   635
Odysseus, equal in resource to Zeus,
Led these, together with twelve red-cheeked ships.   *Iliad* 2.631–7

This passage begins by introducing the Cephallenians, who form Odysseus'
contingent. The following lines specify who these Cephallenians are, by listing
places where they live. The list takes the form of a series of relative clauses:
'Who occupied / lived in . . .'. Some of the verbs in these relative causes
mean 'occupied' ('held possession of'), the others mean 'lived in'. There is no
significance in the choice of verb. Choice is dictated by metre. I have translated
these clauses with an introductory 'from', and not as relative clauses, because
my verse-scheme does not have room for a series of verbs. Nothing is lost. The
verbs are unimportant. Only the names are important.

   Line 635 is misunderstood by commentators and translators. They take
'mainland' and 'region opposite' to be two different expressions for the same
place. Here is a typical translation: 'held the mainland and dwelt on the shores
opposite the isles' (Murray). Of the commentators it will be sufficient to mention R. Hope Simpson and J. F. Lazenby, *The Catalogue of the Ships in Homer's
Iliad* (Oxford 1970) pp. 104–5, and G. S. Kirk, *The Iliad: A Commentary*, vol. I
(Cambridge 1985) p. 221.

   The grammatical structure of line 635 (reflecting the structure of each of
the preceding three lines) shows that this line refers to two different sets of
people and places: inhabitants of the 'mainland' and inhabitants of the 'region
opposite (the mainland)'. The latter expression, properly interpreted, means
'land opposite on the other side (of some intervening space)'. And so we must
find an interpretation of 'mainland' which will allow us to make sense of 'land
opposite (the mainland) and on the other side (from the mainland)'.

   If the mainland is mainland Greece, then the land opposite is the islands.
But we have already had the islands. We cannot have them again, especially
not in such a clumsy circumlocution as 'land opposite the mainland'. In any
case, if the mainland is mainland Greece, what part? Commentators struggle to
find a convincing part of mainland Greece for Odysseus to rule (again, consult
Simpson and Lazenby and Kirk, palpably struggling). So great is the improb-
ability that Odysseus' domain extended to mainland Greece that some have
even condemned line 635 as inauthentic: 'a relatively late addition designed

to rescue Odysseus from the poverty to which the Catalogue condemns him' (D. L. Page, *History and the Homeric Iliad* (Berkeley and Los Angeles 1963) p. 162).

The way to make sense of line 635 is to interpret 'mainland' as E. Cephallenia and 'region opposite' as W. Cephallenia (Ithaca).

I anticipate an objection: that we now have an implausible sequence of names. So indeed we do. Consider the sequence: first (632) Ithaca and its mountain; then (633) Crocyleia and Aigilips (location uncertain); then (634) Zacynthos and Samos (i.e. Zacynthos and Cephallenia); finally (635) E. and W. Cephallenia. Clearly this will not do: we do not want Samos (E. Cephallenia) and Ithaca (W. Cephallenia) mentioned twice. It must not be supposed that line 635 is recapitulating what has gone before – that it is giving us the two broader areas in which the places just mentioned are located. For, even if (what is uncertain) Crocyleia and Aigilips belong to Ithaca, so that we should then have on the one hand Samos (E. Cephallenia), on the other hand Ithaca, Neriton, Crocyleia, Aigilips (W. Cephallenia), this bipartite summary ignores the island of Zacynthos. Furthermore the grammatical structure of the passage proves that line 635 is not recapitulating anything, but is adding a new item, parallel to those which have gone before.

The answer, I suggest, is that line 635 was never designed to stand alongside lines 632–4. It represents an alternative way of describing Cephallenians: occupants of E. and W. Cephallenia. What we have here is a combination of two traditional descriptions of Cephallenians: (i) people associated with Ithaca and Neriton, Crocyleia and Aigilips, Zacynthos and Samos; (ii) people who occupy E. and W. Cephallenia. It happens that a papyrus omits line 635. This is evidence that in antiquity some readers considered line 635 to be incompatible with lines 632–4. If we had more papyri containing this passage, I should not be surprised to find that one of them has line 635 and omits lines 632–4.

Addendum: After writing this I discovered that my interpretation of 635 as referring to E. and W. Cephallenia is anticipated by C. I. Tzakos, *Peri Homerikis Ithakis* (Athens 2002) p. 222, who however supposes that the line amplifies and defines 'Samos' in 634, which is impossible. G. Volterras, *Peri Omerikis Ithakis* (Athens 1903) had already taken 'mainland' to mean E. Cephallenia; but he mistakenly took 'region opposite' to mean the region opposite W. Cephallenia (i.e. the west coast of E. Cephallenia), as well as supposing (like Tzakos) that the line amplifies 'Samos'.

Section D   Doulichion

Gilles le Noan cites an entry from a 'Maritime Itinerary', a semi-official gazetteer of the Roman world, composed in the second to third centuries AD:

Insulae Cephalenia Zacinthos et Dulichia: hic est mons Ithacus, ubi est patria Vlixis.

'The islands Cephalenia, Zacinthos and Dulichia: here is Mount Ithacus, where the homeland of Ulysses is.'[1]

The striking feature of this description is that only three islands are listed. The omission of Ithaca is highly revealing: it is another case of the dog that didn't bark in the night from Chapter 17. Where we might expect a reference to Ithaca, instead we find a reference to Dulichia, which has a mountain called Ithacus on it. And this island is described as the homeland of Ulysses (Odysseus). Nothing could be clearer: as early as the second- to third-century AD Ithaca, the homeland of Odysseus, was identified with Dulichia. And what island was the writer identifying as Dulichia? After mentioning Cephalenia and Zacynthos there is only one island left for him to mention, an island which he cannot possibly omit: the modern Ithaca.

We can trace this identification of Ithaca and Dulichia even further back, as le Noan observes. It is a curious fact that Roman poets from the first century BC onwards frequently associate Odysseus with Dulichia. The earliest example of this is found in Virgil, who describes the ships of Odysseus as 'Dulichian' (*Eclogues* 6.76). An ancient commentator on Virgil (Servius, in the fourth century AD) has the following note: *Ithacenses, a monte* ('Ithacan from the mountain'). In other words, 'Dulichian' means 'Ithacan' because (as we read in the gazetteer) there is a Mount Ithacus on it.[2]

Modern commentators would have done well to listen to Servius. But they think that they know a better reason why 'Dulichian' can mean 'Ithacan'. In two reputable recent commentaries we read that 'Dulichium was part of Odysseus' kingdom in Hom. *Od.* 1.245–6', and 'Odysseus was lord of Dulichium, Same, Zacynthus, and Ithaca (*Od.* 1.246–7)'.[3] That is untrue: these lines are not describing the islands ruled by Odysseus but the islands where the suitors come from. As we have seen, in the *Odyssey* Doulichion is ruled by Acastos, just as in the *Iliad* it was ruled by Meges.

The next example is especially illuminating. Propertius (2.14.4) speaks of Ulysses' delight 'when he touched the shores of dear Dulichia' (*cum tetigit carae litora Dulichiae*). Propertius, like every single reader of the poem from antiquity to the present, knew that there is one island and one island only whose shores Odysseus longed to touch, and one and one only which could possibly be described as 'dear' to him. And that island is Ithaca. So why do Propertius and Virgil, and other Roman poets after them,[4] say 'Dulichia' when they should be saying 'Ithaca'? The answer is clear: by their time there was an island called Dulichia which they and their readers identified with Homer's Ithaca. In other words, by the first century BC Ithaca was no longer an island with an independent existence: in so far as it existed at all, it was Dulichia under another name.

Notes to Section D

1 Le Noan cites this with the reading *Cephaleniae* (rather than *Cephalenia*). The manuscripts and the printed editions (the latest is O. Cuntz, *Itineraria Romana, uolumen prius, Itineraria Antonini Augusti et Burdigalense* (Leipzig 1929)) do indeed have the genitive case *-iae*. But this would entail the translation 'The islands of Cephalenia, namely Zacinthos and Dulichia', which is nonsense. The necessary change to the nominative *Cephalenia* was suggested long ago (see P. Wesseling, *Vetera Romanorum Itineraria, siue Antonini Augusti Itinerarium* (Amsterdam 1735) p. 524).

2 The text may be found in G. Thilo, *Seruii Grammatici qui feruntur in Vergilii Bucolica et Georgica Commentarii* (Leipzig 1927) p. 80. One manuscript adds this fuller explanation: *Dulichium insula est, ubi mons est Ithacus, in qua fertur habitasse Vlixes, eoque et ipse Dulichius et Dulichias habuisse rates dicitur* ('Dulichium is an island, where there is a mount Ithacus, on which [island] Ulysses is said to have lived, and for that reason he himelf is described as Dulichian and as having had Dulichian ships').

3 R. Coleman, *Vergil, Eclogues* (Cambridge 1977), and W. Clausen, *A Commentary on Virgil, Eclogues* (Oxford 1994).

4 A full list of them may be found in *Thesaurus Linguae Latinae, Supplementum, Nomina propria Latina* vol. III fasc. II (1989) p. 268. Tellingly, the entry begins by defining Dulichia as *insula prope Ithacam (uel Ithaca ipsa)*, 'an island near Ithaca (or Ithaca itself)'.

Section E Telemachos' route home from Pylos
(15.28–42, 295–300)

(i)

Choice suitors plan to ambush you in the strait
That lies between Ithaca and rugged Samos,
Intent on murdering you on your way home.   30
It's not to be – the earth will first close over
Those suitors who eat up your property.
So keep your sturdy ship far off the islands
And sail by night and day. Whatever god
Is guarding you will send a following wind.   35
When you reach the first shore of Ithaca,
Send on your ship and comrades to the city.
Yourself, go first to the swineherd, who keeps watch
Over your pigs and is still loyal to you.
Spend the night there, and send him to the city   40
To give the news to wise Penelope
That you are now back safely home from Pylos.   15.28–42

In line 33 I take 'the islands' to mean Ithaca and the three islands which are traditionally mentioned alongside Ithaca: 'Doulichion and Same and wooded Zacynthos' (1.246, 9.24, 16.123, 19.131).

In line 36 the words which I have translated 'first shore' may also be translated 'first headland'. Athene's directions are vague. This is understandable. She has told Telemachos to keep his ship 'far off the islands', and these must include Ithaca, or at least that part of Ithaca where the suitors are known to be lurking. Having kept clear of the danger area he will probably be approaching the safe part of the Ithacan coastline from some distance out at sea, and at night.

So Athene tells him to land as soon as he can, where best he can. And not only are Athene's directions vague. They are also unusually brisk and elliptical. She tells Telemachos to send his ship ahead as soon as he reaches land, and omits to mention that he himself must disembark. The ample and leisurely narrative style of Homer does not normally omit such details. Furthermore, this vagueness over where he is to land is matched by a vagueness over where he does actually land. At 15.495ff he is suddenly described as landing. But the place at which he lands (and how he gets there) is not specified. It looks as if Athene (and the poet) wanted to keep Telemachos' options open.

(ii)

The following passage appears to offer us Telemachos' route:

> They went past Crounoi and past fair-streamed Chalcis.   295
> Then the sun set and all the streets grew dark.
> She made for Pheai, sped by Zeus's wind,
> And passed divine Elis, where the Epeians rule.
> He then aimed for the swift isles, wondering
> Whether he would be caught or escape death.   300
>
>   15.295–300

However, this passage is a magpie's nest. Almost certainly it was not a part of the original text but is a later addition to it.

Line 295 is not found in any manuscript. It is quoted (along with 296–8) by Strabo. It was first put into the text of the *Odyssey* by Joshua Barnes, Regius Professor of Greek at Cambridge, at the turn of the seventeenth century, another of whose contributions to Homeric scholarship was to persuade his rich and pious wife to finance his edition of the *Iliad*, by assuring her that its author was King Solomon. This line is modelled on a line (425) in the *Hymn to Apollo* (composed in the sixth century BC).

Lines 297–8 also appear in the *Hymn* (in reverse order at 426–7). Line 298 also largely repeats 13.275. The formulaic line 296 (it appeared recently in this Book at line 185 and will reappear at line 471) is inept, because we are at sea, where there are no streets to grow dark. The meaning (and identity) of the 'swift isles' in line 299 has been disputed since antiquity. Dispute is idle, since the words 'he aimed for the swift isles', more literally 'he sent forward to the swift isles' (notice, in passing, the abrupt change of subject, from the ship to Telemachos, and the lack of a grammatical object, 'ship', for the verb), are borrowed from *Iliad* 17.708, 'he sent [him] forward to the swift ships' (the object 'him' is expressed earlier in the line), with the substitution of 'isles' for 'ships' (similar-looking words in Greek).

If we take this passage at face value, Telemachos passes Crounoi, Chalcis, Pheai and Elis and then 'keeps his sturdy ship far off the islands' until he reaches the 'first shore [*or* headland] of Ithaca'. In this case he passes north-east of Zacynthos and then heads out to sea towards the west to keep far away from the islands of Same and Doulichion and from the entrance to the straits between Ithaca and Same and the suitors hiding at the Asteris peninsula.

But if (as I assume) these lines are a later addition, and must therefore be set aside, then we may entertain the possibility that Telemachos takes a different route, to the south-west of Zacynthos, so that Zacynthos will now be included among the islands which Athene tells him to 'keep far off'. And this is right and proper, because a bare mention of islands conjures up the traditional trio of 'Doulichion and Same and wooded Zacynthos'.

Section F   Athene meets Telemachos (1.180–6)

'I am the son of wise Anchialos,   180
Mentes, king of the Taphians, rowing men.
I am here with ship and shipmates, bound abroad
Over the wine-dark main for Temese,
In search of bronze. I carry glinting iron.
My ship stands here in the country far from town,   185
In Rheithron bay, below wooded Neïon.'   1.180–6

Lines 185–6 were absent from some ancient manuscripts, and were condemned as inauthentic by Aristophanes and Aristarchus (see my 'Introductory note' above). There are several linguistic details to puzzle us.

First, the use in line 185 of the word which I have translated 'here'. This word is not, in Greek, a local adverb, but is the so-called 'deictic' (i.e. 'pointing') pronoun, and literally means 'this (at which I am pointing or am able to point)'. In this line it is applied to 'ship' and implies 'this ship here'. Exactly the same line recurs at 24.308, spoken by Odysseus to Laertes (the passage is quoted in Chapter 22). The use of the word is perhaps more natural in this later passage, where Odysseus is actually 'in the country' and so presumably nearer to his ship than is Athene to hers, since she is at the palace. None the less, it is possible to imagine Athene gesturing vaguely in the direction of the rural harbour, especially if it is not in fact very far away.

Second, the names Rheithron and Neïon, which appear in line 186, are not found elsewhere in the poem or anywhere else in Greek literature. The name Rheithron is based on the common noun *rheithron*, 'stream'. But the spelling is surprising: *rheithron* is the spelling of the so-called Attic (i.e. Athenian) dialect. Whenever the common noun is used in the poem, it has the spelling of the older Ionic dialect, *rheethron*, as we should expect. We therefore expect the name to be spelt *Rheethron*. Nothing, however, prevents our speculating that the name *was* originally here spelt *Rheethron*, and that this spelling was changed to the Attic form at a later time (there are many Attic spellings in the poem, which should not be there, and originally were not).

The phrase 'below wooded Neïon' clearly shows that Neïon is a mountain. At 3.81 Ithaca is described with a puzzling adjective which may possibly mean 'under-Neïan', i.e. 'under Neïon'. Neïon is curiously similar to Neriton, Ithaca's main mountain.

So lines 185–6 'My ship stands here in the country far from town, / In Rheithron bay, below wooded Neïon' caused puzzlement in antiquity, and some scholars believed that these lines did not belong to the text of the original poem.

Section G   *Amphi*, *chthamale* and *eudeielos* (9.19–26)

> I am Odysseus, Laertes' son, world-famed
> For stratagems: my name has reached the heavens.   20
> Bright Ithaca is my home: it has a mountain,
> Leaf-quivering Neriton, far visible.
> Around are many islands, close to each other,
> Doulichion and Same and wooded Zacynthos.
> Ithaca itself lies low, furthest to sea   25
> Towards dusk; the rest, apart, face dawn and sun.   9.19–26

I begin at the end. In line 26 the directions 'towards dusk . . . dawn and sun' refer to west and east. To refer them (as some have) to north and south (or south-east) does violence to the Greek language and to common sense. It follows that 'around' in line 23 does not mean 'all around Ithaca': because, if the islands encircle Ithaca, then Ithaca cannot be furthest west. Since 'furthest west' is an explicit and unambiguous direction, and 'around' is (in its nature) inexplicit, I take it to mean 'round about, nearby'. *Amphi* regularly means 'near', with proximity its sole implication and no possible implication of encirclement. When the friends of Polyphemos are described as living 'around' him on windy heights (9.399), the meaning is not that they encircle him but that they live nearby.

The word *chthamale* means 'near the ground', in the sense 'low'. The use of the word in Homer is remarkably uniform. It is used of low beds on the ground (*Od.* 11.194); of a rock which is low in relation to another rock (*Od.* 12.101); of a low wall (*Il.* 13.683). Most significantly, it is used to describe the island Aiaia (*Od.* 10.196) as seen by Odysseus from a high vantage-point: it 'lies low', which evidently means that the body of the island is not marked by high ground and lies notably lower than his vantage point. Applied to Ithaca, I take the adjective to mean that Ithaca lies low in relation to the islands nearby. Their mountains dwarf its own. Strabo's interpretation (10.2.12) 'close to the mainland' must be rejected.

In line 21 'bright' is a non-committal translation of an adjective (*eudeielos*) whose meaning is uncertain. It may have something to do with visibility (the literal sense may be 'well-visible'). It is used almost exclusively of Ithaca, and we should expect it to refer to an aspect of Ithaca which distinguishes Ithaca from other islands. It is often translated 'sunny'. But what Greek island is sunless? Line 25 suggests a possible aspect. If Ithaca 'lies low', its mountains may not be high enough to be much troubled by clouds. So perhaps, the idea is 'always fully visible'.

Section H The headlands of Phorcys Bay (13.95–100)

Then the seafaring ship approached the island.	95
On Ithaca there is a bay of Phorcys,	
The old man of the sea: in it, two headlands,	
Projecting, sheared off, crouching from the harbour,	
Shield it from waves whipped up by blustering winds	100
Outside.	13.95–100

The most remarkable feature of this description is the statement in line 97 that the two projecting headlands are 'in' the harbour. One modern scholar has tried to get them out of the harbour by changing *en* ('in') to *ep'* ('over'). If the bay of Phorcys is Atheras Bay, 'in' makes sense. The bay is flanked by two massive headlands projecting out to sea. An observer who stands on the shore of the harbour and looks out to sea sees two smaller headlands, very much closer, projecting into the harbour and creating an inner bay.

Visible above the right inner headland is the high ridge of the outer headland. The left inner headland conceals the left outer headland. In line 98 the headlands are described as 'crouching from the harbour'. This is a plausible, but not certain, translation of an unusual expression. The inner headlands may be imagined as crouching below the outer headlands (the right inner headland visibly does so to the observer on the shore) and as crouching away from the harbour, as they slope down into the sea from the harbour, with their heads (as it were) bent low to seaward.

Section I   Pigfarm and room with a view (14.1–10, 1.425–7)

(i)

He climbed a rugged path up from the harbour,
Along the heights through woods, the way Athene
Pointed him to the swineherd, of all the servants
The most faithful steward of his property.
He found him seated in the porch, on ground   5
Exposed to view all round, where he had built
With his own hands a high surrounding wall,
A fine big wall, for his absent master's swine,
Far from his mistress and the old Laertes,
With quarried stones, topping it with wild pear.   10

14.1–10

The expression which I have translated 'on ground [more literally, 'in a place'] / Exposed to view all round' (lines 5–6) is used elsewhere in the poem to describe the location of Telemachos' bedroom (1.426) and Circe's house (10.211 and 253). It is disputed whether the adjective used in this expression (*periskeptos*) means (a) 'visible around' or 'with a view around' or (b) 'sheltered around'. Either of senses (a) suits the location suggested for the pigfarm. It is on elevated land which commands a view, and is open to view, on three sides. Since only its north side is sheltered (by a wall of rock), sense (b) is not suitable. Support for the sense 'visible around' comes from a similar expression at 5.476, where Odysseus finds a copse 'in a place visible around', i.e. beside a clearing. The verb used there is unambiguous.

(ii)

With much on his mind Telemachos made for bed.
His bedroom was a lofty chamber off
The fair courtyard, in a place with a view all round.   1.425–7

There are two uncertainties here. First, it is uncertain whether 'lofty' refers to the height of the room above the ground or instead to its internal height. Second, the words which I have translated 'in a place with a view all round' are the same ambiguous words which were used to describe the location of Eumaios' Pigfarm. Once again, as with the pigfarm, it is unclear whether the meaning is that Telemachos' bedroom was 'visible from all round' or (what is much the same) 'had a view all round' or that it was 'sheltered all round'. While the latter sense cannot, in this case, be ruled out, both of the other senses are suitable here and they are the only senses which suit the pigfarm.

Section J   Additional notes on the translations

Odyssey

1.169–73

Come, answer me precisely – Who are you?
Whose son? Where are your city and your parents?   170
What ship did you come on? Why did the sailors
Bring you to Ithaca? Who did they claim
To be? For I hardly think you came on foot.

Lines 171–3 recur in 14.188–90 (Eumaios questioning Odysseus) and (for the greater part) in 16.57–9 (Telemachos questioning Eumaios about Odysseus), where they are rather more appropriate. They were omitted here by some ancient manuscripts and were regarded as inauthentic by Aristarchus (see the 'Introductory note' to this Appendix).

2.146–54

So spoke Telemachos. In answer Zeus
Despatched two eagles from a mountain peak.
They flew a while upon the gusting breezes,
Close to each other, pinions at full stretch.
But when they reached the middle of the assembly,   150
They wheeled about, wings beating rapidly,
Stared at the heads of all, death in their eyes,
Clawed with their talons at their cheeks and necks,
And sped off to the right through houses and city.

Lines 152–4 are very oddly expressed and may be a later addition designed to make the omen more sensational. In terms of Greek divination 'to the right' (line 154) means 'to the east'.

2.427–9

The canvas billowed in the wind, and as
She sped the dark wave thundered round the prow.
[Over the waves she ran pursuing her path.]

Line 429 (wholly unwanted here) is omitted by several papyri and manuscripts. It is borrowed from *Iliad* 1.483.

3.79–85

'Great Nestor, Neleus' son, glory of the Achaians,
You ask where we are from: I shall explain.   80

We come from Ithaca beneath mount Neïon.
Our business here is personal, not public.
I search for news of my long-suffering father,
Noble Odysseus, who, they tell me, once
Fought alongside you at the sack of Troy.'   85

For the problematic 'beneath mount Neïon' see the note on 1.186 in Section F of this Appendix.

4.600–8

Your gift should be a treasure I can store: 600
Horses I cannot take to Ithaca.
Here they should stay, for you to glory in.
Your kingdom is a broad plain, with much clover,
Galingale, wheat, oats, glistening broad-eared barley.
Ithaca has no meadows or broad horse-runs;   605
Neither has any of the sea-perched isles.
But there's not one so fair as Ithaca,
Goat-land, more lovely than horse-grazing land.

The line which is numbered 608 in this translation appears in the manuscripts after line 605. The sequence of thought, and the grammatical structure, is improved if we place it at the end of the passage, as a nineteenth-century scholar suggested.

4.660–2

Antinoos, Eupeithes' son, addressed them
[In pain. His heart was black and filled to bursting
With rage, his eyes resembled flashing fire].

Lines 661–2 were condemned (rightly) by Aristarchus (see Section A of this Appendix) as an interpolation from *Iliad* 1.103–4, where the presence of pain (sorrow) alongside anger more appropriately captures the mood of Agamemnon.

4.778–86

He picked out twenty men, the best there were;
And off they went to the swift ship on the shore.
They dragged her first of all into deep water,   780
And then they put the mast and sail aboard
And fixed the oars in leather oarlock straps

[All in due order, and spread out the white sail],
While proud attendants brought them their equipment.
They moored her well out in the water, came   785
Ashore, had supper, and awaited nightfall.

Line 783 (which occurs elsewhere) is omitted by many manuscripts. You do
not spread out sail until you are at sea with a wind behind you. In line 785 the
precise meaning of the words which I have translated 'well out in the water'
is uncertain.

13.344–51

Look how the land lies, then you will believe me –
The bay of Phorcys, old man of the sea,   345
And here a leafy olive at its head
[And nearby a delightful misty cave,
Sacred to the nymphs who have the name of Naiads].
This is the spacious vaulted cave where often
You offered potent hecatombs to the nymphs,   350
And this is forest-clad mount Neriton.

Lines 347–8 repeat lines 103–4 and are omitted by papyri and several
manuscripts. Line 349 is a better introduction to the cave.

13.404–10

Go first of all to the swineherd, who keeps watch
Over your pigs and is still loyal to you   405
And loves your son and wise Penelope.
You will find him sitting with the pigs; they feed
By Raven's Rock and Arethousa Spring,
Guzzling dark water and munching tasty acorns –
A diet that builds up healthy fat in pigs.   410

The expression 'dark [black] water' is well glossed by the Oxford commentary
on 4.359 as 'water from deep places where the light cannot reach'. In addition
to that passage (where it refers to water in a well) it recurs at 6.91 (water
in washing-troughs) and 12.104 (water churned up by Charybdis), also *Iliad*
2.825 (people 'drinking the black water of [river] Aisepos'), 16.161 (wolves
lapping up black water from a black-water spring [the expression 'black-water
spring' recurs in *Od.* 20.158]), 21.202 (river water). Contrast 5.70, Calypso's
springs of 'white [clear] water'.

14.343–354

When, in the evening,
They reached the farmlands of bright Ithaca,
They bound me tight with plaited ropes and left me   345
On board the vessel, while they disembarked
And took a hasty supper by the shore.
But the gods themselves untied the knots for me
With ease. I wrapped the rags around my head,
Slipped down the landing-plank until the water   350
Was chest-high, then struck out and started swimming.
Soon I was clear of them and climbed ashore.
Then I crept inland and crouched down in hiding
In a flowery copse.

For 'bright Ithaca' (line 344) see the note on 9.21 in Section G of this Appendix. The words which I have translated 'flowery copse' (line 354) mean literally 'copse [or thicket] of a flowery wood'. The precise nuance is unclear. Other translations which have been suggested are 'copse of blooming trees', 'thicket of leafy wood', 'thicket of flowering shrubs'.

16.322–30

The sturdy ship which brought Telemachos
And crew from Pylos put in to Ithaca.
As soon as they arrived inside the deep harbour
They dragged the black ship up onto dry land   325
[While proud attendants took away their equipment].
At once they carried off the splendid presents
To the house of Clytios, and sent a herald
To Odysseus' palace with the news for wise
Penelope that her son was in the country.   330

Line 326 is probably a later addition, based on line 360 and 4.784 (quoted above), in both of which the 'proud servants' belong (appropriately) to the suitors. Telemachos' men are unlikely to have been blessed with such helpers. At any rate, they did their own fetching and carrying at 2.414–15.

16.363–70

Antinoos, Eupeithes' son, addressed them:
'Damn it! The gods have snatched him from our clutches.
By day lookouts stood on the windy heights,   365
Shift after shift without break; and when the sun set
We never slept the night on land but waited

For dawn at sea on our swift ambush-ship,
Hoping to catch and kill Telemachos.
But meanwhile some god carried him off home.'   370

'We never slept the night on land'. The word *epeiros* suggests a substantial land mass, whether island or mainland. Dascalion is too small to be described as anything other than 'rock'.

16.465–75

I did not think of going down to town   465
To inquire of that: I wanted to deliver
The message and return here with all speed.
I fell in with a messenger sent by
Your shipmates: he was first to address your mother.
One thing I know: I saw it for myself.   470
By now I had walked up above the city
To the Hill of Hermes, when I saw a ship
Entering our harbour. It was fully manned
And heavy with shields and double-bladed spears.
I took it to be them, but can't be sure.   475

The verb which I have translated 'going down to' (line 465) is commonly mistranslated as 'going through'. It occurs only here in Homer, and only three more times in surviving Greek literature, where it means, as we should expect, 'go down [to]', and could not possibly mean 'go through'. One of these later uses is particularly interesting. Apollonius of Rhodes ('a learned and allusive poet, who is for ever showing how cleverly he can adapt the language of Homer to new contexts and uses', as I have described him in Section B above) applies it (in Book 1, line 322) to people who have 'gone down' from a city to a beach, thus giving a reverse turn to the Homeric expression ('going down to the town' becomes 'going down from the city').

17.22–3

'Go on your way. He'll guide me, as you order,
As soon as I have warmed myself by the fire.'

After 'by the fire' follows the phrase 'and there is heat'. It is impossible to decide whether this refers to the heat of the fire or the heat of the sun.

21.106–9

Step forward, suitors, see the prize on show:
A woman without equal in Achaia –

In holy Pylos, Argos or Mycenae
[Or Ithaca itself or the dark mainland].

This passage is not referred to in the text of this book but is cited here for the sake of completeness, since line 109 might otherwise be regarded as an additional clue. In fact this line is omitted by a papyrus and by many manuscripts. It is made up from the second half of 14.97 and the first half of 14.98 'either on the dark mainland / Or Ithaca itself' (see Chapter 8). It is impossible here, because it makes Ithaca and the mainland, like Pylos, Argos and Mycenae, subdivisions of Achaia (the Peloponnese).

24.223–5

They had gone off
To gather stones for a protecting wall
For the orchard.

The obscure word which I have translated 'stones' might (for all we know) mean 'brushwood' or 'stones and brushwood'.

24.306–8

Some god drove me hither
Off course from Sicily, against my wish.
My ship stands here in the country far from town.

Line 308 repeats line 1.185 (quoted in Chapter 2, Chapter 19 and Chapter 22). See the comments on that passage in Section F of this Appendix.

24.468

The city with broad dancing-places.

This description is also not referred to in the text of this book but it is cited here to explain why the line has not been adopted as a clue. The adjective 'with broad dancing-places' (or possibly just 'with broad places') is applied to five other cities or regions in the *Odyssey*. It tells us nothing specific about Ithaca; only that it was a city of some size.

Iliad

2.625–630

Men from Doulichion and the sacred isles   625
Of Echinai, across the sea from Elis,
Were led by Meges, warrior son of Phyleus,

The horseman loved by Zeus, who quarrelled with
His father and migrated to Doulichion.
Forty black ships sailed under his command.   630

It is impossible to decide, on grammatical grounds, whether 'across the sea
from Elis' describes the location of both Doulichion and the Echinai islands or
of the Echinai alone.

APPENDIX 2 John Underhill: the geology and geomorphology of Thinia

The aim of the geological and geomorphological fieldwork in the Thinia area has been to evaluate the evidence for and against the hypothesis that a marine connection described by Strabo existed in historical times to separate what is now the western Paliki (Lixouri) peninsula from the main body of Cephalonia. The field studies have involved gaining an understanding of the solid (bedrock) geology and the more superficial Holocene (drift) deposits.

Geology

The Thinia area forms a distinctive *c.* 5 km long, NE–SW trending steep-sided valley between Kolpos Agias Kiriaki and Kolpos Livadhiou in NW Cephalonia (Figures A2.1 and A2.2).

Geologically, the region may be separated into two distinct parts: a western area in which a largely stratigraphically conformable, but folded and locally thrusted, succession of Cretaceous and Paleogene limestones overlain by Miocene marly and clastic sediments dips gently eastward; and an eastern area in which Cretaceous and Paleogene limestones dip steeply westward (Accordi et al. 1998; Figure A2.3).

Although its trace is largely obscured by rockfall debris, the boundary, where observable, between the two dip provinces is marked by a reverse (thrust) fault that emplaced the eastern, westerly-dipping Cretaceous–Paleogene limestones on to easterly-dipping Miocene sediments. The thrust plane itself forms the northerly continuation of the Ainos Thrust, a major structure that can be traced for >25 km and which took up contractional deformation as the Hellenide (Pre-Apulian) foreland experienced shortening in Plio-Quaternary times (Underhill 1989).

The steep (45 to >60 degree) westerly dips that characterise the eastern side of the valley (Figure A2.4) result from their forming the western limb of a major hangingwall anticline that lies above the Ainos Thrust and formed as a natural consequence of its emplacement. Many of the bedding planes show evidence (e.g. slickensides) for down-dip (flexural) slip having occurred on them, a fact that originally led other workers to suggest erroneously that the whole region was dominated by extensional faulting rather than contraction (e.g. BP Co. Ltd 1971).

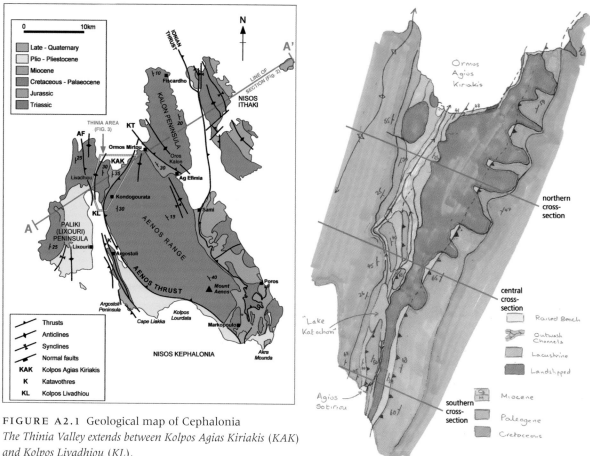

FIGURE A2.1 Geological map of Cephalonia
The Thinia Valley extends between Kolpos Agias Kiriakis (KAK)
and Kolpos Livadhiou (KL).
[Image credits: John Underhill (1989, redrawn).]

FIGURE A2.3
Geological map of the
Thinia area, Cephalonia
The northern, central and
southern cross-sections are
illustrated at Figures
A2.21–A2.23. The dark blue
colour represents landslipped
material.
[Image credits: John
Underhill.]

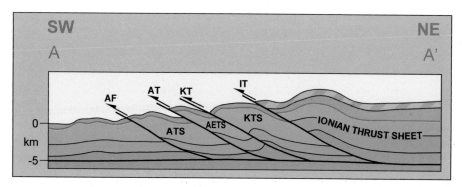

FIGURE A2.2 Regional cross-section through northern part of Cephalonia
depicting the attitude of the main thrust faults affecting the island
Depicts the line of section A–A' shown in Figure A2.1.
AF = Atheras Thrust; AT = Aenos Thrust; KT = Kalon Thrust; IT = Ionian Thrust.
The Thinia valley is located between the Atheras and Aenos Thrust.
[Image credits: John Underhill.]

FIGURE A2.4
View looking south-east towards the village of Petrikata.
The hillside above the village consists of steep westerly dipping Paleogene limestones. The village itself is sited upon degradation products derived from the hillslope behind. The exposures to the right of the image consist of Paleogene limestones thrust over Miocene marl. A detailed photograph of the thrust plane itself is shown in Figure A2.5
[Image credits: John Underhill.]

FIGURE A2.5 Detail of the Agia Sotira Thrust (view looking south-east).
The sharp contact between Paleogene limestones (top left) and Miocene marls (bottom right) represents the easterly dipping Agia Sotira Thrust Fault.
[Image credits: John Underhill.]

FIGURE A2.6
View looking north-east at
the northern end of
Kolpos Livadhiou.
*Development of a major
hangingwall anticline
immediately to the east of
Kolpos Livadhiou*
[Image credits: John
Underhill.]

The general easterly dip seen in the footwall to the Ainos Thrust is, however, complicated by the presence of at least one subsidiary thrust fault, referred to here as the Agia Sotira Thrust, which causes repetition of Paleogene limestones and Miocene sediments in the southern part of the valley (Figures A2.4 and A2.5).

The intermediary thrust may also be the reason for the otherwise anomalous presence of Paleogene limestones midway along the northern coastal section, which has previously been interpreted as an olistolith (Bizon 1967).

Folding and thrusting also occurs further to the west. A major thrust fault termed the Atheras Thrust runs across the north-eastern side of the Paliki peninsula through the village from which it takes its name. A major hangingwall anticlinal fold occurs immediately to the east of the thrust plane and defines the eastern slopes of a palaeo-estuary area at the northern end of Kolpos Livadhiou (Figure A2.6).

FIGURE A2.7 View looking NE of the core and eastern slopes of the Thinia valley
The low-lying area left of centre consists primarily of landslipped material derived from the eastern slopes. [Image credits: John Underhill.]

FIGURE A2.8 Detail of one of the catchment areas along the eastern slopes of the Thinia valley
The products of the drainage form the westerly dipping alluvial cone on which the village sits.
[Image credits: John Underhill.]

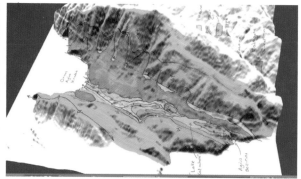

FIGURE A2.9 Digital Elevation Model image of the Thinia valley with draped geological and geomorphological features
The view from the SW highlights both the landslip coverage and the scalloped embayments that characterise eastern hillslopes of the Thinia valley from which that debris was derived.
[Image credits: John Underhill. Data source: DEM data from Hellenic Military Geographical Service. Processing: OziExplorer 3D. Websites: www.gys.gr, www.oziexplorer.com/]

FIGURE A2.10 View looking SSW of the landslipped material that lines the slopes of the steep westerly dipping limestones (left hand side of picture)
The village of Angonas (left of centre) lies on one of the major landslides. The core of the Thinia valley also consists of slipped material lying upon easterly dipping Miocene marls. The western slopes (right hand side) consist of easterly dipping Cretaceous and Paleogene limestones.
[Image credits: John Underhill.]

FIGURE A2.11 View looking east of prominent scarps consisting of in situ bedrock of Miocene conglomerate
Beneath this lie slopes composed of disaggregated landslipped material.
[Image credits: John Underhill.]

FIGURE A2.12 View looking east of the Agia Sotira area at the southern end of the Thinia valley
The hillside in the distance consists of westerly dipping Paleogene limestones and Miocene conglomerates, which are separated by the northward continuation of the Ainos Thrust. The slopes immediately above the low-lying pastures on the right hand side of the image consist of disaggregated landslipped material derived from the eastern hillslopes. A thrust contact occurs between easterly dipping Paleogene limestones and Miocene marls in the immediate foreground.
[Image credits: John Underhill.]

FIGURE A2.13 View looking north of the southern end of the Thinia valley and the coastline immediately to the south
The low-lying area between the sea and the scarp from which this photograph was taken largely consists of slipped and slumped material derived from the eastern hillslopes that border Kolpos Livadhiou.
[Image credits: John Underhill.]

Holocene – recent geomorphological elements

The occurrence of sculpted embayments in the topographic profile is very striking (Figures A2.7 and A2.8) and is analogous to mass-wasting processes that have been seen to operate on steep hillslopes (e.g. Willett et al. (2001); Densmore et al. (1998)). Significant talus fans (Figure A2.9) containing large detached blocks of Paleocene limestone are found immediately down-dip from the scallop-like hillside valleys. The occurrence and derivation of the material combine to suggest that gravitational instability set up by the steep westerly dip of bedding is a major driver in the creation of the present topographic profile (Figures A2.7–A2.10).

Significantly, this phenomenon is not specific to the Thinia area and is something that also characterises analogous structures on the island, most notably on the north-eastern flank of Ormos Mirtou. Consequently, the present valley shape appears to be controlled not only by the underlying solid geology but also by recent geomorphic processes of rockfall and landsliding. The clear implication is that prior to geomorphic degradation, the valley itself was once much deeper (Figures A2.11–A2.13).

FIGURE A2.14 Photograph looking east depicting the drainage channel at the northern end of the Thinia valley (low valley in the foreground)
The channel has exploited soft Miocene marls.
[Image credits: John Underhill.]

FIGURE A2.15
View looking NW of the
Agia Sotira area at the
southern end of the Thinia
valley
*The image illustrates the two
deeply incised drainage
channels that characterise the
area. While the courses of
both preferentially exploit the
more easily erodable Miocene
marl, the more easterly of the
two formed a palaeowaterfall
where it cut across more
resistant Paleogene
limestones.*
[Image credits: John
Underhill.]

Four distinctive narrow, steep-sided valleys occur within the Thinia area, all of which extend to the coast. The northern valleys merge into one, which displays an ever-shallowing gradient and less pronounced incision as it leaves the extent of Paleogene limestone outcrop and approaches Kolpos Agia Kiriaki (Figure A2.14).

The two valleys that drained southward both primarily lie within the extent of the most easily eroded fine-grained Miocene sediments. The eastern tributary appears to have cut a palaeowaterfall (now dry) where it crosses Paleogene limestones before entering the sea at Agia Sotira (Figure A2.15).

A notable flat-lying area lies towards the south of the Thinia valley (i.e. immediately to the west of the small settlement referred to locally as Katochorion: Figures A2.16 and A2.17). The strata lie unconformably above the easterly-dipping Paleogene and Miocene strata and the Agia Sotira Thrust and appear to onlap on to both the landslipped rock debris on its eastern side and on to the headward parts of the drainage channels (described above). The strata consist of horizontal, laminated, fine-grained, poorly consolidated clastic sediments that are interpreted herein to have been deposited in lacustrine conditions.

Flat-lying vegetated areas characterise both coastlines in the Thinia area. A distinctive wave-cut platform also occurs at a height of *c.* 6 m in the north-east of the area, a vegetated terrace occurs at Agia Sotira and a well-defined bay-fill is seen at the northern end of Kolpos Livadhiou (Figure A2.18). All provide strong evidence for uplift having affected the Thinia region. The wave-cut platform may be interpreted to represent a raised beach (Figures A2.19 and A2.20).

FIGURE A2.16
View looking west of the
low-lying area near the
village of Katochori that is
interpreted to have formed
a lake created by closed
drainage
*The break in slope on the
western side of the arable land
is thought to represent the
former strandline to the lake.*
[Image credits: John
Underhill.]

FIGURE A2.17
View looking north-west
from Petrikata
*The image depicts the
northern end of the flat-lying
area thought to define a
palaeolake, 'Lake Katochori'.*
[Image credits: John
Underhill.]

Geomorphological evolution

The stratigraphic relationships between the various geomorphic elements are distinctive enough to enable the following temporal and spatial evolution of the Thinia area to be determined. The valley walls experienced periodic landslips that led to its infill. New drainage pathways were set up as a result of the rapidly evolving, landslip-modified topography leading eventually to

four main outwash channels forming. Further significant landslides below the
Petrikata–Kondogourata area led to channel capture and the development
of internal (closed) drainage with the formation of a lake (Lake Katochori).
Slumping and erosion of the landslipped barrier or sill led to drainage of the
lake.

FIGURE A2.20
Rock exposure along the
north-eastern shore of the
Thinia valley, Kolpos Agia
Kiriaki
*The poorly sorted, angular
clasts and the red iron-rich
infill that form the toesets of
uplifted talus cones are clearly
visible.*
[Image credits: John
Underhill.]

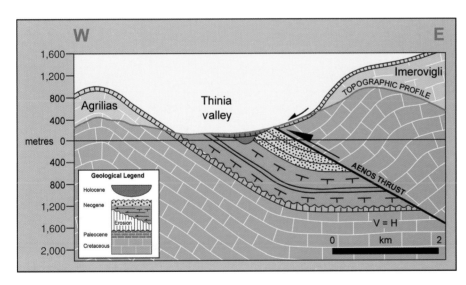

FIGURE A2.21
Northern cross-sectional
profile through the Thinia
area
*Depicts the regional structural
geology and shows the
development of a prominent
hangingwall anticline above
the Ainos Thrust. It is the
steep westerly dips generated
on the western limb of this
fold that set up slope
instability and lead to land
and rock sliding into the
Thinia valley.*
[Image credits: John
Underhill.]

Cross-sectional geometries

In order to address the issue of what form the bedrock profile takes in the
Thinia area and whether these can confirm or refute the possibility that a
marine connection once existed in the area, a series of cross-sections was constructed across the valley (Figures A2.21–A2.24). The most important cross-
sections were those constructed in the highest parts of the valley (where elevations exceed 175 m).

FIGURE A2.22
Central cross-sectional
profile through the Thinia
area
*Shows a detailed section
across the southern area of the
Thinia valley and highlights
the way in which the
unconformable contact
between the resistant
Paleocene limestones and
easily erodable Miocene marls
has been exploited by the
valley and subsequently filled
by debris derived from the
eastern hillslopes. Further
west, a conformable and
easterly dipping succession of
Cretaceous–Miocene sediments
have been transected by one
thrust, termed the Agia Sotira
Thrust.*
[Image credits: John
Underhill.]

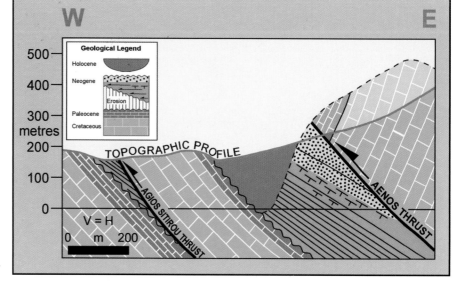

FIGURE A2.23
NW-SE cross-sectional
profile through the Thinia
area (southern end)
*Shows some possibilities for
the geometric projection of the
buried valley sides. Although
high, an easterly dip of 60
degrees and a westerly dip of
68 degrees are consistent with
measured dips along strike
(e.g. Ormos Mirtou and along
the eastern shores of Kolpos
Livadhiou and Kolpos Agias
Kiriakis) and within the
valley itself. Importantly, if
they extend to depth, both dips
are compatible with the valley
having once reached below
sea level.*
[Image credits: John
Underhill.]

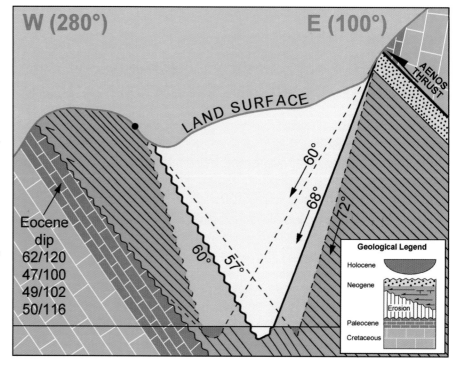

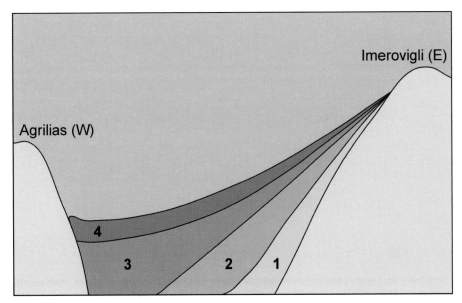

FIGURE A2.24
Hypothetical cross-sectional profiles through the Thinia area to illustrate how successive landslips may have filled the valley profile over time *Whilst there are believed to have been at least four major and discrete earthquake-related uplifting events, these numbered wedges are only schematic and illustrative. Earthquakes that did not lead to co-seismic changes in topography and slopes will also have produced landslides as would natural (aseismic) degradation. Consequently, in detail, there would therefore have been considerably more than four individual valley-filling episodes and the landslides would consist of many overlapping and overstepping lobes.*
[Image credits: John Underhill.]

The results of the cross-section profiles constructed all imply that it is possible that a significant palaeovalley once existed, which was infilled by landslipped and slumped Holocene cover derived largely from the eastern hillslopes. This is likely to have occurred in a succession of landslips (shown schematically in Figure A2.24) rather than in one single valley-filling event.

Significantly, since the bedrock profile projects to a level *at or below sea level irrespective of where it is constructed* along the length of the Thinia valley, the intriguing possibility exists that this palaeovalley formed a narrow marine channel connecting Kolpos Agia Kiriaki with Kolpos Livadhiou, with the present Paliki peninsula therefore having once been an island.

If the valley once extended down to sea level, the most likely reason for its original formation was that it was created by subaerial erosion during the last glaciation (*c.* 30–20,000 years ago) when sea levels are thought to have been more than 100 m lower than at the present day. Sea level rise over the following 10,000 years is a plausible mechanism for its drowning and the creation of a marine connection between Kolpos Agias Kiriakis and Kolpos Livadhiou. Subsequent marine erosion and slope instability caused by seismic events then instigated landslides and the valley became progressively filled.

Dating considerations

Whilst the age of the landslipped material remains imprecise at present, it is possible to place some constraints on its timing from archaeological and historical artefacts found below or within the disaggregated sediments.

FIGURE A2.25
Exposed example of ancient man-made wall covered by landslip material at beach level, Kolpos Agias Kiriakis
The wall is tentatively dated from c. 1500 BC which implies that landslip material has buried it during the last 3,000 years and that sea level has not changed markedly between then and the present day.
[Image credits: John Underhill.]

First, the discovery of a wall buried beneath landslipped material (Figure A2.25) demonstrates that human activity was well established in the area before burial. Importantly, given that its construction has been tentatively identified as being similar to Mycenaean in style (after 1500 BC; Snodgrass pers. comm.) this points to the fact that very significant slippage and burial has occurred over the past 3,500 years.

Secondly, the identification of numerous angular fragments of brick and glazed pottery within the sedimentary cover itself suggests that much of the land slippage is relatively recent (i.e. over the past few hundred years). Deformation and repair of the coastal road highlights the fact that landsliding continues unabated at the present day.

Discussion

The geological and geomorphological evidence provide a sound basis for there previously having been more relief to the Thinia valley. This may have been sufficiently large for a narrow marine connection to have existed between the northern and southern marine bays. However this possibility must remain speculative until definitive age dates constrain each of the geomorphic processes identified.

Notwithstanding this, the discovery of a Mycenaean-like wall under the rockfall material and the evidence for historical land slippage all imply that very significant burial has taken place over the past 3,000 years with much of it occurring in historical times (i.e. over the past few centuries).

The next priority must be to devote further effort into quantifying the dates and rates of the processes that operated. The most significant site for placing an upper envelope on deformation is the palaeo lakebed that covers the drainage channels and onlaps on to the landslips. If carbon-14 age dates for lignitic material derived from the lake sediments should prove to be >3,500 years old then this would mean that Paliki was permanently connected to the rest of Cephalonia during the Late Bronze Age period and therefore also by the time of Strabo as well (*c.* AD 1). However, if the lakebed dates prove to be significantly younger then this will increase the likelihood that earlier landslides infilled the topographic profile and buried a former marine channel that separated Paliki from the rest of Cephalonia during this period.

Conclusion

Whilst the geological and geomorphological data do not refute the possibility that an infilled and buried marine palaeovalley exists on the eastern side of the Thinia valley, definitive evidence for its archaeological and classical significance awaits further geophysical and geochronological tests.

References

Accordi, G., Carbone, F. and Pignatti, J. 1998. 'Depositional History of a Paleogene Carbonate Ramp (Western Cephalonia, Ionian Islands, Greece)'. *Geologica Romana* 34, 131–205.

Bizon, J. 1967. 'Contribution à la connaissance des foraminifères planctoniques d'Epire et des îles Ioniennes (Grèce occidentale) depuis le Paléogène supérieur jusqu'au Pliocène'. PhD thesis, Paris.

British Petroleum Co. Ltd 1971. *The Geological Results of Petroleum Exploration in Western Greece.* Institute for Geological and Subsurface Research Report No. 10, Athens.

Densmore, A. L., Ellis, M. A. and Anderson, R. S. (1998). 'Landsliding and the Evolution of Normal Fault-bounded Mountains'. *Journal of Geophysical Research* 103, 15203–19.

Strabo c. 1. *Geography*, 10.2.15.

Underhill, J. R. 1989. 'Late Cenozoic Deformation of the Hellenide Foreland, Western Greece'. *Bulletin of the Geological Society of America* 101, 613–34.

Willett, S. D., Slingerland, R. and Hovius, N. 2001. 'Uplift, Shortening and Steady State Topography in Active Mountain Belts'. *Amer. J. Sci.* 301, 455–85.

APPENDIX 3 Exploratory technology

This project has relied very considerably on modern technology and it therefore seems appropriate to bring together the relevant tools into a single list. In most cases the brand names listed below are the trade marks of their respective companies and I have accordingly avoided polluting the page with a plethora of symbolic superscripts.

The Internet has been an essential source of reference and insight: the research involved over 1,000 websites, far too many to list as favourites but the Perseus resource of classical texts at *www.perseus.tufts.edu* deserves special mention. Internet-based e-mail was obviously indispensable: over 4,000 messages were generated. Laptop computers and broadband connections made it possible to download, store and process the satellite imagery: the main project files occupied about 20 Gb of storage. The typescript and index were composed in Microsoft Word with the Endnote program used to access and organise the citations and bibliography.

Omnipage OCR and the Anagnostis program were used to scan modern Greek documents into machine-readable text and Systran software then attempted an English translation: despite my abrasive comments in Chapter 18 these generally worked surprisingly well. Google helped with translations from other languages. I dictated some of the text using the Dragon Naturally Speaking voice recognition program although the high proportion of graphic material made this impractical most of the time.

High resolution satellite imagery was acquired from Digital Globe via their Eurimage agency in Rome and this was initially manipulated using the Global Mapper program, which was also used to print out large maps to take to the island. Lower resolution images were acquired from Landsat and other sources as listed. These files were then georeferenced using Oziexplorer which links directly to the Garmin Etrex Vista GPS receiver, enabling waypoints and tracks to be transferred in both directions. Oziexplorer 3D was used for the digital elevation modelling, with altitude data obtained from the Hellenic Military Geographical Service and also from Intrasearch. 1:5000 survey maps were also obtained from HMGS, scanned into TIF images and rotated, cropped and merged using Paintshop Pro. The Leveller program was used to sculpt some of the 3D images to examine the effects of channel infill.

Radarteam's 100 MHz ground-penetrating radar antenna was coupled to GSSI's SIR-3000 and 2000 control units and the resulting data files were analysed by their RADAN software. The Oxford RLAHA facility provided carbon-14 and optically stimulated luminescence dating facilities. The Grant Institute at Edinburgh University provided the auger that was used to extract borehole samples. Alpacka Raft of Alaska was the source of an ultra-lightweight pack raft that facilitated offshore geological inspection.

Over 5,000 photographs were taken using a Nikon Coolpix 5700 digital camera, generally with a wide angle lens and recording on to 1.5 Mb JPG files. The OziPhototool program read the camera file formats and synchronised these with the timestamp on the OziExplorer GPS files, automatically identifying the location of each photograph and marking this on an interactive map. Motorola T6222 walkie-talkies kept the expedition team members in touch while we were measuring distances with a Bushnell Yardage Pro laser rangefinder.

The first expedition in March was professionally filmed by Chris Goodger using a Sony PD150 camera and radio microphones: subsequent visits were captured on a semi-professional basis using Sony DCR-TRV940 equipment. The photograph at Figure 19.1 shows this camera perched precariously on top of a Wimo 18330 glass fibre telescopic tower: somehow it survived the experience.

APPENDIX 4 **A comparison of Homeric theories**

The table that follows these introductory notes summarises the views of twenty-three of the principal theorists since Strabo's time regarding thirty-two of the locations on or near Ithaca that are mentioned in the *Odyssey*. Where a clear opinion on a location is not provided then the corresponding entry in the table has been left blank. Writers who summarise current thinking without adding a new hypothesis and those who focus on the overall voyage rather than on the local topography of Ithaca have been omitted. Also omitted are those imaginative proposals which locate ancient Ithaca in other parts of the world.

The idea of assembling these clues in a spreadsheet emerged in September 2003 and the desire to complete as many cells of it as accurately as possible acted as a spur to locating the relevant publications. I would like to record special thanks to Gilles le Noan and Manolis Pantos who provided hard-to-find copies, some of which are in Greek, Dutch, German or French. I have also been considerably assisted by the comparative reviews contained in several of these books, particularly that of C. H. Goekoop. The analysis represents a joint effort by James Diggle and myself and I would like to acknowledge his painstaking work in digesting some of the more recent theories that have been published only in Greek.

Since the table is provided as an alternative to a detailed textual discussion, the following notes are not exhaustive but are intended only to provide some idea of the historical continuity of this quest and also to emphasise certain key issues and to pay tribute to individual achievements. The name of each publication is in the table and a full reference to each theory can be found in the Bibliography against the name of its proponent.

Strabo's analysis in his *Geography* is remarkably thorough and it has influenced subsequent theorists considerably: his debate about possible alternative meanings of Clue 1 has provided a bolt-hole for many later hypotheses. Ironically Strabo did not appreciate that the isthmus on Cephalonia that he identified as 'often submerged from sea to sea' contained the answer that he was looking for: he thought that ancient and modern Ithaca were the same.

In 1675 Jacob Spon and Sir George Wheler found a town called Dolicha on modern Ithaca, which supports the suggestion that today's Ithaca was ancient Doulichion. However their identification of ancient Ithaca as today's tiny island of Atokos in Spon's 1678 publication *Voyage d'Italie, de Dalmatie, de Grèce et du Levant* was a radical and unpopular proposal.

The modern debate effectively started in 1807 with the publication of William Gell's *The Geography and Antiquities of Ithaca*. He agreed with Strabo that today's island was the same as that of the poet. He proposed that the ancient harbour and city were on the eastern side of the island at or near the present capital of Vathy. He did not regard Dascalion as a credible island for an ambush and instead he suggested that this might have been further south on the promontory of Chelia (now Dihalia), north-east of Sami. He also speculated on the possibility that this promontory might once have been separated from Cephalonia. He had read Strabo's observations on the island and he considered the contribution of Apollodorus, concluding that Homer was mistaken on the matter and that Alalcomenai was located on Ithaca rather than on Asteris.[1]

William Leake travelled to Ithaca in 1806 but it was not until 1835 that he published *Travels in Northern Greece*. He proposed that the ancient city was on the north-western side of modern Ithaca in the Polis Bay–Stavros area, which enabled him to identify Dascalion as the ambush island. Leake had also read Strabo's description and was apparently troubled by it: he says 'As Alcomenæ was certainly not in Asteris, which is too small to contain a town, there is some reason to believe that Strabo mistook the meaning of Apollodorus, and that the latter referred to the situation of Alcomenæ on the isthmus of Ithaca, which is the precise description of Aetó.' Later he adds 'Strabo seems to have a most incorrect idea of Cephalonia, for he states that its circumference was only 300 stades, instead of which it is near 800, and that at the gulf containing the cities of the Cranii and Palenses the island was divided into two parts by an isthmus, so low that it was sometimes covered by the sea.'[2]

William Gladstone's main Homeric publications *Studies on Homer and the Homeric Age* (1858) and *Juventus Mundi: The Gods and Men of the Heroic Age* (1869) cover a wide range of topics including what he refers to as the 'outer geography' – his interpretation of Homer's mental model of the map of the world and Odysseus' voyage upon it. These lengthy analyses do not include a discussion of the local geography of Ithaca but I am indebted to C. H. Goekoop for identifying a pamphlet of Gladstone's which does.[3] In this work Gladstone stuck to the conventional identification of modern Ithaca but he was dissatisfied with Dascalion and he thought that Homer's geography was vague.

Heinrich Schliemann visited Ithaca several times between 1868 and his death in 1890. Like Gell he looked for ancient Ithaca on modern Ithaca near Vathy and in his 1869 publication *Ithaque le Péloponnèse Troie: recherches archéologiques* he attempted to solve the Dascalion problem by suggesting that it had conveniently disappeared.[4] By 10 July 1868 he was confident that he had found not only the royal palace but also the ashes of Odysseus and Penelope, or at the very least those of their near descendants. On 12 July he sat down in a field that he was sure had once belonged to Laertes and he read *Odyssey* Book 24 to an enthralled local audience: 'All eyes were bathed in tears when I had finished my reading . . . They carried me triumphantly to the village.'[5]

Joseph Partsch was a geographer and early geologist: some of the maps of Cephalonia and Ithaca from his 1890 *Kephallenia und Ithaka: Eine geographische Monographie* are still in use today. His main contribution was to dilute the impact of various influential cynics such as Rudolf Hercher and F. A. Wolf, who felt that the *Odyssey* was not the primary work of a single composer but simply an assortment of myths and legends. For them it followed that there was no point in looking for geographic correspondence on Ithaca because the places described were fictitious. Partsch interpreted Homer's 'west' as our north-north-west and he generally supported Leake's proposals, although he differed on the location of Phorcys Bay.

Although Wilhelm Dörpfeld's main publication *Alt-Ithaka: ein Beitrag zur Homer-Frage: Studien und Ausgrabungen aus der Insel Leukas-Ithaka* did not appear until 1927, his theories about Lefkas were formulated from 1900 onwards and articulated in lectures and papers. Writing in 1902 Victor Bérard opposed him vociferously: his theory in *Les Phéniciens et l'Odyssée* was similar to that of Leake and Partsch although he located Doulichion on the small island of Meganisi, south-east of Lefkas.

In 1903 a local historian called Gerasimos Volterras wrote in his *A Critical Study of Homeric Ithaca* 'This isthmus did not exist at the time of Homer, and the peninsula of Pale, commonly known as Paliki, was an independent island; one could perceive that this peninsula was an island at that time because 2,000 years ago the geographer Strabo wrote, quite unambiguously, these words.' Volterras followed this by quoting the relevant passage from Strabo and he added a few pages later that 'In this study we cannot undertake to show how this Homeric island became a quasi-island, because that is the subject of another science, geology, for which such physical phenomena are entirely acceptable and within which one can find copious examples.'[6] Understandably he appears to be in some doubt about how this could have occurred because he later refers to the passage from Riemann that I quote in Chapter 27, that Strabo's suggestion 'seems quite extraordinary because there is not a single place on the island where this could be true'.

Volterras located Phorcys Bay at Atheras Bay and Doulichion at modern Ithaca, but he thought that Asteris was the reef of Vardianoi and he positioned the harbour, city and palace of Ithaca near Lixouri. He realised that Homer's 'mainland' must have been the rest of Cephalonia but he then assumed that the 'region lying opposite' referred to the eastern side of Argostoli Bay opposite Paliki: as James Diggle explains in Appendix 1 in fact it must refer to the region lying opposite ancient Same, i.e. southern Paliki. Volterras' work was not unearthed until after the thesis of this book had been developed but it is fitting to learn that it was a Palikian who predated some of this present research by 100 years. His work does not appear to have been widely circulated and little mention of it occurs in later research. C. H. Goekoop refers to him briefly but the credit for reappraising his contribution belongs to Gilles le Noan (see below).

In 1907 Carl Wilhelm Vollgraff, who had been working with A. E. H. Goekoop, published an article which adhered to the Leake–Partsch–Bérard school of thought that ancient Ithaca was near Polis Bay on modern Ithaca, but he identified Doulichion with Lefkas. Vollgraff had discovered and partially excavated the Polis Bay cave in 1904: it was he who unearthed the votive terracotta inscription referred to in Chapter 33.[7]

Adrian Eliza Herman Goekoop was the grandfather of C. H. Goekoop and as we heard in Chapter 2 he assisted Dörpfeld on Ithaca and Lefkas. In *Ithaque la Grande* in 1908 he published his own theory which was radical in two respects: he challenged the notion that Ithaca itself was an island, maintaining that it was instead a region within a larger island, and he located that region in the south-east of Cephalonia centred around today's imposing castle and hilltop of St George. For A. E. H. Goekoop all the main Homeric locations were on Cephalonia itself: Same was centred around today's eponymous town while Doulichion was a composite name for both Erissos to the north and Paliki to the west. His assiduous study of British Admiralty charts convinced him that Asteris was a partially submerged rock now called the Hydra Bank near a reef called the Montague Rocks between Zacynthos and the Peloponnese.

Dörpfeld eventually published his own magnum opus in 1927. In it as we have seen he proposed that ancient Ithaca was located on Lefkas in the plain of Nidri, that ancient Same was modern Ithaca and that Doulichion was Cephalonia itself. However in view of the lack of a major archaeological find on Lefkas, the fact that Lefkas itself fails to satisfy the 'farthest to the west' requirement and also the need to rename a total of three islands, the theory did not receive widespread support. It did however present the first well-circulated alternative to the status quo and thereafter we find that there are essentially two competing propositions: the conventional Leake–Partsch–Bérard–Vollgraff focus on modern Ithaca versus the radical Dörpfeld solution of Lefkas. This debate became of sufficient interest to merit an appendix of its own in the Loeb edition of Strabo[8] and to be summarised thereafter in most of the leading commentaries.

In the same year of 1927 Lord Rennell of Rodd leapt to the defence of the conventional interpretation with a publication roundly entitled *Homer's Ithaca: A Vindication of Tradition*. His proposal was virtually identical to that of Strabo: he was apparently an insular conservative, disagreeing even with Vollgraff about details such as the location of Doulichion and reverting resoundingly to the classical view. As we heard in Chapter 9 he encouraged the British School of Archaeology in Athens (BSA) to establish an investigation and a team was set up under the leadership of W. A. Heurtley and

Sylvia Benton. The first excavation took place in the autumn of 1930 and was documented in a subsequent BSA report.[9] The overall position, including a description of the tripods in the cave at Polis Bay, was also summarised in an article by Helen Waterhouse published in 1996.[10] The cave and the Pilikata–Stavros area were recently re-examined by Dr C. Morgan of King's College London and Dr A. Soteriou from the 6th Ephorate of the Greek Archaeological Service, and interim summaries have been published by the BSA.[11]

During the 1930s there was continuing activity on the island by Heurtley and Benton and also by Greek archaeologists such as S. Marinatos and M. Oikonomos. A. E. H. Goekoop's widow Dr J. Goekoop-de Jongh defended her husband's theory and added some literary emphasis of her own in a 1933 booklet *La Nesos Homérique* but from a geographical perspective this did not add any new proposals.

The Second World War intervened and the Italians parachuted into Cephalonia on 30 April 1941; on landing they hi-jacked a local bus and took over Argostoli as their headquarters.[12] On 1 August 1943 the Germans occupied Lixouri across the bay, anticipating the signature of the Italian armistice with the Allies on 3 September. Between 15 and 17 September 1943 they mounted a three-pronged invasion of the island from the north, the east and the south-west, using landing-craft and aircraft. The northern group landed at Agia Kiriaki bay on 15 September and proceeded south towards Argostoli and Lixouri, travelling up Strabo's Channel and crossing the mouth of the ancient harbour with tanks and troop transports.[13]

From an archaeological perspective the occupation of the island was not advantageous to the state of the ancient sites in this area and it halted exploration for a long period. The German invasion and the subsequent massacre by the German forces of about 5,000 of the Italian troops after they had surrendered on 24 September has been documented in a recent book by Mark Mazower.[14] The Italian occupation itself was sympathetically portrayed in Louis de Bernières' 1994 novel *Captain Corelli's Mandolin* and the subsequent film of the same name. The activities of the Greek resistance parties were described somewhat less sympathetically and in 2002 Lefteris Eleftheratos of Lixouri published *False Notes from Captain Corelli's Mandolin* to set the record straight. After the Second World War the Greek civil war continued until 1949 and, as Andreas Delaportas explained in Chapter 1, the combination of these two wars and the 1953 earthquake made life on the island very hard: there was consequently mass emigration. In these conditions archaeological field research was not a priority.

In 1965 Dionysios Korkos re-opened A. E. H. Goekoop's hypothesis that ancient Ithaca was located on S.E. Cephalonia, but his work *The Queen of the Ionian Islands* was published in Greek with hand-drawn maps and received little attention.

In 1974 W. B. Stanford and J. V. Luce published *The Quest for Ulysses* and in Chapter 4 we saw that J. V. Luce reviewed the arguments surrounding the location of Ithaca. His views on the main locations were close to those of Vollgraff but he also added some interesting anecdotal material regarding the possible identification of Eumaios' Pigfarm, Raven's Rock and Arethousa Spring, all on the modern island of Ithaca. Luce updated this work with the publication of *Celebrating Homer's Landscapes: Troy and Ithaca Revisited* in 1998 but his theory remained essentially the same.

In 1984 Sarantis Symeonoglou launched an initiative known as *The Odyssey Project* which looked for Odysseus' Palace at the Aetos isthmus of modern Ithaca and thereby reopened the 1807 proposals of William Gell. The 1985–6 issue of *Archaeology in Greece*, the BSA's annual review, commented 'S. Symeonoglou began a reinvestigation in 1984 at Aetos, where a number of buildings dating to the 4th century BC and late Hellenistic times (160–30 BC) are assigned to ancient Alalcomenai (Strabo 10.2.16). Interest attaches to standing Cyclopean masonry, including a wall with doorway recalling structures at Mycenae and Tiryns, identified on Mount Aetos itself.' The identification of Alalcomenai at Aetos appears to follow the proposal made above by Leake in 1835. Work has continued since that time and a current report is available on the project's website.[15]

In 1990 Cees H. Goekoop, the grandson of A. E. H. Goekoop, published *In Search of Ithaca* in Dutch. He adopted his grandfather's proposal that Ithaca was previously a region of Cephalonia rather than an island in its own right, but he reversed the identification of Ithaca city and Doulichion. Whereas his grandfather had located Ithaca city in S.E. Cephalonia and Doulichion in Erissos and Paliki, C. H. Goekoop placed ancient Ithaca in Erissos (at Fiscardo) and Doulichion became the rest of the island apart from that northern peninsula. The suggestion that Ithaca was not an island was a difficult proposition to sell but C. H. Goekoop's methodology and research were outstanding: included in the significant debt that I owe him is an appreciation of the importance of analysing the local geography from the many clues provided in the *Odyssey*. I understand that an English translation of Goekoop's book is currently being undertaken by Manolis Pantos of the Archaeometry Unit of Daresbury Laboratory and his colleagues: further details may be available at the website listed under his name in the Bibliography. There are many good reasons why this book should reach a wider audience: one of them is that Cees Goekoop explains in his Foreword that 'It all started with a question from my daughter Marije.'

In 1998 Nikolas Livadas published a book in Greek that was translated into English two years later under the title *Odysseus' Ithaca: The Riddle Solved*. Although he did not believe that Paliki was once separated from mainland Cephalonia, he located ancient Ithaca harbour and city at the present site of Livadi village on the north-western side of Argostoli Bay, corresponding to the site that I have proposed for Rheithron Bay. He thought that Odysseus' Palace was on the adjacent hilltop of Crikellos that I have identified as Crocyleia and he pinpointed Atheras Bay as ancient Phorcys Bay. Livadas also suggested that by 'the mainland' Homer meant the main land opposite ancient Ithaca, in other words the rest of Cephalonia. Some of his proposals were more fanciful: he noted Strabo's observations but suggested that the isthmus to which he was referring was the now submerged sandbank between Vardianoi island and the south-eastern tip of Paliki, and Doulichion itself was rather surprisingly transferred to the Argostoli peninsula. However Livadas made a significant contribution to this ancient puzzle, one that is especially appropriate in view of his name and his local origins. I should add that I was unaware of his work when I first formulated my own proposals.

Also in 1998 Ourania Tsimaratos, daughter of Evangelos Tsimaratos, a teacher at Lixouri High School, posthumously published her father's manuscript entitled *Which is Homeric Ithaca?*. E. Tsimaratos lived from 1874 to 1954 and his proposition was that Strabo's Channel was once a seaway and ancient Ithaca was on E. Cephalonia, while Paliki was actually Same. Today's Ithaca was Doulichion, Asteris was Vardianoi island and Phorcys Bay was at Fiscardo. It is delightful to learn that Tsimaratos, who lived for so long at Lixouri, was prepared to entertain the possibility that the isthmus near his home town was once a seaway (although he does not propose a geological mechanism for this) but it is strange that he then ceded the advantage of identifying Ithaca as 'farthest to the west' in favour of locating it on the opposite land mass. On the cover of Tsimaratos' book is a copy of a *c.* 1740 map of the Ionian Islands engraved by Tobias Conrad Lotter that identifies Doulichion as modern Ithaca.[16]

In 2000 Henriette Putman Cramer and Gerasimos Metaxas published a book proposing that today's Ithaca was Homer's Same. They suggested that ancient Ithaca was at Poros in S.E. Cephalonia and that Doulichion was on Paliki.

In 2001 Gilles le Noan published *A la recherche d'Ithaque* and he followed this in 2003 with *La ferme d'Eumée*. These were provided on interactive CD-ROM as well as being published in book form and le Noan presented a wealth of supportive research, rare historical texts and maps in support of his case, which is that ancient Ithaca was indeed Paliki but it had never been separated from Cephalonia. After quoting from Volterras (see above) he went on to say 'But contrary to what Volterras imagined, all the geologists consulted on this question are quite categorical: the peninsula of Paliki has been attached to the rest of Cephalonia for a long time and it is impossible that the isthmus could have elevated itself by 180 m in only 30 centuries.'[17]

On the matter of Asteris and Doulichion le Noan and I are in agreement, but he was undecided on the location of Phorcys Bay and also that of the ancient harbour, city and palace. He initially located them towards the northern end of Paliki but in his later work he proposed a more southerly location. Le Noan's researches contain much that is admirable and, as I have recorded in Chapter 21, when I received his CD-ROM in June 2003 it was instrumental in providing a series of historical references. He also obtained and most generously made available to me copies of the publications of Volterras (1903), Riemann (1879) and other relatively inaccessible writers, as well as a splendid analysis of Cephalonian place names written by the eminent local historian Ilias Tsitselis in 1877. James Diggle has combed these works for additional clues but with the exception of the above-mentioned work of Volterras there do not seem to be any further qualitative proposals therein.

As this book was going to print le Noan published a third treatise *Le Palais d'Ulysse* in which he confirms his opinion about Paliki: 'Where his [Volterras'] theory is erroneous is only in so far as having regarded the peninsula of Paliki as an independent island in the time of Homer.'[18] In considering the location of Odysseus' Palace le Noan lists eight candidate hilltops which include Crikellos, Mesovouni and Kastelli before coming to the conclusion that ancient Pale, just north of Lixouri, is the most likely.[19]

In 2002 Matthias Steinhart and Eckhard Wirbelauer published *Aus der Heimat des Odysseus* which provides a well-documented and richly illustrated account of the rediscovery of Cephalonia and Ithaca by travellers and archaeologists from the middle ages onwards. My copy arrived as this typescript was being sent to the publisher and in thoughtful consideration of my non-existent German, James Diggle digested it in record time. He notes that the writers have independently identified material quoted in this book from Buondelmonti, Spon, Wheler, Gell, Leake and others, but its central question is not their concern.

Finally, also in 2002 Christos Tzakos proposed in *A Brief Essay on Homeric Ithaca* that ancient Ithaca and modern Ithaca were one and the same, but he identified Same (correctly) as the mainland. In a previous article he defended Dascalion as Asteris on the grounds that the identification of Homer's description of the ambush location as 'in between Ithaca and Same' fitted this barren reef if the two harbours were located at Fiscardo and Polis Bay.[20] He has made several additional contributions to the excellent Cephalonian annual cultural digest *Odusseia*, including a spirited defence of the reason why the name Kefallinia should always be spelt with a double L. He argues that the word comes from Kefalos, an ancient Achaian warrior, and Ellines (Greeks).[21]

This etymological debate will doubtless run on: indeed it is tempting to suppose that the name of the island is in some way related to the fact that *kefale* means 'head' in both ancient and modern Greek. In the light of the previous chapters perhaps we may empathise with those Cephalonians past and present who secretly regard themselves as Head of the Greeks.

	1	2	3	4	5	6
	Strabo	Spon & Wheler	Gell	Leake	Gladstone	Schliemann
Year published	1 AD	1678	1807	1835	1863	1869
Publication	Geography	Voyage d'Italie, de Dalmatie, de Grèce et du Levant	The Geography and Antiquities of Ithaca	Travels in Northern Greece	The dominions of Odysseus, and the island group of the Odyssey	Ithaque Le Peloponnèse Troie: Recherches Archéologiques
Summary	ancient Ithaca = modern Ithaca; Homer's "west" was different from ours	ancient Ithaka = Atokos	ancient Ithaca = modern Ithaca; city is at Aetos isthmus	ancient Ithaca = modern Ithaca; city is at Polis Bay	ancient Ithaca = modern Ithaca; Homer's geography was wrong	ancient Ithaca = modern Ithaca; Asteris disappeared in an earthquake
1 **Clue 1:** Does Ithaca lie low and to the west, the furthest out to sea of a group of neighbouring islands called Ithaca, Same, Doulichion and Zacynthos?	No: he disputes the meaning of these words [10.2.12]	No	No	No	No	No
2 **Clue 2:** Does Ithaca contain a bay with two distinctive jutting headlands?		No	Debatable	Debatable	Debatable	Debatable
3 **Clue 3:** Can a ship leave Ithaca harbour driven by a stiff following wind from the west?	No: harbour exit faces to the west because "the Cephallenian strait was being guarded by the suitors" [8.3.26]	Yes	With difficulty	No: harbour exit faces to the west	No: harbour exit faces to the west	With considerable difficulty
4 **Clue 4:** Is there a two-harboured island called Asteris in the straits between Ithaca and Same, with windy heights that would enable an ambush to take place?	No: "not even a good anchorage" [1.3.18]	No straits	Not an island	No windy heights	Agrees that there is no double harbour at Dascalion	Disappeared in earthquake
5 Was Strabo's Channel submerged?	"Often submerged from sea to sea" [10.2.15]	No	No	No	No	No
6 Same / Samos	Cephalonia [10.2.10]	Cephalonia	Cephalonia	Cephalonia	E Cephalonia	
7 Doulichion	Echinades [8.2.2, 10.2.10,19]	modern Ithaca	Kalamos, Meganisi or part of Cephalonia	Petala in the Echinades	W Cephalonia	
8 Zacynthos	Zacynthos [10.2.18]	Zacynthos	Zacynthos	Zacynthos	Zacynthos	Zacynthos
9 ancient Ithaca (region)	modern Ithaca [8.3.26]	Atokos	modern Ithaca	modern Ithaca	modern Ithaca	modern Ithaca
10 ancient Ithaca (harbour)	Polis Bay [8.3.26]		Schoenus, Vathy, Dexia and Molo coves	Polis Bay	Polis Bay	
11 ancient Ithaca (city)			Aetos isthmus	Polis (now Stavros)	Polis (now Stavros)	Aetos isthmus
12 ancient Ithaca (palace)			Aetos isthmus			
13 Asteris: ambush bay	Probably Dascalion [1.3.18]		Cape Dichelia (on E Cephalonia)	Dascalion	Homer's geography was faulty	Disappeared in earthquake
14 Asteris: twin harbours	"not even a good anchorage" [1.3.18]		Bays on each side of Cape Dichelia			
15 Asteris: Alalcomenai	Quotes Apollodorus [10.2.16]		Probably at Pilikata	Thought Apollodorus meant Aetos isthmus		
16 Phorcys Bay: location			Dexia Bay	Ikonios (Skhino)	Ikonios (Skhino)	Dexia Bay
17 Phorcys Bay: Cave of the Nymphs	Disappeared [1.3.18]		Fallen in			
18 Telemachos' landfall	W of modern Ithaca [10.2.26]		Near Marathia			
19 Mount Neriton	On modern Ithaca [10.2.11]		Anogi (N Ithaca)	Anogi (N Ithaca)	Mt. Marovugli or Stefano (near Vathy)	
20 Eumaios: Arethousa Spring			Marathia, above Parapegada islet	Below Koraka		
21 Eumaios: Pigfarm			Marathia, above Parapegada islet			
22 Eumaios: Raven's Rock			Marathia, above Parapegada islet	Koraka, N summit of Mt Oxoi		
23 Eumaios: Hollow rock breaking north wind						
24 Eumaios: Hermes' Hill				S. summit of Mt Oxoi		
25 Laertes' farm			Lefki, west of Anogi			
26 Rheithron: Bay				Bay of Afales		
27 Rheithron: Stream						
28 Mount Neïon	Possibly = Neriton? [10.2.11]			Mt Oxoi	Anogi (N Ithaca)	
29 Nericon	"belonged to Leucas" [10.2.8, 1.3.18]		On Lefkas, hilltop S of Lefkas town			
30 Crocyleia	"belonged to Leucas" [10.2.8]			Vathy	Region of Ithaca	
31 Aigilips	"belonged to Leucas" [10.2.8]			Anoi	Region of Ithaca	
32 Scherie (Phaiacians)	"unpardonable to call it Corfu" [7.3.6]					

FIGURE A4.1(a) A comparative table of Homeric theories

	7	8	9	10	11	12
	Partsch	Bérard	Volterras	Vollgraff	A E H Goekoop	Dörpfeld
Year published	1890	1902	1903	1907	1908	1927
Publication	Kephallenia und Ithaka	Les Phéniciens et l'Odyssée	A critical study of Homeric Ithaca	Dulichion-Leukas	Ithaque la Grande	Alt-Ithaka
Summary	ancient Ithaca = modern Ithaca; by W Homer means NW	ancient Ithaca = modern Ithaca; Homer's geography was wrong	ancient Ithaca = Paliki, cut off by a navigable Strabo's Channel	ancient Ithaca = modern Ithaca; Homer's geography was wrong	ancient Ithaca = SE Cephalonia, city is at St George's hilltop	ancient Ithaca = Lefkas
1 Clue 1: Does Ithaca lie low and to the west, the furthest out to sea of a group of neighbouring islands called Ithaca, Same, Doulichion and Zacynthos?	No	No	Yes	No	No	No (Lefkada is not westmost even if it was then an island)
2 Clue 2: Does Ithaca contain a bay with two distinctive jutting headlands?	Debatable	Debatable	Yes	Debatable	Debatable	Debatable
3 Clue 3: Can a ship leave Ithaca harbour driven by a stiff following wind from the west?	No: harbour exit faces to the west	No: harbour exit faces to the west	Yes	No: harbour exit faces to the west	No: harbour exit faces to the west (on Same)	No: harbour exit faces to the north
4 Clue 4: Is there a two-harboured island called Asteris in the straits between Ithaca and Same, with windy heights that would enable an ambush to take place?	No windy heights	No windy heights	No windy heights	No windy heights	No windy heights	No straits
5 Was Strabo's Channel submerged?	No	No	Yes	No	No	No
6 Same / Samos		Cephalonia	Cephalonia	Cephalonia	E Cephalonia	modern Ithaca
7 Doulichion		Meganisi	modern Ithaca	Lefkas	Erissos and Paliki	Cephalonia
8 Zacynthos	Zacynthos	Zacynthos	Zacynthos	Zacynthos	Zacynthos	Zacynthos
9 ancient Ithaca (region)	modern Ithaca	modern Ithaca	Paliki	modern Ithaca	SE Cephalonia	Lefkas
10 ancient Ithaca (harbour)	Polis Bay	Polis Bay	Karabostasi, N of Lixouri, now silted up	Polis Bay	Minies (near airport)	Vlicho bay
11 ancient Ithaca (city)	Polis (now Stavros)	Polis (now Stavros)	Palaiokastron, N of Lixouri	Polis (now Stavros)	Mazarakata	Plain of Nidri
12 ancient Ithaca (palace)					St George's hill	
13 Asteris: ambush bay	Dascalion	Dascalion	Vardianoi	Dascalion	Hydra Bank, near Montague Rocks	Arkoudi
14 Asteris: twin harbours						
15 Asteris: Alalcomenai						
16 Phorcys Bay: location	Vathy harbour	Vathy harbour	Atheras Bay	Dexia Bay	Koroni Bay (SE Cephalonia)	Syvota Bay (Lefkas)
17 Phorcys Bay: Cave of the Nymphs			Melissospelia (N of Atheras Harbour)		Valeriano	
18 Telemachos' landfall					Katelios, SE Cephalonia	
19 Mount Neriton		Mt Stefano (S Ithaca)	Mt. Lakties, by Atheras		Mt Aenos	Elati mountains (Lefkas)
20 Eumaios: Arethousa Spring			Chavdata		Mavrata	
21 Eumaios: Pigfarm			Chavdata		Near Katelios	
22 Eumaios: Raven's Rock			Chavdata		Cape Koroni (SE Cephalonia)	
23 Eumaios: Hollow rock breaking north wind						
24 Eumaios: Hermes' Hill			Vouno (S Paliki)			
25 Laertes' farm			S Paliki			
26 Rheithron: Bay			Karabostasi, N of Lixouri, now silted up		Kutavos (Argostoli inner harbour)	
27 Rheithron: Stream						
28 Mount Neïon					St George's hill	
29 Nericon			Same (E Cephalonia)			Acarnania, opposite Lefkas
30 Crocyleia			somewhere on Paliki			
31 Aigilips			somewhere on Paliki			
32 Scherie (Phaiacians)		Corfu: city = Paleocastritsa				

FIGURE A4.1(b) (cont.)

		13	14	15	16	17	18
		Rennell	Korkos	Luce	Symeonoglou	C H Goekoop	Tsimaratos
	Year published	1927	1965	1974 / 1998	1984	1990	1998
	Publication	Homer's Ithaca: a vindication of tradition	The Queen of the Ionian Islands	(i) The Quest for Ulysses; (ii) Celebrating Homer's Landscapes	The Odyssey Project (website)	Op zoek naar Ithaka	Which is Homeric Ithaca? [posthumous ms 1954]
	Summary	ancient Ithaca = modern Ithaca; city is at Polis Bay	ancient Ithaca = SE Cephalonia	ancient Ithaca = modern Ithaca; city is at Polis Bay	ancient Ithaca = modern Ithaca; Alalcomenai = Ithaca city at Aetos	Ithaca was not an island: it was N Cephalonia	Channel was submerged, Doulichion = modern Ithaca, ancient Ithaca = Cephalonia
1	Clue 1: Does Ithaca lie low and to the west, the furthest out to sea of a group of neighbouring islands called Ithaca, Same, Doulichion and Zacynthos?	No	No	No	No	No (even if Ithaca was not an island, Erissos is not westmost)	No
2	Clue 2: Does Ithaca contain a bay with two distinctive jutting headlands?	Debatable	Debatable	Debatable	Debatable	Debatable	Debatable
3	Clue 3: Can a ship leave Ithaca harbour driven by a stiff following wind from the west?	No: harbour exit faces to the west		No: harbour exit faces to the west	With considerable difficulty	Yes	Yes
4	Clue 4: Is there a two-harboured island called Asteris in the straits between Ithaca and Same, with windy heights that would enable an ambush to take place?	No windy heights		No windy heights	No windy heights; island is too far north for an ambush	No (the two harbours are not on Asteris)	No windy heights
5	Was Strabo's Channel submerged?	No	No	No	No	No	Yes
6	Same / Samos	Cephalonia		Cephalonia		modern Ithaca	W Cephalonia (Paliki)
7	Doulichion	Echinades		Lefkas		Cephalonia excluding Erissos	modern Ithaca
8	Zacynthos	Zacynthos	Zacynthos	Zacynthos	Zacynthos	Zacynthos	Zacynthos
9	ancient Ithaca (region)	modern Ithaca	SE Cephalonia	modern Ithaca	modern Ithaca	Erissos	Cephalonia (Krani-Same district)
10	ancient Ithaca (harbour)	Polis Bay		Polis Bay		Fiskardo	
11	ancient Ithaca (city)	Pilikata (nr Stavros)		Pilikata (nr Stavros)	Aetos isthmus	Fiskardo	
12	ancient Ithaca (palace)	Pilikata (nr Stavros)		Pilikata (nr Stavros)	Aetos isthmus	Fiskardo	
13	Asteris: ambush bay	Dascalion		Dascalion: adjacent coves of Cephalonia		Dascalion: adjacent coves of Cephalonia	Vardianoi
14	Asteris: twin harbours			Dascalion: adjacent coves of Cephalonia		Ithaca & Cephalonia, by Dascalion	
15	Asteris: Alalcomenai				Identifed as on Aetos isthmus		
16	Phorcys Bay: location	Dexia Bay		Dexia Bay		Assos Bay	Fiskardo
17	Phorcys Bay: Cave of the Nymphs	Marmarospilia		Marmarospilia		Assos Bay	
18	Telemachos' landfall			Palia Lugia or Ormos Andri		Vigli, W Erissos	
19	Mount Neriton			Mt Anogi		Kalon Oros, south of Erissos	Mt Aenos
20	Eumaios: Arethousa Spring			Marathia			
21	Eumaios: Pigfarm			Marathia		Between Kalon Oros and Fiskardo	
22	Eumaios: Raven's Rock			Marathia			
23	Eumaios: Hollow rock breaking north wind						
24	Eumaios: Hermes' Hill					Part of the Neïon range	
25	Laertes' farm					Near Antipata, NW Erissos	
26	Rheithron: Bay			Phrikes Bay		NE of Fiskardo	
27	Rheithron: Stream			runs through Phrikes village		Not a stream: refers to high waves	
28	Mount Neïon			Mt Exogi		N Erissos	a ridge of Mt Aenos
29	Nericon					South of Lefkas town	
30	Crocyleia					S Erissos	
31	Aigilips					Part of Cephalonia	
32	Scherie (Phaiacians)			Corfu		Not Corfu	

FIGURE A4.1(c) (cont.)

	19	20	21	22	23
	Livadas	Cramer & Metaxas	Le Noan	Tzakos	Bittlestone, Diggle & Underhill
Year published	1998	2000	2001/2003/2004	2002	2005
Publication	Odysseus' Ithaca: The Riddle Solved	Homeric Ithaca	(i) A la recherche d'Ithaque; (ii) La ferme d'Eumée (iii) Le Palais d'Ulysse	A brief essay on Homeric Ithaca	Odysseus Unbound: The Search for Homer's Ithaca
Summary	ancient Ithaca = Paliki, but it was always joined with Cephalonia	ancient Ithaca = SE Cephalonia	ancient Ithaca = Paliki, but it was always joined with Cephalonia	ancient Ithaca = modern Ithaca	ancient Ithaca = Paliki, cut off by a navigable Strabo's Channel
1 **Clue 1:** Does Ithaca lie low and to the west, the furthest out to sea of a group of neighbouring islands called Ithaca, Same, Doulichion and Zacynthos?	Only if Doulichion was Argostoli peninsula	No	Only if Ithaca itself was a peninsula not an island	No	Yes
2 **Clue 2:** Does Ithaca contain a bay with two distinctive jutting headlands?	Yes	Debatable	Debatable	Debatable	Yes
3 **Clue 3:** Can a ship leave Ithaca harbour driven by a stiff following wind from the west?	Yes		Yes	No: harbour exit faces E	Yes
4 **Clue 4:** Is there a two-harboured island called Asteris in the straits between Ithaca and Same, with windy heights that would enable an ambush to take place?	No windy heights		Yes (Asteris was Argostoli peninsula)	No windy heights	Yes (Asteris was Argostoli peninsula)
5 Was Strabo's Channel submerged?	Yes: but as the reef between Vardianoi and SE Paliki	No	No	No	Yes
6 Same / Samos	modern Ithaca	modern Ithaca	Cephalonia, excluding Paliki	Cephalonia	Cephalonia, excluding Paliki
7 Doulichion	Argostoli peninsula	Paliki	modern Ithaca	Leucas or Echinades or Strophades	modern Ithaca
8 Zacynthos	Zacynthos	Zacynthos	Zacynthos	Zacynthos	Zacynthos
9 ancient Ithaca (region)	Cephalonia, but also Paliki on its own	SE Cephalonia	Paliki	modern Ithaca	Paliki, cut off by Strabo's Channel
10 ancient Ithaca (harbour)	Livadi		W side of Argostoli Bay	Polis Bay	NW end of Argostoli Bay
11 ancient Ithaca (city)	Livadi	Poros	Oikopeda or Pale, N of Lixouri	Pilikata (nr Stavros)	Kastelli
12 ancient Ithaca (palace)	Crikellos Hill, Livadi		Oikopeda or Pale, N of Lixouri	Pilikata (nr Stavros)	Kastelli summit
13 Asteris: ambush bay	Dascalion: adjacent coves of Cephalonia		Argostoli peninsula	Dascalion	Argostoli peninsula at Paliostafida Bay
14 Asteris: twin harbours	On Cephalonia opposite Dascalion		Paliostafida & Makris Gialos	Fiskardo and Polis Bay	Paliostafida Bay & Argostoli harbour
15 Asteris: Alalcomenai	Identified on the reef of Strabo's isthmus				Mount Gerasimos
16 Phorcys Bay: location	Atheras Bay	Gulf of Sami	Atheras Bay or Ag. Kiriaki or Kaloudakia		Atheras Bay
17 Phorcys Bay: Cave of the Nymphs	W end of Atheras Bay	Melissane	Kaloudakia: location unknown		SE end of Atheras Bay
18 Telemachos' landfall	Atheras Bay	Cape Mounda			Agni Bay
19 Mount Neriton	Mt Aenos (on Cephalonia)	Mt Aenos			Mt Lakties, by Atheras
20 Eumaios: Arethousa Spring			Possibly near Lixouri		SE of Atheras below Mt Lakties
21 Eumaios: Pigfarm			Possibly near Lixouri		SE of Atheras below Mt Lakties
22 Eumaios: Raven's Rock		Kotylas near Koronai	Multiple locations considered		Escarpment SW of Mt Lakties
23 Eumaios: Hollow rock breaking north wind					NE corner of Eumaios Pigfarm
24 Eumaios: Hermes' Hill	Crikellos Hill, Livadi	Pierovouni, above Poros			Southern foothill of Mt Lakties
25 Laertes' farm	Between Platies Strates and Halkes		S of Lixouri, poss Lipeda or St George		On Atheras road N of Petani fork
26 Rheithron: Bay	Samoli, S of Livadi	River Vochyna at estuary near Poros			Samoli, S of Livadi and Akro Samoli point
27 Rheithron: Stream	Kleisoura, emerging at Akros Louros				Akro Samoli point, S of Livadi
28 Mount Neïon	Mount Milo	Above Poros			N-S ridge along W Paliki; summit is Mt Milo
29 Nericon	Krani		On Lefkas		On Lefkas, hilltop S of Lefkas town
30 Crocyleia	South of Agios Efemia	Kokylia		Arkoudi	Crikellos hillside
31 Aigilips	Erissos	Pyrgi		Atokos	Katochori hillside
32 Scherie (Phaiacians)	Corfu				Corfu

FIGURE A4.1(d) *(cont.)*

Notes

1 In this view Gell cited Plutarch as his authority: see Appendix 1 Section B for James Diggle's rebuttal.

2 Leake (1835) vol. III, pp. 48, 60.

3 Goekoop (1990) p. 132 n. 21. In his footnote Goekoop refers to Gladstone (1863) and explains that 'This writing of W. E Gladstone was located only with great difficulty. With the help of the Bodleian Library in Oxford, a single known copy was traced to the Public Library in New York, where my collaborator, Ms M. A. van der Vlugt, was able to copy it.' Fortunately a more accessible version appears in the October 1877 issue of Macmillan's Magazine.

4 From Runnels (2002) pp. 25–7 we learn that Schliemann's first publication of this work was in French. The frequently cited German edition was translated by Carl Andress and published later that year.

5 Quoted in Deuel and Schliemann (1978) pp. 138–9.

6 Volterras (1903) pp. 35, 37 quoted in le Noan (2003) pp. 22–3.

7 Payne (1930–1) p. 196.

8 For a discussion and bibliography of 'The Ithaca–Leucas problem' see the Appendix to vol. V, Books 10–12, pp. 523–9 in Jones (1917–32).

9 Payne (1930–1) p. 195.

10 Waterhouse (1996).

11 See Chapter 21 n.9.

12 See www.geocities.com/kumbayaaa/itroyparadropkephalonia1941.html

13 See www.geocities.com/Athens/Agora/6062/travelogues/conflict.html which is an English translation based on the Greek text of 'About Kefalonia' by Kosmas P. Fokas-Kosmetatos. From this we learn that an air raid shelter was constructed on the Spelia hilltop (near the presumed site of Alalcomenai) and a '7 metres deep, 10 metres long anti-tank trench was built in the middle of Kranea Plain' (near ancient Cranioi). See also Randsborg (2002) p. 26.

14 Mazower (2001) p. 150.

15 See Catling (1985–6) p. 55 and Symeonoglou (1984). At Luce (1998) p. 247 we read that 'Symeonoglu [sic] has published summary reports of his work in *Ergon* (1984, 1986, 1987, 1990, 1992) and a fuller account in *Praktika* (1986): 234–40.'

16 Seutter et al. (1744).

17 Le Noan (2003) p. 24.

18 Le Noan (2004) p. 17.

19 Le Noan (2004) pp. 63–5: 'That is why the site of ancient Pale remains the most simple and reasonable site since it is traditionally known as the site of the ancient capital of the peninsula.' On page 72 le Noan adds 'We have however seen that we could possibly also look for the palace of Ulysses on the hills of Crikellos, Misouvouni or Castelli which were perhaps also inhabited in the Homeric period.'

20 Tzakos (1999) p. 95.

21 Tzakos (2000).

The typescript of this book was committed to Cambridge University Press towards the end of 2004 but a few pages were left open here for the addition of late-breaking news. Such news did indeed arrive, in three separate categories. The first was encouraging and the second unexpected: but the third was more terrible than anyone could have imagined.

Preliminary scientific dating

During July and August 2004 Christopher Bronk Ramsey and Jean-Luc Schwenninger of the Oxford Research Laboratory for Archaeology and the History of Art (RLAHA) collected preliminary samples for scientific dating under the scope of John Underhill's permit from IGME, the Institute of Geology and Mineral Exploration in Athens. These pilot trials were performed in order to learn about field conditions on the island with a view to designing a more extensive range of subsequent age assessments.

The scope of the work was not intended to provide a comprehensive test of the proposals of this book: that will come later as part of 'Phase B'. Nevertheless it is thought-provoking that none of the results obtained to date contradict the two main geological hypotheses: that Strabo's Channel was a marine seaway in the late Bronze Age around 1200 BC and that the land mass of Cephalonia was at that time considerably lower than it is today.

Samples were collected from the following areas:

(a) Raised beach north-east of Agia Kiriaki
(b) Palaeolake (Lake Katochori)
(c) Agni Cove
(d) Agia Kiriaki Beach (the presumed northern channel exit)
(e) South of Agia Sotira (the presumed southern channel exit)
(f) Rockfall on road section in Petrikata
(g) Atheras Bay

Samples for radiocarbon dating (C14) included root tissue, plant fragments, shells, limpets, bone material and charcoal. Samples for optically stimulated luminescence (OSL) dating included calcite, soil and some small ceramic fragments. After discarding samples that yielded no results, diagnostic age ranges were obtained for nineteen samples drawn from all locations apart from (g). These are summarised in Figure A5.1 and can be interpreted as follows.

(a) Raised beach north-east of Agia Kiriaki

Inconclusive results: Sample 1 (OSL), a fragment from an embedded rock, yielded a 'Last exposed to light' date of at least 300,000 years ago. This is before the last interglacial period when the beach would certainly have been immersed, so this sample is clearly not reflecting marine immersion in any period. OSL tests involve the average of multiple individual grains from a given sample (see below) and on a raised beach multiple such samples will be needed to provide adequate coverage. Sample 2 (C14), a shell, yielded a date range from AD 1495 to 1670 and was probably thrown up by high waves during the mediaeval period.

(b) Palaeolake (Lake Katochori)

Inconclusive results: Samples 3 and 4 (OSL) were both drawn from the same test pit in the centre of the lake and their dates for last exposure to light agree fairly closely at around 12,500 years 'Before Present' (1950) i.e. about 10500 BC. Sample 5 (C14) was also taken from the test pit and is from within the last few decades, suggesting root penetration or disturbance by burrowing animals.

At first sight the dates for samples 3 and 4 seem to present a problem but in interpreting these it is important to bear in mind the nature of the OSL test process. Each test is performed on an aluminium disc which typically contains around 2,000 individual grains and the resulting age reading is an average across all of these grains. Consequently an average age of 12500 BC for a disc could emerge from an infinite number of possible grain age distributions, including variants such as:

(a) Each of the 2,000 grains was last exposed to light in 12500 BC;
(b) 50% of the grains were last exposed to light in AD 0 and the remaining 50% in BC 25000;
(c) 10% of the grains were last exposed to light in AD 0 and the remaining 90% around 14000 BC.

Outcomes other than (a) typically reflect a mixing process whereby grains of different light-activated age are brought together. John Underhill comments:

The sediments in the lake were deposited subaqueously and so never saw the light of day. Consequently we might expect grains to yield ages of when they last saw light (were exposed) before being deposited in the lake. If those grains were buried (no longer exposed to light at the surface) and then transported subaqueously (by rivers)

Line	Field code	Location	Sample type	Test	Age diagnosis
1	KEF04-02	Raised beach NE of Agia Kiriaki	Bloc sample	OSL	Last exposed to light > 300,000 years ago
2	KEF/H/1	Raised beach NE of Agia Kiriaki	Shell, *pattela vulgata*, 5.4 m a.s.l.	C14	AD 1495–1670
3	KEF04-06	Palaeolake (Lake Katochori) *centre*	Soil from pit 0.5 m deep	OSL	Last exposed to light 12,550 ± 1,250 years ago
4	KEF04-07	Palaeolake (Lake Katochori) *centre*	Soil from pit 1.15 m deep	OSL	Last exposed to light 12,290 ± 3,600 years ago
5	KEF/G/X2157	Palaeolake (Lake Katochori) *centre*	Root tissue or aquatic plant 1.15 m deep	C14	AD 1990–2000 or possibly AD 1955–65
6	KEF04-08	Agni Cove *at intersection of green and red radar scans on Figure 31.1.*	Soil from sampling tube, 0.55 m deep	OSL	Last exposed to light > 65,000 years ago
7	KEF04-09	Agni Cove *at intersection of green and red radar scans on Figure 31.1.*	Soil from sampling tube, 1 m deep	OSL	Last exposed to light 72,300 ± 7,000 years ago
8	KEF/C/1	Agni Cove *30 m inland from shore*	Shell, *columbella rustica*, 5.2 m above sea level	C14	After AD 1830
9	KEF/C/2	Agni Cove *30 m inland from shore*	Shell, *pattela vulgata*, 5.2 m above sea level.	C14	After AD 1950
10	KEF04-10	Agia Kiriaki	Ceramic fragment in beach wall	OSL	Last exposed to light < 150 years ago
11	KEF04-11	Agia Kiriaki	Ceramic fragment in beach wall	OSL	Last exposed to light < 1,390 ± 180 years ago
12	KEF04-15	Agia Kiriaki	Ceramic fragment in beach wall	OSL	Last exposed to light < 100 years ago
13	KEF04-16	Agia Kiriaki	Ceramic fragments in beach wall	OSL	Last exposed to light 390 ± 60 years ago
14	KEF04-19	Agia Kiriaki	Bloc sample from beach wall	OSL	Last exposed to light 1,140 ± 370 years ago
15	KEF/F/04-16	Agia Kiriaki	Bone of dog embedded in beach wall	C14	AD 1655–1950
16	KEF/F/04-17	Agia Kiriaki	Charcoal in beach wall	C14	AD 1680–1950
17	KEF/F/X2169	Agia Kiriaki	Fine roots in situ or reworked	C14	After AD 2000 or possibly AD 1955–60
18	KEF/A/3	South of Agia Sotira	Loose shell – *vermetus triqueter*	C14	After AD 1950
19	KEF04-22	Rockslide in Petrikata	Rockslide bag sample	OSL	Last exposed to light 80,000 ± 5,400 years ago

FIGURE A5.1 Results of scientific dating

into the lake, then it would be expected that the ages would be considerably older than the lake deposition itself. Only the transport of grains from the contemporaneous exposed margins of the lake would give a precise date for deposition within the lake itself, and there may only be a very few of these. Hence, only the youngest grain dates would be important, which means that individual grain age counts matter.

(c) Agni Cove

Consistent results: Samples 6 and 7 (OSL) were collected from a borehole drilled by a hand auger in very hard compacted soil at the intersection of the green and red radar scans on Figure 31.1. This location is above the terrace at which the radar detected salt water inundation and consequently the expected age is the last interglacial period. The result 'Last exposed to light > 70,000 years ago' is consistent with this. John comments:

I am happy with this. I have always expected this bay fill to become progressively younger to the south-west, reflecting progressive beach ridge progradation and burial up until the present day.

Samples 8 and 9 (C14) yielded dates after AD 1832 and although they were located 30 m from the shore it is likely that they were thrown up by waves or transported subsequently.

(d) Agia Kiriaki Beach

Consistent results: Samples 10–17 were collected close to the buried wall of Figure 31.2. The first five of these were OSL and yielded a range of earliest dates between AD 600 and 1940, averaging around AD 1400. The remaining three were C14; the latest of these was on root material likely to date from the last few years and relates to recent plant growth but samples 15 and 16 yielded a date range between 1655 and 1950 and are likely to date landslip events.

These dates suggest that the samples came from landslips that took place during the mediaeval and later periods. It is important to recognise that the surface that we see today in Thinia is the result of a sequence of landslips over a widely spaced period, not a single event. Figure A2.24 in John's Appendix 2 makes this sequence clear and his assessment of these results is as follows:

These Zola beach pottery samples are entirely consistent with historical landslips, something that we know has been happening over the past couple of centuries at least from local accounts. Age ranges such as this are in keeping with the working hypothesis.

(e) South of Agia Sotira

No useful results: Sample 18 is a C14-dated shell which yielded an age after AD 1950 and is therefore a recent marine deposit.

(f) Rockslide on road section in Petrikata

Consistent results: An OSL sample collected in Petrikata (see map at Figure 16.2) yielded a date of *c.* 78000 BC. Further tests in this area will be needed to determine if this result is reliable: if so it may indicate that some of the earlier landslips took place at that time. As John's Figure A2.24 makes clear, such events would not have blocked the channel. Alternatively the date range might reflect the last interglacial sea level maximum, although the altitude of the village is about 300 m so this seems unlikely.

(g) Atheras Bay

No results: None of the samples collected here yielded dates.

NASA World Wind

In the latter half of 2004 NASA launched 'World Wind', a planetary visualisation tool that integrates Landsat imagery with Shuttle Radar Topography Mission (SRTM) elevation data to provide interactive three-dimensional fly-by photographic access to anywhere in the world. To put this achievement into perspective, the task of producing all the Landsat-based images in this book (as at Figure 27.10) which required significant effort and expenditure has overnight become instantaneous, ubiquitous and free.

Unfortunately within a few days of launching the site it was overwhelmed by global demand and became inaccessible. Accordingly I contacted the NASA project team and introduced them to a corporate sponsor willing to provide them with a solution. NASA kindly responded by providing me with priority access to World Wind from late November 2004.

I have been captivated by its capabilities and I understand that by the time this book is published the facility will be publicly available once again. Whatever age and stage of life you are at, I urge you to go to http://learn.arc.nasa.gov/worldwind/index.html and try it (if that is ineffective just type 'World Wind' into your search engine). It will fill you with awe at the beauty of our planet and it is the next best thing to being there. I hope it will also encourage us to preserve it.

It is time for us to say goodbye to Homer's Ithaca. Here is a World Wind composite satellite image of it taken on a sequence of almost cloudless days. In fact by flying over the Mediterranean in this way all of us now have the chance of solving problems that have eluded humanity for centuries. Where exactly did Odysseus travel on his way home from Troy? It turns out that the answer has been staring us in the face.

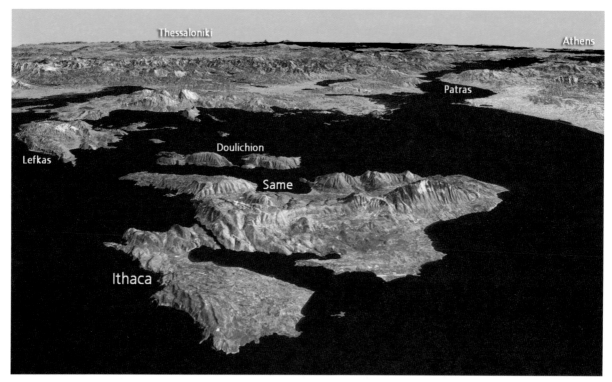

FIGURE A5.2
Ancient Ithaca from the Ionian Sea
False colour NASA World Wind image of the Ionian Islands and Western Greece, showing
former place names and the route of Strabo's Channel. Colour interpretation: as Figure 1.3.
[Image credits: as Figure 3.1.]

Sunday 26 December 2004

For the countless thousands who lost their lives, for the orphaned children and for the families with homes destroyed by the tsunami from the earthquake in Indonesia: we pray that Poseidon may never return to your shores. We pray as well that he may never return to Cephalonia. But in our hearts and our minds we know that he will always be with us. The next time we must be ready.

Bibliography

As well as listing works cited in the text, this bibliography includes the main publications that I have consulted while writing this book. References associated with James Diggle's and John Underhill's appendixes have been retained alongside their own text.

Agassiz, L. J. R. and Agassiz, E. C. 1866. *Geological Sketches*. Ticknor & Fields and J. R. Osgood, Boston.

Aitken, M. J. 1990. *Science-Based Dating in Archaeology*. Longman, London.

Albini, P., Ambraseys, N. N. and Monachesi, G. 1994. 'Materials for the Investigation of the Seismicity of the Ionian Islands between 1704 and 1766'. In *Materials of the CEC Project 'Review of Historical Seismicity in Europe'* (edited by P. Albini and A. Moroni) vol. II pp. 11–26. CNR, Milan. Also at http://emidius.mi. ingv.it/RHISE/ii_2alb/ii_2alb.html

Aldenhoven, F. 1841. *Itineraire descriptif de l'Attique et du Péloponêse, avec cartes et plans topographiques*. Athens.

Andrews, P. B. S. 1962. 'Was Corcyra the Original Ithaca?'. *Bulletin of the Institute of Classical Studies* 9, 17–20.

Antoniou, M. 2003. 'Borehole Drilling in Thinia'. Personal communication, Cephalonia.

Antonova, I. A., Tolstikov, V. and Treister, M. Y. 1996. *The Gold of Troy: Searching for Homer's Fabled City*. Thames and Hudson, London.

Anzidei, M., Lambeck, K., Antonioli, F., Baldi, P., Benini, A., Esposito, A., Nobili, A. and Surace, L. 2003. 'Sea-Level Change from Roman Time up to the Present in Central Mediterranean'. In *Coastal Environmental Change during Sea-Level Highstands: A Global Synthesis with Implications for Management of Future Coastal Change*. International Geological Correlation Programme No. 437, Puglia.

Arnold, M. 1862. *On Translating Homer. Last Words. A Lecture Given at Oxford*. Longman & Co., London.

Åström, P. 1987. *High, Middle or Low? Acts of an International Colloquium on Absolute Chronology Held at the University of Gothenburg 20th–22nd August 1987*. Paul Åströms Förlag, Gothenburg.

Åström, P. and Demakopoulou, K. 1996. 'Signs of an Earthquake at Midea?'. In *Archaeoseismology* (edited by S. Stiros and R. E. Jones). IGME & British School at Athens, Athens, 37–40.

Auriemma, R., Iannone, A., Mastronuzzi, G., Mauz, B., Sansò, P. and Selleri, G. 2003. 'Late Holocene Sea-Level Changes in Southern Apulia (Italy)'. In *Coastal Environmental Change during Sea-Level Highstands: A Global Synthesis with Implications for Management of Future Coastal Change*. International Geological Correlation Programme No. 437, Puglia.

Baker, C., Hatzfield, D., Lyon-Caen, H., Papadimitriou, E. and Rigo, A. 1997. 'Earthquake Mechanisms of the Adriatic Sea and Western Greece: Implications for the Oceanic Subduction-Continental Collision Transition'. *Geophysical Journal International* 131, 559–94.

Bérard, V. 1902. *Les Phéniciens et l'Odyssée*. Armand Colin, Paris.

Besonen, M. R. 1997. 'The Middle and Late Holocene Geology and Landscape Evolution of the Lower Acheron River Valley, Epirus, Greece'. University of Minnesota, Minneapolis.

Bintliff, J. and Snodgrass, A. M. 1988. 'Off-Site Pottery Distributions: A Regional and Interregional Perspective'. *Current Anthropology* 29 (3), 506–13.

1999. 'The Hidden Landscape of Prehistoric Greece'. *Journal of Mediterranean Archaeology* 12 (2), 139–68.

Blackman, D. 2001. 'Archaeology in Greece 2000–2001'. *British School at Athens Archaeological Reports* 47, 44.

Blegen, C. W. and Rawson, M. 1962. *A Guide to the Palace of Nestor*. University of Cincinnati, Cincinnati.

Bolling, G. M. 1925. *The External Evidence for Interpolation in Homer*. Clarendon Press, Oxford.

Boschi, E., Ferrari, G., Gasperini, P., Guidoboni, E., Smriglio, G. and Valensise, G. 1995. *Catalogo dei forti terremoti in Italia dal 461 A.C. al 1980*. Istituto Nazionale di Geofisica e Vulcanologia, Storia Geofisica Ambiente, http://www.ingrm.it/, Bologna.

Bousinos, A., Papazisimou, S., Christanis, K. and Tsellkes, P. K. 2001. 'To "Plouti" Elos tes Limnes Voulkaria (N. Aitoloakarnania) (the "Floating" Mire of Voulkaria Lake (Prefecture of Aitoloakarnania))'. *Bulletin of the Geological Society of Greece* 34 (1), 415–22.

Bowra, C. M. 1933. *Ancient Greek Literature*. Oxford University Press, Oxford.

1972. *Homer*. Duckworth, London.

BP Co. Ltd. 1971. *The Geological Results of Petroleum Exploration in Western Greece*. IGSR (IGME), Athens.

Bradford, E. 1963. *Ulysses Found*. Hodder & Stoughton, London.

Braune, K. 1973. 'Die Rezenten und Pleistozänen Sedimente des Sublitorals von Kephallinia (Ionische Inseln)'. *Senckenbergiana maritima* 5, 99–133.

Bristow, C. S. 2004. 'GPR in Sediments: Recent Advances in Stratigraphic Applications'. In *Tenth International Conference on Ground-Penetrating Radar*, Delft.

Bryce, T. 1998. *The Kingdom of the Hittites*. Clarendon Press, Oxford.

Bull, W. B. and Brandon, M. T. 1998. 'Lichen Dating of Earthquake-Generated Regional Rockfall Events, Southern Alps, New Zealand'. *Geological Society of America Bulletin* 110 (January), 60–84.

Buondelmonti, C. *c.* 1385–1430. 'Liber Insularum Archipelagi'. In *Description des îles de l'Archipel publ. d'après le manuscrit du Sérail avec une traduction française et un commentaire par E. Legrand*. Ernest Leroux, Paris (1897).

Burgess, R. 1835. *Greece and the Levant; Or, Diary of a Summer's Excursion in 1834*. Longman & Co., London.

Butcher, S. H. and Lang, A. 1879. *The Odyssey of Homer*. Macmillan & Co., London.

Butler, S. 1897. *The Authoress of the Odyssey*. Fifield, London.

Camps, W. A. 1980. *An Introduction to Homer*. Clarendon Press, Oxford.

Carlisle, M. and Levaniouk, O. 1999. *Nine Essays on Homer*. Rowman & Littlefield Publishers, Lanham, MD.

Carter, G. A. and Spiering, B. A. 2002. 'Optical Properties of Intact Leaves for Estimating Chlorophyll Concentration'. *Journal of Environmental Quality* 31, 1424–32.

Catling, H. W. 1976–7. 'Archaeology in Greece'. *British School at Athens Archaeological Reports* 23, 55.

1985–6. 'Archaeology in Greece'. *British School at Athens Archaeological Reports* 32, 55.

Cavafy, C. P. and Auden, W. H. 1961. *The Complete Poems of Cavafy*. Hogarth Press Ltd, London.

Cazenave, A., Bonnefond, P., Mercier, F., Dominh, K. and Toumazou, V. 2002. 'Sea Level Variations in the Mediterranean Sea and Black Sea from Satellite Altimetry and Tide Gauges'. *Global and Planetary Change* 34, 59–86.

Chadwick, J. 1958. *The Decipherment of Linear B*. Cambridge University Press, Cambridge (2nd edn, 1967).

1976. *The Mycenaean World*. Cambridge University Press, Cambridge.

Chapman, G. 1616. *Homer's Odysses. Translated according to Ye Greeke by Geo. Chapman*. Imprinted by Rich. Field for Nathaniell Butter, London.

Clark, W. G. 1858. *Peloponnesus: Notes of Study and Travel*. John W. Parker and Son, London.

Clinton, H. F. 1834. *Fasti Hellenici. The Civil and Literary Chronology of Greece from the Earliest Accounts to the LVth Olympiad*. Oxford University Press, Oxford.

Conan Doyle, A. 1890. *The Sign of Four*. Spencer Blackett, London.

1892. 'The Adventure of Silver Blaze'. In *The Adventures of Sherlock Holmes*. G. Newnes, London.

Conyers, L. B. and Goodman, D. 1997. *Ground-Penetrating Radar: An Introduction for Archaeologists*. AltaMira Press, Walnut Creek.

Cosmetatos, H. 1995. *The Roads of Cefalonia*. Corgialenios Museum, Argostoli.

Cramer, H. P. and Metaxas, G. 2000. *Omeriki Ithaki* (Homeric Ithaca). Kaktos, Athens.

Cramer, J. A. 1828. *Description of Ancient Greece*. Clarendon Press, Oxford.

Cutlac, O. N. and Maillol, J. M. 2004. 'Study of Holocene Landslide Deposits by Comparison of GPR, Refraction Seismic and Electrical Resistivity Data'. In *Tenth International Conference on Ground-Penetrating Radar*, Delft.

d'Anville, J.-B. B. 1768. *Géographie Ancienne Abrégée*. Merlin, Paris.

Darwin, C. 1839. *Journal of Researches into the Geology and Natural History of the Various Countries Visited by HMS Beagle under the Command of Captain Fitzroy RN from 1832 to 1836*. Henry Colburn, London.

Davis, J. L. 1998. *Sandy Pylos: An Archaeological History from Nestor to Navarino*. University of Texas Press, Austin.

de Bernières, L. 1994. *Captain Corelli's Mandolin*. Secker & Warburg, London.

Densmore, A. L., Ellis, M. A. and Anderson, R. S. 1998. 'Landsliding and the Evolution of Normal Fault-Bounded Mountains'. *Journal of Geophysical Research* 103, 15203–19.

Deubner, L. A. 1937. *Iamblichi de Vita Pythagorica Liber*. B. G. Teubner, Leipzig.

Deuel, L. and Schliemann, H. 1978. *Memoirs of Heinrich Schliemann*. Hutchinson, London.

Dickinson, O. 1994. *The Aegean Bronze Age*. Cambridge University Press, Cambridge.

Diggle, J. 1994. *Cambridge Orations 1982–1993: A Selection*. Cambridge University Press, Cambridge.

Doblhofer, E. and Savill, M. 1961. *Voices in Stone. The Decipherment of Ancient Scripts and Writings*. Souvenir Press, London.

Dominey-Howes, D. 2002. 'Documentary and Geological Records of Tsunamis in the Aegean Sea Region of Greece and their Potential Value to Risk Assessment and Disaster Management'. *Natural Hazards* 25, 195–224.

Dörpfeld, W. 1927. *Alt-Ithaka: ein Beitrag zur Homer-Frage: Studien und Ausgrabungen aus der Insel Leukas-Ithaka*. R. Uhde, Munich.

Dougherty, C. 2001. *The Raft of Odysseus: The Ethnographic Imagination of Homer's Odyssey*. Oxford University Press, Oxford.

Drews, R. 1993. *The End of the Bronze Age: Changes in Warfare and the Catastrophe ca. 1200 BC*. Princeton University Press, Princeton, N.J.

Durrell, L. 1978. *The Greek Islands*. Faber, London.

EERI. 2003. 'Preliminary Observations on the August 14, 2003, Lefkada Island (Western Greece)

Earthquake'. In *EERI Special Earthquake Report*. Earthquake Engineering Research Institute, Oakland.

Eleftheratos, L. 2002. *False Notes from Captain Corelli's Mandolin*. Tekmiriou, Athens.

Ellis, M. A., Densmore, A. L. and Anderson, R. S. 1999. 'Development of Mountainous Topography in the Basin Ranges, USA'. *Basin Research* 11, 21–41.

Emlyn-Jones, C. J. 1980. *The Ionians and Hellenism: A Study of the Cultural Achievement of Early Greek Inhabitants of Asia Minor*. Routledge & Kegan Paul, London.

Emlyn-Jones, C. J., Hardwick, L. and Purkis, J. 1992. *Homer: Readings and Images*. Duckworth, London.

Evelyn-White, H. C. 1914. 'Of the Origin of Homer and Hesiod, and of their Contest'. In *Hesiod, the Homeric Hymns and Homerica*. Loeb Classical Library (Harvard University Press), Cambridge, Mass.

Fagles, R. 1990. *Homer: The Iliad*. Viking, New York.

1996. *Homer: The Odyssey*. Viking, New York.

Finley, M. I. 1956. *The World of Odysseus*. Viking, New York (2nd edn, 1977).

1977. *The Ancient Greeks*. Penguin, Harmondsworth.

Fitton, J. L. 1995. *The Discovery of the Greek Bronze Age*. British Museum Press, London.

Fleming, I. 1959. *Goldfinger*. Jonathan Cape, London.

Fornara, C. W. 1983. *Archaic Times to the End of the Peloponnesian War*. Cambridge University Press, Cambridge.

Fortey, R. A. 2004. *The Earth: An Intimate History*. HarperCollins, London.

Fowler, R. L. 2004. *The Cambridge Companion to Homer*. Cambridge University Press, Cambridge.

Frame, D. 2004. *Hippota Nestor (Manuscript)*. Center for Hellenic Studies, Washington.

Frazer, J. G. S. and Van Buren, A. W. 1930. *Graecia Antiqua. Maps and Plans to Illustrate Pausanias's Description of Greece*. Macmillan & Co., London.

French, E. B. 1992–3. 'Archaeology in Greece'. *British School at Athens Archaeological Reports* 39, 25.

1996. 'Evidence for an Earthquake at Mycenae'. In *Archaeoseismology* (edited by S. Stiros and R. E. Jones). IGME & British School at Athens, Athens, 51–4.

Freytag-Berndt. 2000. *Cephalonia Road Map 1:50 000*. Freytag-Berndt.

Friedrich, W. L. 2000. *Fire in the Sea: The Santorini Volcano: Natural History and the Legend of Atlantis*. Cambridge University Press, Cambridge.

Galanopoulos, A. 1955. *Seismic Geography of Greece. Ann Geol des pays Helleniques* 6, 83–121.

Gell, W. 1807. *The Geography and Antiquities of Ithaca*. Longman, Hurst, Rees and Orme, London.

Giffard, E. 1837. *A Short Visit to the Ionian Islands, Athens, and the Morea*. London.

Gillings, M., Mattingly, D. and van Dalen, J. 2000. *Geographical Information Systems and Landscape Archaeology*. Oxbow, Oxford.

Gladstone, W. E. 1858. *Studies on Homer and the Homeric Age*. University Press, Oxford.

1863. *The Dominions of Odysseus, and the Island Group of the Odyssey*. Reprinted Oct. 1877 *Macmillan's Magazine*.

1869. *Juventus Mundi: The Gods and Men of the Heroic Age*. Macmillan, London.

Gödel, K. 1931. 'On Formally Undecipherable Propositions of Principia Mathematica and Related Systems', *Anzeiger der Akad. d. Wiss. in Wien (math.-naturw. Kl.)*, 19.

Godley, A. D. 1920–5. *Herodotus: The Persian Wars*. Loeb Classical Library

(Harvard University Press), Cambridge, Mass.

Goekoop, A. E. H. 1908. *Ithaque La Grande*. Beck & Barth, Athens.

Goekoop, C. H. 1990. *Op zoek naar Ithaka*. Heureka, Weesp.

Goekoop-De Jongh, J. 1933. *La Nesos Homérique*. Erven B. van der Kamp, Groningen.

Grandazzi, M. 1954. 'Le tremblement de terre des Isles Ioniennes (août 1953)'. *Bulletin de la Société de Géographie* 43, 431–453.

1968. 'Les derniers jours d'Argostoli'. *Acta Geographica* 71 (Jan.–Mar.), 27–8.

Graziosi, B. 2002. *Inventing Homer: The Early Reception of Epic*. Cambridge University Press, Cambridge.

Greenhalgh, P. and Eliopoulos, E. 1985. *Deep into Mani: Journey to the Southern Tip of Greece*. Faber, London.

Griffin, J. 1987. *Homer: The Odyssey*. Cambridge University Press, Cambridge.

Handrinos, G. and Demetropoulos, A. 1983. *Birds of Prey of Greece*. Efstathiadis Group, Athens.

Harris, H. A. 1964. *Greek Athletes and Athletics*. Hutchinson, London.

Heikell, R. 2003a. 'Chart G12: Nísos Levkas to Nísos Zákinthos'. In *Greece – South Ionian Islands*. Imray Tetra, St Ives.

2003b. *Ionian: Corfu to Zakinthos and the Adjacent Mainland to Methoni*. Imray Laurie Norie and Wilson Ltd, St Ives.

Herodotus *see* Godley, A. D.

Heubeck, A. and Hoekstra, A. 1989. *A Commentary on Homer's Odyssey Vol II Books 9–16*. Clarendon Press, Oxford.

Heubeck, A., West, S. and Hainsworth, J. B. 1988. *A Commentary on Homer's Odyssey Vol I Books 1–8*. Clarendon Press, Oxford.

HMGS. *1:5000 Scale Maps of Greece: Ref 6111, 6112, 6121, 6122, 6132*. Hellenic Military Geographical Service.

Hodgson, J. H. and Cock, J. I. 1955. 'Direction of Faulting in the Greek Earthquakes of August 9–13 1953'. *Canada Dominion Observatory Pub.* 18 (8), 29–47.

Homer *see* Butcher, S. H. and Lang, A.; Chapman, G.; Fagles, R.; Murray, A. T.

Hope Simpson, R. 1965. *A Gazetteer and Atlas of Mycenaean Sites*. Institute of Classical Studies, London.

Hope Simpson, R. and Lazenby, J. F. 1970. *The Catalogue of the Ships in Homer's Iliad*. Clarendon Press, Oxford.

Horden, P. and Purcell, N. 2000. *The Corrupting Sea: A Study of Mediterranean History*. Blackwell, Oxford.

Hornblower, S. and Spawforth, A. 2003. *The Oxford Classical Dictionary*. Oxford University Press, Oxford (3rd edn).

Huxley, G. L. 1966. *The Early Ionians*. Faber & Faber, London.

1969. *Greek Epic Poetry: From Eumelos to Panyassis*. Faber, London.

Iamblichus *see* Deubner, L. A.

IGME. 1985. *Geological Map of Greece – Northern Cephalonia*. Institute of Geology and Mineral Exploration, Athens.

Innes, M. M. 1955. *The Metamorphoses of Ovid*. Penguin Books, Harmondsworth.

Jackson, M. 1997. *The Underground Man*. Picador, London.

Jackson Knight, W. F. 1968. *Many-Minded Homer*. George Allen & Unwin, London.

James, P. 1991. *Centuries of Darkness: A Challenge to the Conventional Chronology of Old World Archaeology*. Jonathan Cape, London.

Jaynes, J. 1979. *The Origin of Consciousness in the Breakdown of the Bicameral Mind*. Allen Lane, London.

John, E. 1954. *Time after Earthquake. An Adventure among Greek Islands in*

August, 1953. William Heinemann, London.

Jones, H. L. 1917–32. *Strabo: Geography*. Loeb Classical Library (Harvard University Press), Cambridge, Mass.

Jones, P. V. 1988. *Homer's Odyssey: A Commentary Based on the English Translation of Richmond Lattimore*. Bristol Classical Press, London.

Jones, W. H. S. 1918–33. *Pausanias: Description of Greece*. Loeb Classical Library (Harvard University Press), Cambridge, Mass.

Kavalieratos, P. A. 2000. 'Historical and Topographical Notes on Kefallonia by Ioannis Karandinos, Written in 1776'. *Odusseia*, 47.

Kavvadias, G. 1984. *Paleolithic Cephalonia*. Fitrakis Publications, Athens.

Keynes, J. M. 1936. *The General Theory of Employment, Interest and Money*. Macmillan, London.

Kirk, G. S. 1962. *The Songs of Homer*. Cambridge University Press, Cambridge.
  1964. *The Language and Background of Homer*. W. Heffer & Sons, Cambridge.
  1965. *Homer and the Epic*. Cambridge University Press, Cambridge.

Kirk, G. S., Edwards, M. W., Hainsworth, J. B., Janko, R. and Richardson, N. 1985–93. *The Iliad: A Commentary*. Cambridge University Press, Cambridge.

Kirkwall, V. 1864. *Four Years in the Ionian Islands: Their Political and Social Condition*. Chapman and Hall, London.

Kitchen, K. 1987. 'The Basics of Egyptian Chronology in Relation to the Bronze Age'. In *High, Middle or Low? Acts of an International Colloquium on Absolute Chronology Held at the University of Gothenburg 20th–22nd August 1987* Part 1. Paul Åströms Förlag, Gothenburg.

Korkos, D. 1965. *I Vasilissa ton Ionion Neson* (The Queen of the Ionian Islands). Metaxa-Metropolou, Patras.

Koumantakis, I. and Mimides, T. 1989. 'Hyperalmyra Nera se Enklovismenous Asbestolithous tes Kephalonias' (Brines in an Enclosed Limestone Body of Kefalonia). *Bulletin of the Geological Society of Greece* 23 (3), 61–76.

Kraft, J. C., Rapp, G., Kayan, I. and Luce, J. V. 2003. 'Harbor Areas at Ancient Troy: Sedimentology and Geomorphology Complement Homer's Iliad'. *Geology* 31 (2), 163–6.

Kuniholm, P. I., Kromer, B., Manning, S., Newton, M., Latini, C. E. and Bruce, M. J. 2002. 'Anatolian Tree Rings and the Absolute Chronology of the Eastern Mediterranean, 2220–718 BC'. *Nature* 381, 780–3.

Lacy, A. D. 1967. *Greek Pottery in the Bronze Age*. Methuen & Co., London.

Laigle, M., Hirn, A., Sachpazi, M. and Clement, C. 2002. 'Seismic Coupling and Structure of the Hellenic Subduction Zone in the Ionian Islands Region'. *Earth and Planetary Science Letters* 200, 243–53.

Lambeck, K. 1995. 'Late Pleistocene and Holocene Sea-Level Change in Greece and South-Western Turkey: A Separation of Eustatic, Isostatic and Tectonic Contributions'. *Geophysical Journal International* 122, 1022–44.
  1996. 'Sea-Level Change and Shore-Line Evolution in Aegean Greece since Upper Palaeolithic Time'. *Antiquity* 70, 588–611.

Lambeck, K. and Bard, E. 2000. 'Sea Level Change along the French Mediterranean Coast for the Past 30,000 Years'. *Earth and Planetary Science Letters* 175, 203–22.

Lambeck, K. and Chappell, J. 2001. 'Sea Level Change through the Last Glacial Cycle'. *Science* 292, 679–86.

Lambeck, K., Esat, T. M. and Potter, E.-K. 2002. 'Links between Climate and

Sea Levels for the Past Three Million Years'. *Nature* 419, 199–206.

Latacz, J. 2004. *Troy and Homer: Towards a Solution of an Old Mystery*. Oxford University Press, Oxford.

le Noan, G. 2001. *A la recherche d'Ithaque*. Editions Tremen, Quincy-sous-Sénart.

2003. *La ferme d'Eumée: nouvelle recherche sur l'Ithaque Homérique*. Editions Tremen, Quincy-sous-Sénart.

2004. *Le Palais d'Ulysse*. Editions Tremen, Quincy- sous-Sénart.

Leake, W. M. 1830. *Travels in the Morea with a Map and Plans*. John Murray, London.

1835. *Travels in Northern Greece*. J. Rodwell, London.

Legrand, E. L. J. and Pernot, H. 1910. *Bibliographie Ionienne. Description raisonnée des ouvrages publiés par les Grecs des Sept-Isles ou concernant ces îles du quinzième siècle à l'année 1900*. Ernest Leroux, Paris.

Liddell, H. G. and Scott, R. 1940. *A Greek–English Lexicon*. Clarendon Press, Oxford (9th edn revised by Sir Henry Stuart Jones).

Livada-Duca, E. 2000. *Kefallonia: The Castle of Saint George*. Odusseia, Kefallonia.

Livadas, N. G. 1998. *Odysseus' Ithaca: The Riddle Solved*. Publications Nicholas G. Livadas, Athens (transl. C. Bisticas, 2000).

Livieratos, E. and Beriatos, E. 2001. *He Heptanesos se Xartes: apo ton Ptolemaio stous Doruphorous* (The Seven Islands in Maps: From Ptolemy to Satellites). National Map Library, Thessaloniki.

Lorimer, H. L. 1950. *Homer and the Monuments*. Macmillan, London.

Louden, B. 1999. *The Odyssey: Structure, Narration, and Meaning*. Johns Hopkins University Press, Baltimore.

Louvari, E., Kiratzi, A. A. and Papazachos, B. C. 1999. 'The Cephalonia Transform Fault and its Extension to Western Lefkada Island (Greece)'. *Tectonophysics* 308, 223–36.

Luce, J. V. 1998. *Celebrating Homer's Landscapes: Troy and Ithaca Revisited*. Yale University Press, New Haven & London.

McKean, J. and Roering, J. 2004. 'Objective Landslide Detection and Surface Morphology Mapping Using High-Resolution Airborne Laser Altimetry'. *Geomorphology* 57 (3–4), 331–51.

Mackendrick, P. 1962. *The Greek Stones Speak: The Story of Archaeology in Greek Lands*. St Martin's Press, New York.

Makropoulos, K. C. and Kouskouna, V. 1993. 'The Ionian Islands Earthquakes of 1767 and 1769: Seismological Aspects. Contribution of Historical Information to a Realistic Seismicity and Hazard Assessment of an Area'. In *Materials of the CEC Project 'Review of Historical Seismicity in Europe'* (edited by P. Albini and A. Moroni) vol. II pp. 27–36. CNR, Milan. Also at http://emidius.mi.ingv.it/RHISE/ii_3mak/ii_3mak.html

Mandelbrot, B. B. 1982. *The Fractal Geometry of Nature*. W. H. Freeman, San Francisco.

Manning, S. 1992. 'Archaeology and the World of Homer: Introduction to a Past and Present Discipline'. In *Homer: Readings and Images* (edited by C. J. Emlyn-Jones, L. Hardwick and J. Purkis). Duckworth, London.

March, J. R. 1998. *Dictionary of Classical Mythology*. Cassell, London.

Marinatos, S. N. 1962. *Cephallenia: A Short Historical and Archaeological Sketch*. Ekdosis TET Cephallenias, Argostoli.

Mastronuzzi, G. and Sansò, P. 2000. 'Boulders Transport by Catastrophic Waves along the Ionian Coast of Apulia (Southern Italy).' *Marine Geology* 170, 93–103.

Mavrogordato, J. N. 1952. *The Poems of C. P. Cavafy*. Hogarth Press, London.

Mazower, M. 2001. *Inside Hitler's Greece: The Experience of Occupation, 1941–44*. Yale University Press, New Haven & London.

Mee, C. and Spawforth, A. 2001. *Greece: An Oxford Archaeological Guide*. Oxford University Press, Oxford.

Meiggs, R. and Lewis, D. M. 1969. *A Selection of Greek Historical Inscriptions to the End of the Fifth Century BC*. Clarendon Press, Oxford.

Méliarakis, B. A. 1890. *Geographia Politiki Nea Kephallinia* (The Political Geography of the Island of Kephallinia). Athens.

Mitford, W. 1808. *The History of Greece*. T. Cadell and W. Davies, London.

Monro, D. B. 1891. *Homeric Grammar*. Clarendon Press, Oxford.

Morgan, C. 2003. *Early Greek States beyond the Polis*. Routledge, London.

Moritz, L. A. 1958. *Grain-Mills and Flour in Classical Antiquity*. Oxford University Press, Oxford.

Morkot, R. 1996. *The Penguin Historical Atlas of Ancient Greece*. Penguin, London.

Moschona-Maragaki, E. 2000. 'Seismoi Phoverotatoi' (Terrible Earthquakes)'. *Odusseia*, 35–9.

Moulinier, L. 1985. *Quelques hypothèses relatives à la géographie d'Homère dans l'Odussée*. Publication des Annales de la Faculté des lettres, Aix-en-Provence.

Müller, K. O. 1839. *History and Antiquities of the Doric Race*. Collingwood, Oxford.

Münster, S. and de Belleforest, F. 1575. *La Cosmographie Universelle de tout le monde*. M. Sonnius, Paris.

Mure, W. 1842. *Journal of a Tour in Greece and the Ionian Islands*. Blackwood, Edinburgh.

Murray, A. T. 1919. *Homer: Odyssey*. Loeb Classical Library (Harvard University Press), Cambridge, Mass. (rev. G. E. Dimock, 1995).

1924. *Homer: The Iliad*. Loeb Classical Library (Harvard University Press), Cambridge, Mass. (rev. W. F. Wyatt, 1999).

Murray, G. 1897. *A History of Ancient Greek Literature*. Heinemann, London.

1924. *The Rise of the Greek Epic: Being a Course of Lectures Delivered at Harvard University*. Clarendon Press, Oxford.

Murray, W. M. 1982. *The Coastal Sites of Western Akarnania: A Topographical-Historical Survey*. University of Pennsylvania, Philadelphia.

1983. 'The Ancient Harbour of Palairos'. In *Harbour Archaeology: Proceedings of the First International Workshop on Ancient Mediterranean Harbours* (edited by A. Raban). BAR International Series 257. Centre for Maritime Studies, Haifa University, Haifa, Israel.

1985. 'The Weight of Trireme Rams and the Price of Bronze in Fourth-Century Athens'. *Greek Roman and Byzantine Studies* 26, 141–50.

1986. 'The Ancient Harbour Mole at Leukas, Greece'. In *Archaeology and Coastal Changes, Proceedings of the First International Symposium on Harbours, Port Cities and Coastal Topography* (edited by Raban, A.). BAR International Series 404. Centre for Maritime Studies, Haifa University, Haifa, Israel, 101–18.

1993a. 'Ancient Sailing Winds in the Eastern Mediterranean: The Case for Cyprus'. In *Proceedings of the International Symposium, Cyprus and the Sea*, Nicosia.

1993b. 'Polyereis and the Role of the Ram in Hellenistic Naval Warfare'. In *5th International Symposium on Ship Construction in Antiquity* (edited by H. Tzalas). *Tropis V*. Hellenistic Institute for the Preservation of Nautical Tradition, Nauplia.

Myres, J. L. and Gray, D. 1958. *Homer and his Critics*. Routledge & Kegan Paul, London.

Nagy, G. 1996. *Homeric Questions*. University of Texas Press, Austin.

— 2001. 'Reading Bakhtin Reading the Classics: An Epic Fate for Conveyors of the Heroic Past'. In *Bakhtin and the Classics* (edited by R. B. Branham). Northwestern University Press, Evanston, 71–96.

— 2003. *Homeric Responses*. University of Texas Press, Austin.

Newman, H. and Newman, J. O. 2003. *A Genealogical Chart of Greek Mythology*. University of North Carolina Press, Chapel Hill.

Niebuhr, B. G. 1853. *Lectures in Ancient Ethnography and Geography*. Walton and Maberly, London.

Nur, A. 2000. 'Poseidon's Horses: Plate Tectonics and Earthquake Storms in the Late Bronze Age Aegean and Eastern Mediterranean'. *Journal of Archaeological Science* 27, 43–63.

— 2002. 'Earthquakes and Archaeology'. In *International Handbook of Earthquake and Engineering Seismology* 81A.

Olalla, P. and Priego, A. 2002. *Mythological Atlas of Greece*. ROAD Editions, Athens.

Onians, R. B. 1988. *The Origins of European Thought*. Cambridge University Press, Cambridge.

Orrieux, C. and Schmitt-Pantel, P. 1999. *A History of Ancient Greece*. Blackwell, Oxford.

Ovid *see* Innes, M. M.

Page, D. L. 1955. *The Homeric Odyssey. The Mary Flexner Lectures Delivered at Bryn Mawr*. Clarendon Press, Oxford.

— 1973. *Folktales in Homer's Odyssey*. Harvard University Press, Cambridge, Mass.

Pakenham, T. 2002. *Remarkable Trees of the World*. Weidenfeld & Nicolson, London.

Palmer, L. R. 1961. *Mycenaeans and Minoans. Aegean Prehistory in the Light of the Linear B Tablets*. Faber & Faber, London.

— 1963. *The Interpretation of Mycenaean Greek Texts*. Clarendon Press, Oxford.

Pantos, M. 2003. *The Ithaca Question*. http://srs.dl.ac.uk/people/pantos/the-ithaca-question/in-search-of-ithaca.html.

Papadopoulos, G. A. 2001. 'Tsunamis in the East Mediterranean: A Catalogue for the Area of Greece and Adjacent Seas'. In *Proceedings of the Joint IOC–IUGG International Workshop: Tsunami Risk Assessment Beyond 2000: Theory, Practice and Plans*. Institute of Geodynamics, National Observatory of Athens http://www.gein.noa.gr/services/tsunami.htm.

Papazachos, B. C., Comninakis, P. E., Karakaisis, G. F., Karakostas, B. G., Papaioannou, C. A., Papazachos, C. B. and Scordilis, E. M. 2000. *A Catalogue of Earthquakes in Greece and Surrounding Area for the Period 550bc–1999*. Geoph. Lab., Univ. of Thessaloniki http://lemnos.geo.auth.gr/the_seisnet/en/catalog_en.htm.

Paradissis, A. 1999. *Fortresses and Castles of the Greek Islands*. Efstathiadis Group, Athens.

Parry, A. M. 1971. *The Making of Homeric Verse: The Collected Papers of Milman Parry*. Clarendon Press, Oxford.

Partsch, J. 1890. *Kephallenia und Ithaka: eine geographische Monographie*. Justus Perthes, Gotha.

Pausanias *see* Jones, W. H. S.

Payne, H. G. G. 1930–1. 'Archaeology in Greece'. *Journal of Hellenic Studies* 51 (Part II), 16.

Peter, Y. F. 2000. 'Present-Day Crustal Dynamics in the Adriatic–Aegean Plate Boundary Zone Inferred from Continuous GPS-Measurements'. Swiss Federal Institute of Technology, Zurich.

Pfeiffer, R. 1968. *History of Classical Scholarship: From the Beginnings to the End of the Hellenistic Age*. Clarendon Press, Oxford.

Piozzi, H. L. and Johnson, S. 1786. *Anecdotes of the Late Samuel Johnson LI.D. during the Last Twenty Years of his Life. By Hester Lynch Piozzi. The Third Edition*. T. Cadell, London.

Pirazzoli, P. A. 1996. *Sea-Level Changes: The Last 20,000 Years*. Wiley, Chichester.

Pirazzoli, P. A., Laborel, J. and Stiros, S. C. 1996. 'Earthquake Clustering in the Eastern Mediterranean during Historical Times'. *Journal of Geophysical Research* 101 (B3), 6083–98.

Pirazzoli, P. A. and Pluet, J. 1991. *World Atlas of Holocene Sea-Level Changes*. Elsevier, Amsterdam.

Pirazzoli, P. A., Stiros, S. C., Laborel, J., Laborel-Deguen, F., Arnold, M., Papageorgiou, S. and Morhange, C. 1994. 'Late-Holocene Shoreline Changes related to Paleoseismic Events in the Ionian Islands, Greece'. *The Holocene* 4 (4), 397–405.

Plafker, G. 1965. 'Tectonic Deformation Associated with the 1964 Alaska Earthquake'. *Science* 148, 1675–87.

Pocock, L. G. 1965. *Odyssean Essays*. Basil Blackwell, Oxford.

Polybius *see* Shuckburgh, E. S.

Porcacchi, T. 1576. *Isole Piu Famose del Mondo*. S. Galignani et G. Porro, Venice.

Powell, B. B. 2004. *Homer*. Blackwell, Oxford.

Price, S., Higham, T., Nixon, L. and Moody, J. 2002. 'Relative Sea-Level Changes in Crete: Reassessment of Radiocarbon Dates from Sphakia and West Crete'. *Annual of the British School at Athens* 97, 171–200.

Pucci, P. 1987. *Odysseus Polutropos: Intertextual Readings in the Odyssey and the Iliad*. Cornell University Press, Ithaca, N.Y.

Randsborg, K. 2002. 'Kephallénia: Archaeology and History – the Ancient Greek Cities'. *Acta Archaeologica* 73 (1, 2).

Redfern, R. 2000. *Origins: The Evolution of Continents, Oceans, and Life*. Cassell, London.

Rennell, J. R. 1927. *Homer's Ithaca: A Vindication of Tradition*. Arnold, London.

Riemann, O. 1879. *Recherches archéologiques sur les Iles Ioniennes: ii Céphalonie*. Thorin, Paris.

Robinson, A. 2002a. *Lost Languages: The Enigma of the World's Undeciphered Scripts*. McGraw-Hill, New York.

2002b. *The Man Who Deciphered Linear B: The Story of Michael Ventris*. Thames & Hudson, London.

Robinson, A. R., Theocharis, A., Lascaratos, A. and Leslie, W. G. 2001. 'Mediterranean Sea Circulation'. In *Encyclopedia of Ocean Sciences*. Academic Press, London, 1689–706.

Rohl, D. M. 1995. *A Test of Time*. Century, London.

Runnels, C. N. 2002. *The Archaeology of Heinrich Schliemann: An Annotated Bibliographic Handlist*. Archaeological Institute of America, Boston.

Runnels, C. N. and Murray, P. M. 2001. *Greece before History: An Archaeological Companion and Guide*. Stanford University Press, Stanford.

Runnels, C. N. and van Andel, T. 2003. 'The Early Stone Age of the Nomos of Preveza: Landscape and Settlement'. In *Landscape Archaeology in Southern Epirus, Greece*, I (edited by J. Wiseman and K. Zachos). American School of Classical Studies at Athens, Athens.

Russo, J., Fernández-Galiano, M. and Heubeck, A. 1992. *A Commentary on Homer's Odyssey Vol III Books 17–24*. Clarendon Press, Oxford.

Rutherford, R. B. 1996. *Homer*. Oxford University Press, Oxford.

Sakellariou, M. B. 1958. *La migration grecque en Ionie*. Institut Français d'Athènes, Athens.

Savant, J. 1953. 'Le drame des Isles Ioniennes'. *La revue des deux mondes* 1 Sept. 1953.

Schaeffer, C. F. A. 1948. *Stratigraphie comparée et chronologie de l'Asie Occidentale*. The Griffith Institute, Oxford.

Schein, S. L. 1996. *Reading the Odyssey: Selected Interpretive Essays*. Princeton University Press, Princeton, N.J.

Schliemann, H. 1869. *Ithaque le Péloponnèse Troie: recherches archéologiques*. C. Reinwald, Paris. 1880. *Ilios: The City and Country of the Trojans*. John Murray, London.

Schmidt, M. 2004. *The First Poets: Lives of the Ancient Greek Poets*. Weidenfeld & Nicholson, London.

Schuchhardt, C. and Schliemann, H. 1891. *Schliemann's Discoveries of the Ancient World*. Avenel Books, New York.

Seferis, G., Keeley, E. and Sherrard, P. 1995. *George Seferis: Complete Poems*. Anvil Press Poetry, London.

Seutter, G. M., Seutter, A. K. and Lotter, T. C. 1744. *Atlas Minor*, Augsburg.

Severin, T. 1985. *The Jason Voyage: The Quest for the Golden Fleece*. Hutchinson, London. 1987. *The Ulysses Voyage: Sea Search for the Odyssey*. Hutchinson, London.

Shannon, R. 1999. *Gladstone: 1809–1865*. Penguin, London.

Shelley, P. B. 1820. *Prometheus Unbound. A Lyrical Drama in Four Acts*. C. & J. Ollier, London.

Shipley, G. 1987. *A History of Samos, 800–188 BC*. Clarendon Press, Oxford.

Shipp, G. P. 1961. *Essays in Mycenaean and Homeric Greek*. Melbourne University Press, Melbourne.

Shive, D. 1987. *Naming Achilles*. Oxford University Press, Oxford.

Shuckburgh, E. S. 1889. *Polybius: Histories*. Macmillan, London.

Skarlatoudis, A. A., Margaris, B. N. and Papazachos, B. C. 2004. 'Recent Advances in Greece on Strong-Motion Networking and Data Processing'. In *The Consortium of Organizations for Strong-Motion Observation Systems (COSMOS) Workshop*. University of California at Santa Barbara (UCSB).

Smith, C. F. 1919. *Thucydides: History of the Peloponnesian War*. Loeb Classical Library (Harvard University Press), Cambridge, Mass.

Smyth, H. W. 1922. *Aeschylus, with an English Translation*. W. Heinemann, London.

Snodgrass, A. M. 1967. *Arms and Armour of the Greeks*. Thames & Hudson, London.

Sorel, D. 1976. *Etude neotectonique dans l'arc Egéen Externe Occidental*, Académie de Paris, Paris.

Soteriou, A. 1995. 'Kastelli Region'. *Archaiologikon Deltion* 50 (B1), 246.

Souyoudzoglou-Haywood, C. 1999. *The Ionian Islands in the Bronze Age and Early Iron Age, 3000–800 BC*. Liverpool University Press, Liverpool.

Spon, J. 1678. *Voyage d'Italie, de Dalmatie, de Grèce et du Levant, fait aux années 1675 & 1676 par Jacob Spon et George Wheler*. A. Cellier, Lyon (see also Wheler).

Stanford, W. B. 1954. *The Ulysses Theme: A Study in the Adaptability of a Traditional Hero*. Blackwell, Oxford.

Stanford, W. B. and Luce, J. V. 1974. *The Quest for Ulysses*. Phaidon Press, London.

Steiner, G. and Fagles, R. 1962. *Homer. A Collection of Critical Essays*. Prentice-Hall, Englewood Cliffs.

Steinhart, M. and Wirbelauer, E. 2002. *Aus der Heimat des Odysseus: Reisende, Grabungen und Funde Auf Ithaka und Kephallenia Bis Zum Ausgehenden 19. Jahrhundert*. P. von Zabern, Mainz am Rhein.

Stiros, S. C. 2001. 'The AD 365 Crete Earthquake and Possible Seismic Clustering during the Fourth and Sixth Centuries AD in the Eastern Mediterranean: A Review of Historical and Archaeological Data'. *Journal of Structural Geology* 23, 545–602.

Stiros, S. C. and Jones, R. E. 1996. *Archaeoseismology*. IGME & British School at Athens, Athens.

Stiros, S. C., Kontogianni, V. A. and Drakos, A. G. 2002. '20th Century Versus Long-Term Deformation Rates in the Aegean Region: Evidence from Analysis of Coastal Change Data'. In *Wegener 2002*. NTUA, Athens.

Stiros, S. C. and Papageorgiou, S. 2001. 'Seismicity of Western Crete and the Destruction of the Town of Kisamos at AD 365: Archaeological Evidence'. *Journal of Seismology* 5, 381–97.

Stiros, S. C., Pirazzoli, P. A., Laborel, J. and Laborel-Deguen, F. 1994. 'The 1953 Earthquake in Cephalonia (Western Hellenic Arc): Coastal Uplift and Halotectonic Faulting'. *Geophysical Journal International* 117 (3), 834–49.

Strabo *see* Jones, H. L.

Symeonoglou, S. 1984. *The Odyssey Project*. http://www.artsci.wustl.edu/~artarch/sections/FACULTY/fac_symeonoglou.htm

Symonds, J. A. 1893. *Studies of the Greek Poets*. Black, London.

Synolakis, C. E. 1991. 'Green's Law and the Evolution of Solitary Waves'. *Physics of Fluids* A, 3 (3), 490–2.

Talbert, R. J. A. 2000. *Barrington Atlas of the Greek and Roman World*. Princeton University Press, Princeton.

Taylour, W. 1983. *The Mycenaeans*. Thames and Hudson, London.

Thalmann, W. G. 1998. *The Swineherd and the Bow: Representations of Class in the Odyssey*. Cornell University Press, Ithaca, N.Y.

Thucydides *see* Smith, C. F.

Tomlinson, R. A. 1995–6. 'Archaeology in Greece'. *British School at Athens Archaeological Reports* 42, 16.

Toynbee, A. J. 1969. *Some Problems of Greek History*. Oxford University Press, Oxford.

Tozer, H. F. 1873. *Lectures on the Geography of Greece*. John Murray, London.

Tsagarakis, O. 2000. *Studies in Odyssey 11*. F. Steiner, Stuttgart.

Tsapanos, T. M., Papadopoulos, G. A. and Galanis, O. C. 2003. 'Time Independent Seismic Hazard Analysis of Greece Deduced from Bayesian Statistics'. *Natural Hazards and Earth System Sciences* 3, 129–34.

Tsimaratos, E. 1998. *Poia I Omeriki Ithaki?* (Which Is Homeric Ithaca?) Etaireias Meletes Ellenikes Historias, Athens.

Tsitselis, I. 1877. *Onomata Theseon en Kephallenia* (Names of Places on Kephallenia). Athens.

Tzakos, C. 1999. 'Concerning Homeric Ithaki: Asteris'. *Odusseia*, 95.
2000. 'Kefa-ll-ines Kefa-ll-inia Kefa-ll-onia'. *Odusseia*, 70–2.
2002. *Ekthesi Synoptiki peri Omerikis Ithakis* (A Brief Essay on Homeric Ithaca). Angelos Eleutheros, Athens.

Tzanis, A., Vallianatos, F. and Makropoulos, K. 1999. 'Seismic and Electrical Precursors to the 17-1-1983, M7 Kefallinia Earthquake, Greece: Sigatures of a SOC System'. *Phys. Chem. Earth* (A) 25 (3), 281–7.

Underhill, J. R. 1989. 'Late Cenozoic Deformation of the Hellenide Foreland, Western Greece'. *Geological Society of America Bulletin* 101 (5), 613–34.

van Andel, T. 1994. *New Views on an Old Planet: A History of Global Change.* Cambridge University Press, Cambridge.

— 1998. 'Paleosols, Red Sediments and the Old Stone Age in Greece'. *Geoarcheology* 13 (4), 361–90.

Vellacott, P. H. 1961. *Aeschylus: Prometheus Bound.* Penguin Books, Harmondsworth.

Ventris, M. G. F. and Chadwick, J. 1956. *Documents in Mycenaean Greek.* Cambridge University Press, Cambridge.

Vollgraff, W. 1907. 'Dulichion-Leukas'. *Neue Jahrbücher fur das klassische Altertum* 19, 617–29.

Volterras, G. 1903. *Kritiki Meleti peri Omerikis Ithakis* (A Critical Study of Homeric Ithaca), Athens.

Vött, A., Brückner, H. and Handl, M. 2003. 'Holocene Environmental Changes in Coastal Akarnania (Northwestern Greece)'. In *Aktuelle Ergebnisse der Küstenforschung* (edited by A. Daschkeit and H. Sterr) 28. Berichte aus dem Forschungs- und Technologiezentrum Westküste der Christian-Albrechts-Universität zu Kiel, Büsum, 117–32.

Wace, A. J. B. and Stubbings, F. H. 1962. *A Companion to Homer.* Macmillan, London.

Waddington, C. H. 1977. *Tools for Thought.* Cape, London.

Wade-Gery, H. T. 1952. *The Poet of the Iliad [the J. H. Gray Lectures for 1949].* Cambridge University Press, Cambridge.

Waterhouse, H. 1996. 'From Ithaca to the Odyssey'. *The Annual of the British School at Athens* 91, 301–17.

Webster, T. B. L. 1958. *From Mycenae to Homer.* Methuen & Co., London.

Wheler, G. 1682. *A Journey into Greece, by George Wheler Esq., in Company of Dr Spon of Lyon.* William Cademan and Robert Kettlewell, London (see also Spon).

Whitley, A. J. M. 2001. *The Archaeology of Ancient Greece.* Cambridge University Press, Cambridge.

— 2002–3. *The British School at Athens: Annual Report of Council.*

— 2003. 'Archaeology in Greece 2002–2003'. *British School at Athens Archaeological Reports* 49.

— 2004. 'Archaeology in Greece 2003–2004'. *British School at Athens Archaeological Reports* 50.

Wiener, M. H. 2003. 'The Absolute Chronology of Late Helladic III A2 Revisited'. In *The Annual of the British School at Athens* (edited by A. J. M Whitley) 98. British School at Athens, Athens, 239–50.

Willett, S. D., Slingerland, R. and Hovius, N. 2001. 'Uplift, Shortening and Steady State Topography in Active Mountain Belts'. *American Journal of Science* 301, 455–85.

Williams, D. W. 2002. *Admiralty Sailing Directions: Mediterranean Pilot Volume III (11th Edition).* United Kingdom Hydrographic Office, Taunton.

Winchester, S. 2001. *The Map that Changed the World: The Tale of William Smith and the Birth of a Science.* Viking, London.

Wiseman, J. and Zachos, K. 2003. 'Landscape Archaeology in Southern Epirus, Greece'. American School of Classical Studies at Athens, Athens.

Wood, D. W. and Bjorndal, K. A. 2000. 'Relation of Temperature, Moisture, Salinity, and Slope to Nest Site Selection in Loggerhead Sea Turtles'. *Copeia* 1, 119–28.

Wood, M. 1985. *In Search of the Trojan War.* BBC Books, London.

Wyse, T. R. H. S. and Wyse, W. M. 1865. *An Excursion in the Peloponnesus in the Year 1858.* Day & Son, London.

Homeric index

Quotations from the *Iliad* and the *Odyssey* are listed here by their book and opening line references (based on the Greek text of the poems), followed by an introductory extract from the quoted passage. Alternative translations of the same line give rise to multiple entries. The translations are by James Diggle except where otherwise indicated.